Hollywood East

Hollywood East

Louis B. Mayer and the Origins
of the Studio System

By Diana Altman

A Birch Lane Press Book
Published by Carol Publishing Group

A Birch Lane Press Book
Published by Carol Publishing Group
Birch Lane Press is a registered trademark of Carol Communications, Inc.
Editorial Offices: 600 Madison Avenue, New York, N.Y. 10022
Sales & Distribution Offices: 120 Enterprise Avenue, Secaucus,
    N.J. 07094
In Canada: Canadian Manda Group, P.O. Box 920, Station U, Toronto,
    Ontario M8Z 5P9
Queries regarding rights and permissions should be addressed to
Carol Publishing Group, 600 Madison Avenue, New York, N.Y. 10022

Carol Publishing Group books are available at special discounts for
bulk purchases, for sales promotions, fund-raising, or educational
purposes. Special editions can be created to specifications. For
details, contact: Special Sales Department, Carol Publishing Group,
120 Enterprise Avenue, Secaucus, N.J. 07094

Manufactured in the United States of America
10 9 8 7 6 5 4 3 2 1

Library of Congress Cataloging-in-Publication Data

Altman, Diana.
    Hollywood East : Louis B. Mayer and the origins of the studio
system / Diana Altman.
        p.   cm.
    "A Birch Lane Press Book."
    Includes bibliographical references and index.
    ISBN 1-55972-140-5
    1. Motion picture industry—United States—History. 2. Mayer,
Louis B. (Louis Burt). 1885-1957. I. Title.
PN1993.5.U65A47   1992
384'.8'0973--dc20   92-20883
                                                          CIP

FOR RICHARD

The verb TO FILM having gained currency, it must be graciously admitted to the language. It will soon be in the "advanced" dictionaries and it must be recognized. The old idea of protecting the English language from invasion is extinct. To *film* means to make a picture for a *movie* show. *Movie* is a tolerably new word, too, but all the elite use it.

—*New York Times*, May 1914

The policy is to give as much as you can for the money. I suppose that is the secret of success in the show business.

—Sidney R. Kent, 1927
  General Manager,
  Paramount-Famous-Lasky Corporation

And I will sing of heroism from an American point of view.

—Walt Whitman

Contents

Preface

T HE MYTH is that Louis B. Mayer was a colossus with a vol-
cano inside instead of a heart. After a childhood as squalid as
his rotten personality deserved, so the tale goes, he sprang
into Hollywood where he strode around doing whatever he
wanted.

Truth is, he was middle-aged before people noticed that he
had made a difference. The first film history, *A Million and
One Nights* by Terry Ramsaye (1926), mentioned the forty-year-
old Louis B. Mayer only twice: first, in a list of officers of the
1915 Metro Picture Corporation, "Louis B. Mayer of Boston,
secretary," and second, as the also-ran company that Marcus
Loew acquired when Metro and Goldwyn merged—"Marcus
Loew, once a New York newsboy, now holding the incorporated bouquet entitled Metro-Goldwyn-Mayer, taking its
name from two companies and Louis B. Mayer of Boston. . . ."
The author devotes many pages to men he thought were really important: Otway Latham, Mark Dintenfass, Richard

Rowland, and others posterity seldom mentions.

Far from ruling Hollywood, Louis B. Mayer, as head of production at the Metro-Goldwyn-Mayer studio in California from
1924–1951, was answerable to his boss in New York, first Marcus
Loew, then Nicholas Schenck. Metro-Goldwyn-Mayer was just
one of 124 subsidiary companies owned by Loew's Inc., a multi-
billion dollar concern with headquarters in Times Square.

Until the sixties the film industry in America had two capi-
tals, Hollywood and New York. New York was the financial center of the industry and conducted the lucrative foreign export
trade. Decisions about budgets and product were made at corporate headquarters on the east coast, not at the studios on the
west coast. Clark Gable may have posed for cameras in Culver
City, but his paycheck was signed at 1540 Broadway, across the
street from the Camel Cigarette sign blowing smoke rings.
When Adolph Zukor, the founder of Paramount Pictures, went
to work in the morning, it was to an office in the Paramount
building on Broadway. Marcus Loew, the founder of M-G-M's
parent company, Loew's Inc. lived on Long Island and went to
work in his office in Times Square. Albert Warner, one of the
brothers, ran Warner Bros. headquarters in New York, as
David Sarnoff ran RKO's headquarters there. William Fox,
who founded the Fox part of Twentieth Century-Fox, had two
offices in New York, one at the Roxy Theater and the other at
his newsreel factory on Tenth Avenue and Fifty-fourth Street.

Yet recent film histories discount the influence of New
York, mentioning it merely as some small speck connected to
Hollywood by a telephone wire. If Hollywood had collapsed,
the film industry in America could have continued pretty
much as it was, simply setting up studios in some other sunny
place. But when New York collapsed, the whole industry
changed completely.

In recent film history, Marcus Loew, Adolph Zukor, the
Warner brothers, and William Fox have all become isolated
from the corporations they founded and have grown into
mythical giants who made arbitrary decisions based on their
personal needs, as if every decision came from being holed

up somewhere in isolation. As if they, all by themselves, could make a product that interested the whole world.

All corporations have a life of their own, and the film corporations were no different. Except that the public, through dozens of censorship organizations, including the powerful Legion of Decency controlled by the Pope in Rome, exerted an outside influence that is not usually so immediate in corporate life.

Because of his genius for self-promotion, Louis B. Mayer has emerged as the Zeus of film pioneers. He's probably laughing in his grave. He started out in his youth as an entrepreneur, but he ended up an employee—an internationally famous, politically powerful employee. Which is to say, he could be fired. And he was.

Louis B. Mayer-bashing is a current fad. Fact is, there were people so loyal they worked for him thirty and forty years. My father was one of them.

Al Altman was a talent scout for Metro-Goldwyn-Mayer from the time the company was founded in 1924 until the early sixties, when the headquarters moved out of New York and the New York talent department was dissolved. My father and Louie Mayer met in Boston when Al was nineteen and Louie was about thirty. Their satisfying relationship lasted until Louie died at age seventy-two. They were both prudish men; they were both devoted to their mothers. They knew what it was to grow up poor and how wonderful it was to finally be able to afford to dress well. They were both showmen and had an eye for quality. They kept in close touch though Al worked in New York at the home office and Louie was at the studio on the west coast.

The founders of the film industry in the United States were the men who invented the machines—the projectors and cameras. But it was the men who loved "the show business" who made the American film industry dominant in the world. They began as theater owners who grew to love their audience and to believe that, where entertainment is concerned, "the public is never wrong."

Acknowledgments

THE FOLLOWING people were most generous with their help:

Gregory Laing, head of special collections at the Haverhill Public Library, has such a profound knowledge of Haverhill he made doing research there fun. When he suggested I try the corn chowder at Haverhill's A-1 Deli, I did, and discovered the best restaurant in Massachusetts. Thanks to Lynda's mother, Elaine Demerritt, who introduced me to Beatrice Malbon, whose father was an usher at the Cozy Nickel. Thanks to Dee Doucett and Redd Slavit, whose fathers knew Louis B. Mayer when. Bertha Woodman has written the definitive book about Haverhill's early Jewish community and understood how much encouragement writing a book requires. David Joyall at the Northeast Document Conservation Center was a doll to give me a break on the price of restoring an old photo, and Charles Hillner, III, whose grandfather played piano in Louie Mayer's theater, was generous with his enthusiasm for my project.

Thanks to Myer Levin and his sister, Edna Grace, who spoke to me for a long time about their father, Louis B. Mayer's first production partner. Dr. Arthur Linenthal, who has written a great history of Boston's Jewish hospitals, became my friend while I was doing this book. Thanks to Betty Gordon in California, who put me in touch with Marion Bever in Cambridge, whose father was Mayer's Boston partner in the theater business.

At the Glen Gove Library on Long Island, thanks to Jim Brown. At the Huntington Historical Society, thanks to Mitzi Caputo, and at the Newton Free Library, thanks to the entire staff, especially Cathy Garoian and Ernie Kruhmin. Brian Smarsh at the Georgetown University Library selected many of the photographs used on these pages. He found them in the fabulous Quigley Collection donated by Martin Quigley, Jr., who was generous with his time.

Thanks to Howard Bass at the New York Jockey Club, who probably doesn't remember how much time he spent researching Louis B. Mayer's racehorse history for me. Thanks to Karl Fasick for lending me that Dore Schary book and telling me about his days as a salesman for M-G-M. And Russell Merritt, the film writer, probably forgot that long telephone conversation we had years ago in which he encouraged me.

Speaking of encouragement, thanks to my brother-in-law, Jerry E. Bishop, the *Wall Street Journal* reporter, who made me realize that just saying what I knew about the early days of the film industry would be plenty interesting.

Thanks to photographer Barrett Gallagher and his wife, Timmie, for their willingness to share their photographs, and to Anne Grossman for introducing me to the late Irene Selznick. At the Dana Farber Cancer Institute, thanks to Regina Vild and Hallie Baron.

Jerry Spindel, my friend for more than twenty years, always said I should write about the film industry, and when I began, was there with advice and good cheer. My friend Michaele

Weissman helped edit the finished manuscript, a very above and beyond thing to do.

Thanks to my agent, Barbara Lowenstein, and my editor, Allan J. Wilson.

Todd Luspinski, who introduced hundreds of people in Boston to the stars of the silent screen with his monthly "Silent Movie Night" shows, died before he could see his name here. He was such an ardent fan, his beloved Mary Pickford and Lillian Gish corresponded with him, their letters beginning, "Dearest Todd," though they had never met him. We all miss him. Thanks to his companion, Michael Emley, for making Todd's library and papers available to me and for being such a good pal.

ONE

Louie Jumps In

Haverhill, Massachusetts, a small city north of Boston, is forlorn and in a perpetual state of waiting. The red-brick mills seem shrunken, embarrassed by the "For Lease" signs on their doors. Stores on Merrimack Street are abandoned, their windows bandaged with plywood. The atmosphere in Haverhill is full of mourning for a time long ago.

Once there were dozens of passengers at the train depot, hiring the horse-drawn cabs that waited on the cobblestone street. Visitors sniffed the air and recognized leather. That perpetual hum was the sound of steam-driven machinery coming from the open windows of red-brick factories. Smoke rose from chimneys in a big, prosperous way, and the factory whistle blasted the time of day. Store windows on fashionable Merrimack Street were artistically arranged to show off hats and collars, butter and eggs, jewelry, penny candy, and furniture. Bolts of fabric were snapped open in several tailor shops, and in the barber shops there was a man in every chair. The Merrimack River flowing alongside the city was a busy thoroughfare full of barges piled high with leather goods bound for markets in Europe and Asia. Haverhill was the "Slipper Capital of the World."

The population was forty-five thousand souls who lived clustered together according to the language they spoke and the amount of money they had. The very wealthy lived by Lake Saltonstall, in mansions full of intricately carved furniture made in London and Philadelphia, silver articles from Boston, and silken stuff from Asia. The most spectacular mansion was "Birchbrow," a thirty-three-room gothic mansion on the shore of the lake, stone pillars in front, gargoyles sticking out above the porte cocher. It was built in 1880 by Thomas Sanders, founder of the Bell Telephone Company. His son was the deaf boy whom Alexander Graham Bell was tutoring when the "speaking telephone" was invented.

Other mansions were owned by the descendants of railroad presidents, real estate entrepreneurs, bankers, coal traders, shipbuilders, and shoe manufacturers. They attended the North Congregational Church. If they happened to be male, they were members of Haverhill's Pentucket Club, where there was a library, reading room, resident chef, and bowling alley in the cellar.

In 1907 Louis B. Mayer, age twenty-two, arrived in Haverhill broke. He was a short man with a torso made bullish by a childhood full of physical labor. A softness deep in his eyes showed how easy it was to hurt him, but his abrupt and choppy manner kept others at a distance. His walk was so rapid his wife, with their two baby daughters, had to run to keep up with him as he led them to the poor section of town, where factory workers lived many to a room. Foreign-looking underwear flapped on clotheslines. Louie and his wife Margaret rented a room and settled their babies in.

He had decided to go into the photoplay business. Trade papers were full of the successes of men similar to Louie, immigrants with little formal education. *Variety*, which was then two years old, and New York's *Daily Mirror* carried stories of William Fox, age twenty-eight, who already owned a half dozen picture houses in Brooklyn and Manhattan. His Dewey Theater on Fourteenth Street, a former legitimate house that could seat one thousand, had twelve uniformed ushers who escorted patrons to upholstered seats. The show, consisting of motion pictures and vaudeville acts, lasted two hours.

Marcus Loew, age thirty-seven, and his partner Adolph Zukor had started with penny arcades and were acquiring theaters all over New York. They bought a dump in Brooklyn, a burlesque house called Watson's Cozy Corner, renovated it, and changed the name to the Royal. Their first show was an opera put on by an Italian company, which gave the theater class.

Carl Laemmle in Chicago owned picture houses and had already branched out into distribution. Harry Cohn in Pittsburgh was making money from films, and in Boston Nathan Gordon was opening picture houses as fast as he could buy old theaters.

Louie said he regretted quitting school when he was twelve. He should have quit when he was ten. That way everyone would not have had a head start on him.

What brought Louie to Haverhill was a small theater on the sleazy side of town, a run-down wooden structure with warped floors and tobacco-spit stains on the walls. The official name of the theater was the Gem, but people in town called it the "Germ" and the "Garlic Box." Louie had purchased it for six hundred borrowed dollars. The town mothers and fathers had been trying to close the place down for years.

In truth the burlesque program at the Gem was quite tame, by today's standards. Willard G. Cogswell remembered the Gem in a paper he presented to the Massachusetts Historical Society:

The tickets of admission (soiled by use over and over again) cost, I think, fifteen cents each. The aggregate take-in was consequently low, and permitted the engagement of only local talent, mostly funny-boys and throaty "fallen women."

I remember one night [in 1898] when a scrawny, middle-aged, bony-kneed harlot was doing the split. In the climax of her act a lout in the back row guffawed loudly; and the poor awkward she-wretch turned her thin face viciously towards him and, one leg straight out in front of her and the other straight out behind, thumbed her nose at him for a full venomous half-minute, a female in the most graceless of all possible postures.

Yet I recollect little actual obscenity done there. Most of the acts were comic, acrobatic, or sentimental. What made them attractive to us boys was, of course, that they were strictly forbidden to us. We had to sneak into them, and lie about it afterwards. . . .

The dramatis personae were: the piano-player, a dark sallow young gent who performed rattlingly, but with an air of contemptuous superiority to his surroundings; the announcer, a florid fleshy stranger from the great city, with yellow hair parted in the middle and plastered with hair-oil, a long mustache carefully waxed, a plaid waistcoat; the singer, young but, alas, not beautiful.

The Announcer intones (in cadences he had picked up in the grander music halls of the Bowery): "Miss Blanche Fernandez will now sing 'White Wings.'" A vulgar fellow in the rear shouts: "Blanche Fernandez is a whore!" Announcer blandly rejoins: "Nevertheless, Miss Blanche Fernandez will now sing 'White Wings.'"

Louie's intention was to convert the Gem into a motion-picture hall. He knew that the Gem had a bad reputation, but like most boys whose mothers never insult them, he was full of confidence in his abilities. His mother in Canada said that she was sure he would accomplish big things, and his wife thought so, too. His wife, so Louie's mother told him, had come to him from heaven, and Louie's mother was so grateful a good woman would be looking after her son that she once kissed the hem of Margaret's skirt.

Haverhill was a good choice for launching a career in show business. It was not a mill town, had not grown up because of the mills, but had existed since colonial times, long before there were any shoe factories there. Social status was not determined by one's place at the factories but by how long one had lived in Haverhill. The old families set the city's tone. They supported a local orphanage, felt a constant obligation to help the poor, and believed adamantly in public education. They were sophisticated people with money to travel to Europe and Asia, to dress well, and to see the great cultural events of the day.

The most important legitimate theater north of Boston was located in Haverhill. The Academy of Music was a mandatory stop on the circuit of all well-known performers. The theater, built in 1884, had capacity for fifteen hundred customers. There were twelve dressing rooms, and eleven exits opened onto four streets, enabling an audience to empty the building in three minutes. The carpets and curtains were red, the walls were light salmon, and there was a crystal chandelier hanging from the ceiling containing ninety gas jets. Famous performers arrived at the Haverhill depot, their luggage plastered with foreign labels. Ethel Barrymore and her brother John played there, and so did Douglas Fairbanks and Maggie Kline. Edwin Booth, whose unbalanced brother shot Abraham Lincoln, was paid $1,000 for a performance of *Othello*.

Haverhill was known as a "show city." The circus set up tents there and brought elephants, lions, and clowns to town. Buffalo Bill brought his Wild West show to Haverhill. He arrived with eight hundred performers and five hundred fifty horses. The hundreds of Indians in his troupe set up tepees on the fairgrounds. Fifteen thousand people sitting under the tent on River Street cheered as they watched Mexicans mounted on horseback throwing lariats. Skilled riders galloped around the arena barely clinging to the saddle to demonstrate how the pony express used to operate. Buffalo Bill, in his sixties, sun-tanned, his white hair down to his shoulders, his goatee white, and dressed in buff suede with fringe at the cuffs, rode a prancing white horse and was as exotic and dignified as an old tree come to life.

Mark Twain, then known as a humorist rather than an author, lectured in Haverhill, and so did Lieutenant Robert E. Peary, the intrepid arctic explorer. Peary, who hoped to raise money for his next voyage on his ship, the *Roosevelt*, told of his trips to the North Pole and showed stereopticon slides of his dogs freezing to death and his men with icicles in their beards.

When Louie Mayer moved to Haverhill from Boston, where he had been living with his wife's parents, there was only one photoplay theater in town, the Bijou, a former dry-goods store. Display shelves were still on the walls. Three hundred chairs were set up in front of a screen.

A hand-painted sign over the entrace to the Bijou proclaimed "High Class Motion Pictures & Illustrated Songs. New Ideas. New Novelties. Coolest Theatre North of Boston." On the sidewalk was an easel supporting a sign that read "Coming Next. Charlie's Ma-in-law. You'll laugh for half an hour!" A phonograph record blasted a barker's message to everyone on the sidewalk: "Step right up, folks, come inside. Step right up, folks, come inside."

Next to the screen was an upright piano with some of its teeth missing. At the back of the theatre was a fireproof metal booth that enclosed a projector known as the Vitascope Special. There were one-hundred-twenty patented machines similar to the Vitascope Special under one hundred twenty different names. The manager of the theater had to crank it by hand, and when he got tired the action on the screen slowed down. The audience was mostly made up of immigrants. Children shouted in English to friends on the other side of the room, then switched languages to answer their mothers in Italian, Armenian, Polish, Russian, German, and Yiddish.

When the Bijou's manager pulled a switch to dim the house lights, the automatic barker was turned off in the middle of its sentence, "folks, come. . . ." He dropped a song slide into his slide projector, and lyrics flashed onto the screen. Then he projected the words "Please read the titles to yourself. Loud reading annoys your neighbors." To thread his projector he had to turn on the house lights, and that started the automatic barker on the sidewalk: "Step right up, folks, come inside." A slide on the screen reassured the audience that "We Aim to Present the Pinnacle of Motion Picture Perfection."

Motion pictures flickered on the screen for about six minutes average and showed what were called "local actualities," such as the Yale football team at practice, a steam shovel digging the New York subway, Coney Island lit up at night, a locomotive being stoked with coal, a circus elephant being electrocuted because it had killed two men. There were travelogues featuring an Australian ostrich farm where feathers were plucked for hats, pygmies building a vine bridge over an abyss, gondolas in Venice. And rudimentary story films: *The Hold-Up of the Rocky Mountain Express,* which showed bandits robbing a train; *Terrible Ted,* which showed an obnoxious, overweight child getting into trouble and then being kicked and slapped by adults. There were also trick pictures like *Smashing a Jersey Mosquito,* in which a mosquito grew until it was the size of a blimp and killed the man who was trying to swat it; and another in which an innocent man had his clothes mysteriously removed and then put back on. His chair moved and his pipe flew out of his hand.

Between reels, slides were projected onto the screen: "You Wouldn't Spit on the Floor at Home, So Please Don't Do It Here;" "Ladies and Gentlemen May Safely Visit This Theatre as No Offensive Films Are Ever Shown Here;" "Please Remain;" "Just a Moment, Please, While the Operator Changes Reels;" and "Ladies, We Like Your Hats, But Please Remove Them."

Though the audience at the Bijou lacked education and the experience of speaking English, they would not have been caught dead at the Gem Theater.

Much to Louie's dismay, another photoplay theater came to town before he had a chance to open. An abandoned music hall on Winter Street, slated for demolition, had collapsed in

on itself from neglect. The owner of the structure had expected to take a loss and was amazed when he was contacted
by eight different parties who wanted to save the theater from
the wrecker's ball in order to convert it to a motion-picture
hall. Photoplays were becoming the rage. William Furber
changed the theater's name to the Cozy Nickel, and the local
newspaper carried the story of its remodeling:

> On Monday all roads will lead to the new place of amuse-
> ment. There is always a great desire to see something
> new by almost every one. Those who have been in the
> new house say it is going to be a dandy. That may be
> rather a slang word to use, but it tells the truth all the
> same. . . . The Cozy Nickel has not been built just for a
> little while and then after the craze of moving pictures is
> over shut up and abandoned, it has come to stay and will
> become a family resort, where parents can send their
> children to learn more in a few minutes of the manners,
> customs and scenery of foreign lands than they can learn
> from their school books in hours of study.

Haverhill's story was being repeated in towns across America. The demand for motion pictures had increased three-
fold. Most theaters, changed their programs at least every
other day. Orders for films from all over the United States
poured into the film factories, mostly located in New York,
which were able to sell everything they produced.

There were dozens of them: Pilot Film Corporation in
Yonkers, Eclectic Film Company on Fortieth Street, Chey-
enne Feature Film Company on Broadway, Ambrosio Ameri-
can on East Twenty-sixth, Solax in New Jersey, U.S. Film
Corporation on West Forty-fifth, Great Northern Special Fea-
ture Film on East Fourteenth, Monopol Film Company on
West Forty-fifth, Gaumont Company in Flushing, Thanhouser
Film Corporation in New Rochelle, and many others.

The Cozy Nickel in Haverhill was scheduled to open in December 1907. Louie declared that his theater, its name now
changed from the Gem to the Orpheum, would open a whole
month earlier, on Thanksgiving Day. He thought that if he

put the word *Thanksgiving* next to the words *Orpheum Theater* the association would be beneficial. The opening picture, *The Life of Christ From the Annunciation to the Ascension in 27 Beautiful Scenes*, would be accompanied by an all-girl orchestra.

What Louie did not realize was that Thanksgiving was a most important holiday in New England. Gifts were exchanged after a large family dinner. Haverhill shut down completely on that day. Volunteers brought turkeys, buckets of cranberries, sweet potatoes, pumpkin pies, and apple pies to the thirty-five children who lived at the Elizabeth Home for Destitute Children, on Main Street. Even orphans and those children at the Home who were victims of abuse or were waiting for parents to get out of jail stayed in on Thanksgiving to eat a big dinner.

Louie's wife Margaret took her place in the box office at the Orpheum and got ready to sell tickets. She was a high-school graduate and was Louie's bookkeeper and secretary. In a ledger book she had divided the pages into columns, one headed Debit and the other, Credit. Each day she planned to enter on the debit side such expenses as electricity, film rental, slides, advertising, and salaries. On the credit side would be earnings.

The Orpheum looked much more like the old Gem than Louie had intended. The floor was still warped, and the tobacco stains on the walls had not been entirely covered by two coats of paint. He had specified a marquee that could hold four thousand bulbs and would extend over the sidewalk to protect patrons during rain, but there was no money for it because the fire chief insisted that Louie install another exit in front. So Louie had to announce his next attraction, *Bluebeard, the Man With Many Wives,* on a sign propped on an easel on the sidewalk.

People not only stayed away from the Orpheum on Thanksgiving Day but on all the other days, too, because the theater was still the "Garlic Box" to them.

The Cozy Nickel opened in late December, and even though it was snowing there were lines waiting to get in. People still remembered "Zola the Contortionist" who had once delighted them when the theater was the Music Hall. By the time Louie's theater opened, the Bijou on Merrimack Street had been renovated and no longer resembled a store. The new Bijou could seat five hundred in cushioned, collapsible leather seats. There were uniformed ushers and a ladies' "retiring room." At night the front of the New Bijou was illuminated with five hundred electric lights.

Louie took to his bed, his sinuses flaring. Margaret served him chicken soup and made sure no light came in at the windows. He had promised Maggie that they would never again have to live with her parents, and now it seemed he would have to break that promise. He owed money. Maybe they would have to retreat to Louie's childhood home in Canada, where Louie's father would gloat over his son's defeat.

Louie decided to lay his case before the citizens of Haverhill. There were dozens of organizations in town that helped new arrivals who came to work in the shoe factories. The organizations were social clubs as well as charities that loaned money, found rooms, and translated for the immigrants when they went to the doctor. Louie spoke in Yiddish to the Jewish organizations, to the members of The Workmen's Circle, the Independent Order of B'rith Abraham, the Haverhill Zion Lodge, the Blossoms of Zion, and the Ladies Helping Hand Society. He said that he was aware of the bad reputation of his theater but that he had two children of his own and would never show any pictures that he thought were dirty or that showed bad people getting away with doing bad things. He said that moving pictures were a good way to teach children American manners and that they would learn to read by wanting to read the title cards. He asked his audience to come see for themselves, and then he pledged money to the Beth Jacob Synagogue, where the Ashkenazic Jews worshipped, and to the Ahavas Synagogue, where the Sephardic Jews prayed.

He spoke, with translators, to the Italian organizations and pledged money to the Saint Anthony Day Parade, and to the

Germans, the Poles, and the Armenians. He screwed up his nerve and spoke in his best English to the ladies of the Garden Club and the John Greenleaf Whittier Society, a literary club named after Haverhill's native son. Louie told the women his dreams, how he wanted to bring the finest of entertainment to Haverhill. The ladies said that moving pictures were not good for the health of children, that fresh air was what children needed, that they agreed with the judge in Chicago who said motion pictures caused juvenile crime, and that Jane Addams of Hull House, the great social worker, was correct in her drive to regulate what children could see on the screen. They said they understood Mayor George B. McClellan of New York City, who had started a war on "store shows" to close them by canceling their licenses.

Louie agreed that there were offensive pictures being manufactured: *Gaieties of Divorce, Old Man's Darling, Beware, My Husband Comes,* and *The Bigamist,* but for every sensational picture there was an agreeable one like *Cinderella, Quaint Holland, Wonders of Canada,* and *The Passion Play.* He said that the fight to ruin the reputation of picture houses was being lead by men of the legitimate theater who were beginning to feel the pinch of competition from motion pictures. Big money, for the men of the speaking stage, was in the road show that followed a successful run on Broadway. Motion-picture houses in the small towns across the country were stealing audiences from road shows. It was theater men who alerted town officials of the dangerous moral character of motion pictures. Louie said that if the women of the Garden Club would just give him a chance he would prove to them that he was in the business of delighting, not offending.

Louie, who was then about the age of a college senior, was such a mixture of confidence and awareness of his own shortcomings: he could barely read and had a thick accent and coarse manners, that he inspired in others a desire to help him. People felt that if they didn't help him he would fall flat on his face. His success would be their own personal triumph.

So they gave him a chance. The Orpheum Theater began to prosper and earned enough in its initial season for Louie to be able to convince his backer to invest more to really spruce the place up. His backer was Charles Clayton Chase of the Chase & Laubham Corporation, which owned most of the stores, barrooms, and pool halls neighboring the Orpheum. Mr. Chase knew that a decent theater would bring a higher class of people to Essex Street and that expensive shops might follow. He invested $28,000 in the Orpheum. The New Orpheum opened in September 1908 with a seating capacity of nine hundred and a marquee that extended over the sidewalk.

Louie enlisted the help of local reporters. He gave them free passes and promised to introduce them to celebrities who might appear on his stage. "Always be good to the men who write" was his philosophy. They wrote their hearts out for Louie, making news out of just about anything. The *Haverhill Gazette* reported in September 1908:

> A grand piece of work has been accomplished of which the city as well as Manager Mayer may justly feel proud. It is not a moving picture house enlarged, but an actual theatre, conforming in every degree with the state laws and state police regulations, licensed for the production of anything in the theatrical line, and the finest structure of its class this side of Boston. No expense has been spared in making for Haverhill theatre-goers a model playhouse. . . . Louis B. Mayer, prominently identified with local theatrical enterprises, will offer a new and up-to-date line of entertainment of such a class as will speak for itself, no expense to be spared in securing for patrons exactly what they want. Vaudeville and moving pictures will comprise the bill and the latest and best in each class will be the only offerings of the house which proposes catering to the best people in the city.

The reporter from the *Sunday Record* wrote:

On the stage walls are the big ventilators supplying 1500 cubic feet of fresh, pure air every minute. . . . The heating is by steam, radiators being mounted on the side walls throughout the house and in the various rooms, steam being supplied from the latest model of Syracuse boilers, which are situated beneath the stage and enclosed within the fire walls, the boiler weighing more than three tons. . . . In the opening of the present season Manager Mayer has the wishes of no end of friends and acquaintances in this city for a most prosperous season during the next few months.

The owner of the competing New Bijou began to think that his own theater manager was too lethargic. Since Louie Mayer had arrived in town, fewer customers frequented the New Bijou. At the New Orpheum audiences could see stage acts as well as motion pictures, and Louie Mayer managed to have his photograph in the newspaper all the time. He ran contests at his theater, went out speaking to civic organizations. Three months after Louie's New Orpheum opened, he was asked to take over the management of the New Bijou. The *Record* reported in November 1908:

One of the greatest changes in local theatrical circles that has ever taken place occurred yesterday when the New Bijou theatre on Merrimack Street changed hands. Louis B. Mayer the popular manager of the New Orpheum, assuming control. . . . The name New Bijou will be no more, for the theatre is to be christened the Scenic Temple, and it is the idea of the proprietors that the theatre will be everything that its name implies. . . . Although the New Orpheum and the Scenic Temple will be under the same management there will be a different entertainment at each house in every way. . . . Manager Mayer has gained numberless friends since his appearance here a year ago, and those who are acquainted with the New Orpheum have watched its progress from practically nothing to one of the finest playhouses in New England. Everything possible will be done to make the Scenic Temple as great a success as the New Orpheum.

This will surely be forthcoming now that Manager Mayer has taken hold, as he has earned the reputation of the "Hustling Manager," which he justly deserves.

Louie and his family moved out of their one room into a triple-decker house on Temple Street. Now when Louie walked down the street, people in town greeted him. He took the train to Boston to attend conventions of motion picture theater owners where film salesmen sold their wares. Here he was, just starting out and already the manager of two theaters. But Louie's eyes were bigger than his stomach, and he was mortified to discover that he was not up to managing two theaters. His New Orpheum began to deteriorate immediately, and the staff at the Scenic Temple resented him. It was a fiasco, and after only two months Louie had to back away. The Scenic Temple was sold.

But by now Louie was pals with all the reporters in town, and they made his failure sound like a victory. Mr. A. Benjamin, who bought the Scenic Temple, hardly figured into the news at all:

It was with pleasure that the large number of New Orpheum patrons learned of the change, as they readily understand the betterness of the programmes that will be offered now that Manager Mayer can devote his whole time to "The Little Theater Round The Corner," as the New Orpheum is called, as the house is a popular one, having grown in popular favor from the day that Mr. Mayer opened. With that progressive manager devoting all his time to the improvement of the amusements they feel that their wants will be happily satisfied and that the entertainments will be the best in town.

A picture of Louis B. Mayer, not Mr. Benjamin, accompanied the article.

Louie settled into Haverhill with his one successful movie house, paid his debts, and watched his babies, Irene and Edith, grow. Secretly he feared that he did not have what it took to accomplish the big things his mother expected of him. He had bouts with a nasty rash the color of a baboon's bottom, and he often had to pinch the sides of his nose to stop his sinuses from paining.

His dream was to build a grand theater for motion pictures and big-time vaudeville, a showplace right on Merrimack Street. He would bring world-class performers to the people of Haverhill: Gertrude Hoffman, the dancer; Blackstone the Magician; J. Robert Pauline, the hypnotist; Felix Honey, the comedian; and the Lauder Brothers, minstrels.

On the other side of town, at the Cozy Nickel, William Furber presented a motion picture entitled *The Runaway Engine*, which showed two large locomotives tearing toward each other on the same track. When the engines collided, the audience screamed, and William Furber had to go on the stage to calm everyone. Folks were calling it the most thrilling picture ever shown in the city. For a week everyone was talking not about the New Orpheum but about the "near riot" at the Cozy Nickel.

William Furber secured the "eighth world wonder" for his patrons, Daylight Pictures. The only place people in Massachusetts could see Daylight Pictures was at Keith's Theater in Boston. Now Furber was going to bring them to Haverhill, and nothing Louie advertised could compare. Darkened houses were going to be a thing of the past. No more stumbling to one's seat; no more blindness upon coming out of the theater into the sunshine. Women no longer would have to fear being molested in the dark. That problem was so bad, women in several states were urging that laws be passed to require a separate seating area in theaters for women only. Daylight Pictures did not flicker and had no scratches on them. They were altogether superior.

Louie's competition grew. A fourth motion-picture house opened in Haverhill, the Majestic Theater, on Washington Street. Managed by Max Slavit, who also owned the popular restaurant the Star, the theater could seat six hundred, had hot and cold water in the dressing rooms, and promised the people of Haverhill an innovation—noon shows every day.

In 1908 profits to film manufacturers in the United States were $75 million. Distributors, the middlemen who took the films from the factories to the theater owners, earned $4 million. Theater owners earned $8 million, and customers spent $65 million at the box office. Entrepreneurs who went into the business thinking to make a quick buck and then get out when the fad ended now began to take another look. And those who had been in on the thing from the start began to try to keep others out.

*   *   *

The first men in the business were those who invented the machines—the motion picture cameras and projectors. Thomas Edison, famous not only for his inventions but also for the naps he took in the middle of meetings, now began to resent that others were getting rich from the devices he invented in his New Jersey laboratory. He demanded that those using his machines pay him a fee. Some thought his demand reasonable; others—Thomas Armat, William Kennedy Laurie Dickson, and Sigmund Lubin—claimed that the machines they were using to manufacture photoplays were not invented by Edison. Many theater owners claimed that their projectors were not invented by Edison, and they refused to pay him a licensing fee. There ensued a patents war, with thousands of dollars spent battling in court. The "Big Ten" producers: Edison, Biograph, Vitagraph, Kleine, Selig, Essanay, Lubin, Kalem, Méliès, and Pathé, controlled about 85 percent of all motion-picture patents. About the time that Louie landed in Haverhill, the "Big Ten" decided to stop fighting and join together to keep newcomers out of their pot of gold. They entered into an agreement whereby they forced other manufacturers to buy licenses from them for the use of their cameras, and exhibitors to pay a $2-a-week fee for running their pictures on patented projectors.

Marcus Loew, in New York, was one of the few exhibitors who did not balk. He paid his fee for licensed projectors and went on expanding his business. That's how he was. Whatever he had to do to get along, he did. But there were others in the business who refused to pay fees to the new Motion Picture Patents Company. William Fox was one of them. He was used to fighting, having supported himself from the time he was a child on the Lower East Side. One day William Fox would face-off against Louis B. Mayer, but at this time Mayer did not exist for Fox, who had already risen from the ranks of the hundreds of anonymous small theater managers in America.

His feisty personality made him the one chosen by other nickelodeon showmen in New York to fight for their rights when Mayor George B. McClellan declared war on picture houses. William Fox was suspicious of everyone except his wife Eve and was quick to take offense. He seldom smiled, he seldom rested, he never wore a watch. His face, though mobile and expressive, showed permanent worry. His eyes were heavy-lidded and full of sorrow, his nose was big, his lips were crooked, and one side of his mouth pulled in close to his teeth. His wife Eve described him as a slave. "The only way I could ever have a husband was to go and be a slave with him. We hardly ever got home from the studio before three o'clock in the morning, and the canary bird in our home adjusted its hours and sang for us at whatever hour we returned."

That Mayor McClellan was going to close down the business that was making Fox rich was not to be tolerated. If nickelodeons closed in New York, the idea would spread to the rest of the country. Fox asked the film men to donate $25 each so he could begin a legal campaign against the mayor's shut-down order. After much fighting in court, nickelodeons were allowed to stay open in New York, but only after exhibitors agreed to some form of censorship of the pictures they presented.

The idea of censorship was taking hold. In Chicago the city council passed an ordinance of censorship. Legislators in California passed a law prohibiting moving pictures from showing girls with skirts flying in the wind, and in Ohio a law was passed that prohibited showing anyone pulling off a girl's skirt.

The mayor of Boston, Honey Fitzgerald, was orchestrating a war against the advertising banners displayed in front of Boston picture houses. The banners depicted scenes of robbery, safecracking, murder, suicide, and other crimes which Mayor Fitzgerald thought would excite the minds of passersby. He demanded that all exhibitors submit their advertising banners to his office for approval, or he would revoke their licenses.

Producers began to make pictures guaranteed not to offend: *Jesus of Nazareth, The Visiting Nurse,* scenes from the life of one, *A Day at West Point Military Academy, Educating the Blind,* and *Annual Celebration of School Children in Newark,* which offered views of four thousand children in outdoor exercises. The market became flooded with educational films like *Pictures in Chemistry, The Bud, Leaf, and Flower, Sea Birds and Their Haunts,* and *Examination of the Stomach by X-Rays.* That pictures on a screen could influence behavior was taken for granted.

William Fox decided to battle the Patents Company because they were trying to shut down his fledgling distribution company. The "Big Ten's" stated aim was a complete monopoly of production and distribution. They had formed a distribution company called the General Film Company, which tried to buy out other distributing companies. If the owners would not sell, they found they could not get any pictures from the "Big Ten," pictures which were, at that time, the ones most in demand by audiences. This sad notice from the *New York Dramatic Mirror* was typical:

KINETOGRAPH SELLS OUT. General Film Company Buys Entire Stock of Films on Hand. Trouble between the General Film Company and the Kinetograph Company was ended last week when the latter concern went out of business and sold its stock of films to the General Film Company. This action will end the dispute over the Detective Burns picture, "Exposure of the Land Swindlers." The amount of money involved in the transaction is not known, but it is supposed to have been a large sum, as the Kinetograph Company had a big stock of pictures on hand. After a few weeks, during which the affairs of the company will be settled, the Kinetograph offices will be closed.

When the General Film Company revoked William Fox's license on the grounds that he had shown some of their films in a whorehouse (which was a lie), Fox retaliated by bringing a lawsuit against the Patents Company for $6 million, saying the companies involved constituted a trust in restraint of trade, thereby violating the Sherman Antitrust Act. Fox was a bulldog yapping at the heels of an elephant:

> William Fox, owner of many theaters and president of the Greater New York Film Rental Company, was the chief witness at the hearings in the Federal suit against the Motion Picture Patents Company, resumed at the Hotel McAlpin, last Thursday, with Edward N. Hacker as special examiner. Attorney Edward P. Grosvenor and Joseph R. Darling, special agent of the Department of Justice, represented the Government. Mr. Fox testified at length to the effect that the defendants had brought pressure to bear in the effort to induce him to sell his business. A.H. Sawyer, manager of the sales department of the Kinemacolor Company of America, was the first witness called on Friday. He told of the experiences of the company he represented with the Patents Company.
> —*New York Dramatic Mirror,* March 5, 1913.

Fox was not the only independent film man to fight the Trust. Carl Laemmle, a tiny, agreeable man who would one day found Universal Pictures, decided to fight the Patents Company in the press. He put cartoons in the trade papers; one showed the Patents Company as a big fat man taking money from angry theater owners: "Every week I bring thee two simoleons." The fat man, standing on a pile of coins that represented $1 million a year, replies, "Every little bit helps." The Patents Company took out cartoons against the independents, portraying them as junkmen hauling junk pictures around.

Carl Laemmle found himself with no product to show in his many theaters because the Patents Company would not rent him any pictures. So he imported pictures from Europe and produced his own at a studio in rural New Jersey. Carl Laemmle advertised for players:

> We want novelty stunts! Dumb acts! One-act skits! To pose for moving pictures. . . . If you have a rattling good snappy act that has never been shown in motion pictures and you want to make good extra money during off hours, write immediately.
> —*New York Dramatic Mirror,* March 5, 1913.

Laemmle's first production, made in 1909 while the battle with the Trust was raging ("You can bet it's classy or I wouldn't make it my first release"); was *Hiawatha,* a sixteen-minute dramatization of Longfellow's poem. The picture boasted a cast of "150 full-blooded Indians." The Patents Company hired hoodlums to smash Laemmle's cameras and throw stones at his actors. Carl Laemmle shipped his players, including Mary Pickford, to Cuba for safety. They remained there for three months.

To escape the Patents Company goons, other producers fled to California. The first studio in Hollywood opened. The Centaur company, owned by two Englishmen, had been making westerns in Bayonne, New Jersey, one-reel pictures such as *Indian Raiders,* featuring real Indians. The weather in California was so dependable that Centaur could churn out one picture after another. Producers in the east took notice. Within months fifteen other companies were shooting in and around Hollywood.

*   *   *

In Haverhill, obscure to the rest of the country, Louie's business had grown. He now had a publicity agent, a secretary, a stage manager, and a chauffeur to drive his Model T. When some old wooden stables on Merrimack Street came up for sale, he convinced two prominent Haverhill businessmen to help him make his dream of a new theater come true. One investor was George Clement Elliott, in the coal business on River Street and a charter member of the exclusive Pentucket Club, who said, years later, "Louis was a worker. He never sleeps, you know, and he was always scheming up something." The other partner was Charles Howard Poore, an attorney. The three men bought the site of the stable but had to wait for the lease to expire at the adjoining Clamshell restaurant before they could acquire that property and start construction.

The Colonial Theater would be one of the largest theaters in New England, seating about fifteen hundred people, with a foundation big enough to support a ten-story building.

The lobby of the new theater was finished in old rose, with frescoes of green set off with studs of electric light clusters. Several oil paintings decorated the walls, including one that Louie had commissioned. For some reason he had wanted a painting of a recumbent lion. He liked the painting so much he gave it a place of honor over the fireplace in the theater lobby.

The floors at the Colonial were carpeted, and the stage was big enough for a large road show. There was a balcony with a marble staircase leading up to it.

The opening of the Colonial, "a sumptuously appointed palace of amusement," was a gala event in 1911. "It was an opening," said the local paper, "that was attended by people in all walks of life, city officials, theatrical managers from New York, Boston, and other cities." A local citizen who was there recalled, "Men and women for miles around swarmed into the Colonial. They were treated to a spectacular display of showmanship which only Louis B. Mayer could present."

The Colonial orchestra opened the program with a rendition of the "Colonial March," composed expressly for the occasion by a local composer. Then followed five acts of vaudeville and motion pictures.

Haverhill's Mayor Edwin Moulton was called to the stage,

and the orchestra played "Hail to the Chief." The mayor spoke of Haverhill's industrial and commercial development during the past few years and concluded with a tribute to the zeal of the man who was giving to Haverhill a theater "that was a pride to everyone who beholds it." The audience stood and applauded. The mayor introduced a little girl who was carrying a cornucopia of roses. These she flung about the stage as she christened the theater the Colonial. Then, in her piping little voice, she called Mr. Louis B. Mayer to the stage.

"He needed no further introduction," the newspaper reported the next day, "for since entering the amusement field he has become a leader in it, and he was greeted with applause that attested the appreciation of thousands of playgoers who have now been provided with a theater to their liking. Mr. Mayer told the audience, "The Colonial is the zenith of my ambition."

TWO

The Feature Craze

To BRING grand entertainment to people without the means to go and get it for themselves was the goal of the men who rose to prominence in the early days of the American film industry. This is what Louie had in common with men he had yet to meet.

Still obscure in Haverhill in 1912, though a bit less so because the program at the Colonial Theater was printed each week in the New York trade papers, Louie knew that his neighbors in double-decker houses on muddy streets had the same longing for beauty as those across town in manicured mansions. His mission, so he believed, was to open the world to those closed in by circumstances. Since they could not go to Boston to see the opera, he would bring the opera to Haverhill.

Everyone said he couldn't do it; the Boston Opera Company would never travel to Haverhill. There was scenery, cos-

tumes, a full orchestra, and singers to transport on the train.
Why would the Boston Opera Company bother? Haverhill
factory workers didn't care about opera. But Louie was possessed by the idea and guaranteed that all the seats would be
sold. He raised money from Haverhill citizens and prepaid
every seat in the house.

Customers camped out the night before to make sure they
were at the box office when it opened. Every seat was sold, all
standing room was sold, and people on the sidewalk were
begging to get in the night of the performance. The audience
stood and applauded for nearly fifteen minutes at the conclusion of Puccini's *Madama Butterfly.*

There was a biography of Louie in the opera programme
that took up twice as much space as the biography of the
prima donna:

> Mr. Louis B. Mayer whose inspiration and ambition it
> was to make grand opera in his home city a possibility,
> and through whose energy tonight's performance was
> made possible, is undoubtedly as well known in
> Haverhill and its suburbs as any man in public life. His
> business career in Haverhill has been successful; he has
> won friends in legions, and his sincere interest in giving
> to his home city and his fellow citizens the best that
> drama and music can provide is an achievement of more
> than ordinary merit.
> Mr. Mayer has striven to uplift the field of good, whole-
> some entertainment in Haverhill. He has provided the
> best in all fields of entertainment and has labored un-
> ceasingly toward the end that his playhouses may afford
> to the theatre-going public everything that is desirable.
> . . . Successes in dramatic and vaudeville endeavors have
> elevated Mr. Mayer to a plane equal with the most suc-
> cessful of theatrical men in New England; and Haverhill
> can boast, among other things, of having a citizen who is
> to be depended upon for those things which are neces-
> sary to enjoyment, with an assurance that everything is
> of the best, and it is of him that the authors of this souve-
> nir program express their appreciation.

In New York Adolph Zukor felt the same passion that Louie did. Zukor's idea was to bring famous plays with their original casts to motion-picture screens, so that people living outside of large cities might have a chance to see greatness. He thought that the current one-reel motion pictures were mostly beneath the intelligence of almost everyone. Charlie Chaplin described Zukor as "a sweet, small man, with a vivid personality."

Adolph Zukor dissolved his partnership with Marcus Loew, sold most of his Loew's stock, and took a chance. He said to his skeptical friends when they met in the evening at Shanley's Grill in Times Square, "Think how intimately all the great figures in stage history—Shakespeare, David Garrick, Kemble, Macready, Edwin Forrest, Mlle. Rachel—would be revealed to us. The light of their genius would be imperishable and shine as brightly for us today as it did in the heyday of their glorious careers."

Zukor heard that, in France, Sarah Bernhardt was posing for a motion picture version of her successful stage play, *Queen Elizabeth.* Adolph Zukor paid $40,000 for the rights to import the resulting four-reel motion picture, which he planned to show not in a nickelodeon but in a legitimate theater. There would be a gala opening night and a two-dollar admission price.

Zukor's former partner and lifelong friend, Marcus Loew, believed that photoplay audiences could not sit still for two hours and warned Zukor's wife that Adolph had lost his head and soon he would lose all his money. "I reassured my wife," the future founder of Paramount Pictures said, "by pointing out that Marcus was interested chiefly in the business end of the theaters. He was always looking around for new properties and better ways of management. Also, he relied chiefly on vaudeville at the box office. . . . I told my wife, 'I know pretty much what I am doing.'"

Zukor set up a studio, a 100-by-200-foot space at 213–227 West Twenty-sixth Street, between Seventh and Eighth Avenues, in New York, and announced his intention to photograph famous players in famous plays. The problem was that stage actors and producers were contemptuous of motion pictures. But Daniel Frohman, one of the great theatrical producers of the day, a cultivated, aristocratic man of sixty, was able to see the future. He agreed to help Zukor. "My brother Charles tells me," Daniel Frohman said to Zukor, "that transferring plays to the screen is a ridiculous and quixotic dream. I'm not sure that I agree with him."

Frohman thought the major problem would be convincing those who owned plays to sell movie rights, because once a play was made into a motion picture, audiences would no longer pay to see the play performed by stock and touring companies. Frohman predicted that motion pictures would ruin stock, and he turned out to be correct. As for players, enough money and the chance for immortality made most famous actors agree to give pictures a chance.

Frohman went into business with Zukor and offered his Lyceum Theater on Broadway for the premiere of Sarah Bernhardt's *Queen Elizabeth*. No major legitimate theater had ever before been given over to a film showing. What was spectacular about the film *Queen Elizabeth* was not just that Sarah Bernhardt, who was almost seventy, had agreed to pose for the "flickers," or that the picture required that an audience sit still for almost two hours, but that Adolph Zukor was charging "Broadway prices."

Nearly every member of the audience had seen Sarah Bernhardt live on the stage. Consequently there was a disappointed feeling at the beginning, because the picture was silent and the audience missed hearing her famous voice. It was evident that she was not at home before the camera; her gestures were too exaggerated. The *New York Herald's* critic wrote, "While it can add nothing to Mme. Bernhardt's fame that she has acted before the motion picture camera, future generations will be grateful to her that she has done so."

Sarah Bernhardt's performance went a long way toward breaking down the prejudice of theatrical people toward the screen. But the next obstacle was motion-picture theater men, who were now asked to pay a higher rental for a picture with a great star. "That is outrageous," Marcus Loew shouted. "No picture can be worth fifty dollars a day." But he showed the picture anyway. Gradually exhibitors realized that the public would pay increased admission prices for famous players in famous plays. And they saw that a new type of audience, wealthier and more educated, could be attracted to photoplay theaters.

In his Manhattan studio, helped by the prestige of Daniel Frohman, Adolph Zukor produced *The Prisoner of Zenda*, starring the matinee idol of the day, James K. Hackett, who had created the role on the stage. Using the costumes of the *Prisoner of Zenda* stock company and props collected from various wrecking crews, and having hired a publicity man, a man to run the film laboratory, and a salesman, Zukor began his career as a producer. "I shoveled all the money I could find onto the small blaze," Zukor wrote in his memoirs. "I hired more directors and cameramen, and searched frantically for scripts. I knocked on the dressing-room doors of stage stars, and, waving money as if I had a lot of it, begged them to come before the cameras."

The motion-picture industry was now wide open. William Fox had won the fight against the Motion Picture Patents Company, so anyone with stamina and imagination could now advance.

Louie in Haverhill was restless. He converted his first theater, the New Orpheum, to a legitimate theater, rounded up some New England actors, formed the Louis B. Mayer Stock Company, and put on plays for $2 a ticket. He brought his brother Jerry from Canada to manage the New Orpheum. His Colonial Theater prospered; Bill "Bojangles" Robinson danced there, and so did Fred and Adele Astaire. He rented the theater to local organizations when they wanted to raise money. The post-office department put on *The Governor's Lady* to aid the Postal Clerk's Mutual Benefit Association.

"The Colonial was successful all right," Louie's partner George Elliott recalled, "but it was an idea of Louis's that really made our organization worth some money." They formed a new company, the American Feature Film Company, and went into the business of distribution.

Distribution involved delivering films to theaters after they arrived by rail in fireproof tins from New York; being responsible for the repair, renovation, and replacement of the films; getting rental contracts from exhibitors for specific dates; and advertising the film to theater owners through trade papers and to the public through posters and newspapers. Louie and his partners would show each film first at the Colonial and then rent it at whatever the traffic would bear to other moving-picture houses.

Louie set up an office in downtown Boston and hired Fanny Mittenthal to run it for him. She knew how the distribution business worked. She wrote a letter to theater owners in New England telling them that Louis B. Mayer was offering the best in new, high-quality films. If any of the theater owners wanted these films, they should write.

Louie took the few letters he received to New York and showed them to various motion-picture manufacturers to prove that he did have customers. A company that made comedies took a chance. Louie distributed their pictures in New England, and his business got under way.

In 1913 a new producer named Jesse Lasky needed a distributor. Lasky had been a moderately successful producer of vaudeville shows on Broadway. His brother-in-law, Sam Goldfish, nagged him until he agreed to try the motion picture business. Goldfish (who later became Goldwyn), was tired of the glove business and wanted to find a new venture. Together they hired a young director named Cecil B. De Mille. With $20,000 borrowed from their various brothers-in-law, they went out to Flagstaff, Arizona, to find authentic scenery for their first picture, *The Squaw Man,* starring the famous and well-nourished stage actor, Dustin Farnum. The photoplayers were so chubby, an author put this caption under a still from the film: "Whatever squaw men died of in those days, it wasn't starvation."

Based on the stage success of the same name by Edwin Royal, *The Squaw Man* was one of Hollywood's first feature-length pictures—five reels. When Lasky's picture played in New York, at Marcus Loew's theaters, it was advertised, "Five-Reel Motion Picture, First Time in Any Theater" and "Doors Open One Hour Earlier." The customers figured that it was such a big show it had to start earlier. Actually, it ran about the same length, except the audience got three fewer vaudeville acts.

Louie Mayer and his partners purchased exclusive rights in New England to Lasky's first six feature-length productions. The second production was *Brewster's Millions*, another gold mine. According to Louie's partner George Elliott, "That was the picture that did the trick. The American Feature Film Corporation played the movie for several weeks at the Colonial and then let it out for months at a handsome profit. *Brewster's Millions* was the *Gone With the Wind* of its day."

At the Colonial, as well as at theaters across the country, people saw Woodrow Wilson's inauguration in 1913.

> Americans will see this year for the first time moving pictures of the administration of the oath of the President of the United States. The strict rules which have hitherto limited occupation of the "battery stand" facing the inaugural platform to photographers representing large newspapers were suspended by the Congressional Inaugural Committee, and an addition was built at each end of the platform to accommodate operators from eight motion picture concerns.

That same year a photoplayer dared, for the first time, to appear in person before the public. Handsome Francis X. Bushman defied the current wisdom which said that the public would feel let down if it saw a star in the flesh. "When photoplayers appear in the same old way as stage actors, I think the average person feels a great disappointment," said the vice president of Vitagraph, the hugely successful Brooklyn-based production company. "One of the keynotes of the success of the film stars with the picture-loving public is the element of remoteness. They are mysterious abnormal personages."

Francis X. Bushman went on a lecture tour. He could do what he wanted not only because he was the highest-paid screen lover at the time, $750 a week, and was voted by the readers of *Ladies World* magazine as the man who most approximated a "typical American hero," but also because he was working for himself. His studio, Quality Pictures, was in New York. After his tour, Bushman reported that he could not have been received in a more gracious, hearty, and enthusiastic manner if he had been a royal prince.

Florence Turner, a great star of the day, quit the Vitagraph Company and formed Turner Films. The first thing she did was to go out and meet her public. She was an actress and needed to hear applause. She was suprised to find how knowledgeable people were about the film industry and how eager they were to meet her.

> Neither Lent nor the depressing influence of a big clothing strike, she reported from Rochester, New York, served to diminish the size of the audiences. I played to capacity. The programs they offer here, all for five cents, are astonishing. On the bill with me were a singer and a family of eight musicians. In addition to vaudeville attractions, four licensed pictures are shown, three first-runs and one of the previous day.

In April of that year *Quo Vadis?* was imported from Italy and opened at the Astor Theater on Broadway, a legitimate house where motion pictures had never before been shown. This story of the life of Nero, filmed in Rome with three thousand Italian and French actors and produced by an Italian company, had nine thousand feet of film on eight reels. *Quo Vadis?* startled the amusement world by playing a run of twenty-two weeks on Broadway.

The promoter of the film, William E. Raynor, sent *Quo Vadis?* traveling from town to town, from legitimate theater to opera house, as a regular theatrical attraction, carrying complete equipment with advance agents and billing similar to the method used in the legitimate theatre. The profits were tremendous.

Marcus Loew took cameras to the Polo Grounds and photographed the 1913 World Series, Giants vs. Athletics. Audiences saw the game three hours later in Loew's nineteen theaters.

Sound pictures were introduced that same year. Thomas Edison's latest invention, the Kinetophone, was introduced in New York at four Keith Theaters. "New York Applauds the Talking Picture," the *New York Times* reported in 1913. "Only Drawback is When the Talk Falls Behind the Picture." There was no story to this talking film, it was just a display of synchronizing sound to picture. A man appeared on the screen in a drawing-room setting and talked enthusiastically about Edison's invention. As his lips moved the words sounded from a big machine behind the screen. He broke a plate, blew a whistle, and dropped a weight. Then he brought on a pianist, violinist, and soprano, who performed "The Last Rose of Summer." Finally, the scope of kinetophonic powers was further illustrated by a bugler's efforts and the barking of some collies.

New York soon tired of talking pictures because they were so imperfect. "The talking picture film has been forced upon vaudeville audiences in New York for several weeks," reported *Variety*, "excepting at Hammerstein's. This house, not exhibiting them at all, has been doing the biggest business of any variety theater in town."

But Haverhill welcomed the new invention. William Furber got the exclusive rights in Haverhill to show talking pictures. Hundreds of people went to the Cozy Nickel. From the first show until the last the house was crowded.

Some say that Louie, tired of being tied to his Colonial Theater, asked William Furber to manage it for him. Furber was the sort of ambitious manager Louie needed. But William Furber had no desire to leave the Nickel. He loved it as much as Louie loved his theater.

No one has ever explained what started the fire at the Cozy Nickel. Haverhill fire horses galloped through the streets, buckets clattering on the wagon behind them, but they were too late. The theater burned to the ground.

Louis B. Mayer announced that he was going to give up the management of the Colonial and that he had hired William Furber to take over for him. William Furber claimed, when interviewed by local reporters, that he had always wanted to manage a big theater like the Colonial. "The financial interests controlling the theater have assured me that I will have their support in presenting as big and costly attractions as I demand, and, if the local public will rally to the support of the house by an increased patronage, my convictions will be verified. If bigger and better attractions than ever before will spell success in my new venture, it is already mine."

Louie now spent his days in Boston, where B.F. Keith, Nathan Gordon, and other theater men were buying legitimate houses to convert to picture houses. It surprised everyone that audiences were willing to pay top dollar for just a movie, even if it was a long one. Movie patrons began to rank theaters according to size and quality. They were willing to pay more just to sit in luxurious surroundings. The same picture that cost ten cents to see in Max Slavit's Majestic Theater in Haverhill cost fifty cents to a dollar to see in Nathan Gordon's rococo Olympia Theater in Boston's Scollay Square.

On Broadway, Mitchell Mark built an elegant three-thousand-seat theater designed specifically for showing pictures. The Mark Strand at Forty-Seventh Street was the first theater built from the ground up for the purpose of showing only films. There were no live acts, except that musicians did play for patrons when they strolled on the mezzanine during intermission. At the gala opening an audience of celebrities wearing formal attire watched *The Spoilers,* a nine-reel adventure story about the Alaskan gold rush, presented in three acts with a prologue.

The film, based upon a 1906 novel by Rex Beach and produced by Colonel William N. Selig for his Selig Polyscope

Company, marked the first time that an author received a cut of the box-office take. Rex Beach demanded $2,500 for his story, but Selig refused to pay that much. Instead he offered Beach a royalty arrangement which proved to be much more profitable to the author. *The Spoilers,* besides bringing fame and fortune to its star, William Farnum, who had never appeared in a motion picture before, was the first picture to show a violent fistfight. Screen fights had been limited to short scuffles, a few punches and some shoves, but the fight in *The Spoilers* was prolonged and caused a sensation. The year was 1914, and directors did not yet know about breakaway furniture, actors' doubles, quick editing, and other elements of deception. William Farnum and his rival, Tom Santschi, really did fight, and the audience could see that it was authentic.

Marcus Loew watched three thousand people pack into the Mark Strand Theater on Broadway and wondered what to do. His first interest was vaudeville, not pictures. If he started showing long pictures the vaudeville schedule in his chain of theaters would be turned upside down. He truly did not believe that most people could absorb a long movie. He thought the average brain just wasn't capable of it. But when he saw all those people pouring into Mitchell Mark's theater day after day and night after night, he knew he had to do something. He made a deal with Charles Ebbets, who owned the then new Ebbets Field. They split the profits. Twenty-one thousand people went to the ball park on a June night, sat outside and saw a wild west show, tumblers, dancers, jugglers, and Thomas Ince's six-reel drama, *The Wrath of the Gods.* After that, Loew joined his colleagues and began to buy up legitimate houses to convert to movie theaters.

In 1914 the longest picture ever shown in America became a smash hit. Ten reels long and produced by an Italian company, *Cabiria* was considered good enough to be shown at the White House. Woodrow Wilson, his family, and members of his cabinet watched *Cabiria* as music, especially composed for the occasion, accompanied the moving pictures of Rome burning and Nero fiddling. It was a sign of the times that an Italian picture was the first one presented at the White House. No American picture was yet worthy of that honor.

European filmmakers were much more sophisticated than American producers. While Europeans had once enjoyed American pictures, now they found them tedious. They were always chase pictures, or childhood sweetheart pictures, in which some young girl with long curls was put upon, or westerns, Indian films, and comedies in which some poor fool got into a mess of circumstances (water, mud, dogs, runaway motor cars) then continued his contortions across the screen ad nauseam. Now Europeans were demanding Italian feature films about love and passion, French films about the "eternal triangle," and English productions of old classics. The world began to turn its back on American motion pictures.

But many American producers and distributors still believed short films were the best. One exchange man, Jules Burnstein, proclaimed in the New York *Daily Mirror*, "The backbone of the moving picture industry is the single-reel picture, and I believe that it will continue to be so for many years to come. There is nothing startlingly original in this assertion; it is only the repetition of a great truth."

The same month that President Wilson sat on the White House lawn and watched *Cabiria*, Louie took the train to New York to attend the International Motion Picture Exposition at the Grand Central Palace. For four days more than a thousand exhibitors met to discuss the motion-picture business. They were entertained by photoplay stars, fed luncheons, and heard a lecture from a scientist about moving-picture screens. After the lecture a resolution was passed, much to Louie's amazement, in which the motion-picture exhibitors expressed their disapproval of the production of multi-reel pictures. Multi-reel pictures, they asserted, greatly depreciated the quality and artistic value of all films. William H. Wright, of the Kalem Company, stood up and said that brevity was the soul of a picture. The short photoplay was the model for success tomorrow, the next day, and the day after that. "One- and two-reel films can be improved," he said, "but dragging them into five or six reels isn't an improvement." Ignoring the declining market for American one-reel pictures abroad, he claimed that foreign buyers and the rank and file of exhibitors at home both looked askance at pictures that took an hour or an hour-and-a-half to run. Motion pictures were supposed to be like short stories, not novels.

The exhibitors at the convention resolved that, in order to maintain the artistic standard in moving pictures, producers should no longer manufacture films of various lengths for commercial purposes, but should reduce all long films to five hundred feet. A film that was any longer, they claimed, was full of unnecessary matter.

About twelve days after American exhibitors met together and showed their lack of foresight, the Archduke Francis Ferdinand, heir to the Austrian throne, and his wife were assassinated in Sarajevo. Germany declared war on Russia and France and invaded Belgium. Britain declared war on Germany; Austria declared war on Russia; Serbia and Montenegro declared war on Germany; Britain and France declared war on Austria; Russia declared war on Turkey and so did France and Britain.

Outside Louie's office window overlooking the Boston Common there was an antiwar demonstration organized by Samuel J. Elder, president of both the Boston Bar Association and the Massachusetts Peace Society, a man nicknamed "Dr. Sunshine" by the press. Ten thousand marchers gathered to hear Mr. Elder proclaim from a raised platform decorated with American flags, "The world will soon say 'lay down your arms.' Armaments must be limited and no longer be a menace to the peace and comfort and progress of the world."

The major address of the rally was given by Boston's Mayor Curley:

It is my opinion that the best and surest way to stop this war is for the American nation—North and South—to place an embargo on food products. No man can be a good soldier with an empty haversack. As Napoleon put it, the "army travels on its belly." Sooner or later wheat will be more valuable to our friends across the sea than cannon. If you should ask my advice, it would be that we adopt resolutions today favoring the appointment of a commission to work with President Wilson and Secretary of State Bryan to bring together the presidents of the South American republics in an agreement to establish an absolute embargo on every necessary of life while the war continues.

One of the consequences of the fighting abroad was that motion-picture production came to a standstill in Europe. America's steady supply of feature-length motion pictures dried up. Film studios in France, England, and Germany, once full of scenery and cameras, were now stocked with ammunition and weapons. European actors wore uniforms instead of costumes. There were bloody bodies lying on fields where there had once been fairy-tale scenery.

Theater men in America who had invested in grand movie palaces now found themselves with no product to show. In order to keep their expensive buildings operating, they were forced to charge high prices at the box office. Patrons began to complain. They were paying top dollar for slapstick comedies, one-reel westerns, and short dramas. Exhibitors began to beg American manufacturers to produce feature-length pictures. European theater owners begged Americans to produce pictures with some substance because, war or no war, Europeans still went to the movies, and product was needed.

THREE

America Goes Multi-Reel

W HO KNOWS if the American film industry would ever have taken the lead from Europe if it were not for World War I? Europeans understood that motion pictures were a new art form long before Americans did. Had events allowed them to proceed uninterrupted, it is likely America would never have caught up. The absence of European movies and the pressure exerted on American producers were the spurs needed to urge American film men to take some chances.

Always ready to do just that was William Fox, the man most responsible for shaping the American film industry. He is remembered today in an offhand way, as the "Fox" part of Twentieth Century-Fox and as the man for whom the Fox Television Network was named. He scorned personal publicity and presented himself in such an acerbic way that reporters were not attracted to him. It is a perfect example of the power of personality that Louis B. Mayer became more famous than

William Fox. "William Fox?" recalled Martin Quigley, Jr., the former publisher of the *Motion Picture Herald,* "He was the one no one liked."

The eldest of thirteen children, only six of whom survived their infancy, Fox left school at age eleven to help support his family by working in a sweatshop. From the moment he launched his theater business, around 1904, when in his mid-twenties, William Fox was innovative. He was the first nickelodeon owner to use song slides.

In those days before radio, the songwriters of Tin Pan Alley sent "pluggers," usually young men, to music halls to sing new songs. If people liked the song they would buy the sheet music. Irving Berlin, as a boy, plugged the songs of the Harry von Tilzer firm from a seat at Tony Pastor's Music Hall, but other boys sang wherever there was a piano. There was always one in the nickelodeons.

An electrician from Brooklyn invented a new way of plugging songs. He made up slides which dramatized the song pictorially and flashed the words of the lyric. A set of those slides was manufactured for a song, "The Little Lost Child," and the inventor went from nickelodeon to nickelodeon trying to interest theater owners. Only one exhibitor took a chance. William Fox used the slides in his Union Square motion-picture house. Now when the song plugger arrived, the audience could sing along. Fox's community sing so delighted his audience that more song slides were manufactured. Illustrating them became a new career for artists in New York. The slides were purchased by theater men far from Tin Pan Alley, who hired local talent to lead the sing-alongs. William Fox originated what became the standard nickelodeon program in the United States.

He next changed the industry when he sued the Motion Picture Patents Company and made it possible for independent film men to prosper.

When Europe went to war he opened a studio, on Staten Island, to make feature-length pictures. His first, *Life's Shop Window,* cost $4,500. The result, he thought, was pedestrian, but the public loved it, and he earned enough money to continue producing. In 1915 he changed the industry again by being the first film producer to create an entirely made-up personality for a movie actor. He invented the "star build-up."

Fox realized that the public went to pictures to see not stories or the work of particular directors but favorite players. Other producers believed that people went to the movies to see a story and that conveying the story depended more upon the director than the actors. There were no movie scripts back then. The director had a rough idea of the story and improvised as he went along. He told his players exactly where to move and what to say. An actor wrote in 1913:

> The difference between the regular stage and the moving picture rehearsal is that the stage manager, or author of the legitimate, reads his play to the company, after which the parts are handed out and a rehearsal takes place. Business of the piece is written in. This goes on until the actors are conversant with their lines, then parts are discarded, and the real acting takes place; for it is impossible to feel a part until such time that one is dead-letter perfect. The moving picture rehearsals are vastly different.
>
> The director calls his company around him, and with scenario in hand calls the ladies and gentlemen by their names, first mentioning what the wordless play is. "Mr. _____, you are a lover. Miss _____, you are his affianced bride. Mrs. _____, you are the mother. Mr. _____, you are the father. Mr. _____, you are a villain" and so on. Thus the different scenes are rehearsed without parts, the director explaining the business, and, as the playlet proceeds, he elaborates and builds up situations and sensations that the author never dreamed of.

Producers believed that any player given good material and a competent director would please an audience. Films were the result of teamwork, so there was no reason to emblazon an actor's name.

The biggest name on motion-picture advertising banners was the name of the studio, even if the photograph on the banner was that of the star. Mary Pickford was advertised as the "Biograph Girl," Florence Turner as the "Vitagraph Girl." The dainty Anita Stewart, who became a major star at the age of sixteen, still did not have her name displayed on marquees after appearing for Vitagraph in more than twenty-one sold-out pictures. Audiences learned the names of their favorites by searching for them in the film credits.

When popular photoplayers began to make public appearances, producers realized the futility of keeping the players' names secret and cashed in on their value. Press agents were hired to feed the public's appetite for personal information. The idea of making up a bogus biography and phony character traits entered no one's mind, except William Fox's.

Having grown up in New York, he was well-acquainted with the ballyhoo of vaudeville impresarios who lied to the press for fun and the money there was in it. William Hammerstein, owner of the hugely successful Victoria Theater, had his own star, Gertrude Hoffman, arrested. Subsequent headlines said that she was warned by police to wear more clothes.

In 1914 William Fox acquired the screen rights to the stage play, *A Fool There Was*, about a woman who had such powerful sex appeal she could ruin happy marriages and change self-reliant businessmen into spineless weaklings. The play was loosely based on Rudyard Kipling's poem, "The Vampire:"

A fool there was and he made his prayer
(Even as you and I!)
To a rag and a bone and a hank of hair
(We called her the woman who did not care)
But the fool he called her his lady fair
(Even as you and I!)

Fox decided to follow the lead of vaudeville producers. If Willie Hammerstein could invent a personage known as "Abdul Kadar, Court Artist of the Turkish Sultan," who arrived in New York with "three wives," really one wife and two grown daughters, who all sank to their knees and prayed to Allah when reporters asked them questions, then Fox could invent a vamp, a woman so mysterious and bad the whole world would rush to see her.

Fox found his vamp in Cincinnati, Ohio, a tailor's daughter. She had had some acting experience in stock. Fox changed Theodosia Goodman's name to Theda Bara, and she achieved world fame as the woman whose appeal was irresistible.

Fox told the press that Theda Bara, born on the sands of the Sahara, was the daughter of a French artist and an Arabian mistress. She was foreign so she couldn't help being wicked. Theda Bara drove to press conferences in a snow-white limousine attended by "Nubian" servants. The room where she received reporters was dimly lit, draped in velvet, and perfumed with incense. Reclining in gossamer clothes, surrounded by human skulls and crystal balls, and speaking in hushed tones, the tailor's daughter, who was, in fact, a simple, good-hearted girl who winced when married women sent her angry letters, told of her exotic childhood along the Nile and her triumphs on the stage in Paris. Reporters whispered their questions to her. The money poured in. Theda Bara made about forty vamp pictures for Fox. At a time when other producers were still debating whether or not to feature the names of their photoplayers and thought it generous to give them $150 a week, William Fox was paying Theda Bara $4,000 a week.

*   *   *

At the time that war broke out overseas, Adolph Zukor and Jesse Lasky were already producing multi-reel pictures. As orders for them escalated, they realized they could make more money if they distributed their own films. The *New York Times* reported:

> The Famous Players Film Company and Jesse L. Lasky Feature Play Company and Bosworth, Inc., three well-

known moving picture producers, have formed a new corporation to be known as The Paramount Pictures Corp. for the distribution of the feature films manufactured by the three firms. The Bosworth concern produces film versions of Jack London's fiction works. The new Corp. will distribute 104 film productions a year. (May 21, 1914).

Mack Sennett was another producer who surged ahead because of the war. He had been an actor and director for Biograph Studio but left to found Keystone, a company that specialized in slapstick comedies. After his initial success with *Tillie's Punctured Romance*, a six-reel comedy starring Marie Dressler and the then unknown Charlie Chaplin, Mack Sennett told the press, "The day of multiple-reel comedies is just dawning. I believe that the public demand for the full evening's programme, represented by a successful comedy production, is just as great as it is for the dramas. I am pioneering the five- and six-reel comedy and will attempt to prove that there is a place near the top for such productions."

Klaw and Erlanger, legitimate stage producers, decided to enter the moving-picture field "on a large scale, producing films made from their successful plays" which would be shown in their circuit of theaters. "A corporation is about to be formed," the *New York Times* reported, "by Messrs. Klaw & Erlanger for the purpose of exploiting by means of moving pictures, the plays which these managers own and are interested in. The organization will be known as the Protective Amusement Company. . . ."

A film salesman working for Adolph Zukor quit to go into business for himself in 1914. Al Lichtman reasoned that, if several independent distributors got together and pooled their money, they could finance the production of feature-length films. They would have exclusive rights to sell the pictures they financed. Each man would have his own territory. The company would be called Alco Film Corporation, after Al.

Lichtman approached the distributor Louie Mayer of the

American Feature Film Company in Boston and asked if he wanted to buy into the new company. It would cost $40,000, and Louie would have exclusive rights to the New England territory. It seemed a good idea to Louie, but, while he was trying to raise the money, the Alco Film Corporation died in litigation.

But the idea of distributors pooling their money to make movies was so good that some of the men stayed together to start a new company, Metro Pictures Corporation. Metro hoped to acquire one new film per week, each film costing between $15,000 and $20,000. Executives of the new company put the following ad in "Moving Picture World" magazine:

> Responsible producers possessing or contemplating features of quality . . . desiring immediate marketing, wide distribution, through an organization composed of exchange men of acknowledged standing . . . submit their products to . . . 1465 Broadway.

Several independent producers signed contracts with Metro, including Francis X. Bushman. Mack Sennett's Keystone, which had already made thirty-five films with Charlie Chaplin, signed a contract to produce several comedies.

Louie in Boston needed someone to back him. He did not have the $40,000 required to become a part of Metro, but what he did have was the ability to convince anyone of anything. While he paced in his office figuring out how he'd handle this challenge, the greatest suffrage parade Massachusetts ever saw took place on the street below.

The sidewalks were crowded with well-wishers who waved yellow flags at the passing parade. Men and women dressed in historical costumes marched along carrying signs. A decorated float pulled by a motorized truck inched along the street carrying a woman dressed as Victory in a white satin robe and royal purple wings. A cavalry drill team with all the riders in uniforms pranced along with each rider carrying the yellow banner of the suffrage movement. Behind them were women dressed alike in business suits carrying a banner, "Newspaper Women of America Unite!" A contingent of marchers wearing caps and gowns carried a yellow banner, "College Women For Equal Suffrage." Several buildings and houses along the parade route were draped with yellow ribbons. Peddlers on the street sold "Votes for Women" badges.

The anti-suffrage people were also out in force waving red banners and taunting the marchers with red streamers. One woman carried a picket sign that said, "I am not afraid of the masculine woman, but I have grave fears for the woman who confuses the work of man and woman and attempts to do both." Birds flew to the horse manure left on the cobblestones, had a few pecks, then flew up in alarm when the next group, dozens of girls on black horses, vibrated the street. The girls, wearing riding clothes, carried a yellow banner, "Daughters for Equal Suffrage."

Alice Stone Blackwell, president of the Massachusetts Suffrage Association and the daughter of Lucy Stone, appeared at the parade. So did Helen Keller. She arrived in an open motor car seated next to her secretary, Pauline Thompson, and her teacher, Mrs. J.A. Macy. She carried a yellow balloon in one gloved hand and did not hear the speaker on the platform say, "We are honored today by the presence of one of the truly great women of America, a champion of women's suffrage, Miss Helen Keller." The crowd cheered. "Miss Keller wishes to thank the governor and the mayor for their support. She sends this message: Every soldier who was ever brought into the world came at the risk of some woman's life. Every soldier who today lies dead upon the battlefield of Europe is some mother's son. We have won the vote in ten states, and we will not rest until we win the vote here." The crowd went wild, but Miss Keller didn't know that until her teacher played a message on her hand. Then Helen Keller waved her yellow balloon.

* * *

The man Louie convinced to back him was Nathan Gordon,

who owned the largest chain of theaters in Boston. Gordon did not like the young Louie Mayer, thought him crude, but he believed him to be competent, and he wanted exclusive rights to Metro pictures for his theaters. Gordon invested in Louie and made him secretary of Metro Pictures, an odd office for a man who had so much trouble reading and writing.

As a young man Nathan Gordon came to America from Poland. At the time Louie contacted him, Gordon was already wealthy, living in a mansion with maids, chauffeur, and governess for his children. Two years after Metro was formed, Nathan Gordon became a founder of First National Exhibitors Circuit, a motion picture production and distribution company, which became a major force in the industry until Warners absorbed it in the twenties. Gordon's daughter recalled:

> He was a powerhouse, an impossible father and not a very good husband, but he was terribly, terribly intelligent. He never owned a house until he was sixty. He rented those huge places already furnished, and Mother would have to accommodate herself. My poor mother! She was very smart and knew how to run the house. We had the most elegant afternoon teas. One of the biggest houses was in Jamaica Plain. It had a bowling alley in the garage. And you know that painting by John Singer Sargent of the three young girls, *The Daughters of Edward D. Boit?* We lived in that house for a while. On either side of the girls are urns, and we lived with those urns. The misery of my mother worrying about those damn urns!

Nathan Gordon and Louis B. Mayer formed the Gordon-Mayer Theatrical Company, which booked talent for Gordon's theaters and distributed Metro's pictures. Metro's first were *Satan Sanderson, The Heart of a Painted Woman, Shadows of a Great City, The Song of a Wage Slave,* and *An Enemy to Society.* They must have been pretty good because Metro made enough to invest in more pictures.

Nathan Gordon was married to a kindhearted, determined woman to whom he felt superior. "She was terrified of him," their daughter said. "They didn't see eye-to-eye on anything. He read and read, went to museums, knew about art and music. He was an intellectual. He was an anti-Zionist from the word go. He was miscast. He wished he'd been a Cabot or a Lowell. When Mother's family came to visit, he went fishing."

Sally Gordon was a registered nurse and had run away from home as a teenager so she could go to nursing school, an unusual thing for an Orthodox Jewish girl to do. As the wife of a wealthy man, she was continually contacted by fundraisers. It was pointed out to her, in 1911, that the Jewish immigrants who were flooding into the port of Boston were at a terrible disadvantage when they became sick. They had to go to the large Boston hospitals, Massachusetts General, Carney, and St. Elizabeth's, where the doctors and nurses did not speak Yiddish, and the food was not kosher.

> The poor Jew surrounded by strangers whose food he hesitates to eat, whose language he does not understand, who, with all the willingness in the world, cannot really sympathize with him, is suffering more than the normal misery that the ordinary sick person [suffers]. He, therefore, rushes at the suggestion that he can leave the hospital before he is cured, and the results are that incidental sickness is readily turned into chronic invalidism.
> —From *First a Dream*, Arthur Linenthal, M.D.

Sally Gordon kept one of her kitchens kosher, though her husband thought such customs ridiculous. When it was suggested to her that Boston needed a Jewish hospital, she agreed. Mt. Sinai had existed in New York City since 1852. Together with other wealthy Boston women and several doctors, she founded the Beth Israel Hospital Organization in 1911 and pressured her husband and his friends until they contributed. She shamed them by pointing out that the three large hospitals in Boston were supported by private Catholic and Baptist charities. While Jews used the hospitals they did not contribute to those charities. The argument was persuasive, and soon there were 231 charter members of the Beth racial particularity at the altar of a superior American identity, substituting the terms of one strain of nationalism for the priorities of another.

By this common ritual of national identity, for instance, the Irish, Poles, Italians, and Jews have been absorbed into a universal image of common citizenship. But the transformation of black cultural identity is often poorly served by this process, impeded as much by the external pressures of racism and class prejudice as by internal racial resistance to an "inclusion" that would rob blacks of whatever power and privilege they already enjoy in their own domains.

As further testimony to the contemporary black quest for a secure racial identity, gusts of racial pride sweep across black America as scholars retrieve the lost treasures of an unjustly degraded African past. This quest continues a project of racial reclamation begun in earnest in the nineteenth century, but recast to fit the needs of end-of-the-century utopian nationalists, including followers of Louis Farrakhan and Leonard Jeffries, and proponents of certain versions of Afrocentrism.[18]

Louis Farrakhan has caused a firestorm of controversial reaction to his anti-Semitism and to his support of the content of racist, sexist, and homophobic remarks made by former aide Khalid Abdul Muhammad at an infamous speech at Kean College in 1993. Leonard Jeffries has gained wide attention because of his allegedly anti-Semitic remarks about Jews' financing of the slave trade and his allegedly bigoted beliefs that Italians and Jews had collaborated in Hollywood to stereotype and denigrate blacks.[19] Both Farrakhan and Jeffries are beloved and celebrated among many blacks, however, because they speak their truth to the white powers-that-be without fear of punishment or retaliation. And the Afrocentric movement has quickened the debate about multicultural education and cast a searching light on the intellectual blindness and racist claims of Eurocentric scholars, even as it avoids acknowledging the romantic features of its own household.[20]

Malcolm's unabashed love for black history, his relentless pedagogy of racial redemption through cultural consciousness and racial self-awareness, mesh effortlessly with black Americans' (especially black youths') recovery of their African roots. As rapper KRS-One summarized a crucial feature of Malcolm's legacy, black children will "come to know that they come from a long race and line of kings, queens and warriors," a knowledge that will make them "have a better feeling of themselves."[21]

Perhaps above all other facets of Malcolm's heroic stature is his unfettered championing of the politics of black masculinity (a theme I will pursue more fully in the next chapter). Few other aspects of Malcolm's rejuvenated appeal have been as prominently invoked as Malcolm's focus on the plight and place of black men in American society. In light of the contemporary cultural status of black men, particularly young black males, it is easy to comprehend his heroic status as a defender of black men.

Although established black males like Bill Cosby, Michael Jordan, and Bryant Gumbel enjoy enormous success and broad acceptance because of their superior talent and clean-cut images, young black male hard-core rappers such as Dr. Dre, Tupac Shakur, and Snoop Doggy Dogg continue to face sharp criticism because of their "vulgar" language, their toughened images, and their run-ins with the law. Moreover, young black male rappers are obsessed with the terms and tensions of black manhood, often employing women and gays as rhetorical foils in exploring what they think is authentic masculinity.

Too often, though, a crude reductionism on the part of its critics hampers a truly insightful engagement with gangsta' rap. Like any art form, gangsta' rap allows the creation of a musical persona, an artistic convention honored in opera and even the Tin Pan Alley gangsterism of Frank Sinatra. This convention has been observed in many antecedent black oral traditions, from the long, narrative poems known as toasts to the explicitly vulgar lyrics of Jelly Roll Morton (whose music, by the way, is stored in the Library of Congress) and the ribald and rambunctious reflections of many blues artists.

The wide distribution of recorded music has allowed technological eavesdropping on what formerly were tightly contained communities of vulgar discourse circulated within secular black gatherings. (Note, too, Chaucer's *Canterbury Tales* are strewn with the day's vulgarities; might this mean Snoop Doggy Dogg's "What's My Name" will be read with great reverence, with an eye to imitation, in American classrooms in a couple of centuries?!) These oral traditions, rife with signifying practices, symbolic distortions, and lewd language, must be kept in mind in comprehending and justly criticizing the troubled quest for an enabling black masculinity expressed in much of gangsta' rap.

In this light, the recent attacks on gangsta' rap as fatally misogynistic and deeply sexist by prominent black women like political activist C. Delores Tucker and entertainer Dionne Warwick must be qualified considerably.[22] Gangsta' rap is neither the primary source nor the most nefarious expression of sexism or misogyny, in either society at large or black communities in particular. That honor belongs to cherished branches of our national culture, including the nuclear family, religious communities, and the educational institutions of our society. Black bourgeois civic life, religious communities, and educational institutions have certainly not been immune. These cultural centers that reflect and spread sexist and misogynist mythology—especially the black church, black civil rights organizations, and the black family—much more effectively influence black cultural understandings of gender than does gangsta' rap.

Also, most attacks on gangsta' rap not only continue the widespread demonization of black male youth culture— its alleged out-of-control sexuality, pathological criminality, and sadistic preoccupation with violence—but conceal an attack on black women. Accompanying the wails and whispers of complaint aimed at black males throughout the United States are the detrimental accusations that black males are shaped as they are by black women in single-parent, female-headed households; by welfare queens; or, in the vicious logic that Tucker and Warwick are right to point to, by black mothers who are the bitches and ho's named in many rap lyrics. But Tucker and Warwick often miss the larger point about how their conservative allies in their struggle against gangsta' rap have similarly, but more subtly, demonized black women. (And besides, like most critics, Tucker and Warwick don't mention the homophobia of gangsta' rap; is it because like many mainstream critics, they are not disturbed by sentiments they hold in common with gangsta' rappers?)

The most just manner of criticizing gangsta' rap is by juxtaposing salient features of black culture—such as moral criticism, sage advice, and common-sense admonitions against out-of-bounds behavior—with a ready appreciation of black oral practices like signifying and distorting. By doing this, we can powerfully criticize gangsta' rap for its faults while skillfully avoiding the move of collapsing and corresponding rhetoric and art to reality. Also, we can criticize the conceptions of black masculinity that are prevalent in hip-hop culture without making rappers the scapegoats for all that is seriously wrong with gender in our culture. In the process, we might more clearly see and name the real culprits.

The difficult personal and social conditions of most young black males make Malcolm's rhetoric about the obstacles to true black manhood and the virtues of a strong black masculinity doubly attractive. Indeed, blacks from the very beginning of Malcolm's career have accented his focus on a virile black manhood denied them because of white racism as a primary contribution of his vocation.[23] As Ossie Davis stated in his beautiful eulogy at Malcolm's funeral, "Malcolm was our manhood! This was his meaning to his people."[24] From gang members to preachers, from college students to black intellectuals, Malcolm's focus on black men has made him a critical spokesman for unjustly aggrieved black males plagued by sexual jealousy and social fear.

But if the reemergence of black nationalism and Malcolm's explosive popularity go hand in hand—are duplicate images of response to the continuing plague of an equally rejuvenated racism—then not only their strengths, but also their limitations are mutually revealing. In this regard, two aspects of Malcolm's legacy are striking: the troubling consequences of his focus on the black male predicament, and the ironic uses of black nationalist discourse by a black middle class often closed from nationalism's most desperate constituency—the black ghetto poor.

Malcolm's brand of black nationalism was not only a fierce attack on white Americans, but a sharp rebuke as well to black women. Malcolm went to extremes in demonizing women, saying that the "closest thing to a woman is a devil." Although he later amended his beliefs, confessing his regret at "spit[ting] acid at the sisters" and contending that they should be treated equally, many contemporary black nationalist advocates have failed to take his changed position on gender seriously. Malcolm, Patricia Hill Collins notes, died "before Black feminist politics were articulated in the 1970s and 1980s," but his

> Black nationalism projects an implicit and highly prob-
> lematic gender analysis. Given today's understanding
> of the gender-specific structures of Black oppression
> . . . his ideas about gender may be interpreted in ways
> detrimental not only to both African-American women
> and men but to policies of Black community develop-
> ment. . . . Malcolm X's treatment of gender reflected
> the widespread belief of his time that, like race, men's
> and women's roles were "natural" and were rooted in
> biological difference.[25]

Like the early Malcolm and other 1960s nationalists, contemporary black nationalists have defined the quest for emancipation in largely masculine terms. Such a strategy not only borrows ideological capital from the white patriarchy that has historically demeaned black America, but blunts awareness of how the practice of patriarchy by black men has created another class of victims within black communities.

Further, the strategy of viewing racial oppression exclusively through a male lens distorts the suffering of black women at the hands of white society and blurs the focus on the especially difficult choices that befall black women caught in a sometimes bewildering nexus of kinship groups assembled around race, class, and gender. Reducing black suffering to its lowest common male denominator not only presumes a hierarchy of pain that removes priority from black female struggle, but also trivializes the analysis and actions of black women in the quest for black liberation. Given Malcolm's mature pronouncements, his heirs have reneged on the virtues of his enlightened gender beliefs. It is these heirs, particularly young black filmmakers, whose artistic meditations on black masculinity I will explore in the next chapter.

The cultural renaissance of Malcolm X also embodies the paradoxical nature of black nationalist politics over the past two decades: those most aided by its successes have rarely stuck around to witness the misery of those most hurt by its failures. The truth is that black nationalist rhetoric has helped an expanding black middle class gain increased material comfort, while black nationalism's most desperate constituency, the working class and working poor, continues to toil in the aftermath of nationalism's unrealized political promise.

Ironically, talk of black cultural solidarity and racial loyalty has propelled the careers of intellectuals, cultural artists, and politicians as they seek access to institutions of power and ranks of privilege, even within black communities, as esteemed vox populi. The trouble is they are often cut off from the very people on whose behalf they ostensibly speak, the perks and rewards of success insulating them from the misery of their constituencies.

The greatest irony of contemporary black nationalism may be its use by members of the black middle class—for instance, black intellectuals and artists thoroughly insulated in niches of protection within the academy—to consolidate their class interests *at the expense* of working-class and poor blacks. By refusing to take class seriously—or only half-heartedly as they decry, without irony, the moves of a self-serving black bourgeoisie—many nationalists discard a crucial analytical tool in exploring the causes of black racial and economic suffering. If Malcolm's brand of black nationalism is to have an even more substantive impact on contemporary racial politics, his heirs must relentlessly criticize his limitations while celebrating his heroic embrace of issues, like class and opposing white nationalism, long denied currency in mainstream social thought.

This is not to suggest that nationalism's vaunted alternative, bourgeois liberal integrationism, has enjoyed wide success, either, in bringing the black masses within striking distance of prosperity, or at least to parity with white middle and working classes. Commentators usually gloss over this fact when comparing the legacies of Malcolm X and Martin Luther King, Jr. For the most part, Malcolm and Martin have come to symbolize the parting of paths in black America over the best answer to racial domination. Although Malcolm's strident rhetoric is keyed in by nationalists at the appropriate moments of black disgust with the pace and point of integration, King's conciliatory gestures are evoked by integrationists as the standard of striving for the promised land of racial harmony and economic equity.

In truth, however, King's admirers have also forsaken the bitter lessons of his mature career in deference to the soaring optimism of his dream years.[26] King discerned as early as 1965 that the fundamental problems of black America were economic in nature and that a shift in strategies was necessary for the civil rights movement to become a movement for economic equality. After witnessing wasted human capital in the slums of Watts and Chicago, and after touring the rural wreckage of life in the Mississippi Delta, King became convinced that the only solution to black suffering was to understand it in relation to a capitalist economy that hurt all poor people. He determined that nothing short of a wholesale criticism and overhaul of existing economic arrangements could effectively remedy the predicament of the black poor and working class.

This is a far cry from contemporary black capitalist and business strategies that attempt to address the economic plight of black Americans by creating more black millionaires. Highly paid entertainers and athletes participate in the lucrative culture of consumption by selling their talents to the highest bidder in the marketplace—a legacy, we are often reminded, of King's and the civil rights movement's vision of a just society where social goods are distributed according to merit, not color. King's willingness, toward the end of his life, to question the legitimacy of the present economic order and to challenge the logic of capitalism has been obscured by appeals to his early beliefs about the virtues of integration.

The relative failure of both black nationalist and integrationist strategies to affect large numbers of black Americans beyond the middle and upper classes raises questions about how we can expand Malcolm's and Martin's legacies to address the present crises in black America. What is the answer? I believe the best route for remedy can be found in a new progressive black politics anchored in radical democracy.[27]

Black progressive intellectuals and activists must view class, gender, and sex as crucial components of a complex and insightful explanation of the problems of black America.[28] Such an approach provides a larger range of social and cultural variables from which to choose in depicting the vast array of forces that constrain black economic, political, and social progress. It also acknowledges the radical diversity of experiences within black communities, offering a more realistic possibility of addressing the particular needs of a wide range of blacks: the ghetto poor, gays and lesbians, single black females, working mothers, underemployed black men, and elderly blacks, for instance.

Black progressives must also deepen Malcolm's and Martin's criticisms of capitalism and their leanings toward radical democracy. The prevailing economic policies have contributed to the persistent poverty of the poorest Americans (including great numbers of blacks) and the relative inability of most Americans to reap the real rewards of political democracy and economic empowerment. A radical democratic perspective raises questions about the accountability of the disproportionately wealthy, providing a critical platform for criticizing black capitalist and business strategies that merely replicate unjust economic practices.

A radical democratic perspective—which criticizes capital accumulation and the maximization of profit for the few without regard to its effects on the many, advocates an equitable redistribution of wealth through progressive taxation and the increased financial responsibility of the truly wealthy, and promotes the restructuring of social opportunities for the neediest through public policy and direct political intervention—also encourages the adoption of political and social policies that benefit all Americans, while addressing the specific needs of h'   is universal health care.

At present, black A·   • gly rep-resented among the   r nation. A radical democratⁱ   ..ion that pays over $820 biⁱⁱ   .ent ot the GNP, for the well-insured caʳ   ,ιstribute its wealth through a progressive tax on thc .   ithiest 2 percent (and a fair tax on the top 50 percent) to help provide the $50 or $60 billion more needed to provide universal health coverage.[29] By refusing to take class seriously, many black nationalists undermine their ability to completely explain and understand racial and economic suffering.

The quest for black racial and economic justice has been heavily influenced by black religious conceptions of justice, charity, equality, and freedom. During the civil rights move-ment, King articulated black Christian conceptions of justice through the language of human rights and the political lan-guage of civil religion. Likewise, Malcolm X expressed his conceptions of divine retribution for racial injustice, and the religious basis for healthy self-esteem through black Islamic, and later orthodox Islamic, belief that accorded with black secular ideas about racial self-determination and cultural pride. A radical democratic perspective encourages the broad expression of conceptions of justice, equality, and po-litical freedom that are tempered by regard for the widest possible audience of intellectual interlocutors and political participants, including those trained in the rich traditions of black social protest.

Finally, black progressives must make sensible but forceful criticisms of narrow visions of black racial identity, especially after the Clarence Thomas–Anita Hill debacle. That wrenching drama provided a glimpse of the underdeveloped state of gender analysis in most black communities and provoked a serious reconsideration of the politics of racial unity and loyalty.[30] In reflecting on Thomas's nomination to the Supreme Court, black Americans were torn between fidelity to principles of fairness and justice. Many blacks agonized over his qualifications for office and troubled over whether blacks should support one of their own, despite his opposition to many of the legal principles cherished by black communities.

The introduction of Hill's perspective into this already complex calculus ripped open ancient antagonisms between black women and men. The Hill–Thomas affair also affirmed the need for black progressives to pay special attention to the roots of sexism and misogyny in our communities, instead of hitting easy targets like gangsta' rappers. Black progressives must address the pitiful state of gender relations reflected in the lyrics of hip-hop culture, while also addressing the pernicious consequences of the economic misery and social collapse in which they live.

Malcolm X and the Resurgence of Black Nationalism

In a public and painful manner, the hearings forced many black Americans to a new awareness of the need to place principles of justice above automatic appeals to race loyalty premised exclusively on skin color. Many Americans, including many blacks, came to a clearer understanding of the idea of the "social construction of racial identity" (which argues that race extends beyond biology to include psychological, cultural, and ideological factors), recognizing that black folk are by no means a homogeneous group. The differences that factors such as geography, sexual preference, gender, and class make in the lives of black Americans are too complex to be captured in a monolithic model of racial unity.[31] Progressive blacks share more ideological and political ground with white progressives such as Barbara Ehrenreich and Stanley Aronowitz, for instance, than they do with conservatives of the ilk of Clarence Thomas, or even Anita Hill.

For black leaders, the political and social significance of this fact should further the building of bridges across the chasm of color in the common embrace of ideals that transcend racial rooting. Progressive blacks must join with progressive Latinas and Latinos, gays and lesbians, feminists, environmental activists, and all others who profess and practice personal and social equality and radical democracy. The relative absence of sustained progressive black political opposition, or even a radical political organization that expresses the views of the working class and working poor, signals a loss of the political courage and nerve in the United States that characterized Malcolm and Martin at their best.[32]

In the end, Malcolm and Martin are in varying degrees captives of their true believers, trapped by literal interpreters who refuse to let them, in Malcolm's words, "turn the corner." The bulk of each man's achievements lay in his willingness to constantly consider and employ new tactics in chiseling the best route to social reconstruction and racial redemption. Their legacy to us is the imagination and energy to pursue the goals of liberation on as wide a scale as the complex nature of our contemporary crises demand and our talents allow.

One segment of black cultural artists in particular— young black filmmakers—have fashioned intriguing and often troubling responses to the issues of thwarted liberation that Malcolm X so boldly raised, especially as they engage the politics of black masculinity and understandings of the ghetto. It is the accomplishments of these artists that I will now explore in seeking to gauge Malcolm X's impact on their lives, most powerfully and painfully in their obsessions with what it means to be a black male in racist white America.

4
IN MALCOLM'S SHADOW: MASCULINITY AND THE GHETTO IN BLACK FILM

> I'm the man you think you are. And if it doesn't take
> legislation to make you a man and get your rights rec-
> ognized, don't even talk that legislative talk to me. No,
> if we're both human beings we'll both do the same
> thing. And if you want to know what I'll do, figure out
> what you'll do. I'll do the same thing—only more of
> it.
>
> Malcolm X, in *Malcolm X Speaks: Selected Speeches
> and Statements*

The emergence of contemporary black cinema and hip-hop culture marks the wide influence of black popular culture on American life.[1] The work of contemporary black filmmakers embodies the important effort to portray the complexities and particularities of black life. Through the images, symbols, and themes it explores, the new black cinema promises artistic visions of black life that shatter the troubled zone of narrow white interpretations of black culture.

Several recent black films investigate the politics of black masculinity and its relationship to the ghetto culture in which ideals of manhood are nurtured. Debates about masculinity abound in black communities, driven by a need for blacks to understand and address the often tragic circumstances—from high percentages of infant mortality and AIDS infection to staggering rates of imprisonment—that plague black boys and men.[2] Because of the strong link in Malcolm's thought between loyalty to the race and the responsible representation of a disciplined, dignified manhood, he presaged—and continues to influence—the work of contemporary black filmmakers.

Indeed, without the sustained hero worship of Malcolm X, contemporary black cinema, often dubbed New Jack cinema or ghettocentric film, is almost inconceivable. By examining the work of contemporary black filmmakers—the themes they treat, the styles they adopt, the moods they evoke—I seek to gauge Malcolm's ongoing impact on a generation that has driven and seized on his heroic return. In this chapter, I will examine several films as examples of the failure or success in treating the relation between the ghetto and black manhood in powerful and productive ways.[3] In the process, I hope to characterize the manner in which these films engage or distort issues of black female identity.

In his 1991 debut film, *Straight Out of Brooklyn*, director Matty Rich desolately rejects the logic of liberal democracy:

that individuals can act to realize themselves and enhance their freedom through the organs of the community or the state. For the inhabitants of Brooklyn's Red Hook Housing Project, the possibilities of self-realization and freedom are severely reduced by the menacing ubiquity of the ghetto.

The suppressed premise of Rich's film is a rebuke to all pretensions that the ghetto is not a totalizing force, that it is possible to maintain the boundaries between geography and psychic health implied by the expression: live in the ghetto, but don't let the ghetto live in you. It is precisely in showing that the ghetto survives parasitically—that its limits are as small or as large as the bodies it inhabits and destroys—that *Straight Out of Brooklyn* achieves a distinct niche in black film while contributing to black popular culture's avid exploration of black urban (male) identities.

After disappearing from the intellectual gaze of the American academy and being obscured from mainstream cultural view by the successes of *nouveau riche* yuppies and the newly prominent black middle class, the ghetto has made a comeback at the scene of its defeat. The reinvention of American popular culture by young African-American cultural artists is fueled by paradox: now that they have escaped the fiercely maintained artistic ghetto that once suffocated the greatest achievements of their predecessors, black artists have reinvented the urban ghetto through a nationalist aesthetic strategy that joins racial naturalism and romantic imagination. That the most recent phase of black nationalism is cultural rather than political indicates how successfully mainstream politics has absorbed radical dissent, and betokens the hunger of black youth culture for the intellectual sources of its hypnotic remix of pride and anger.

Mostly anger, and little pride, stirs in the fragmented lives of teenager Dennis Brown (Lawrence Gilliard, Jr.); his younger sister, Carolyn (Barbara Sanon); and their parents, Frankie (Ann D. Sanders) and Ray (George T. Odom). Each of the family members is the prisoner of a personal and ecological misery so great that distinguishing its impact on their lives appears impossible.

The exception to their equally shaded misery is the extraordinarily acute condition of father and son. The black male predicament is first glimpsed in the cinematic chiaroscuro of Ray's descent into a Dantean hell of racial agony so absurd and grotesque that its bleakness is a sadistic comfort, a last stop before absurdity turns to insanity. Ray's gradual decline is suffered stoically by Frankie, a throwback to an earlier era when the black-woman-as-suffering-servant role was thrust on black women by black men, themselves forced to pay obeisance to white society. These same men, when they came home, expected to claim the rewards and privileges of masculinity denied them in the white world. Another model of female identity engaged by black women consisted of an equally punishing (and mythic) black matriarchy that both damned and praised them for an alleged strength of character absent in their feckless male counterparts. Thus the logic of black communities ran: as the black man's fate goes, so goes the fate of the family.

Straight Out of Brooklyn's narrative line ties generously into the fabric of this argument, its dramatic tension drawn from the furious catastrophes that sweep down on its black male characters, the defining center of the film's raw meditation on the angst of emasculation. Ray's frequent beatings of Frankie are rituals of self-destruction, her brutally bloodied countenance a sign of his will to redefine the shape of his agony by redefining the shape of her face.

Ray's suffering-as-emasculation is further sealed by his denial of desire for white women during a Lear-like verbal jousting with an imaginary white man, a deus ex machina produced by his search for an explanation of his suffering, and a dramatic ploy by Rich that ascribes black suffering to the omnipotent white bogeyman. And Dennis's soliloquies about his quest for money to reverse his family's collapse in the presence of his girlfriend, Shirley (Reana E. Drummond), underscores a deeper need to redeem black masculinity by displaying his virility, his desire to provide for his family allied disastrously with his gratuitous desires to "get paid."

A different tack is pursued, of course, in John Singleton's 1991 debut, *Boyz N the Hood.* Singleton's neorealist representation of the black working-class ghetto neighborhood provides a fluid background to his literate script, which condenses and recasts the debates on black manhood that have filled the black American independent press for the past decade.[4] Avoiding the heavy-handed approach of racial didacticism, Singleton instead traces the outline of the morality play in recognizable black cultural form. All the while, he keeps his film focused on The Message: black men must raise black boys if they are to become healthy black men. Thus Tre (Cuba Gooding, Jr.); his father, Furious (Laurence Fishburne); Ricky (Morris Chestnut); and Doughboy (Ice Cube), the four black males whose lives form the fabric of Singleton's narrative quilt, are the films's interpretive center. Reva (Angela Bassett), Brenda Baker (Tyra Ferrell), and Brandi (Nia Long), the mothers of Tre and of Ricky and Doughboy, and Tre's girlfriend, respectively, occupy the film's distant periphery.

As in most cultural responses to black male crisis, Singleton's film is an attempt to answer Marvin Gaye's plea to save the babies. He focuses his lens especially on the male baby that he and many others believe has been thrown out with the bathwater to float down the river, like Doughboy and one out of four black men, into the waiting hands of the prison warden.

Singleton's moral premise, like so many assertions of black male suffering, rests dangerously on the shoulders of a tragic racial triage: black male salvation at the expense of black female suffering, black male autonomy at the cost of black female subordination, black male dignity at the cost of black female infirmity. In jarring fashion, Singleton's film reveals the unintended but deadly alliance between black cultural nationalists and the cultured despisers of black women. His thinly veiled swipe at black women fuses easily with the arguments of conservative cultural commentators who bash poor and working-class black women as promiscuous welfare queens. Furious's brilliant presence as a redemptive and unswerving North Star and Brenda's uncertain orbit as a dim satellite are the telling contrast in Singleton's cinematic world.

Singleton's moral premise would seem outdated—the warmed-up leftovers of black macho posturing painfully evident in strains of 1960s black nationalism—were it not for its countless updates in black youth culture. Such sentiments are also expressed in rap lyrics, for instance, that denounce white racism while glorifying black males' sexual and material mastery of black women. Of course, the quest for black manhood is everywhere apparent in black culture—note its evocation as well in the upper climes of respectable bourgeois life as the implicit backdrop to Clarence Thomas's claim of betrayal by Anita Hill, his charge communicated in the racial code of his undertone: another *sister* pulling a *brother* down. But it is with the reemergence of the ghetto in popular culture and its prominence in a resurgent black nationalist cultural politics that lionizes Malcolm X that for better and worse the images of black masculinity find an intellectual home.

This circumstance is especially true of black film and rap music. The politics of cultural nationalism has reemerged precisely as the escalation of racist hostility has been redirected toward poor black people. Given the crisis of black bourgeois political leadership and a greater crisis of black liberal social imagination about the roots of black suffering, black nationalist politics becomes for many blacks the logical means of remedy and resistance. This explains in part the renewed popularity of Malcolm X, whose uncompromising focus on nationalist themes of unity and authentic blackness help secure his heroic niche in black youth culture. Viewed in this way, black film and rap music are the embodiment of a black populist aesthetic that prevents authentic blackness from being fatally diluted.

Rap music has grown from its origins in New York's inner city over a decade ago as a musical outlet for creative cultural energies and as a way to contest the invisibility of the ghetto in mainstream American society.[5] Rap remythologized New York's status as the spiritual center of black America, boldly asserting appropriation and collage as its primary artistic strategies. Rap developed as a relatively independent artistic expression of black male rebellion against a black bourgeois worldview, tapping instead into the cultural virtues and vices of the so-called underclass. Male rap artists romanticize the ghetto as the fertile root of cultural identity and racial authenticity, asserting that knowledge of ghetto styles and sensibilities provides a Rorschach test of legitimate masculinity.[6]

The styles and sensibilities encouraged in the hip-hop aesthetic have found expression in many recent black films. Mario Van Peebles's 1991 directoral debut, *New Jack City,* for instance, boils with the fusion of ghetto attitude and style that expresses a substantive politics of culture among young black males. As in *Boyz N the Hood* with Ice Cube (Doughboy) and *Juice* with Tupac Shakur (Bishop), *New Jack City* appeals directly to the ironic surplus of hip-hop culture by drawing on a main character, rapper Ice-T, to convey the film's thinly supplied and poorly argued moral message: crime doesn't pay.

Thus Ice-T's "new jack cop" is an inside joke, a hip-hop reconfiguration of the tales of terror Ice-T explodes on wax as a lethal pimp, dope dealer, and bitch hater. The adoption of the interchangeable persona of the criminal and "the law" in hip-hop culture is taken to its extreme with Ice-T's character. Although he appears as a cop in *New Jack City,* Ice-T on the soundtrack as a rapper detailing his exploits as a "gangsta'" blurs the moral distinctions between cops and robbers, criminalizing the redemptive intent of his film character (even more so retroactively in light of the subsequent controversy over his hit "Cop Killer," recorded with his speed metal band).

115

Van Peebles's cinematic choices in *New Jack City* reflect a mode of exaggerated cultural representation that characterizes many ghetto films of old. His ghetto is a sinister and languid dungeon of human filth and greed drawn equally from cartoon and camp. Its sheer artifice is meant to convey the inhuman consequences of living in this enclave of civic horror, but its overdrawn dimensions reveal a cinematic pedigree traced more easily to 1970s blaxploitation flicks than to neorealist portrayals of the ghetto in recent black films.

As a black gangster film, *New Jack City* reveals the Cagneyization of black ghetto life, the inexorable force of woman bashing and partner killing sweeping the hidden icon of the people to a visible position larger than life. Thus criminal Nino Brown (Wesley Snipes) reigns because he tests the limits of the American Dream, a Horatio Alger in blackface who pulls himself up by forging consensus among his peers that his life is a ghetto jeremiad, a strident protest against the unjust material limits imposed on black males. As Nino Brown intones with full awareness of the irony of his criminal vocation: "You got to rob to get rich in the Reagan era."

But it is the state of black male love that is the story's unnarrated plot, its twisted pursuit ironically and tragically trumped by boys seeking to become men by killing one another. Thus when a crying Nino clasps his teary-eyed closest friend and partner in crime, Gee-Money, on the top of the apartment building that provides the mise-en-scène for the proverbial ode to an empire destroyed by the fatal winds of undisciplined ambition, he avows his love even as he fills Gee-Money's belly with steel as recompense for disloyalty. It is the tough love of the gang in action, the logic of vengeance passing as justice in gang love's fulfillment of its unstated obligations.

The mostly black and Latino gang, of course, has also recaptured the focus of American social theory and journalism in the past decade. Urban sociologists such as New York's Terry Williams in *Cocaine Kids* and Los Angeles's Mike Davis in *City of Quartz* have written insightfully about the economic and social conditions that have led to the emergence of contemporary black and Latino gang culture.[7] And model turned journalist Leon Bing has interviewed Los Angeles gang members who speak eloquently about their own lives in words as moving for their emotional directness as their honesty about the need for affection and comfort that drives them together.[8] In *Straight Out of Brooklyn* and in Ernest Dickerson's *Juice,* the theme of black male love expressed in the ghetto gang looms large.

In *Straight Out of Brooklyn,* Rich presents a loosely associated group of three black male teens, Dennis, Kevin (Mark Malone), and Larry (played by Rich), who are frustrated by poverty and the stifling of opportunity that lack of money signifies. In *Juice,* the crushing consequences of capital's absence are more skillfully explored through the interactions between the characters (its damning effects as subtly evoked in the threads of anger, surrender, and regret weaved into the moral texture of the film's dialogue as they are dramatically revealed in the teens' action in the streets); in *Straight Out of Brooklyn,* money's power is more crudely symbolized in the material and sexual icons that dominate the landscape of desire expressed by Dennis and his friends: big cars, more money, and mo' ho's.

The lifelessness of the ghetto is represented in the very textu(r)al construction through which *Straight Out of Brooklyn* comes to us. Although it's in color, the film seems eerily black and white, its crude terms of representation established by its harsh video quality and its horizontal dialogue. Of course, the film's unavoidable amateur rawness is its premise of poignancy: after all, this is art imitating life, the vision of Matty Rich, a nineteen-year-old Brooklyn youth with little financial aid committing his life to film. This is the closest derivation in film of the guerrilla methods of hip-hop music culture, the sheer projection of will—onto an artistic canvas composed of the rudimentary elements of one's life—in the guise of vision and message. .

In *Straight Out of Brooklyn,* the trio of teens is not a roving, menacing crew engaging in the business of selling crack rock and duplicating capitalism's excesses on their native terrain. Rather, they are forced by desperation to momentary relief of their conditions by robbing a dope dealer, an impulse that is routinized in the crack gang, where rituals of gunplay and death feed on the lives of opponents out to seize their turf in the harrowing geopolitics of the drug economy.

The anomie produced by everyday acts of surrender to despair, and the spiraling violence of his father, Ray, force Dennis from his family to affectionate camaraderie with Larry and Kevin, and with Shirley. All other hints of family are absent, except Larry's barber uncle, who unwittingly provides the ill-named getaway car for their even more ill-fated heist. But the vacuum at home for Dennis is made more obvious by Ray's attempt to preserve the disappearing remnants of a "traditional" family: he angrily reminds Dennis after he misses dinner that his empty plate on the table symbolizes his membership in the family. But Rich shatters this icon into shards of ironic judgment on the nuclear family, as Ray breaks the dishes and beats Frankie each time he becomes drunk.

Dennis's only relief is Shirley and his crew. When Shirley disappoints him by refusing to buy into his logic about escape from the ghetto by robbery, he turns to his crew, who, in the final analysis, leave Dennis to his own wits when they agree that they have stolen too much cash ("killing money," Kevin says) from the local dope dealer, an act whose consequences roll back on Dennis in bitter irony when the heist leads to his father's death. The film's inescapably dismal conclusion is that black men cannot depend on one another, nor can they depend on their own dreams to find a way past mutual destruction.

In *Juice*, the crew is more tightly organized than in *Straight Out of Brooklyn*, though their activity, like that of the teens from Red Hook, is not regularized primarily for economic profit. Their salient function is as a surrogate family, their substitute kinship formed around their protection of one another from rival gangs, and the camaraderie and social support their association brings. But trouble penetrates the tightly webbed group when the gangster ambitions of Bishop threaten their equanimity. Of all the crew—leader Raheem, a teenage father; GQ, a DJ with ambitions to refine his craft; and Steel, a likable youth who is most notably "the follower"—Bishop is the one who wants to take them to the next level, to make them like the hard-core gangsters he watches on television.

Viewing Cagney's famed ending in *White Heat*, and a news bulletin announcing the death of an acquaintance as he attempted armed robbery, Bishop rises to proclaim Cagney's and their friend's oneness, lauding their commendable bravado by taking their fate into their own hands and remaking the world on their own violent terms. Dickerson's aim is transparent: to highlight the link between violence and criminality fostered in the collective American imagination by television, a medium whose images compete with the Constitution and the Declaration of Independence for supplying the unifying fictions of national citizenship and identity. Television is also the daily and exclusive occupation of Bishop's listless father, a reminder that its influence unfolds from its dulling effects in one generation to its creation of lethal desires in the next, twin strategies of destruction when applied in the black male ghetto.

Like the teens in *Straight Out of Brooklyn*, *Juice's* crew must endure the fatal consequences of their failed attempt at getting paid and living large, two oft-repeated mantras of material abundance in the lexicon of hip-hop culture. After Bishop's determination to seize immortality leads him to kill the owner of the store his crew robs, the terms of his Faustian bargain are more clearly revealed when he then kills Raheem, destroying all claims of brotherhood with a malicious act of machismo, succeeding to Raheem's throne through murder.

Dickerson, who has colorfully photographed most of Spike Lee's films, uses darker hues in *Juice* but nowhere near the drained colored canvas on which *Straight Out of Brooklyn* is drawn. Dickerson's moral strategy is to elaborate to its fatal ends the contradictory logic of the gang as a family unit, a faulty premise as far as he is concerned because it overlooks the gang's lack of moral constraints and the destructive consequences it breeds. Dickerson's aesthetic and directorial strategy is to move the cameras with the action from the observer's frame of reference, borrowing a few pages from Lee's book without mimicking Lee's panache for decentering the observer through unusual angles and the fast pace of editing. Like Rich in *Straight Out of Brooklyn*, Dickerson wants the impact of his message to hit home, but his methods are not as harsh as Rich's. Instead, he draws us into his moral worldview with an invitation to view the spectacle of black male loss of love by degrees and effects.

The ghetto working-class family in *Juice* is much more visible and vital than the one in *Straight Out of Brooklyn*. Mothers and fathers wake their children in the morning for breakfast and make certain they take their books to school. The notion of extended family and "fictive kin" is even given a nice twist when GQ fetches a gun from one of his mother's old friends, a small-time neighborhood supplier.[9] And Dickerson subtly draws attention to the contrasts between the aesthetic and moral worldviews of the generations, and the thriving of an earlier era's values among the younger generation, at the dinner at Raheem's family's house after Raheem's funeral.

As snatches of gospel music float gently through the house, GQ and Steel pay their respects to Raheem's family. But when Bishop arrives, the rupture between generational values forces to the surface the choice each of the remaining three crew must make. GQ and Steel are offended at Bishop's effrontery, his mean-spirited hypocrisy leading him to violate Raheem's memory with this latest act of machismo and pride. For them, the choice is clear. The religious values signified in the quiet gospel music seem no longer foreign, providing a gentle counterpoint to the hip-hop aesthetic of violent metaphors used in the service of greater self-expression.

Instead, the gospel music and the world of black respectability that it symbolizes carry over into GQ's and Steel's grieving acknowledgment of the bonds between them and their departed friend, a sure sign that religious consciousness survives in them no matter how distant the teens appear to be from its redemptive effects. Bishop's desecration of Raheem's memory and family signify the depth of Bishop's moral failure, embodying the reckless abandon to which his acts of violence have given cruel expression. Unlike the black teens in *Straight Out of Brooklyn*'s ghetto, the black males can depend on one another, but only after being encouraged to acknowledge their debts to the moral vision of an older culture, and only after discovering the limits of their freedom in destructive alliance with one another.

In sharp contrast to *Juice*—which portrays the pernicious effects of generational decline and narrates the carnage of fratricide from within the arc of traditional black morality—the Hughes brothers' brilliant, disturbing 1992 debut, *Menace II Society*, unblinkingly unveils the absurdity and terror that cloak young black male ghetto life. Their terse, lean script—complemented by the cast's surprising economy of emotional expression, given the genre's tendency to trumpet more than whisper—counterpoints the unwieldy realities the film brutally reveals: postindustrial urban collapse, the ravaging personal and social effects of underground drug economies, the sheer violence of everyday life in the ghetto, and the destruction of black male life.

From the opening scene, where "Old Dog" (Larenz Tate) makes his childhood friend (Tyrin Turner) an unwitting partner in crime by murdering the Korean owner of the store they visit, to the film's finish, where Turner's character is gunned down as he attempts to escape Los Angeles and enjoy a more promising life in Atlanta with his girlfriend and her son, *Menace II Society* exposes the contradictory impulses of black male life that fuel its hope even as it ensures its destruction. *Menace II Society*, even more than *Juice* (or the Oliver Stone–produced *South Central*), registers the raw realities of black ghetto life in the message that black men are both one another's greatest allies and most lethal enemies. Turner's narration throughout the film— bringing coherence to a world, and his own life, fragmented by the forces of violence and retribution that mark the rhythm of urban existence—reveals an ironic hopefulness and even a muted moral passion that redeem young black life *on its own terms.*

The contemporary debate within black culture about black film and its enabling or destructive representations of black males and black females started with the meteoric rise of Spike Lee. With Lee's groundbreaking *She's Gotta Have It,* young black men laid hold of a cultural and artistic form—

the Hollywood film—from which they had with rare exception been previously barred. In gaining access to film as directors, they began to seize interpretive and representational authority from what they deemed ignorant or insensitive cultural elites whose cinematic portrayals of blacks were contorted or hackneyed, the ridiculously bloated or painfully shriveled disfigurements of black life seen from outside black culture. Lee's arrival promised a new day beyond stereotype.

What we get with Lee, however, is Jungian archetype, frozen snapshots of moods in the black male psyche photographed to brilliant effect by Ernest Dickerson. Lee's mission to represent the various streams of black life denied cinematic outlets has led him to resolve the complexity of black culture into rigid categories of being that hollow his characterss' fierce and contradictory rumblings toward authentic humanity.[10] And after *She's Gotta Have It*, black women became context clues for the exploration of black male rituals of social bonding (*School Daze*), the negotiation of black male styles of social resistance (*Do the Right Thing*), the expansion and pursuit of black male artistic ambitions (*Mo' Better Blues*), or the resolution of black male penis politics (*Jungle Fever*).

Lee's cinematic representations of black male life occasioned sound and fury over his most important project to date: his film biography of Malcolm X. As a reigning icon of black popular culture, Malcolm's autobiography is the Urtext of contemporary black nationalism. Because his legacy is claimed by fiercely competing groups within black America, Lee's film was a hard sell to some factions. More important, since Malcolm's complex legacy has only recently been opened to critical review and wider cultural scrutiny, his admirers and detractors have rushed forward to have their say once again.

To many, however, Malcolm is black manhood squared, the unadulterated truth of white racism ever on his tongue, the unity of black people ever on his agenda, the pain of black ghetto dwellers ever on his mind. Thus the films that I have discussed, which also represent the visual arm of black nationalism's revival, bear in many ways the burden of Malcolm X's presence in every frame, his philosophy touching every aspect of the issues they deal in: drugs, morality, religion, ghetto life, and, especially, the conditions of being a black man. For many, as for his eulogist Ossie Davis, Malcolm embodied the primordial, quintessential Real Man.

But as with the films of Dickerson, Lee, Rich, Singleton, and Van Peebles, this focus on black masculinity spells real trouble for black women. Perhaps only when more major-studio black films begin to be directed by black women will the repertoire of identities that black women command be adequately represented on the large screen. Powerful gestures toward black female–centered film exist in the work of Julie Dash in *Daughters of the Dust* and especially in Leslie Harris's *Just Another Girl on the IRT*. But until the cultural and economic barriers that prevent the flourishing of films by black women are removed, such works threaten to become exceptions to the rule of black male film.

In the meantime, black male directors remain preoccupied, even trapped, by the quest for an enabling conception of male identity. Such an enterprise will continue to be hampered until black male filmmakers explore masculinity's relationship to black women, promoting ideas of black masculinity that dissolve its links to the worst traits of Malcolm's lethal sexism. (John Singleton's 1993 *Poetic Justice*, however, failed dismally; its attempt to explore the life of a young black female [Janet Jackson] was fatally frustrated as the film's center turned quickly, and unapologetically, to the struggles of her male companion [Tupac Shakur]). Gestures of Malcolm's new attitude survive in the short hereafter Malcolm enjoyed on his escape from Elijah Muhummad's ideological straitjacket. Malcolm's split from the Nation of Islam demanded a powerful act of will and self-reinvention, an unsparing commitment to self-critical reflection, a trait that led him to reject his former hostility to (black) women.

But this is not the aspect of Malcolm most remarked on by his contemporary imitators who champion his return to prominence. Is this the Malcolm who emerges in Spike Lee's cinematic portrait of the slain leader? This question, of course, entails many others. What are the costs of presenting Malcolm's complexity on screen? Can Lee break the mold of severely limited female agency that characterizes his work and the work of his black film contemporaries up to this point? What happens to Malcolm when his life is treated by a cultural nationalist who is also a bourgeois black artist? I turn my attention now to Lee's film biography of Malcolm, the most important cultural representation of the black cultural hero yet created, in search of answers.

5
SPIKE'S MALCOLM

> When you teach a man to hate his lips, the lips that
> God gave him, the shape of his nose that God gave him,
> the texture of the hair that God gave him, the color of
> the skin that God gave him, you've committed the
> worst crime that a race of people can commit. And this
> is the crime you've committed. . . . This is how you im-
> prisoned us. Not just bringing us over here and making
> us slaves. But the image that you created of our moth-
> erland and the image that you created of our people
> on that continent was a trap, was a prison, was a chain,
> was the worst form of slavery that has ever been in-
> vented by a so-called civilized race and a civilized na-
> tion since the beginning of the world.
>
> Malcolm X, in *Malcolm X: The Last Speeches*

Malcolm X's intellectual legacy and his representation in
popular culture are often, not surprisingly, at odds with
each other. Although the stated point of analytical investigations of Malcolm's life is to probe the roots of his thought
and action with critical sophistication and intellectual rigor,
artistic treatments of Malcolm's career encourage a greater,
freer use of the imagination. Although art may occasionally
dispense with "fact" (since, at its best, art reveals cultural
biases that shape radically opposed interpretations of
events), it has an obligation to tell, if not *the* truth, then *its*
truth.

In Malcolm's case in particular, making choices about how to portray him on film are indivisible from the long, bitter struggle to bring his life to the screen at all.[1] As David Bradley argues, Hollywood "didn't keep firing writers from the 'X' project because the scripts were wrong. They kept firing writers because the *story* was wrong."[2] If Malcolm's story, then, was too controversial to bring to the big lights, too prickly for bourgeois formulas about racial problems and their smooth, painless removal, then what kind of Malcolm worth anything could possibly survive Hollywood's pulverizing machinery? And of the Malcolms being advanced by conflicting cultural constituencies for a starring role—including Malcolm as symbol of racial hatred and violence, Malcolm as black nationalist, Malcolm as newly minted American cultural icon, Malcolm as revolutionary internationalist, Malcolm as weak integrationist, Malcolm as reborn humanist—which one would ultimately make the cut?

These questions barely graze the interpretive and cultural complexities that Spike Lee confronted as he set out to make history and *his* film on Malcolm X. From the start, Lee was embroiled in controversy as he sought to seize control of the project from white director Norman Jewison. whom Lee believed categorically incapable of telling the story of not just any black man, but the quintessential Angry Black Man and, by extension, the urban black American. Lee played the politics of racial privilege with cunning, but barely before his success had settled in, he in turn came under attack for his anticipated mistreatment of Malcolm.

Even before filming began, writer and social critic Amiri Baraka drew blood in a war of words with Lee, asserting that Lee's poor history of representing black men meant that he would savage the memory of Malcolm X—a memory, by the way, to which Baraka presumed to have special access—loading onto Malcolm's historical frame Lee's own bourgeois distortions. This battle between the two diminutive firebrands, ironic for its poignant portrayal of the only logical outcome of the politics of more-black-nationalist-than-thou—a game Lee himself has played with relish on occasion—was but a foretaste of the warfare of interpretation to come because of Lee's portrait of Malcolm.

Besides these considerations, Lee's shrewd and, at times, crass commercialization of Malcolm's memory—plus his grandstanding public-relations stunts meant to make his film a guaranteed draw (for instance, telling children to skip school to see his film on opening day)—raised serious questions about his integrity in doing the film. Lee's merchandising of Malcolm memorabilia led many to conclude that he was hustling Malcolm's history to his own financial advantage. Plus Lee's methods of promotion appeared to some a bourgeois exploitation of black nationalist politics severed from a real commitment to the working-class and poor constituency Malcolm loved. And ironically, Lee, who has often been perceived in the white media as a hotheaded film-maker and racial firebrand, became, in the eyes of many, the vehicle for the mass production and dilution of Malcolm X as an acceptable, easily packaged, even chic commodity that Lee sold in his film and in his 40 Acres and a Mule Shops.

In light of these realities, and the inherent difficulties of cinematically representing a man whose life has been reconstructed by webs of myth and romance, however, Lee's *Malcolm X* is still an often impressive, occasionally stunning achievement. It is a richly textured and subtly nuanced evocation of the life and times of a supremely American paradox: a onetime racial particularist whose fame has been shaped to display his belated, if confusing, universal appeal.

Lee's Malcolm is inevitably a creation of Lee's own oversized ambitions. He has reframed the racial themes of his earlier work around the shadow figure at its spiritual core.[3] In *School Daze,* Lee ridiculed the petty but pernicious politics of skin color that abound within black culture, an echo of Malcolm's warnings against the ubiquitous threat of black self-hate. In *Do the Right Thing,* Lee dashed the easy sentimentalism that often prevails in integration-minded talk about racial progress and harmony, a favorite rhetorical trump in Malcolm's shuffling and dealing of the racial deck. And in *Jungle Fever,* Lee explored the fatal conflicts that can ensnare interracial romance, which in his view and in the view of the early Malcolm is a chasm of pathology.

132

In *Malcolm X*, Lee's racial ruminations, which have often spun out of control, have found their artistic apotheosis. The last time Lee integrated Malcolm into one of his films, Malcolm's words about violence in aid of black liberation served as a textual coda to *Do the Right Thing*, his sentiments set in black and white, much like the image Lee conjured of Malcolm in that context. But Lee's understanding of Malcolm has matured since Malcolm was used to supply a stylized signature to Lee's own racial reflections.

The genre of *Malcolm X*—the epic—and the film's real-life subject impose historical limits, aesthetic constraints, and artistic conventions that work wonders for Lee's treatment of the complexities of race. The field of fire sparked before filming began by his battles with the writer Baraka and others over the "correct" representation of Malcolm made Lee's job virtually impossible. Satisfying the varying constituencies that have a stake in shaping the memory of Malcolm is no small task, and it is the sort that few directors have faced. The directors of comparable epic films—David Lean (*Lawrence of Arabia*) and Sir Richard Attenborough (*Gandhi*)—confronted nothing like the scale of attack that Lee endured in the battle over Malcolm's legacy.

The three hours and twenty-one minutes Lee takes to explore Malcolm's life are divided between the three major stages in his career: as street hustler and criminal; as devotee of Elijah Muhammad and preacher par excellence of black nationalism; and as an independent black leader who formed two organizations, the Muslim Mosque and the Organization of Afro-American Unity, to reflect his changed religious and political views after his departure from the Nation of Islam and his pilgrimage to Mecca. Lee seems to rush through the last stage with dizzying and distorting speed, leaving largely untouched Malcolm's visit to Africa and the substantial broadening of his ideological perspective. Lee's pace may be unintentional, but it is nevertheless effective in dramatizing the almost desperate improvisation that Malcolm displayed. He lived less than a year after his break with the Nation of Islam, and no matter how much we want to fill in the blanks, a definitive account of his latter days is hard to come by.

The tripartite division of the life follows faithfully the lineaments of Malcolm's various emergences and conversions as detailed in his autobiography (as told to Alex Haley), *The Autobiography of Malcolm X.*[4] That text itself has been criticized for avoiding or distorting certain facts. Indeed, the autobiography is as much a testament to Haley's ingenuity in shaping the manuscript as it is a record of Malcolm's own attempt to tell his story. The profound personal, intellectual, and ideological changes Malcolm was undergoing near the end of his life led him to order the events of his life to support a mythology of metamorphosis and transformation that bore fruit in spiritual wisdom. But that document bears deep traces as well of Malcolm's attempt to fend against the inevitable vulnerabilities revealed in the process of recalling and reconstructing one's life. In simple terms, this means that Malcolm's claim that he was expelled from West Junior High School in Lansing, Michigan, for instance, is inaccurate; he slid through the seventh grade there in 1939. In a more profound manner, however, Malcolm never mentions his meeting with the Ku Klux Klan in 1961 to see if that group, which like the Nation of Islam espoused racial separatism, could help Elijah Muhammad and his followers obtain land to implement their beliefs.[5]

As with most autobiographies, Malcolm's recollections were an effort to impose order on the fragments of his experience. The story of his escape from functional illiteracy, his exodus from mental and social slavery, and his conversion to true belief—only to have that belief betrayed by the father figure of his faith—is a narrative whose philosophical pedigree draws on Augustine, Booker T. Washington, Frederick Douglass, and Sigmund Freud. To the extent that Lee embellishes the historical account, he is being faithful in a way to the spirit of self–re-creation that Malcolm evidenced in his colorful telling of his own life.

Oscar-winning actor Denzel Washington invests the early Malcolm, then known as Malcolm Little and eventually as Detroit Red, with a canny and charismatic mix of steely determination and unpolished naïveté. He plays perfectly Malcolm's entree into the black hustling world at the awkward age of fifteen. The mix of awe and aspiration is captured on Washington's face when he is spotted and wooed by Sophia (Kate Vernon), a white woman at the ballroom where he and his partner Shorty (played by Lee) are jitterbugging. In *Jungle Fever*, Lee cluttered his examination of interracial love with diverting, confusing stories about drugs and adultery. Here Malcolm's experience places a cinematic loop around Lee's treatment. The moral of the story is the same as in Lee's earlier coverage: interracial love is lethal and self-destructive. But the historical context and racial rationale of that moral is given a denser treatment. Lee's version is drawn from Malcolm's early and middle rhetoric, not from his later declarations to James Farmer and others that interracial love is a personal, not a political, choice.

Lee evokes the criminal phase of Malcolm's career with a vibrant and dream-time palette of colors that suggests the hustling life's attraction to people of color in the 1940s and 1950s. All too often, cinematic treatments of black street life are reduced to an appendage of chic white goings-on (as in Francis Ford Coppola's *The Cotton Club*) or a cartoonish colored approximation of a parallel white street buffoonery (as in Eddie Murphy's *Harlem Nights*). With Lee, we feel the pulse and passion of the streets through a hodgepodge of crafty and stylized characters who possess intelligence and dignity. Later in the film, however, Lee addresses the brutish and seedy underside of that life, which gets canned and canonized as black cultural pathology in the lazy eyes of social theory in journalistic dress, and gets viewed as the harmful and insidious symptom of white racist neglect in the black puritanism of the Nation of Islam that Malcolm preached.

West Indian Archie, played with smooth and seductive equanimity by Delroy Lindo, is the embodiment, in both the autobiography and Lee's film, of the misled ingenuity that betrays the citizen of the street when his or her life is severed from a black religious mooring. Although he takes the young Malcolm under his wing, it is he who, after a dispute over money in his numbers racket, eventually forces Malcolm to flee Harlem and return to Boston, the scene of his earliest hustling, before his fateful turn in prison. West Indian Archie is both father and foil to Malcolm, and thus a foreshadowing of the treachery he will confront in Elijah Muhammad.

Here and throughout his film, Lee conflates characters: West Indian Archie (mentioned in the autobiography) and his cronies stand in for Sammy the Pimp and others in the autobiography who befriended Malcolm and showed him the ropes of hustling. In the prison sequence, Lee produces a fictional character named Baines (Albert Hall), who accomplishes the work of both the disciplined prisoner Bimbi in the autobiography (who told Malcolm that he "had some brains" and should use them) and his brother Reginald, who along with his other brother, Philbert, had become a member of the Nation of Islam. Reginald advised Malcolm that if he didn't "eat any more pork" or "smoke any more cigarettes," he would show Malcolm how to get out of prison.

Lee's tactic finds precedence in Malcolm himself, who conceded that Shorty was a composite of characters. And as in Malcolm's case, perhaps, Lee's strategy allows him to avoid dealing with some painful truths. By making Baines the source of Malcolm's conversion, Lee doesn't have to unravel the messy ironies involved when Malcolm observed the enforced shunning of Reginald, the very brother who had introduced him to the faith. And by making Baines the traitor to Malcolm because of his (and other Nation ministers') resentment of Malcolm's prominence in the white media, Lee avoids laying the blame for the jealousy at the feet of its likely source, Elijah Muhammad, whose quirky resonances are deftly presented in the charming and gnomish bearing of Al Freeman, Jr. Lee escapes as well explaining the betrayal and renunciation of Malcolm by two of his brothers in the Nation after his assassination.

Lee's choices make sound cinematic sense for the most part, especially in his treatment of Malcolm's slow awakening from an unconscious worship of the white world. Lee takes his time, allowing us to watch the unraveling of layer upon layer of resistance to the truth that Elijah Muhammad brought: that the white man is a "devil," that black people are the true masters of the universe, that white culture has throughout the world left death and destruction in its wake.

This was strong brew for a black male barely out of his

teens whose "conked" hair style reflected his esteem for the white world. "It look white, don't it?" he asks after getting his hair processed for the first time, seeking the approval of other black men who had endured the painful process of relaxing their stiffened manes.

Lee is especially effective in portraying the profound spirituality that marked Malcolm's mature years and that was the source of an eerie poise in the midst of social upheaval and personal crisis. The markers of black spirituality have been dominated by the Christian cosmos; the themes, images, and ideas of black spiritual life are usually evoked by gospel choirs enthralled in joyous praise or a passionate preacher engaged in ecstatic proclamation. Never before in American cinema has an alternative black spirituality been so intelligently presented. One montage of Malcolm's rhetorical ripostes and verbal volleys extends, incredibly, for several minutes. And throughout Lee's treatment of Malcolm's Nation of Islam stage, his words, thoughts, and ideas and those of the Nation are vigorously presented. This is no small achievement in our anti-intellectual environment, which punishes the constituency that has made Malcolm its hero: black teens and young adults.

Lee portrays Malcolm's extraordinary self-possession when, without words, he waves away the followers who have collected to make certain that justice will be rendered by white New York police after a beating of one of the "brothers." The police captain both acknowledges and la-ments Malcolm's quiet authority, saying, "That's too much power for one man to have." Malcolm's balance would eventually collapse under the threat to his life posed by Nation loyalists who resented Malcolm's rebuff of Elijah Muhammad and who hatefully hounded him during his last few months, inducing in Malcolm a psychic vertigo that Lee only barely captures.

By contrast, and in keeping with the hagiographical tendencies of all epic films, Lee presents Malcolm near the end as harried but hushed, a man of saintly moral attainment. Lee's intent to portray Malcolm as having it all together on the inside while his world crumbles around him not only is romantic, but does a disservice finally to the greater truth that Malcolm continued to work even in the midst of the palpable premonition of his quickly approaching death.

The murder scene is one of the most brilliantly staged film accounts of the emotional pitch and pandemonium surrounding an assassination. As is true throughout the film, Lee's choice of period music is haunting and effective. As Malcolm glides toward death at Harlem's Audubon Ballroom in his sleek Oldsmobile 98, the sweetly agonizing verse of "A Change Is Gonna Come" (penned and sung by former gospel great Sam Cooke, another black genius killed in his prime) captures Malcolm's impossible predicament. Cooke's pathos-brimmed melisma reminds us that though it's been "too hard living," he's "afraid to die."

Although Lee's Malcolm is more subdued, even softer, than many had wished—possessed less by strident rage than by hard-won wisdom—he survives the Hollywood machinery and remains a provocative, valuable figure. Still, Lee's Malcolm speaks rhetoric that is a far cry from the volatile, incendiary talk that the police and government feared would be spewed by Malcolm's character and that would incite riots in theaters on opening night. That fear, as with Lee's earlier *Do the Right Thing,* reflects a tragic lack of awareness about the dynamics of racial rage and the suitable targets of its expression. Such racial paranoia prevented many filmgoers from viewing the film in its theatrical release.

Interesting as well is Lee's portrayal of Malcolm's finely nuanced relationship with his wife, Betty Shabazz, whose mellow thunder and independent temperament are sketched with revealing concentration by Angela Bassett. Shabazz was alternately supportive and sternly self-willed (she left Malcolm after the birth of each of their first three children). But Shabazz's affectionately sparring relationship with Malcolm, especially over gender roles, is only slightly acknowledged in the film.

There are other absences. Chief among them is Louis Farrakhan, former calypso singer, Malcolm's onetime associate turned enemy, and the current leader of the Nation of Islam. The bad blood between Malcolm and Farrakhan and the Nation of Islam continues to this day, despite Farrakhan's moderation of his sentiments expressed in the

141

1964 statement that "a man such as Malcolm deserves to die." Absent, too, is the figure of Muhammad Ali, who was led into the Nation by Malcolm and was a huge attraction to young black men. The two had a falling-out over Malcolm's departure from Elijah Muhammad's ranks. A few years later, though, Ali himself would be straitjacketed by the Nation, leading to his eventual passage into the precincts of orthodox Islam.

One might also quibble about the unnecessary didacticism of the film after the assassination. In this part, staged in classrooms in the United States and South Africa, children repeat, "I am Malcolm X," to indicate their inheritance of the fallen leader's legacy. This move is Lee's attempt to solve cinematically a perplexing condition: how to get black youth to identify with the redemptive message of Malcolm's racial edification. It comes off as needlessly contrived and facile, but it reveals just how difficult the task of reaching black youth really is. Still, Lee's failed attempt at least forces us to concede how our most desperate attempts to address the problems of black youth, either through law and order or by appealing to an ethical norm in a golden past of black tradition, have likewise failed.

The appearance of Nelson Mandela, before his ascent to the presidency of South Africa, is at once riveting and revealing. In an ironically poignant coda, Mandela's presence reinforces for our eyes the difficult lot of *living* heroes, his well-worn visage registering complexities of fate that in figures like King and Malcolm are swept away by the sacred wash of early martyrdom. At the end of Mandela's speech about Malcolm and black freedom, it is not Mandela's voice but Malcolm's that utters the widely quoted and more widely misunderstood phrase "by any means necessary." One senses at that moment, albeit ever so slightly, the loss of heroic authority that marks our era and that sends millions back to the words of a dead man for hope.

Like *The Autobiography of Malcolm X,* Lee's work avoids uncomfortable questions about Malcolm's alleged homosexual alliances during his hustling days, the ambiguous events surrounding the burning of his Nation-owned home (and allegations that Malcolm himself set the fire), doubts about whether Malcolm's father died at the hands of revenge-minded white racists (a scenario Lee reproduces), and Malcolm's skillful manipulation of white media fascinated by his rhetorical excesses.

Nevertheless, Lee has rendered the life of an American original in terms that are both poignant and insightful. Above all, in taking the risk of defining and interpreting a figure entwined in racial and cultural controversy, he has sent us back into our own memories, or to books and documentaries, in search of the truth for ourselves. And he has done more than that. He has set the nation talking about a figure whose life deserves to be discussed, whose achievements deserve critical scrutiny, and whose career merits the widest possible exposure. Many great films have achieved considerably less than that.

Lee's film has contributed significantly to the renewed heroism of Malcolm X among black and other Americans. But the enormous buildup to his film has also, ironically, contained and capped the interest in the leader it has inspired. Now the real work of intellectual and political recovery and reconstruction of Malcolm's legacy must begin.

What are the most powerful, liberating uses to which Malcolm's legacy can be put? What is Malcolm's meaning to the black males who have invested heavily in his heroic return, especially as their fortunes continue to decline? And how will the progressive vision of race encouraged by Malcolm's mature philosophy fare in the age of Clinton? I will attempt to answer these questions in the final chapter.

6
USING MALCOLM: HEROISM, COLLECTIVE MEMORY, AND THE CRISIS OF BLACK MALES

> It's not wrong to expect justice. It's not wrong to expect freedom. It's not wrong to expect equality. If Patrick Henry and all of the Founding Fathers of this country were willing to lay down their lives to get what you are enjoying today, then it's time for you to realize that a large, ever-increasing number of Black people in this country are willing to die for what we know is due us by birth.
>
> Malcolm X, in *Malcolm X: The Last Speeches*

Malcolm X's heroism not only is linked to the resurgence of black nationalism and a revived racism to which it forcefully responds, but draws as well from a grand tradition of black heroism that dates back to slavery. A significant feature of historic black heroism is the stimulation and preservation of cultural achievement through collective memory.[1] Thus the achievements of heroes and movements from the black past were ceaselessly evoked in black communities in oral and written form as an inspiration to continued thought and action in the same vein. The logic of such strategies hinged on the belief that if other blacks in the past could perform heroic activities, and often under brutal circumstances that defied adequate description, then blacks in succeeding historical eras could surmount obstacles to racial achievement.

Another closely related function of collective memory was its use as "an instrument of survival."[2] Through the stories black folk have always told one another about a history filled with accomplishment and failure—tales about incredible feats performed against inhuman odds as well as bitter accounts of justice denied, of opportunities missed, and of dreams and lives cut short prematurely—they have managed to negotiate the treacherous terrain of American life with their lives intact.

The celebration of Malcolm's memory, then, has cultural and racial precedent. I want to examine briefly the roots of an African-American heroism that illumines Malcolm's legacy, while exploring varieties of collective memory in suggesting how Malcolm's memory may be useful now. I will also examine the progressive vision of race inspired by Malcolm's latter-day humanist philosophy. Perhaps the greatest use of Malcolm's memory today can be in dissolving the links that connect the tragic triangle of self-hatred, violence, and racism that plagues the constituency most invested in Malcolm's cultural return: young black males. Because the collective morale of young black males is threatened, I will suggest helpful ways to think about their vexing problems.

In African-American culture, heroic traditions have usually developed in response to forces of oppression, especially white racism in various forms: chattel slavery, black codes, Jim Crow, separate-but-equal laws, lynching, castration, and the like. During slavery, heroes were seen as figures who resisted racial dominance through slave insurrections, plantation rebellions, work slowdowns, or running away.[3] Leaders like Denmark Vesey, Gabriel Prosser, Harriet Tubman, and Nat Turner acquired mythic stature as heroes because they defied white rule during slavery.

After slavery, when African-American society faced enormous obstacles in reshaping a culture that had been deliberately undermined by the forces of white racism and vulgar capitalism, heroic action consisted of the continued battle against racist oppression in various forms. Most notably, black heroism was viewed in autobiographical stories of escape from slavery, the rehabilitation of African-American culture through political action, and the remaking of the moral life of African-American communities in religious affiliation and spiritual devotion.[4] Figures like Frederick Douglass, Henry Turner, Sojourner Truth, and Henry Highland Garnett became heroes during Reconstruction.

147

From slavery until the present, African-American heroes have been instrumental in preserving the collective memory of black culture against the detrimental consequences of racial amnesia while fighting racism in American public culture.[5] The collective memory of black Americans countered the racial amnesia represented in the selective memory of the recent American past in white America. As Michael Kammen has pointed out, selective memory expresses the desire for reconciliation—through strategies of depoliticization and amnesia—by dominant traditions that obscure or distort the collective memory of minority traditions.[6]

In discussing the heroic use of collective memory by African-Americans, Kammen describes how selective memory "kept African-Americans outside the mainstream of retrospective consciousness," leading to blacks' perpetuating their own heroic "traditions and memories." From "the mid-1880s onward, therefore, African-Americans largely celebrated their heroes and pursued their own historic occasions alone."[7] African-Americans' "collective memory of slavery remained vivid," and "what they chose to emphasize by means of traditional activities each year was the memory of gaining freedom."[8]

Frederick Douglass in large measure carved out his heroic niche in African-American culture by advocating a tradition of collective memory that fought racial amnesia:

It is not well to forget the past. Memory was given to man for some wise purpose. The past is . . . the mirror in which we may discern the dim outlines of the future. . . . Well the nation may forget, it may shut its eyes to the past, and frown upon any who may do otherwise, but the colored people of this country are bound to keep the past in lively memory till justice shall be done them.[9]

It is the quest for social justice in a racist society, along with the preservation of collective memory, that has forged a powerful connection between earlier expressions and contemporary varieties of black heroism. Malcolm X fits easily into this tradition. Both progressive and conservative views of collective memory may be useful in viewing Malcolm's life.

In discussing twentieth-century studies on collective memory, Barry Schwartz makes a distinction between two views. The first view, a progressivist or constructionist one, "sees the past as a social construction shaped by the concerns and needs of the present."[10] This approach draws on the work of George Herbert Mead and Maurice Halbwachs in showing how conceptions of the past are drawn from contemporary problems and how collective memory reconstructs the past by adapting the images of past beliefs to present historical needs.[11]

The second perspective on collective memory, a conservative one, "is distorted in a different direction: It is the past that shapes our understanding of the present rather than the other way around."[12] This perspective draws on the work of Emile Durkheim and Edward Shils in contending that commemoration rites reproduce the past, while offering an understanding of a stable tradition that transmits a common heritage.[13] As Schwartz maintains, the conservative view "draws attention to continuities in our perceptions of the past and to the way these perceptions are maintained in the face of social change."[14]

Both views have relevance for African-American uses of collective memory in preserving heroic images of Malcolm and in combating paralyzing forms of political and racial amnesia. The contention that the past is constructed from present historical needs contains a powerful—if partial—insight about the function of contemporary struggles in not merely preserving, but also re-creating, memories of Malcolm. This view accents the agency of contemporary participants in the heroic tradition of response to racism that he so imaginatively represented.

This view also actively includes the intellectual contributions of contemporary participants in reshaping a tradition of heroic response to racism given to them by Malcolm. It confirms, too, the flexibility of traditions of social protest, encouraging the rejection of literal interpretations of heroic figures that make narrow notions of loyalty to their ideas a prerequisite for participation. This view provides welcome relief from heroic celebrations of Malcolm that turn on strict and selective interpretations of his social and historical meaning. A constructionist approach to the collective memory about Malcolm stresses the ongoing evolution of understanding about his career that acknowledges the many uses to which his memory may be put in reaching the goals he expressed.

Finally, this understanding encourages the expansion of social criticism and moral vision that Malcolm represented, inviting criticism of aspects of his legacy that undermine the needs of contemporary participants. For example, Malcolm's sexism is a significant blight on his achievements. Principled opposition to his gender blindness actually encourages the observation of broader principles of fairness and justice that Malcolm cherished.

The more conservative approach to collective memory, though, ensures an attention to historical detail that guards against romantic fictions and unrestrained myths that so easily attach to Malcolm's career. This conservative approach emphasizes the historical character of Malcolm's career, linking present observations about his heroism to interpretations of his rhetoric, practice, and behavior in accounting for his enduring racial significance.

This perspective also encourages a more lucid explanation of the complex positions Malcolm adopted throughout his career and an exploration of how his radical transformations of thought reflected a self-critical posture.

The Malcolm that has often been lost in hero worship is the Malcolm who could be critical of himself as well as the society that treated black people with fundamental disrespect. This is the most promising dimension of Malcolm's legacy that we can extend: a willingness to see the errors of our ways, to acknowledge that without sometimes severe self-criticism black folk will never achieve the true measure of our intended greatness as a people.

The conservative view of collective memory carries with it a rebuke to all who believe that they have the *definitive* view of Malcolm X without critically engaging his life and thought. Those who spare Malcolm from criticism do his legacy the most harm. For his best ideas and most powerful insights to flourish in our present historical context, they must be subjected to thorough examination. Only then can we understand and measure his true greatness, acknowledging his accomplishments and failures as we assess his place in our national history.

Among the most helpful ways that Malcolm's memory may be used in our contemporary moment is to develop a powerful defense of radical democracy and a sharp criticism of race and racism in the age of Clinton. Malcolm's antiracist speech anticipated the sort of keen, no-nonsense analysis and action we must undertake, especially when our nation's political condition seems to favor, on its surface, the interests and aspirations of most African-Americans. But as Malcolm so clearly understood, it is just such a "favorable" political climate that may encourage the worst offenses against black interests, because those figures in violation of black progress shield themselves from attack under cover of an often unmerited black loyalty. As Malcolm might muse, a political wolf in sheep's clothing often does more harm to black folk than an explicit enemy.

President Clinton's policies and actions so far indicate that he may be just the sort of political figure Malcolm often warned us against. Clinton's public positions on race encourage clever but often unprincipled manipulations, even distortions, of racial rhetoric in our national life. A brief look at recent racial history will help illuminate the hopes of racial progress that Bill Clinton has come to embody and, I think, annul in his time in office.

For the past twelve years, fateful changes in American culture have sapped our nation's ability to speak about race with informed passion. The collapse of the will to undo the legacy of past racial injustice with immediate intervention, through either governmental sponsorship or the beneficent public action of the private sector, has left a gaping hole in the patchwork of remedies that at our most hopeful moments we imagined could remove the bruising inequalities that continue to haunt us.

Also, the fierce rivalry among previously despised or ignored groups for a visible stake in the politics of public attention has masked the source of their anxieties: that too often, social goods are parceled out as so many concessions to demands by the strongest group in a system of reward held hostage by zero-sum thinking. African-Americans, women, Latinos and Latinas, and Asian-Americans are often pitted against one another in a battle for scarce resources—a sour arrangement indeed, for they aren't the source of one another's primary pains. In this light, all the noise about "special interest groups" seems a disingenuous denial of the factors that led minorities to adopt competition as their stock-in-trade to begin with.

Moreover, the thinly veiled contempt for racial minorities during the Reagan and Bush administrations unleashed a racist backlash, the worse effects of which had been held in check by the gains of the civil rights movement and the altered social landscape it brought into existence. For those who point out that even that arrangement was dishonest (that it simply shifted racism underground, concealing the persistence of bigotry that conforms the American character to its ugly, irrational image), a word of caution is in order. To paraphrase Ernest Becker, the American character may be a lie, but it's a *vital* lie. Some forms of restraint that protect the possibility of rational dialogue and humane behavior must be retained as we work through the occasionally deadly consequences of reordering our unjust racial practices.

To this end, the election of Bill Clinton promised a breath of fresh air, and in some ways, his presidency has been refreshing. The hoopla surrounding his ascendancy marked a return to the rituals of public participation in power largely absent since the gilded mythology of John Kennedy's Camelot, and more narrowly glimpsed in the cowboy captivity of Ronald Reagan's reign. Clinton's charm with the media, his crafting of a persona as the American everyperson who invites his constituency to become partners in reshaping American democracy around the common good, and his revival of a vocabulary of national service have all combined to make his appeal larger and more humane than that of his Republican predecessors.

Clinton's cabinet appointments reflected his stab at a new direction. Undeniably, Clinton was plagued early on by his asleep-at-the wheel handling of the attorney general "nanny-gate" affair, which both betrayed his ignorance of the average citizen's perspective and documented his insensitivity to child-care issues. Overall, however, Clinton pulled in racial minorities and women to make his official advisers "look more like America" than before. But his bristling at pressure to appoint more women, as he responded that he wouldn't "count beans," revealed that he is more closely allied with George Bush's principles of gender and race relations than was initially believed. Clinton's unprincipled about-face on the Haitians coercively sequestered at Guantanamo Bay and his vicious repatriation of Haitians seeking asylum from political tyranny (a policy on which he finally relented only after Randall Robinson's hunger strike and protest from the Congressional Black Caucus) only reinforce this suspicion.

The real danger of race in the age of Clinton is a cautionary tale about "friendly fire," the unintended wounds inflicted by alleged friends, not the deliberate assaults of enemies. (No one knows this more painfully than Clinton's friend Lani Guinier, whom Clinton proposed to head the Civil Rights Division at the Department of Justice. Clinton's abandoning of Guinier after she was unfairly dubbed a "quota queen" by the *Wall Street Journal,* and his refusal to permit her a fair hearing before the Senate after the tide of public opinion turned against her, only reinforced the perception that Clinton was quite willing to sacrifice loyalty for popularity.)

During his campaign, Clinton expanded the influence of the conservative Democratic Leadership Council, a group composed of disgruntled neoliberals formed after the collapse of traditional liberalism within the Democratic party. Signs of this conservatism, especially in regard to race, flashed during the presidential campaign when Clinton employed the code phrase "winning back the suburbs." By using this phrase, Clinton implicitly distanced himself from the pain and perspectives of the working class and the ghetto poor. The gesture not only smacked of hubris—the premise was that he didn't need poor blacks and Latinos and Latinas, and that middle-class minority support was already sewn up—but further endangered the racial goodwill that many citizens, especially progressives, had expected from Clinton.

Such hopes of racial goodwill were dealt a further blow with Clinton's exploitative treatment of Sister Souljah, aping the rancid public-relations maneuvers associated with the late Lee Atwater's symbolic manipulation of white suburban angst in the infamous Willie Horton affair. Clinton's cynical and opportunistic response to rapper Sister Souljah's comments that blacks should harm white folk during the urban rebellion in Los Angeles revealed the flawed character of much liberal thought about race in America. Perhaps Clinton was seeking to generate moral revenue by investing in Dan Quayle's school of shallow ethical analysis or looking to bolster his sagging campaign, but the timing and venue of opportunity for Clinton's remarks suggested something tragically awry.

Why did Clinton wait so long before responding to Sister Souljah's comments? On the face of it, his camp's contention that swift reaction by Clinton would have been viewed as gratuitous seemed to wash. But it is more likely that neither Clinton nor his handlers had any idea of Sister Souljah's existence before she made her observations. Her sole importance to Clinton derived from Sister Souljah's symbolic worth in his quest to make a highly visible, if unprincipled, moral gesture. Moreover, by making his remarks at the Rainbow Conference, where Sister Souljah had ap-

peared the previous day, Clinton distanced himself ideolog-
ically from Jesse Jackson and rang the register of race
suspicion while appearing to practice racial fairness.

But his gain was the American citizenry's loss. Clinton
blew a prime opportunity to become a public moralist, to
move beyond the treacherous insinuations and finger-
pointing that abound in discussions of race and to teach us
something genuinely useful about the ethical consequences
of racial desperation. Sister Souljah's statements certainly
warranted careful critical commentary. But Clinton might
have as easily acknowledged the extreme difficulty of adequately responding to social forces that have made Los Angeles a powerful symbol of the postindustrial urban crises
that fueled the riots and evoked the rapper's sharp observations. By drawing attention to Souljah, Clinton chose an
easy target. He also avoided the more challenging task of
addressing the futility embodied in Souljah's sentiments
and in the cultural expression of many young blacks, especially hip-hop artists.

What Clinton failed to grasp—a trait he shares with
many American intellectuals and leaders—is that, like Malcolm, rappers channel black rage and defiant rhetoric at the
conditions that make life hell for urban residents. At its best,
rap entails a refusal of silent complicity in the social and
political destruction of black life by offering sometimes rude
rebukes to the white and black powers-that-be. Of course,
rap is sometimes intoxicated with its own candor and right-

ness of cause, leading to rhetorical excesses that are sometimes more desperate passion than hateful harangue.

Had Clinton played to his announced strengths of sharp social and political analysis, he could have challenged Sister Souljah's understanding of the political utility of violence by linking a discussion of the Los Angeles rebellion with previous incarnations in Detroit and Watts. This turn of conversation might have led to an insightful discussion of the loss of political will and imagination around remedying the problems generated by race and class. And where better to launch such a project than at the Rainbow Conference. Standing on Jesse Jackson's political terrain and going toe-to-toe in a much needed debate about these issues?

Instead, Clinton shrank moral ambiguity and racial desperation to simplistic terms. He searched through the fortuitous arrangements of a lately lackluster schedule to seize a golden, if gratuitous, opportunity to shine. In so doing, Clinton betrayed his desire to broaden liberal political debates about race beyond hackneyed phrases, contemptuous posturing, and stifling opportunism. That such debates are sorely needed is demonstrated by the character of most cultural criticism expressed in the aftermath of Clinton's attack on Sister Souljah. Praising Clinton for his righteous rhetorical ripostes to Souljah's sentiments, lauding his jettisoning of Jackson from the moderate ship of liberalism that Clinton sails, or condemning Jackson for his condemnations of Clinton, most commentary was moralistic and narrow. The real moral tragedy is that neoliberal race theorists and practitioners have underplayed or misdiagnosed the urban blight, social hopelessness, and thinly veiled anger that give rise to raw and sometimes misdirected statements like those made by Sister Souljah.

Young black ghetto residents, a major constituency of rap music, have remained invisible to the Bill Clintons of the world until they serve useful political purposes that have nothing redemptive to say about their painful predicament. By playing to the greatest fears of disaffected, dropout white Democratic voters at the expense of loyal black Democrats (and only after the primaries were over), Clinton displayed the ugliest sort of political opportunism.

When she appeared on the "Phil Donahue Show" in the winter of 1991, Sister Souljah revealed that she had grown up on welfare in the Bronx, escaped poverty, studied in Spain, and won a scholarship to Rutgers. Her ridiculous statement about harming white people—after all, most people who died in the riots were people of color—was a departure from her severe but articulate defense of black nationalism. Of course, Bill Clinton didn't know this, because he used her for his small purposes and not our larger learning.

Despite these signs of a lapsed faculty for principled debate about the future of race, there is lingering hope that Clinton can recover moral ground and begin to speak and think about race in complex and productive ways. Equally important, there is still hope that the new era he aspires to embody will encourage the elaboration of radical democratic tendencies within our culture. Such activity can help lift the veil of fear and ignorance about racial difference, a veil that reinforces the structural political and economic inequities already eroding the lives of many minorities.

For now the end of the Reagan–Bush era, more than the beginning of the age of Clinton, contains the seeds of hope for radical democrats and other progressives and antiracists. Because we are losing a clear target to aim for—one of the virtues, after all, of outright opponents is that they encourage outright opposition—radical democrats must become even more vigilant in clarifying the terms of antiracist struggle in our culture. Inspired by the example of the mature Malcolm X, and the radical democratic views he began to express near the end of his life, such a project can find a broad base of support.

One of the major forms such struggle should take is continued opposition to the pernicious stereotyping of black women as the symbol bearers for the afflictions of the welfare system. Conservatives like Charles Murray contend that if we could somehow improve poor black women's initiative, their will to upward mobility, we could solve the problem of a congenital welfare syndrome. Most conservative analyses of welfare dependency and initiative (to which Clinton seems inclined) are notoriously one-sided, neglecting the structural factors that prevent black women from flourishing.

For instance, initiative is often dependent on the amount of reward one receives for it. One's motivation to continually seek employment will not be high when there is little prospect of finding it. In this scenario, initiative expresses the relation between expectation and reward. What kinds of jobs are available? What kinds of education or training does the employment seeker have? To what kinds of education or training has she or he had access? What are the structural changes in the economy that affect the viability of the kind of work the person does? What are the chances for education or retraining? What is the person's relation to the informal network of information that often influences employment chances? These are simply a few of the questions that must be pressed in assessing the level of initiative present and in understanding how one can relate initiative to a larger range of factors.

A radical democratic rethinking of such questions, buttressed by investigations of the social causes behind the fragile place of poor black women in the economy; an understanding of the sexist employment force, in which women continue to earn only 70 percent of what men make for comparable work; and an explanation of the dominance of the service industry over manufacturing, which has eroded the wage base of poor black women, compromising their ability to support their families, might help place initiative in a more illumined framework. Further, comprehending the effects on women of the casualization of labor and honestly acknowledging the disincentives to initiative contained in regulations that bar women from supplementing their welfare incomes with work would chasten those who call for simpleminded workfare solutions that tie welfare benefits to employment.

The radical democratic antiracist struggle must continue to oppose racist violence, manifested most recently in the Rodney King beating in Los Angeles. While the riot that followed the acquittal of the police officers who savagely assaulted King is a complex phenomenon, the conditions that provoked that social rebellion remain buried in poor communities across the United States. For the past decade, rap artists—who as informal ethnographers of black youth culture translate the inarticulate suffering of poor black masses into articulate anger—have warned of the genocidal consequences of ghetto life for poor blacks. Their narratives, though plagued by vicious forms of misogyny and homophobia that merit strong criticism, communicate the absurdity and desperation, the chronic hopelessness, that festers inside the postindustrial urban center. Police brutality is a recurring theme of rap narratives, generated by young black males victimized by the unchecked exercise of state repression. Radical democrats must take the lead in criticizing the actions and rhetoric of prominent figures who help shape a national climate where racist violence, particularly police brutality, seems a plausible or unpunishable action.

The radical democratic antiracist struggle should, in Malcolm's spirit, oppose all forms of oppression while constantly forging links with other progressive peoples and organizations. Religion, for example, continues to play a significant role in the lives of Latinos and Latinas and of African-Americans, and it remains a major route of entry into a common politics of opposition to racism within their communities. Given the erosion of moral community across our nation, religion continues to provide moral strength and insight for millions of people through narratives of personal transcendence, ethical responsibility, and spiritual nurture. Especially within minority communities, where issues of meaning and morality are often fused with politics in prophetic religious practices, religion can provide a means of personal stability and social criticism. Radical democrats must continue to overcome antireligious sentiment if we expect to connect with many African-Americans, and Latinas and Latinos, for whom it is relevant to talk of God while speaking of human community.

Particularly within African-American communities, the fight against racism has centered in black religion. With their noble articulation of the norm of fundamental human equality and their strong insistence on black worth, black religionists (Christian and Muslim) are suspicious of secular ideologies that deny the validity of religious experience. Conversely, the strength of radical democratic philosophy and practice has been its unblinking description of the ills associated with forms of thought and political practice shaped by unjust forces, some of which were maintained by religious belief.

These mutual suspicions may be put to good use as black religionists and radical democrats join forces in the reconstitution of the civic order and the reconstruction of political practice. Radical democratic thought can provide a rich vocabulary of social criticism to engage the varied forms of social inequality that prevail in black communities across America. And black religion can offer a needed emphasis on the moral dimensions of political practice and social criticism. Black religionists can insist on anchoring such practice and criticism in a perspective that values human life and asserts the priority of meaning as a fundamental goal of human life.

Given Bill Clinton's identification with the politics of meaning, and his advocacy of the virtues of placing discussions about the common good at the center of American political discourse, radical democrats can make headway by pushing him to broaden his understanding of the problems of race. Radical democrats must urge Clinton to live up to his inaugural-ceremony rhetoric about springtime in the United States. Otherwise, the calamitous consequences of racial domination and violence will make it the long winter of our nation's discontent, especially for a population hit hard by these forces—black men. Malcolm's memory can help us understand and combat the precarious predicament of young black males in America, even if by only forcing our nation to acknowledge its role in their condition.

Urban America is living through an epidemic of violence that has targeted and viciously transformed black male life.[15] With chilling redundancy, black men are dying at the hands of other black men. The mutual harming of black males is a thematic mainstay of the contemporary black films I discuss in Chapter 3. Such films portray the cruel consequences of urban collapse on black male life. The situation for black men, especially juvenile and young adult males, is now so fatally encrusted in chronic hopelessness that terms usually reserved for large-scale social catastrophes—terms like "genocide" and "endangered species"— are now applied to a wide variety of black males with troubling regularity.[16]

Many cultural critics, especially conservative commentators, have concluded that black male violence is the exclusive result of pathological cultural tendencies working themselves out with self-destructive fury. On this view, black male aggression is part of a larger black cultural malaise manifest in welfare dependence, criminal lifestyles, gang activity, and other morally impaired behavior associated with an ominously expanding "underclass." And even when more reasonable critics, especially politically liberal figures, weigh in on the causes and consequences of black male violence, their analyses often skid dangerously close to reductionist cultural arguments that blame the victims of violence for its existence.

Because the situation of black males has become so formidably complex, the horizon of clarity often recedes behind vigorous yet confusing attempts to understand and explain their predicament. Can Malcolm X's example and memory in any way help black men past mutual destruction and the threat of social annihilation? How should we proceed in thinking about these highly charged, complex issues?

In combating the crisis of black males, we must first comprehend the staggering array of difficulties that hound and hurry them from the cradle to the grave. Malcolm was keen on scrupulously documenting the truth of black life, a trait that led him to combine common-sense observation and critical investigation in detailing the plight of African-Americans. In this vein, the extent of social injuries to black male life is indexed in the virtually mind-numbing statistics whose mere recital is the most powerful testimony to a hydra-headed crisis.

Black males are more likely than any other group to be spontaneously aborted. Of all babies, black males have the lowest birth weights. Black males have the highest infant mortality rates. Black males have the greatest chance of dying before they reach age 20. Although they are only 6 percent of the U.S. population, blacks make up half the male prisoners in local, state, and federal jails. Thirty-two percent of black men have incomes below the poverty level. Fifty percent of black men under 21 are unemployed. But it doesn't end here.

Between 1980 and 1985, the life expectancy for white males increased from 63 to 74.6 years; for black males, only from 59 to 65. Between 1973 and 1986, the real earnings of black males between the ages of 18 and 29 fell 31 percent, as the percentage of young black males in the work force plummeted 20 percent. Suicide is the third-leading cause of death among young black men. And as noted earlier, black-on-black homicide is the leading cause of death for black males between the ages of 15 and 34, as young black males have a 1-in-21 lifetime chance of being killed. This is not new; in 1987 alone, more young black men were killed within the United States in a single year than had been killed abroad in the entire nine years of the Vietnam War. This deadly pattern of problems, which accumulates without apparent abatement and taxes black male mortality beyond expected limits—makes it difficult to view the black male condition as the product primarily of black cultural failure.

Next, we should place black male suffering in a historical framework that illumines how black males, far earlier than their recent troubles suggest, have been culturally fashioned as a "problem" category. From the plantation to the postindustrial city, black males have been seen as brutishly behaved, morally flawed, uniquely ugly, and fatally oversexed. The creation of negative black male images through the organs of popular culture—especially in theological tracts, novels, and, more recently, film and television—simply reinforced stereotypes of black males as undisciplined social pariahs, citizens of a corrupt subculture of crime, or imbeciles. Add to that the influence of scholarly portrayals of black males, particularly those contained in ethnographic studies that have both aided and undermined the cultural status of black men, and one gets a hint of the forces challenging a balanced interpretation of their condition.

Finally, we must pay attention to the structural factors that spawn black male suffering. As Malcolm preached a year before his death, "Unemployment and poverty have forced many of our people into [a] life of crime."[17] The shift of the labor base of black males from high-wage, low-skill jobs to scarcer service employment; the expanding technical monopoly of information services; the part-timing of American labor (leaving workers without employee benefits); and the wrenching of the U.S. economy by crises in global capitalism all bode ill for black males.[18] These changes, coupled with cycles of persistent poverty, the gentrification of inner-city living space, the juvenilization of crime, and the demoralization of poor blacks through cultural stereotypes about widespread loss of initiative, only compound the anguish of an already untenable situation for black males.

I am not suggesting that we can reduce the black male crisis to its economic or social determinants. Nor do I contend that black males are without responsibility for elements of their condition. Indeed, the example of Malcolm's black moral puritanism—which promoted self-reliance, rigorous self-discipline, a strong work ethic, and law-abiding behavior—is a rebuke to black males who profess to follow his example while shirking personal and moral responsibilities to their families and communities.

I am simply arguing that the debate about black males must become much more complex and sophisticated, that its participants must be more honest in unearthing the roots of black male agony. It is much easier to damn black males for being irresponsible, immoral, or even criminal than to own up to how American cultural traditions and economic practices have contributed to their plight. Malcolm believed that

> the real criminal is the white man who poses as a liberal—the political hypocrite. And it is these legal crooks, posing as our friends, [who are] forcing us into a life of crime and then using us to spread the white man's evil vices among own people. Our people are scientifically maneuvered by the white man into a life of poverty. You are not poor accidentally. He maneuvers you into poverty. . . . There is nothing about your condition here in America that is an accident.[19]

Although Malcolm's conspiracy theory of history ascribes too much responsibility to individual whites, his words un-

Using Malcolm

derscore an understanding that American society bears significant responsibility for the plight of black males.

This is perhaps most tragically true of the spiritual fatigue and psychic trauma occasioned by racism, and the black male self-hate that it engenders, most viciously expressed in black-on-black homicide, but also insidiously present in less conspicuous gestures of mutual black male contempt. After all, black males have not been immune to the destructive influence of negative cultural messages about themselves, fatally absorbing surface and subtle reminders that their lives are perishable and expendable, less valuable than white lives, and not as useful as those of famous figures like Michael Jordan and Bill Cosby. Malcolm poignantly described the self-hatred that sits at the heart of black-on-black crime:

> We hated our heads, we hated the shape of our nose . . . we hated the color of our skin, hated the blood of Africa that was in our veins. And in hating our features and our skin and our blood, why we had to end up hating ourselves. . . . It made us feel inferior; it made us feel inadequate; made us helpless.[20]

Neither have young black males resisted the seductions of violence; the addictive character of aggression is symptomatic of American popular culture from hockey to Hollywood. It is this combination of violence, racism, self-hatred, and economic desperation that makes black male

171

life vulnerable to confused and often unfair criticism. But if we are to solve the problem of violent black males, we must solve their problems. To paraphrase the great Catholic social prophet Dorothy Day, we must work toward a world in which it is *possible* for black males to behave decently.

Malcolm's memory may yet help save an entire generation of black males buffetted by brutal forms of racial and class antagonism from outside black culture, and beseiged by internal demons and temptations, from drug addiction and violence directed against one another, from within. His wise, salvific offer of comfort to black males—that they are worthy of the highest measures of respect and love—came wrapped in poignant demands of self-discipline and racial uplift. And his heroic example of relentlessly questioning his own unjust thoughts and deeds, leading him to reject narrow racialism and blind gender scapegoating, remains the truest and most meaningful monument to black manhood. Perhaps more than when he first spoke and lived them, Malcolm's words and deeds carry profound import for black males at the dawning of our first full century of American freedom.

Malcolm X's words and deeds can also spur us on to great efforts: they can move us to build on his most valuable ideas even as we are encouraged to transcend his failures and weaknesses. We can confirm his true significance as a prophetic orator and fearless spokesman by acting to en-

flesh the ideals of humane community and progressive political action he didn't live long enough to see become a
reality. By this measure, the greatest achievements of the
heroic tradition Malcolm X participated in remain in the
future.

AFTERWORD
TURNING THE CORNER

> The only person who can organize the man in the street is the one who is unacceptable to the white community. They don't trust the other kind. They don't know who controls his actions. . . . The greatest mistake of the movement has been trying to organize a sleeping people around specific goals. You have to wake the people up . . . to their humanity, to their own worth, and to their heritage. The biggest difference between the parallel oppression of the Jew and the Negro is that the Jew never lost his pride in being a Jew. He never ceased to be a man. He knew he had made a significant contribution to the world, and his sense of his own value gave him the courage to fight back. It enabled him to act and think independently, unlike our people and our leaders.
>
> Malcolm X, in *Malcolm X Speaks:*
> *Selected Speeches and Statements*

Since Malcolm's death in 1965, black Americans have witnessed the arrival of pretenders and wannabees to his throne of rage. There have been many lesser incarnations of Malcolm's prophetic spirit and rhetorical passion, men and women who believed that all that was in Malcolm's bag of tricks was loud speech and hateful harangue. (Khalid Abdul Muhammad's ad hominem attacks on black leaders and Jews is only the most recent example.) Although Mal-

175

colm's withering words would sometimes transport vicious verbal assassinations of other black leaders—and though he could be stubbornly, willfully blind to the truth of a situation that stared him straight in the face—he learned, finally, to make his rage work for the best interests of black folk. That included learning to work with people—like Martin Luther King, Jr., and other leaders of a civil rights movement that he grew to respect for its masked radicalism— with whom he didn't always agree, in fact to whom he'd formerly been vehemently opposed.

Malcolm also came to believe that real leadership was empowering people to lead themselves, to eventually do without the mortal suffering that he had endured at the hands of charismatic but corrupt leadership. Malcolm's push near the end of his life was for people to learn and grow as much as they could in the struggle to free mind and body from the poisonous persistence of racism and blind ethnic loyalty, as well as economic and class slavery. He apologized for his former mistakes, took his lumps for things he'd done wrong in the past, and tried to move on, even though, as he lamented, many devotees (and enemies) wouldn't allow him to "turn the corner." For Malcolm's sake, and for the sake of our survival, black folk must turn the corner.

But what does turning the corner mean for us now? It means that we must turn away from the easy scapegoating of other minorities and ethnic groups in assigning blame for our pain. The problems between blacks and Jews, for instance, are much ballyhooed and bemoaned. Of course, with countless pressing problems facing black communities, we must ask why the media has given so much attention to black–Jewish relations.

In large measure, the media has exploited conflicts between blacks and Jews by imbuing them with an almost surreal intensity and by helping to construct black anti-Semitism as a much more pervasive and virulent phenomenon than empirical research can support. The media has fanned the flames of alleged black discontent with Jews by irresponsible reporting that fails to place relations between the two groups in historical and political perspective. While the fractures of spirit and face suffered by aggrieved parties on both sides are significant, the deeper truth is that these tensions are part of a broader conflict between African-American communities and other groups. Because the black–Jewish compact is certainly among the oldest and most enduring intergroup relations for both sides, the black–Jewish conflict is undeniably a complex, special case; but there are also black–Korean conflicts, black–Latina and –Latino tensions, and black–Chaldean rifts, of shorter duration, of course, though hurtful nonetheless.

The ready temptation is for commentators and critics to chide black folk for being ethnosaurs, upholders of ancient forms of racial complaint against every other group that has come to America and made it over us. The real story, of course, is that as black folk we *have* been stepped on and passed over. As Toni Morrison has eloquently reminded us, it is on the "backs of blacks" that America has been fashioned in such splendid economic privilege and cultural glory. So when I say black folk should turn the corner on the easy route of blame-the-Jew or blame-the-Korean, I don't mean we shouldn't raise tough questions. We should simply move from finger-pointing to serious analysis in discovering the source of our suffering.

When Kahlid Abdul Muhammad, former spokesman for Louis Farrakhan, finds a Jew behind every problem that plagues black folk, he is engaging in a highly imitative move ripped off from the worst proponents of black conspiratorial thinking throughout our history. That his verbiage is vicious is obvious, though he still strikes a chord in desperate black people who want to find some concrete reason for their plight. Why? Because we haven't done our homework.

While Muhammad manipulates the understandable human emotion to name the demon that vexes us—and when you're in bad shape, any demon will do—we fall farther from the truth of our condition. Jews are not our problem. Koreans are not our problem. Latinos and Latinas are not our problem. And though we have legitimate gripes with each group (as they do with blacks), what conscientious blacks have in common with conscientious Jews, Koreans, and Latinos and Latinas is much more interesting to ponder and exploit.

By forging alliances between such groups, substantive issues get debated and dealt with in ways that don't make the destruction of our opponents the way we gain cachet in our communities. And real conflicts surface that have much more to do with how power is distributed, how wealth is circulated, how influence is shared than with how your last name ends. The case of blacks and Jews is instructive. Blacks question why powerful Jews have sided with conservative southern politicians in opposing the renewal of the Voting Rights Act and important redistricting measures that would bring enhanced political power to black citizens. And blacks ask Jews why there is no outcry against these conservative Jews, nor is there a demand for Jews to renounce the potentially racist policies of their brothers and sisters.

Thus Jews ask blacks why their constant love affair with conspiracy makes them vulnerable to claims by some black intellectuals and leaders—from Leonard Jeffries to Louis Farrakhan—that Jews are the major roadblocks to black progress. Jews ask blacks why any criticisms of affirmative action are viewed automatically as racist, why blacks emotionally chafe when any suggestion that alternative strategies for black improvement are proffered. And Jews and blacks ask each other about the hierarchy of pain that grants privilege for each group's collective suffering, viewed in the Holocaust-versus-slavery debate, which often turns ugly and irrational. The point here is that we turn the corner

179

on the acrimonious assaults on each other, and turn to more serious conflicts whose resolution might relieve the need of glorified pettiness on both sides.

But turning the corner also means that black folk have to come to grips with how we do one another in. Not simply in the ghettos of urban America, where black-on-black crime is much lamented and commented on, even if in ridiculously racist and sexist manners. The black-on-black crime I'm speaking about happens at the highest levels of intellectual and organizational endeavor. The deep distrust we harbor for one another—we still think white folk have some magic that black folk don't possess, whether in medicine or in marketing—makes us liable to vicious forms of professional backbiting and jealousy. It's the same for preachers and professors, lawyers and doctors, and journalist and judges. We kill with the pen as swiftly as we do with the Uzi.

This impulse to hurt those with whom we disagree, and with whom we share the greatest resemblance, is an ancient passion, a form of intolerance that only intimate contact can ignite. It's what killed Malcolm, this inability to disagree close-up without destruction. And there is so much at stake in our fights—identity, loyalty, passion, and love, as well as hatred, dissemblance, treachery, and betrayal.

We can turn the corner on the impulse to destroy what's black only by affirming the best of what's black—by offering simple economic measures that circulate black dol-

Turning the Corner

lars in black communities; by taking a chance on black brothers and sisters in a professional service blacks have need of; by black parents insisting on excellence from their children in their schoolwork and social life; by refusing, consciously, to destroy the reputation of a brother or sister by speaking false or irresponsible words; and by heeding edifying, enabling criticism. This sounds, of course, so naive as to be incredible; but the ministration of a daily political ethic of care for fractured black bodies and spirits, as well as the sort of profound structural analysis and radical democratic social activity that I have advocated, is like Poe's purloined letter, made invisible because it lies hidden in full sight.

Such a political ethic of care might have saved Malcolm's life, might have enabled his promethean will to self-improvement and re-creation to be extended vastly into our bewildering wastelands of lost hope and surrendered faith. He was, after all, a holy man, a troublesome formulation to declare because religion—and rightfully so in many cases—is viewed with increased suspicion in our nation. But his hardheaded insistence on enlivening a black public theodicy, on delineating the shape and limits of black angst and rage against racial and economic injustice, makes his vision just right for our times.

If we are to turn the corner in earnest, ordinary black folk and leaders—local and national alike—must stop bashing young black people. The perennial evocation of a golden age of black ethical achievement, when the fabric of our common moral and social life was magically knit together, is certainly produced out of the whole cloth of utopian reverie. At every stage of our sojourn on American soil, black folk have appealed to a time, largely mythical and unquestionably romantic, when we were better than we are in whatever age in which we happen to be struggling. This understandable strategy of moral regeneration by harkening to past ideals is sometimes helpful and, as we're now discovering, sometimes quite harmful.

The present generation of young blacks has been rebuked and reviled for its fateful loss of a moral compass that had been bequeathed from one black generation to the next since slavery. They have been called a "lost generation," and damned for their violent self-destruction. Their hip-hop music has been scorned and attacked in a manner virtually unprecedented in our nation's history, and their culture has been viewed as damaged and pathological.

In turning the corner on our views of young blacks, we must acknowledge the incredible assault on mind and body that they have endured in ways hard to imagine for most adults. Although they are the victims of violence more than any other population, they are blamed for its vicious expression. Although they are caught in cycles of poverty that begin before they are born, their indigence is laid at the feet of their stubborn refusal to work. Although they are often born into families hardest hit by the postindustrial collapse and restructuring of industries that once provided stable work, their turn to informal economies to survive is viewed in coldly animalistic terms. And not just by white folk.

Most young black people want to do well, are afraid of a violent world, spurn self-destructive behavior, and aren't pathological. As we continue to demand the best of our young people, as we listen to them and *learn* from them, as we shed tears for them as they make mistakes while we recall our own foibles and failings, and as we continue to affirm their value as worthful human beings hampered from their best in a world determined, often, to snuff out their lives, we can help them survive to witness their children's prospering. Not without, however, a radical reorientation in our willingness to criticize capitalism and classism, and not without a willingness to sacrifice the comforts of our bourgeois, conservative black culture for a deeper analysis of why so few have so much while so many have so little.

Malcolm's greatest contribution to us is to think for ourselves, to learn to help ourselves when others refuse, and to demand a world in which such help is not the preserve of the privileged, but the domain of the masses. Malcolm's example still invites us to ask hard questions of ourselves, to renew ourselves at the altar of rigorous sacrifice and a shameless love of black folk. With the broad, humane vision that powered Malcolm's final days, African-American life can surge forward against the incredible odds we presently face. We can continue to reinvent ourselves as Malcolm reinvented himself. By our willingness to think and do the impossible in the name of the inextinguishable hope that moved our ancestors to dream and act with great boldness, we too can triumph, like Malcolm, by any means necessary.

NOTES

Chapter 1

1. Bruce Perry, *Malcolm: The Life of a Man Who Changed Black America* (Barrytown, N.Y.: Station Hill Press, 1991).
2. Louis Lomax, *To Kill a Black Man* (Los Angeles: Holloway House, 1968); Perry, *Malcolm.*
3. Malcolm X, with the assistance of Alex Haley, *The Autobiography of Malcolm X* (New York: Grove Press, 1965).

Chapter 2

1. These personal and political understandings can be described as paradigms, or theories that explain evidence or account for behavior, that shift over space and time. For a discussion about paradigm shifts in the history of science, see Thomas Kuhn, *The Structure of Scientific Revolutions,* 2d ed. (Chicago: University of Chicago Press, 1970). According to Kuhn, revolutions in science occur when a given paradigm fails to account for an increasing degree of disconfirming evidence, called anomalies. Failure of the paradigm creates a crisis, and can be resolved only with the emergence of a new scientific paradigm. For an application of Kuhn's work to moral philosophy and religious experience, see Jon Gunnemann, *The Moral Meaning of Revolution* (New Haven: Yale University Press, 1979).
2. The lack of a significant body of scholarly literature about Malcolm reveals more about the priorities, interests, and limitations of contemporary scholarship than about his importance as a revolutionary social figure. There is no dearth of interest in Mal-

colm, however, in the popular press, and though cultural curiosity about him is now undoubtedly at a peak, he has unfailingly provoked popular reflection about his life and career among journalists, activists, and organic intellectuals since his death in 1965. This is made abundantly clear in two book-length bibliographies on Malcolm: Lenwood G. Davis, with the assistance of Marsha L. Moore, comps., *Malcolm X: A Selected Bibliography* (Westport, Conn.: Greenwood Press, 1984), and Timothy V. Johnson, comp., *Malcolm X: A Comprehensive Annotated Bibliography* (New York: Garland, 1986).

3. For an illuminating discussion of the philosophical issues and problems involved in understanding and explanation in the humanities, see Charles Taylor, "Interpretation and The Sciences of Man," in *Interpretive Social Science: A Reader*, ed. Paul Rabinow and William M. Sullivan (Berkely: University of California Press, 1979), pp. 25–71.

4. For the notion of thick description, see Clifford Geertz, "Thick Description: Toward an Interpretive Theory of Culture," in *The Interpretation of Cultures* (New York: Basic Books, 1973).

5. Michael Eric Dyson, "Probing a Divided Metaphor," in *Reflecting Black: African-American Cultural Criticism* (Minneapolis: University of Minnesota Press, 1993), pp. 115–128. For discussion of Malcolm's motivations for his autobiography, and Alex Haley's role in shaping the narrative of Malcolm's life, see also Arnold Rampersad, "The Color of His Eyes: Bruce Perry's *Malcolm* and Malcolm's Malcolm," and Robin D. G. Kelley, "The Riddle of the Zoot: Malcolm Little and Black Cultural Politics During World War II," both in *Malcolm X: In Our Own Image*, ed. Joe Wood (New York: St. Martin's Press, 1992), pp. 117–134, 155–175, respectively.

6. For more of my comment on other books about Malcolm, see Dyson, "Probing a Divided Metaphor," pp. 115–128.

7. For a good overview and discussion of these groups, see Raymond Hall, *Black Separatism in the United States* (Hanover, N.H.: University Press of New England, 1978).

8. For an excellent discussion of the links between Malcolm

X and the Black Power movement, of which he was a precursor, with discussions of SNCC, CORE, and the Black Panthers, see Robert Allen, *Black Awakening in Capitalist America: An Analytic History* (Garden City, N.Y.: Doubleday, 1969), pp. 21–88. For a discussion of the economic programs and comparisons of the social visions of each group, see Hall, *Black Separatism in the United States*, especially pp. 139–196.

9. See especially John Ansbro, *Martin Luther King, Jr.: The Making of a Mind* (Maryknoll, N.Y.: Orbis Books, 1982); Stephen B. Oates, *Let the Trumpet Sound: The Life of Martin Luther King, Jr.* (New York: Harper & Row, 1982); and David Garrow, *Bearing the Cross: Martin Luther King, Jr., and the Southern Christian Leadership Conference, 1955–1968* (New York: Morrow, 1986).

10. John Henrik Clarke, ed., *Malcolm X: The Man and His Times* (1969; Trenton, N.J.: Africa World Press, 1990).

11. Charles Wilson, "Leadership Triumph in Leadership Tragedy," in *Malcolm X*, ed. Clarke, pp. 36–37.

12. James Boggs, "The Influence of Malcolm X on the Political Consciousness of Black Americans," and Wyatt Tee Walker, "Nothing but a Man," in *Malcolm X*, ed. Clarke, pp. 52, 67.

13. Albert Cleage, "Myths About Malcolm X," in *Malcolm X*, ed. Clarke, p. 15.

14. Oba T'Shaka, *The Political Legacy of Malcolm X* (Richmond, Calif.: Pan Afrikan, 1983); Malcolm X, *The End of White World Supremacy: Four Speeches by Malcolm X*, ed. Benjamin Karim [Goodman] (New York: Arcade, 1971).

15. T'Shaka, *Political Legacy of Malcolm X*, pp. 244–245.

16. Ibid., pp. 57, 118.

17. Karim, Introduction to Malcolm X, *End of White World Supremacy*, pp. 21–22.

18. Gordon Parks, "Malcolm X: The Minutes of Our Last Meeting," in *Malcolm X*, ed. Clark, p. 120.

19. On his repudiation of the white devil theory, see Malcolm X, with the assistance of Alex Haley, *Autobiography of Malcolm X* (New York: Grove Press, 1965), pp. 362–363. For Malcolm's

desire to meet Robeson a month before his death, see Martin Duberman, *Paul Robeson* (New York: Knopf, 1988), p. 528.

20. I take up this issue in "Beyond Essentialism: Expanding African-American Cultural Criticism," in *Reflecting Black*, pp. xiii–xxxiii.

21. The debate about cultural and racial authenticity as it relates to who is able to interpret Malcolm's legacy legitimately has most recently occurred in writer-activist Amiri Baraka's attacks on Spike Lee about Lee's film portrait of Malcolm X before his film appeared. Implicit in Baraka's charges that Lee would not adequately or accurately represent Malcolm is the belief that Baraka's representation of Malcolm is superior. Baraka's hagiographical recollections of Malcolm and his refusal to concede that Lee's claims and representations of him may be equally valid are a prime example of the often insular intellectual climate surrounding debates about Malcolm. The irony here, of course, is that of all current black directors, with the possible exception of John Singleton, Spike Lee appears most suitably disposed to represent a vision of Malcolm that jibes with Baraka's cultural views, given Lee's Afrocentric film and aesthetic vocabulary and his neonationalist cultural perspective.

22. Malcolm X, "Answers to Questions at the Militant Labor Forum," in *By Any Means Necessary: Speeches, Interviews, and a Letter, by Malcolm X*, ed. George Breitman (New York: Pathfinder Press, 1970), pp. 22–23.

23. See Henry Young's two-volume study, *Major Black Religious Leaders* (Nashville: Abingdon Press, 1977, 1979).

24. Louis E. Lomax, *When the Word Is Given: A Report on Elijah Muhammad, Malcolm X, and the Black Muslim World* (Cleveland: World, 1963), and *To Kill a Black Man* (Los Angeles: Holloway House, 1968); James H. Cone, *Martin and Malcolm and America: A Dream or a Nightmare?* (Maryknoll, N.Y.: Orbis Books, 1991); Peter Goldman, *The Death and Life of Malcolm X*, 2d ed. (1973; Urbana: University of Illinois Press, 1979). For a discussion of moral saints, see Susan Wolf, "Moral Saints," *Journal of Philosophy* 8 (1982): 419–439, and Robert Merrihew Adam's response to her essay in

Notes

The Virtue of Faith and Other Essays in Philosophical Theology (New York: Oxford University Press, 1987), pp. 164–173.

25. Of course, the classic treatment of the Black Muslims during the leadership of Elijah Muhammad and Malcolm X is C. Eric Lincoln, *The Black Muslims in America* (Boston: Beacon Press, 1961, 1973). Also very helpful is E. U. Essien-Udom, *Black Nationalism: A Search for an Identity in America* (Chicago: University of Chicago Press, 1962). For a treatment of the Nation of Islam under Elijah Muhammad and Malcolm X, and it transition to orthodox Islamic practice and belief under Wallace Muhammad as the World Community of al-Islam in the West, see Clifton E. Marsh, *From Black Muslims to Muslims: The Transition from Separatism to Islam, 1930–1980* (Metuchen, N.J.: Scarecrow Press, 1984). For a historical and analytic treatment of the Nation of Islam, including its history under Muhammad and Wallace Muhammad, and its separate revitalization as the second incarnation of the Nation of Islam under Louis Farrakhan, see Martha F. Lee, *The Nation of Islam: An American Millenarian Movement* (Lewiston, N.Y.: Edwin Mellen Press, 1988).

26. Lomax, *When the Word Is Given,* pp. 87, 68.

27. For an extended review of Cone's book, see my essay "Martin and Malcolm," in *Reflecting Black,* pp. 250–263.

28. Of course, Malcolm's life and thought represented and addressed various aspects of both religious and revolutionary nationalism. In this regard, see John H. Bracey, Jr., August Meier, and Elliott Rudwick, eds., *Black Nationalism in America* (Indianapolis: Bobbs-Merrill, 1970), p. 505. Also see Essien-Udom, *Black Nationalism.* For a fine historical treatment of the heyday of black nationalism, see Wilson Jeremiah Moses, *The Golden Age of Black Nationalism, 1850–1925* (Hamden, Conn.: Archon Books, 1978).

29. Cone, *Martin and Malcolm and America,* p. 151.

30. Ibid., p. 170.

31. Other works explore the relationship between King and Malcolm, along with comparative analyses of other intellectual and religious figures, in a religious and social ethical context. For

two fine examples, see Peter Paris, *Black Leaders in Conflict,* 2d ed. (Louisville: Westminster Press/John Knox Press, 1991), and Robert M. Franklin, *Liberating Visions: Human Fulfillment and Social Justice in African-American Thought* (Minneapolis: Augsburg, 1990).

32. Ralph Ellison, quoted in Robert B. Stepto and Michael S. Harper, "Study and Experience: An Interview with Ralph Ellison," in *Chant of Saints: A Gathering of Afro-American Literature, Art, and Scholarship,* ed. Stepto and Harper (Urbana: University of Illinois Press, 1979), p. 458.

33. For insightful treatments of Du Bois, see Arnold Rampersad, *The Art and Imagination of W. E. B. Du Bois* (Cambridge, Mass.: Harvard University Press, 1976); Gerald Horne, *Black and Red: W. E. B. Du Bois and the Afro-American Response to the Cold War, 1944–1963* (Albany: State University of New York Press, 1986); Manning Marable, *W. E. B. Du Bois: Black Radical Democrat* (Boston: Twayne, 1986); and, of course, the definitive treatment of Du Bois to date, David Levering Lewis,*W. E. B. Du Bois: Biography of a Race, 1868–1919* (New York: Holt, 1993). For the definitive treatment of Booker T. Washington, see Louis Harlan's two volumes: *Booker T. Washington: The Making of a Black Leader, 1856–1901* (New York: Oxford University Press, 1972), and *Booker T. Washington: The Wizard of Tuskegee, 1901–1915* (New York: Oxford University Press, 1983).

34. Lomax, *To Kill a Black Man,* p. 10.

35. George Breitman, "More Than One Way 'To Kill a Black Man,'" in *The Assassination of Malcolm X,* ed. George Breitman, Herman Porter, and Baxter Smith (New York: Pathfinder Press, 1976), pp. 131–144.

36. Robert Franklin also makes use of Goldman's notion of public moralist in his excellent book *Liberating Visions,* a comparative study of Booker T. Washington, W. E. B. Du Bois, Malcolm X, and Martin Luther King, Jr.

37. There is a swelling literature on the possible plots and theories of how Malcolm was murdered. While the close study of this literature is beyond my purposes here, it certainly constitutes an intriguing category of debate around Malcolm. See, for ex-

ample, Breitman, Porter, and Smith, eds., *Assassination of Malcolm X*, and Karl Evanzz, *The Judas Factor: The Plot to Kill Malcolm X* (New York: Thunder Mouth Press, 1992).

38. For arguments that Goldman's views about Malcolm's assassination support the official government story, and that the CIA and the Bureau of Special Services (BOSS)—the name of the New York secret police agency at the time of Malcolm's death—were implicated in his assassination, see George Breitman, "A Liberal Supports the Government Version," in *Assassination of Malcolm X*, ed. Breitman, Porter, and Smith, pp. 145–166.

39. Goldman, *Death and Life of Malcolm X*, p. 191.

40. Martin Luther King, Jr., quoted in David Halberstam, "When 'Civil Rights' and 'Peace' Join Forces," in *Martin Luther King, Jr: A Profile*, ed. C. Eric Lincoln, rev. ed. (New York: Hill & Wang, 1984), p. 202.

41. Clayborne Carson, "Malcolm and the American State," in *Malcolm X: The FBI File*, ed. David Gallen (New York: Carroll & Graf, 1991), p. 18.

42. Ibid.

43. See George Devereux, *Basic Problems of Ethnopsychiatry*, trans. Basia Miller Gulati and George Devereux (Chicago: University of Chicago Press, 1980); Frantz Fanon, *The Wretched of the Earth* (New York: Grove Press, 1966), and *Black Skin, White Masks* (New York: Grove Press, 1967); Erich Fromm, *Beyond the Chains of Illusion: My Encounter with Marx and Freud* (New York: Simon and Schuster, 1962); Christopher Lasch, *The Culture of Narcissism* (New York: Warner Books, 1979); Bruce Brown, *Marx, Freud, and the Critique of Everyday Life: Toward a Permanent Cultural Revolution* (New York: Monthly Review Press, 1973); Margaret MacDonald, ed., *Philosophy and Analysis* (Oxford: Blackwell, 1954); and relevant work of the Frankfurt school, including Theodor W. Adorno, Walter Benjamin, Erich Fromm, Max Horkheimer, Herbert Marcuse, and Jürgen Habermas. For a collection of essays by these authors, see Andrew Arato and Eike Gebhardt, eds., *The Essential Frankfurt School Reader* (New York: Continuum, 1982). For a treatment of their work in relation to psychoanalytic theory, see C.

Notes

Fred Alford, *Narcissism: Socrates, the Frankfurt School, and Psychoanalytic Theory* (New Haven: Yale University Press, 1988).

44. Richard Lichtman, *The Production of Desire: The Integration of Psychoanalysis into Marxist Theory* (New York: Free Press, 1982), p. ix.

45. Ibid., pp. ix–x.

46. Erik H. Erikson, *Gandhi's Truth: On the Origins of Militant Nonviolence* (New York: Norton, 1969). For a more controversial psychobiographical treatment of a historical figure, see Erikson's study of Protestant reformer Martin Luther, *Young Man Luther* (New York: Norton, 1958).

47. Eugene Victor Wolfenstein, *The Victims of Democracy: Malcolm X and the Black Revolution* (1981; London: Free Association Books, 1989).

48. Ibid., pp. 1–2.

49. Ibid., p. xiii.

50. For an important historical examination of white working-class racism, see David R. Roediger, *The Wages of Whiteness: Race and the Making of the American Working Class* (London: Verso, 1991).

51. Other Marxist, socialist, and progressive approaches to race theory and racism attempt to theorize race as a socially, culturally, historically, and politically constructed category that undergoes change over space and time. See, for example, Cornel West, "Marxist Theory and the Specificity of Afro-American Oppression," in *Marxism and the Interpretation of Culture*, ed. Cary Nelson and Lawrence Grossberg (Urbana: University of Illinois Press, 1988), pp. 17–33; Lucius Outlaw, "Toward a Critical Theory of 'Race,' " in *Anatomy of Racism*, ed. David Goldberg (Minneapolis: University of Minnesota Press, 1990), pp. 58–82; Michael Eric Dyson, "The Liberal Theory of Race," and "Racism and Race Theory in the Nineties," in *Reflecting Black*, pp. 132–156; Leonard Harris, "Historical Subjects and Interests: Race, Class, and Conflict," and Lucius Outlaw, "On Race and Class, or, On the Prospects of 'Rainbow Socialism,' " both in *The Year Left 2: An American Socialist Yearbook*, ed. Mike Davis et al. (London: Verso, 1987); and Michael

Notes

Omi and Howard Winant, *Racial Formation in the United States: From the 1960s to the 1980s* (London: Routledge & Kegan Paul, 1986).

52. See Thomas Gossett, *Race: The History of An Idea in America* (Dallas: Southern Methodist University Press, 1965).

53. Wolfenstein, *Victims of Democracy*, p. 37.

54. Bruce Perry, *Malcolm: The Life of a Man Who Changed Black America* (Barrytown, N.Y.: Station Hill Press, 1991).

55. Ibid., p. ix.

56. Ibid., p. x.

57. Ibid., pp. 41–42.

58. Ibid., p. 54.

59. For further discussion of this subject, see Dyson, "Beyond Essentialism," pp. xiii–xxxiii.

60. For insightful discussions of the predicament of black intellectuals, see, of course, Harold Cruse's pioneering *The Crisis of the Negro Intellectual* (New York: Morrow, 1967); Cornel West, "The Dilemma of the Black Intellectual," *Cultural Critique*, no. 1 (Fall 1985): 109–124; and Jerry Watts, "Dilemmas of Black Intellectuals," *Dissent*, Fall 1989, pp. 501–507.

61. Christian ethicist Katie Cannon writes about the "white academic community's flourishing publishing monopoly on the writing of black history, black thought, and black world view. Black scholars did not abdicate their roles in these fields to white academicians. Blacks have written monographs, theses, conference papers, proposals, and outlines for books on various aspects of black reality since the 1700s, but white publishers did not give them serious consideration until the 1970s" ("Racism and Economics: The Perspective of Oliver C. Cox," in *The Public Vocation of Christian Ethics*, ed. Beverly W. Harrison, Robert L. Stivers, and Ronald H. Stone [New York: Pilgrim Press, 1986], p. 121).

62. William James, *The Varieties of Religious Experience* (1902; New York: Penguin, 1982).

63. Lomax, *To Kill a Black Man*, p. 142.

64. Goldman, *Death and Life of Malcolm X*, p. 189.

65. George Breitman, *The Last Year of Malcolm X: The Evolution of a Revolutionary* (New York: Pathfinder Press, 1967); Malcolm X,

Notes

Malcolm X Speaks: Selected Speeches and Statements, ed. George Breitman (New York: Pathfinder Press, 1965); *By Any Means Necessary;* and *Malcolm X: The Last Speeches,* ed. Bruce Perry (New York: Pathfinder Press, 1989).

66. Breitman, *Last Year of Malcolm X,* p. 69.

67. Malcolm, X, *By Any Means Necessary,* p. 159.

68. Breitman, *Last Year of Malcolm X,* p. 65.

69. Malcolm X, *By Any Means Necessary,* p. 159.

70. Given the variety and complexity of black nationalist thought, Malcolm could have accommodated and advocated such changes had he had sufficient time to link his broadened sense of struggle to the subsequent social and political activity he inspired. It is important, however, not to overlook the tensions between groups like SNCC and Malcolm while he lived. As Lomax says: " . . . Malcolm was never able to effect an alliance with the young black militants who were then plotting the crisis that is now upon the republic. His trip to Selma was arranged by SNCC people but no alliance resulted. The Black Power people would later raise Malcolm to sainthood but they would not work with him, nor let him work with them, in life" (*To Kill a Black Man,* pp. 157–158).

71. Breitman, *Last Year of Malcolm X,* p. 27.

72. Ibid., p. 34.

73. Malcolm X, *Malcolm X Speaks,* p. 128, quoted in Breitman, *Last Year of Malcolm X,* p. 35.

74. Malcolm X, "The Harlem 'Hate-Gang' Scare," in *Malcolm X Speaks,* ed. Breitman, p. 65.

75. Ibid., p. 69.

76. Malcolm X, *By Any Means Necessary,* pp. 159–160.

77. See Leon Trotsky, *Leon Trotsky on Black Nationalism and Self-Determination* (New York: Pathfinder Press, 1978).

78. C. L. R. James, interview in *Visions of History,* ed. MARHO (New York: Pantheon, 1984), p. 270.

79. I do not mean to rule out other genres in which Malcolm's life and accomplishments may be examined. For an example of a science fiction approach to his life and thought, see Kent Smith, *Future X* (Los Angeles: Holloway House, 1989),

Notes

which appears to have been influenced as much by Schwarzen-negger's *Terminator* films as by ideological currents in African-American culture.

Chapter 3

1. For insightful treatments of black nationalism, see John Bracey, Jr., August Meier, and Elliot Rudwick, eds., *Black Nationalism in America* (Indianapolis: Bobbs-Merrill, 1970); Wilson Jeremiah Moses, *The Golden Age of Black Nationalism: 1950–1925* (Hamden, Conn.: Archon Books, 1978); and Alphonso Pinkney, *Red, Black, and Green: Black Nationalism in the United States* (London: Cambridge University Press, 1976).

2. For useful treatments of the various stages and varieties of black nationalism, see Moses, *Golden Age of Black Nationalism;* John Bracey, Jr., "Black Nationalism Since Garvey," in *Key Issues in the Afro-American Experience,* ed. Nathan Huggins, Martin Kilson, and Daniel M. Fox (New York: Harcourt Brace Jovanovich, 1971), vol. 2, pp. 259–279; and Mary Frances Berry and John Blassingame, *Long Memory: The Black Experience in America* (New York: Oxford University Press, 1982), pp. 388–423.

3. Clayborne Carson, *In Struggle: SNCC and the Black Awakening in the 1960s* (Cambridge, Mass.: Harvard University Press, 1981); Raymond Hall, *Black Separatism in the United States* (Hanover, N.H.: University Press of New England, 1978); Robert Allen, *Black Awakening in Capitalist America: An Analytic History* (Garden City, N.Y.,: Doubleday, 1969); James Cone, *Black Theology and Black Power* (New York: Seabury Press, 1969); William Van Deburg, *New Days in Babylon: The Black Power Movement and American Culture, 1965–1975* (Chicago: University of Chicago Press, 1992); Hugh Pearson, *The Shadow of the Panther: Huey Newton and the Price of Black Power in America* (Reading, Mass.: Addison-Wesley, 1994).

4. Cited in "Malcolm X," *Newsweek,* November 16, 1992, p. 72.

5. See especially, Lawrence Levine, *Black Culture and Black*

195

Notes

Consciousness: Afro-American Folk Thought from Slavery to Freedom (New York: Oxford University Press, 1977).

6. I realize that there are divisions in hip-hop culture and music, including hard-core, pop, black nationalist, and gangsta' rap. I am referring primarily to the black nationalist expression phase of rap, though Malcolm's influence is by no means limited to this subgenre of hip-hop.

7. Quoted in "A Tribute to Malcolm X" [special issue], *Black Beat Magazine*, 1992, p. 15.

8. Ibid., p. 13.

9. Ibid., p. 48.

10. The phrase is from Derek Bell, *Faces at the Bottom of the Well: The Permanence of Racism* (New York: Basic Books, 1993).

11. I am not suggesting that King was, by himself, the civil rights movement or that his accomplishments exclusively define its scope of achievements. I am suggesting that he is the most powerful symbol of the movement, however, and as a result was often the most visible target of Malcolm's attacks on its strategies, goals, and methods.

12. Quoted in "Tribute to Malcolm X," p. 13.

13. Ibid., p. 12.

14. C. Eric Lincoln, quoted in "Malcolm X," pp. 71–72.

15. C. Eric Lincoln, *The Black Muslims in America* (Boston: Beacon Press, 1961, 1973). Max Weber defined "theodicy" as the perception of incongruity between destiny and merit. In strict theological terms, theodicy has to do with justifying the ways of God to human beings, especially as a response to the problem of evil. As I use the term here, I view theodicy as the attempt by Malcolm X and the Nation of Islam to explain the evil of white racism and the suffering of blacks, by reference to an elaborate demonology of whiteness and a justification of the Nation of Islam's superior moral position in relation to white people.

16. Malcolm X, quoted in "Tribute to Malcolm X," p. 50.

17. Ibid, p. 49.

18. For my take on Jeffries, see my essay "Leonard Jeffries and the Struggle for the Black Mind," in *Reflecting Black: African-*

196

Notes

American Cultural Criticism (Minneapolis: University of Minnesota Press, 1993), pp. 157–163.

19. Ibid., p. 157.

20. I realize that Afrocentrism is a complex intellectual movement composed of many strands. However, I have in mind here primarily the views of its founder, Molefi Asante. For a sampling of Asante's views, see his *Afrocentricity: The Theory of Social Change,* 2d ed.(Trenton, N.J.: Africa World Press, 1990).

21. Quoted in "Tribute to Malcolm X," p. 12.

22. C. Delores Tucker, Dionne Warwick, Congresswoman Maxine Waters, and I, along with music professors and critics, testified before the U.S. Senate on gangsta' rap in 1994. I am basing my comments about their positions on their written testimonies, in possession of the author, delivered that day.

23. "Malcolm X," p. 70.

24. Ossie Davis, eulogy of Malcolm X, in *Malcolm X: The Man and His Times,* ed. John Henrik Clarke (1969; Trenton, N.J.: Africa World Press, 1990), p. xii.

25. Patricia Hill Collins, "Learning to Think for Ourselves: Malcolm X's Black Nationalism Reconsidered," in *Malcolm X: In Our Own Image,* ed. Joe Wood (New York: St. Martin's Press, 1992), pp. 62, 78.

26. For more comment on this aspect of King's legacy, see my op-ed "King's Light, Malcolm's Shadow," *New York Times,* January 18, 1993, p. 19.

27. I hope to sketch out briefly in this chapter and in Chapter 6 what I mean by radical democracy. Suffice it say the term seeks to accent the emancipatory elements of political practice, signifying a broad emphasis on popular participation in the affairs of the citizenry. For me, radical democrats view issues of race, gender, sexuality, the environment, the workplace, and the like to be crucial spheres where the negotiation over identity, equality, and emancipation takes place. My radical democratic principles commit me to a relentless quest for the sort of political behavior, economic arrangements, and social conditions that promote a full, productive life for the common citizenry. For a powerful vision

Notes

of radical democracy, and a defense of this term to express and unite a wide range of progressive politics, see Stanley Aronowitz's "The Situation of the Left in the United States," *Socialist Review* 23, no. 3 (1994): 5–79. See also the lively exchange between Aronowitz and several capable interlocutors, including Amarpal Dhaliwal, Barbara Ehrenreich, Barbara Epstein, Richard Flacks, Michael Omi, Howard Winant, and Eli Zaretsky, on pp. 81–150.

28. By now, of course, "sex," "race," and "class" are viewed as hackneyed terms meant to invoke an automatic knowledge of the problems to which they refer. The strategy of some critics is to dismiss the seriousness of these issues because of a terminological or ideological impasse. This strategy, I believe, is disingenuous and fails to account for the bleak persistence of sexism, racism, and classism. Indeed, I would argue that it is not that we have tried to employ sophisticated notions of the relationship between these spheres of social identity and theory, and public struggle, and they have failed, but that they have never been really tried, actually implemented. The debate over multiculturalism and its opponents has encouraged reactionary elements to seize the upper hand in the battle to describe our contemporary social landscape. But often, these critics fail to highlight either their own direct complicity in racism, sexism, or classism, or their participation in traditions of thought that supply the (sometimes subtle) rationale for these problems' bleak persistence.

29. See Uwe Reinhart, "Cut Costs? Of Course," *New York Times,* June 12, 1994, sec. 4A, p. 8.

30. For instance, see Toni Morrison, ed., *Race-ing Justice, Engendering Power* (New York: Pantheon, 1992).

31. I take up this issue in "Beyond Essentialism: Expanding African-American Cultural Criticism," in *Reflecting Black,* pp. xiii–xxxiii.

32. This does not deny the importance of forms of social activity and group behavior manifest in cultural activity such as play that represents subtle political resistance. For a highly creative analysis and application of a broadened notion of politics, especially among working-class black folk, see Robin G. D. Kelley's

Notes

brilliant *Race Rebels: Culture, Politics, and the Black Working Class* (New York: Free Press, 1994).

Chapter 4

1. On black popular culture, see Gina Dent, ed., *Black Popular Culture* (Seattle: Bay Press, 1992). See also my section on black popular culture in *Reflecting Black: African-American Cultural Criticism* (Minneapolis: University of Minnesota Press, 1993), pp. 1–111; Manthia Diawara, ed., *Black Cinema: Aesthetics and Spectatorship* (New York: Routledge, 1992); Mark Reid, *Redefining Black Film* (Berkeley: University of California Press, 1993); Ed Guerrero, *Framing Blackness: The African American Image in Film* (Philadelphia: Temple University Press, 1993); and Thomas Cripps, *Making Movies Black: The Hollywood Movie from World War II to the Civil Rights Era* (New York: Oxford University Press, 1993).

2. For my take on black men, see ''The Plight of Black Men,'' in *Reflecting Black,* pp. 182–194. See also Jewelle Taylor Gibbs, ed., *Young, Black, and Male in America: An Endangered Species* (Dover, Mass.: Auburn House, 1988).

3. A slew of recent films, from *Above the Rim* to *Inkwell,* also treat aspects of black male life. My analysis here is not an exhaustive engagement with the genre of male-centered films. Rather, I am attempting to provide a reading of dominant interpretive strategies within selected black films that address black masculinity.

4. For a discussion that provides the context for debates about black males, and the role the black independent press has in both fostering the debate and influencing black film, see my essay ''Between Apocalypse and Redemption: John Singleton's 'Boyz N the Hood,' '' in *Reflecting Black,* pp. 90–110.

5. For more extensive commentary on the history of hip-hop, and critical discussion of rap's moral and political vision, see my *Reflecting Black,* pp. 1–22, 167–179, 276–281.

Notes

6. Of the many raps that explore these themes, see rap group Naughty by Nature's song "Ghetto Bastard."

7. Terry Williams, *Cocaine Kids: The Inside Story of a Teenage Drug Gang* (Reading, Mass: Addison-Wesley, 1989); Mike Davis, *City of Quartz: Excavating the Future in Los Angeles* (London: Verso, 1990).

8. Léon Bing, *Do or Die* (New York: HarperCollins, 1991).

9. For the notion of fictive kin, see Carol Stack, *All Our Kin: Strategies for Survival in a Black Community* (New York: Harper & Row, 1974).

10. For more on Lee's move from stereotype to archetype, and its consequences for his artistic vision and his treatment of film character, see my essay "Spike Lee's Neonationalist Vision," in *Reflecting Black,* pp. 23–31.

Chapter 5

1. See David Bradley's discussion of this struggle, and his role as one of the many hired and fired writers of the screenplay of Malcolm's life, in "Malcolm's Mythmaking," *Transition* 56 (1992): 20–46.

2. Ibid.

3. For an exploration of some of the themes of Lee's earlier work, see my essay "Spike Lee's Neonationalist Vision," in *Reflecting Black, African-American Cultural Criticism* (Minneapolis: University of Minnesota Press, 1993), pp. 23–31.

4. Malcolm X, with the assistance of Alex Haley, *The Autobiography of Malcolm X* (New York: Grove Press, 1964).

5. Bruce Perry, *Malcolm: The Life of a Man Who Changed Black America* (Barrytown, N.Y.: Station Hill Press, 1991). Malcolm confesses to this act not in his autobiography, but in a speech delivered a week before his death. See Malcolm X, "There's a Worldwide Revolution Going On," in *Malcolm X: The Last Speeches,* ed. Bruce Perry (New York: Pathfinder Press, 1989), pp. 122–123.

Notes

Chapter 6

1. I use the term "collective memory" in the way it is employed in contemporary historical and sociological scholarship. Barry Schwartz says that collective memory is "a metaphor that formulates society's retention and loss of information about its past in the familiar terms of individual remembering and forgetting. Part of the collective memory is, in fact, defined by shared individual memories, but only a small fraction of society's past is experienced in this way. Every member of society, even the oldest, learns most of what he knows about the past through social institutions—through oral chronicles preserved by tradition, written chronicles stored in archives, and commemorative activities (making portraits, statues, and shrines, collecting relics, naming places, observing holidays and anniversaries) that enable institutions to distinguish significant events and people from the mundane, and so infuse the past with moral meaning" ("Iconography and Collective Memory: Lincoln's Image in the American Mind," *Sociological Quarterly* 32, no. 3 (1991): 302.

2. Mary Frances Berry and John Blassingame, *Long Memory: The Black Experience in America* (New York: Oxford University Press, 1982), p. x.

3. Ibid., especially chaps. 1, 5.

4. Eric Foner, *Reconstruction: America's Unfinished Revolution, 1863–1877* (New York: Harper & Row, 1988), pp. 78–123.

5. I am not suggesting that these are the only expressions of heroism in African-American culture, but these two elements of African-American life are certainly the central poles of African-American heroic achievement.

6. Michael Kammen, *Mystic Chords of Memory: The Transformation of Tradition in American Culture* (New York: Knopf, 1991), p. 13.

7. Ibid., p. 122.

8. Ibid.

9. Frederick Douglass, quoted in ibid., pp. 121–122.

10. Barry Schwartz, "Social Change and Collective Memory:

Notes

The Democratization of George Washington," *American Sociological Review* 56, no. 2 (1991): 221.

11. George Herbert Mead, "The Nature of the Past," in *Essays in Honor of John Dewey*, ed. John Coss (New York: Holt, 1929), pp. 235–242; Maurice Halbwachs, *The Collective Memory*, trans. J. Ditter, Jr., and Vida Yazdi Ditter (New York: Harper Colophon, 1980).

12. Halbwachs, *Collective Memory*, p. 222.

13. Emile Durkheim, *The Elementary Forms of the Religious Life* (1912; New York: Free Press, 1965), pp. 415, 420; Edward A. Shils, *Tradition* (Chicago: University of Chicago Press, 1981), pp. 31–32.

14. Schwartz, "Social Change and Collective Memory," p. 222.

15. I am working on an ambitious project to wedge beneath stereotypes and statistics to deliver a complex, sophisticated analysis and interpretation of black males in *Boys to Men: Black Males in America* (New York: Random House, forthcoming [1997]).

16. See, for instance, Robert Staples, "Black Male Genocide: A Final Solution to the Race Problem in America," *Black Scholar* 18, no. 3 (1987): 2–11; and Jewelle Taylor Gibbs, ed., *Young Black and Male in America: An Endangered Species* (Dover, Mass.: Auburn House, 1988).

17. Quoted in James Cone, *Martin and Malcolm and America: A Dream or a Nightmare* (Maryknoll, N.Y.: Orbis Books, 1991), p. 89.

18. William Julius Wilson, *The Truly Disadvantaged: The Inner City, the Underclass, and Public Policy* (Chicago: University of Chicago Press, 1987); Mike Davis, *Prisoners of the American Dream: Politics and Economy in the History of the U.S. Working Class* (London: Verso, 1986).

19. Quoted in Cone, *Martin and Malcolm and America*, p. 89.

20. Malcolm X, *Malcolm X Speaks: Selected Speeches and Statements*, ed. George Breitman (New York: Pathfinder Press, 1965), p. 169.

INDEX

Aerosmith, 84
Aesthetic, black populist, 114. *See also*
    Art, and truth; Artists, black
Affirmative action, 179
Africa, trips to, 69
African-Americans, religious practices
    of, 164. *See also* Culture, African-
    American
Afrika Bambaata, 83
Afro-American, The, 74
Afrocentrism, 91–92, 188, 197n.20
AIDS infection, 108
Alexander, Elizabeth, 19
Ali, Muhammad, 142
Ali, Shahrazad, 73
Amnesia, racial, 148–149, 150
Amsterdam, News, The, 74
Anger
    of black male students, xx
    Malcolm's articulation of, 9
    in rap music, 86, 123
    and rhetorical resistance, 47
Anti-intellectualism, 60
Anti-Semitism, 91–92, 177
Aronowitz, Stanley, 105
Arson, of Malcolm's home, 58,
    143
Art, and truth, 129. *See also* Music
Artists, black
    cultural, 106
    filmmakers, 106, 107, 108
    ghetto reinvented by, 109
    rap, 93, 158, 163

Assassination, of Malcolm, 47, 82,
    190n.37, 191n.38
Attenborough, Sir Richard, 133
Atwater, Lee, 157
Audubon Ballroom, Malcolm's speech
    at, 69
Augustine, 135
Authenticity
    debate about, 188n.21
    politics of, xii, xiii
Autobiography of Malcolm X, The, 13,
    23, 55, 134–135, 143, l86n.5

Baccdafuccup, xx
Backlash, racist, 154. *See also* Racism
Baraka, Amiri, 131, 133, 188n.21
Bassett, Angela, 112, 141
Becker, Ernest, 154
Bibliographies, on Malcolm, l85n.2
Bigotry, ethnic, xxii
Bilalian News, 74
Bing, Leon, 117
Biography, film, 125–127. *See also*
    Psychobiography
Black Legionnaires, 4
*Blackman's Guide to Understanding the
    Blackwoman, The* (Ali), 73
Black men, 165
    in American society, 92–93
    causes of death among, 168
    crisis of, 167
    in film, 199n.3
    and Malcolm's legacy, 169

203

Index

Black men (*continued*)
  mutual contempt among, 171
  negative images of, 168–69
  violence among, 166–169, 171–172
  young, 147, 166
Blackness
  of Malcolm, xi
  and strength, 57
Black News, 74
Black Panthers, 25, 81, 82
Black Power movement, 25, 81, 186n.8
Black studies, 60–61
Blues artists, 93
Boggs, James, 30
Bonding, black male rituals of, 125
Bourgeoisie, black, 5
Boyz N the Hood (Singleton), 111, 115
Bradley, David, 130
Brainwashing, religious, 74
Break dancing, 83
Breitman, George, 65–69
Brown, James, 85
Brown v. *Board of Education*, 7
Brown University, Malcolm X seminar at, ix–x, xi, xvi
Burglary, 6
Bush, George, 154, 155
Businesses, racial antipathy of, 74
Busy Bee, 83
By Any Means Necessary: Speeches, Interviews, and a Letter (Malcolm), 3, 65, 71, 79

Cagney, James, 121
Canonization, of Malcolm, 73
Capitalism
  black, 25
  criticism of, 183
  global, 169
  King's challenge to, 45, 100–101, 102
  Malcolm on, 70, 102

Care, political ethic of, 181
Carmichael, Stokely, 25, 81
Carson, Clayborne, 49
Carson-Newman College, xviii
Charity, black religious conception of, 103
Chestnut, Morris, 112
Child-care issues, 155
Childhood, Malcolm's, 56
Christianity. *See also* Religion
  in African-American culture, 37
  Malcolm's challenge to, 46
Church
  in African-American culture, 36–37
  misogynist mythology of, 94
Cinema, new black, 107. *See also* Filmmakers, young black
Citizenship, national, 121
City of Quartz (Davis), 117
Civil disobedience, nonviolent, 9, 26
Civil Rights Division, at Department of Justice, 156
Civil rights movement, 8, 28, 88
  church as base of, 16
  gains of, 154
  King as symbol of, 196n.11
  shift in strategies of, 100
Clarke, John Henrik, 29
Class, and black America, 101–102
Class antagonism, 49
Class differences, and black nationalism, 99
Classism, 183, l93n.28
Class prejudice, and search for identity, 91
Cleage, Albert, 29, 31, 65, 69
Clinton, Bill, 152, 153, 154–161, 165
Clinton, George, 85
Cocaine Kids (Williams), 117
Coexistence, social, 46
Cold Rush Brothers, 83
Collins, Patricia Hill, 97
"Colonial dilemma," xxii

Index

Index

Index

Goldman, Peter, 38, 46–48, 59, 65, 69
Gooding, Cuba, Jr., 112
Goodman, Benjamin, 34
Gospel music, 122–123
Graffiti, 83
Grandmaster Melle Mel, 83
Greer, Sonny, 57
Guinier, Lani, 156
Gumbel, Bryant, 93
Guns, as metaphor, 84

Hadj. *See* Mecca
Haitians, and Clinton policy, 155–156
Halbwachs, Maurice, 149
Haley, Alex, 13, 23, 55, 134, 186n.5
Hall, Albert, 137
Hampton, Lionel, 57
Harlem, 5
"Harlem 'Hate-Gang' Scare, The"
    (Malcolm), 70
Harlem Nights (Murphy), 136
Harmony, racial, 44–45
Harris, Leslie, 126
Health care, universal, 103
Hero, Malcolm as, 24, 29–30, 79, 82,
    139, 145, 150, 172
Heroism, in African-American culture,
    147, 201n.5
Hero worship, 74, 126, 140
Hill, Anita, 104, 105, 113
Hip-hop culture, 74, 82–83, 158
    attacks on, 182
    beginnings of, 83–84
    and black films, 115
    black masculinity in, 96
    divisions in, 196n.6
    gender relations in, 104
    lexicon of, 121
    rage in, 87
History, African-American, 61, 75
    black, 62, 92, 193n.61
    conspiracy theory of, 170
    writing of, 193n.61

History of the Russian Revolution
    (Trotsky), 71
Hollywood, and film on Malcolm, 130
Holocaust-versus-slavery debate, 179
Homeboy-from-the-hood
    backgrounds, xix
Homicide, black-on-black, 166, 168.
    See also Violence
Homophobia, xxii, 14, 58
    of gangsta' rap, 95
    of rap culture, 163
Homosexuality, Malcolm's alleged, 58,
    143
Horton, Willie, 157
Households, single-parent, 95
Human rights, 103
Human rights advocate, Malcolm as,
    14–15
Hustling tactics, Malcolm's, xv, 5–6,
    133, 135, 136, 137

Ice Cube, 112, 115
Identity
    black female, 108
    erosion of communal, 80
    male, 58
    national, 121
Identity, racial
    narrow visions of, 104
    search for, 90–91
    social construction of, 105
Identity politics, x
"I Have a Dream" (King), 27
Imprisonment, of black men, 108
Inequality, religious resistance to, 37.
    See also Equality
Infant mortality, 108
Influence, sharing of, 179
Injustice
    economic, 181
    religious resistance to, 37
Integration, vs. separation, 44
Integrationism, 44

Index

Index

Index

Index

Index

Racism, 198n.28
  American, 13, 37–38, 88
  black resistance to, 37–38, 79
  and black teens, 83
  cultural, 74
  heroic response to, 150
  impact of, on African-American
    culture, 36–37
  meanings of, 54
  permanence of, 88
  resisting, 15
  resurgent, 87
  revived, 145
  and search for identity, 91
  Trotskyist views of, 71
  and young black men, 146–147
Racism, white, xv, 4
  black bourgeois protest of, 89
  and black manhood, 126
  cultural costs of, 10
  evil of, 90
  and heroic traditions, 147
  resistance to, 75
Radicalism. *See also* Democracy,
    radical
  black, 26
  of Malcolm, 45
  masked, 176
Radio stations, of Nation of Islam, 7
Rage, black, 87, 158. *See also*
    Anger
Rainbow Conference, 157, 159
"Raising Hell" (Run-D.M.C.), 84
Rap artists
  as ethnographers, 163
  rage and, 158
  young black male, 93
Rap culture, 82, 83. *See also* Gangsta'
    rap
  black nationalist expression of,
    196n.6
  form in, 85
  and Malcolm's legacy, 88–89

Rap music
  development of, 114–115
  lyrics, 113
Reagan, Ronald, 27, 154, 155
  era of, 116
Received view, of Malcolm, 35
"Reciprocal bleeding," 9
Reconstruction
  and black nationalism, 80
  heroic traditions during, 147
Record industry, 93–94
Religion
  and black nationalism, 89
  misogynist mythology of, 94
  moral cohesion provided by, 54
  and racism, 164
Religious conversions, Malcolm's, 6,
    22, 64
Republic of New Africa, 25
Revolutionary figure, Malcolm as, 24,
    68–69, 130
Revolutionary leaders, black Christian,
    37. *See also* Leadership, black
Rhetorical resistance, 15–16
  Malcolm's, 47, 87
  of rap culture, 158–159
  sermons, 16
Rich, Matty, 108, 117, 118, 122, 126
Riots
  in Los Angeles, 163
  of 1967, 15
Robeson, Paul, 34
Robinson, Patricia, 31
Robinson, Randall, 156
Role model, Malcolm as, 86
Roxbury, Massachusetts, 5
Run-D.M.C., 84
Rust Belt, 8

Saint, Malcolm as, 24, 25–36, 73
Salvation, black male, 112–113
Sampson, Frederick, G., 16
Sanders, Ann D., 110

212

Index

Sanders, Stephan, xxii
Sanon, Barbara, 110
Scapegoating, x, 176
School Daze (Lee), 125, 132
Schwartz, Barry, 149, 150
Science fiction approach, 194n.79
Self-awareness, racial, 92
Self-criticism, of Malcolm, 17
Self-defense, 3, 31
Self-destruction, 56, 182
Self-determination, black, 9, 25, 80,
    103
Self-discipline, 170
Self-hatred, 146–147, 171
Self-realization, and ghetto
    experience, 109
Self-reliance, 170
Seminar, on Malcolm, viii–x, xi, xvi
Senate subcommittee, U.S., testifying
    before, xxi
Separatism
    advocation of, 6
    definition of, 66
    ideology of, 33
Sermon, black, 16
Sex, and problems of black America,
    101
Sexism, 198n.28. *See also* Gender
    differences; Misogyny
    Malcolm's, 151
    roots of, 104
Sex life, Malcolm's, 58–59
Shabazz, Betty, 19, 141
She's Gotta Have It (Lee), 124
Shils, Edward, 150
Signifying practices, 94, 95
Sinatra, Frank, 93
Singleton, John, 111, 113, 126, 127,
    188
Sister Souljah, 157–158, 159, 160
Slavery, 80
    collective memory of, 148
    heroic traditions during, 147

Snipes, Wesley, 116
Snoop Doggy Dogg, xxi, 93, 94
Social action, Malcolm's, 22
Social criticism
    of radical democrats, 164, 165
    sexual hierarchy of, 43–44
Social dislocation, 75
Social goods, 36, 153–154
Socialism
    black nationalism and, 67, 68–69
    cooperative, 25
    Malcolm on, 70
Socialist movements, 13
Socialist Workers Party, 65
Social protest, 89, 150
Social reconstruction, 106
Social revolution, 49
South Central (Stone), 124
Speeches, Malcolm's
    at Audubon Ballroom, 69
    rhythms of, 85
Spirituality, black, 89, 139
Stereotyping, x
Stone, Oliver, 124
Straight Out of Brooklyn (Rich), 108–
    111, 117, 118–120, 121, 122,
    123
Student Nonviolent Coordinating
    Committee (SNCC), 25, 81–82
Students, black female, xix
Survival, and collective memory,
    146
Symbol, Malcolm as, 130

Television, violence on, 120–121. *See
    also* Violence
Temples, of Nation of Islam, 7
Theodicy
    black public, 89–90, 181
    definition of, 196n.15
Theological premises, Malcolm's, 90
Thick description, 23, 186n.4
Thomas, Clarence, 104, 105, 113

Index

Index

NOTES FROM TOYOTA-LAND

AN AMERICAN ENGINEER IN JAPAN

DARIUS MEHRI

FOREWORD BY ROBERT PERRUCCI

ILR PRESS
AN IMPRINT OF
CORNELL UNIVERSITY PRESS
ITHACA AND LONDON

First published 2005 by Cornell University Press

Printed in the United States of America

Design by Scott Levine

Author photograph by John Woo.

        Library of Congress Cataloging-in-Publication Data

Mehri, Darius.
    Notes from Toyota-land : an American engineer in Japan /
Darius Mehri.
      p. cm.
    Includes bibliographical references and index.
    ISBN-13: 978-0-8014-4289-6 (cloth : alk. paper)
    ISBN-10: 0-8014-4289-3 (cloth : alk. paper)
    1. Automobile industry and trade—Japan—Management.
2. Work environment—Japan.   3. Industrial relations—Japan.
4. Corporate culture—Japan.   5. Toyota Jidōsha Kabushiki
Kaisha—Management.   6. Mehri, Darius—Travel—Japan.
I. Title.
    HD9710.J32M43 2005
    338.7′6292′0952—dc22
                              2005011566

Cloth printing   10 9 8 7 6 5 4 3 2 1

for Meilin

CONTENTS

FOREWORD

In 1990 I was conducting research on Japanese automobile plants that had recently been built in six Midwestern states ("the *transplants*"). Japanese corporations invested billions of dollars to build the plants, and the six states combined provided about one billion dollars in incentives to attract the transplants to their states. Because Japanese auto plants in Japan were believed to have a distinctive organizational approach ("lean production"), one of my research objectives was to see how they would transfer their work arrangements ("teams") and work processes ("continuous improvement") into the American setting. I wanted to study how the Japanese companies were training American production supervisors to implement lean production methods.

With the help of a university vice-president who had a liaison role with the local transplant, I was able to meet with the CEO of the transplant to present my research proposal. The meeting was held in a company conference room with me and my university sponsor on one side of a long table, and on the other side, the Japanese CEO, a Japanese vice-president for production, an American vice-president for human resources, and two Japanese secretaries who took notes during the meeting. After polite introductions and exchange of business cards, I was asked to make my presentation. I spoke for about twenty minutes, outlining a two-part project that involved first studying the transplant's training program for American team leaders, and second a survey of American production workers ("associates") concerning their reactions to team leaders after start-up of production. When I finished, I thanked everyone for the opportunity to present my proposal. All attention turned to the CEO who sat opposite me. He spoke: "Thank you for your interesting proposal. Now tell me, how do you feel about labor unions?"

I was taken aback by this unexpected question and immediately suspected that he had made inquiries into my politics and my pro-labor sympathies. I proceeded to describe the role played by organized labor in improving working conditions in the twentieth century, and I acknowledged labor's contributions to our economy. I closed my reply to the CEO by reassuring him that my research has nothing to do with unionization, and if his workers unionized it would have more do with him than me. The CEO stood up, thanked me, and said they would soon respond to my proposal. When we left the meeting, my university sponsor said that my closing remarks were not helpful. He said that I was "too direct." A week later the transplant VP of Human Resources informed me that the company decided not to approve my request to study their training program.

Darius Mehri's memoir is a rare account of an insider's view of working in an automobile company in Japan. If I had access in 1990 to his detailed description of everyday work-life in Japan, I would have responded to the Japanese CEO's query about unions with the knowledge of Mehri's description of the subordinate and ineffective role of Japanese company unions. I would also have framed my reply to the CEO within the context of *tatemae* ("what you are supposed to feel or do") and not *honne* ("what you actually feel or do"). Mehri provides an absorbing detailed account of working and living in Japan. His memoir has the feel of exceedingly rich and detailed field notes provided by an experienced ethnographer. Students of Japanese organizations and work patterns will be provided with rich day-to-day descriptions of the abstract concepts that are used to characterize the Japanese approach to work and organizing. Readers will come to recognize *kaizen* as something more than "continuous improvement" and will learn what Japanese professional employees think about "lean production," and how under the guise of "teamwork" and the importance of the work group, Mehri and his colleagues are subjected to great work intensity and pressure to produce. We also get a first-hand look at how the office without walls, which is supposed to symbolize equality, is used to provide markers for who is on the way up and who is on the way out.

In Mehri's third year at Toyota an economic downturn leads the company to begin downsizing. The Japanese approach to this unpleasant task differs from the American experience, and reveals the way that the "family" of companies (the *keiretsu)* is used to buffer job loss. The efforts to use voluntary means to downsize ("who wants to take a challenge leave?") and shared wage reductions also provide interesting contrasts to the two-week notice in the U.S.

In addition to the informative accounts of what it is like to work at Toyota, the memoir also provides a picture of Japanese life that extends beyond the workplace while still intimately connected to the workplace. The descriptions of after-work drinking and eating sessions are amusing and revealing; Japanese dating and gender relations, viewed through the eyes of a foreigner, provide interesting contrasts with the American experience; and the family life of *salary-men* provides an image of the how the long arm of the job reaches into all segments of daily life.

ROBERT PERRUCCI

Purdue University

PREFACE

This book is a memoir about my life in Japan, where I worked from April 1996 through June 1999 as a computer simulation engineer at a Toyota automobile company. Every night, alone in my tiny company apartment, I recorded the day's events. What began as the usual expatriate journal became something more complex when the Japanese economy, in trouble since 1990, took a drastic downturn in 1997. Then I saw Japan's management system—highly touted and imitated in the United States and elsewhere—placed under desperate stress. My entries recorded group dynamics, health and safety issues, gender relations, restructuring, and the company involvement in local elections.

My vantage point was unusual. Many observers have written books about new management methods in the office, in the Japanese factory, and in the so-called transplants (Japanese factories located in the United States), but until now no American engineer has described the Japanese white-collar experience.

I was able to experience the 1997 recession and the company's response to it from several perspectives. I worked with Japanese engineers on product design teams, and I was fortunate to be included in their drinking parties and other social occasions. But as a foreign worker, I also had many friends among foreigners on the assembly line. I learned from them about the hazards of lean production in the factory, particularly as line speeds increased during the economic downturn. I also learned how management coped with the economic emergency by using foreign workers and by outsourcing within the Toyota conglomerate.

My journal soon became a record of the company's culture and its managerial adaptations during the economic downturn. Later in my stay, I became absorbed by the company's close involvement in a local election, and the activists I met during that campaign taught me how business affects politics in Japan. This topic is not well enough understood in the West.

The company that I worked for is called Nizumi in this book, and while descriptions of people and processes are drawn from my journal and from interviews, I have changed names and certain nonessential details to respect the privacy of my former colleagues and the proprietary nature of my engineering work for Nizumi.

Nizumi is an upper-level Toyota group company. It employs more than seven thousand workers, maintains more than five offices and factories throughout Japan, and its 2002 sales were over $5 billion. It also maintains a number of sales offices and factories in foreign countries. Nizumi is an original manufacturer of products for Japanese and foreign markets and has its own distribution network. The company also supplies parts for Toyota Motors, and like most companies within the Toyota industrial pyramid (the *keiretsu*), it relies on connections with Toyota to maintain and expand its market share. Although Nizumi is an independent company, it has been an official Toyota *keiretsu* affiliate for several years, and as a result has adopted the Toyota style of management. Nizumi workers have been thoroughly immersed in the various practices of the Toyota Production System (TPS), such as just-in-time and pull manufacturing, which I will discuss later.

To maintain control over its companies and to ensure implementation of the TPS, Toyota manages the daily activities of Nizumi through Nizumi's top managers, president, and board of directors, many of whom come directly from Toyota. The enterprise unions are another organ of control, and the whole system has surprising connections with the political system at various levels. The complexities of this total system are not evident at first, and this book is both a description of the system and an account of how it revealed itself to me and my colleagues.

I worked with other computer simulation engineers like myself, and we all worked alongside CAD (Computer Animated Design) engineers, scientists, and technicians with a variety of educational backgrounds. Many had college degrees, but some did not. A few had Ph.D.s, but some had entered the company directly after high school or with a two-year degree from a technical college. Some were temporary, contract workers, but most were full-time regular employees of the company.

What I enjoyed most about my job was that I was doing sophisticated engineering design. My job as a computer simulation engineer in the analysis department for advanced design involved cutting-edge technology, and I felt I was making meaningful contributions to improving vehicle efficiency.

I also enjoyed starting to understand Japan. When you work in a foreign country, you become immersed in its society. Every day when I came to work in the morning, filled my ceramic cup with coffee, and walked over to talk with my boss, I knew I would soon be learning something new about Japanese society and the famous Toyota Production System. I took every opportunity to learn and record as much as I could. By the time I left Japan, my journal amounted to more than 250 single-spaced pages. I documented every detail so that I could create a full picture of what life was like at the company.

People who work in Japan and write about the culture often go through three phases: experiencing Japan as an alien environment, "going native," and finally becoming more critical. These shifts were especially pronounced in my case because the economic recession put the contradictions and tensions of the system into high relief, both for foreign workers like me and for my Japanese colleagues.

My Japanese colleagues often talked to me about a distinction which is fundamental to understanding Japanese culture and business: *tatemae* (what you are supposed to feel or do) and *honne* (what you actually feel or do).

Imagine getting a haircut in Japan. When the barber begins cutting, you notice he is making many mistakes. When he is finished, your hair looks terrible. Yet when the barber asks "How is the haircut?" you respond, "It looks great." You refrain from criticizing or confronting the barber because it is bad behavior in Japan to embarrass someone in public. You leave the barbershop and swear you will never return again.

In this case the *tatemae* was your response that the hair "looks great" when in fact your true feeling, the *honne*, is that you are furious because it looks awful.

In Japan, if two employees disagree with each other, it is considered bad behavior to be confrontational. You are supposed to fake a good-natured relationship and not show your true feelings. In my interviews with workers, I would often inquire about the management's behavior and in case after case, *tatemae* and *honne* were used to explain company policy. The company's policies were *tatemae,* and the underlying realities were *honne.*

As a foreigner I was challenged by the inherent *tatemae/honne* contradiction, but I believe that the Japanese experience both the *tatemae* and the *honne* simultaneously and without hypocrisy. Japanese workers who had spent some time working abroad, however, seemed almost as baffled as I was about the complex levels of meaning in the culture they were rejoining.

I believe that international enthusiasm for the Toyota Production System results from Western observers' failure to discern the *honne* within the *tatemae.* It has been easy (but erroneous) to accept the *tatemae* as given, and to write about it without regard to the Japanese realities or to any possible losses in translation. But *tatemae, honne,* and other phenomena of the Japanese workplace release their meanings only to observers who spend time in the culture.

This book is the story of my time in Japan and the gradual understanding I acquired there. What emerges is a detailed account of the Toyota Production System and contemporary life at a Japanese car manufacturing company.

ACKNOWLEDGMENTS

I have many people to thank for the publication of this book. I was fortunate to meet a number of academics and activists who were just as passionate as I am about Japanese work issues. I would first like to thank Narumi Hasegawa who introduced me to a larger world outside the company. I am grateful to Dr. Shinya Yamada, Dr. Masaki Saruta, and Shozo Sasaki of the Aichi Labor Institute for their many conversations in helping me understand Japanese work, society, and labor issues and to the Zenroren Federation of Unions for their many discussions about Japanese labor.

Many thanks to Laurie Graham and Robert Perrucci who read my journal and initial chapters and encouraged me to continue writing. Heidi Gottfried provided invaluable help writing the prospectus and advising me about gender issues. Her encouragement and enthusiasm about work issues greatly helped me to continue to shape my journal into a book. Frances Benson showed interest early in the project, and her enthusiasm helped in motivating me to complete the book even though it was not always clear that it would eventually make it into print. I thank Paul Adler and Steve Babson for reviewing the manuscript and offering excellent advice on ways to improve its focus and restructure the narrative. Reiko Goodwin and Hidemasa Yamakawa supplied me with excellent translations, and Terry McKiernan gave me many creative suggestions which improved the manuscript. Thanks to my brother Cyrus of Mehri and Skalet and to John Richards of Essential Information for their legal advice. Thanks to my father, who spent many hours proofreading the original manuscript. Thanks to Edward Ching who did an excellent job of preparing the illustrations for publication. Catherine Hiller did a wonderful job as a development editor in restructuring the manuscript and providing stylistic advice. Without Catherine, this book might not have been published.

Finally, I thank my parents and my wife, Meilin, for their love and support throughout.

DARIUS MEHRI

NOTES FROM TOYOTA-LAND

INTRODUCTION

My first ideas about Japan came from the Japanese movies I watched as a child. I loved sitting on the living room couch on a Sunday afternoon, watching Godzilla breathe fire as he tromped through Tokyo, wreaking havoc. I was thrilled when the models (even as a child I could tell that they were fakes) were tossed about as if they were toys.

I was always fascinated with models and was very skilled at putting them together. My friends where impressed when I was able to rapidly assemble them without even looking at the directions. Perhaps even then I was something of an engineer. I would put models together, take them apart, put them together again. When I was bored I would throw them against the wall or light them on fire, just like Godzilla.

My next thoughts about Japan were inspired some years later by Toyota.

I grew up in Connecticut, the son of an ophthalmologist and a housewife, both naturalized American citizens from Iran. Every three years, my father would drive a new Cadillac into the garage. These cars were huge; when my siblings and I got into the back seat, it was as if we had entered our own private house, replete with all the luxuries, including the most comfortable leather sofas that I have ever sat upon—to this day. But the neighbors were starting to buy Japanese cars. In the late 1970s, our next-door neighbor purchased a blue Subaru. I remember that car because I saw him driving it around for at least ten years. He was always bragging about its mileage and quality.

My father, however, loved American cars. He had aspired to them even as a child growing up in Iran. It wasn't until he bought a Pontiac station wagon for my mother in the early 1980s that his opinion began to change. He felt that the Pontiac had quality, design, and safety problems. Furthermore, it was so underpowered that with the pedal to the floor it could barely climb a hill. Within a few years, my parents sold the car for almost nothing.

My dad was also becoming disenchanted with his beloved Cadillacs. The last Cadillac my father purchased was a Seville with a diesel engine. It had the worst handling of any car in which I have ever ridden. When my father made turns or sudden stops, the car would wobble as if it was an egg floating on water. One day, the Seville broke down while my father was on his way to work. He asked the mechanic about the problem and he was told that the engine was shot. The car was barely two years old! Cadillac agreed to replace it at no charge, but my father had had enough.

And so Toyota came into our lives: my father came home with a 4Runner. It was a funny change. The man who used to dress in suits and drive flamboyant Cadillacs now wore woolen sweaters and drove a pickup truck. From then on, my dad only bought Toyotas. "The best cars ever made," he would say. As a doctor, he needed a vehicle that was reliable. A delay on the road could mean the difference between whether a patient could ever see again or not.

This was the era in which Japan was coming into its own. Its products were considered the best in the world. I remember seeing a news story on Japanese technology in which a woman cut a piece of paper with a pair of ceramic scissors. I was greatly impressed. Not only can they make great cars, I thought—they can even make ceramic scissors.

When I entered the University of Rochester, I intended to study engineering, but I found the program to be too stifling, and I had other interests. I changed my major to history with a specialty in Asian studies and anticipated a career in business. At the time, Japan was becoming famous for its industrial system. Automobiles, bullet trains, miniature electronics, televisions—the Japanese were manufacturing some of the best and most innovative products in the world.

By the mid 1980s, when the Japanese economy was growing at a steady clip and its work system was relatively unknown, books on the Japanese economy and workplace were becoming more popular. The most notable books on the subject include James Abegglen, *The Japanese Factory: Aspects of its Social Organization* (1958); Robert Cole, *Japanese Blue Collar* (1971) and *Work, Mobility and Participation* (1979); Ronald Dore, *British Factory, Japanese Factory* (1973); Thomas Rohlen, *For Harmony and Strength* (1974); and Rodney Clark, *The Japanese Company* (1979). Focusing on the organization and social structure of the corporation, these books emphasize Japan's "corporate welfare."

Corporate welfarists claim that Japanese companies have a unique labor-management relationship: they function as social support institutions where workers are engaged in an interdependent relationship with management. This relationship requires workers to be loyal and cooperative. In return, the company provides stable employment and worker participation through consensus decision-making.

According to the corporate welfare school, the company works as a benevolent family. Labor policies benefit both workers and management, employment is guaranteed for a lifetime, team work is pervasive, and the wage structure is based on seniority. Some have claimed that as a result of lifetime employment, a "community of fate" develops among employees, resulting in an intense loyalty to the firm. These claims have created a pervasive belief that in Japan employees work in an environment which functions more like a nurturing family than like a highly competitive profit-making entity. Cole (1979), Abbeglen (1958), and others have written about familial ideology and its impact on worker behavior. Some say that the reason the Japanese are such disciplined workers is because of this familylike environment.

One notable book by a native Japanese, Satoshi Kamata's *Japan in the Passing Lane* (1973), offered an alternative view of life at a Japanese company. Kamata demonstrated the hardship of life on the line at Toyota and claimed the company was more interested in high productivity than in the welfare of its workers. But Kamata's book remained largely overlooked. It certainly was not required reading in any of my courses.

The program at the University of Rochester required me to study Japanese, so I attended an intensive Japanese language program at Yale University in the summer of 1988. There, I met the wife of a professor, and when I went to Japan on graduation from Rochester, I ended up staying with her friends in Tokyo for many months. Their daughter, Akiko, was interested in studying in America, so in exchange for helping with her English, I got a place to live in the most expensive city in the world.

Akiko was a pretty and serious young girl of seventeen. I was a curious student of twenty-four. We never felt romantic about each other, but we got along very well. We often spoke about movies, life in Japan, and what it was like to study in America. The family was prosperous: the father worked as an engineer, and they lived in six luxurious rooms in Tokyo.

At that time, Japan's economy was at its peak, and everyone seemed very happy. Any time I entered a pub, Japanese people whom I had never met would invite me to their tables and offer me an abundance of food and drink. Perhaps they, too, were interested in practicing their English—but I didn't mind.

During my postcollege year in Japan, I came to value Japanese industriousness and ingenuity. Everywhere I went, I saw hard workers and advanced Japanese products. And I fell in love with Japanese food. The way they baked fish was out of this world—not too spicy, not too bland, just perfect. It was the first time in my life I had eaten fish that wasn't soaked in butter.

But I couldn't stay in Japan eating baked fish and speaking English with Akiko for the rest of my life. I had to start preparing for my life's work. By now, I felt that a career in business would not suit my personality. I returned to my initial ambition to become an engineer, and when I returned to the United States, I enrolled at the City College of New York to study mechanical engineering. Then I spent two years at the University of Wisconsin in Madison, getting a masters degree in the subject.

When I told my classmates about my experience in Japan, they would often say that with my engineering degree and knowledge of the Japanese language, I could "write my own ticket" in pursuing an engineering career. I thought their comments to be interesting but not relevant since I had no intentions of moving back to Japan. I just wanted to become a highly skilled engineer.

At this time, many people attributed the Japanese manufacturing success to a unique organizational structure called the Toyota Production System or "lean work." The Toyota Production System claims to improve quality and productivity while respecting workers' rights.

When I arrived in Madison in the early 1990s, the Toyota Production System had already proliferated throughout the United States, particularly in the manufacturing heartland of the Midwest. A 1992 study of organizations with fifty or more employees found that nearly 80 percent had adopted practices associated with TPS (Osterman, 1994). A separate study conducted among organizations of all sizes in 1993 reports that more than 40 percent had some experience with adopting TPS practices.[1]

---

[1] Mark Brenner, David Fairris, and John Russer, "Flexible Work Practices and Occupational Health and Safety," Political Economy Research Institute, Working Paper Series, no. 30, 2002.

But the TPS has now reached far beyond manufacturing to include the service industries. John Price writes: "Lean production has inspired a resurgent quality movement in North America that has spread from the factory to the warehouse and even into health care and educational facilities. Often appearing under the labels Total Quality Management (TQM) or Continuous Quality Improvement (CQI), the quality movement is based largely on the model of lean production."[2] Despite the economic troubles that Japan has experienced in the past decade, it remains an economic powerhouse and its production system has been studied and admired.

Many Westerners find it perplexing that a country with so few natural resources should produce such a plentiful amount of high-quality goods. Much of the literature purports that the Toyota Production System manages to achieve maximum production and quality while it maintains a harmonious and humane workplace. Popular literature by economists and business writers have lauded the Toyota success story and touted what others can learn from it.

Terry Besser has dubbed this line of thinking the "production technology" school. Its adherents believe that the Japanese miracle owes much to "just-in-time manufacturing," where parts are delivered on time to reduce inventory costs, and "pull manufacturing," a process where a worker can stop the line if he or she sees quality problems.

Praise is given to "mechanisms for total quality control, plant layout and design for quick changes and retooling."[3] Besser also notes the Japanese emphasis on continuous improvement (*kaizen*) and design detail.

While I was at Madison, the most prominent book from the production technology school was published: *The Machine that Changed the World* by Womack, Roos, and Jones, based on research funded by GM and the IMVP consortium at the Massachusetts Institute of Technology. The authors explain that the Japanese production system departs from the Henry Ford assembly line techniques known as Taylorism. They claim that if a company adopts the Toyota Production System techniques they refer to as "lean pro-

    [2] John Price, *Japan Works: Power and Paradox in Postwar Industrial Relations* (Ithaca, NY: Cornell University Press, 1997), 2.
    [3] Terry Besser, *Team Toyota* (Albany: State University of New York Press, 1996), 20.

duction," the organization will not only foster superior production but will also provide "challenging and fulfilling work for employees at every level."[4]

However, I didn't read the book until much later, after I had spent three years working in Japan, at which point I was in a good position to judge its accuracy.

While I was finishing the masters program, my adviser at Wisconsin introduced me to a senior researcher at Japan's National Mechanical Engineering Laboratory in Tsukuba, Japan. I was still excited about living abroad, so when this researcher offered me the opportunity to work with him in Tsukuba, I jumped at the chance.

At the laboratory in Tsukuba, I developed further contacts, including a senior engineer who worked for Toyota. Contacts are everything in Japan, and my contacts helped me obtain a position as a research and design engineer at Nizumi. I was thrilled to get the job. Japanese companies rarely hire foreigners to work within the company alongside their key engineers, particularly when they are involved in designing proprietary technology. My contract was for three years.

I decided that I would document my experience working at a Japanese company. I had heard wonderful things about working for Japanese companies—especially about how they valued the team. I heard that one of the reasons American cars were falling apart was the lack of teamwork in their production.

During my first few months working in Japan, I had many discussions with a Ford manufacturing engineer named Steve. He was in Japan on an American grant, funded by the Japan Technology Management Program (JTMP) based at the University of Michigan. The program enabled Steve to work at Nizumi for a few months to gain experience about lean work. He asked if I had read *The Machine that Changed the World*. When I said "no," he looked at me in dismay. Here I was, an American engineer living in Japan and working at a Toyota group company—and I had not educated myself about its revolutionary production system! Steve said it was an "amazing" book and that I would learn a lot by reading it.

I had already read a number of books about Japanese companies that I had found to be inaccurate, and I wondered if I should bother reading yet another book about Japan, so I put it off until after my return to the States,

---

[4] James P. Womack, Daniel T. Jones, and Daniel Roos, *The Machine that Changed the World* (New York: Harper Perennial, 1991), 225.

when an academic named Laurie Graham suggested I read it to understand the origins of lean work in America. When I finally read it, I shook my head in disbelief that a supposedly scholarly book from one of the most prestigious technical universities in the world could be so terribly inaccurate and misguided.

The inaccuracies of the *Machine that Changed the World* further motivated me to provide my viewpoint about work at a Japanese company. For instance, one of the supposed benefits of lean work is that it requires only half the manufacturing space of traditional, Taylorite manufacturers. But the reason lean work consumes less space is not because of a superior production system but as a result of gross negligence by the company, which subordinates the safety of its workers to lowering plant costs. At Nizumi, I was shocked to find machinery jammed into every square inch on the line, creating constant safety hazards.

Books like *The Machine That Changed the World* just look at the numbers without any regard to the human costs of lean work implementation. They talk about high productivity and extol the fast assembly-line speeds. But on these lines, workers must work every second of every minute, without a moment for a break.

After leaving Nizumi, I was introduced to the director of the Aichi Labor Institute in Nagoya, who sat me down with a fifteen-year veteran of Toyota Motors. I asked this worker about lean work, and he replied that the line speeds are so fast that "workers do not even have a second to wipe the sweat off their faces."

Some workers that I knew were considering what they would do when their Nizumi contracts expired. They considered working at the Toyota factory where SUVs were manufactured, but one of them told me that although the pay was good, he refused to work in such a dangerous environment. The lines were even faster at Toyota plants than at the group companies—and they were much too fast even at Nizumi.

In the 278 pages of *The Machine that Changed the World* there is not a single quote from the people who work within the system—the employees who dedicate their lives to hard work on the line and in the office. While the book is highly influential, it has also been criticized by scholars around the world as a gross misrepresentation of the Japanese work system and as a threat to trade unions everywhere.

For the majority of American workers, the Japanese work system had an entirely different effect than the idyllic life portrayed in the *Machine that Changed the World*. The flood of Japanese products in the 1980s and the resulting trade deficit led the Japanese to compensate for the loss of American jobs by locating Japanese factories in the United States. Automobile "transplants" resulted: first in Ohio by Honda, then in Tennessee by Nissan, then in California and Kentucky by Toyota. With these plants came a supposedly new form of organization based on the Japanese concepts of empowerment and the team. Management claimed that there was no need for unionization because the Japanese way involves cooperation, not confrontation, to resolve work issues. American trade unions naturally viewed that as a sham and a threat.

Parker and Slaughter's *Choosing Sides: Unions and the Team Concept* (1988) defines lean work as "management by stress" that exposes workers to a high degree of exploitation. Fucini and Fucini's *Working for the Japanese* (1990) condemns lean work as being insensitive to the needs of workers. Other publications that show a more realistic side of the Japanese miracle are Laurie Graham, *On the Line at Subaru-Isuzu* (1995); Terry Besser, *Team Toyota* (1996); and Rinehart, Huxley, and Robertson, *Just Another Car Factory* (1997). These books are localized studies of the basic techniques of the Toyota work system that has dominated the "new" lean way of automobile manufacturing in the past two decades. Although Womack, Roos, and Jones claim that the fundamental principles of "lean work" can be applied to any industrial organization with the will to incorporate new and innovative techniques, more recent scholars claim that "lean work" is a regression to the old practices of Taylorism.

In actuality, lean work has little to do with improving the lives of workers and much to do with producing vehicles with the least amount of money in the quickest time. Recent studies show similar conditions to those Satoshi Kamata documented at a Japanese Toyota factory in 1972, and his book is now held in high esteem.

Notes from Toyota-land introduces a new theory of work at a Toyota company. This theory holds that a "culture of rules" determines what goes on in the Japanese workplace. All rules fall into three major categories. The first category is the written rules that are distributed in company booklets or are printed and hung on company walls and bulletin boards. The second category comprises unwritten rules that the employee learns through observation or experience at the company, particularly in his or her section or team.

In the third category are rules that are learned culturally, simply by being Japanese or living in Japan. These rules include the proper language and gestures to be used in speaking to a superior.

Rules were also of two different types: formal and informal. Formal rules were those that could be enforced through social mechanisms of control or by management. Informal rules were those that could not be enforced, such as slogans or mottos. Some rules overlapped categories and types, but collectively all the rules help construct an expected code of behavior. A culture of rules coerces employees to share attitudes, values, and goals as defined by the group, the team, or the entire corporation.

The company hierarchy and relationships within the groups provide the organizational structure within which the culture of rules is communicated and enforced. The family ideology of the company defines management as parents and employees as children—an embedded hierarchy that binds workers, management, and their rules. Breaking a rule leads to punishment in which the errant employee is used as an example to the others. Employees learn about these rule infringements and their consequences through drinking parties and company gossip. Social mechanisms of control such as monitoring and bullying help keep the workers in line. Monitoring provides the information for the bullies to use. Bullies are typically members of an old boy group who have developed a close relationship to an important and powerful manager. The open-space office at Nizumi (and most Japanese companies) facilitates both monitoring and bullying. It is important that the employee who is the subject of harassment be humiliated in front of other members of his group.

Employees are expected to follow all rules and obey the prescribed code of behavior that exists at the company. Rules at Nizumi are generally context-oriented in that they apply to the section, team, or group whose leaders create and implement them. At times the rules are vague, allowing management the flexibility to blame the workers at will. The future of the employee depends on how well that person follows the rules his boss has laid down. The most powerful rules are unwritten and can only be learned by observation. Breaking an unwritten rule, however, can expose a worker to harassment and punishment.

Although recent studies provide valuable insight into work at Japanese companies, they focus on work either in the office or on the assembly line. *Notes from Toyota-land,* however, examines both kinds of work. The TPS is certainly lean, but it is also unhealthy and dangerous. This book questions the very fundamentals of the lean work system. In the office, "lean" means engineers are overloaded with tasks. In the factory, it means that workers on the line are continuously at risk of being seriously injured. It is not coincidental that none of the employees at the company, neither at the office nor in the factory, have an effective union. The Japanese enterprise union system is merely another way management controls workers.

Notes from Toyota-land also undertakes a thorough examination of familial ideology that is often heralded by the "corporate welfare" school. I suggest that this ideology is used to bind workers to the culture of rules, and I argue that the reason the Japanese are diligent and disciplined workers is not because they feel an obligation toward a company that provides them with many benefits, but because they are working within rules that tightly control every aspect of their behavior. Workers acquiesce to the demands of management simply because they have no choice. In observing and documenting the role of women at Nizumi, I also saw how women are coerced into traditional gender roles.

Notes from Toyota-land demolishes the myth of the generous, paternalistic Japanese company. Above all, this book shows how the famous Toyota lean production system has been devastating to its employees.

Notes from Toyota-land is based on my years as a covert participant-observer at Nizumi. In addition to the direct observation I recorded in my journal, I also conducted more than seventy-five interviews with employees, politicians, lawyers, labor scholars, and members of the community. The interviews ranged in duration from ten minutes to two hours. About three-quarters of those interviewed were Nizumi workers. I interviewed temporary laborers, contract employees, and mid- to high-level managers. I interviewed engineers and union leaders and workers on the line. Some 20 percent of the workers I interviewed were foreign, temporary workers, while the rest were permanent Japanese workers. I conducted approximately two-thirds of the interviews on company grounds. These were informal talks. The remaining third were held outside the company and were more formally structured.

To give the reader a look at the corporate culture, I have included quotations and illustrations from the thousands of newsletter pages I received at the company. It is customary for Japanese companies to deluge its employees with literature. The company distributed at least a half a dozen regular monthly or bimonthly newsletters and many annual newsletters and booklets. All of this material was for workers to take home to read, but I was probably the only worker to retain every page.

I have not included anything in this book that I did not personally observe or that did not come from at least two sources. My own observations and experiences have almost always been confirmed by those of my interviewees. In the chapter on women in the company, however, I depended solely on my own experience and the company literature. In Japan, it is very difficult to talk to others unless formally introduced. When I first entered the company, I spoke to a few male workers without an introduction and they reacted with surprise and discomfort. It was only after a formal introduction with a defined reason for our communication that they opened up freely. Except for an occasional conversation with a woman worker—typically a drafter, a technician, or an office lady (a Japanese term for a young woman assigned menial job functions, such as distributing newsletters or serving tea to visitors)—I did not have the opportunity to work with women. Had I approached a woman to talk about work without a formal introduction, she would have reacted with suspicion and alarm.

FIRST YEAR

INITIAL IMPRESSIONS

On my first day at Nizumi, I got off the train at Yashima at 8:34 and began walking to company headquarters. Yashima is a medium-sized industrial city by American standards, with a population of 170,000, but Japanese friends of mine had told me it was a place where country bumpkins lived. I wondered about this as I walked a mile along the winding streets amid the rush of traffic.

The company was located in an unassuming part of town. As with many manufacturing companies in Japan, the Nizumi engineering offices and the main factory were in the same location. When I approached the entrance, I saw that the grounds were surrounded by a tall cement wall. The air was sooty from vehicles passing on a nearby avenue.

I had expected the company surroundings to be typically Japanese, bustling with life and full of mom-and-pop stores, so I was surprised to find the streets in the immediate area to be mostly empty. There were a few working-class noodle shops, but the most visible attractions were a Denny's restaurant and a 7-11 store. It was early April, and the area's bleak industrial look was softened on the side streets by the bright pink flowers of the blossoming cherry trees.

I entered the company gate, where a Human Resources representative, a young woman dressed in a pantsuit, was awaiting me. While engineers, factory workers, and technicians hurried along to begin the day, I was escorted through more rows of cherry trees to the building where I would begin my orientation. The cherry trees seemed right out of classic Japanese poems—

symbols of promise or regret. But a different cultural reference came to mind. The division director who had interviewed me a few weeks before had said with a smile, "You will start working on April Fools' Day."

The main office, a wide, five-story building, was located close to the main entrance of the company. The modern structure and its clean façade contrasted sharply with the drab factories on the grounds. Many of the factories looked like large aircraft hangers. They were built of corrugated steel and were full of loud machinery. A peek inside one of the doorways gave me my first view of the line, with some workers driving forklifts at a fast clip to deliver parts. During my time in Japan, I would form close friendships with many of the men who worked in these factory buildings.

Another five-story building housed the engineers, and several smaller cement buildings were clustered directly behind the engineering building. (Later I would learn that tests on the company's products were conducted there.) The clanging sounds of manufacturing filled the air, and workers in soiled uniforms walked around the company grounds. Large pipes, open garages, and grease were all part of the surroundings. There was a pleasing intimacy about the layout, with workers making products that had been designed by the engineers next door. It was truly a blue-collar work environment, and I was comfortable in it. It reminded me of how as a child fascinated with the way things were built, I was always playing in the dirt with the models I had created.

Most of the workers in the factory were Japanese, but I would find that quite a few were Peruvians or Brazilians of Japanese descent who worked on contract. At the time I arrived, a group of Africans were also hired to work in the factory.

The only building that was clean enough for a Japanese businessman was the main building, to which the Human Resources person now accompanied me. I was escorted to a small room in the Human Resources office. I sat alone for a minute or two. Then another foreigner suddenly came into the room: a thin young Italian with shoulder length black hair. He shook my hand and said, "I'm Erberto." He said he had come to Japan for graduate school and was staying in the country so he could work at Nizumi. A woman manager joined us and introduced herself. I was surprised: I had heard that at Japanese companies, women worked only as secretaries.

The woman gave us a general orientation covering such topics as opening a bank account, receiving a paycheck, and getting a Japanese signature stamp (*hanko*) with which to sign official documents. Japanese people do not sign official documents by hand, but use a wooden object upon which the Chinese character of their last name is carved. This *hanko* is dipped in ink and stamped onto official papers. (Mine is reproduced as the section-dividing symbol in this book.)

At all times, employees were required to wear a badge with their name, division, and section. In the *hanko* and the company badge, traditional Japan met the modern Japanese workplace.

When the woman handed us our company badges, Erberto looked at his. It said, "Design Division." Erberto began arguing with her. Then he turned to me and said, "I was supposed to be assigned to the Research Division!" This was the section I was in. After an awkward silence, he shrugged his shoulders and said he would talk to his new boss about the mix-up.

Soon we were whisked away to a small meeting room on the fifth floor of the other large building. Four Japanese men, Erberto, and I were seated at a long table. When Erberto took his seat, he placed his hands on the table, bowing deeply and elegantly to the older gentleman sitting in the center. At the time, I did not know that this man was Kurata, the director of the Design Division—a person of tremendous importance. Kurata returned Erberto's greeting by bowing slightly. Seeing Erberto bow, I did the same, but my bow was neither as deep nor as graceful as his, and Kurata did not acknowledge me.

Kurata talked for a few minutes about the division and then introduced Erberto to his boss, Nishida, and me to mine, Higuchi. Higuchi was a little chubby, almost completely bald, and significantly younger than the other men. To my surprise, he spoke very good English, although he had never lived in an English-speaking country.

After the introductions, he and I walked over to our section and sat down at a small table in a huge, makeshift office created from a warehouse by fitting it with desks and lights. I was amazed at its size—it was absolutely enormous and completely open. There were no interior walls. The sections were organized into separate entities by desks jammed close together, carving out a space on the floor and a narrow path through which employees could pass. Although the office was open, there seemed to be complete order, with employees communicating politely and efficiently. With managers and their subordinates working shoulder to shoulder in a space without walls, it seemed that the office had been designed to embody egalitarianism. It would take me a while to learn otherwise.

Uno, our section manager, approached the table where I sat with Higuchi and introduced himself. He said that for now I would work on improving a part of the drivetrain but if my Japanese improved, I could work on other projects. During the discussion, Higuchi sat still, but when Uno left, Higuchi gave me some advice. "We have had two other foreigners work for our section," he said. "One was an American named Jeff who really liked living in Japan. He tried to learn the Japanese culture, and he could speak Japanese very well." I was happy to hear that an American had attempted to fit in. "The second was an engineer from Ireland named Sheila. She didn't like Japan at all and refused to speak Japanese. If you are like Jeff, you will do well. If you are like Sheila, you will not." His deep voice cut through the silence of the section, and I wondered how many other people had heard this little talk.

We talked briefly about the details of my first job assignment, and he finished by saying, "The most important thing is for you to get good results."

I asked Higuchi about Erberto. I was very curious about him, since we were the only two white foreigners working in the office. "I hear he is a graduate of Hokkaido University," he said. "He has been living in Japan for many years, and I believe he has a Japanese wife." (Later I would learn that Erberto's wife was actually Brazilian, although of Japanese descent.) Higuchi went on. "There is another foreigner working on this floor, a Chinese named Chen, who is working in the same section as Erberto. I will introduce you to him later, but now we must go to a department meeting, where you will give a short speech."

"Uh—what kind of speech?" I was not prepared to speak spontaneously to an entire department.

"Oh, it is just an introductory speech, it's not important."

"Well, what should I say?"

"Talk a little about yourself, where you went to school, your hobbies, your home town and its claims to fame. That will be enough." It seemed manageable.

We left through the main corridor of our floor, where there were posters and pictures on the bulletin boards. Many had detailed cartoonlike illustrations that instructed workers on particular tasks. I remember thinking that these posters were useful. They were simple and easy to understand—just one look at the cartoon and the task it illustrated, and you immediately knew what to do.

Finally we came to the meeting room and walked in. Higuchi brought me to the front of the room. Before me, about a hundred employees from various sections in the division were standing in silence, wearing their company uniforms and soft-brimmed hats. A few older men wore company blazers as well. Abe, the director of the division, made a few announcements, while I and a few other young recruits listened respectfully. Abe was a short, balding older man who seemed cordial and polite. Then the recruits gave their introductory speeches.

Soon, it was my turn. I went through the list of things that Higuchi had suggested, but when I got to my hometown in Newtown, Connecticut, I couldn't think of anything to say about it. Finally, I came out with, "Connecticut is where they make nuclear submarines." Then I blushed, remembering Hiroshima and Nagasaki. No one seemed to think I had made a grievous mistake, however, and when I finished, everyone clapped. Higuchi asked me to give the same speech to my section.

While on my way back to the office with Higuchi, I noticed photographs on small bulletin boards beside the sections, showing workers on company trips, often with their families and colleagues. I arrived at my desk and saw that a number of newsletters had already been placed there for me to read. I flipped through one and noticed many articles and pictures of company employees. Many of the photos were of groups of employees with their colleagues or with friends and family engaging in a hobby or talking about work. One article titled "My Favorite Pet" was about an employee's relationship with his dog. Written in the first person, the employee describes how his dog likes to be treated as a member of his family. I thought that Nizumi seemed like more than just a place to work. It was like a community, with all of the social support systems that a family provides.

Higuchi introduced me to Shiina, a bespectacled man with a thin face who spoke impeccable English. He had been sent by the company to an engineering lab in California for four years. "I consider California my second home," Shiina said. "When I met Americans they always thought I was Mexican! It was really odd." He offered to answer any questions I might have, and this was very helpful, for he was seated right beside me and informal communication would be easy. Shiina became a valuable source of information to me.

I sat at my desk for no more than a few minutes before Higuchi asked me to help him fill out some documents. These were my official company documents and would be used as a record of my employment at the company.

They would include a yearly write-up by management about my performance. I was surprised when Higuchi told me that if I were a Japanese employee, I would need to provide the name of the town where my family's name was registered. Since I was a foreigner, however, Nizumi did not need the information.

During the meeting, I noticed a wiry fellow with slick, greased-back hair sitting directly in front of Higuchi's desk. He talked so quickly that I was surprised that even a native Japanese speaker could understand him. Higuchi introduced me to him as Takanashi, a member of the analysis team. Higuchi, Takanashi, and I were all part of the same group. When I talked with Takanashi, I immediately noticed his agitated demeanor, but it would be months before I understood why. Higuchi then gave me a company blazer, a soft brimmed hat, and safety shoes for work outside the office. He also told me that the next week I would be attending a tour of the company for new recruits.

At the end of the day, I was brought to my apartment in the company dormitory, a fifteen minutes' walk from corporate headquarters. The company offered subsidized housing to employees in their first few years at the company. The subsidy was substantial and required an additional payment from me of only $120 a month, which the company automatically deducted from my paycheck.

The room was quite small, hardly six tatami mats. This was a standard way to measure living space in Japan, with a mat equaling an area approximately two feet by five feet. The space was so small that when I stepped out of the bathroom, I was in the kitchen, and a mere two steps from the kitchen brought me to the bedroom.

When we walked into the hallway, the dormitory supervisor handed me the list of dormitory rules. The rules prohibited nonresidents from staying overnight and stated that all residents were required to return to the dormitory before 11:00 P.M. The dorm manager also said that no male resident was allowed to have a woman in his room. He then handed me some forms to fill out when I took vacation. These forms required employees to provide their company identification number, their section and job, what transportation they would take, whether it was a four- or two-wheel vehicle, and the address and relationship of the "person(s)" with whom they would be staying while on vacation. Since the dorm housed employees who were adults and not students, I found these rules and questions perplexing.

STRIVING FOR PROFIT AND POWER

The next day, I woke up at 7:00 A.M. The company had a dress-down policy for engineers, so I put on a pair of trousers and a button-down shirt with a collar. I wasn't prepared to cook my own breakfast, so I decided to eat at the company cafeteria on company grounds. I put on my slippers and walked toward the shoe room. Residents were not allowed to wear shoes in the dorm, so we stored our shoes in small lockers by the entrance. In Japan, it is customary to leave one's shoes at the door of a house.

As I entered the shoe room, I saw many posters about dormitory life. One poster encouraged us to greet each other. Entitled "The Oasis [*Oashisu*] Movement," it defined the meaning of the *Oashisu* acronym: O for *Ohiyō* (Good Morning), A for *Arigatō* (Thank You), Shi for *Shitsurei Shimasu* (Sorry to Bother You), and Su for *Sumimasen* (Excuse me). The bottom of the poster proclaimed, "Let's exchange greetings and have a fun dormitory life." Another poster showed a man throwing his clothes in the washer and sweeping the floor. I couldn't help smiling at the cynical response such posters would receive in America.

When I left the dormitory building, I noticed two small farms located nearby. One grew fruit, the other vegetables. On my way to work, I passed small stores, noodle shops, vegetable stands, and a high school. When I approached the high school, I heard a choir rehearsing in the yard. This sweet sound contrasted with the roar of helicopters and military transport planes flying toward a nearby Japanese base supplied with American equipment.

When I approached the gate, I took out my Nizumi identification card and showed it to the guard, who wore a Western-style officer uniform. For some reason, he saluted me as I walked through. Later on, I observed that he only saluted foreign engineers and high-level managers, but never regular employees or workers on the line.

As soon as I walked through the gate, I immediately passed one of the factories, inside of which I could see machinery and workers rushing to deliver parts. All this speed was exhilarating. It made the factory feel alive.

I entered the engineering building and went straight to the cafeteria on the ground floor. They were serving a traditional Japanese breakfast, including a choice of fish served with rice, or *natto. Natto* was a sticky paste of fermented soy and raw egg which gave off such a horrible smell that I wouldn't even taste it.

After breakfast, I headed upstairs and entered the locker room. I noticed that employees changed from their street clothes into the clothes they wore for work. This puzzled me, as both kinds of clothes were casual. I simply dropped off my jacket and headed for my desk. I walked down a long hallway, passing through a very smoky section. The hallway at the entrance of the office was a designated smoking area, and I soon learned to hold my breath when walking down this passage. Since smoking is popular in Japan, particularly among the men, the hallway was always full of employees who sat on leather sofas and puffed away during their break. As I entered my section, I flagged my name on a large name board as being "in the company"— as opposed to on a business trip or at home. Now everyone knew I was here.

When I sat down, I noticed a purple, pocket-sized pamphlet on my desk. It was titled "This Year's Company Goals." A short slogan beneath the title read, "Working Together towards Nizumi's Goals in the 21st Century." The first page of the pamphlet stated three of Nizumi's long-term goals. The first was to "create a flexible and robust corporate structure, which is able to respond to the changing corporate environment, and an attractive corporate culture, in which employees experience the joy of working, based upon mutual trust between labor and management." The second goal was "to unite all of Nizumi's strength to continue inventing new values and to strive for a profitable and powerful existence in the 21st Century." And the third goal was "to contribute to a prosperous and comfortable society in harmony with the global environment and the community." I was pleased to be working at a company with these lofty goals.

The body of the pamphlet discussed goals for the fiscal year, such as cutting costs and implementing the "Mid-Term Management Plan." The last page listed the standard of conduct employees were expected to follow. Workers were to "recognize the value of bonding with society and becoming good citizens." All morning, I saw purple pamphlets poking out of the pockets of managers but most employees just left them on their desks.

As an analysis engineer, I was responsible for using computer tools to improve the design process and coming up with innovative ideas that could be incorporated into new products. Since I worked in the Research Division, my daily life involved working with CAD models on the computer and using numerical tools to evaluate the design of specific parts. When I sat behind the computer, the part I was working on hung in 3D space on the computer screen. Its finely machined edges and exotic curves were amazingly true to life.

A CAD object is composed of many parts. There are analytical parts such as cylinders or cubes as well as parts made out of complex surfaces. With a click of the mouse, a cylinder can be used to cut a cube, creating a virtual part that would cost thousands of dollars to make in the shop. Lines in 3D space are called "splines." Splines are used to make the backbone of the object, and the surfaces are wrapped around the splines like the outer shell of a tent tightly fitted over its poles. The most time-consuming part of my job was to put all of these complex surfaces and analytical parts together to make a final object.

It was a painstaking process. I would click, make changes to a dimension, click again. Sometimes, I would make that last key click and I would end up with the part I needed. Many times however, I would make a bad decision, make a dimension too small or too large, or simply click the wrong button. Then the part would explode onscreen like a firecracker, and the result would be a mangled mess that would take me hours to fix. Behind the screen, the computer was solving many complex mathematical equations, and when one of the equations could not be solved, I ended up with a problem. The objective was to make an optimal part that could be validated with experimental results. Heat, constant movement, and many years of use and abuse could cause the part to degrade or to fail.

I was soon immersed in the company design process, but for me the most striking aspect of being at Nizumi was not my actual job but the work environment. For one thing, there was a total lack of privacy. Since every section was entirely open, there was not one place in the whole office that could not be seen by all members of the section. All desks were arranged in blocks of four and they all faced inward. The managers' desks were located on the outer edge of each section making a large rectangle that surrounded the inner blocks. Each manager's desk faced the lower-ranked workers. The resulting formation meant that everyone could see what each other was doing, and in many cases, what they were reading as well.

There was one minor exception for my section only. Each desk was separated from the next by a partition nine inches high from the desktop of the desk, partially blocking what the others could see. I surmised that since we were the research division some of our information was proprietary. Nevertheless, I always felt I was being watched. As I sat at my desk, the top of the wall was at eye level, so when I looked up, I always saw the eyes of my facing colleagues over the top edge of the wall.

As an American socially conditioned to value privacy, I was uncomfortable with the lack of walls, but what made me even more anxious was the way I was constantly being monitored by my colleagues. It was common practice for employees to look over the shoulders of their colleagues and to poke their noses into their computers or personal documents. Members of the section commonly opened each other's desk drawers and read each other's notes, letters, and papers. Nothing was private. My mild-mannered boss, Higuchi, would routinely approach me from behind and stick his face directly into my work to see what I was doing. This was standard management practice.

This monitoring unnerved me. At first, I would frequently go to the toilet to be in the one place where I could have privacy, if only for a few minutes. However, since a restroom is not a pleasant place, particularly when it is being used by others, I soon abandoned these temporary escapes. Erberto was more philosophical about this constant monitoring, simply claiming that Japan was a "spy society."

The computers in my section were not at our desks. Rather, all the computers were shared and were placed at one side of the room. Most of my time, I spent at the computer.

Our section took a one-hour lunch break at noon, and we could spend the time any way we wanted, as long as we did not leave company grounds.

Lunchtime was signaled by a melodic series of notes from the loudspeaker embedded into the wall. I saw a group of men who sat close to the section manager leave at once. Then Higuchi approached and asked if I wanted to join him and some other employees in the section for lunch. Of course, I said yes.

The food in the main section of the cafeteria consisted of white rice and miso soup, a choice of a main meal—pork, fish, chicken, or tempura—and a side dish such as a Western style salad or pickled vegetables. Another section was dedicated entirely to serving curry rice, and another to serving ramen. I chose the fish, miso soup, and pickled vegetables and wended my way through the crowded cafeteria to sit with Higuchi and the other men. One of the men asked, "Don't you like eating meat?" I told them I preferred fish, and they were surprised. They thought most foreigners preferred red meat. I scored points with my lunch choice; it indicated that I could adapt to Japanese ways. Although the cafeteria meal was inexpensive, it was also rather tasteless.

I sat across from someone who was wearing a badge with an acronym written on it. I asked Higuchi about the badge, and he said that the man, Kurasawa, was the assigned union leader for our section. I inquired about the acronym and he said it was a slogan of the union meaning "Creation, Inspiration, and Passion." I told Higuchi that I was surprised that white-collar employees were in the union and he responded, "That's the way it is in Japan." I remember thinking that I hadn't realized that Japanese unions had this much power.

My colleagues ate very quickly, and while I ate my food at a steady pace, they were all finished before me. But they waited until I was done, and we headed back to the section together, where we found a number of employees napping at their desks (the fluorescent light above each desk could be manually turned off.) One employee had lined up the chairs at the meeting table to make a small bed where he lay down for a snooze. I thought this was odd, but nobody else did. At one o'clock, another series of notes came over the loudspeaker, and we all started working again.

When Higuchi wanted to talk to me he would approach me at my desk or at the computer, and we would sit at the small meeting table in the section. Now he told me Uno had canceled my tour of the company. I wondered why, but I didn't inquire. I thought I could probably go on a tour some other time. Then Higuchi told me about the rules related to working hours. My working hours were from 9:00 A.M. to 5:30 P.M. with an unpaid hour for lunch. Like most employees, I was also required to work 40 hours of overtime per month at 1.3 times the normal hourly wage.

Higuchi explained that the base pay at the company was extremely low, accounting for only about 40 percent of the total salary. The remaining 60 percent was obtained from overtime work and yearly bonuses. An average yearly bonus ranged from 3 to 6 times the monthly salary and was received biannually. If one's salary was $1,000 per month and the yearly bonus was $5,000, then one would receive a lump sum of $2,500 twice a year. Since the bonus depended on company performance as a whole, overtime was the only way an employee could increase his or her paycheck on an individual basis.

I thought about the overtime rules and did a quick calculation. These rules would require me to stay at work as late as 8:30 or 9:00 P.M. on at least three out of five weekly workdays. Luckily, there was also a flextime policy. As long as they put in their hours, employees could come and go anytime during the day except during core time, between 10:00 A.M. and 3:00 P.M. If workers wanted to take a day off during the week they could work on a Saturday.

Higuchi explained that not all employees were required to work overtime. There was a new policy in place called *sairyō rōdōsei*. This based the employee's paycheck entirely on performance and the annual company bonus. It did not require the employee to receive the bulk of his or her paycheck by working overtime. Unfortunately, since I was a first-year employee, I was not allowed this option. According to Higuchi, many of the employees with seniority in my section worked on a *sairyō rōdōsei* basis.

I was not at all happy about my overtime requirement but felt relieved when Higuchi encouraged me to leave work at 5:30 that second day. However, I noticed that despite what Higuchi said, I was the only person leaving at 5:30. When I returned to my desk to pack up my things, all the employees in the section were still working hard, and when I walked out there was total silence. I felt as if everybody was staring at me.

THE COFFEE MACHINE INCIDENT

On my third day at work, I unintentionally revealed myself to be a troublemaker. I came into work and saw Abani, our section office lady, talking with

Takanashi. Takanashi was wearing the same fluorescent yellow pants he had worn the day before, and the day before that. I got bad vibes from Takanashi, but I'd enjoyed talking to Abani, who'd been a helpful guide through the elaborate paperwork. Abani always smiled and giggled when I spoke to her. I came to learn from my colleagues that she had the typical personality of a woman from the countryside.

"Abani," I asked that morning, in all innocence, "Does our section have a coffee machine?"

She shook her head, looking embarrassed and flustered. I felt like I had made some huge mistake. But what was the big deal? It was just a coffee machine—every office in America had one.

I knew that even in Japan coffee machines were not expensive, so I blundered on, "Well, is it okay if I buy one and bring it in?"

The excitable Takanashi shouted something incomprehensible.

I looked at Abani for help. She obliged. "He says, 'Where would we put it—and who would be allowed to use it?'"

Now I became confused. I replied, "How about we put it in the *kitchen*? And since I'm paying, I'll let *everyone* use it!"

My generosity did not impress him. Takanashi snarled, "We have a vending machine in the hall that serves instant coffee and tea."

This was true; I had used that machine. One small cup of instant coffee was 100 yen (about 80 cents), and it wasn't very good. So I replied, tactfully, I thought, "I think instant coffee is a bit tasteless."

Silence. All the employees in the area looked up. At this point, I realized I had said something terribly wrong, so I suggested that Takanashi and I talk to our boss, Higuchi, when he was available. I walked to my computer with a lowered head, chin to chest, baffled.

A few hours later Higuchi approached me and said, "I hear you don't like instant coffee." I nodded cautiously. He said we could buy a machine—no problem. In fact, there was money in our research budget for this—but the most important issue was where to put it and who would use it. I couldn't believe it! The same nonsensical response!

At this point, I wanted to abandon the issue, so I said, "Why don't we just forget the whole thing? I'll drink the instant coffee and tea, it's fine."

No, Higuchi refused to forget it. He insisted, with a show of cordiality, that we would discuss it later on.

At this point, I was totally baffled, so I went to consult with Erberto. Erberto had lived here for three years as a student, so he had much more experience with the ways of Japan than I did. I told Erberto what had happened, and he burst into hysterical laughter. He gasped, "You got yourself into big trouble, man!" More shrieks of mirth. Finally, when he had calmed down enough to speak coherently, he told me that there were three important lessons to be learned from my experience.

First, when I'd said instant coffee was "tasteless (*mazui*)" I was not just criticizing the coffee but the entire company—especially those who drink instant coffee. As it happens, *mazui* is a very strong word and also translates as "disgusting" or "putrid." Erberto explained, "What you really said to them is something like, 'I think instant coffee is foul and I don't understand how all of you can drink this crap!'"

"Oh, my God—I didn't mean it like that! So what happens next?"

"Well, they'll make a decision about buying the coffee machine, but it will take a couple of weeks because all the managers in our division have to be part of the decision-making process. So Higuchi will talk to his boss and he will talk to his boss and it will go all the way up to the top. Then, once the decision is made, it will come all the way down again. Here's your second lesson: decisions by consensus take a while. Third, don't say *anything* about the coffee machine until the decision is made. And during this time, don't drink any instant coffee because that would show that you *can* drink it, sending them mixed signals."

I took his advice. During this time, communication with my colleagues suffered, and some refused to talk to me. Higuchi tried to organize an informal drinking party for me with some of his colleagues, including Uno, the section manager, but no one wanted to come. When we finally went out, it was just me and Higuchi. He advised me to start appreciating the Japanese culture. I protested, "But I do, I do!"

One morning, weeks later, I came into my section, and my colleagues approached me enthusiastically. "Hey, Mehri *san*. Come over here. Look at this." And there it was on the section conference table—a big, beautiful coffee machine! Later that morning, Higuchi announced the rules for using the machine. He said that anyone interested in drinking brewed coffee would chip in on a monthly basis to pay for it. An employee had been assigned to collect the money and buy the coffee. Sugar and milk would be bought by another employee, and yet another would clean the machine every night. I was amazed at how organized and detailed the whole thing had become, but

I said not a word, happy that the issue was resolved and that my colleagues felt it was safe to talk to me again.

COMPANY ISSUES AND THE DEPARTMENT MEETINGS

The day after I had first asked about the coffee machine, I attended my first section meeting. At this point, I felt quite intimidated, so I decided keep my mouth shut and just observe.

Uno, our section manager, announced the meeting from his desk, and we all trooped over to a meeting room. Section meetings were held every Thursday and were attended by all employees of our section, no matter what their position (except for Abani, the office lady, who never attended the meeting, whether by choice or not, I never found out). There were about thirty people in my section. The meeting room did not have doors, so anyone walking by could overhear the proceedings. The section manager sat at the center of the table and was flanked by some of the higher-level managers.

Most of what we did at that first department meeting was listen to summaries of the three managers' meetings held earlier in the week: the general section meeting, the Technical Research Lab meeting, and the R & D meeting.

In the general section manager meeting, worker evaluations had been discussed. How were the managers supposed to fill out evaluation forms? What criteria were being used to evaluate the workers? Those who had not taken their accrued paid vacations were advised to do so quickly. The managers were told to contribute to the education of the employees at the company, perhaps by a lecture on management.

The Technical Research Lab meeting featured the monthly update about market share. Nizumi's Product A was at 27.5 percent, slightly down from previous month. Product B, at 28.9 percent, was slightly up. Nizumi had exported thirty-one thousand products in the past month: principally to Thailand, Indonesia, and Taiwan. They also discussed a Nizumi worker who had won a special prize. Finally, it was announced that the competitor's benchmarking results would be displayed all week from 9:00 A.M. to 5:00 P.M. All employees are required to attend the display at their convenience. Benchmarking means the careful comparison of different designs to see which one is best.

The R&D meeting was devoted to many topics. Although the competitor had significantly increased market share, the president of Nizumi was confident that the sale of Nizumi products would increase that year. Mr. Okuda, the president of Toyota Motors, had suggested that we look at Korean products and vigorously benchmark them. There was a discussion of just-in- time manufacturing and the next product cycle, with comments from the director. Apparently, the design specifications were poor and quality control had to be improved. Finally, the managers were asked to please turn off certain auxiliary lights at lunchtime.

My colleagues looked bored to tears, but I was fascinated by these synopses. I was especially impressed by the wide-ranging nature of the discussions and by the value placed on improving quality at the front end of the design process. I was also impressed by the emphasis on market share and product quality instead of stock values and company profits.

Hearing about these meetings reinforced my initial impression that the company thrived on the free exchange of information and did its best to support its employees. I decided that the coffee machine incident was just an aberration, caused by my insensitivity to the culture.

The meeting ended with several announcements. Professor Tekechi's presentation on new engineering materials would be held that afternoon. A talk about Toyota's Vehicle Stability Control (VSC) would be presented the next day. Next Monday, there would be a lecture by the police about driving. This year's seminar by the Technical Research Laboratory was going to involve three presentations about vehicle technology.

When we returned to our desks after the Thursday meeting, there were envelopes on them so that we could easily donate money to someone in our group who had lost a member of his family. Later that day, I saw one of the engineers hand out neatly wrapped Japanese apples to each member of our section. I asked a colleague why he was doing this, and he said that his family had been in Kobe during the earthquake. Everyone in our section had donated money to support his parent's family while they rebuilt their house, and as a way of thanking us, his parents provided us with an annual gift. Again, I was impressed with the system. The company seemed so supportive and helpful.

POSITION WITHIN THE HIERARCHY

During these early days, almost everything charmed me, even the distribution of information: announcements, technical specifications, and accident reports. A sheet stapled to each document listed all the employees' names and, if a name was crossed out with a red marker, that document would not be circulated to that person. If the name was not marked off, it was to be circulated to that individual and he or she was required to read it, check off his or her name, and then pass it on to the next person. When all the names were checked off, the document was given to Abani, who would either file it or trash it. There was something quaint and old-fashioned about this system, and it certainly cut down on paper use.

I was not as delighted by the importance of hierarchy on the job. Even in the elevator, the hierarchy governed behavior. Higher-level managers stood in the middle of the elevator and walked off first, while younger employees stood in the back or at the corners. If an office lady entered the elevator, she positioned herself behind the control panel, asking riders what floors they needed, and pushing the buttons with a deferential smile.

As I felt Higuchi and I were rather stiff with each other, I listened attentively to how my colleagues interacted with their superiors. I quickly gathered that the only proper response to orders given by superiors was *hai, wakarimashita* ("yes, I understand" or "yes sir!"). As we worked in an open space, all day long I heard *hai, wakarimashita.* A manager would yell out the name of an engineer, and the subordinate would drop what he was doing and rush to his desk. Their exchange would be loud enough for everyone in the section to hear. Once in a while, the subordinate brought up an issue with the manager, but mostly he listened deferentially. Finally, the boss gave an order and the engineer gave a *hai, wakarimashita.*

In my first week at work, my boss pulled me away from my desk to the section meeting table. He took out a pad and pencil and drew a diagram showing the company hierarchy (I've laid out this hierarchy in a chart at the back of the book.) All regular employees are referred to as *seishain,* meaning they are permanent employees of the company. Contract or temporary workers are referred to as *keiyaku shain.* This was my category.

I was amused to learn that first-year employees, permanent or temporary, are called *ferushuman.* After five to seven years at the company, if a worker demonstrates ability, he is promoted to the lowest rank of management, called *kakarichō. Kakarichōs* typically manage a few subordinates and work directly under a *kachō,* who occupies the next highest level. It takes about fifteen years for an employee to become a *kachō.* A *kachō* typically manages a group of four to six engineers and occupies the position (at several intermediate levels) for another ten to fifteen years, before being promoted to a *buchō*. Section managers are at least at the *buchō* level but it is not required for a *buchō* to manage an entire section. If you show great talent, you became a *jichō,* responsible for managing two or three sections. Finally, you might become a *jōmu* or division director: manager of the entire division. The *jōmu* is a person of great power and reports directly to the vice president and the president of Nizumi, as well as to the top company directors, including senior members of Toyota Motors. For engineers, the most esteemed position in the company was the *gikan.* A *gikan* is a semiretired executive who has held a high position at the company and who is widely recognized for his technical achievements.

The steel name board reified the hierarchy. The names of all the employees in the section were printed on thin magnets. On entering or leaving the company, you moved your magnet to a column showing whether you were in the office, at home, or away on business. The names were arranged vertically by rank. The section manager was placed at the top of the board, with his direct subordinates placed under him, and under that the other employees. The name board reflected some of the subtleties in the system. Since I was the newest member of the section, I was placed toward the bottom—but higher than Kume, a technician who had been there for several years, but who was part of a lower-ranked subsidiary company. Abani, the office lady, was at the lowest position on the name board.

At the factory there was a similar grid to indicate whether you were at work or not, and there was a similar hierarchy. A regular worker at the lowest level is an *ippan rōdōsha*. The *ippan rōdōsha* work in a group and are managed by a group leader or *hancho*. The *hancho* works on the line as well as monitoring the *ippan rōdōsha.* report to group leaders called *kumichos.* The manager of the entire section is the *kochō.*

On my first day off, I went to a bookstore that sold books in English. I decided that I should avoid further "coffee machine mistakes" by reading up about Japanese business. I bought *The Japanese Company* by Rodney Clark. This was an informative book, but it provided little information about how Japanese behave within the corporation. I picked some books I had read as an undergraduate such as Ezra Vogel's *Japan as Number One* and Reischauer's *The Japanese,* but these books did not yield the job insights I needed. Finally, I turned to a book popular amongst foreign businessmen who seek to learn about Japanese business behavior, *The Book of Five Rings: The Bushido Warrior Code* by Musashi Miyamoto. The idea was that if you studied the tradi-

tional samurai warrior code, you could learn about the behavior of corporate managers. It was an interesting thesis.

One day, I brought the book to work and opened it during our lunch break. Shiina asked me why I was reading it, and I explained. He laughed and said, "You're not going to learn anything about Nizumi from that!"

I replied, indignantly, "There must be *something* about Japanese traditions that will give me insight into the company."

"Nothing" he said. "Nothing at all. Learn by observation and experience."

Stubbornly, I kept reading *Warrior Code,* but as the days passed and I did not find anything of use, I abandoned it.

THE DRESS-DOWN CODE

By the end of the first week, I noticed something interesting about the way people dressed. Everyone usually wore the same clothes from one day to the next. Some wore company work suits, others wore flannel shirts with jeans, some wore blue-striped shirts with khakis—but everyone wore more or less the same thing everyday.

In bewilderment, I asked Erberto, "I don't get it! Why does everyone wear the same thing every day?"

He smiled and said, "Katachi."

"Form?" That *was* the translation, wasn't it?

He nodded. "It's just good form here." He himself wore black trousers and a striped shirt each day, and he advised me to pick a "uniform" so I would not stick out and be thought of as some goofy foreigner.

Once again, I thought it best to play safe and so I chose a basic outfit and stuck to it. From then on, I always wore light brown dress pants and striped shirts. I began to understand why most employees kept their work clothes in their lockers and changed when they arrived at work. On some level, they regarded their chosen dress-down clothes as an official company uniform, and it didn't seem appropriate to wear it anywhere else but at work.

You can imagine my shock when a few weeks later, I ran into Erberto in a brightly colored, flowered Mexican shirt. Erberto, of all people! I inquired about his radical change in dress. He told me that he'd received the shirt as a gift from his Brazilian wife and was wearing it to work no matter what anyone thought.

I was amazed at this boldness. "You're crazy," I said. "Everyone's going to stare at you all day!"

And they did—but Erberto didn't care. It was a gift from his wife, and he wanted to wear it.

Most of the engineers and managers, however, wore either the company uniform (a company jacket and pants), or dark slacks and shirt and tie. The office ladies and technicians were sometimes more flamboyant. One office lady often wore a Dallas Cowboy T-shirt with a big, bright silver star sewn on the front. A young technician in the section wore a Reggae T-shirt, which displayed a Rastafarian with the traditional long dreads smoking a cigar-size marijuana spliff. I was surprised he chose this shirt to wear at Nizumi. I went closer to get a better look at this amazing shirt, and I saw it was an advertisement for a Jamaican head shop. Next to the Rastafarian were a marijuana bong, the words "Bong Section," and an address. Another guy in our group sported long Bob Marley dreads.

VISITING TOYOTA AND HOKKAIDO UNIVERSITY

One day, Higuchi asked if I would be interested in attending a conference at Toyota Motors at their largest and most prestigious laboratory. I was excited. I looked forward to engaging in technical discussions about the latest in research and development. Employees of the Design and Research divisions were all invited. We left on a weekday and when we arrived, we checked into the hotel, and Erberto and I took an *onsen* bath. Water from natural hot springs ran into a large bath. I found it interesting that in a society that is considered conservative, it is the norm for a group of men to take a naked bath together. Erberto and I enjoyed a long night of food and drink with Kurata, one of our hosts for the evening. Kurata was dressed in the traditional *yukata,* a white robe with prints of tradition Japanese designs. He had a chiseled face with many sharp edges, and Kurata expressed interest in our backgrounds and asked many questions about our education and our work.

The next morning Erberto and I entered the Toyota compound together and got to observe something extraordinarily: the morning drill called the *chōrei.* A large group of company employees were lined up, military-style, shouting company slogans. They were all dressed in Toyota company uniforms of one-piece jumpers and soft brimmed hats. The hat was the same style used by Japanese soldiers during World War II, and it was standard issue for all employees at the company.

One employee stood at the front directing the drill. He would shout out a slogan and the group would shout back in unison. This display of group obedience reminded me of old films of the Japanese military. "But why here?" I wondered. "Why would a company need to engage in military drills?"

We entered a large lecture room. Most of the attendees were seated either in the center or toward the back of the room. Toward the front of the room was a section for older participants. We all sat silently as they entered the room. They bowed deeply to each other, exchanged a few words, and were escorted to their designated seats. More came, one after the other, some bowing more deeply than others. Finally, a short, white-haired, much older gentleman entered the room. He seemed very important because all who greeted him bowed very, very deeply. This most important man was seated in the center of the first row.

I asked Erberto what was the deal with the octogenarian group. He replied that they were all members of upper-level management, and the important guy sitting in the center was Ikegami, professor at prestigious Kyoto University. Ikegami was the most famous professor (an *erai sensei*) in the Japanese automobile industry. It was interesting observing the close relationship between the car industry and the academic world, which is not common in America.

That morning, we heard one lecture after the other. They were all delivered as monologues without pause. At the end of each lecture, a few people would ask one or two very specific questions, but there was no debate or deep discussion. At the end of the morning, Ikegami was formally introduced, and everyone stood and bowed in unison. A few other *erai sensei* were also introduced, but none of them were as distinguished as Ikegami, who gave a ten-minute speech about how much he has enjoyed his long relationship with Toyota. When he finished, everyone bowed again.

As noon approached, I looked forward to lunch and the possibility of talking shop with the Toyota engineers. This discussion, however, did not occur. We all sat in the cafeteria and ate one of the most silent lunches of my life. Everyone looked very serious, and there was no talk at all.

After lunch, Erberto and I walked around the grounds in the summer heat. I asked him why everyone had been so silent at lunch, and he replied, "Japanese engineers just don't share information with each other. They're afraid you'll steal their secrets." I noticed a large group of men in shorts running around a field. I wondered why they would be running in the middle of the day in the sweltering heat. I asked Erberto, and he told me that they were new recruits. I marveled to learn that this exercise was part of their training.

A few weeks later, Shizumi *gikan* of Nizumi invited me to accompany him to Hokkaido University on his annual recruitment trip. A couple of the professors at Hokkaido University had studied at the graduate program at the University of Wisconsin, and they wanted to show me the campus. The professor who most pressed the *gikan* to have me visit was named Koga. He was very well known in his field—another *erai sensei.*

When we arrived at the university, Shizumi *gikan* gave a lecture about the history of the company and his role in developing technology. Shizumi *gikan,* who was retired, was an ex vice president of the company, a charismatic and sophisticated person with graying hair. He was a fine speaker who scattered his lecture with a few good jokes. I took some pictures.

After the lecture, Shizumi disappeared, and Professor Koga came up to greet me. He was a very nice graying older man with fond memories of his stay in America. He showed me around the university, speaking with pride about its distinguished history. Then he brought me to the office of a young professor who had also studied at the University of Wisconsin. He was quite handsome in his slick double-breasted suit. In excellent English, he introduced himself cordially and offered me a seat at a table. He picked up a box of chocolates and offered me one. After the brief introduction, he began talking about the university and its research in the field. He asked if I wanted a tour of the labs, and I was happy to accept his offer. As we walked from one experiment to another, he explained each project. I was impressed with his knowledge and his insight.

After the tour, I was invited to dinner with Shizumi, the professors, and the managers of Nizumi who ran the operations in Hokkaido. In order for the company to obtain good engineers and for the university to send their graduates to well-known companies, it was important to maintain good connections. The company had rented a private traditional tatami room in which high-quality black lacquer utensils were neatly arranged on the table. As they greeted each other, the younger professors and managers all bowed very deeply to Koga and Shimizu *gikan.* Since we were in a tatami room, everyone was already on their knees, and when they greeted Koga and Shimizu *gikan,* the younger professors and managers bowed so deeply their faces almost hit the ground. It was as if they were praying at a temple. I noticed that the bows to Koga were deeper than those to the *gikan*. The two venerated old men sat across from each other in the center of the table and began talking like old friends about the latest in automobile technology.

Koga then began a long tirade about the decline of Japanese engineers over the years. He said that they did not know as much as he did when he was young. I was interested in hearing more about this, when the debonair young professor suddenly asked if I liked to drink. I responded with a definite "yes," and he enthusiastically poured me a glass of beer. He wanted to talk to me about something. During his stay at the university in America, he had become good friends with Williamson, an American professor, but he was perplexed about his behavior. Once when they met at an annual Society of Automotive Engineers meeting in Detroit, the young Japanese professor had invited Williamson to a strip club just over the border in Canada, a well-known hangout for men of all nationalities. Williamson had refused with some anger, and the incident had apparently strained their relationship. I had to smile, because I knew Williamson, and he was definitely not interested in such activities.

The other guys in the room became excited about our conversation and began joking and giggling to each other about their experiences at this well-known Canadian hot spot. According to the young professor, it was common for groups of men to go there together and have a great time because "shame will be forgotten for the night." I was surprised that they would talk so openly and casually about such behavior with their business associates—just as the Japanese professor was surprised that Williamson had indignantly turned it down.

When I returned to work after my trip, I slipped into my old routine. I had been at Nizumi for only a few weeks, and I was still learning how to use the software. I thought that I would stay late only when necessary but when I left early my colleagues would give me a sour face and say "otsukare sama deshita." There is no equivalent translation in English, but it literally means "Thank you for working hard [for our group]." At times, an employee would say it more loudly than usual while bowing slightly. It was clear that they were sending me a message to work late with them, so I decided to stay late whether I had overtime or not. Early on, this did not bother me much, since I was still in the learning mode and wanted to impress my superiors with good results.

Strangely, I would not receive a good-bye of any sort when I stayed late.

IMPROVING THE FLAGSHIP PRODUCT

After I had been at Nizumi a few weeks, Higuchi called me to his desk. The upper-level managers had decided on using CAD to improve one of the company's flagship products, the XT37—part of the drivetrain. Higuchi explained my role in the project and what he expected of me. He was confident that I had acquired the skills to begin working on my first assignment. I was pleased to be getting my career off the ground and excited that I would be learning how to design in Japan, where they made the best products in the world.

Getting my career moving in Japan, however, required me to adjust to the Japanese way of doing things. I learned early on that Higuchi was my only source of information about the technology I was using. On-the-job training by one's immediate superior was the norm for all engineers at the company. As my boss, Higuchi was responsible for educating me. That meant we needed to develop a traditional Japanese relationship where the superior functioned as the mentor, or *senpai,* and the subordinate was the *kōhai.* As a *kōhai* and a new recruit, I was very dependent on Higuchi. Since much of the information was proprietary, only Higuchi, with his in-house experience at Nizumi, could provide the education I needed to design the part.

According to Higuchi, improving the XT37 was vital to the drivetrain our section was responsible for developing. He wanted me to create many models of various designs. Then we would choose the best among the many options available. The aim was to design a part with the highest efficiency while keeping manufacturing costs down. During the design process, we were required to sit down with engineers in production who explained the manufacturing process and costs.

Perhaps you don't know what a drivetrain looks like, so imagine designing an automobile tire. Designing even something relatively simple like a tire can be very complex. You need to design a tire that can be used in all weather conditions—the dry heat of a road in Sudan, the snow and ice on an Alaskan highway, or the drenched autumnal streets of New York City. You need to design a tire that can brake on a hill and veer at high speed. You need to make sure that the driver is safe and that the vehicle meets its fuel consumption goal. To design a good tire, you have to be able to solve one problem after another.

During the contentious weekly technical meetings Uno convened every

Friday, I learned how Japanese engineers approached problem-solving. To arrive at the best design, the engineers would gather huge amounts of information, comparing new designs with previous designs. If the technology unearthed by their research could benefit the product in any way, they would include it in the many alternatives they were considering.[1] I would soon learn that set-based design was used extensively at the company. Comparing one design to another was considered the best way to evaluate the advantages of each.

Abe once distributed a memo called "The Vision Method." This was a step-by-step directive about engaging engineers in the set-based process. One of the steps was "Deciding the Subject": "To achieve the goal, you must think about as many ideas as you can and write them down. Then you must choose the best idea from all of the ideas."

Although my relationship with Higuchi was congenial, working as an American-educated engineer was not without its frustrations. The way I learned from him and discussed the technology was very different than the way I learned in the West. I would frequently ask him questions about design considerations. He would respond with very specific answers, never discussing the concepts abstractly. All discussions about technology were concrete. While I would always begin my talks with a discussion of basic ideas, he would immediately focus on the details. Once when I brought him 3D pictures of a design I was considering, Higuchi bent forward and put his head right up to a small part of the model. He said, "What about this?"

"What?"

"*This,*" he said, pointing to a tiny speck on the model. I thought he was pulling my leg—but he was serious. I was beside myself that he would consider such a small detail while ignoring the beauty of my overall design. But remembering I was a *kōhai,* I just said I would look at it and went back to work.

I did express my disagreement sometimes, but this was invariably frustrating and time-consuming. Higuchi was usually surprised that I would

---

[1] Sobek, Ward, and Liker's research describes Toyota's approach to product development as set-based design where "designers think and reason about sets of design alternatives. Over time, these sets are gradually narrowed as the designers eliminate inferior alternatives until they find a final solution" (Durward Sobek, Allen Ward, and Jeffrey Liker, "Toyota's Principles of Set-Based Concurrent Engineering," *Sloan Management Review* 40, no. 2 (winter 1999): 67–83). They claim this method differs from the conventional practice of choosing a single design early on and iterating to improve it until a solution is obtained. See also Jeffery Liker, Jon Ettlie, and and John Campbell, *Engineered in Japan: Japanese Technology Management Practices* (New York: Oxford University Press, 1995).

question his wisdom at all, and we would discuss the issue at length, arguing back and forth, with me focusing on the abstract and him on the details. In the end, he wouldn't budge, so we would end up right where we had started.

In retrospect, most of the time he was correct. After all, he was the more experienced engineer. But what I found irritating was the assumption that there was only one way to approach the design project—his way: focus on the concrete. He always remained affable and patient while hearing me out, but I soon saw that our discussions were mostly a way for me to get things off my chest. Unless I had concrete results to show him, he wouldn't even consider what I had to say. However, if I could prove my ideas with results, he would affably and easily change his mind. Higuchi was open to new ideas—as long as I could prove them.

I observed a similar emphasis on detail during Uno's Friday technical meetings. A debate about the basic physics of the engineering phenomena rarely occurred. Only concrete information that could be validated through experiments or through previous designs was considered acceptable for discussion.

As I worked on designing the part for the new drivetrain, I became frustrated by the lack of information that Higuchi provided. I always received information on a piecemeal basis. At times it was as if he was giving me secret "hints" about the technology, and when he finished, there was often an awkward silence as I waited for more information that never came.

Even the engineers in my section were not as forthcoming as I expected. One day Erberto came to my desk and told me that Kurata was holding a contest to come up with the best new drivetrain designs. At the meeting to discuss the details, I was surprised when Kurata, who was a highly placed director of the Design Division, bluntly stated that the company's foreign competitors had moved ahead of Nizumi. When I returned from the meeting, I approached members of my section and asked them what they thought about the new designs. To my surprise, they reacted defensively and avoided discussion, as if I was trying to steal their secrets.

Because of my frustrations with Higuchi, I was interested in learning how my colleagues interacted with their bosses, so I observed them closely. They would talk about the issue—usually loudly enough for everyone in the section to hear. Although the engineers would sometimes raise issues and make objections, in the end, they deferred to what their bosses said. Finally, the superior would give the subordinate a direct order and the engineer would respond with a "hai, wakarimashita" and walk away. Both sides avoided a direct clash of ideas. Now I saw why Higuchi was surprised at some of my objections. Although I was only trying to create the best design, I was breaking the rules of social conduct.

The concept of "the team" is supposedly central to Japanese business and manufacturing, but from working at Nizumi, I find the term *group* to be a more accurate description. In my section, all the engineers worked in groups of three or four. Each group was composed of engineers who had specific skills. We all worked on projects of little relevance to the others in our group, yet we were all supposed to be working on the same product.

I belonged to the analysis group—composed of myself, Higuchi, and Takanashi. The goal of the analysis group was to provide the corporation with the latest in advanced computer simulation technology. Far from feeling like a member of a "team," I worked alone on most projects and simply reported to Higuchi with the results. Our group was even less cohesive than the others. The irascible Takanashi rarely talked to Higuchi, and when he did, he always seemed agitated. As for Takanashi and me, we rarely communicated at all, which was fine with me, as he was so personally abrasive. I worked on designing products while Takanashi worked on developing high-end software that the management hoped would eventually be used by other engineers at the company. Although we were both part of the analysis group and happened to be improving the same product, our tasks were not related.

TECHNOLOGY EXCHANGE

I enjoyed it when foreigners visited the company to give technical presentations, because unlike the Japanese, Westerners were always interested in sharing information, particularly when they wanted to make a sale. Many of the companies were funded by venture capital and owned by brash young entrepreneurs. I met my first American from a software company at a conference we attended. He was a lanky, well-dressed young Californian who tied his long, blond hair in a neat ponytail. He wore a diamond earring in one ear, which added a bit of exotica to his progressive American persona. He came to Japan to talk about how his company's innovations would change the industry. The technology allowed engineers to design the drivetrain dynamically using 3D CAD. The drivetrain, along with the vehicles' many parts, could be placed on the computer where it could be analyzed in depth. It was a beautiful example of technology integration.

The Californian gave a brief introduction and then said, "Okay, now I would like everyone to take off their ties." Clearly, he thought this was a way to make his clients relax, as they might have done in America. When the Japanese did not respond at all, I saw him hesitate. But he shrugged, smiled, and continued. Everyone listened attentively, for he said that his company would no longer be selling its source code, since many engineers in America had been incorporating it into their own software and selling it as their developments.

All computer software contains "source code" that tells the computer how to implement tasks, such as drawing a picture on the computer. At times, a software company allows users to have access to the code in what is called "open source" so that they can customize it to their own needs. "Open source," however, permits engineers who are developing similar software to copy the source code and implement it in their own software.

I saw Higuchi quietly laugh. Stealing technology and industrial espionage frequently came up during conversations with him and other employees at the company.

Then the Californian did a demo that knocked the socks off the attendees. The computer program simulated the motion of the vehicle as it rode over bumps on rough terrain. The program could create a stunning animation and was able to analyze the entire dynamics of the drivetrain design. It enabled you to create graphs on the fly comparing various design parameters. The information could also be used to program the little computer that controlled the vehicle. It was high-end technology, and the Californian loved showing it off.

He came back to the company the next day to coax Higuchi into buying his company's software. He handed out promotional material on the latest in simulations and talked openly about which company was buying their software and how they were using it. He also showed us graphical results of simulations on specific products that had been improved using the software.

Higuchi obviously enjoyed this free flow of information, since Nizumi was incredibly secretive about sharing technology. Not a single bit of information about a product could be sent out without approval from above. In most cases, even if the products were already in production, the management refused to share the information. Even during meetings where they could clearly benefit from an open discussion, the engineers always remained guarded.

Ultimately, the American with the ponytail and the diamond in his ear was able to make the sale, even if he had not been able to get the Japanese to loosen their ties.

For days, I thought about how Higuchi had laughed when he heard that the Californian company was protecting its source code, but I didn't fully understood the extent of industrial espionage until a few weeks later, when Higuchi and I attended the annual Tokyo Motor show. The management required all engineers to attend, and upon our return, we would fill out a document about significant developments at the show that were relevant to Nizumi's products.

As Higuchi and I walked around the large hall, he pointed to some important exhibits that I should investigate. At the show, each company had a booth where smiling women, neatly dressed in company uniforms, greeted the visitors. The new technology on display forced the engineers at the booth to discuss the latest developments, but they never revealed very much. They spoke enthusiastically about their products, but tried desperately to conceal any technical information that could be used by their competitors. Everything was sterile. None of the engineers engaged in open conversation, and they traveled in small groups, keeping to themselves. I noticed one group of engineers suddenly pause to examine the shape of a certain part. The engineer at the booth watched this group closely.

When I returned to Higuchi, he said that a few years ago the Motor Show had been more open. Then a group of engineers from Honda entered a Toyota car on display and made measurements of the entire vehicle. "For what reason?" I asked.

"To copy it," he said. A few months later Honda came out with an exact copy of that car!

INTIMIDATION AT WORK

After I met Scarface, I decided I was lucky that Higuchi was my boss. Scarface was a senior engineer at the company, a heavy man with a deep scar running down the side of his face. Scarface was close with Uno, the section manager, which gave him free license to bully anyone in the section. He would abruptly approach an employee from behind, commandeer his chair, then harass him about his work, reading some of his data out loud and asking hostile questions. When the employee responded, Scarface would yell, "So why is that? What do you mean? Why didn't you use this procedure?"

Some engineers maintained their composure, but others stuttered and their faces turned bright red. These incidents always occurred when other members of the group were present, as Scarface's goal was to publicly humiliate his target. When Scarface walked into our section with his wrathful gaze, the atmosphere became tense. Everybody feared him, and he relished this.

I was not spared his attentions. I hated when he poked his eyes into my work, but I answered his questions as accurately as I could and without fear. Indeed, I would almost chuckle inside. Being a foreigner, I had not been conditioned to react to public humiliation the same way as my Japanese colleagues, so instead of inducing shame, Scarface's harangues struck me as strangely comic.

The engineers were also harassed and humiliated during the technical meetings convened by Uno every Friday. I was told that the meetings were held so that the engineers could share their results with the group. Each of us would make a presentation and the others would ask questions. I initially thought that this was an excellent way for us to learn about each other's research. However, I quickly learned otherwise. The presentations were followed by marginal discussions at best, and I saw that these meetings were merely opportunities for Uno and his close subordinates to receive a report from each group. Some of the men closed their eyes and took quick naps as they sat at the table.

When an engineer presented his material, Uno's face would contort in anger as he waved his index finger up and down. Then he would question some technical detail. While listening to the answer, Uno would put his glasses on the table and place both of his hands on his face as if he was praying at a temple until the engineer stopped talking. When the engineer fell silent, Uno came back to life to ask more questions. Sometimes Scarface would add to the inquisition in his loud and penetrating voice. His arms were always crossed as he embarrassed the chosen victim.

It was rare for an engineer to put up resistance, but one time the drilling turned into a tit-for-tat exchange that became quite heated. Even as Uno tried to invalidate his reasoning, the engineer stood his ground. Uno shook his finger and yelled over and over, "You still haven't answered my question! Why did you do that?" The time allocated to the meeting eventually expired without any resolution to the issue. I walked away stunned, wondering what could have caused Uno to be so hardheaded and what could have made the young engineer courageous enough to stand up to him. This was a highly unusual situation, and it did not occur again.

After about two months, it was my turn to present my research at the Friday technical meeting. Naturally, I was nervous, so I had spent much time preparing my data so I wouldn't fumble. I made my presentation with a chart showing which configuration would produce the best results within the design constraints. Higuchi had taught me how to design the chart. The horizontal axis represented the different XT37 designs, Design A, Design B, and the rest, and the vertical axis showed the efficiency of the design according to the part of geometry that had been tweaked for optimization. All other engineers reported their data in a similar fashion. It was a very effective way of showing which design was the best among the many alternatives.

I expected to be put through the grinder, but Uno merely asked me a few quiet questions. None of the other men said a thing except a short, wildhaired manager with thick eyeglasses. He cracked a couple of jokes and laughed maniacally to himself, as he always did. As for Scarface, he sat at the table as usual, with his hands folded on his chest, but to my surprise, he didn't say a thing. Perhaps they treated me more gently than the others because I was a foreigner. They may have been afraid that under pressure I might react differently than a Japanese.

After I had worked for several months at Nizumi and produced some good engineering results, Uno organized a drinking party to welcome me into the section. About time, I thought. I had heard that welcoming parties typically occurred within the first two weeks of an employee's arrival. Higuchi explained that Uno was a very strict section manager, and his purpose in postponing my welcome party was to let me know that my primary purpose in the section was to produce good engineering results. My introductory tour of the company, which would have consumed a day's work, had been cancelled for the same reason.

When the welcoming party was eventually organized, it was indeed a grand event. I knew it was an important affair since Abe, the manager of the Technical Research Division, was also invited. An expensive restaurant that served an esoteric Japanese cuisine had been chosen, and every participant was required to pay eighty dollars out of his own pocket for the dinner.

The dinner was held in a tatami room, where we all sat on the straw mat floor at a long, narrow table that nearly spanned the length of the room. A balcony, accessible by walking through the *shōji* screen (a sliding door made of light wood and paper), overlooked a large, well-manicured Japanese garden. We made ourselves comfortable with several bottles of beer and various small snacks. Soon bottle caps hissed as they were pried open, and the beer began to flow. Each of us sat patiently until everyone was served a small glass of beer. Ienaga, the leader of the party, made a short speech welcoming me to the company and we all said "cheers" as we drank our first glass of the evening.

Abe sat opposite to me and asked about my hobbies, what food I liked to eat, and so on. He professed surprise that I could use chopsticks adeptly, and he talked about how some high-level managers at Nizumi were connected to the University of Wisconsin. After Abe completed his information-gathering, Mochida, a young engineer, asked if I liked to drink. When I said I did, he seemed very pleased. He, too, complimented me on my skill with chopsticks, turning to his neighbor to say, "Isn't it great how good Mehri *san* can use chopsticks!"

As we ate and drank, the laughing and talking became louder. A great fuss was made about the exact way to serve of one of the exotic delicacies from a small town in Kyushu. Eventually, the proper way was determined, and Abani, the only woman in the group, served the delicacy, as well as all the other dishes in the meal. The dinner ended amicably and Mochida suggested that we attend a second party, but the other members were not up to it, and so the party ended early. When I talked with Shiina about the party the next day, I learned that some employees were upset about the high cost of the meal and how they would explain it to their wives.

When I returned to the dorm that evening, Erberto knocked on my door. "Hey, man, the American engineer from Ford has arrived." We had been expecting him for weeks. I was particularly interested in getting to know a fellow countryman, because I sometimes became homesick and longed for someone with whom I shared a common culture. All I needed was to exchange an American colloquialism or a joke now and then. Erberto and I knocked on his door and we introduced ourselves. The American said, "My name is Steve." He gave each of us a confident and robust handshake then invited us into his room. We made small talk for a while, but Erberto always became impatient with talking about trivial things. He loved contentious discussions, so he said, admiringly, "I hear that the United Auto Workers are very strong in America." At the time a number of UAW auto strikes in America had made the news in Japan.

"They're a bunch of animals," Steve responded in his loud, Midwestern voice. "They're so goddamn lazy. I came to work one day and I saw a bunch of them just laying around doing nothing, and they refused to work." I felt embarrassed for him. He had come all the way around the world to live in a country radically different from his own and one of the first things he did was to put down his fellow countrymen.

I was curious as to why he had come to Japan, and he told me that to move into a management position these days you needed to have international experience. I suspected that a man with his confidence would rise to a high position at Ford, but I wondered how Steve would interact with Japanese. His thoroughly rough, overconfident personality might prove too abrasive to a group of mild-mannered folks who rarely showed their feelings. I was disappointed to realize Steve was not going to be a good friend of mine, as I didn't find his personality appealing. However, his many years of experience in the American auto industry would prove useful in providing me with a frame of reference.

"WHO IN THE OFFICE DO YOU LIKE?"

By now, I was recognized as an important part of the department, and this was very satisfying. Nonetheless, I began to feel the effects of staying late on the job. As the days passed, the more hours I worked, the more tired I became. I had no social life during the week because I returned home from work too late to do anything, and during the weekends I was too tired to have any fun. I was lonely and fatigued. Since my work evaluations were good and I was putting in the proper overtime, I decided to stop staying late at the company unless it was required by either my job or my paid overtime. I did not want to spend the rest of my days in Japan alone and exhausted—I wanted to enjoy my life.

Soon, however, the negative signals from members of my section began to reappear. During lunchtime they would ask me about what I was doing in the evening, was I busy, was I seeing a woman, and other such prying questions. At the end of the day, when I was leaving, some colleague or other would put me on the spot by remarking, "You are going home early tonight Mehri *san*." Still, I held my course. To avoid direct confrontations such as these, I modified my exit strategy by leaving the office, head down, to avoid all eye contact.

At this time, I began to copy some of the others and take short naps at my desk during lunch break. Although it helped reduce work-related stress in the afternoon, I was still exhausted every Friday.

One day after a meeting, I passed Mochida, the young engineer, who was reading a trade magazine about the auto industry. It featured the industry's leaders discussing corporate policy. I asked Mochida about the magazine and he responded that it was "full of lies." I laughed and said in the United States we had magazines like that, too. He suggested that we go out to eat some time soon with Kurasawa, an engineer in our section and our section union leader. These two were close friends, and Kurasawa had introduced Mochida to his wife.

When I met Mochida, he had just returned from a three-year stint at a joint national lab where all the companies in the country are forced by the government to work on "national" projects. Mochida said that nothing was ever accomplished because the engineers, who were all from competing companies, refused to share any information. "Most everyone wasted their time reading comics and drinking beer while living in fear of sharing company secrets." Three valuable years of his life had been wasted doing nothing.

Mochida asked me what restaurants I was frequenting while in Japan. I told him that I liked the *kaiten* sushi restaurants, where the sushi passes before you on a conveyer belt. Mochida grinned and twirled his hand. "The sushi goes around and around," he said. The next day, Kurasawa approached my desk and asked if I would join him and a few of his friends in a drinking party.

I was excited about the possibility of an evening out with the boys. I had been at the company for close to six months and I had yet to make friends in my section. Although I was constantly surrounded by people on the floor—some only an arm's length away—I felt isolated because they kept to themselves. I also felt alienated because of the lack of genuine emotional interaction. Neither their voices nor their expressions revealed their true feelings. Even if they were very angry, they would not show it. It was as if everyone was wearing a mask. If I got together with my colleagues outside the office, perhaps I could learn what lay under the mask: discover the *honne* behind the *tatemae.*

We left the company after work on Friday evening, walked toward the station, and packed ourselves into a train filled with other groups of company men who had planned a similar ritual. The trains were always crowded at that time of the day, so we stood pressed against each other while conversation and body odor filled the air. We traveled to the next town, which had plenty of small pub-restaurants.

We entered a *kaiten* sushi restaurant in a crowded section of town and sat on low bar stools at a narrow Formica table while the plates of sushi went past us. We started the meal by simply reaching over and grabbing a plate. Each plate contained two pieces of sushi and sold for about a dollar. We took one plate after the other—tuna, octopus, fish eggs. When I took a plate, the others were sometimes surprised at what "the foreigner" was eating. Then, as if to test me, Mochida asked if I would like to try *natto* sushi. From my first morning at the company cafeteria, I had been revolted by *natto,* a slimy concoction of soybean and raw egg, but now I did not want to refuse his offer. As he looked around on the conveyer belt hoping one would pass by, Kurasawa commented upon how well I used chopsticks, picking up one piece of sushi after the other without a hint of trouble. By now, I had learned the proper response to a compliment is to humble yourself, so I responded, "No, my use of chopsticks is not very good."

"Aha!" said Mochida, reaching out and grabbing a plate of *natto* sushi. "Here it is!" He passed the plate to me, and I took a piece of the disgusting sushi. I made sure to dip it thoroughly into the soy sauce to mask its flavor. The guys watched me intently when I popped it in my mouth. It was a test. I tried to get it down quickly—but as it turned out, it wasn't so bad. Eventually, I even grew to like it.

After the sushi, we went to an *izakaya* to drink and nibble on snacks. Often built into the basement of an office building, an *izakaya* is a loud, smoke-filled pub where businessmen drink, eat, and talk about company matters. The male bonding for salarymen typically lasts late into the night and involves stopping at several pubs before returning home drunk and foul-smelling. We sat at a table in the center of the room. I was squeezed into a wooden seat and frequently moved my tiny chair aside to let the quickly moving waitresses go by. Many were college students working part time to make ends meet.

I looked over to the adjacent table and saw two women serve their male colleagues by sorting the small dishes of food on the table, pouring beer, and lighting cigarettes, all the while childishly giggling and deferring to male opinion. Although the *izakaya* are mainly for men, women come along during official drinking parties, which are typically organized by their boss.

After my colleagues had filled my tiny glass with beer again and again, I warmed to the conversation, which was mainly about work. They were curious about how I had ended up at Nizumi and asked me several background questions, always joking and pouring more beer. They asked how old I was, and when I told them I'd been born in 1965, they told me it was time to find a wife. As our conversation continued, our chopsticks picked up bits of baked squid, pickled vegetables, radish salad, and fried chicken from the small, neatly arranged dishes on the table. Suddenly, the topic changed to the manager with the long, scraggly hair and the maniacal laugh. I learned that he was universally known as Dr. Zombie. They hated the guy! Nobody could understand his orders, and he was so bizarre looking, with his wild hair and thick, black-framed glasses. They joked that he'd been born during the Japanese Edo period, about 250 years earlier, and had been transformed into a zombie due to an accident in the lab. They also spoke of another manager in our section, Hiraga, who didn't do much but yawn, stroke his hair, take smoking breaks, and walk down the office corridors. They envied me in having Higuchi for a boss, because he was easygoing.

Kurasawa then told me how his boss, Ebisawa, had lied to him. "I was working for a smaller supplier company," he said "when Ebisawa called me about a job at Nizumi." Ebisawa had also worked at the smaller supplier company and had recently started working at Nizumi. He needed to build an engineering team for a new project. "He made many promises, but when I started the job, I found out that the hours were much longer and the pay was not as good as he had told me." He said Nizumi was "big and famous" but he had made a mistake—his old job had been much better. He paused for a moment, then said, "On the other hand I have made some good friends at Nizumi, like Mochida."

I was surprised to hear such open criticism of senior-level managers at the company. It was the first time that the relationships between superior and subordinate took on a human dimension, and I saw that it was not unusual for employees to criticize their bosses or vent their anger at the system, especially when they left company premises. There was a moment of silence after Kurasawa's complaints, but he quickly revved up the party again by asking me, "Do you like Japanese women?"

My contact with women had been limited to brief conversations about company matters with a few ladies at work. I found their behavior to be childish. When I spoke they would giggle, cup their hands to their mouths, and speak coquettishly in high-pitched voices. I was often confused as to whether I was talking to a twelve-year-old girl or a grown woman. I did not find their behavior appealing, but I knew the correct response. I said, "Of course, I like Japanese women."

"So, who is your favorite office lady?" Kurasawa asked.

I really didn't have any favorites but thought I should name one or two to avoid questions about my masculinity. During a cherry-picking company trip, I had had a brief but pleasant chat with a nice young woman, so I decided to name her as the one I liked. "The one that with the long hair that curves down to her shoulders."

"Oh, you mean the one that works for Kurata?"

"Yeah, that's the one. And there's another who's really attractive—Ms. Iida."

He looked surprised. "That's strange," he said. "Don't you find her too clever?"

"Not really."

Most Japanese men don't like women who are clever. Ms. Iida was a graduate of the prestigious Tokyo Institute of Technology and was on a three-month rotation in our section to see if she fit in the group. Would they think I was peculiar, I wondered, if I liked a woman that did not play the role of a traditional woman? Iida was smart, educated, and somewhat assertive. She seemed fine to me.

Kurasawa broke the awkward silence by saying, "I hear she likes playing tennis. Maybe Higuchi could organize a tennis match with you and Iida."

"That would be nice," I said and thought nothing more of the matter.

When I finally returned to the dorm, Steve, the Ford engineer, was at my door. We would occasionally pop into each other's rooms for a short chat. He was interested in learning as much about the Japanese system as possible. He was especially interested in verifying what he had read in *The Machine that*

Changed the World. I was confused when he spoke about such things as the wonders of "team work" and consensus, because I had yet to experience these ideals.

Much has been written about consensus decision-making by scholars of Japanese companies, but throughout my time in Japan, I did not experience or hear about a single case of genuine consensus. Consultation was typically the norm, but it depended entirely on the manager in charge. Ideally, he consulted with lower-level employees, asking them for feedback on technical issues, but the extent of his consultation varied considerably. I heard about, but did not experience, consensus on the upper levels.

Steve came in that evening talking glowingly about *kaizen*. "It is great what they do to improve safety," he said. "When a worker gets into an accident, they write up a report and hang it on the bulletin board so that workers can learn how to make improvements." I had seen those accident reports but had not looked at them closely. I was tired that night, so I politely asked him to leave.

When I arrived at work the next day, I felt the atmosphere in my group had changed. What it was I did not know, but I soon found out. During lunch, Higuchi asked me if I wanted to play tennis one day with Ms. Iida. "There are a few tennis courts near my house," he said, "I'm not sure if I can make a reservation but maybe one day we can get together to play tennis with Ms. Iida." Although I felt embarrassed and surprised that he knew about my conversation with the boys, I could not turn down his kind offer.

I felt awkward about imposing myself on someone whom I had casually called "attractive," and I was hesitant about starting a relationship with a woman in the office. But apparently the news that I fancied Ms. Iida had spread all around the office, so I had no choice but to face the consequences. Sure enough, during the next company outing, Uno asked me to join him and a few others, including Ms. Iida, of course, for a tennis match. It was fun, but, as I'd expected, nothing came from our encounter.

Although the rumors about me and Ms. Iida soon ceased, general curiosity about me and Japanese women never seemed to fade. Raucous discussions about me and Japanese women were a staple of our drinking parties. I was sometimes asked, "How many times have you had sex in one day?" And I was often asked about the size of my penis. I had heard from my Japanese colleagues that some Japanese women liked being with foreigners because they were well hung, so I knew these questions came from the guys' insecurity.

Nevertheless, they often expressed a sincere interest in my happiness by saying that it was lonely (*sabishii*) being single. They said it would be a good idea for me to find a kind Japanese wife. After I returned from my first trip back to the States, Uno asked me if my parents were worried that I was still unmarried. I jokingly responded, "My mother sure is!"

Uno smiled. Then he asked, "What are your chances of getting married this year?"

"Christ, no chance at all!" I thought to myself, but I merely responded, "Who knows? I'm still dating—maybe some time next year."

I was both touched and irritated by this interest in my private life.

The topic of finding a proper Japanese woman to ease my *sabishii* never stopped interesting my colleagues. One day, Shiina suggested that if I wanted to meet new women at the company, the safety newsletter was a good place to start. "The women's articles in the safety newsletter are mainly there to introduce young women to men at the company," he explained. "There is an article about a new woman every month, and many of them work right here in the office." He pointed his finger in the direction of the office ladies.

Matching available women with appropriate men is such a part of the working culture that marriages resulting from company contact have their own special word: *sankon.* In Japanese, *san* means "three" and *kon* means "marriage." So *sankon* translates roughly as, "marriage three meters away from a desk." Men are often so busy at work that the only way to obtain a bride is to pursue a woman within his immediate surroundings.

Shiina's comments piqued my curiosity, so I picked up an edition of the safety magazine lying on my desk. It included several articles about safety at the company and a small section titled "The Women's Group." This section included articles about women who worked in the office and on the line. One woman wrote, "I am always careful about two things—to greet punctually and to smile as much as possible. Everyone loves me because of these things." Another article read, "Happy New Year! Ms. Nakamura started work last year with her feet on the ground and can do many things at the company. She wants to put in her best effort to make this year a substantial one." The accompanying photograph showed a woman dressed in a *furisode* kimono (with long hanging sleeves and bright colors) that only single women wear.

Many of the articles involved women talking about their social lives, such as an article that read, "These days, having a meal with my elementary school friends once a month is an important pleasure for me. The contents of our discussions are about our school days, work, and love." The articles usually included flattering photos of the women. At times, they were also pictured with family or friends. In effect, Nizumi encouraged the women to run free personal ads to catch a company man.

A few months after our tennis match, Ms. Iida quit her job. When I asked Shiina why, he said, "She was impatient, and she did not give the company the chance to offer her the position she wanted." I had seen Iida spending much of her lunchtime chatting with the two other women engineers who were senior to her. One of the women had entered the company three years earlier, after graduating from a well-known university with a degree in chemistry. Instead of receiving a position in her field, she was given a job as a mechanical design drafter with the Advanced Design Group, a job that was not only unrelated to her educational background but did not even require a college degree. Once she complained to me, "I hate my job, it is so boring. I want to be transferred." But she was never transferred. The other woman was a Ph.D. who worked hard to obtain good results, but she was never allowed to publish a technical paper like her male colleagues. I suspected that Ms. Iida was not really "impatient"; she probably saw what would happen to her career if she stayed on at the company.

MOVING UP

At Nizumi, a worker did not quietly get a promotion. Promotions and job changes were very public: something of a semiannual ritual. I experienced this for the first time in September of my first year at Nizumi. In the middle of the working afternoon, the entire company stopped working and converged to the center of the room in front of Kurata, the august director of the Design Division, to listen to the changes. The office ladies stood in a row close to him, behaving obediently and coquettishly, while the men quietly stood nearby.

Our section was at the corner of the floor. Although we were located on the same floor, we belonged to an entirely different division and hence we had our own transfer meeting held by Abe later in the afternoon. Nonetheless, we came to listen to these changes since managers in the Design Division could potentially influence our work.

Kurata introduced the promotions and job changes—one name after the other—sometimes laughing as he mispronounced a name. Some of the men, particularly the higher-ups who were being shifted to another section, gave a greeting or a good-bye speech about some of the things they had accomplished and the relationships they had developed.

That evening, Steve popped his head into my room again. This time, he seemed somewhat chagrined. "I can't believe how retarded the casting plant is," he said. "They're using technology from the 1920s!" He also said that he had discovered that an exhaust pipe for vehicle testing had been broken and was now directing toxic gas back into the building. "I can't believe it," he said. "There's no way in hell we would allow people at Ford to work in such conditions."

A few weeks later, Steve was back at my door. He told me he had met a worker that day who had lost a finger on the line. Steve said, "In all of my years working at Ford I never met a worker who lost a finger in a factory." I could tell that he was shocked. He kept shaking his head in disbelief.

Steve left the company a few months later to start a three-year stint at the Mazda plant in Hiroshima. I very much doubt that he continued to invoke *The Machine that Changed the World*.

THE ADVANCED DESIGN PROJECT: "WE CAN DO ANYTHING"

After I had been on the job for several weeks, Higuchi informed Uno that I was obtaining good results. A stack of CAD pictures and detailed graphs showed the design optimization. Higuchi showed these to Abe, along with the results of other engineers in my section.

With the recent increase in the computational power of our computers, the skills of the computer simulation engineers like myself became particularly useful to the company at large. I was now assigned to work on a project with the Advanced Drivetrain Design Section of the Design Division. The role of the Advanced Section was to develop innovative products to be put into production three to five years from inception.

Kurata, who managed the Advanced Drivetrain Design Section, wanted to design a completely new product within a year, so he sent his subordinate, an elegant man named Saiki, to meet with us. Saiki was tall, with a perfectly sculpted face and piercing eyes. He had a smooth, quiet voice, and I was sure that he made many a woman in the office swoon. Saiki had gathered engineers from various groups. Since the Advanced Design Section was a branch of the Design Division, Erberto's entire group was assigned to the project, while I was the only engineer from my section, the Technical Research Division.

Our first meeting was lively indeed. Many engineers wondered whether we could meet the new deadline without improvements in the design tools, but instead of addressing the issue, Saiki leaned back in his chair, as if he was tanning himself on a beach, and responded in his velvety voice, "We're Nizumi, we can do anything." One engineer after another pleaded for an alternative design approach, but Saiki rejected all such talk, even when important technical issues were raised.

When I told Higuchi about the speed of the project, he said, "I don't think it is a good idea." I asked him what Uno thought, and Higuchi replied, "He doesn't think it is good either." Erberto said that his boss, Oda, felt the same way. I attended a few more meetings, then received an assignment to improve the design of the Advanced XT37 on the computer. Initially, it was unclear what my job would be. If the managers did not send down an order, Higuchi and I could only make an educated guess—or talk with people in another group who might know.

To figure out what was going on, I approached a lower-level manager I had known through my CAD work. Although I found Inoue to be technically competent, he was one of the oddest employees at the company, notorious for playing the clown. Instead of working, he spent his days making jokes and fooling around. Whenever he cracked a joke, his group roared with laughter. I found all this to be very annoying since I was seated close to the group and was constantly distracted from my train of thought. Inoue would swirl in his chair while making funny noises, like a child on an amusement ride. Or he would sit on the floor sorting out various office items. Once when a colleague did not understand him, Inoue actually jumped onto the man's desk and put his mouth close to his ear so that he could hear him. Higuchi explained this peculiar behavior by saying that Inoue had spent many years working at Toyota and had been terribly overworked, but physically he seemed as healthy as anyone else.

Anyway, Inoue told me that my job was to design the part on the computer, while Genda, an Advanced Design engineer, would work to improve the same part by running experiments in the technical center. Like all the other men working on the project, we had to produce a viable product in about half the necessary time, so we had to work very long hours. When I reached the end of a long day, I felt as if my bloodshot eyes were burning two holes straight through my skull, and long-dormant skin allergies began to flare up. Once in a while, Genda would poke his puppylike face out of the lab, but usually I didn't hear from him for days.

Higuchi asked me to talk with the Advanced Design Group, so I visited the section. By automating the tedious complex surface creation, I had written a CAD program that reduced the time of one engineering process from about two weeks to two hours. I showed it to Inoue and he got so excited he called Kurata over to have me show him the technology. No more exploding parts with this program!

Although the engineers in the Advanced Design Section seemed to be competent about the technology, the managers were terribly disorganized. About once a week Kurata and the managers in the Design Division would make major changes to the design and pass their decisions down to us. Every time they came up with a new design, all the CAD models had to be redone, all the parts had to be changed and the entire product had to be updated. This was tremendously time-consuming and tedious. As a result, all the workers assigned to the project were terribly overworked. In Erberto's group alone, at least three workers were forced to work a hundred hours of overtime per month: about five hours of overtime per day.

The way I learned about changes in the product design was through my good friend Erberto. His round, wire-frame glasses and long hair made him look like a studious college student. With his thick, dark hair and slender body, he could have passed for a Japanese if not for his Western features: a long skinny nose, sculpted lips, and a well-defined chin. As an employee inside the Design Division, Erberto was privy to details of the design and to important gossip within his group. We used to love squirreling away during the day to discuss various company issues.

As an Italian college student, Erberto had become fascinated with Asia when he had traveled to Thailand with his friends. He loved the landscape and the women. He was attracted to their ready smiles and petite bodies. "I had to marry an Asian woman," he told me. "They're just so cute." He made plans to go to graduate school in China, but after Tiananmen Square, he decided to go to Japan. He met many women in graduate school, but felt that the cultural gap was too wide for him to marry a native Japanese. So he married a Brazilian woman of Japanese descent who was working toward a Ph.D. in architecture.

Erberto came to my desk one day with a smile on his face and told me he had some news. We went down to the company café, Erberto's hair swinging. He always wore his hair loose on his shoulders, and when he walked it would swing from side to side. I enjoyed the contrast between his flamboyant Latin style and the quiet stoicism of our Japanese colleagues.

As soon as we settled onto the bar stools, he turned to me and said in a stage whisper "Hey, beware of spies!" I looked over my shoulder and saw Saiki with his subordinates walk by. Erberto laughed; he loved catching me off guard. After Saiki had passed, Erberto said, "They're going to change the design again."

"What!" I cried in outrage. "*Again*?" It must have been the sixth or seventh time the managers had changed the design.

"They want to add a couple more parts. They're afraid that the competition will release a more advanced product." He rolled his eyes upward.

"What did Nishida have to say?" Nishida was his boss.

"He attended an all-day meeting and concluded that it would actually save more time to make the changes than to resist the management."

I shook my head in exasperation. There was nothing to be done.

"GO MARRIAGE!"

More days passed as we ploughed away on the Advanced Design Project. My allergies became worse, and I was constantly scratching my body. The dry skin sometimes broke.

Once when Hiraga came back from one of his many coffee breaks he approached me saying "What happened, Mehri *san*?"

"What do you mean?" I responded, looking into his glassy eyes. Hiraga always looked like he was high on something.

"Your shirt," he said. I looked over my shoulder and saw blood stains blooming on my back. I told him it was nothing.

Erberto also had skin allergies, and his conclusion was that they were caused by the food in the cafeteria. "They put chemicals in it," he said. I ignored him at first, but as my condition became worse, I decided to test his hypothesis. I observed that the men who did not eat in the cafeteria ate lunch at their desks. Some bought lunch from the sandwich shop on the first floor, while others ate neatly packed combinations of rice, vegetables, and meat from their *obento* boxes.

When I left work, I went to a small mom and pop store and picked up an *obentō* box, which came with a convenient airtight lid and a pair of plastic chopsticks. That evening I made my own lunch and packed it into the box.

A few days passed. Then Mochida approached me to ask, indirectly, where my *obentō* was coming from. When I told him I had made it myself, I thought he would faint. "No! Really?" he said, eyes wide. "I thought one of your girl-friends was making it for you. I'm surprised you know how to cook!" To me it was no big deal. I merely cooked up some rice in my automatic rice cooker and stir-fried some vegetables and tofu. That was all.

But all the other guys were equally shocked. Each of them came to my desk while I was eating and looked at my *obentō*, expressing amazement that I could cook for myself. I took another look around the office during lunch, and, it was easy for me to distinguish between men who were married and men who were not. If they had a homemade *obentō* they were definitely mar-ried since it was obviously rare that a Japanese man had the skill or inclina-tion to make it himself. Those who ate sandwiches at their desks or who ate in the cafeteria were probably single.

Although these lunches were delicious, my skin allergies did not go away. I had been wrong in blaming them on the cafeteria food.

During lunch, I would sometimes approach Kurasawa for a short chat. He had a round, childlike face, yet his eyes were mournful. As the designated union leader for our section, he was a good source of information about the company. He seemed to get a kick out of hearing about my life in Japan. His sad eyes would light up when I told him about my love life, particularly when I spoke about the International Adventure Club—a mixed foreign and Jap-anese outing organization that sponsored hiking trips throughout Japan. When I told him that many of the Japanese who attended were single women who had studied abroad, he and Mochida would joke, "Yeah, I bet the best part of those trips is when you get to the top of the mountain!"

Sometimes, Kurasawa would puzzle me by saying, "Let's go drinking again with Ishii." Ishii had organized the welcome party for me. According to Kura-sawa, he was a homosexual in a fake marriage. I remembered how Ishii had once reached over to touch me. I had ignored him.

As I got to know Kurasawa better, my friend Akiko, whom I had met during my yearlong stay in Japan after college, began asking me about meeting some of the men in my office. Akiko had graduated from a famous Japanese junior college, and had moved to the United States to attend Boston University. Upon graduation, in the early 1990s, she had returned to Japan, but had found it hard to reassimilate into society and find a job at a Japanese company. By the late 1990s she was approaching thirty and was eager to get married before being considered too old to find a suitable husband. In Japan, an introduction through a connection is an important way to establish a relationship with someone whom you do not know. I was the perfect person to introduce her to available men at the company.

I approached Kurasawa one day to tell him about Akiko's request, and he immediately proposed that I organize a *gōkon*. The word is the short form of *godo-conpa, godo* meaning "joint" and *conpa* meaning an informal drinking party. A number of the guys in our section were suffering from severe loneliness. Returning home to an empty apartment after a twelve-hour work-day was the norm for single men in our section.

I talked with a member of Kurasawa's group named Chiba one day about dating. Chiba was single and had a gaunt-looking face. He told me he sometimes frequented a brothel to relieve his pain. "I wake up in the morning, go to work, and return home at around eleven at night, and do the same thing the next day, so I do not have time to meet women," he said. "When I go to the whorehouse and have sex it feels good for about an hour, but afterwards I feel lonely once again. I need to find a wife."

Then there was Ienaga. He made it clear to others in the section that he was looking for a wife, and his colleagues joked about his failed attempts to meet women. One sign of his desperation was that when he was asked to leave the company dorm (after his allotted four years in the subsidized housing ran out), he moved *two hours away* to a town with a well-known women's junior college. "It is far," the others said, "but now he has the opportunity to meet women."

Kurasawa quickly organized five bachelors in our section, and in turn, Akiko invited five of her single friends whom she knew from her school days.

Gossip about the *gōkon* spread throughout our section. At last! The men finally had a chance to meet single women. Ienaga was certainly excited about the encounter. Once he and Kurasawa asked if I had a picture of the women they would meet. I shook my head. Kurasawa pointed to Ienaga's pants and said, "Ienaga is hard and is about to explode!" Ienaga's face flushed red—and we all laughed.

Takanashi was another lonely man. He was well into his forties and still a bachelor. Given his antisocial nature, it did not surprise me that he remained unmarried. He wore his bright yellow pants with an impeccably clean white shirt and shuffled around the office as if his shoes were slippers. His computer was located beside mine, and I would often see him swivel in his chair, legs crossed in a lotus position, pen shoved under his lower lip, as he stared, stone-faced, into the screen. If I ever asked him a question, he would react angrily, as he had about the coffee machine, or tell me to ask Higuchi. Nevertheless, I had sympathy for him, as I did for all men who were lonely. There were various times in my life when I did not have female companionship, sometimes for months on end.

When Kurasawa and I were deciding which guys to invite, I asked if we should ask Takanashi. I thought that if Takanashi had a good time, it might help us bond. After all, we were in the same group. But Kurasawa said that if Takanashi came along it would be the end of it for all the men. When I asked why he said, "He likes making love to horses."

Takanashi was the ringleader of the horse-betting group in our section. A group of the boys would get together during the lunch break to talk about horses. Mochida was heavily involved and would often talk about the latest bets with Takanashi. They even had a spreadsheet to analyze who in the group had made the most profitable bets. I didn't want to sour the *gōkon,* so I abandoned the idea of inviting Takanashi.

I thought it was strange that many of the men found themselves in such need of a date when there were more than a few single office ladies available for them to meet. The company had no restrictions on co-workers dating; indeed, they encouraged it. So I asked Kume, who sat across from me—a good-looking technician who was fully integrated in the section but belonged to separate subsidiary company—why the men couldn't just meet the office ladies. Kume responded that Kurata was responsible for selecting the women who worked on our floor, and he tended to like women who were spoiled. They were *ojōsan,* he said and were not approachable. *Ojōsan* translates roughly as a pampered woman who is naïve about the world.

I turned to Shiina for some answers. "Most men do not have the chance to meet women," he said. "Many are from the countryside far from the city and they live alone." He explained that in the old days, young men had more opportunity to meet women because they could be introduced to them by older women in the village in which they grew up. He concluded, "A lot of guys who work around here are single, even the older ones in their forties.

It's a lonely life." To compensate for the lack of social support, modern Japanese society created the *gōkon*, which was essentially a modified version of the arranged meeting.

The day finally came for the *gōkon*. Kurasawa had made reservations at an Italian restaurant, and when the women arrived, he immediately ordered hors d'oeuvres, beer, and red wine. When the food and drinks arrived, the women began serving the men, pouring beer and arranging small plates of food for each one. The men sat and answered questions about the company, their jobs, and company life. They seemed to be having a good time. For most, it was a rare occasion to spend the evening with the opposite sex and to escape from the drudgery of overtime.

After about twenty minutes, Kurasawa suddenly yelled out, "Everyone switch."

"Switch?" I said, "What do you mean?"

"Change positions!" he replied. "Every man move down one seat!"

And so a new conversation began, with a fresh face for each to explore. I was surprised at how each woman tried to demonstrate that she would make a good Japanese housewife. Everything that I had learned as an American made me feel uncomfortable with the women's nonstop ritual of pouring beer, serving food, and lighting cigarettes in an giggling, self-effacing manner. I was also bored with the silly and superficial conversation. "What would I do with such a woman?" I thought to myself. The cultural gap was too wide for me to enjoy a serious relationship with a Japanese woman, but I did not want the men to know, so I continued to show interest.

Akiko arrived late. From the beginning she seemed uncomfortable and out of place. She sat next to Ienaga who quickly began to chat her up.

"I heard you lived in America," he said. "You must speak good English, especially with Mehri *san*?"

"No, I have forgotten my English," she replied, "I speak with him only in Japanese."

I was shocked at her response, which was completely false. We always spoke in English, and her communication skills were impeccable. The only reason for her to deny her knowledge of English was to protect herself from being considered nontraditional and thus reducing her chances of getting a husband. I was surprised at how Akiko behaved and wondered if this was expected of good wives of Japanese businessmen. Later, I was told that this self-effacing, childish behavior on the part of Japanese women was only *tatemae*—a superficial way it was necessary to behave in order to get a husband.

After all the men completed their rotations, it was time to pay the bill. Kurasawa figured out how much each should pay, but told me, "The men will pay more than the women, this is the Japanese way." So we all paid about 50 percent more than the women and then we went off to sing karaoke. When we got to work the next day, I learned that none of the men had been able to obtain a single phone number from any of the women. Still, they were pleased to have had the night out.

The day after the *gōkon,* I asked Akiko what she thought. She said that although all the men were nice, they were not her type: too traditional and too nerdy. She persisted in asking me if I knew someone she would like. She had experienced a number of formal introductions through her parents' *omiai* that did not work out, because "most of the men who do *omiai* are unattractive geeks."

I thought Kume, the technician sitting across from me, might be a good match for Akiko. When I first met him, he asked if I listened to Eric Clapton. I had listened to Eric Clapton a lot as a teenager but hadn't picked up one of his albums for years. Sensing what was required, I said "yes" enthusiastically (*tatemae,* not *honne*), and we became friends.

Kume was shy but he seemed very nice. He was also attractive, with shining hair and large eyes, so I told Akiko that I had a candidate for her. When I mentioned her to Kume, he responded enthusiastically. I asked Akiko if she would give me her *omiai* information: her hobbies, family history, where she and her parents went to school, the positions they held, what town they were from, and a photograph.

I showed the information to Shiina and he gasped. "Wow, she's from a very high-level family. Her father is a graduate of Kyōto University and is the director of a famous company! She is too high level for anyone in this section." He shook his head and handed me back the *omiai* information. And that was that. I realized that any discussion about breaking the hierarchical barriers would be futile. I had really goofed! I had planned to set up a daughter of the elite with a humble technician.

The next day over lunch, Erberto said, "By the way, I overheard a conversation today. Apparently, Genda is saying your results are not good—so take care." I couldn't believe my ears. Weren't Genda and I working on the project together? While he looked like a puppy, he acted like a snake. I was furious, so I approached Higuchi and discovered that Genda and I were actually in competition with each other so the management could see who had the superior technology. I thought the plan was ridiculous and felt if they were really interested in designing a great product we should all be working together. After all, weren't Japanese companies known for working well in teams? The incident shattered that myth.

At the next Friday morning technical meeting, I presented the results of the ongoing analysis and vented some of my grievances. They all sat and listened with quiet, drawn faces, nodding in agreement. These were serious problems, I said: the entire company could be jeopardized if the end product was flawed. Uno listened, but he merely said, "That's not good." Higuchi then mentioned the impossible time constraints, and all the men laughed. But that was it. I thought of a comment I had heard earlier, "The managers don't care about anything, as long as they get their paychecks."

MEETING FOREIGNERS IN THE COMMUNITY

I was happy to have some escape from work. The company provided foreign employees with six months of language lessons, and when the lessons expired, I discovered that the city gave free language classes. I rode my bike through the narrow streets to the small community center. When I got to the entrance of the classroom, I saw a scrawny Indian man sitting at the desk. He introduced himself as Bhanu and said he was in charge of managing the program. He had me take a Japanese test, then assigned me to level three. He pointed to the room where the class met. I walked through the door and introduced myself, and the teacher asked me to take a seat. I sat next to an African man.

When the lesson was over, a small group of older women arranged rice crackers and prepared green tea so we could socialize for a little while. I approached the African, whose name was Kofi. He told me he worked at the Nizumi factory. I had seen a number of foreigners at the plant, but since I worked in the office, I hadn't had the opportunity to meet any. Now I had my chance, so I asked Kofi about his background and how he had made it to Japan. He said he was from Ghana and had met his wife in Africa. They had married in Ghana and come to Japan a few years earlier to live in his wife's hometown, three hours to the north, where his wife and daughter still lived.

Kofi had moved to Yashima after getting the job at Nizumi, so he saw his family only on weekends. His daughter had asthma and it was thought that the air in Yashima would be poor for her health. Kofi had to leave immediately after the class but we exchanged phone numbers so we could meet again.

I mingled with the other foreigners. A few other Africans, a number of Chinese, and a group from Southeast Asia were also attending the class. Most worked in factories in the area or were spouses of Japanese men or women. Bhanu circulated in the group, and then he asked me out for dinner.

We wound our way through the streets, hearing the humming of train wheels on the tracks. Close to the train station were several *izakayas,* and we made our way into one on the third floor of a very skinny building—only a couple of dozen yards wide. I used to wonder about these buildings, but I soon learned that everything in Japan was packed into very small spaces. Bhanu ordered a few dishes in his impeccable Japanese. Soon we were drinking beer and eating bits of fried squid while talking about our lives in Japan.

"When I came to Japan I used to work for Nizumi," he said. "But they didn't offer me a permanent job so I quit." He had worked in production and his job had good pay and benefits, but he was married to a Japanese woman and had children, so he needed a more stable job. He subsequently got a job at a smaller company that did not provide the same benefits as Nizumi, but it was a permanent position. To make some extra money, he had worked as a manager at the community language school.

Since Bhanu had worked at Nizumi for several years, I asked him what it was like when he was there. He said that although the benefits were good, the working conditions were terrible. "They worked people so hard that some guys had to work a thirty-six- to seventy-two-hour shift. One guy on a seventy-two-hour shift fell asleep on the line, which is certainly understandable. But while he was sleeping, he was cut in half by a machine. We couldn't believe it! But the company covered it up. There was no mention of his death in the newsletter, no safety warnings about it, nothing at all."

I wasn't sure whether to believe him or not. I didn't think the factory could be all that dangerous. I thought that perhaps Bhanu wanted to vent his anger because he hadn't been offered a permanent job. The evening wound down, and Bhanu reminded me about an International Friendship meeting at the City Hall that weekend.

As I approached City Hall that Saturday, I noticed a crowd gathered in front of the main building. I moved to the front of the crowd and saw an older man with a large mallet pounding a white sticky paste in a large wooden bowl which was carved into the trunk of a tree. He paused to rest for a moment and asked if I wanted to give it a go. He wrapped a ceremonial *hachimaki* on my head and threw a large handful of moist white rice into the bowl. He handed me the wooden hammer and told me to raise it over my head and swing it down onto the rice. I obeyed, and the hammer made a large wet thud when it hit. I looked at him expectantly, and he cried out, "You can't just do it *once,* you got to keep going!" I hammered the rice a few more times, and it began to turn into a gooey paste. A group of older ladies then picked the white paste out of the bowl to make small oval cakes with a sweet red bean center. The cakes were quite good: perhaps a little bland, but not overly sweet, as American pastries often are.

Suddenly I noticed Bhanu in the crowd. He called out "Hello," and I went to his side. "Meet Ms. Kondo," he said. "She also works at Nizumi." Kondo was a middle-aged woman who worked as a drafter in the Design Division. Kondo called to her friend Rie, a much younger woman with long, wavy hair. Rie was a violinist, and we had an interesting conversation about music. We exchanged phone numbers, and she suggested we get together with some of her friends.

A few days later Rie and Kondo asked me to come for dinner and suggested that I bring a friend. To compensate for my mismatching him with Akiko, I brought Kume with me. This was a fine idea. Kume had a great time with Rie and continued to see her.

AN INDEPENDENT WOMAN

I stayed in touch with my new friends and would occasionally bump into Kondo on the company grounds. Despite the stench from the casting factory, the grounds were quite nice, with rows of cherry trees in front of the drab buildings. One day, Kondo handed me a postcard and a Kuroyume CD. Kuroyume, meaning "black dream," was one of Japan's best-known punk rockers. Kondo asked me to listen to the album and to write on the postcard how I felt about the music.

The album was called Corkscrew, and on the cover, written in English was the following crude message: "I found that I cannot be only myself as I used to be, let's fuck up all the rules." The CD cover featured Kuroyume gashing his arm with a knife and smiling while he looked at the blood. The album contained such songs as "Knees to Break," "Spoon and Caffeine" and "Screw Mix." The lead song was called "Masturbating Smile."

I brought the album to my desk, put it into a laptop computer and pressed "play." A loud scream came from my speakers—and all my colleagues turned their heads. I quickly turned it off. Then I asked Kurasawa if this sort of music was popular in Japan, "I don't like it," he said, "but it is becoming more popular. It is bad for young people and bad for society."

I filled out the card as Kondo had requested and gave the CD a two-word review: "masturbating smile." I popped the card into the mail and thought no more of it.

A few weeks later. Kondo told me that Kuroyume was touring Japan and was planning to give a concert nearby. Did I want to see the show with her? I was puzzled about why a fifty-something-year-old woman would like such rubbish, but I was also intrigued. I couldn't turn down what might be a once in a lifetime opportunity—so I went.

We walked into a theatre packed with young teenagers, including many so-called "Shibuya" girls. They are called "Shibuya girls" because they were first seen wandering through the busy Shibuya Station in downtown Tokyo. These young women dress up in the most outlandish way. Tanning their skin dark brown and dying their hair blonde, they wear exaggerated 1970s clothes including gigantic bell-bottom pants and twelve-inch-high platform shoes. They brush layers of makeup on their faces, particularly around their eyes. They wear sparkling eye shadow and long strokes of bright eyeliner that flow back from the corners of their eyelids. Many carry mini Hello Kitty dolls and small, childlike vinyl purses.

I thought they looked like a bunch of freaks from a low-budget, 1970s American monster movie. I wondered if they dressed up that way to rebel against Japanese female social traditions or because they felt they looked attractive. Kondo thought they looked absurd, but perhaps the young guys disagreed.

A group of these excited young women almost knocked me down getting to their seats. When we finally arrived at our own seats, we found ourselves surrounded by a large group of rowdy teenagers. The show began. The music was bad, and it was so loud that I had to cover my ears with my hands. To make matters worse, the woman sitting directly behind me felt it necessary to scream into my right ear when Kuroyume played her favorite songs. Soon, to my surprise, Ms. Kondo was standing up and pushing her way to the aisle.

She began to dance. It was a strange sight—a middle-aged woman dancing to punk rock. I called her back, but she kept on moving, eyes closed, deaf to my entreaties.

Not all men thought that women needed to follow traditional social norms. Opinions about the role of Japanese women varied from the staunch traditionalists to the progressive. Kurasawa had conservative views, and often criticized the independent behavior of modern women as adversely affecting Japanese society. When I told him about the Kuroyume concert he frowned and said that Kondo was strange.

On the other hand, some, like Shiina, had spent years abroad and returned either with English-speaking Japanese wives or with foreign wives. These men tended to be more open-minded in their attitudes toward women. Of all of the men in my section, Higuchi was the most progressive. Once after a dinner at his house, he complained about the traditional role of women. "My wife wanted to talk with us more but she spent most of the evening preparing food," he said, "I'm sorry for this." He continued, "In Japan it is a bad situation for women working in the home. They must spend most of their time in the kitchen preparing food and do not spend much time socializing."

The company newsletters occasionally printed articles reflecting women's independence. In a Women's Group article one woman writes, "I think spring is a good time for motorcycle riding. Although I don't have a license to ride a motorcycle, I want to get a license this year and obtain a large 400cc bike someday."

Despite a few articles that reflected independence, the overwhelming majority depicted women in traditional roles. One sixteen-page company newsletter contained thirty-three photos where seventeen were of female employees or wives of male employees. Among the seventeen pictures of women, ten were pictured with their friends in casual nonwork clothes, three showed them dressed as housewives, and three showed them with their children. Only one woman was shown on the job. Thirteen of the sixteen male photos included an article about their work abroad, offering general advice, or in discussing the latest market conditions. The men were always dressed in suits or work clothes.

The newsletter contained a series of articles titled "Our Favorite Food at

Home" in which female employees shared their favorite "home" recipe. One article was titled "My *Nabe* House." (*Nabe* is a traditional Japanese stew of vegetables and meat.) It began: "We would like to introduce a very unique *nabe* that you can make to warm you up to fight against cold during winter."[2] Before leading into a detailed discussion of the recipe, the article stated the woman's name and department. It included a picture of the woman with her husband and child as well as a color picture of the dish. Scattered among these articles were the following illustrations.

Another group of articles was titled "My Family." One of the articles described a female employee's relationship with her mother: "My mother and I have a difference of height of around 15 cm but I am very much like my mother. Recently cooking with my mother has become a custom." She goes on to explain that although her mother has physically become smaller her mental abilities have increased. She concludes by saying, "There is a proverb that says when children become old, parents must obey. My mother speaks

---

[2] In Japanese *shoogatsu*. New Year celebrations in Japan typically last four or five days. During New Year the company would close the plant for ten days of vacation and allow time for the factory to retool.

timidly, but sometimes she acts thoughtlessly. However, she still is well and is always kind hearted."

THE PRICE OF OBEDIENCE

Every New Year, everyone was required to give a short speech about the projects they had worked on and the results they hoped to achieve in the coming year. Hiraga said he would work hard to make sure that Nizumi stayed on top of the market. Hearing that from a man who spent most of his days sitting at his desk staring into space was amusing. Mochida said he would be going to Hokkaido University again to engage in research activities, but would like spend more time drinking with the professors. Everyone laughed. I said I would continue to work on developing the Advanced XT37. I noticed that Takanashi was not present so I turned to Higuchi and asked where he was. "He does not come to these meetings," he said. "He makes sure he is absent." I was surprised that this eccentricity was tolerated.

In the Design Division, we were still required to put in impossible hours, and the entire project suffered for it. The quality of our work deteriorated, and morale was low. But every time we approached an upper-level manager, the response was the same: "We can do anything!"

Aizawa, in particular, was deteriorating in front of us. While at the computer, this tall engineer would suddenly lean backward and shut his eyes as if he were going to pass out—then quickly throw himself forward to face the screen again. It happened repeatedly throughout the day: every few minutes, up and down. He was shutting off, if only for a few moments, so he could slog through the tedious assignment. He sat there day after day, redesigning the product according to the whims of upper management, staying as late as midnight and catching the last train home. Then back to work at nine the next day, always behind the computer, that damned computer. Erberto and I were appalled at the company's indifference to his health. Furthermore, Aizawa was the designated union leader for his section. Erberto remarked, "If they keep working him like this, he'll be dead by forty."

Fortunately, since I was essentially "on loan" from the Research Division, my experience was not as brutal. Higuchi was considerate enough to thwart many demands on my time from the project leader. One day Saiki asked Higuchi if I would work on a project that Genda was supposed to have worked on, but Higuchi refused. When Higuchi told me of Saiki's request, he said that Genda had been a very hard worker until he'd been sent to work at a national laboratory to work on a collaborative industrial research project. "All he did there was play golf all day." Now he had become lazy. Again and again, I heard that the national labs where joint research was conducted were a total waste of time.

As we tried to get things done within absurd time constraints, I couldn't understand why the engineers in the Design Division were so docile, meekly accepting the bad decisions of a small group of upper-level managers. Higuchi explained: "Once a decision is made from above, everyone follows. No one will complain or stand up to authority, even if they know the decision is wrong." Once in a while, a person will voice a grievance, as was the case during my first design meeting, but the overwhelming majority of engineers do not say a word against management policy, even if it is a failure.

For instance, I discovered that the efficiency of the XT37 could be dramatically improved if an adjoining part could be moved 5 millimeters. When I told the key engineer about this, he said that nothing could be done. I asked Shiina the reason for this and he responded: "The 'reason' is that someone important has made the decision and no one will question it. So now it a rule that is not questioned." According to my experience, not all decisions were as rigid, but Shiina's comment highlighted the authoritarian way design decisions were made.

In Japan, to an even greater extent than in the United States, if a subordinate wants to move up, he has to do what his superiors request. When I approached upper-level managers about design alternatives, none of them would listen to what I had to say, because my position was lower than theirs. Rank was more important than reason.

VENTING DURING DRINKING PARTIES

The careless way that the Advanced Design managers conducted the project naturally caused concern among employees at the company. The company would provide them with a livelihood for most, if not all, of their working careers, so they were anxious about the project. If the company went down, many of the older employees would not be able to jump ship.

Drinking parties were a way for the engineers to allay their anxieties and express their concerns, even in the presence of their superiors.

During a good-bye party organized by Mochida and Kurasawa, we all sat on tatami mats while the boys distributed a generous amount of beer. The manager of the Tech Center sat in the center while his close subordinates flanked him. Most of the engineers were young, in their mid twenties. As soon as I sat down, a technician named Kanegawa began talking with me about sports. He said his favorite hobby was beach ball. I found this amusing, for he was a big man with a deep voice. I couldn't imagine him dressed in a swim suit, tossing a ball around on a beach. Suddenly, he said, "We've been doing some tests on the product and the results are not very good. Is there any chance you can redesign the part?"

"I doubt it."

Kanegawa slowly nodded and his eyes flared with passion, "You know, the biggest problem with the company is that everyone works on their own and does not communicate with other groups. If we work together we can design a much better part."

I said, "I totally agree."

But this didn't appease him. He began a tirade about the company's organization. It became apparent that he saw our section as an elite organization, whose members should not be burdened with trivial technical problems.

Mochida defended us, "Our section exists to provide advanced technology for the whole company."

The discussion became lively, even acrimonious.

What I found interesting was that all this took place in the presence of some important mid-level managers. (The high-level managers were not present.) You were allowed to let off steam, and I never heard of anyone being punished for saying something that angered management during a drinking party.

The day after the drinking party, a meeting was called to compare my results with Genda's. We had each made charts and CAD pictures to show how we were progressing. A manufacturing engineer was present to discuss any issues that could arise in production. We had both made significant improvements, but Genda claimed his design was the best. We were discussing various details when the manufacturing engineer interrupted and said, "It can't be made, manufacturing can't cast it." He pointed to a defect in Genda's design. The meeting suddenly became deathly quiet. Genda stroked his chin in disbelief, and his hands began to shake. They ended up choosing one of Genda's other designs, to my chagrin. I had created a very efficient design, but it did not meet one of the design criteria, which once again management had recently changed. To my mind, this alternate design of Genda's had only one virtue: it could, in fact, be cast.

ENDURE THE PAIN!

My medical condition continued to worsen. Allergies were not new to me; I'd had bouts of eczema for several years in the States, but now the severity of my skin allergies had become intolerable. Erberto thought my eczema was caused by air pollution. He said, "In Japan, allowable dioxin levels are the highest in the world, about 400 times what's permitted in Europe." He, too, suffered from eczema. There were times when his entire face was covered with dry flakes.

But my condition was even more severe. The allergy had spread over most of my body, leaving large, red patches. My legs were swollen and bloody. The dormitory cook wondered if there was too much dust in my room. Her friend thought I had insects under my skin. I said, "Maybe it's the incinerator burning trash at low temperatures." The cook assured me the air in Japan was clean. She offered to help and told me to see her in a few days. The next time I saw her, she called me into the cafeteria to give me two small containers of cream for my skin, saying. "It's good, it's from the dermatologist." I thanked her. She said, "By the way, when your skin itches, don't scratch yourself—slap your skin instead."

As I expected, the cream did not work. Nor could I get myself to slap my skin instead of scratching when it itched. My condition deteriorated further.

I received much sympathy from my colleagues about my allergies. Some were sincerely concerned and suggested measures I could take. Others, however, just said fatalistically, "Japan is a dirty country, and nothing can be done."

My co-workers lamented the unhealthy conditions at the company. Takanashi was especially outspoken. With his legs folded in lotus position on his chair, he said, "It's the filth in the air coming directly from the factories, particularly the casting plant." Placing his hands on the desk, he swiveled his chair back and forth. "When I started working here, I noticed that a number of workers had chronic coughs because of the pollution from that factory. See the soot coming from the vent?" He pointed his finger upward. I looked up at the air conditioner vent and saw that the surface covered with black soot. Takanashi continued angrily, "This place is filthy! I don't think they even have air filters here." According to him, the company had never cleaned the air conditioners. Nor were they planning to.

By law, the company had to provide its employees with health benefits. These included a yearly checkup—examination of eyes, ears, throat, and chest and blood tests.

A myriad of newsletters from the union instructing us on how to stay healthy dropped onto our desks. One article titled, "Checking Bad Teeth," used cartoons to illustrate each problem. One cartoon showed a man in pain holding the side of his mouth. The caption read, "You feel pain when you drink cold water."

In addition to literature, the union provided each employee with an annual medicine kit containing several kinds of remedies: pills for stomach aches, sore throats, colds, and nausea. Still hoping for relief from my allergies, I handed Shiina the package of pills for the common cold and asked him to translate the writing. Shiina said, "It reads 'all purpose medicine'—but 'all purpose' really means 'no purpose.'"

I decided to see the company doctor, but my colleagues told me not to bother—he was useless.

Higuchi told me that the health system in Japan was fundamentally flawed. "The problem in Japan is that doctors do not charge their patients fees. Under the national health care, they receive a salary from the government. Most of their money comes from pharmaceutical companies, who pay the doctors according to how much medicine they prescribe. The pharmaceutical companies deliberately weaken the medicine to increase their own profits because that way, more medicine needs to be prescribed. What you receive from the doctor is a quick examination and lots of medicine, which is usually too weak to help you. The health system in Japan is terrible."

Higuchi had a son with severe asthma, so he had much experience with the medical system. One of the doctors he consulted told him to buy an American house, one without tatami mats. The mats are made out of straw and are notorious for collecting dust. A home without them would greatly reduce the chances of an asthma attack. Higuchi decided to take the doctor's advice, but now he was puzzled. In an American house, he would need an American sofa. "But what is its function?" he asked.

"To sit on," I said, "Americans usually put them in the living room."

"That's all?"

"Yeah."

"Oh." He was puzzled. "But what if they want to take a nap?"

"They go to the bedroom."

"All the way to the bedroom? That's so inconvenient. In Japan, all you have to do is move the table and nap on the tatami mats in the living room."

I assured him that he could also take a nap on the couch, but he didn't seem happy with the idea.

Nor was he happy with my continued allergic reaction. Once while I scratching myself in agony (slapping had not proved to be a doable strategy), he came over to me and said, "This place is dirty, the dust is terrible. Look up at the air conditioner—it's full of dirt." I nodded, as I had done when Takanashi had pointed this out. Higuchi went on, "But allergies are your problem. Something is wrong with you."

Nothing helped my eczema. Erberto told me to drink bottled water and eat only organic fruits and vegetables, and I constantly cleaned my room to remove the dust and soot, but my allergies persisted. If I had an attack during the night, I couldn't sleep, so the next day I would be more tired than ever.

I decided to see the company doctor and request a generic antihistamine. It might ease the allergy, and it might also make me drowsy enough to sleep at night. As I sat in the medical chair, the doctor barely glanced at my chapped, bloody body. He shook his head at my request. "I don't want to give you medicine. If you are itchy and feel you must scratch, just be patient and endure the pain." He clenched his fists, raised them in front of his chest, then shook them violently, illustrating the strength I should muster. He said over and over, "Endure, endure." I didn't think I would obtain much relief by practicing the ancient Japanese virtue of *gaman* (to endure), so I left the clinic in despair. My colleagues were right. The company doctor was useless.

The next time I visited the States, I saw an allergist who prescribed Zyrtec and cortisone cream and told me to take cold showers. It worked; the swelling went down, my red patches faded, and my ordeal was over. I was sure some good allergists existed in Japan, and no doubt they could have prescribed something equally effective, but as long as I worked at the company, I would not have the chance to see one, because you cannot miss work to go to the doctor.

THE COMPANY AS FAMILY

Over the months, Kurasawa and his group became good friends of mine. They were fun and we would always joke around. I felt free to talk to them about work-related issues. Their boss, Ebisawa, also seemed like a very nice guy. He was always cheerful, and when he arrived each day, he would say good morning to everyone in the section.

One day, Kurasawa and Mochida asked me to go drinking with them. We started the evening at a small *yakitori* spot in the city frequented by many Nizumi employees. *Yakitori* places were plentiful in Japan since they primarily exist to provide inexpensive food and drink for male workers. The place we attended had a flavor all its own. The owner had a little barbecue grill (*hibachi*) that he set outside so his clients could grab a bite to eat while standing in the street with their buddies. We placed our bags on the street, huddled around the warm *hibachi,* and engaged in small talk. Inside, the restaurant was so narrow that there were no tables, just a counter. A TV set hung at the corner and beer ads decorated the wall with pictures of large-breasted women in bathing suits, holding that special can of brew. Mochida had received some money from his wife, which he was happy to spend on food and drink for us all. I felt extremely comfortable with Kurasawa and Mochida. I knew I could share my *honne* feelings with them and not worry about the formality of a *tatemae* relationship.

The cozy *yakitori* restaurant provided a good atmosphere for confidences. Kurasawa talked about his relationship with his wife and child. He was tired of spending so much time away from his newborn baby, and his marriage was becoming difficult, with frequent quarrels. He found his job too demanding, and he was unhappy working at Nizumi. When he was at work he always felt bad and wanted to quit. And he was enraged at the seemingly pleasant Ebisawa. He felt he had been cheated because during the job interview Ebisawa had not explained his job responsibilities in detail. Mochida explained the situation. Ebisawa was intent on rising in rank, and as a result, he worked Kurasawa and his group extremely hard. At each weekly meeting, Uno would assign each group more work than it was possible to complete, and while other managers would deflect some of the assignments, Ebisawa never did. As a result, all workers in the section were terribly overworked. Kurasawa was known to disdain his boss, so Ebisawa reacted by assigning the most work to him. Some of his assignments were virtually open-ended, with no chance of completion.

I shook my head in sympathy. Kurasawa poured me another beer. Suddenly, a drunken middle-aged man in a long overcoat walked into the restaurant from the bar next door. My colleagues knew him and greeted him by name, Ichiro *san*. Ignoring them, he approached me and stared right into my eyes. This is something some inebriated Japanese men do on seeing a foreigner to show they are surprised and dumfounded. He stood there eyeballing me, and I could see the interconnecting rivers of blood in the whites of his eyes. He asked where I was from. When I said "America," his face wrinkled up in confusion. "No," he slurred in disbelief. I told him again I was American, and he gave me another incredulous look. Then he asked what division I worked for, and when I said the Research Division he said, "No that can't be right!" He couldn't believe (1) that this dark-haired, brown-eyed foreigner could actually be an American and (2) that I worked as a research engineer. As he kept denying both my nationality and my job, the encounter became confrontational. Ichiro began to yell at me and call me names, until Mochida told him I was not a "low-level" foreign troublemaker: I was "elite" (*elito*).

This changed everything. Ichiro began grabbing my arm to pull me toward a snack bar. In Japan, snack bars are places where men eat, sing karaoke, and are served drinks by pretty women whose main job is to flatter their male guests. I found snack bars to be unappealing places where poor Asian women in miniskirts babied lonely, middle-aged men who sang corny country and blues songs (*enka*) and sipped whisky and water. I had no interest in spending anytime at all with this drunken fool, much less in a snack bar, so I resisted his attempts to drag me along as his companion. He insisted that I go drinking with him. Again, I refused. My colleagues seemed embarrassed and tried their best to pull Ichiro away from me, but he would not be deflected. Finally, I decided that the best way to defuse the situation would be to go along with him for a little while and then catch up with the boys later on at another *izakaya*. They agreed, and Ichiro and I went in and out of a few places nearby. In every place we visited, all the waitresses knew him. I engaged in some small talk with Ichiro but as soon as he was distracted, I escaped. I reappeared at the *izakaya* where Mochida and Kurasawa were waiting. When I sat down with them there was an awkward silence. The first words out of their mouths was that Ichiro was lonely.

The party began to pick up again. The boys had had a few more drinks while I'd been entertaining the crazy drunk. Naturally, it was time for the usual questions about my love life. Who was I dating? Where did we meet? Was she pretty? How old was she?

In fact, I was dating someone: the Japanese language teacher the company hired for us. She was a little older than I, and I was drawn to her because she did not behave childishly like the other Japanese woman.

The question that always shocked me was "How big is your penis?"

I cringed at this question. I had various ways of responding. This time, I took the macho route and said, "*big*." The boys looked at me, intrigued. How could a Japanese woman accommodate a big, foreign penis? One of the guys wanted to know how many centimeters mine was. As I had never measured it, I couldn't say. But he kept on badgering me, so I pointed to a very large bottle of sake Kurasawa had ordered and said "It's about that big."

"Really" he said, eyes widening to the point of idiocy. "That's amazing."

Mochida cut it short. "He's just kidding, you fool."

Suddenly, everyone became silent. Ebisawa appeared in the doorway and entered the *izakaya*. He sat opposite Kurasawa and tried to strike up a conversation, but it remained flat. Kurasawa resented his boss's intrusion. I could read it all over his face. So could Ebisawa, who felt slighted. I had learned that it is very important to include all members in group activities. The other men smoothed things over with banter and jokes. Ebisawa tried a little small talk with Kurasawa but was rebuffed.

Soon, Ebisawa stood up to leave, first giving us ten thousand yen (about eighty dollars) toward the bill. Kurasawa was happy with the money and happy to see him leave. As soon as he was gone, everyone started complaining about him, calling him Uno's dog and vilifying him for the hours he made them work. They wondered how he could have known about the party. Kurasawa said Ebisawa must have discovered the map he had left on his desk with directions to the *izakaya*. I couldn't imagine an American boss following his subordinates to a bar so he could crash their drinking party.

The next day when I came to work, Ebisawa said good morning as usual in his polite and affable way. He seemed like such a nice guy. But now I knew he was utterly spineless and wanted promotion more than anything else, even if it meant working his men to the ground.

Thinking of Kurasawa's situation, I picked up some pages that Abe had written and given me when I first started working: "The Vision Method." This document purports to tell you how to go about working as an engineer at the company. It didn't make much sense to me, so I handed Shiina the piece and asked him what he thought. He sat silently for a moment and said, "It means nothing."

"What do you mean?"

"Let me put it to you more clearly." He adjusted his eyeglasses. "Nizumi is like a labyrinth. When you walk in, you cannot walk out since you cannot find the exit. At best, you become stupid, at worst, you lose your life."

"You mean you die from overwork?" I asked skeptically.

He nodded. "I saw a man die from overwork in front of my own two eyes. We went out to lunch one day, and he just collapsed, he couldn't get up."

"Why was he so overworked?"

"He was assigned to a very important project that had a strict deadline, and he was a serious worker, so he put in too many hours. Many of us at Nizumi thought his family should have filed it as a death by overwork case to get compensation from the government, but for some reason they did not."

During New Year's vacation, Chiba, the gaunt-looking member of Kurasawa's group, began vomiting blood and discovered that he had an ulcer.[3] "The reason I am sick," he told us, "is because I work too hard. I wake up in the morning, go to work, and come home at eleven. And the very next day I do the same."

I refused to put in this kind of workday. Since I was a foreigner, the social mechanisms designed to make me work long hours were not very effective. When I was tired, I simply packed up my belongings and got out—straight onto the street and into my dormitory bed. I continued receiving negative feedback from my co-workers, but I didn't give a damn.

One night before leaving, I looked at the engineers in the Design Division. With their uniforms full of grease and their faces worn and tired, they looked like a ragtag group of defeated soldiers. I told Kurasawa he looked terrible

---

[3] Familial ideology has historically played a significant role in labor relations in Japan. See Andrew Gordon, *The Evolution of Labor Relations in Japan* (Cambridge: Harvard University Press, 1988); Robert Cole, *Japanese Blue Collar* (Berkeley: University of California Press, 1971) and *Work, Mobility, and Participation* (Berkeley: University of California Press, 1979); and Yoshio Sugimoto, *Introduction to Japanese Society* (New York: Cambridge University Press, 1997).

and suggested he go home early. "If you rest," I said, "you'll be healthier and get better results."

He responded, "I have so much work it won't make any difference. Besides, I must stay late with the others, this is the Japanese way, I must endure [*gaman*]." The group-dependent orientation required members to help each other if anyone fell behind. And since each member was very overextended, many got sick, leaving huge amounts of work for the rest of us. The work was endless, relentless.

Nizumi, like most Japanese companies, is deeply attached to the idea of the company as family. This familial ideology is manifest in the newsletters. Many stories portray managers as parents and employees as children. High-level managers offer advice to employees about the rules of social conduct. In one article, written about coming of age (a ceremony which customarily takes place when one turns twenty), the company president encourages young employees to challenge themselves and not to fear failure. "Do not behave like spoiled children," he writes, "you must challenge again! There are plenty of opportunities to recover from failures." Employees should never give up and must learn from failures because "youth is a special privilege." One young man responded that he had two goals now that he was twenty. The first was to "absorb only good things from my seniors." The second was to "enjoy my days with a good frame of mind."

Kurasawa agreed that the company functioned like a family. "In our section the *kachō* is like the father, the *buchō* is like the mother, and all the workers are like children." The basic premise is that workers are like children, naïve and dependent, and their behavior should be molded by management, who function as wise parents.

MY INTRODUCTION TO LIFE IN THE FACTORY

Although I was fully immersed in Japanese society and had made friends with some of my Japanese colleagues, as a foreigner I felt a need to bond with other foreigners who could understand my frustrations about life in Japan. I had become good friends with Erberto. We saw each other on a daily basis and got along very well. We both loved to discuss Japanese society and politics, and we learned a lot from each other. He would engage in any discussion just for the fun of it.

One day Kofi gave me a call and invited me to for dinner. I invited Erberto to accompany us, and we ate at a Chinese restaurant. Kofi and Erberto hit it off at once. Machines were in their blood, and they both loved to talk about vehicles of all types: the newest small cars to agricultural tractors. When you live as a foreigner in Japan, class boundaries do not confine you the way they might in the West. No matter what your educational level or job status (Kofi worked on the assembly line), you can be friends because as foreigners, you share similar experiences. Shared anxiety binds you together.

Kofi, who came from west Ghana, had had a fascinating life. He'd received a postsecondary technical degree at a vocational school in his country, and on graduation, he'd gone to England and Holland for further education. Before coming to Japan, he'd worked for an American company as a heavy machinery specialist on an irrigation project in Libya.

When he first came to Nizumi, he worked in the rust-coating body-parts section. Parts would come from the fabrication section onto the line. Kofi's job was to hang the part on the conveyor belt, dip it in the solution, remove it from the conveyer belt, and send it to the assembly area. He was a fast worker, and he didn't feel the line speed hampered his ability to perform. His job was not physically strenuous, but he was constantly exposed to dangerous chemicals, particularly during the quarterly cleaning of the coating containers. He had to oversee the process on a holiday, usually a Saturday, and would be exposed to large quantities of ammonia fumes. His clothing consisted of a jump suit, apron, hat, gloves, and safety shoes.

Although the pay was good, he was unsatisfied with his job. He felt he'd been sent to the coating section because of the color of his skin. The company assigned undereducated workers to the unskilled jobs, and since he was African, they'd assumed Kofi did not have an education. When they discovered he was a highly skilled worker with a technical degree in welding, they sent him to the drivetrain fabrication section. Now Kofi was responsible for riveting and welding various products within a flexible manufacturing system. He was delighted with the job change, which gave him the opportunity to use his education and improve his skills.

Kofi complained about what he called the jungle bunny mentality. Many Japanese assumed that all Africans lived in primitive environments and were ignorant of the modern world. When his boss met Kofi for the first time, he was surprised to learn that in Ghana people lived in modern houses with electricity and plumbing. His boss told Kofi he thought Africans lived in tree houses.

Like most foreigners, Kofi could not escape the stereotypes. He, too, was bombarded with intimate inquiries—how big was his penis? How many times did he have sex in one day? And so on. We marveled at these obsessions.

Another night, as Kofi and I walked to a workingman's *izakaya,* a couple of Japanese salary men addressed us mockingly in rudimentary English. We were glad to get inside. It was very homey: the chubby owner also functioned as bartender and cook. Factory workers, truck drivers, and welders could grab a bite to eat, drink beer, and talk shop. Many statues of Buddha sat on top of the refrigerator. We ordered our favorite dish: a long, slender fish cooked on the hibachi and eaten with shredded radish and soy sauce. Kofi loved this fish and claimed since he was from the Gold Coast of Ghana, where fish were a staple, he knew good fish. This, he said, was the best in all Japan. We ordered a tall beer, and in typical Japanese style poured each other a glass and began talking.

Inevitably, we talked about work. I had fun telling him about the coffee machine incident and he told me he had also been labeled a "troublemaker." For his first job at Nizumi, they provided a three-hour training session, where workers basically learned about their jobs via pictures. A safety engineer discussed the use of crash helmet and goggles and showed them where they were allowed to walk on the line. The entire factory floor was painted to show employees where they could and could not go.

Kofi and the other contract workers were upset about the small amount of training they had received. Since they had recently arrived, most could not speak Japanese, and hence could absorb little of it anyway. Kofi demanded that the information be provided in English. He wanted to understand his job so he could avoid having a serious accident. But management labeled him a troublemaker, given to "inappropriate behavior."

Since the training he received was inadequate preparation for working on the line, Kofi had to rely on intuition. "The first day, they talk with you, tell you what to do. But the next day, hey, I had to use my own sense." He also made use of the instructive cartoonlike illustrations drawn on posters. These hung on the line showing the workers how to perform their jobs. These pictures would show what rivet to use with a certain thickness of steel, how to grip a tool, proper body position, and other information about the assembly line.

Kofi paused from discussing his work history to look at my plate. "You're not from the Gold Coast, you don't know how to eat your fish. You must eat the head, too."

The Japanese also ate the head, considering it the best part of the fish. I looked down at that small head, its left eye looking up at me. I said, "Why don't you have it?" He took it from my plate and continued talking about training.

Permanent workers received months of high-level training, while contract workers received just a few hours. They are not introduced to any new techniques or job opportunities. Furthermore, many foreigners do not understand Japanese. The company does not offer language classes to the factory workers, so they have a hard time learning new skills.

Hearing Kofi talk, I felt embarrassed at the contrast between our experiences. The coffee machine incident was an innocuous misunderstanding in a clean, safe office, while the dispute between Kofi and management over training concerned the risk of death or injury while working with heavy machinery.

I had been at Nizumi a full year, and once again it was time for the semiannual transfer meeting. This was the end-of-year meeting that was held in April. Kurata stood in the center of the room and announced who would be coming and going. Inoue, the CAD clown, would no longer manage the CAD group; now he would manage the office ladies. It was a public humiliation and a dramatic demotion. Erberto got a kick out of this, and a lot of other workers were pleased as well. I certainly was. We had all worked very hard, and we'd resented Inoue, who did nothing but joke and fool around all day.

Now Kurata announced that Erberto's group would have a new manager, Oda, who had long, graying hair. I didn't know Oda well, but occasionally loud laughter would come from his group during their morning meetings. Erberto was not happy with the change. He really liked his current boss and was sad to see him go.

My job was also up for review. After consulting with Abe, Uno, and Higuchi, Human Resources offered me another contract, which I signed. A few days later we met with Abe. He was always exceptionally nice to me and he often complimented my work. He had a soft voice and baby face. Higuchi explained my work to him in detail, saying what I had accomplished and what we were planning to do in the New Year. Higuchi even showed a short video about the engineering work I had done. I had figured out a way to automate one of the important CAD processes—the creation of complex parts. Higuchi told Abe that I had developed the new technique entirely on my own. Abe said that it was an extremely powerful tool which he wanted me to develop further.

Then Abe told us he used to design drivetrains as well: he had stood in my shoes many years ago. I looked around his office and saw his wall, full of engineering awards and photographs of famous people. We had a very amiable chat, then I stood up to leave. Just as we were at the door, he said that his son lived in America and was handicapped. Although he was wheelchair bound, he worked for Sun Microsystems in California. I wondered if his son's experience in America had had any influence on Abe's feelings toward Americans, and whether that was why he had always been especially kind to me.

SECOND YEAR

THE CONSULTANT

One day, Higuchi told me that an engineer from the well-known German consulting firm ATN would be coming to the company to discuss our project. I was confused: why would a German engineer be working with us, privy to proprietary information? Later that day, Erberto raced to my desk, hair over his brow and onto his face. He pulled it back over his shoulders so he could look directly into my eyes and said, almost panting, that Nizumi had hired ATN to design the product. "It's just crazy," he said, "ATN is gong to be working on the design!"

"What? But we're already designing it!"

"The plan is to have ATN design their own version of the drivetrain while we design it independently."

I couldn't understand why they would go to such trouble. Why spend the extra time and money to design it in-house when the product was being designed by an outside firm?

I went with Erberto to the meeting, eager for the chance to chat freely about the project with a knowledgeable Western engineer. I saw a short bald man sitting at the desk surrounded by a number of Advanced Design engineers: Saiki, Hoshino, Aizawa and a technician. (Genda, however, was conspicuously absent.) The short man had large teeth and a face carved into wrinkles. He had an earthy, gritty personality. In heavily accented English, he introduced himself as Rolf. Westerners in Japan always insist upon being called by their first names.

Saiki and Hoshino presented their designs, laying out CAD drawings of the assembly showing every bolt, curve, and surface. The level of detail was impressive, but Rolf asked how the parts could work together without major malfunctions. His idea of the product was different from theirs. He presented a fundamental reason why they should design it his way, but they did not agree. Rolf gave another reason, and they argued back and forth. During the discussion, Saiki and Hoshino would always drag Rolf into talking about the details. Rolf, however, would discuss the basics of the design, backing his reasoning with fundamentals. His voice got louder and he began acting agitated.

I empathized with him, because for months I had experienced the same frustration. Saiki and Hoshino argued with Rolf, back and forth, for every component in the product.

Then the German began talking about the Advanced XT37 design. He pointed to a part of the design that would dramatically reduce its efficiency, offering logical reasons why it would not work well. Saiki asked, "How do you know it will be inefficient if you don't have any data?"

"I don't need data!" Rolf was getting angry. He explained yet again what was wrong. "You're going to have to pray at the temple for this to work!" he said. He clasped his hands together in the prayer position.

My Japanese colleagues laughed, as they do when chagrined, adding an element of absurdity to the encounter. They were obviously trying to cover up an embarrassing incident. Rolf, too, tried to smooth the situation over, actually touching Saiki and Hoshino on their arms to show he really meant well.

The German turned to me, asking why the XT37 was not well designed. I told him that the fault lay with casting. He proceeded to criticize the entire casting technology at Nizumi and advised how we could improve overall efficiency if we made certain changes. Then he listed all the German companies that would be happy to sell us the products necessary for these essential improvements. Hoshino told him in Japanese, "We can't buy foreign products." Rolf didn't understand a word of this, so one of the managers who spoke English translated for him: "We'll think about it." Management had no interest in buying foreign products, so the proposal to improve our casting plant went nowhere.

I found it significant that a company world-renowned for its products remained dependent on the West for its basic technology. From what I had experienced at Nizumi—the emphasis on secrecy, the lack of creativity, the stifling work environment—I could understand why the company hired the consultants. The managers in Advanced Design needed their expertise. They did not have the organizational or educational creativity to come up with their own advances, and they knew that the European products were far more innovative than any Japanese products on the market. It was a clever strategy. They were able to obtain key technology for the Japanese market that had already been designed for the European market.

After Rolf's dramatic visit, Higuchi called me to his desk. He said that Genda reported that the results for the chosen design were excellent while Hoshino said they were atrocious. "Well, someone's not telling the truth," I told Higuchi. He agreed. I was vindicated, knowing that the heat would be put on Genda for his apparent dishonesty.

THE GROUP AND SOCIAL MECHANISMS OF CONTROL

After this, my role in the Advanced Design project was over. I was happy to go back to working on the ongoing project in my section. I was making good progress with the automation tools, and this success impressed management and allowed me to go home on time unless I had to fulfill my overtime requirements. The men in my section, however, were not happy that two days a week I was leaving work at five thirty.

One morning I passed Kurasawa's desk and asked how he was doing. He said that the previous evening I had missed a drinking party. When I asked why I hadn't been invited, he merely said, "You went home early." There was a short silence: a hint of his displeasure. I had learned that in Japan, direct confrontation is rare. Instead, the Japanese use silence and body language to convey a message. Colleagues communicated their displeasure with a physical response—a chagrined expression, a bow, a suspended action. I had learned to ignore such signs, so I simply replied to Kurasawa, "That's too bad." Similarly, I did not react at all when my colleagues gave me looks of disbelief and displeasure when I left "early" at the end of the day.

By now I had learned that the importance of the group is deeply embedded in the Japanese character. From their earliest school years, Japanese children learn to work in groups. All classes are divided into groups of five or six students, and each group has a team leader, or *hanchō*. The *hanchō* is responsible for distributing information, making sure the group achieves its daily assignments, and generally managing the group. Although members of the group do not do homework together, they each pressure the others to get the assignments done on time. Each group receives a performance ranking. If one person is deviant, it may cause the group to sink in its ranking. Hence the children learn to monitor each other for the good of the group.[1]

On trips sponsored by the company or the Japanese class, the tour leader would hold a small flag aloft so participants could walk from one site to the other *as a group*, without getting lost. On these trips, we always sat and ate together, making sure that our conversation was such that everyone could participate. No one was ever left alone, and the group organization made it highly unlikely that anyone would display antisocial behavior.

"The problem is," said Shiina, "Japanese will group up and not share information with members of an outside group. The group becomes extremely tightly knit, creating its own rules, with no one quite sure how or why they were created. But the rules determine how the group behaves." These rules become a way for a group to bond and conform to a distinct pattern of behavior that sets it apart from other groups.

"Groups at the company are defined according to divisions and sections," Shiina went on. "These groups are well known. But there are also other groups that are invisible yet very powerful, and these hidden groups create their own rules. Often you do not know about these groups. It's very complicated. You must observe closely, for that is the only way to find out about these hidden groups."

A few days later, Higuchi silently approached my desk. He told me he was reading a book by a famous Japanese psychoanalyst who was making comparisons between the American and the Japanese. He said the doctor wrote that the American system was better than Japan's because American infants are raised in a very severe environment: they are left all alone in their rooms to sleep at night. Higuchi asked me whether this was true, and I replied that it was. Higuchi seemed confused. "You mean it's like a dormitory? Everyone is separated in their own rooms?" He was puzzled because in Japan, children sleep with their parents from infancy until puberty.

Initially, I thought this explained why Japanese preferred to work in groups rather than as individuals. Later, I came to realize that groups are a way for Japanese companies to get employees to work harder. You are coerced into longer hours by your very colleagues.

Nicholi, a Romanian factory worker, who wore a bandana around his

---

[1] From an interview with Mr. Yamato Kobayashi, the secretary general of the Research Institute of Democracy and Education, January 2000, Tokyo, Japan.

neck, attested to the importance of the group on the line as a force for social coercion. To his surprise, it was the working group instead of his boss that functioned to control workers. He had left Romania in 1990, thinking he had left his communist past behind, but he told me, "There are a few things I learned in Japan about controlling workers that I could teach the communists back in Eastern Europe!"

Nicholi had had an exciting life. Escaping Romania, he had stowed away on a ship to Toronto, where he had married a Japanese woman of Korean descent. Now they had returned to her native land and had two small children.

Nicholi brought me to the attendance board that stood between the office and the line. A large grid listed the names of each worker in the factory, and the dates of the year. Each box represented a particular workday and held a small outline of a human figure.

"When a worker arrives in the morning," Nicholi explained, "he must fill in the drawing with a colored pencil: green for well, yellow for not so well, white for a little sick, and red for very sick. It is a very efficient way to control workers." It was public way of revealing who was ill or absent so the group, punished by having to work harder, could exert social pressure upon the culprit. I was familiar with social disapproval, as I experienced it every night I left work at a normal hour, but for a Japanese person, social disapproval is much more disturbing than it is to me.

Nicholi's experience on the line mirrored mine in the office. "Workers are always watching each other and looking over each other's shoulders," he said. "I feel like I am at home because people are watching me all the time. The only difference is that in Eastern Europe, it was a dictatorship, so people worked hard because they were forced to. Here, the group makes you work hard: workers on the line are forced to monitor each other for their own self-interest."

If, for example, a quality or safety problem arose, despite the fact that it could be traced to an individual, the entire group would be punished. This created an environment in which members of the group monitored each other's performance to ensure that work ran smoothly and the group as a whole was protected from punishment.[2]

---

[2] Laurie Graham, *On the Line at Subaru-Isuzu* (Ithaca, NY: Cornell University Press, 1995), and Dorrinne Kondo, *Crafting Selves: Power, Gender, and Discourses of Identity in a Japanese Workplace* (Chicago: University of Chicago Press, 1990), also experienced monitoring while working on the line at a Japanese company.

I asked Shiina why groups were so important at Japanese companies. "To be a member of the group is crucial," he said. "Every member of the group is like a part of the body, each has his own role, and those who come in as outsiders are not accepted because they have no role. It's like having an extra arm or leg with nothing to do, for you only need two legs to run, not three."

Shiina pushed up his glasses and continued. When he'd returned from America with a new set of skills, he was looking forward to joining a group of other engineers in his field. Management was interested in using his knowledge to make improvements in technology. However, management disagreements about the details of the new team and the appointment of the supervisor complicated the formation of the group. Some managers thought he was being given special treatment and felt jealous, while other managers wanted the new group in their own sections. A power-struggle ensued, and the formation of the new group was abandoned.

When he returned to the Research Section, his colleagues did not show any interest in him. "They would smile and say something nice but it was not sincere." In spite of his desire to contribute, they didn't want his knowledge. "I had been out of the company for over four years, and they had established a world without me." So he approached a colleague who had helped him in the past and requested a transfer to another department. The colleague was indignant. "What? You want to move without returning anything to this department?" Shiina had been very embarrassed.

As a result of Shiina's alienation, he felt dissatisfied with his work and lagged behind others in his performance. He felt that Uno was patient and he did not blame him for his failures until one day during his evaluation he said, "I didn't want to force my son to study too hard when he entered junior high school but now he doesn't study hard at all. I wonder if my decision was correct." Other managers who wanted Shiina to join their group approached him, but he felt they had no intention of using his knowledge but merely wanted one more subordinate. The upshot was that Shiina ended up working alone, without any group, simply reporting to Uno. This was a great tribulation to Shiina.

One advantage of being a member in good standing of a group is protection. Higuchi told me a story that illustrated this. One day, it became known that a high-level manager from Toyota wanted to talk to Higuchi about a technical issue. Since Uno did not know exactly why the Toyota manager wanted to speak to Higuchi, first he sent Hiraga, who was ignorant about the issue, to speak with him in the hope of learning more. Hiraga returned from his meeting without any information about the issue—having been humiliated, to boot. Then Uno sent Dr. Zombie to talk with him. He was also scolded and sent back without any relevant information. Uno continued to send one warm body after another to talk with the Toyota manager until there was no one left to send except Higuchi. At this point, Higuchi was terribly worried and had no other choice but to face the fire. As it turned out, the Toyota Manager simply wanted to know why he had spent so much money on an expensive design tool. Higuchi presented him with a satisfactory reason and the issue was resolved. This incident shows how managers protected their subordinates from outsiders.

Typically, an engineer at Nizumi—particularly in the research and design departments—was introduced to the company by his professor or by an alumni connection. If the engineer had a specialty, particularly a graduate degree, he would be assigned to a group that specialized in his field. Those with only undergraduate degrees were assigned to any department. On joining a work group, it was important for the *kōhai* to establish a smooth and long-lasting relationship with his *senpai* or he could not be taught the skills he would need to be promoted.

It seemed odd that you needed to be accepted by your group to learn important information about your job, and the company did distribute some reports to help engineers obtain needed skills without relying on a *senpai*. These reports, however, often lacked substance or were too specialized for easy understanding. Shiina's problems were twofold: he lacked a *senpai* who could help him develop his skills, and he lacked a group that needed his expertise.

The entire system was dependent on relationships. Although the variety of groups in a section worked on the common goal of increasing the efficiency of the product, little communication existed between groups unless they worked on joint projects, or unless individual members were introduced to one another through their connections.

When new employees entered the section, I watched closely to see what would happen. I saw that other members of the section kept to themselves and were not at all friendly to the newcomers. The new members spent much of their time observing and digesting group behavior so they were better able to learn the rules. Even those who had been at the company for several years did not find it easy to develop friendships within the section. Each employee at most had only a few good friends at the company with whom he could share his true feelings (the *honne*) as opposed to interacting in the world of day-to-day superficial relationships (the *tatemae*).

An important characteristic of the group was permanence. Human Resources allowed an employee to transfer to another group, but in general it was very rare. Developing an engineering or technical specialty, particularly if it required years of education and experience, meant you tended to stay with your group. It was common to assign employees to "lend help" to departments that needed more personnel on a short-term basis, but in most cases, employees remained in their initial groups, within the same section, for their entire careers.

Because of the closed nature of the organization, it was very important to maintain close relationships with upper-level managers (*erai hito*) and even to professors (*erai sensei*) outside the company. I remembered when a well-known professor from the Tokyo Institute of Technology visited the company to give a presentation. He was given a royal welcome. When he arrived, he was ushered into a conference room, where office ladies served him green tea. Selected managers (Uno, Scarface, Shiga) chatted respectfully with him. Then a general announcement about the lecture was broadcast over the loudspeaker system, inviting all employees to attend the presentation. After the professor was introduced, everyone bowed deeply in unison. When the professor talked about his research, the managers and employees reacted to every bit of technical information as if it was the word of God—bowing their heads deeply and murmuring, "Oh, is that so." After the lecture, the section manager and two other managers brought the professor to a very expensive five-star restaurant.

THE POWER GROUP AND BULLYING

After I had been at Nizumi a while, I noticed the existence of a tightly knit group that seemed to be a power center. Scarface was extremely close to Uno, the section manager. I frequently saw him attend the high-level meetings sitting beside Uno. Scarface was a skilled engineer, so his input was valuable, but his close personal relationship with Uno determined his position within the hierarchy. Scarface was also close to two other lower-level managers named Shiga and Jimbo. Both were also overweight, spoke in very deep voices, and were graduates of high-level universities whose professors were *erai sensei*. Scarface was particularly close to Shiga, whose professor was the *erai sensei* from the Tokyo Institute of Technology who had visited Nizumi. Scarface and Shiga often enjoyed daily conversation during the smoking break, a ritual that occurred at twelve thirty immediately after they returned from lunch. I would often see them sitting among the others in the smoking room, talking in deep authoritative voices and laughing only with each other.

I asked Shiina why Scarface was so close to Uno, and the answer was simple: "He is the one whom Uno trusts the most." For one thing, both were graduates of Keio University. For another, Uno respected Scarface's technical expertise. So Scarface was Uno's right-hand man, and as an employee who worked alongside the other engineers, he was responsible for making sure the workers were performing their duties while Uno attended to his higher-level job functions.

In Japan, there is no real equality: either someone is above you or they are below you.[3] So I wondered how Scarface's relative youth and lower rank affected his relationships with the high-level managers in the section who were not part of the inner circle the way he was. After all, Dr. Zombie and Hiraga were a lot older than Scarface and had a higher ranking. But Scarface had greater decision-making power about product design, and he was a man moving up, while Zombie and Hiraga had reached their highest level.

I asked Erberto about his group, and he said that Oda also had a young subordinate with whom he was close. His name was Matsuki. I began observing his behavior and noticed that Matsuki wore clothes similar clothes to Oda's, talked in a loud voice like Oda, and laughed just like Oda. It was as if he was copying his behavior. No wonder Oda felt at home with him. Superior and subordinate had a shared way of thinking (*kangaekata*) as a result of close personal contact.

What I found upsetting about the power group in my section (Uno, Scarface, Shiga, and Jimbo) were the methods they used to establish discipline. Harassment, or what in Japan is referred to as bullying (*ijime*), was routine, and some unfortunate individuals were bullied on a daily basis.

Ienaga was assigned to work with Uno's power group, and he initially seemed well acclimated. Although he had a quiet, introverted personality, he would often joke and laugh when the others made suggestions or comments

[3] See Chie Nakane, *Japanese Society* (Berkeley: University of California Press, 1970).

about his work. As the weeks passed, however, these suggestions became pointed, and the criticism was more like harassment. Ienaga became nervous and withdrawn, keeping his head down as he sat at his desk. Once at a drinking party, Ienaga ordered a mixed drink. When Jimbo saw that it came with a bright red cherry, he growled that Ienaga should be drinking beer.

When Scarface or Uno asked Ienaga questions during department meetings, he often seemed shaken. His face would turn bright pink as he stuttered out a reply. Once while we were at a meeting, Uno asked whether certain members of our section would attend a seminar. When his name was called Ienaga hesitated for a few seconds. The room became still as everyone waited for his response. Finally, he replied in a shaky voice, "I plan to take it." This behavior was designed to let Uno know he was unhappy, yet Uno did nothing about it.

It was obvious that Ienaga had the wrong *kokoro* for the group. A person's *kokoro,* how one feels and thinks, was highly important in developing long-term relationships with co-workers.[4]

THE WEEKEND RETREAT

Socializing after work was intended to strengthen bonds among employees. This was why the drinking parties were so important. In our section, at least once a year we also spent a weekend together. This was called the *shain ryoko,* in which all the members of our section spent the weekend at a company hotel. We traveled to the hotel in assigned vehicles, Ienaga riding with Uno. I thought this arrangement curious since it was well known that Ienaga was upset with Uno's bullying. When everyone arrived, we sat down for dinner, but Uno and Ienaga did not appear. We waited a few minutes, then Dr. Zombie decided we should eat without them.

Shiga was the only member of the power group at dinner that night, and I suppose he thought it necessary to strut his stuff. Tonight, the person in his sights was Ishii. Shiga sat at the center of the table and said that Ishii's pre-

---

[4] Nakane, in *Japanese Society,* makes an insightful observation about the nature of the relationship between two individuals in a senior and subordinate position in Japanese society. Often referred to as the *oyabun-kobun* relationship, the *oyabun* is the employee who obtains the status of parent and *kobun* of that as the child. "The essential elements in the relationship are that the kobun receives benefits or help from his oyabun, such as assistance in securing employment or promotion, and advice in the occasion of important decision making." The relationship is one that develops over many years. Within the context of work, the *kobun* also functioned as an *oyabun* to a subordinate whom he can "trust" establishing a line of hierarchy.

sentations during the Friday technical meetings were inferior and that Iishi should learn more from the meetings. Iishi responded in his high-pitched voice, saying that when he'd entered the company he hadn't known anything about the technology, but he'd since learned a lot. His effeminate voice contrasted with Shiga's deep voice. Shiga spoke as if he was god in heaven speaking to a lesser mortal. Dr. Zombie joined Shiga in the attack on Ishii. Ebisawa defended him. Nonetheless, Ishii left the dinner table in anger.

Now it was my turn. Dr. Zombie began talking about patents and said it was important to publish more patents. He turned toward me, "So what's up with your patent Mehri *san*?" I assured him that I had already developed a patent and that I was in the process of submission.

As we sat at the long table in a dark room, drinking and eating small bits of neatly prepared food served on a myriad of small dishes, the conversation began to lighten up. Dr. Zombie would crack a joke then burst into maniacal laughter. His thick black-rimmed glasses and wiry Einsteinlike hair made him look like an intoxicated professor, and I found him quite amusing.

After dinner we headed upstairs for the *nijikai,* where we waited for Uno and Ienaga. We sat on the tatami mats and began to drink and talk, but they still did not arrive. The person who organized the event was the youngest member of the section, and he poured the drinks and organized the food. Naturally Shiga sat in the center of the room, self-positioned as the leader of the party. It was well known among the guys that he was a heavy drinker and would often drink himself into a stupor. Now he began a monologue about himself and his connections to a famous professor at the Tokyo Institute of Technology. We listened without interruption to stories we had often heard before. Although he was a skilled engineer, Shiga's accomplishments were less important than his connection to a high-level, well-respected professor at Japan's number-one technical university.

Finally, Uno and Ienaga arrived, and we were all relieved. The guys immediately poured Uno some beer, but he did not drink much. Ienaga said the reason they were late was that they had had an important meeting with a large company that ran longer than they had expected. Now I speculated that Uno's choosing Ienaga as his traveling companion was an indirect atonement for Ienaga's earlier mistreatment.

Shiga suddenly announced that he wanted to sing some karaoke. A half dozen other men and I joined him. Dr. Zombie sang his favorite song, "Diana"—not once, but several times: "Oh, please, stay with me—Diana!"

I sang, as I often did, Frank Sinatra's version of "My Way." Then the guys begged me to sing a traditional Japanese *enka* song. Japanese country and blues songs (*enka*) are particularly popular during karaoke. I resisted, but finally decided to give it a go. After all, *enka* songs had catchy melodies. Ishii sang along with me, helping me read the Japanese characters on screen. After a few beers, he had relaxed and forgotten his earlier anger at Shiga and Dr. Zombie.

Chiba approached me and said he would like to go on a trip with the International Adventure Club. "I once traveled across Japan in a van by myself," he said, perhaps to establish his credentials as an adventurer. I encouraged him to come, for I thought a day in the mountains with other singles would be healthier than an evening at a whorehouse.

The party continued upstairs. The upper-level managers went off to play mahjong in the other room, while the younger engineers and lower-level managers remained behind. As we continued to drink, Shiga became increasingly boisterous. He turned to me and slurred that famous question "So, Mehri *san,* do you like Japanese woman?"

The room became quiet as all the men turned to me, anticipating my response. I had been asked this question so many times I knew exactly what to say. Although I found their coy behavior displeasing, I said, as usual, "Oh, yes. Japanese women are so kind-hearted [*yasashii*]."

"Compared to American women, Japanese girls are very sweet," he said.

Then Shiga began to wrestle with Ienaga. He started with a few harmless holds, but gradually became rougher, tossing Ienaga about and making him look like a fool in front of his colleagues. As they continued to wrestle, Uno came in to grab a drink and saw the two men rolling about on the straw mats like a couple of school children. He laughed and went back to playing mahjong. It looked like Ienaga was in for more physical abuse.

I felt bad for Ienaga and angry at Shiga. His bullying made me remember some unhappy times I'd had as a teenager. I was extremely awkward and shy at that time, so I was often the victim of bullying. I eventually grew into a mature and sociable adult but those memories did not fade. A little drunk myself, I suddenly found myself down on the floor wrestling with Shiga. Ienaga rolled away gratefully. Shiga pinned me down pretty quickly. We wrestled again, and he won again. As we continued to wrestle, I began to learn his moves and put up a better defense. We occasionally took short breaks to drink a little more, and then we would continue our brawl. Although the fight was not serious, I wanted to pin him down to get some payback: if not for Ienaga then for myself. I needed to relieve the frustration that had been building up in me.

Finally, I was able to pin him down. I felt a tremendous sense of victory. Shiga, however, became extremely angry, like a child bully who'd been embarrassed in the schoolyard. He asked if I was fighting for real. I replied that I was just having fun. He said that if he hadn't known me, he would have wanted to kill me. I was surprised at the violence of his emotions, but again I assured him that I wasn't serious. I must confess, however, that I felt satisfied: even elated. Someone had finally humbled the bully.

SERVICE OVERTIME AND COMPANY RULES

I returned to the dorm that Sunday and entered the shoe room. As I placed my shoes into the locker, I heard "Hey man!" I turned around and saw a tall, lanky Japanese man named Fuse. We had met a few months earlier during a dormitory get-together. I should specify that we had not met over green tea, casually saying a few words to each other; rather, we'd been formally introduced to each other by the dorm manager. Fuse had lived in America for a year in high school and now worked as a salesman at Nizumi. He had once invited me to his room, and to impress me, he'd played "Top Gun" on his VCR. When I told him I hadn't seen the movie, he'd been shocked.

Now he asked me if I wanted to join him for dinner, and although I had a slight hangover from the weekend retreat, we headed to a local family restaurant. Family restaurants were popular in Japan and typically featured "Japanized" American food, such as hamburger or chicken cutlet—served, however, with rice and not potatoes.

"I'm learning Spanish now," Fuse said. "The company wants me to work for the sales division in Central America."

"Wow, that's great," I said.

"Yeah, I suppose. But my *senpai* lived there for three years, and he said there was a big problem with violence."

"In what way?" I asked

"People kill each other just for sport."

I told him there were some problems with violence but that killing for sport was probably just a rumor. Soon, he began complaining about work. "I hate my job," he said, "I'm so busy and I always have to do service overtime."

"Service overtime? What do you mean?"

"It's a rule at the company," he said, "You've never heard of it? In Japanese it's called *sābisu zangyō*. *Sābisu* is from the English 'service' and *zangyō* means overtime in Japanese. The rule requires you to do overtime work without pay. I hate it, and my boss doesn't like it either, but his boss requires it."

Suddenly, I realized why my leaving work "early" always upset my colleagues. Although I had spent over a year at the company, not a single person had told me about *sābisu zangyō*. I couldn't believe that Higuchi had neglected to tell me about this important part of the Nizumi culture.

"Who told you about this rule?" I asked Fuse.

"Nobody. I followed what my co-workers did. Maintaining harmony related to overtime is important at Japanese companies. If you don't do what others do, the group will punish you."

Sābisu zangyō! When I first started working at Nizumi, I thought employees stayed late because of loyalty. Later, I thought it was because they had too much work to do in too little time. But all along, whether employees had to work on a demanding project or not, *sābisu zangyō* was a company rule. I now knew why my colleagues showed their displeasure when I left before they did. I was supposed to do as they did, but I wasn't following the rule.

Uno was a strong believer in service overtime. As a result, most employees would stay late most nights, whether or not they had fulfilled their required paid overtime. Although for some reason Uno had never reproached me for my hours, I felt angry that the system was cheating the other workers.

Rules play a significant role in controlling the behavior of Japanese people from an early age. "There are hundreds of rules at Japanese schools," said Yamato Kobayashi when I interviewed him later. Some rules include socks of a certain length and hair of a certain style. One function of the rules is to force students to conform to group norms. For example, there is a rule that if your hair is curly, you will need to straighten it to look like other students.[5]

I returned to work on Monday not knowing how Shiga would behave after our heated wrestling bout. To my surprise, he approached me and said he was sorry. I told him there were no hard feelings.

I was curious about what the guys thought of the wrestling match. I told Shiina what had happened, since he hadn't been at the Shain Ryōkō. He

[5] From an interview with Mr. Yamato Kobayashi, the secretary general of the Research Institute of Democracy and Education, January 2000, Tokyo, Japan.

smiled and said, "I heard all about it." The news had already spread. Since I had humiliated a bully, my colleagues were pleased, which was a great relief to me.

Having only learned the rule about service overtime after a year at Nizumi made me think that perhaps there were other rules I knew nothing about. I walked over to Erberto's area to ask him about rules. He shook his head, and his hair rippled over his shoulders. "There are rules for everything in Japanese society. It's crazy! There is even a rule that tells workers how to urinate."

"Get out of here!"

"If you don't believe me, go take a look."

So I walked into the bathroom and saw a small sign hanging above the urinals that read, "Take one step forward." The bathroom walls held a number of such small postings. One told employees how to behave during an earthquake "Guard yourself from falling objects. If a fire occurs, put it out."

When I returned to Erberto, he said, "Did you hear about the parking rules?"

"No."

"Here, take a look." He handed me a list of instructions about proper use of parking permits. One rule prohibited any employee of Nizumi to park a non-*keiretsu* car in the company parking lot. I was surprised by this rule since so many people in Japan owned cars not made by Toyota. Later on, I discovered that anyone breaking the parking rules would be punished. What I found most interesting thing about the parking rules was that they were phrased in the language of morality: justice and injustice, good and bad. An employee who uses the parking lot without permission commits "an injustice to the company. From now on if there is a person who does this we will severely punish that person, so please obey the rules on this document (do not be a bad member of the company)."

I asked Shiina about the rules at Nizumi, and he pointed to a thick book lying on my desk that explained many of the company rules. One day I would read portions of it at length, but for now I just asked him to show me the page about service overtime. He shook his head: that was an unwritten rule. I asked him how employees were supposed to learn about these rules if they were unwritten. He fiddled with his glasses for a moment, then said, "At Japanese companies you are supposed to learn by absorbing through your skin." When I asked him what he meant, he confirmed what Fuse had said the night before—one has to observe and copy other employees' behavior.

Shiina said that rules at Nizumi were extremely important, and he told me a personal story about what had happened when he broke a cardinal rule.

Upon returning home from his stay in America, he was eager to publish his research results in an engineering journal. First, he approached his old boss and asked him about submitting a paper for publication. He was told it was a good idea. Then he asked Uno. But when Uno discovered that Shiina had gone to his former boss before talking with him, Uno angrily rejected his request.

The result was that after many years of hard work, Shiina never received the opportunity to publish his paper, which might have contributed to a substantial promotion. He said that after living in America, he had forgotten this important company rule,[6] a rule that mandated that one must always report to one's direct superior before approaching anyone else. By making an example of Shiina, Uno was telling all the employees in the section to obey the rules, written and unwritten.

I felt sorry for Shiina. Not only was he having a rough time at the company, but his wife was ill. He never told me what sickness she had, and I didn't want to pry, but he often said she wasn't happy with her life in Japan. She was Japanese, but she was having a difficult time acclimating to Japanese society after living in America for ten years.

One day, Erberto came to work and went to his morning meeting. To his surprise, he found that his group had adopted a new rule—you must take off your shoes before entering the section. A line had been drawn on the carpet showing the boundaries of the workspace. When you crossed that line, your shoes had to come off. Japanese custom requires a person to take off his or her shoes before entering a house, a temple, or any place with a straw mat floor. However, before this, no working areas inside the company had been designated shoeless areas. The reasons were obvious. In many sections of Nizumi, there was heavy machinery; indeed, some workers were required to wear steel-tipped shoes.

Erberto was angry at having to take off and put on his shoes when entering and leaving his section. He couldn't understand the purpose of the new

---

[6] Japanese often have problems relearning rules of the company on returning from abroad. Some companies provide employees and their families with retraining so that they can relearn social conduct, language, and the rules of how to reassimilate within Japanese society.

rule; he said it wasn't rational. Furthermore, it directly violated safety rules, since large and very heavy parts were located on a table in the section. If a chunk of cast iron fell off the table, it could seriously damage a foot. Erberto's manager, Oda, responded that the rule had been decided—and that was that.

CRUDE BEHAVIOR

One day, during the morning break, Erberto and his colleague Chen asked me to join them for a stroll. Chen was a chubby, mild-mannered Chinese man with a large round face. When he smiled, he bore a striking resemblance to the Pillsbury Dough Boy. Erberto had come to work that day dressed in his company blazer. I thought his irreverence made him an unlikely candidate for the typical company man, but he looked sharp in his attire. Since the office was hot and stuffy from computers that functioned as space heaters, I was happy to take a break in the fresh air.

We strolled in the courtyard, and Chen talked about his group. He said some strange things happened when he went on drinking parties with them. "Tell us!" asked Erberto. Chen gave a smile that consumed most of his face. He told us that during one drinking party, a young technician suddenly removed his sock and put it in the *nabe* that was boiling in the center of the room.[7] He cooked his sock in front of his group, then poured the sock-cooked stew into a small bowl. Then he asked his immediate boss to drink from the bowl! His boss refused, of course, but the young man was relentless. He sat on his knees, bowed to the ground and screamed over and over again "onegai shimasu, onegai shimasu [please, please, do me a favor]." He seemed to be having a hysterical fit. Embarrassed at this adolescent behavior, the boss caved in and drank from the stew.

"How bizarre!" said Erberto.

Chen told us about even more peculiar evenings. At another drinking party with his colleagues, including one woman engineer with a Ph.D., members of Chen's team became so drunk they stripped down and ran through the bar fully naked. They threw up, made lewd remarks to other patrons, and insulted their boss. When I inquired about the woman, Chen said that she was embarrassed but had not been forced to join in.

---

[7] *Nabe* is a traditional Japanese stew of vegetables and meat that is placed on a burner to cook continuously while people freely eat from it using chopsticks.

During yet another party, the men in Chen's group got so zonked they put cigars up their rear ends and began smoking with their butt cheeks. After each took a few puffs, they passed the stogy around to smoke it in their mouths. They ended the party with a macho game that involved pouring hot sake on each other's crotches followed by cold water and a punch in the chest. According to Chen, Oda would usually instigate this crude behavior and cheer on his subordinates. The group members forget their usual social conduct in favor of these new group norms encouraged by their boss.[8]

Never before had Chen experienced such terrible foolishness. Furthermore, he was upset about the cost of such evenings: from about $80 to $100 for each person. At the end of the month, it added up to a lot of money, but Oda reveled in the drinking parties and required group members to attend them frequently.

My colleagues continued to resent my early leave-taking. Even though I now knew about *sābisu zangyō*, I pretended I did not. So I continued to defy the group. This led to some odd results. Once while I was talking to Shiina about joining foreign organizations, I jokingly commented, "Yeah, and there are lots of pretty, single women."

He responded, "Just don't rape any of them."

I initially regarded this as a joke, but then I felt something more serious was going on. So I asked Shiina why he had made this crude remark. He said, "In Japan, if you do not do what others do, they will look upon you with suspicion. Be careful—that's all." Apparently, the lunchroom talk was that I spent the evening hours (while they were still at work) chasing down young women in an unsavory part of town. My colleagues wanted to modify my aberrant behavior by spreading rumors and making me feel guilty. I was angry at their scurrilous talk, but I refused to give in to them.

A few months later, Erberto told me that Chen was being bullied by Oda and his group.

I asked, "For what?"

"Because he's not attending drinking parties anymore, and you know how Oda is about that."

I could well imagine. It's all right to refuse the occasional drinking party, but to refuse twice in a row will worry your group members, and a third re-

[8] The scholar Takie Lebra refers to this behavior as "social nudity," where a participant's self is "stripped of all face or social mask." Takie Lebra, *Japanese Patterns of Behavior* (Honolulu: University of Hawaii Press, 1976), 116.

fusal signals that something is definitely wrong. When an individual rejects the rules, he or she will experience the displeasure of the group as well as the wrath of his boss.

My sympathies were entirely with Chen. He simply did not want to spend his rare free time and hard-earned money with a group of raucous, drunken fools. Oda saw things differently and interpreted Chen's actions as a refusal to bond with the group and to obey his own authority. Oda tried to bully him into attending the drinking parties, but Chen held his ground and refused to attend. Soon, Chen discovered that one of his colleagues was reporting his daily behavior to Oda. Chen's determination had made his own group—as well as management—deeply suspicious of him. Chen just hoped the whole thing would blow over and he would again gain the favor of the group.

CONTRACT WORKERS IN THE FACTORY

During the day, Erberto and I often got restless. We sat long hours at our computer screens, and our backs, necks, and eyes felt the strain of our fixed positions.

One day a little before three, Erberto suggested that we visit Kofi in the factory. That would be a welcome change of scene. I hesitated at first, thinking management might not like foreigners poking their noses into the production area, but Erberto assured me it wouldn't be a problem.

Kofi worked from 8:00 A.M. to 4:55 P.M. with a fifty minute lunch break at noon and two ten-minute breaks at 10 A.M. and 3 P.M. All factory workers had a similar schedule. If Kofi did not finish the day's quota, or if there was a quality problem or an accident, he had to work overtime. The three o'clock break, however, was sacrosanct, and no one worked through it.

Erberto and I strolled through the courtyard toward the factory. He had taken to wearing the company blazer, and today he also wore the soft-brimmed company hat, pulled down to his eyebrows, his long black hair fanning out beneath it. We walked along, talking and cracking jokes. Kofi worked on the second floor of the factory, so we walked up a tiny steel stairway and into the factory clamor. Erberto and I both loved the loud sounds of the machinery. Since it was still before three, we waited for Kofi near a small room where men could watch television or break for a cigarette. For some unknown reason, there were always one or two guys sitting there while the others were busy working.

I could see Kofi working on the line. He was dressed in typical factory clothes: a greasy jumpsuit and a cap. Kofi was not large, but he was all muscle. He moved quickly from one portion of the vehicle to the other, welding each component. I enjoyed the irony. Here I was, ten thousand miles from my home, and an African was making the Japanese vehicles so many Americans loved.

Finally, the three o'clock bell sounded, and Kofi came over and greeted us. There was a big smile on his dark, leathery face. This brief opportunity with us allowed him to vent some of his grievances, and he spoke freely of his work on the line. He said that one product after the other came through while he welded them. He showed me the numbering system on the wall, which indicated the amount of products made per day. Kofi said, "When a worker makes a mistake, the line stops, and we find a solution."

The worker pushes one of three lights to signal the danger level: a green light means no danger, a gold light means the worker needs mild assistance, and a red light means that the worker is in danger and needs help right away. When the gold light goes on, maybe one person comes to help, but many more rush over if the light is red. If the *andon* cord (which stops the line) is pulled for quality problems, a team pulls the vehicle over to work on it while the line starts up again. After the problem has been fixed, a top quality-control (QC) supervisor goes to the floor to inspect the vehicle.

As we continued to talk, Kofi walked over to a large sink where the men were cleaning their hands. He introduced me to Romone, a Peruvian of Japanese descent. We had been in the Japanese language class together, but had never spoken to each other. Now we said hello as if we were old friends. Romone had worked at Isuzu before coming to Nizumi, so I asked him how the two compared. He told me that what immediately struck him when he arrived at Nizumi was its policy of hiring workers of different races and nationalities. At Isuzu, the policy was totally discriminatory. Romone said, "You will not be hired if you're black or if you're white, and the only foreigners they hire are of Japanese descent." Isuzu had been recruiting labor from Japanese communities in Peru, and Romone went to the Japanese Embassy and applied for a position. After an extended interview, he was one of the few Peruvians to be offered a job. In the past, many companies in Japan, including Nizumi, refused to hire whites or blacks, but today most Japanese companies have a more enlightened policy. Nizumi became more inclusive in its hiring when the demand for workers in Japan increased during the bubble of the late 1980s, and they had to tap alternative sources of labor.

I brought up the issue of *kaizen* with Kofi. "Improvement meetings are vital to the way Japanese work," he said. "It's like communism, everyone shares their views."[9] He said it was a job requirement for all workers in his group to meet every Tuesday after work to discuss improving safety and production. Management would ask for suggestions, but since Kofi was only a contract, or temporary, worker, they never gave him credit for his ideas, even when they implemented them.[10] It was rare for temporary workers at the company to become permanent employees. According to Kofi, all foreigners in the factory were contract workers, even if they were married to Japanese women, as he was, and had permanent residences in Japan.

He went on to talk about unequal workloads between Japanese and foreigners. He said that the Japanese would work in groups that were fully staffed, while foreigners were often required to do the same job with fewer people. For example, if a job required a working group of three people, the Japanese workers would get three people for the job, while the foreigners would have to do the same job with only two people in their group. According to Kofi, the company was "testing" the foreigners to see what they would endure. Not only did foreigners receive less training than Japanese workers, they continually suffered from discrimination related to job assignments. "Lazy Japanese workers at the company are always trying to push work onto foreigners because they feel they can get away with it," Kofi said. "They said to me 'You're a foreigner, so you don't get overtime.'" Overtime work at Japanese companies accounts for 30 to 40 percent of a workman's total pay, so it's hard to earn a decent living without it. According to Kofi, Nizumi is very afraid of losing permanent, Japanese workers to other companies so they give the permanent employees the more pleasant and less dangerous tasks. Nat-

---

[9] On the line, safety *kaizen* meetings were called KYT, in Japanese *kikken yochin* training, meaning danger awareness training.

[10] In her study on the Subaru-Isuzu plant in Indiana, Laurie Graham also observes a tension between the permanent and temporary workers. Although they did not have job security or full benefits, temp workers were an integral part of the work system, even though they were considered as second-tier workers who could obtain a full-time position as an "associate." "Temps are part of the psychological tension created by the Japanese model because they represent both a threat and a promise to the Associates." Although psychological tension existed between the temp and permanent workers at the company, it manifested itself in the form of discrimination related to race and compensation. See Graham, *On the Line.*

urally, this leads to some friction between the two groups, with the foreign workers of Japanese descent occupying the middle ground.

Then Kofi told me about the hierarchy of favoritism among foreigners. "The Japanese Brazilians are on top. They're considered the closest to the Japanese so they're treated best." The Japanese Peruvians are ranked lower, since they've lost favor in recent years. A few have been arrested for crimes, and all Peruvians are in disrepute after the hostage crisis in Peru, so recruitment efforts in Peru have fallen sharply. Other foreigners—Chinese, Koreans, Iranians, Bangladeshi—are ranked lower.[11] Naturally, education, strength, and language ability are also used to determine what type of job a worker will be assigned. The strongest and least educated guys are sent to the casting plant.

Romone approached me to ask if I would be going to the Japanese language class this week. I said I was and asked him to tell me about himself. Romone had come to Japan in the early 1990s to work at the Isuzu factory. "Safety at Isuzu was terrible, the lines were so fast and the work was so hard that at the end of the day my body hurt all over. And all they gave us was a safety helmet—for the rest, we were on our own."

While on the line at Isuzu, Romone had watched a friend die when a vehicle frame fell from its supports and crushed him. That's when he decided to go back to Peru. He needed two years off to make a complete recovery from the work-related injuries he'd experienced at Isuzu and the trauma of seeing his friend die brutally. But because he could not get work in Peru, he ended up back in Japan, this time working for Nizumi.

The bell sounded, and our visit was over. Erberto and I returned to the white collar world. I entered the office and sat down at my desk. I sifted through the papers that had recently been placed on my desk. Thinking about the men in the factory, I picked up one of the accident reports and saw a drawing of a man on a conveyer belt. I could read a little of what was written, for my knowledge of Japanese characters was limited, so I asked Shiina

[11] In his study of Japanese-Brazilian immigrants working in Japan, Takeyuki Tsuda, a social science professor at the University of Chicago, claims that the hiring policy and job placement that the foreigners obtain at most Japanese companies is based on race, as the comment of one employer that he interviewed illustrates, "When it comes to hiring foreigners, there are clearly several levels based on like and dislike. We feel closest to the Nikkeijin, so they work at the best firms with the best wages. Then come Chinese and Koreans, whom we find less preferable and therefore, they work in less desirable jobs. At the bottom are the Bangladeshis and Iranians, who work in the smallest companies and are paid the lowest wages. We avoid interacting with Middle Easterners the most, so they get the worst jobs. It really shouldn't be this way, but it just is." See Takeyuki Tsuda, "The Permanence of Temporary Migration," *Journal of Asian Studies* 58, no. 3 (August 1999): 698.

to translate. He said that the man had climbed onto the conveyer belt when it was operating and had been killed. "It happened at Toyota," he said, "It's not unusual for someone to lose their life in a factory in Japan." He handed the report back to me and I took a closer look. The man's head had been crushed between the car and the frame of the conveyer belt machine.

A SAFETY MESSAGE FROM THE FAMILY

I learned more about conditions at Toyota when I went to a dinner party with Kume. The party was held at Rie's apartment. Kondo was there, and so were her friends Jorge and Octavio, two Peruvian foreigners of Japanese descent. Jorge was outgoing, warm and friendly, with a spontaneous laugh and a dashing personality. Octavio was a muscular man who was somewhat more reserved. I had often seen them standing outside the company store during their lunch break, talking, smoking, and joking around. For this dinner party, Jorge and Octavio had prepared a Peruvian meal. My Japanese friends wanted to know each detail of Peruvian dinner etiquette: where the dishes should be placed, when to serve each dish, how much sauce should be placed where. The easygoing Jorge became irritated when they forced him to discuss these details. "Do it any way you want," he told them. "I don't care as long as the food's good." The Japanese looked shocked at this indifference to presentation and detail, but they did enjoy the food.

It was fun having Jorge and Octavio at the party. At dinner parties with my Japanese friends, we always huddled around a single table and only spoke about topics common to us all, so that everybody could participate. No one would dare walk away from the table to talk privately with a friend, for this would be to isolate themselves from the group. I liked the warm feeling of inclusion, but conversations would often remain superficial. If, after all, we all needed to participate, and our interests diverged, topics for dinner conversation were limited. With Jorge and Octavio around, things were quite different. The meal was much more informal, and they joked and laughed like it was the last festival on earth. At the end of the party, everyone was satisfied.

Whether in America or Asia, good food, good drink, and good company make a great party.

When Kondo, Octavio, Jorge, and I approached the elevator, I noticed that Kume stayed behind with Rie. I was delighted to see that they were getting close. We reached the train station and said good-bye to Kondo. Then Octavio and Jorge asked me to join them at a restaurant called La Bamba. I couldn't believe they were still hungry after all we had just eaten. When I walked in with them off the noisy Japanese street, the owner, a skinny man with long graying hair pulled into a ponytail, greeted us warmly. I heard a cacophony of "hola, como estas" from their Hispanic friends. There was a small mariachi band playing in the corner, and I felt as if I was in Mexico. We ordered beer and appetizers, and I asked Octavio to tell me about himself.

He initially came to Japan on his own in 1992 and learned about Nizumi when he struck up a conversation with a group of Japanese Peruvians on a train in the city. The very next day he applied for a job and was soon working on the Nizumi line. He told me, however, that he'd recently begun working at the Toyota plant. I asked why he'd changed jobs, and he told me the money was better. However, high pay came at a price. He rolled up his sleeve and showed me his arm, which had burn marks on it from spot welding. He said he worked with inadequate equipment and that he was not provided with proper welding clothes. The molten metal had burned right through his shirt.

I was surprised to hear Octavio's story about working at Toyota. It was one thing to occasionally have a serious accident and quite another to have reckless safety policies. Toyota was so profitable that they often boasted about their $21-billion cash reserve. Couldn't a company that was so wealthy provide their workers with basic safety clothing and better working conditions? Not only that—Octavio told me that the line was so fast it was almost impossible *not* to injure yourself. He had to work constantly, sixty full seconds for every minute on the line, with not a moment to rest. At that speed, accidents were unavoidable.

The partying went on until late in the evening. I saw Bhanu and some of the folks from the Japanese language class. Then a man from Thailand introduced himself to me as Sanan. Sanan was married to a Japanese woman whom he'd met on the island of Phu Khet in Thailand when she was on vacation. "Living in paradise," I said to him. "Man, that sounds great!" But Sanan had eked out just a meager living making canoes, so his wife convinced him to come to Japan. After searching hard and long, the only job he could find was as a waiter at a Thai restaurant. He was looking for better wages, so he was applying for a job on the line at Nizumi. He was happy because Nizumi had a branch in Thailand and perhaps he could move back to his home. I could see how this would be a great option, especially if conditions in the Thailand plant were safer than they were here.

A couple of weeks passed, and I heard from Kume again. He invited me to a performance of Mozart's Requiem, in which he was singing and Rie was playing first violin. I made plans to go with Jorge. It was a beautiful Saturday afternoon, with the sun shining brightly, so we walked to the concert hall. The trees were just beginning to turn green. We arrived early, so we grabbed a cup of coffee. I asked Jorge what had brought him to Japan.

When Jorge graduated from college with a business degree in marketing, he spent a year working in Peru. Then President Fujimori took power. According to Jorge, the previous ruler in Peru had been corrupt, so there were few jobs, but when Fujimori took over, he fired the congress and created turmoil. This put many more people out of work, and Jorge was one of the casualties. Life in Peru was unstable and uncertain, so when he read in a local newspaper that Isuzu was looking for employees of Japanese descent to work at their factory in Japan, he applied to work on a factory floor.

I asked Jorge about safety on the line. That year, Nizumi was designated the third most dangerous auto company in Japan. The government ranked all of the large automobile companies according to safety based on accident reports. We all knew about the safety ranking system because the report was distributed onto our desks and discussed during meetings. One of the objectives of the report was to "shame" companies into improving safety. I asked Jorge what they had done to improve the situation, and he said that the managers now checked the equipment before work. According to Jorge, the rule seemed like a preventive safety measure, but in reality, it helped relieve the company from providing compensation to injured workers. "Workers who are injured get compensation only if they can prove that the condition of the machine was at fault," he told me. "If they are to blame, they receive nothing. But it's often difficult to decide who was at fault, the machine or the worker."

"So who's ultimately responsible for safety?" I asked.

"Managers are supposed to be responsible for safety, so if something happens, they get in trouble. So the rule is—injured workers keep their mouths shut. Workers who break this rule are often threatened with dismissal. The only time they do not cover up accidents is when someone is seriously injured, if they lose a finger or hand, and there are witnesses. In actuality, the workers themselves are responsible for their own safety."

Articles in the company newsletters supported Jorge's claims. They often discussed safety problems within the context of human error. An article titled "Meeting of the Safety and Hygiene Committee" quoted the need "to implement safety control keeping in mind that human beings are liable to act unsafely."

To further reinforce the perception that safety is the responsibility of the workers themselves, the company recruited the workers' own families. Every edition of the safety newsletter included a section titled "Message from the Family," which featured a letter written by a child to his father who worked in the factory. Many of the letters included a plea from the child asking his father to be safe on the line. One letter read: "To my father. Father, you work until late at night. Work hard and please do not catch a cold or get into an accident. During the holidays I want to have a good time with you."

Posters that hung on the company walls also used images of the family to reinforce a safety message.

I thought about the idyllic work system that I had heard so much about and wondered why *kaizen* had not been implemented. After all, if workers had the ability to improve the system, certainly the company would benefit. So I asked Jorge about this. They did go through the motions of *kaizen*. When an accident occurred, many would converge on the site to study exactly what had happened. Someone would write up a report, but usually it changed nothing.

Jorge added, "We have *kaizen* meetings twice a week to try to improve safety, and sometimes they are very useful. Mostly they are not, so no one pays attention—we sleep or smoke cigarettes."

So much for *kaizen*.

We eventually made it to the theater and we saw our friends perform. After the concert we went to a coffee shop and socialized. Kondo and a friend of hers joined us. She handed me a book titled *The Writings of Nichiren Daishoshin* and asked if I would read it. They were both active in the Sokka Gakkai, one of Japan's largest new religions, basically a fusion of Nichiren Buddhism and Christian Humanism. I wondered if loneliness had driven Kondo into this religion.

ACCIDENT REPORTS AND HIDING INJURIES

The next evening, I saw Kofi on the street, standing in front of a small juice stand operated by a Japanese woman. Kofi and I shook hands, and I asked him if he wanted to grab some dinner. I kept thinking about the health and safety issues at Nizumi, and I wanted to do some further investigation. We found our way into a small *yakitori* joint where the smell of a charcoal grill wafted into the air. On our way to the restaurant, I told him what Octavio had said to me about the Toyota plant. Kofi had worked with Octavio at Nizumi. Kofi said, "Man, if Octavio thinks Toyota is tough, it must be very tough. Octavio's one of the hardest workers in the plant."

Kofi said many accidents occur because of lack of training. He told me about an incident where both a Japanese and a foreign worker handled a piece of heavy machinery. While they were lowering it, the foreigner's hands got stuck between two large pieces of metal, and when the guy screamed, the Japanese guy didn't hear him.

"Why? What the hell happened?"

"He was wearing head phones to block the noise," Kofi said. "but he wasn't supposed to wear head phones while doing a job like that."

"Don't they enforce the safety rules?"

"Not until an accident happens," he said. "Then they enforce some rules for a short time before abandoning them again. They're only interested in getting the work done."

I wondered how the company was able to keep its image clean. How could it get away with such reckless behavior? Kofi confirmed what Jorge had told me a few days earlier. Although Kofi had worked for more than six years at the company, and either saw or heard about many accidents, he did not know of a single incident in which the company was blamed for the problem, even if the worker received compensation. If the worker was temporary and he couldn't return to work because of his injuries, he was immediately dismissed. If his injuries were not that severe, he would not be immediately dismissed but his contract would not be renewed. Even if he wasn't injured, if a contract employee was involved in an accident, no matter whose fault it was, his contract was unconditionally terminated. No exceptions were allowed.

Even if the machine was defective, the worker got blamed. Once when a conveyer belt brought a batch of parts, there was a power failure, and a worker injured his heel. The worker was blamed for the accident. Another time, an employee was late for work, and while running to his section, he slipped on oil that had been previously spilled on the floor. He injured his knee. "There was blood all over the place—it was so bad that an ambulance came to the factory," Kofi said. That worker was not allowed to renew his contract.

When an accident occurred, accident reports were completed and distributed to employees. In the office, they were passed to our section and in the factory they were hung on bulletin boards. They always included a detailed illustration showing how the accident occurred. According to Kofi, accident reports were often modified in favor of the company, especially if the worker was a regular employee. When a regular worker was injured, lower-level supervisors would modify the reports for fear of punishment by upper-level managers. If a contract worker was injured, however, it didn't matter as much, so those reports were more truthful. After the worker recovered, he was rushed back on the line to work a light duty job, and when he obtained full strength, he returned to his section.

The management continually piled accident reports onto our desks, not only about those that occurred at Nizumi but also about those that occurred at a number of Toyota-group-related companies. By law, when an industrial accident occurs, Japanese corporations must provide a report to the Ministry of Labor. Those reports always included illustrations showing in gory detail workers losing body parts, getting their hands trapped in machinery, break-ing bones, or getting burned. There seemed to be no end to these reports. We received them on a weekly basis, sometimes a few at a time. In many cases, a dozen or so were stapled together and dropped on our desks.

A typical example of a report discussed the injury to a twenty-four-year-old employee. It stated the date of the accident and the extent of the injury: "a compressed chest that lead to serious lung injuries." The injury occurred when the worker stepped off a floor mat to pick up an instruction board that had dropped. The mat was connected to a switch that controlled the ma-chinery, and when it was activated it caused the machinery to disengage. The worker's body was trapped between a heavy piece of machinery and a build-ing pillar.

What was the real purpose of these reports? The reports could certainly reduce accidents by instructing workers to learn from the mistakes of others, but I questioned whether that was the company's true intention. After I left the company, I talked with Dr. Shinya Yamada, a Japanese labor specialist.[12] I mentioned the case of the young man with the lung injury, and he said the accident could have been prevented had they not located the machinery so close to the wall. Furthermore, he said that the machinery had a serious de-sign flaw, because when the worker gets off the mat the pause is released. A safer design would have involved a way to activate the pause with a button so when he reached down to pick up the instruction board he would not have been at risk. "It's likely they implemented the current design to keep the line moving as quickly as possible."

Dr. Yamada derided the preventive measures management suggested to workers in the accident reports. In one report, the preventive measure read, "Don't work if you know it is dangerous." Another read, "Anything in oper-ation is dangerous, and the more you are accustomed to work, the more care-ful you must be. Don't touch equipment in operation." By looking at the preventive measures with Dr. Yamada, I saw the true intention of the corpo-ration, the *honne* behind the *tatemae,* and that was to blame workers for accidents.

According to Dr. Yamada, hiding injuries is a long-standing, pervasive, and hidden rule at most corporations in Japan. He explained that companies have an economic incentive to hide injuries. "The financial management for

---

[12] Dr. Yamada is emeritus professor of the Faculty of Medicine at Nagoya University and one of Japan's leading occupational health and safety experts.

workman's compensation is strictly separate from the National Health care. If a worker experiences a private injury and he goes to a local hospital, he is covered by National Health Care Insurance, and the company is required to pay 50 percent of the cost. However, if the worker obtains workman's compensation, the company must provide full payment for all medical expenses."

According to Kofi, management forced many workers involved in accidents to hide their injuries to improve the safety record and to ensure that they would have work in the following months. "Workers who are in accidents are told not speak about where we got our injuries when we are sent to the hospital. One guy was working on a stamping job when the hammer hit him hard on the ankle. He didn't tell anyone, but it was a bad injury, and soon he went to a hospital outside the company. I told his boss what had happened. The next day his boss told me not to say anything about it to anyone."

In an interview with Satoshi Kamata that I conducted after leaving Nizumi, we discussed his job as a Toyota seasonal worker. He told me, "All workers, whether they were seasonal, contract, or full time employees, would hide their injuries for fear of embarrassing the *hanchō,* the boss responsible for safety." As an American, I was surprised that the fear of embarrassing somebody else would keep them silent about their injuries and the dangers they constantly faced.

Every line worker I spoke to said the factory was *abunai*—dangerous. I asked Higuchi about it. When he first entered the company, he had to work on the line for six long months, and he concurred. Shiina agreed that the factory was dangerous, but he pointed out that the workers have danger awareness training. "It's a process where workers learn from example. They are shown pictures and told of the accident results. It's a good idea, but managers don't implement it. Either they're too busy or they simply don't care anymore, so accidents at the factory are going up."

THE THIRTY-SIX-HOUR SHIFT

I often saw Kofi at the juice stand, chatting with the woman who ran it. I asked him about her. He said she was thirty-eight years old and had a daughter. She was married, but her husband lived with his girlfriend in another house. The husband saw them on weekends, and after his wife made dinner for him, he spent time with his daughter. Then he returned to the girlfriend.

Kofi was very upset about the situation. "These people are sick, how can they live like this, aah, no." I wondered why the woman didn't just get a divorce. But this was Japan, and many things were mysterious here. Kofi wrinkled his dark, sad face and said, "You never know what the Japanese are thinking. Society forces them to hide their feelings, so they keep it all inside."

I had a hunch that the juice woman was interested in being more than just friends but when I asked Kofi, he said he was not at all interested. He was, after all, going through a horrible divorce of his own. He changed the subject quickly and asked if I knew that there were Iranians working at Nizumi. I did not. I heard that many Iranians worked in Japan in the early 1990s, but I thought that most had been sent home.

I obtained a phone number of one of the Iranians, and I immediately gave him a call, for I was eager to connect. In all of my time in Japan, I had yet to meet an Iranian. Later that week, I met Mehdi for lunch. He was a balding man with a buglike face and a friendly smile. He began talking to me in Farsi, but he was disappointed that I could only speak a few words. I was born and raised in America and had only visited Iran once in my life, before the revolution. As an American, visiting Iran immediately after the revolution was out of the question. My parents were thoroughly assimilated and had not taught me Farsi. Mehdi thought it was strange that my Japanese was better than my Persian, but we got along well. I was fascinated to learn about his life.

"Originally I came here on a three-month visitors' visa, but I just stayed on. At that time, during the bubble, it was easy to get a job, so I trained to be blacksmith."

Since the early 1990s, Mehdi had worked at a small Nizumi-related company repairing machinery. Anytime the plant's equipment malfunctioned, they fixed it. Mehdi's company was a typical small Toyota *keiretsu* business employing only fifteen workers. In Japan, more than 57 percent of all companies have thirty workers or less, and more than 73 percent have one hundred workers or less.[13] The Toyota group has been able to increase its profits by outsourcing manufacturing to small group-related companies. These companies are expected to serve the parent company by supplying work or parts only to *keiretsu*-group related companies. At Mehdi's company, none of the employees was permanent except for the president and his son.

Mehdi's life was difficult. "I fix so many things, and I work so hard! But it

[13] *The Year Book of Labor Statistics,* Policy Planning and Research Department, Minister's Secretariat, Ministry of Labor, Japan, 1997.

is the only way I can stay in this county." As an overstayer, he always risked
being caught. "If I am caught I must spend ten weeks in jail and two weeks
in immigration, and then I will be sent back home. We call this jail the 'Royal
House,' and is not a good place. I had an Iranian friend who was also an overstayer, and he was caught and sent there. They bullied and beat him and at
the end of his time he was given a one-way ticket back home."

Mehdi was paid three thousand dollars a month, which enabled him to
live comfortably and to send money to his family in Tehran. He wasn't happy
about being an overstayer and breaking the law. "I don't like to lie, I'm an
honest person, but I have no choice. I must try to help my family. The cost
of living in Iran is so expensive. Some of the money goes to my brother and
sister who are in school, and the rest goes toward food and clothing for my
parents."

From his looks, he seemed to be about my age and so I was curious to
know if he had fought in the Iran-Iraq war. "Yes," he said. He paused for a
moment, and his eyes looked straight into mine. "I didn't want to go, my parents did not want me to go, but I had no choice, I was drafted into the army
and I could not say no."

He spoke defensively, as if he was ashamed. "All Iranians that I know in
Japan fought in the war," he said.

"How was it?"

"I was sent to the front, and within just a few months I had lost two of my
good friends. It was terrible, I didn't want to die, and so I did what I could to
stay alive. I asked to be transferred into the training school where I could
teach other soldiers how to use weapons. Fortunately, my transfer was
granted, and in this way I was able to stay away from the front."

He was in the army for two years, and when he returned home, he had
trouble finding a job. So, like many Iranian war veterans, he came to Japan.
I told him how I had landed at Nizumi, and then it was time to go back to
work. He invited me to his apartment, and I soon took him up on the offer.

When he opened the door, the smell of turmeric was in the air—a familiar scent in Iranian homes. Mehdi led me to the living room, and we sat on
a Persian rug while I chatted with his colleague and roommate, Hossein. As
I made myself comfortable, Hossein talked to me about how he had been
fighting for a pay raise for many weeks. His boss had promised him a raise
many months earlier but had reneged on his pledge because of worsening
economic conditions. After a few weeks of staying home, Hossein had re-

turned to work. As an overstayer, he simply had no other place to go. Although he was barely thirty, he had the face of a rugged middle-aged man. The brutal Iran-Iraq war and Hossein's equally brutal job had aged him beyond his years.

Since Mehdi and Hossein were overstayers, they did not have health benefits, and their health risks were high, since conditions were so dangerous on the floor. "The Japanese people at the company are not bad to me, and some of them are very kind. The main problems are the working conditions and the working hours. It is so dangerous, and if I slack off some days because I am tired, my boss will get angry with me. Sometimes I must work a twenty-four- to thirty-six-hour shift when he needs me. I am always, always tired."[14]

I was shocked to hear that anyone would be forced to work for so long. I asked, "What is it like to work a thirty-six-hour shift?"

"It's tough," he said. "There are times when a worker just walks off the job. That usually occurs during the eighteenth hour—that's the time when the body begins to give out."

"Do you get any breaks?"

"About every six hours we get a break. But at the end we are so tired, so very tired."

His boss showed little sympathy. "My boss benefits from my hard work because I am a good worker and stronger than most Japanese who work on the floor. But he does little to protect me, and he provides little safety equipment." It was obvious that the workers at the small companies were the grunts of the Japanese auto industry, sweating away at jobs that are the most dangerous and least secure.

"SAFETY NUMBER ONE!"

While I was wandering around the grounds one day, I bumped into Sanan, the former canoe builder from Thailand. We made our way into a local pub, ordered *yakitori*, and began chatting about life on the line. Like Kofi and the other contract workers, he received only brief training and was immediately

---

[14] According to the ministry of labor, small companies in Japan are especially dangerous. Statistics show that in the transportation industry, companies of thirty to ninety-nine employees have more than four times the accident rate of companies which employ eight thousand people or more. See the *Year Book of Labor Statistics,* Policy Planning and Research Department, Minister's Secretariat, Ministry of Labor, Japan, 1997.

immersed in the Toyota Production System. His job on the line was to fabricate a part of the drivetrain, and his general duties involved spot-welding the inner and outer portion of the part in repetitive steps. He would first put the frame on a jig, spot-weld other parts, and then glue on the outer shell. Then he placed the product on a tray where it was shipped to another location to be press welded. Since Sanan worked on a flexible manufacturing line, he was responsible for five different kinds of products. Like most contract workers, he felt his job was not different from that of Japanese workers. He participated in all group activities including *kaizen* meetings, QC circles, and safety drills.

On Sanan's line, each section was divided into several work groups, each responsible for manufacturing a part of the product. Sanan worked in a group of eight, of which three, including himself, worked on the left-hand side of the product. Another three, opposite him, worked on the right-hand side. The other two workers were responsible for various group-related jobs. The group leader, who did not work on the line, would check the quality of the products.

I began to wonder about the concept of the "team" that I had heard so much about with reference to the Japanese workplace. There was certainly no teamwork in my job, and none of the workers I interviewed talked about teamwork either. So I asked Sanan about teamwork. He said in most cases the employees did not function as a team. If something happened on the line, if someone needed assistance from another group member—nobody helped. "Everyone just does their own work. When you start out at the factory, if you have questions, people help you, but not after you've learned your job." According to Sanan, the most direct manifestations of group activity were the safety drills, meetings, and competitions. In the morning, Sanan and his team would engage in drills by shouting out a safety slogan. These slogans included such silly statements as "Safety is thinking of a clean shop" or "Keeping danger awareness in your heart and mind will result in zero accidents." After the slogan everyone in unison would shout "*Yosh!*" In Japanese, *yosh* means "let's do it!" *Yoshi* is the formal term. According to Sanan, these drills "did not help with safety, they meant nothing—it's just the Japanese style"

"Safety number one!" The slogan was ubiquitous. It hung over the entrances to the factory, it appeared in the dozens of pages of literature we all received every month, and one day when I came to work I saw that all the managers were wearing "Safety Number One" arm badges. I asked Higuchi about these badges, and he told me that Kurata had ordered them to be worn because of a recent accident in the factory. An employee had been hit on the back of the head by a piece of machinery and had been sent to the hospital. However, the person injured wasn't an ordinary assembly line worker. He was a college-educated engineer on his obligatory six-month assignment to the factory.[15]

Kurata ordered all managers to begin a new safety training program, and to show that they were serious, they were ordered to wear arm badges. Apparently, Kurata took this action because he feared possible retribution from the government after this high-profile accident. According to Higuchi, a few years earlier, a worker had died in the factory, and the government had forced the company to close down the entire manufacturing operations for a full week to investigate why the process was so dangerous.[16]

A couple of weeks later, I bumped into Mehdi in the factory while on my way to the motor pool to look at some parts. A large banner hung on the inside of the main factory building reading "It's safety week, let's work hard to make our shop clean and safe." Beside the slogan was a large green cross symbolizing safety. I thought that the company was actually implementing a real safety program. Surely management wouldn't bother hanging this large banner if they weren't serious, would they?

Mehdi grabbed my shoulder to pull me away from a forklift that was being driven at high speed saying, "Be careful, it's dangerous around here."

I pointed up to the banner and yelled over the din, "What's this about?"

"It's because of the shareholder meeting. The company wants to make a good impression." Laughing, he continued, "Every week is safety week at Nizumi—but it makes no difference, nothing will change."

There was one way, however, that the workers were actively involved in improving safety during safety week. They all participated in a poster contest, and the winners were published in the safety newsletter. Shown here are some of the winning posters, all hand-drawn by employees at Nizumi.

---

[15] During their first year of work, all engineers at Japan's largest companies are required to work six months in the factory.
[16] Higuchi told me about this incident but I could not independently verify it.

Sanan said that he had one safety meeting a week, during which all members of his group were supposed to participate to improve conditions. "The team leader will say that you have to clean the machine, if you don't, it will be dangerous. And the supervisor will hold up illustrations showing how to be safe. Of course, this doesn't help. Every day before we start working, these leaders tell us to be careful, but they never tell us *how* to be careful. They just show pictures of injured workers, like they're trying to scare us."

The safety newsletter covered the work group competitions. The group that had the fewest accidents would win the monthly safety medal. A write-up of the winning team appeared in the monthly safety magazine under the title, "We Are the Team with Zero Accidents." Here is a typical write-up: "Our most important concern is to prevent accidents. The average age of our group is twenty-seven years old. Most of us are very young. Sometimes we feel that we do not have much experience, but we try to understand our deficiencies. Every morning we have a safety meeting where we chant our safety slogan, 'Safety is watching your step to prevent accidents.'" According to Sanan, most workers did not care about winning the safety medal. "No one on the line cares about the safety competition," he said. "Only the team leaders care."

I wondered what happened if someone on the line was sick or injured. Sanan told me that the groups just made do without the injured member unless the job physically could not be accomplished. Sanan said, "If someone is sick, they do not replace him, but if two people are sick then we cannot do the job." Within the section, a small number of highly skilled workers can replace the lost worker in an emergency situation. In many cases, however, these workers are pulled from other work groups, so other teams are burdened that day.

Sanan reiterated what everyone had told me, that the line was *abunai*. The line speed was the main danger. "Working with heavy machinery is always dangerous, but the problem is they work the line so fast that accidents are frequent. Many guys at the company have lost their fingers."[17] On a theoretically average day, Sanan's team was required to make a total of 120 products, which meant spending three minutes on each product. However, the quota was often raised to 132 products, or more, so the production time was correspondingly reduced per product, leading to a faster pace, and accidents.

Flexible manufacturing sounds like a good idea, for it requires each

---

[17] According to Shuzo Sasaki of the Aichi Labor Institute, an organization with more than thirty years of experience studying Toyota and their group-related companies, the largest contribution to accidents on the line is the fast line speeds. "Fast line speeds contribute greatly to work related accidents and health problems. We have noticed a high blood pressure rate, heart problems, work-related injuries, and death directly related to fast line speeds. About 50 percent of all workers have work related illnesses but are still forced to work" (interview in Nagoya, July 2000). The institute has recorded line speeds as fast as 58 seconds per minute but many workers claim they have not even one second to rest.

worker to use a number of skills in the course of the day. But it also makes working with fast line speeds more dangerous because it increases the overall time necessary to finish the day's quota. Sometimes the employees are required to work on products they don't make often and for which they have received little training, and this, too, creates safety problems.

Although Sanan and his group engaged in morning safety drills and *kaizen* meetings, the line was still unsafe, not only because of its speed but also because of the factory layout. The workplace was crowded and stocked with poorly designed equipment, so there wasn't enough room to move around on the line. Sanan complained about the jig, which is a machine to mechanically hold and move the position of parts during assembly. Sanan said, "When you work the jig, it turns, and sometimes your body touches the buttons which control the tools."

I asked if this had ever caused an accident.

"One guy was seriously injured. He had to put a very small part on the drivetrain, and it dropped inside the jig. When he reached down to pick it up, he bent his other arm back and accidentally hit the button. The jig crushed his hand."[18]

Sanan put down his chopsticks and told me about a time he'd injured himself on the line. "I had burned my arm from the welder and it got infected. I had to go to the company hospital and the doctor put my arm in a large bandage. When I went back to work the group leader was angry with me! He yelled at me and sent me back on the line." I was amazed that he had been forced to return to the line.

If a worker was seriously injured and couldn't possibly go back to the line, he would receive compensation. However, the worker was required to come in to work, even if his injuries prohibited him from doing his job. This was perplexing: the injured workers just sat in a room all day and did nothing. Now I understood what I had seen the day I had visited Kofi on the line: a room with a few men in it watching television.

In a later interview with Yoshiatsu Sato of the Aichi Labor Institute, I learned that Toyota and its group-related companies have institutionalized this hidden rule for many years. "At Toyota, even if a worker's accident is so

---

[18] Yoshiatsu Sato, a union activist with fifteen years' experience at Toyota whom I interviewed later, agreed with Sanan: line speed and crowding are the major causes of accidents. "The problem at Toyota is that the factories are very crowded and the workplace is very, very busy to meet the daily quota. Many accidents occur when workers drop parts while the line is running." Interview with Sato in Nagoya, Japan, July 2000.

severe that he loses a body part, he must come to the company and sit and do nothing."[19] In this way, the company avoids recording injuries and the management can project a safe image of itself to the Japanese people.

Shortly before leaving the company, I learned about a terrible accident in the factory. An employee was testing an auto part when the power went out. So he took the tester to the power box—and 3,000 volts went through his body, burning his chest, face, and limbs. The maximum capacity of the tester was 450 volts, and the worker had not been educated on how to handle electricity. Furthermore, the high voltage system was unlocked when it should have been locked, and the high voltage sign that should have been near the power box was nowhere to be seen. The worker was only twenty-three years old, and he suffered permanent neurological damage.

The company had provided neither training nor safeguards and was obviously negligent. But government inspectors hadn't been allowed to check for safety violations because proprietary technology was in place, and Nizumi had received permission to deny them entry.

EMPLOYEE EVALUATIONS

As September approached, Uno told our section to seriously consider participating in a plan called Hopes. (This did not apply to me since I was a contract employee.) Hopes was new to the pay-by-performance policy. A few years earlier, the pay-by-performance policy had become an option when the company announced that it wanted to change the old Japanese-style policy of "seniority"-based pay and promotion. Theoretically, instead of rank determining an employee's salary, the base pay would rise every year as long as an employee's results were good.

An added benefit of pay-by-performance allowed employees to begin and end their workday when they chose. It was expected that this flextime would allow workers to spend more time with their families. Under pay-by-performance, there was no paid overtime, but the plan still seemed attractive. As long as their performance was good, workers would be fairly compensated, and they could come and go as they pleased. Some of the guys in my section were in the pay-by-performance plan, but they didn't seem too happy with it.

---

[19] Ibid.

Shortly after the meeting, I noticed that Takanashi was twitching and turning in his seat like an injured bird trying to fly. "What's the matter?" I asked.

Takanashi was highly indignant about Hopes. He had enrolled in the pay-by-performance plan sometime earlier, and now, with the Hopes addendum, he would be required to write a self-evaluation. "Hopes really means hopeless," he said. "There is no light at the end of the tunnel. Can you see the exit? No! The 'smile' of 'Hopes' comes from Human Resources. They want to make the plan look good, but it is hopeless. I would leave if I could, but no one would hire me with the economy down like this. The problem with Japanese engineers is that we are too narrowly specialized. If we are shifted from one company to another, we don't do as well, so we are not motivated to move, even if we are unhappy with our situations."

I switched the conversation over to the evaluations, for all the men were busy getting things together for their presentations to the directors. Takanashi was cynical about the whole process. "The idea is for workers to get more motivated for their jobs, but most people at the company feel they will never be judged fairly."

"Why is that?" I asked

"Because there aren't any criteria," he said. "Hopes is hopeless," he said once again.

I realized he was right. The pay-by-performance policy, seemed logical and appealing. However, it required employees to forfeit paid overtime and meant that more work was assigned to each employee. Because of service overtime, the advantages of flextime were largely theoretical. Higuchi told me that since there were no objective criteria for the evaluations, in many cases management did not give a positive assessment because they want to get more work from each worker for less money.

Employee review was on all of our minds, so I asked Kurasawa about it. "I don't think I will get a good review," he said. He pointed his finger to the power group and said, "Those guys will be moving up in the company. That is why they sit in the center of the section. But I sit on the outside." It was true: his desk was located toward at the outer edge of the section. Those who had the power were located toward the center of the section, close to Uno, and those who were least important were seated at the edge. So it was clear to all who was an inside member of the old-boy network and could expect to move up and become a future leader and who was an outsider destined to remain on the periphery of power. Everyone was well aware of the geography of the desks and what it denoted.

So my initial impression of the office space symbolizing egalitarianism had to be revised. The lack of walls certainly facilitated communication, particularly during technical discussions, but it also demonstrated distinctions of rank and facilitated worker control.

All those who were connected to the line of power moved up or down within the company when the superior at the top was either promoted or demoted. This type of organizational structure emphasized loyalty to one's superior and the group to which one belonged. In return for Scarface's loyalty, for instance, he would move up with Uno and his close associates, maintaining a close-knit chain within the hierarchy.

When a manager was promoted or shifted to another group, however, his desk remained in the section, even if he no longer used it. Although Abe had worked in a separate office for the last ten years, his desk still occupied a space in the section. All the contents of the desk remained in the drawers, and according to Kurasawa, only Abe had the key. When I asked about the purpose of this, Kurasawa just smiled and said, "It is his style." Since the section suffered from space limitations and the desk could not be removed, it was used as a tabletop for a printer.

One day shortly after the mid-year transfer meeting, I noticed something peculiar at the Advanced Design group, which was located adjacent to our section. The entire section of about two dozen employees had moved downstairs and left an engineer named Hirama sitting all alone with just one other employee, who was known to be unproductive.

I remember when I'd first met Hirama. I was in the benchmarking shop looking at the scattered components of a competitor's product, and a short, stocky older man pulled me over and said in English "You see this part. It has a good design." Hirama discussed the merits of the design and then said, "I used to work for the boss of your section many years ago." In mid-career, he had been switched to the design division, where he worked as a benchmark engineer, collecting information about competitor products for technology improvement.

Now I asked Kurasawa why Hirama was sitting alone in the section, and he responded, "There is no place for him at the company anymore." I initially thought that he would eventually move downstairs with his group, but several more days passed and he and the other employee remained all alone in that huge open space.

HARD TIMES: RESTRUCTURING BEGINS

During the Asian boom, Thailand had become the company's largest export market, buying more than twelve hundred products a month. Then came the Asian crash.[20] In November 1997, the section manager released information on monthly sales. In October, Thailand had bought a mere twelve products.

The company immediately began cutting back on expenses. A couple of weeks after the crash, Uno announced that overtime and the next bonus would also be cut. This caused great consternation since approximately 60 percent of an employee's salary comes from overtime work and the bonus.

There was also worry about the fall of Yamaichi, one of Japan's oldest and largest securities[21] companies. The news of the bank's debt was the main story in all the media. Higuchi said, "All the employees at Yamaichi will be fired from the company, which is very rare in Japan." He frowned and looked despondent. Higuchi always looked concerned when talking about anything related to making a living.

Kurasawa said he was thinking about sending his savings to America. I was surprised; as an American, I never knew that my country's financial institutions were considered especially secure. The very fact that Kurasawa would consider such a move showed he had lost faith in the Japanese economy.

At the next department meeting, Uno announced that the company would be cutting back on research and development. Management also an-

---

[20] Due to international capital flows the Thai economy soared until early 1997. To fuel their economy, Thai businessmen found that they could borrow money at lower interest rates overseas in dollars. By late 1996, however, the economy accumulated too much foreign debt and suffered from large trade deficits and a banking system weakened by unpaid loans. Foreign investors began to worry that their loans could not be repaid so they rushed to move their investments out of Thailand. The Thai government responded by raising interest rates, which consequently caused the value of the Thai *baht* to plummet and the economy to crash. Investors saw similar problems throughout the region so they began pulling their money out of South Korea and Indonesia and as a result the crisis traveled throughout Asia. See Suk Kim and Mahfuzul Haque, "The Asian Financial Crisis of 1997: Causes and Policy Responses," *Multinational Business Review* (spring 2002): 37–44.

[21] Yamaichi was one of Japan's oldest and largest securities companies.

nounced that it expected employees to arrive earlier each morning in the hope of increasing productivity. We received this news in silence.

After the meeting, I went to see Higuchi. As I approached his desk, I saw through his window that dramatically large snow flakes were drifting down once more. I knew that they would probably melt upon touching the ground, for Japanese winters were much milder than the brutal winters I had experienced in Madison, Wisconsin.

I asked Higuchi about what we had just heard at the meeting. Would employees really start their work day earlier? He shrugged. "Our problems are much too deep to be solved with these silly measures." He looked pensive. We both knew that more service overtime would not contribute much to our productivity for the engineers were already working long hours.

So what could be done? "Since the company cannot fire the full-time workers everyone will get a pay cut," he said. "That's the first step. Next, we will buy less new equipment. And we'll let some of our contract workers go, including a number of farmers who work at Nizumi during the winter when they cannot work in the fields."

Cutting back on contract workers meant that I might be fired, so I asked him about my job. He said that my job was safe because I was a special case.

I walked downstairs to grab some lunch. (Months ago, I had abandoned making my own *obentō* lunch since it took too much time.) I ran into Kofi on the ground floor, and he clasped my hands warmly and asked, "Hey brother, what's up?" Many of my colleagues would see us greet each other warmly, and I sometimes wondered what they thought about this friendship between an American engineer and an African factory worker. We chatted for a bit. I told him about the stringent economic measures management was proposing, and I asked how things were in the factory. He confirmed what Higuchi had said. Many of the contract workers, both foreign and Japanese workers, would not have their contracts renewed. Because he was such a valuable employee, however, Kofi's own job was safe.

When I returned to my desk, once again I asked Shiina to help me understand company policy. I wondered why the unions didn't do more to defend our rights, for at Nizumi, the union represented white collar workers as well as the workers on the line. Shiina said that the union was useless. He said a labor dispute was recently settled in which the company agreed to union demands to extend vacation days by one day a year. Not much of a victory, I thought, considering that most of the company had been coerced to work overtime without pay—but better than nothing. Then I heard the details. Instead of giving everyone another day's vacation, management cut five minutes from each working day by changing the official quitting time to 5:25 instead of 5:30. Over the working year, those five minutes added up to one day. "Did you notice that now the bell goes off at 5:25 instead of 5:30?" Shiina asked. I hadn't noticed the change, but we both agreed that this supposed labor victory was useless since the company rule of service overtime required an employee to stay well beyond official hours.

LOCAL POLITICS: THE COMPANY SUPPORTS A CANDIDATE

One day, I saw campaign posters for a local candidate on the company bulletin boards. A slogan beside his picture read "For a city with a warm heart." Who was this man and why was his picture being displayed here? I asked Shiina about it. "He's an employee who has been chosen by the company to run for a seat on the city council. I think it's illegal but they do it anyway."

I was surprised that the company was overtly involved in local politics. I wanted to learn more, so I asked, "Do you think I could join the campaign?"

Shiina laughed. "Sure. All the employees in our section who live in the city, including myself, have been asked by Human Resources to join the campaign—but I don't plan on doing it, of course. Why would you care? You're a foreigner, you can't even vote!"

"I just think it is interesting," I said. "I'm curious about local politics."

"Well, if you're serious, the office is right over there." We walked to the window, and he poked his fingers into the shade to open a small crack. "See? It's over there, across the street." And there it was, right on company property: the campaign office. A large banner stood in front of the entrance: "Create a city that is warm and green."

That very afternoon, all employees at Nizumi received a pamphlet entitled, "The Ishida Yoshiharu Support Club Newsletter." It included a photograph of the candidate alone and another of him playing volleyball with a group of women, for he was the coach of a "mama" volleyball team. The pamphlet discussed his platform and said he wanted to act as a "conduit between the residents and the city government." Ishida wanted to build a happy, green city "through heart-to-heart communication."

I decided to investigate the role of the company in local politics, so I planned to sit down with the company candidate and talk to him face to face. Erberto warned me against this course of action, but I was determined to learn more about Nizumi's involvement in local government.

Ishida's office occupied a room in an abandoned factory building. The factories at Nizumi are large, arched buildings where workers weave through constantly humming heavy machinery. Since Ishida's building was slated for destruction and replacement, his office was eerily quiet. I walked through the door and bowed to a man sitting alone, smoking at a table. He was an older man with a large crop of slick, graying hair combed neatly back. He was dressed in a company uniform with a tie and white shirt that could barely be seen beneath his industrial jacket. He seemed surprised to see me—and even more surprised when I told him I wanted to speak to the candidate. "He's not here now," he said in a hoarse voice reminiscent of the Brando character in *The Godfather.* "He should be here in a few minutes."

I sat patiently, examining a detailed drawing of a campaign van on a chalkboard behind him. The van had several loud-speakers and a roof podium. The older man asked me about my job and section. Then he asked, "So why are you interested in the candidate?"

"Well," I said, "I'm just interested in local politics."

"Is that so?" he asked suspiciously. "Have you ever worked on a campaign?"

"Yes," I told him. "I've worked on some local campaigns in America."

"You know," he cautioned, "elections in Japan are not like those in the United States. In Japan, the candidates don't debate. They just speak to their supporters, and the voters decide who they like."

I thought that this was rather odd. If there was no debate, then how could citizens evaluate the candidates? But I just asked, "What party does the candidate belong to?"

"He's an independent. He represents the people of Nizumi."

I thought it was strange for someone who was relatively unknown to get his start in politics as an independent. I asked if I could read about the candidate while I was waiting for him. But beyond the pamphlet I'd already received, there was no information about the candidate in the campaign office. This surprised me, as the election was a mere two months away.

Finally, Ishida returned. He was a tall, husky man who projected an air of strength and confidence. A flowered tie peeped out from under his company uniform. As he sat down, he grabbed a cigarette from the inner pocket of his jacket, picked up an engine piston lying on the table, and turned it upside down so he could use it as an ashtray. The older man introduced us, telling him I was an American engineer. Ishida bowed slightly. His face lost its smile and his eyes remained still. "So what section do you belong to?" His voice reverberated in the isolated office.

I told him the section name, and he responded that I belonged to the "elite." He picked up the company phone book and began naming the managers in my section. He wanted me to understand that he had a special relation to them. Then he asked me about my work, but he was clearly bored. His eyes wandered around the room and he got out of his seat. He walked to the coffee machine and offered me some coffee. I took him up on his offer, but as he handed me the cup, there was an awkward silence. I felt as if I could read his mind: "Of all the employees in this company, why is this one foreigner interested in my campaign?"

I asked if I could attend one of his campaign rallies. "Of course," he said. Then he pointed his thumb down and added, "but if you attend you must not boo—only cheering is allowed." I assured him I would only cheer and inquired about the next rally. He said he hadn't decided on it yet. I asked if he had any campaign material, but he had none beyond the basic pamphlet we'd all been given. As I walked out the door, he said he would contact me when he knew about his next campaign speech, but I had my doubts about this.

THE CAMPAIGN RALLY

Weeks went by, and despite Ishida's apparent cordiality, he never did contact me about his campaign. He must have felt uncomfortable about having a curious foreigner monitor company affairs, especially if what Shiina had said was true, and that a company's running a candidate for office was an illegal activity. I later found out that he was right: it was unlawful for Nizumi to directly sponsor a candidate. So although company management at its highest levels managed and financed Ishida's campaign, they claimed he was being supported by the union, who was his official sponsor.

I soon discovered the extent of management's concern about me when one of the campaign managers approached me while I was walking on company grounds. "I hear you're interested in the campaign," he said. "Why? You can't vote, and you're not Japanese."

"I'm interested in local politics," I said stubbornly.

"Stay away from the campaign," he warned. "It's not for you."

I felt as if I had come up against a mobster dressed in the Nizumi uniform. Stay away . . . or what? Would they rub me out? But I did not live and work in the underworld. This was a corporation, and as a hard-working employee, I felt I had the right to inquire about the company's support of the candidate.

A few days later, upper management asked all employees to attend the corporate campaign rally. As the event was announced over the loud speakers, Erberto and Chen asked me to join them. We packed ourselves into the elevator and walked into the Public Relations Center where hundreds of other employees were gathered. Most employees wore their company hats and uniforms, but some were dressed casually. At the entrance, a handful of young "campaign girls" wearing neatly fitting uniforms greeted us politely in girlish voices and handed out flyers for the candidate. Each flyer had a large image of Ishida with his fist in the air symbolizing *ganbarō*.[22] Under the photograph was the meaningless personal mission statement: "I am working hard to become a councilman with renewed resolutions and a sense of crisis in mind." Then the flyer listed how if elected Ishida would improve the welfare system, extend the athletic center, and work to create a city that was "happy and green." A single sentence described each policy. I didn't see anything controversial in this platform—nor anything that would be of particular benefit to Nizumi.

At the front of the hall, a purple velvet curtain with the company emblem was draped over a large podium. Soon, the candidate and his staff walked in and sat down. The mayor of the city entered and took a seat beside the candidate, followed by half a dozen city councilmen. The campaign manager kicked off the campaign rally by saying we should work to win as many corporate seats as possible in the coming nationwide election. The mayors and city councilmen also spoke, each stating his desire to expand corporate influence in city government. Representatives from Human Resources, the union, and the Board of Directors also gave short speeches asking employees to vote for Ishida Yoshiharu for the betterment of the company. One manager exhorted us to ask our families and friends to vote for this wonderful man.

Finally, Ishida spoke. He stood tall, his body stance reflecting his confidence, his broad shoulders indicating his strength. At ease and charismatic, he began with some small talk about the company. Then he spoke about his

---

[22] *Ganbarō* in Japanese translates as "let's work hard," or "let's give it our best," and is used in many work rituals in Japan such as the military-style campaigning described above.

platform. He proposed cutting the local government tax on Nizumi, which at the time amounted to 15 percent of company profits, to help the company in the hard economic times that were now upon us. He spoke about expanding the company parking lot, so that more people who drove to work could park. (This policy meant nothing to the average worker, since only managers were allowed to park in the company lot anyway.) Finally, he spoke about the community at large. He said he would extend medical assistance for the elderly, expand the local hospital, support recycling in the community, and work to get more toilets in the local parks. We all just listened. There was no opportunity to ask questions or raise issues.

The event ended with a ritual reminiscent of wartime Japan. A dozen men stood in front of the audience wearing white *hachimaki* headbands. The large, red rising sun of the Japanese flag was painted in the center while the two characters for "victory" were painted to the right and left side of the *hachimaki*. They raised their fists in the air and swung them upward in unison as they shouted "Victory for Ishida, Victory for Ishida!" In response, the crowd returned the slogan in unison shouting "Victory for Ishida!" For the first time in almost two years at the company, I felt uneasy. Only in old black-and-white war films had I seen such fanatic group control.

After the rally, I approached Higuchi to ask his opinion about the campaign and the role of the company in the community. "I have no interest in this campaign," he said, "and wouldn't vote for Ishida even if I lived in town."

Higuchi asked me about the role of corporations in American politics. "Do employees at the Big Three run for Congress in America?"

"Corporations have a lot of influence on American politics," I said, "but they don't choose company employees to run for office. Instead, they influence politics through large campaign contributions to one or both candidates running for national office or congressional seats."

OPINIONS OF THE CANDIDATE

Management saturated us with publicity about the campaign. Flyers were distributed onto the desks of workers, newsletters and magazines featured articles about Ishida, and posters of the candidate were hung on the bulletin boards. None of this contained detailed information about the candidate or his policies. In attempting to learn more about the candidate, I asked some of the employees if they knew Ishida. Virtually no one had heard of him—

he was certainly not popular at Nizumi. All the employees I asked told me they didn't know him, they would not vote for him, and that he did not "represent any ideas." I dug into the company literature, and I found only one article by Ishida: in an edition of the safety newsletter, "Cheers," he compared the drinking culture of Japan to that of Taiwan.

I asked Higuchi about the rationale of selecting a largely unknown company employee to run for public office. "That's why they chose him!" he told me. "It makes it easier for employees to vote for him." In Japan as elsewhere, a long public record could be an election handicap.

Kurasawa told me that if Ishida was elected to the city council, he would get two salaries: one from the company and another from the city government. I hadn't realized that if elected, Ishida would stay on at Nizumi as an employee. "What will he do on the council?" I asked.

"He will work against activists who want to change the pollution laws," Kurasawa said indignantly. "This time, the union is going too far. Our managers are trying to get us to vote for him, and that isn't right."

I asked Shiina about why Ishida was running for office. "He's running because he's been ordered to do so. He was probably chosen by the previous city councilman."

"Well, what will he do when he's in office?"

"I don't know! Hang out with the Board of Directors? He's just a company puppet."

To ensure that Ishida would get elected, Human Resources was actively recruiting workers in the office or on the line to get involved in the campaign. At our weekly department meeting, Uno exhorted the four employees in our section who lived in town to become involved in the campaign. The company also compiled a list of names of all employees who could vote in the town election and distributed this list to the entire company. Presumably, we were all supposed to pressure these people into voting for the company candidate.

In December, Ishida came to our dormitory Christmas party. Although less than 1 percent of the Japanese population is Christian, Christmas is often celebrated as a general holiday. While the dorm residents were mingling and chatting, Ishida, dressed in his company clothes, walked to the front of the room and began addressing the group. Most people became quiet while he spoke, but a few continued to talk as if the candidate did not exist. I almost felt sorry for him, speaking to a crowd that seemed basically uninterested in what he had to say. He finished with a cheer and everyone began drinking and talking again. Then came the bingo. One of the "Christmas" events was a bingo game in which winners could choose among a broad selection of gifts, ranging from Nintendo games and videocassettes to air filters. Meanwhile, sashimi, fried chicken, a white Christmas cake, and strawberry champagne stood waiting on long tables in the center of the room. Once Ishida left, it ended up being a pretty good party.

At lunchtime about a week later, I headed over to pick up some sandwiches only to behold the candidate, incongruously dressed in a tuxedo, greeting employees as they entered the cafeteria. He had a large banner draped over his shoulder that read "Ishida Yoshiharu." I stood back to observe the interaction. Ishida bowed and politely asked the workers to support his candidacy. Most ignored him completely. A few bowed. Of the hundreds of employees that passed by, only one stopped to shake his hand.

Toyota Motors, along with hundreds of other large, well-known companies in Japan, had candidates running at both local and national levels, always through the subterfuge of union support. During the 1997 nationwide city elections, four candidates from Nizumi were running for various seats throughout the district.

With the campaign in full swing, work continued as usual. I was assigned to work on a short project with a pleasant young engineer in production, and he came to visit me to talk shop. One of Toyota's New Friendship party pamphlets fell out of his shirt pocket. He ripped it into shreds and threw it into the garbage. "I don't need that!" he said with disgust.

As the production engineer and I continued talking, Shiina approached me and said, "Mehri *san,* you haven't put your working time into the computer yet. Do it now!"

"Now?"

"Yes, now, right now!"

He was clearly upset, so I said good-bye to the production engineer and immediately went to the computer and filled in my hours. All employees were required to record their projects and the amount of time it had taken to complete them on an old Toshiba computer with a Japanese operating system. In my section, we had to provide this information at the end of the month. Other sections required daily or weekly reports, depending on the manager. Higuchi had told me when I started working at the company that this rule was not so important. I did not really have to fill in the time sheet at the end of the month, as long as I did so ultimately. It was well known that what Uno cared most about was results, not record-keeping, so most of us in the section simply punched in our numbers when we remembered to do so, although the information was usually inaccurate or exaggerated. I thought this self-reporting was unnecessary and cumbersome, especially on this tricky old computer, so sometimes I forgot all about it for months on end, until an office lady reminded me.

I was surprised that Shiina would even ask me about something I thought our section basically ignored, so after reconstructing my hours and recording them into the Toshiba, I returned to my chair and asked Shiina, "So what's the big deal about recording our work time?"

"Abe looked at the time sheet and became furious because no one was taking it seriously. He told Uno that he wanted everyone to start filling it in correctly. The problem is that if one person doesn't do it the entire section could be punished." I felt uncomfortable that my laziness could lead to the punishment of the entire section but I was not surprised. I had come to realize that social mechanisms of control were one of the primary ways to get workers to follow rules.

GETTING OUT THE VOTE

On the Saturday morning before the election I walked out of my dorm and heard a cacophony of sounds emanating from dozens of campaign vans. To introduce themselves to citizens of the city, the candidates had rigged vans with large bullhorns and would ride around town blaring their messages. I walked down the street a few blocks and noticed a large bulletin board on the side of the street which contained a total of forty pictures, one for each candidate.

On Monday of election week, Ishida was still working hard to bring his message to the company employees. It was an unusually cold and snowy day. The sky was gray, and large snowflakes floated down. During lunch hour, a few dozen Ishida supporters gathered outside our building. Some men from Chen's group and I looked down from the fifth floor of our building, waiting for Ishida to arrive. I asked one of Chen's engineers whether he thought Ishida would win the election. He replied stiffly, "He is the best candidate for the position and will try his very best," he said. I was not surprised at this company rhetoric since Oda's group was extremely obedient.

Suddenly, Ishida arrived in a caravan of cars driven by his campaign staff. One of the vehicles was a campaign van while the others were the new, super-aerodynamic Toyota vans. Men wearing bright silver jumpsuits stepped out and escorted Ishida to a little portable platform. This group stood in a line facing the building. I wondered why they were wearing such peculiar outfits. A routine campaign event became hilarious to me when I regarded these "space men" and realized that they probably thought they looked cool. Now Ishida, in his black tuxedo and white gloves, approached the podium. Once again he spoke about cutting the corporate tax, which led into his unchanged litany of political goals.

At the weekly department meeting, Dr. Zombie read from a document that fully embraced the Ishida platform. He said there might be a good chance of reducing local income taxes if Ishida was elected. He named the four employees in our section who lived in the city and said he expected them to vote for Ishida. One of them cracked a wry smile, but the others were not present.

Erberto and I were on our daily break when we walked by the building that contained Ishida's office. I told him I wanted one last visit with Ishida before the election.

"You're crazy to go in there!" he said

"What can they do to me?" I replied, "Fit me with a pair of cement shoes and throw me in the river?"

I walked into the office and saw the reincarnation of the Godfather whom I had met during the first visit sitting with a half a dozen other campaign members at the table. They had exchanged their silver space suits for bright green jumpsuits. They looked bored, as if there was nothing to do. Some delivery trucks from the factory drove by, and the room shook loudly. "The Godfather" greeted me with a congenial smile, as if he was happy to see an old friend. He introduced me to the staff and told them my name and section. And then there was an uncomfortable silence.

"So when is the next speech?" I asked

"There's one this evening," he said in his distinctive hoarse voice. He smiled and showed me a detailed map on the wall. He pointed to the exact location where Ishida would speak. I told him I couldn't attend because of work and asked if he had any other information about the week's activities. He replied that he had none. I asked with surprise, "You mean you have nothing else lined up for this week?" After all, it was the week before the election.

Reluctantly, he walked back to the local map and said, "Okay, if you really want to know, he will be speaking at this town, the one over here—and that one too. And this one, and that one." He smiled and nodded his head slightly as he showed me each town where Ishida planned to speak. When he finished, he stood in silence. It was obvious he did not want me there spoiling their show, so I thanked him and walked toward the door. As I was leaving, he nodded, smiled and said "Please come again."

This was typically Japanese. What he really meant was, "Please do not come back again. We told you to stay away—there is nothing of interest for you here." I told myself I would not return, and I didn't.

I asked Kurasawa what he thought of the elections.

"The problem is in Japan there is very little information about the candidates so I don't know who's good and who's bad," he said. "But I do know that there are many candidates who blame America or China for Japan's problems. In the old days one would choose oneself as the scapegoat. It must have been beautiful," he said without irony. "You would kill yourself if you brought shame to your master."

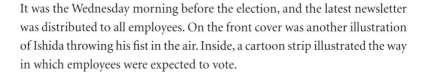

It was the Wednesday morning before the election, and the latest newsletter was distributed to all employees. On the front cover was another illustration of Ishida throwing his fist in the air. Inside, a cartoon strip illustrated the way in which employees were expected to vote.

The City Congressional Election Ballot on February 22

ISHIDA YOSHIHARU

For a smiling, green city, he will work hard with all of his power. Please don't forget to vote.
There is an absentee ballot available for those who cannot vote on Election Day.

I was surprised to see such emphasis on the absentee ballot—until Chen approached to tell me that the voting had already begun.

"What?" I said, confused. "The election is four days away."

"I know, but the company is forcing employees to obtain absentee ballots and vote today. They even hired a bus service to bring them to City Hall."

"You're kidding!"

At that time of the day Chen's team usually had a group meeting, but when I looked over his shoulder, the desks were empty. Chen shook his head in sorrow and said, "I don't think they do this even in China!"

Erberto's group was also bussed to City Hall. However, one of the men in the group did not board the bus. Erberto said, "He either forgot or he wasn't interested in the election. So Human Resources called him and said, 'Now you must vote!'"

The guy had no choice. He got on the next bus.

The results of the election were tabulated quickly, and the company wasn't shy about showing the results. They posted them everywhere—even on the vending machines. Ishida Yoshiharu had won by a landslide. Furthermore, all the other four company candidates (from Toyota, Toshiba, Fuji Electric, and Konica) had won office in our district, with these candidates receiving the highest number of votes, although the four corporate councilmen represented little more than 10 percent of the legislature.

In every city where a large company maintained a factory or a large corporate office, they funded and promoted a candidate for city council. And with the kind of support that the companies were able to offer, the company candidates almost always won.

THE PRESIDENT SPEAKS

By February, Nizumi had a surplus of ten thousand products waiting to be sold. That's an inventory of about $60 million. We gasped when Uno told us about this at the next department meeting. Then he announced that all paid overtime work would be cut. (As usual, there was no mention at all of service overtime.) He read aloud from the company newsletter an article with the headline: "The Tightest Condition since the Establishment of the Company, Now Is the Time for the Trial!" This summarized the president's speech at the annual management meeting, the purpose of which was to talk about the current crisis. The president said both labor and management must gain "a common recognition of the surrounding conditions, economic situation, and the present status and future of Nizumi to establish confidence between labor and management."

It was not a comforting speech. Domestic and export sales had plummeted. Demand for product by Toyota was way down. Government-funded construction had been greatly reduced, which meant Nizumi's profits would also fall. Projections for the coming year were also grim. The president ended his

speech on a dismal note: "Even if we implement every possible countermeasure, we must prepare for the worst situation we have ever seen." The union newsletter printed the president's speech along with these illustrations.

COMPETITION BETWEEN DIVISIONS

Meanwhile, I became eager to spread some of the technology I had developed to other departments in the company. The method I had devised to automate CAD part creation dramatically sped up the design process, and I thought it would be of use to the Design Division. Erberto's boss, Oda, was a lively fellow who showed tremendous enthusiasm for his work. According to Erberto, when technical problems arose, he always encouraged his engineers to find ways to adopt new technology. On top of that, he was also a smart engineer who had won an industry award for his patent on part of the drivetrain. If I could convince Oda to work with me on a project perhaps my ideas might spread throughout the company.

My only connection to Oda was through Erberto, so I decided to pay him a visit. I walked to the entrance of his section and bent down to untie my shoes. I could never slip them on and off as the Japanese did. They had a technique by which they could take off their shoes without untying them, but I always had to kneel down and fiddle with my shoe laces.

While I was fumbling with my shoes, Takagi passed and gave me a smile.

Takagi had an interesting story. She had been an office lady, but one day her boss (Nishida, Erberto's first boss) noticed that she was good with numbers. Since he was short of staff, he decided to train Takagi as an engineer. She learned quickly. She became so skilled that many of the college-educated engineers would approach her with their problems. Once during a company trip, I asked a young engineer from whom he had learned his computer skills. "Ms. Takagi," he said, "We all go to her for computer help." Occasionally I had asked her questions myself, and she had always known the right answers. Once Takagi had solved a tough engineering problem that had stumped several professional high-level engineers, and Nishida had showered her with accolades. She was simply outstanding. Now she sat behind the computer using finite element analysis to determine the strength of materials for advanced product design.

Working as an engineer set Takagi apart from the rest of the office ladies. She stayed at the company until late at night while the other office ladies left for home at five. She worked on engineering problems while the others carried out menial tasks. She spoke in a deeper voice than the others: directly, without giggling. Her new job, however, still retained elements of her old one. She was dressed as an office lady, in a skirt and vest rather than dressing casually like the other women engineers.

I asked Erberto to see if Oda was interested in working on a project with me. Erberto was happy to do so, since by using my technology, everyone could save time. He felt hopeful that Oda would want to work with me, since it was generally felt that Oda dealt with people too directly and was too critical of their work. "So he really likes foreigners," said Erberto. "They have the same mind-set." Japanese managers were often more passive and indirect in their relationships, so although Oda was known to be an excellent engineer, he didn't get along with many of the managers at the company.

While I waited to hear from Erberto, I approached my own boss, Higuchi. He was relaxing in his chair, looking out of the window, with his hands folded on his stomach. It was a clear, sunny day and Higuchi was staring through the window at the mountain. The heavy winds blew a stream of snow from the top of the mountain, and this plume was white against the bright blue sky.

Without turning to me, Higuchi said, "Did you know it's very dangerous to fly near that mountain? Once a jet flew too close to the top, and it was caught in the wind surrounding the mountain and crashed."

I expressed my sympathies for the deceased. There was an awkward silence while I tried to think of a natural way to turn to the topic of interest to me, but I couldn't find it. So I just blurted out: "I'd like to work with Oda and show him the new technology."

Higuchi looked worried. "Those design engineers never listen to my advice. Whenever I have anything new to tell them, they've always been too busy to listen." I told him if the technology was successful that I wouldn't mind starting our own CAD group within the section. Higuchi seemed even more upset with this suggestion. "The problem is if you work on one of their projects, they will ask you to work on another, and another, and then you will be too busy to do our work." I promised him that wouldn't happen, but he continued to resist. I was eventually able to convince him to let me give a simple demonstration of the technology to the Design Section.

Although Higuchi allowed me to meet with Oda, he continued to be negative about working with Oda's group. I wondered why there was all this fuss about what seemed to be a harmless project. I turned to the ever-ready Shiina for answers. He said that the managers in the Design and Research Division did not get along. "Once I worked on a project with the Design Department and Uno found out and got very angry with me," he said. "In a meeting with my group, he pointed his finger at me and yelled, 'Don't you ever work with the Design Department again!' Since then, if it's necessary to work with them, I just do it secretly."

According to Shiina, the conflict started in the mid 1980s when the *gikan* decided that the company needed a separate research department. Previously, research and design existed as one department. When many top engineers were recruited from the design sections, funding became a serious issue, and the research team established itself as an "elite" group. As a result, the two groups spent much time and energy vying for power instead of spending time improving the technology. Communication between the sections practically ceased.

The *gikan* was an extremely powerful manager who provided the company with a technical "vision." The technology he developed had made him a nationally known engineer and industrial leader. His accomplishments were so significant that he received a Blue Ribbon medal from the Japanese government at the Imperial Palace. At Nizumi, he ruled with total authority, making all the major decisions and ordering his subordinates to carry them out without question. The *gikan* was instrumental in Nizumi's success, but when he had retired, it had created a power vacuum, and the design and research directors had intensified their competition for power.

Shiina warned me, "Don't try to build bridges between the two groups." He seemed to think I was casting myself into the role of the troublemaker again, but I was convinced that things would run smoothly. I arranged a meeting with Oda, Erberto, and other engineers from the section. I demonstrated the technology to them, and Oda said, "That's really wonderful, Mehri *san*." Oda became so excited he immediately conferred with Kurata. The plan was for me to write a program that could be used to design the part. When it was complete, I would have another meeting with Oda and his engineers, and then we would talk about the next step.

It took a couple of weeks to develop the technology, and when I made the presentation, Oda again showed incredible interest. He said, "That's great!" and "You are so smart, Mehri *san*."

After the demonstration, Chen, who was one of Oda's favorites, said that

Oda wanted me to join his group. I was flattered, but told him that I wasn't interested, for I had come to like working with Higuchi. Later on, when I talked with Oda about the project again, his plans were vague. I didn't hear from him for several days, and every time I approached him to hold a design meeting, Oda evaded the subject. Finally, I realized that Shiina had been right, after all: you had to choose a division, you could not be in both.

THE CLEVER THIEF

It was the afternoon break, and I was taking my usual stroll with Erberto and Chen on company grounds. I had rolled down my sleeves and folded my arms on my chest in an attempt to fend off the cold. I'd been working with Oda that week, and I felt increasingly uneasy, so I asked Chen about his boss. Chen was not shy about sharing his own frustrations with Oda and his group. For one thing, he was fed up with the barriers to shared information within his work group.

Chen said, "Anytime my colleagues want information, they never come directly to me, they always go to Oda first—even if it's someone in my own group."

The hierarchy required employees to consult with the superior in charge when obtaining technical information or while working on joint projects. In my case, any time an engineer from another section or division needed me to provide them with technical expertise, they always had to talk with Higuchi first. What was odd was that even members of Chen's own group had to contact Oda before talking to Chen.

Chen's field, tribology, was multidisciplinary, so he often had to interact with many engineers from different sections rather than just working with his group. Consequently, Chen often felt isolated. If Shiina had not made his disastrous mistake on returning from America (asking his old boss and not his new one about publishing a technical paper) and if there had not been a power struggle between upper management, Shiina and a few other engineers would all have been working with Chen, which would have made everyone happier. As it was, Chen was constantly frustrated in his attempt to get necessary information from other groups.

I asked, "Why do you think they're so secretive?"

Chen said, "Perhaps it has something to do with Japanese society as a whole. It's all about groups, and if they give information to an outsider, they're afraid it will somehow damage their group."

Erberto and I exchanged wry smiles. We had been similarly frustrated, and we'd thought it was because as Westerners we'd been used to an environment with a much freer flow of information. Since Chen was Chinese, we'd thought he'd been having an easier time at Nizumi, but now he seemed just as frustrated as we were.

Chen went on with his grievances—chief among them, Oda.

"He's such a bully!" interjected Erberto. "When we don't have the right answers to technical questions, he just yells at us, saying we're stupid."

"So why do you always laugh during meetings?" I asked. "It seems like your group is having such fun."

Chen smiled, his pudgy face bulging at the sides. "It's because we're afraid," he said. "When Oda tells a joke, we all feel we must laugh along with him."

After this, I made a point to observe them more closely, and it was true: their laughter was both forced and flat.

"At least Oda's smart," I said now, as we rounded the corner of our building. Oda was known to be innovative and inventive, and he had just won an award from the Japan Society of Automotive Engineers for his contribution to the industry. "Isn't his name on a patent for a drivetrain?"

Chen shook his head in disgust. According to Chen, Oda had actually obtained the idea for the drivetrain while in conversation with an engineer at a conference in Europe. The company that had come up with the idea had patented it in the 1950s but had ignored it ever since. Oda learned that the patent had expired, so he went to the patent office to obtain a copy. He brought it back to the company, developed it further, then obtained a Japanese patent.

"How did you discover this?" I asked Chen.

"At a meeting. The company that had originally patented the technology came to Nizumi to ask if they could license the patent. They didn't know that they themselves had developed the technology many years ago, so Oda told them. You should have seen their faces! They were in shock."

I had to smile imagining that moment. Then we all went back to work.

That afternoon, Yasui, one of Oda's subordinates, appeared at my computer with a problem. He showed me his work, and I was absolutely amazed at how much he had progressed since our last meeting. Yasui had remembered and applied every step I had told him.

I remembered what Erberto had once told me, "The Japanese are data collectors with an incredible memories—but they don't think. They're like computers: you just input the data and they spit it back out at you."

Yasui asked for further information, but I was evasive and said I was busy with another project. After what I had just heard, I didn't want Oda to get hold of everything I was working on. But Yasui was persistent. He approached me the following day to show me a very specific problem with his program. Then he brought mine up and began comparing the two.

I was surprised, since I hadn't given him a copy of my program. Nor had he asked for it. He had just gone into my directory and copied my files without my permission. Abruptly, I got up and found Higuchi. I said I was very unhappy at how Oda was handling the project—sending Yasui over to steal and copy my work.

Higuchi was confused. "Why is that a problem? It's a good way for Yasui to learn."

Now I was confused. I returned to my desk and asked the ever-accommodating Shiina for an explanation. Shiina said, "One thing you have to understand is that in Asia there is very little understanding of confidentiality or of individual rights as related to original ideas. Most ideas are associated with a group, and if you do not claim them as your own, then they belong to the group."

I shook my head, bewildered.

Shiina continued. "But you're right to watch out for Oda. He's notorious for stealing other people's ideas. A lot of people think he's a great engineer, and there's no doubt that he is highly skilled, but he's not world class because he has moved up in the company mostly by stealing technology."

"From who?"

"Mostly from parts manufacturers but also from other Nizumi engineers. I think he may even steal at night when there's no one around." He waved his hand across our section.

I was appalled. "If he steals from engineers at the company—what do they *do*?"

"Usually nothing—because it wouldn't make any difference. Oda's most useful trait is he's able to produce results very quickly for the top managers, so they like him and don't care what he does."

"But how about the parts suppliers?" I asked in dismay. "Won't they refuse to sell to the company if he keeps stealing from them?"

"They don't trust him, but if he guarantees that they can sell parts to the company, then they don't really mind. He's good for their sales reports."

After my discussion with Shiina, I thought about my interaction with Oda over the weeks and realized I had been conned from the very beginning. Oda had tried to get me to join his group, but when I rejected this idea, he had told Yasui to learn the technology so Oda could claim it as his own. In the meantime, Oda had made sure that I remained compliant and happy by flattering me in front of management.

The technology could not have been patented, and I understood that any of my innovations at the company would be shared. What bothered me was the deception.

Shiina suggested that in order for others to know that I had developed the technology, I should write a report about my work and circulate it around the office. This struck me as a good idea, so I wrote the report for my own protection.

BRAINSTORMING AND MINING FOR NEW IDEAS

Soon after I finished working with Oda's group, Abe asked to "borrow" me for one of his projects. Uno wasn't happy about it, but he had no choice. Abe outranked him.

I was assigned to work with a young engineer named Suzuki. He had no experience in this field, so he was very grateful to have me join his group. When we first met, he bowed deeply and said, "Onegai shimasu." This translates literally as, "Please do me a favor," but it really means "Thank you very much."

We engaged in friendly conversation, and I learned about his background. His father had worked at a Japanese trading company in Tanzania, and as a child, Suzuki had lived in Africa for three years. To this day, he missed Africa—the beautiful countryside, the kindness of the Tanzanians, the easygoing life. He asked if I liked my life in Japan. I said I did. He was incredulous. "Really? Life here isn't so great. The city is crowded, the air is polluted, and the cost of living is so high."

By now I felt much the same way, but I always said I liked living in Japan— it was the *tatemae* reply.

I was excited to be working on this new project with Suzuki. It involved designing a device to reduce the aerodynamic drag of the vehicle. The aerodynamic drag is the amount of force pushing against a vehicle in the opposite direction to which the car is moving. Reducing the drag results in better gas mileage. Although drag reducers existed in the industry, Nizumi had never designed one, so we would have to start from scratch (or so I thought).

For inspiration, I consulted my fluid mechanics textbook. I thought about the basic physics of the design problem and worked out some equations. After a few days, I approached Higuchi with my ideas. (Although this was Abe's project, since Higuchi was my boss, I had to go to him.) Higuchi looked at me askance and demanded, "How do you know this? We've never designed a drag-reducer before."

Now I was confused. Hadn't he expected me to use my engineering education and experience to develop a creative design? No, he had not. The next day I discovered the approach he preferred. Suzuki walked into the office with a large cardboard poster showing pictures of all of the drag-reducing products currently used in the industry. He'd gotten these pictures from industry magazines. Higuchi got very excited and studied each one, while Suzuki looked on proudly. It was an excellent display; the color photographs revealed every detail of the products. We discussed the merits of some specific designs, then Higuchi told us to create CAD models and analyze them using computational fluid dynamics (CFD) software on all of them so we could compare them and see which was best.

Many companies were using CFD as a way to simulate the physics of fluid flow on products to improve efficiency before building prototypes. For example, if you were to design the outer shell of an automobile, you would analyze the shape to ensure that the drag was low. A car that is boxy has a higher drag than a car that has many smooth curves. In the past, engineers had to rely entirely on wind tunnels to measure the drag. This process was very costly because it required building many prototypes. With the increase of computer power, the model could be tested using CAD models to investigate its shape before building a prototype for the wind tunnel. This process dramatically reduced costs and an added benefit was that we could see the airflow around the model using 3D graphical displays to pinpoint exactly where problems occurred.

The process of comparing designs is commonly referred to as benchmarking. Benchmarking was the topic of the next department meeting. Uno announced we would benchmark a European competitor's product, which was rumored to incorporate the most advanced technology in the industry. Erberto was thrilled at the prospect. After the meeting, he insisted I accompany him on a walk while he talked about various design possibilities. He often asked me to escort him at times like this, when he paced and thought aloud and illustrated his ideas with his hands. On these occasions, I learned much about automobile design, for Erberto's passion for car engineering far surpassed my own, and he would discuss every detail with utter fascination. As a child, I had been intrigued by how things were put together, but as an adult I was more excited by computer technology.

When we entered the chop shop later that day, my mouth dropped. Enormous effort had been expended in displaying how the European design compared with the Nizumi's and other competitor's similar products. Large, excruciatingly detailed charts filled the walls, comparing efficiency, gas mileage and other indicators. All the relevant parts had been cut up and placed on a table for us to examine. Each part was compared with the corresponding parts of the competition's products. The benchmark was so thorough that there was even a comparison of the number of bolts used to put the products together. All parts on display were documented and filed on the intranet so that any engineer in the company could have access to the information at any time. Erberto and I were amazed.

At Nizumi, benchmarking was a crucial part of the design process. During design meetings, each engineer was required to show the main design parameters for the optimal design of the product. For example, if product efficiency was the main criterion, the chart would be a spreadsheet consisting of the design parameters in the columns and the manufacturer's design of that parameter in the rows, with each cell containing the numerical efficiency. Each design parameter was graded according to efficiency, cost, and ease of manufacture. From this information, a preliminary prototype was produced, and after further investigation, the final prototype made. Then the engineers would improve the design in the technical lab or on the computer by tweaking various design parameters and adding new technology when needed. After further testing, the part was then manufactured.

Benchmarking was used at all levels of product development: in research and development, in product design, and in market analysis. It was not necessarily used to copy other products but was thought to speed up the design process. Analysis of and experiment on an existing product was the basic approach to designing a new one. There were several technicians at the company, such as Hirama, whose only job was to take apart the competitor's products, test them, and write up the results for engineers.

Abe was planning a brainstorming meeting for the new drag reducer Nizumi would produce. I spent many days thinking of the basic physics of the product and engaging in analysis. When the day came, Abe called on each of us to present our new product designs. I was surprised when all the other engineers brought in designs of products that had already been developed or manufactured by other companies. Suzuki and another engineer showed a design that came from a company's brochure. When my turn came, I presented some novel ideas based on my analysis alone. My proposals were not as clever as some of the others, but they were certainly more original.

After my recent experience when I had designed something from scratch, thereby shocking Higuchi, I should not have been surprised when the other engineers took me to task for doing it now. Their approach to problem solving was completely different from mine. They had been educated to engage in an inductive process, while as an American-educated engineer, I had been trained to use deduction. Deductive reasoning and abstract ideas were crucial to who I was as a Westerner. Engineers at Nizumi, however, had to rely on previously documented engineering results when they set about creating a new design.

It occurred to me that the inductive process, along with the authoritarian hierarchy and a disinclination to engage in debate, was one reason why Nizumi was rarely innovative. When it came to the details of a design, the Japanese were brilliant, but when it came to creativity, they were disappointing. Several Japanese engineers themselves agreed that they were "good at manufacturing products but terrible at innovation."

Although genuinely new ideas were rare at the company, management policies theoretically rewarded innovation, and we were often pressured to produce patent submissions. Uno talked about the heat he was receiving from Abe, who was pressing for more submissions from our section. He intended to use these to evaluate us as workers. A bitter look came to Higuchi's face, and the excitable Takanashi jumped up and started arguing with Uno. Takanashi was unique in that he did not fear speaking his mind. On and on he went, cheeks flushing as he jabbered one confusing remark after the next. But I understood his drift. His work was to develop computer code, so he would never be submitting a patent, and he didn't want this to hurt his evaluation.

Suzuki asked me one day if I had submitted any patents. I told him I had been too busy working on my computer programs, but he told me it didn't have to take much time. He reached into a folder and showed me one of his patent submissions. He said he had plucked the idea for it off the internet.

As we buddied up and talked more about company matters he asked me how I got along with Higuchi.

"He's a nice guy," I said. This was true. I genuinely liked Higuchi, although he wasn't ambitious or adventurous. He just wanted to do his job, get paid, and go home.

"My boss and I don't get along," Suzuki said. "Watanabe is truly a good person but he is not very patient." I had sensed there was something amiss with Suzuki. There were times when he did not show up to work on time or was absent. Once while preparing data for a meeting, he came to me and said, "I must leave the company early, I am feeling sick." This happened quite often, and since I didn't understand the severity of his problems, I complained to Higuchi because I had been left to prepare for the meetings on my own. Another time when Suzuki was getting ready to go abroad with his boss, I asked Higuchi why Suzuki seemed so anxious. "It's the first time that Suzuki has ever gone abroad," Higuchi said. I knew this was not the true reason for Suzuki's anxiety. His problems began when he'd been transferred from the electronics to the mechanical engineering department. He worked at a job in which he had received little training and, under the new company policies of judging employees according to their performance, he was not doing well.

The next day, I discussed the issue of patents with Higuchi. He said that the company required each engineer to submit three patents a year, but most of the submissions weren't any good. "You, Mehri *san,* don't have to submit anything," he told me, "but if you do submit a patent, just make sure it is viable. Hirama once submitted a patent for a vehicle that had two dimensions. It was long while it was being driven, but it could become smaller when it was time to park." He laughed loudly, tilting back in his chair so his stomach rubbed against the edge of his desk. "That was really stupid," he gasped between bursts of laughter. His hilarity was infectious, and soon we were all laughing with him, even those who hadn't heard what he had said.

One thing which surprised and pleased me at Nizumi was everybody's eagerness to embrace new technology. Management always urged us to incorporate the latest technology in the drivetrain product. Although Abe was a high-level manager, he actively researched the new technologies. His primary sources of information were Western consulting firms, American and European universities, and technical conferences. Western consulting firms helped Abe decide which technologies to develop, and he handed this information to his subordinates, who determined whether the technology was viable for the manufacturing process. It was as if learning new technology was the duty of every Nizumi engineer, and the organization supported this attitude for fear that the competition would gain market share. This forward-looking policy, however, did not apply to all departments—as witness the notorious casting plant.

"FLOWERS IN THE SHOP"

One day, Erberto came to my desk and told me that Takagi was quitting the company. We were not surprised. Although she had worked as an engineer for nine years, since she had started work as an office lady and had no university training, it was unlikely that she was properly compensated. Perhaps that was why she still dressed like an office lady. Company gossip was that she wanted to move back to the small village where she had been raised to take care of her aging parents. In Japan, children have an obligation to look after their elderly parents, so this may have been the case. But no one really knew the truth. Takagi may have just been leaving an unrewarding situation.

I had always been fascinated by Takagi's unique position at the company, so I asked Higuchi what he thought of her. "She's a hard worker," he said. "I heard that although she always had to work late, she qualified for technical diplomas in a variety of fields. She must be very smart."

Takagi came by to say good-bye to those she had worked with. Her office lady colleagues bought her a bouquet of roses, and a group picture was taken in which they surrounded Takagi and her flowers. Later that day, Oda took her and the engineering group out to a farewell drinking party where her teammates gave nostalgic speeches about working with Takagi.[23]

Company literature at Nizumi revealed interesting gender distinctions. The newsletter included a regular section titled "Becoming a Working Person." This was a short question and answer write-up of both women and men of the company. In one newsletter, the three women questioned responded to the mandate "Introduce Yourself" by saying "I look shy but I am really courageous," "I look like a man, but I am really a woman," and "I am cheerful and merry." The two men queried responded with "I am a sportsman" and "I am striving to be a responsible person." They were all asked: What would you like to experience as a member of society? In response, one woman discussed her love for the piano and said she wanted to "touch many people's hearts through music." Another woman responded that she in-

---

[23] Current research has revealed how Japanese companies effectively coerce women to leave their positions. The policy exists as an unwritten rule. An office lady is expected to quit the company at about age of twenty-five to marry a company man. "One example was the custom for a clerical-track woman to leave the company upon marrying a fellow banker," writes Yuko Ogasawara in her study of the office ladies at Tozai Bank. When she asked the office ladies whether it was a company rule to marry young and quit work, they responded that it was "expected" behavior. See Yuko Ogasawara, *Office Ladies and Salaried Men* (Berkeley: University of California Press, 1998), 33.

tended to show gratitude to her parents who had taken care of her until she was an adult. The responses of the men were quite different. One man said, "I have learned from my *senpai* that my purpose in life is to be a wonderful and responsible person." The other man said, "I would like to receive various certificates for business and challenge myself to do many things at the company." The male answers were significantly more goal-oriented and concerned with their long-term position at the company. These responses are not surprising since most women were not expected to stay long at the company and hence were more inclined to seek personal fulfillment elsewhere, often as a good wife, mother, and daughter.[24]

I had observed the role of women at the office ever since starting work at Nizumi, and I had noticed that some women with engineering degrees were not assigned jobs commensurate with their credentials. What about the women who worked in the factory? Were they working up to their potential?

The safety newsletter featured a kimono-clad factory-worker in a temple with her hands in prayer position. It read "Welcome all freshman, at the beginning of the year we are all praying for no accidents."

---

[24] Mary Brinton provides quantitative data to show the severity of sex segregation at large Japanese companies such as Nizumi. See Mary Brinton, *Women and the Economic Miracle* (Berkeley: University of California Press, 1993), 156.

Women in the line, of course, neither wore kimonos to work nor spent their days praying in temple. What was their life really like?

Suzuki and I took a trip to the factory. On the way, I saw a petite young woman driving a large truck. She had a ponytail that hung down from under a baseball cap onto a soiled one-piece company overall. Suzuki said that female factory workers were increasing in numbers because "women in Japan are becoming stronger." I thought the more likely reason was the high cost of living in Japan. As in America, one breadwinner per family was no longer enough. We arrived at the factory, and we looked at a few parts. I saw a couple of women working on the line, and they seemed to be doing much the same kind of work as the men.

The newsletters reveal that these women have a double mandate. They are supposed to do the job as well as men (except in a few jobs requiring great physical strength), and they are also supposed to display their femininity. An

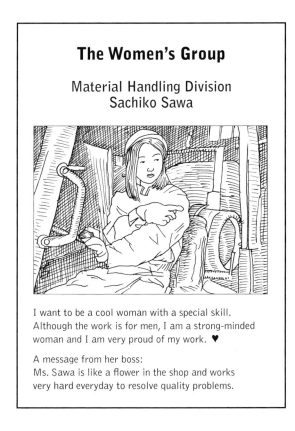

The Women's Group

Material Handling Division
Sachiko Sawa

I want to be a cool woman with a special skill. Although the work is for men, I am a strong-minded woman and I am very proud of my work. ♥

A message from her boss:
Ms. Sawa is like a flower in the shop and works very hard everyday to resolve quality problems.

example is the article from the Women's Group that appeared in the safety magazine.

In another newsletter story, a female factory worker is described as "a very good worker because she uses her sensitivity to solve work-related problems." The newsletter often praises women workers—and patronizes them—by concentrating on their innate feminine characteristics rather than on their work skills.

Women in the factory have to overcome the stigma of working in a traditionally male environment. In one article, a new recruit writes, "When I first started working here, although I did not know, I was called 'monkey,' but I now have learned how to deal with it." At first she had trouble with the physical work and often used the transceiver to call for help. "Now I am able to carry a pipe wrench, which is two-thirds of my height." She says she still gets dirty on the factory line, but "those who think I am no longer a woman are very wrong. In fact, I take care of my skin with cream."

The monthly company newsletter always included an article about an employee who worked on the line. Among all the issues I received, only a few featured a woman worker. One was about a woman who worked in the materials department. She had trouble with some of the physical demands. "Regardless of having the knowledge about my job, sometimes there are situations where I do not have the power to lift heavy material," she said. Luckily, "everyone works in a very friendly atmosphere. For example, if there is a heavy part that I cannot lift, a male employee will carry it for me." Many women factory workers need occasional assistance because they do not possess a man's body, a recurrent theme in the newsletter. To me, the emphasis of this problem in the newsletter implies management belief in the inherent weakness of women. The stories are designed to make one wonder whether or not women should be working on the line at all.

All the stories about female factory workers reveal the same pattern: low self-esteem, problems with heavy work, and difficulties in engaging in the "process" of work. Being teased or called "monkey," and being "scolded by my boss" are elements of on-the-job-training that indicate the difficulty of working in a basically male environment. Some women factory workers feel the need to apologize for being female. They try to be "cool" women (attractive and popular) as opposed to "strong" women (brash and aggressive). In contrast, in the same series of articles, male employees talk about their work with confidence and assume that they will be productive long-term Nizumi employees. They do not worry about being cool.

I wondered about the impact of the women workers on the male employees and whether the women were treated with respect. I asked Suzuki about it. Suzuki seemed more sensitive and less overtly manly than the other men. He was tall and lanky with a skinny face, and he did not speak in a deep voice the way so many Japanese men did.

Suzuki said, "Sexual harassment is a big problem at Japanese companies. Recently, our own Human Resources Department opened a hotline where women can discuss sexual harassment issues in confidence. If a man sexually harasses a woman, he is given a warning. If he does it again, he is fired."

When I first started working at Nizumi, the Mitsubishi sex scandal in Normal, Illinois, was making headlines in America. In 1996 a group of women working on the line at the Mitsubishi plant filed a lawsuit against the company for lack of regard to protect their rights against sexual harassment. My friends from back home had to tell me all about it, because Japanese media initially did not consider it to be important. Shiina said that in Japan, human rights are not thought to be of major importance.

Still, the union at Nizumi was interested in learning about the extent of the problem, and it distributed a questionnaire to all union members, publishing the results in the union newsletter. An act of harassment in the office was defined as a male employee staring at or touching a woman, or hanging up nude pictures in the office. The results showed that 75 percent of the women and 62 percent of the men surveyed said they knew of someone who had experienced sexual harassment. In response to the question "Have you experienced sexual harassment?" 52 percent of the women and 17 percent of the men said yes. While most of the harassment incidents involved rude jokes and sexually oriented questions, a quarter involved being touched, and 4 percent of the women said they had been forced to have sex with a superior.

The questionnaire asked, "After experiencing sexual harassment, with whom did you consult?" Virtually none of the workers consulted with the union; most replied that they spoke about harassment only to their close friends. The union exhorted victims of sexual harassment to contact the union and stressed the importance of saying "no" when sexual harassment occurs. The article maintained that men in a high position engage in sexual harassment because of their "need to use power. Many women can't protest because their harasser may be highly placed at the company." The responses to the questionnaire reveal that occasionally a woman cannot get a raise or a promotion unless she has sex with her boss.

ON THE EDGE OF A NERVOUS BREAKDOWN

As we worked on the drag reducer together, I got to know Suzuki and gain his trust. Soon the young engineer was telling me his problems. Before he spoke, he always said, "Please do not tell others." I assured him he could talk to me in confidence. He said he was receiving help from the Mental Health Clinic because he was having troubles with his boss, Watanabe, who showed little interest in developing Suzuki's engineering skills. Suzuki had been trained as an electronics engineer, so he knew little about mechanical engineering. He had tremendous difficulty getting up to speed with the basics because of his failing relationship with Watanabe, who should have functioned as his mentor. (Indeed, I had to do most of the work Suzuki should have done.) Frustrated and depressed, Suzuki claimed his boss spent too much time criticizing him and not enough time teaching him.

The plan proposed by the doctors was that Suzuki would continue to see them and, if necessary, have counseling with Watanabe to discuss their problems together. "Watanabe's boss thinks this is a good idea," Suzuki continued. "They will not move me to another group unless my condition worsens or I indicate that I want to kill myself." I was naturally taken aback by this mention of suicide, which seemed rather extreme as a response to office politics.

Maintaining mental health among the employees was an important management issue at Nizumi. The Department of Health and Safety distributed a brochure to all workers titled "Relax Go Go." It said that the theme of the month was to "relax." There were many ways to relax, it said. "Watching videos and seeing the seven weeds of autumn will allow your mind to heal." The brochure said that the best videos were those that showed scenes of ocean life, for "the movement of the waves makes humans feel comfortable, and the blue ocean has a calming effect on our minds." The "seven weeds of autumn" were defined as "objects of appreciation" that could be found in the temples, gardens, and flower parks in the ancient cities of Japan. The brochure ended with an exhortation—"Let's forget our busy life and relax our mind to find the seven weeds of autumn."

I don't know whether Suzuki found the seven weeds of autumn, but his situation continued to deteriorate. They moved his desk to our section so he could experience a change in environment. Some of the men introduced themselves to him, and he felt fairly comfortable. Shortly afterward, however, he moved back to his earlier section because he thought he might get along better with Watanabe, now that Abe and Human Resources personnel had spoken to him. But Suzuki was wrong, and he kept on being bullied. One day, he pulled me out to the hall and told me, as he had several times before, that he was going to take the rest of the day off to rest. By now, Suzuki had lost a lot of weight and had developed a terrible twitch in his left eye.

As in all design projects at Nizumi, designing the drag reducer involved analyzing many different existing options. Once we obtained the benchmark results, we used the information to create a set of new designs, which we narrowed down to a few possibilities. At this point, Suzuki contacted Abe, and we all sat down for a discussion. One good thing about working at Nizumi was that an engineer could always talk with a superior right away about engineering results. Abe asked Suzuki for the CAD pictures of the designs and the aerodynamic simulation results using the CFD software. He placed them on the table in the order of best to worst.

Looking at each design in detail, Abe sighed. He turned at me and said, "It's too bad that the winner is our chief competitor." I was amazed at his frankness. Abe said to me, "Take this data and think of a better design. Don't talk to Higuchi about it—do it on your own."

Naturally, I was thrilled to be given this task. He wanted to tap into my creative ability, which my American training had fostered, and I was ready for the challenge.

Alas, Suzuki had not made as good an impression with Abe as I had. Abe had expected Suzuki to be conducting most of the analyses, but he hadn't been educated to do so, and Watanabe had never offered to train him.

Suzuki's problem highlighted a number of important issues at Nizumi. When engineers entered the company, they were relatively ignorant. I once befriended a young engineer while we worked on a project. He felt embarrassed because he was fumbling with the technology. He explained that the reason he lacked good engineering skills was that he had not studied in college. I was surprised because all engineering students in America have to work hard to get through their programs. I asked my young friend what he had done during his four years in college instead of studying. "I played tennis and mahjong," he said. He claimed it was typical of college students to live a relaxed and pleasant life. What surprised me further was that he was a graduate of Keio University, one of Japan's top universities.

I turned to Erberto and Shiina, who had each experienced university systems in both Japan and the West. They both said that Japanese universities offered terrible training for engineers. Shiina said, "In Japan there is little discussion and no debate at all. A student is supposed to learn by memorization alone. You don't ask questions, and you are supposed to applaud and be grateful to your superiors."

I asked, "If you don't ask questions, how can you learn?"

Shiina laughed. "You are supposed to learn by absorption through your skin."

Nonetheless, college life was so congenial that "most students don't want to graduate early or even on time. They want to stay in school as long as possible. It's not unusual for a student to take six years to graduate. I once had a classmate who wanted to stay in school another year. He decided to flunk all his courses, so he went into his exams, signed his name and turned the exams into the professors without writing a thing—but they passed him."

"What? They passed him?"

"Yeah. The school doesn't want students to stay around too long. They needed to get rid of him." I was flabbergasted. Shiina had also graduated from a high-level university, one of best in Japan. I thought his example was probably extreme, but it showed that you could get your degree without being qualified in your field. Therefore, it was especially important to have a healthy relationship with your mentor at your company, the person who could actually teach you how to do your job.

It was obvious why Japanese college students wanted to stay in school as long as they could. What kind of life did they have when they left and got a job? Twelve-hour workdays with an hour commute in the morning and an hour commute at night—and little chance of a break for the rest of their lives. Life was hard at a Japanese company.

THE PURPOSE OF TECHNICAL MEETINGS

One day, Watanabe called a group of us together to discuss the drag reducer. He brought in the analysis information that Suzuki and I had worked on. A design manager contributed extremely detailed drawings showing exactly how the product should be designed. An engineer from the industrial design group brought in his own set of drawings.

It was Watanabe's project, so he directed the meeting and spoke first, presenting the analysis information. Then the design manager took the floor and we discussed his drawings. A technician remarked that a design would be difficult to include because of noise problems. Other engineers wanted a feature that would benefit the customer, while the design guys wanted to make the vehicle more efficient. The meeting went on and on as we discussed in minute detail every aspect of the product—while continually making comparisons to competitor products.

Watanabe took out a chart showing the number of vehicles that would include the drag reducer and the number that would not. He held up another detailed chart, comparing the drag reducer with all the other products Nizumi made. Both charts were incredibly beautiful, with neatly drawn, detailed illustrations of the drag reducer.

Finally, Watanabe pointed to pictures on the chart and said, "O.K., let's try this one, that one, and this one." I was glad we were finally getting somewhere.

Toward the end of the meeting, a design engineer asked me to do a calculation to decide an optimal radius for the product. He showed me a 2D drawing and said, "We're thinking of changing the radius 0.5 mm." He pointed to a picture of a competitor drag reducer product and said, "We think maybe this radius is best, but we're not sure."

In fact, changing the radius of our project a mere 0.5 mm would have little affect on the aerodynamic drag. I thought he was nuts, but I was working with Japanese engineers, and I was no longer surprised when they got bogged down in minutiae while overlooking basic physics. Instead of trying to demonstrate why the calculation was not worth pursuing, I decided to take the middle ground. I said, "Look, I'll check out this 0.5 mm change, but modeling it in 3D is going to take too much time. What if we do it in 2D?" He agreed. My many months of working with Higuchi had taught me not to argue with superiors, especially if our basic methodology diverged.

Uno's technical meetings were as tedious as ever. All members of the section were required to attend, and I hated having to drag my body to a two-hour meeting that was almost entirely useless. Week after week, our meetings followed the same pattern—a young engineer would make a presentation, then Uno and his close subordinates (Scarface, Shiga, and Jimbo) would mock his mistakes in the hopes of shaming him to become a better engineer. It was very Japanese to use embarrassment as a management tool. What should have been amiable conversation about technical issues always became a personal assault.

I sometimes wondered why I myself was never bullied at one of Uno's meetings. Was it due to my excellent job performance? I finally learned that it was related to the hierarchy and to Uno's insecurity about being younger than most of the managers one level below him. Most of them had once been his superiors, so to exert his present authority, now he mocked their underlings. But my boss, Higuchi, was younger than Uno and therefore posed no threat, so I was not harassed.

Hiraga, however, did pose a threat to Uno. Once when he had just returned from a conference in America, he reported on what he had seen of the latest technology. During his presentation, he seemed a bit confused about which technique had enhanced which vehicle. Uno interrupted Hiraga's presentation to point this out, and they argued back and forth. Hiraga stood his ground and rebutted whatever Uno said. Back and forth it went without cease. I was amazed at how long the argument lasted—I timed it at exactly one hour. It surprised me to see a junior manager arguing heatedly with his boss, and I wondered whether it would aid or hurt Hiraga's position at Nizumi.

When I returned to my computer to get back to work, I noticed that Hirama was now sitting all alone at his section. The other unproductive employee had been moved away from Hirama. I asked Kume what he thought about Hirama and he said, "I feel sorry for him." I sat down at my computer but I could not keep Hirama off my mind. That day, a young technician from an outside group came to me for advice about computer simulation. I told him what had happened to Hirama and pointed him out, all alone in a sea of desks. The young technician got up, walked over, and had a good look at Hirama. Upon his return, he just smiled and said, "It's the Japanese way."

HOW MANAGERS ARE CHOSEN

The day for the end-of-year promotions and rotations was announced, and I asked Higuchi what would happen.

"There will be some shifting around in the company but not much in our section," he said. Managers were sometimes shifted around when their skills were needed in another department.

I asked, "How is one selected to become a manager?"

"The selection process is decided from above, and at Nizumi, like at all

Japanese companies, it is done behind closed doors. These meetings are not like engineering meetings which are open to everyone responsible."

"Who chooses the section managers?"

"The company directors. And after they are chosen, the section managers are given almost complete freedom to run their sections. If they do good work they will continue to move up in the company."

Higuchi was becoming impatient with my questioning, but I was able to squeeze in one more question about how employees are notified that they will be promoted to a managerial position.

Higuchi said, "After the decision has been made, the employee will usually be told a few months in advance so he can prepare." If he is being shifted to another group or section, he has to finish his project and write a final report, and if he is sent to another city, he has to find an apartment as well. Higuchi continued, "But he is told not to tell anyone else in the company so as not to create confusion and jealousy among his co-workers."

"By the way," he said, "a new engineer from Germany will be entering our section. He's a graduate of the Tokyo Institute of Technology."

I was pleased to hear this, as diversity always made life at work more interesting.

Higuchi's prediction proved correct—only one engineer was shifted to another position. Baba was being sent to Toyota, to work on engineering projects that were important for both firms. In addition, a few engineers were promoted. After the meeting, we all returned to our desks, and I asked Shiina about his own position. After he returned from America, Shiina's work at Nizumi had suffered, which was not surprising since he was basically working on his own in a company (and a country) where working in groups was the norm. Shiina was disappointed that a number of people of his age were being promoted while he remained static. He knew it was because he wasn't part of a group.

END-OF-YEAR DRINKING PARTIES

Naturally, a good-bye party was held for Baba, who was being sent to a Toyota research lab in another part of Japan. He would probably be gone from Nizumi two or three years and he would be working two hundred miles away. If an employee had to relocate, his family typically remained behind, so Baba would have to live far from his home during the week. This living arrangement is called *tanshin funin*. Baba might be able to visit his family on weekends, but this was by no means guaranteed.

Baba had worked on a project in Hiraga's group for more than two years. He'd had no formal training for this kind of work, and as a result his progress had been nil. I had often seen him at the computer, scratching his head in frustration, and he had sometimes come to me for advice on the most basic concepts. Fortunately, he'd been reassigned to a project for which he was prepared, but at the cost of exile from his home.

During the party, each of us made a good-bye speech. When it was Hiraga's turn, he recalled meeting Baba and working with him. He ended by saying (rather cruelly, I thought), "If you stay away from your daughter too long, she will forget you." Mochida, who was sitting near me, turned to a few of us and said, "His wife will forget him, too." He gave a cynical laugh. "One day, he will travel all that distance to be with his wife, and he will find her making love to another guy!" The men laughed, but soon became somber. They knew that one day they too could be sent away, far from their wives and children.

Abe suddenly entered the party, holding a big silver bowl full of sake. It was so large that he carried it carefully with both hands to make sure it wouldn't spill. He made a good luck speech, took a swig from the bowl, and passed it on. Each of us took a swig and passed it to the next person, but suddenly, Sawa, a manager from another section in our division, grabbed the bowl and upended it. In one breath, he drank all the remaining sake. His face flushed red, and he mumbled unintelligibly. Then he sat beside Uno, who was not at all friendly to him. Although Sawa had behaved like a boor, I was surprised to see Uno being so rude. I asked Kurasawa about it. Apparently Uno and Sawa were rivals, and it was very likely that in the future they would battle each other to head the division.

Shortly after the good-bye party, Hans, the German, arrived on the scene. He started work on April Fool's day, two years to the day after my own arrival. Hans was mild mannered and obedient—certainly in comparison to a "trouble-maker" like me! He had been working at a university in Japan and had been introduced to the company by his boss, a famous professor who had a close connection to the company. Hans was assigned to Hiraga's group, and Hiraga organized a welcoming party, which occurred in a more timely manner than mine had. I was curious as to what kind of relationship they would have. Hans seemed to be a very serious engineer, and the match up with casual Old Droopy Eyes, as Hiraga was sometimes called, might not work out well.

When I arrived at the party, Dr. Zombie told me I was late. "But by only five minutes," I replied. Things were a bit awkward, because it turned out that Hans did not drink—not a drop. They thought it was strange that he abstained, and some thought he must be allergic to alcohol, as some Japanese are. Others thought he might be a former drinker and be judgmental about what we drank. Nevertheless, the party soon became lively.

We all took turns introducing ourselves in a jocular manner. Laughter erupted from one part of the room or another, as the men interrupted the speakers to tease them. Then the party organizer popped a video into the karaoke machine. I took the opportunity to tease Dr. Zombie about his liking the song called "Diana." I warbled words from the song—"I'm so young and you're so old." He gave one of his wonderful, robust laughs. It filled the room with festivity. I had come to realize that Dr. Zombie could sometimes be very convivial. Then it was my turn to speak. I said a few words, and then Dr. Zombie began asking me about my love life (of course).

"Tell us about your girlfriend," he said

"Ask one of my colleagues," I responded, "They know more about it than I do."

"Tell us what you like about living in Japan."

"Kaiten sushi," I responded. Laughter filled the room. The boys found my liking for *kaiten sushi* to be hilarious, for these are budget restaurants.

"What about your private life, what have you been doing?"

"Climbing mountains," I said. "In fact I saw you on top of Mount Yakone a few months ago." It was true. Dr. Zombie and Hirama attended an English language school, and they had gone on a group excursion with the class. Dr. Zombie and Hirama were apparently good friends and liked studying English together.

Hiraga burst into song, imitating Tony Bennett's version of "I left my heart in San Francisco."

An unknown man from the party next door suddenly shouted "Ahhh ooooh." This was immediately followed by the thud of a falling body. More screams from the party next door, which had reached a sort of festive rage, clapping and singing. Our group was not the only rowdy one that night.

When Hiraga finished his song, he remarked that the company was *katai* (tough). Perhaps there had been some repercussions from that hour-long argument he had had with Uno.

After a little while, Hiraga asked if anyone wanted to go to a "snack bar." "I know a place filled with pretty Filipino women," he said, blowing smoke out from his nostrils, as he sometimes did. Until now, I had rejected such offers, but I thought it might be interesting, so this time I went with a handful of others.

The "snack bar" was located on a quaint side street. As we approached, Dr. Zombie reminisced about frequenting it as a young man. His wiry hair swung in the strong breeze, so it looked as if Bozo the Clown had walked into a hurricane. Then we walked in. The manager was an older woman wearing a flamboyant, purplish robe and sparkles on her face. Christmas tree lights and tinsel hung on the upper corners of the walls. The place reminded me of some of the old blues joints I frequented while living in New York City. I looked around for the pretty women, but they weren't there—not that night, at least.

Soon, Dr. Zombie was singing his favorite song. One of the men bought a bottle of *shōchū*, a potato-based liquor with such a strong punch that it is undrinkable unless mixed with tea or juice. We talked and laughed and drank for hours more.

I walked home through the winding streets, intoxicated and exhausted. Passing trucks coated my sweaty body with soot from their exhaust. It was late April, and the cherry trees would soon blossom.

THIRD YEAR

CHALLENGE LEAVE

When I arrived at work the next day, Suzuki and I had to go to the technical center to look at the prototype that was being built for the experiments for the drag reducer project. As we walked into the courtyard, Suzuki outlined a new cost-saving plan announced by the company. It was called "challenge leave." As a result of the economic downturn, the company was trying to retrench, so they offered any interested employee over the age of thirty the chance to leave the company and receive 60 percent of his or her pay for one year (not including the annual bonus) toward education for a new job. If enough employees did not take the "challenge leave" (and "enough" was never defined), management said that a 60 percent pay cut would be applied to all employees at the company.

Suzuki said that, if not for his wife and two children, he would take the challenge leave and go to America to learn English; now he felt stuck at Nizumi. He said that it was likely that many of the younger employees would take the challenge leave and get jobs at other companies. However, the older employees (above age of thirty-five) would probably stay, as they would have trouble finding new jobs.

"But why?" I protested. "If these people are skilled they would certainly be valuable to another company."

"It isn't like that," said Suzuki. "Many of them do not have high-level skills that will land them good jobs at other companies. The average salaryman does not focus on one job, but works on many projects throughout his career. This allows him to obtain a broad experience—but nothing he can transfer to another company." The situation was especially grim because Japanese companies don't hire anyone from a competitor. So even if you are a specialist, designing, say, drag reducers, there are only a handful of other companies that make a similar product, and they are all competitors. Your only real option is to work at a small parts company within the *keiretsu* but that almost always means getting a pay cut and receiving fewer benefits.

Another consideration when changing jobs in Japan is that your bonus is based upon your seniority. If you find a job at a new company, your many years of work at your previous job are not taken into consideration, nor the time you have taken to build up your skills. This was another reason workers dreaded restructuring, which was usually just another word for "downsizing."

"Anyway," said Suzuki, "in this depression, who's hiring? I wish I knew."

When we returned to the office he asked me, as he often did, not to tell others about our conversation.

That afternoon, I asked Higuchi about the company's problems. He said that management had overestimated the profits for April and May and so had no choice but to reduce costs by 35 percent more than planned. The board of directors started to meet every month to find ways to cut costs. The Toyota directors decided to inspect the technology in each Nizumi division to evaluate current production capabilities. How many jobs they would cut was inversely related to how much they liked the technology.

Higuchi asked if I would make a display of my work to show the directors when they came to our company. I was happy to oblige. One project I could show them was my automatic CAD programs.

The day of the visit, Oda behaved like a schoolboy attending his first sports game—and like the coach, as well. Kurata personally approached me about showing my work, and Oda was very impressed. For the rest of the morning, he joked with me, and he placed my presentation beside his. I took out a sandwich and unwrapped it. As I bit into it, Oda said, "jokingly," "You don't want to get caught eating a sandwich when the Toyota directors come around to see our work."

"Just give me some warning," I said, "and I'll swallow the mouthful and hide all the evidence."

"Ha, ha, ha." Then he said, in alarm, "Look, they're coming now!" I hid the sandwich in a drawer, and Oda told his subordinates, "Hurry up, get into position."

Oda greeted the Toyota delegation with extreme deference. He really knew

how to flatter those in power, which was one reason he maintained his position. I bowed deeply to the group of old men and showed them my work.
They watched with serious looks on their faces, said nothing, and moved on
to the next presentation. I waited until they were out of sight before finishing my sandwich.

To reduce costs immediately, management required all employees to work
Saturdays and Sundays to save on electrical expenses, so the weekend holiday was switched to Monday and Tuesday. This was a great hardship for families, but we heard not one squeak of resistance from the union. Higuchi had
to quit being a soccer coach because he could not attend weekend practices.

RESPECT FOR ELDERS

The drag reduction project finally bore fruit, and a prototype was built to our
specifications. Now the product would be tested in a wind tunnel. Higuchi
told me that Abe wanted me to travel out to the lab to view the experiment.
Since the wind tunnel was very expensive, the company had rented the lab
equipment from a national institute many miles away.

Watanabe picked me and Suzuki up at the bus station, and drove us to the
lab. He told us that there had been an accident that had damaged the prototype. This had caused some delays, but the equipment had been repaired and
the experiment was now expected to run smoothly. While the men were busy
preparing the prototype for the experiment, Watanabe talked to me about
the upcoming experiment and drew some detailed illustrations on a black
board in the center of the room. "A large vortex may form off the back," he
said. A vortex is a swirl of air, and when formed behind a drag reducer, it can
reduce efficiency and increase instability. He seemed to like chatting with me,
and I enjoyed his company, too, as he seemed like a nice guy who knew a lot
about his field. Of course, he had treated Suzuki deplorably, but perhaps he
was angry that Suzuki had so little expertise.

Three managers were assigned by Abe to run the experiment: Watanabe
from the Technical Research Center, an engineer from the Design Division,
and an older man who was a technician. Many other people were there as
well. We ran a few experiments, then broke to rearrange the apparatus for the
next round. Suddenly, a fight broke out between Watanabe and the engineer
from the Design Division. Each one wanted to experiment on a certain part

of the prototype that was beneficial only to his department. They argued loudly about this for several minutes. The other men did not interfere—most just left the room. Suzuki turned to me and muttered, "This is what happens when you get three managers together to work on a project." He, too, made a quick exit.

The older technician tried to soothe the other two, saying, "Okay now, both of you guys take it easy, bring it down." He waved his hands gently up and down in an effort to calm the situation—to no avail. The others continued to fight like a couple of alley cats and didn't give a damn what the old man said. Finally, someone suggested they call Abe to resolve the situation. Abe made a decision, and the experiment finally continued.

It was distressing. Precious time and thousands of dollars had been wasted in a battle about which manager would succeed in promoting the interests of his group. As for the much-vaunted Japanese respect for age, I saw that since the old technician had no power over the younger managers, his peace-making efforts had been completely ignored.

A few weeks later, Watanabe invited me to the design division mock-up presentation of the product. Abe attended, along with many engineers who had been assigned to the project from design and research. It was a major presentation, with many speeches by many managers. They all used charts to explain the product design. Engineers from production were also at the meeting, discussing issues related to manufacturing cost. They documented these on a sheet that was attached to a bulletin board for all of us to see. There was also a display of diagrams to illustrate various problems that had been solved. The detailed drawings showed exactly what parts of the design had been discussed, and how the technical issues had been resolved. These were now crossed out with a red pen. The entire meeting was very interesting and a sharp contrast to the closed-door nature of the Advanced Design group.

RESTRUCTURING ON THE LINE

One day in the company courtyard, I ran into Sanan, the former canoe maker from Thailand. I asked how things were going on the assembly line since the Asian crash. He said that orders had plummeted but that back-ordered vehicles were still being produced. Management was trying to reduce costs while keeping daily production numbers high, so naturally the workers bore the burden. In Sanan's group, two workers of an original four were fired. Since the group was still required to produce 132 drivetrain components a day, the remaining two workers had to work twice as hard. Unpaid overtime was also increased by two hours a day.

Seeing many of his colleagues get the ax, Sanan thought his own job might soon expire, but to his surprise, the company extended his contract another six months. Then he learned why. Nizumi was shipping in cheap labor from Thailand, and management wanted Sanan to stay on as a go-between for the new recruits. During the month of April, twenty Thai workers came to one division and another twenty were scheduled to arrive in May. Sanan said the company announced the new trainees were receiving the typical salary of 14,000-yen a day ($115), but "the company is lying. After taxes, these guys from Thailand are only getting 3,500 yen ($30) a day, and they are forced to work overtime without pay," he said. A typical day for these workers lasted about twelve hours. They received a six- to twelve-month contract for what the company called a "training program," and they were provided with a room in the dorm and transportation to and from Thailand.

Sanan said that the Thai workers had to do the most tedious and dangerous jobs on the line, jobs made especially onerous now that one or two workers had to produce what three or four had done earlier. I wondered about their future after their contracts came to an end. According to Sanan, some would work for Nizumi in Thailand but others would just be let go.

I hadn't seen Kofi in a while, so I decided to give him a call. Life had not been kind to the African. A few months earlier, his daughter had died during an asthma attack, and Kofi blamed his wife. Instead of taking the little girl to a specialist, she had brought her to a family friend who was a doctor. After the child died, the divorce proceedings had turned bitter.

Kofi and I met at our favorite *izakaya,* the one where the chubby owner cooked fabulous fish. Kofi's daughter was still on his mind. "That doctor wasn't an asthma specialist," Kofi said again and again. He thought that the doctor had accidentally given the child a drug overdose, but his wife's family didn't want to pursue the matter further. Kofi didn't understand why they wanted to drop the case without bringing the doctor to justice. "They don't even want to investigate it," he said angrily. Finally, he shook his head despairingly and said, "Oh, the Japanese!"

At that moment, a couple of salarymen stumbled into the *izakaya* and asked if we would have a drink with them. Kofi was in no mood to chat with

Japanese strangers, so he looked them in the eye and said in perfect Japanese, "Yes, but I'm a cannibal."

Our potential hosts responded in confusion. "Uhhh?"

"I like humans," said Kofi. "I want to eat you, I'm a cannibal!" And he bared his teeth.

They hurried away, embarrassed and confused. I couldn't help chuckling at the sight of these Japanese businessmen, in their blue suits and ties, scurrying away when a very dark black man played into their preconceptions by acting the role of the wild African.

I had a certain sympathy for them, for they had tried to be friendly, but they had no idea how frustrating it was to be a foreigner in Japan. My experience in Japan had shown me that the average Japanese salaryman was not interested in developing a friendship with a foreigner but just wanted to practice his English and reinforce his own notions of the peculiar ways of other nationalities. Your price for a drink was a series of questions (especially about your love life) that made you feel alienated and disparaged.

Kofi and I started eating our fish, and he told me how restructuring had changed things in his factory. "All contract workers are being fired," he said. "The company is becoming a graveyard." I was curious about what happened to the foreigners who'd been let go. Kofi said that some of the men from South America had found work at a Toyota plant that had the highest manufacturing speed in the world. He said he would never work at that plant. "Workers going crazy with speed," Kofi said.

Then he relayed a surprising development. The company had started filming workers on the line. "They were filming me last week, I am telling you, the camera—I saw it!" Without prior consultation, they had filmed his every move. Since he was not told about the purpose of the filming, Kofi could only conjecture—was it because he was not a good worker? Was it because he was African? No, the company was just implementing a new improvement plan. Shortly after filming him, the company said that they liked his work and that they would extend his contract an extra six months.

JOINING THE UNION

In mid-August I stopped receiving union and company information. No more newsletters, pamphlets, or safety sheets descended onto my desk. On our way back to the dorm one day, I spoke about this to Kurasawa, who was the union leader in our section. I told him I had been receiving the information since the day I entered the company. He responded that since I was not in the union I did not need the information—"and besides, the information is not very interesting so it is not worth reading."

I turned to my colleagues to discuss the possibility of joining the union. They just laughed at me. Why would I want to pay monthly dues to an organization that did nothing to protect workers' rights?[1] I said that joining the union was my right. I told Higuchi that I insisted on joining the union, and he was baffled. "The primary role of the union is to agree with policy promoted by the management." I persisted in my demand, so he passed my request up through the proper chain of command.

Ultimately, I received my response. If I wanted to become a union member, I would have to change my status from a *keiyaku shain* to a regular *seishain* because contract workers were not allowed to join the union.

Later, I discovered that according to the Japanese constitution, all workers are allowed to organize and be part of a labor union. Most companies simply ignore the law because the government does little to enforce it.

The next time I walked home with Kurasawa I asked what exactly he was doing as a union leader. "Nothing but passing out information" he said. "The unions in Japan are different from those in the rest of the world. They are very weak, and the reason is that the people who are chosen to be high-level company managers must first become union leaders. Naturally, they do not oppose management policies. It's not like America, where unions are radical, like the UAW, going on strike like they did just a few months ago. Japanese don't like radical organizations."

I had visited Korea for vacation and had witnessed a violent labor rally, so I said, "Maybe you should learn from the Koreans. Those guys are radical."

"Yeah," he said, his eyes wide, "but Japanese culture is very different. In Korea, they have a history of exchange with other people, and their country has gone through many upheavals. Japan is much steadier. It's related to the group orientation of our society. Everyone has to do what others are doing or they will be ostracized, so there is much more stability here and not many radicals."

I joked, "Well, if you want to change things, maybe *you* should be a radical."

---

[1] When regular employees began working for the company, they immediately became members of the union and were forced to open an account in the *keiretsu*-affiliated bank. The company automatically deducted the monthly union fee from their paychecks.

He jolted his head backward in shock and said, "No, I don't want to do that."

Even if Kurasawa had wanted to change things, he couldn't risk being punished by the company. Being in his late thirties with a wife and two kids, what could he do? He wouldn't get another job easily.

I sympathized with his situation, so I just asked him to distribute union literature to me as before. When he remained silent, I threatened to complain to Higuchi. The threat worked, and the very next day, I began getting union newsletters and pamphlets again.

REFRESH LEAVE

Cost cutting continued at Nizumi. Older men were encouraged to take early retirement. Management made budget cuts in every division and category. They even lowered the beverage allowance for company parties. When I arrived at Nizumi, we used to drink Chivas Regal, but now we were drinking Nikka, a cheap Japanese whisky. Only eighty employees out of seven thousand had taken challenge leave—mainly employees from small towns who wanted to return to a simpler life. The union newsletter announced which employees took challenge leave and printed the following illustration:

Despite the company's efforts, further reductions were needed. On September 1, Uno called a meeting to announce a new plan. This plan was called *rifureshu* (refresh) leave, and it offered an employee the chance to leave the company temporarily for a full year, at 60 percent pay. The company promised to preserve the vacated position until the employee returned. As Uno spoke, the men sat looking downward, not making a sound. Uno told us that upper management had decided that one person in our section had to take *rifureshu* leave, and he asked, then pleaded, for a volunteer. No one said a word. Finally Uno begged us to think about it and said there would be another meeting the following week.

After the meeting, Higuchi told me he would consider refresh leave if he didn't have to make large mortgage payments on his new house. "But maybe next year I can go," he said. "Do you know the best way to obtain good computer skills? Maybe I should join a small cutting-edge American company. I could learn the most advanced techniques—you can't get that at a university." He was thinking aloud, and he wondered how someone of his age, forty-five, would be received. What sort of job could he really get during his *rifureshu* year? He concluded that he would either end up in a software sweatshop, where he would be put down by whiz-kid programmers with American Ph.D.s—or forced into sales. Within seconds, the *rifureshu* dream was gone.

Nonetheless, I didn't see why the younger men would refuse to take what seemed like a great opportunity. Why not take a year off, go back to school, and return to Nizumi well rested and better qualified? My colleagues saw it differently.

As always, Takanashi was the most outspoken because he was the least "refined," so he didn't hesitate to express his opinions about company motives. "People don't want to volunteer for refresh leave because they feel that the company is lying," he said. He swiveled in his chair and moved his head in jerky motions while he spoke, "What they really want to do is restructure, and the employees who go away for a year may never get their jobs back again. When they return, they will find their desks moved to some other department or their responsibility reduced. Nizumi may need to cut more jobs next year, and the year after that—who knows? So being away for a year is too risky. Maybe it would be good for a month or two, but for one entire year—no way."

I thought about what Takanashi had said and reflected on how jobs were defined at the company. No permanent employee at the company had a contract, and an employee's job was not defined according to a specific position or job description. Upper-level managers exercised authoritarian power, and agreements were verbal, not written. It was a system in which jobs could be manipulated and changed at will,[2] so an employee had to constantly protect his position. Takanashi was right: being away might well expose an employee to harsh penalties.

Furthermore, since connections were all-important to success at Nizumi, being away for a year could weaken whatever important associations you had made. When you are physically out of the office for an extended period of time, you can lose your personal contacts. Workers also feared that taking re-fresh leave would damage their personnel records. At some future time, they might not get promoted if a manager thought they'd been lazy and had taken time off for their own pleasure.

Day after day, the company announced further restructuring plans, and the union did nothing about it. Nobody I interviewed had anything positive to say about the union. Everybody felt weak and disenfranchised.

At the next department meeting, Uno showed a chart of each section and the money they were saving through challenge leave. He read off the names of five people in our division who had taken challenge leave, and the meet-ing buzzed with surprise and speculation. Then Uno said he was still look-ing for someone in our section to take refresh leave.

We all looked around, but no one came forward.

LEARNING ABOUT LOCAL POLITICS

It was mid-September, and the first item on the agenda at the weekly de-partment meeting was a discussion about sponsoring a corporate candidate for another local city council election. The candidate would run in a nearby town where Nizumi had a factory. Uno distributed a list of employees who lived in that town and who were expected to cast their vote for the company candidate. Erberto told me that the list was being used in his section to co-erce employees to vote for the candidate. Employees were also being re-quested to ask their family and friends to vote for the company man. It was clear that the second election I observed was going to be a repeat of the first.

It was time for the mid-year transfer, and I waited to hear what would hap-

---

[2] None of the employees at the company has a written contract and when a person enters the company it is Human Resources in consultation with upper-level management that decides the section and division to which they belong.

pen to the much-abused Suzuki, whose condition was still deteriorating. Finally I learned that Suzuki was going to be transferred to the Nizumi High School, where he would become a teacher of electronics. I asked Higuchi why Suzuki had been transferred. Higuchi said, "His performance is low and he does not get along with Watanabe. Watanabe is aggressive, like an American. Suzuki is more kind, so I think he is afraid of Watanabe."

I asked, "Do you think he will be happy there?"

"I don't think he will enjoy his work at the Nizumi School, but he has no choice." Much later, just before I left the company, I saw Suzuki on the street. He gave me a big smile and told me he liked his new job a lot. He seemed healthy again—he had gained weight, and his twitch had disappeared. I was pleased to see that my sensitive colleague had found a position more suitable to his personality than the one he had held at Nizumi.

I wanted to further investigate Nizumi's political involvement, but to learn more I needed to have a connection. At a dinner party at Erberto's, I was able to make the contact I needed. Adrian was from Switzerland. He was studying at a local university and living with his professor and his family. His professor was active in local politics. Adrian and I talked about the election while sipping beer and eating a bowl of *feijoada*—black beans and pork stew prepared by Erberto's Brazilian wife. As the evening ended, Adrian said he would soon leave the country—and did I want his scooter? I took him up on the offer, and he said that when I came to pick it up, I could chat with his professor about the election.

The professor's house was located in the suburbs of the town, near a famous Buddhist temple. Japanese suburbs are much more densely packed than those of Western countries and are typically accessible by narrow, winding roads. With map in hand, I approached his house and made my way through the front gate. Like most houses in Japan, and in much of Asia, it was surrounded entirely by a wall, so only the upper floor and roof could be seen from the road. The professor's wife welcomed me into her home. I untied my shoes at the door, put on a pair of slippers, and entered the kitchen area. She prepared a pot of green tea and placed a few cakes on the table. We began talking about my life in the city, and soon I was telling her about the company campaign. She sat silently and listened to every word I said.

In a little while, her husband came home from the university and joined us at the table. He was a tall, older gentleman who seemed at ease talking openly about politics. Soon, he was questioning me about American military policy. He told me he was upset with the American involvement in Kosovo and criticized Japanese companies for supplying parts for the American military machine. We talked for a few more minutes, then his wife turned to him and said, "You have to hear about what Nizumi did in the last election."

So I told him, too.

The professor was not surprised. "A lot of groups, including those that exist in the city and village, work the same way. Members of the group are practically forced to vote for a particular candidate. It's a hard thing to fight. There is very little information on the candidates, and no one knows who to vote for—so many people just follow the group's 'recommendation.' A few years ago, the city government used to sponsor open discussions and debates, but not anymore."

He suddenly walked to the other side of the room and grabbed a pamphlet on the table. He held the document up to me. I saw an old World War II black-and-white picture of a Japanese soldier with his comrades standing, arms outstretched, celebrating a bonzai victory in a battle in Manchuria. He pointed to a set of flags at the bottom and said, "Look—these are the flags of the fascist countries that fought in World War II. This is the German flag that has changed from the Nazi flag to the German union flag. The Italian flag has also changed—but look at the Japanese flag." Each of the prewar flags was in one column on the left, and the postwar flags were in a column on the right. I looked down at the Japanese flag. The right column contained an empty, dashed rectangular outline where the new flag should have been. "Nothing has changed," lamented the professor. At the time, I was puzzled as to why he thought that this was so significant.

The professor's wife said that members of a local independent political organization called the Open Society would be interested in learning about my experience at the company. The professor and his wife introduced me to Araki Toyama, a social activist and professor of law at a local university.

Toyama said, "We used to have a progressive mayor in the city named Sasaki, but now we have a conservative mayor from the Liberal Democratic party." The progressive coalition lost city power when Mayor Sasaki decided not to run for another term. The electorate became divided due to infighting when they were choosing who would replace the mayor.

We continued to talk about local politics, occasionally bringing the small, cylindrical cups to our lips for a sip of green tea. The company elections were on my mind. I asked how Nizumi was able to get its employees to vote before election day. He told me that the absentee ballot rules had recently changed. "Voter turnout was becoming so low in Japan that it was decided that anyone could vote ahead of time without needing to provide any explanations about why they could not vote on election day." The hope was that this would increase citizen participation, but it gave Nizumi a new opportunity to exploit. The company was able to arrange massive absentee ballots for its employees without giving any reason at all.

At the end of our conversation, Toyama invited me to a Open Society meeting and told me that he could introduce me to a number of people who lived in town.

RUNNING THE CITY LIKE A CORPORATION

A few weeks later, I hopped onto the scooter that Adrian had given me and drove down from the company dormitory to the meeting place. I weaved through hundreds of pubs, mom-and-pop shops, and fast-food restaurants. When I entered the room, Toyama introduced me to Shirai, the city councilman from the Open Society party. Shirai was an affable man in his late forties. He wore glasses and smoked incessantly. The group quickly got down to business and began discussing policy. The city was experiencing many changes imposed by the new conservative government. Due to the lack in tax revenue because of the economic slowdown, the administration claimed that they needed to cut back on social services. Now they were trying to privatize school lunches. Under the old mayor, the schools had hired their own nutritionists and had used homegrown vegetables from local farmers. The new plan involved outsourcing meal production to a corporation and cutting back on the number of school nutritionists. The Open Society denounced the new plan. A second item on the agenda was the draft of a letter to be sent to the education board protesting a principal who had openly used racist comments about Koreans in the school.

After the meeting, Shirai invited me to a restaurant pub where the members of the group converged for drinks. The pub, called the Red Samurai, was located on a relatively isolated street a few blocks from the meeting place. A large billboard with Shirai's name and slogan ("power to the citizens") stood on the sidewalk beside the entrance. Trucks at high speed drove on a highway bridge a few hundred meters above the pub. It was a traditional pub, and the owner, Koizumi, stood in the center and cooked. Patrons sat at low stools at a counter that wrapped around the small cooking space. To the side, a group of men sat cross-legged on tatami mats vigorously eating, drinking, and laughing. Smoke from a grill cooking *yakitori* wafted into the air while 1950s bebop American jazz filled the room. I sat with Shirai at the end of the counter.

Koizumi asked us what we wanted, and Shirai responded "*Shōchū* and an order of *yakitori.*" Shirai was famous for enjoying rice wine. Koizumi grabbed Shirai's *shōchū* bottle and brought it to the table. Shirai introduced me to Koizumi and gave him some background information about me. "So you work for Nizumi," he said, "Do you know Nakaya?"

"Yes," I said nervously. Nakaya was a senior executive.

"He comes here a lot. He's the one who looks like a member of the Japanese mafia."

I had to laugh. With his expensive suits and slicked back hair, Nakaya did look like a prosperous criminal. But I was also was dismayed. If Nakaya came in and learned about my involvement with the Open Society, management would not be happy at all. Koizumi threw some *yakitori* on the small coal grill, and Shirai walked over to small electric heater located at the entrance and filled our small glasses with hot water. He poured some *shōchū* in our glasses, lit a cigarette, and we began drinking and talking.

"Education is a big problem in Japan," Shirai said. "The schools are allowed to pack up to forty students in each classroom. And we have a real problem with bullying."

The media had recently covered several suicides that were blamed on *ijime.* Shirai said, "Large classes contribute to bullying."

A carpenter sitting in a seat beside us chimed in with his view. "I disagree—the bullying is the parents' fault. If they don't raise kids properly, then they are going to be bullied, and that's that!" Shirai tried to explain his point, but the carpenter wouldn't let him speak. "If the kid goes to school and other kids think he is strange, whose fault is that? It's not the school's fault, it's the parents!'"

He continued in this vein for several minutes. I thought it was odd that he kept blaming the bullied child and his parents and never blamed the bullies. Finally, Shirai interrupted.

"Can I speak," he said, "Is it okay now?"

"Yeah, go ahead," said the carpenter.

"Are you sure?"

"Yeah, go ahead, speak all you want, go on!"

"First of all, fathers in Japan can't spend that much time with their kids because of overwork, right?" said Shirai.

"Okay, go on."

"Okay, even if they could spend time with kids how can a single teacher possibly control forty children in a class? Groups form in the classroom and pick on kids who don't fit in. If they reduce class size, there's a chance that teachers can prevent bullying. Instead, all the schools do is impose more and more rules, and it doesn't do a damn thing to help the problem."

The carpenter grumbled a bit, and the two men kept talking. I was thrilled by the open way members of the Open Society expressed themselves. It was such a change from the stifling atmosphere at Nizumi! The Open Society included a variety of social activists who worked to improve the conditions for city residents. They engaged in combative argument, but their spirits were high, and there was a happy ambience. They welcomed me warmly into the group.

Shirai and I settled into conversation as more people arrived and squeezed themselves into a small spot for drinks and conversation. Koizumi was an excellent cook, so I kept nibbling away at the tasty Japanese food.

I asked Shirai what policies the corporations and their candidates promoted in the city council.

"They really have no policy," he said

"What do you mean?" I said. "There must be a reason for all this political activity."

"The primary reason corporations have a councilman is so they can sell their products to the city," Shirai replied.

I asked him to explain the procurement process.

"The city council is supposed to open bids to all companies, but it is rigged," he said. "The entire system in Japan is based on bid-rigging (*dango*) and the whole *keiretsu* system is involved. The big companies supply the smaller *keiretsu* companies with contracts, and it goes down from there."

"Can you give me an example?"

"Oh, there are plenty of them," he said. "We were putting up a new hospital, and we put the project up for bid. A construction company was chosen, and that construction company chose its own subsidiary to supply the electrical system. But the electrical supplier had been decided already—it was one of the four corporations who have factories in city."

Similarly, Toshiba has a factory in the city, and as it happens, they have supplied the elevators in every public building for the past twenty years. Shirai listed off many more examples. I was curious about whether people in the community knew about *dangō*. "The city government does not disclose that information, so no one really knows," he said. "Every year the mayor prepares the budget and then presents it to the city council, and the council either accepts or rejects it. The project suppliers are not listed."

We drank and talked late into the evening. He invited me to a karaoke bar next door, and we sang, drank, and ate for another hour. Shirai said, "If you really want to know about corporate policy in the city council, you can refer to the City Council Notes. And you may want to talk to a few other city council representatives."

Shirai was right. The City Council Notes showed that the corporate councilmen were promoting restructuring in the city government. In one discussion, Ishida even proposed running the government like a Japanese corporation.

I interviewed half a dozen members of the city council, and they all confirmed what Shirai had said about *dangō* and corporate interests. I asked a councilwoman about Ishida's policies in the city government, and she said, "Ishida suggested that the city plant flowers in the places where the old garbage boxes used to be. We all thought that was a good idea, but somehow nothing was done about it."

Nizumi's campaign on Ishida's behalf had paid off handsomely. Toyota got a large contract for the company, and Ishida did what he could to cut city jobs, support big business—and suggest that the city plant a few flowers. Ishida's New Year Message appeared in the company newsletter. He extended his deep appreciation from "the bottom of my heart for your continuing warm encouragement and cooperation." He said he was trying to understand the problems facing the city, especially the bad economic situation. "Under these circumstances I would like to continue to create a green city with lots of smiles." It was the usual meaningless sloganeering.

If he had been honest, Ishida's message would have read:

Happy New Year. Thank you very much for your support in electing me to the city legislature. Through group control and coercion, we were able to ensure that many employees of the company who lived in the city voted for me. Since we knew that many of you were not at all interested in the election, in order to ensure your cooperation, we bussed you to the city hall to fill out special absentee ballots, which we obtained through our connections to the administration. Those of you who did not participate in this enforced voting were punished.

On behalf of Nizumi, I have been happily involved in the dismantling of the welfare system through privatization. No matter the impact on the environment or the community, my role in the city council is to sell company products and to support big business on all issues. One of my recent successes involved obtaining a large company contract through bid-rigging. I was able to obtain this deal through Nizumi's special relationship with the mayor. In return for this favor, you, employees of Nizumi, are expected to vote for the mayor in the next election. Recently, the city has been facing financial trouble, so I have proposed a business plan to improve efficiency, which involves running the government like a private corporation and insisting on financial restructuring. As at Nizumi, this plan involves firing many employees and piling more work on those who remain.

Remember, your role as an employee is to obey company policy. In the next election, you will vote for me or suffer the consequences. I wish everyone a healthy and happy year.

DEATH BY OVERWORK

After the Open Society meetings, we would often go to the Red Samurai to unwind. Professor Nagano often came with us. He was a handsome, distinguished-looking professor with gray hair who sometimes came to meetings wearing a beret. I always enjoyed talking to him. He had been involved in city politics for more than thirty years and had spent a couple of his sabbaticals studying politics in America. We sipped our *shōchū*. "Those who have power in Japan are funny," he said. "They sit on their ass, look around the room, and bow their head—but you have no idea what they're thinking. But in Japan, when you drink, you can learn what people are really thinking. So when a politician asks me out for a drink, I make sure to keep my mouth shut. I let him do the talking."

One reason I went to Red Samurai and engaged in vigorous discussion with Open Society members was to get away from the rules. The ambiance at Red Samurai was free and the talk was lively. I was excited about my new discovery, and I wanted to share it with my foreign friends, so I invited Erberto to Red Samurai. We made ourselves comfortable and started talking about local politics—when a man sitting next to us interrupted our conversation.

"So where are you from?" he asked Erberto.

"I'm from Italy," Erberto responded.

"Oh, I thought you were English!" He laughed, his face cringing to show gums bare except for one remaining tooth in his lower jaw. He poured some of his beer into our glasses and asked me my name. "Oh, that is the name of a dog, ha ha, that's so funny!" he cried out.

In Japan it is common for pets to have American names such as "Mary" or "John." Did he think my name was Mary? He was clearly intoxicated.

Then Mrs. Hara walked in and sat down with us. She had just returned from visiting her husband who was on life support since collapsing on the job many years ago. Now he is little more than a vegetable. Seeing Mrs. Hara, the one-toothed drunk began making negative comments about a woman being in an *izakaya*.

The owner, Mr. Koizumi, put down his cutting knife and interjected. "Stop it! This lady's husband is in the hospital because his company worked him into a coma!"

"What are you talking about!" said the drunk. He continued to argue with Koizumi. I picked myself up from the bar seat and headed toward the bathroom to allow the boisterous argument to cool down.

When I returned, I asked Mrs. Hara how she was doing. I felt sorry for her: her life had become lonely and painful since her husband's collapse. She attended the Open Society meetings, often with her son, and she frequented Red Samurai for community support. Since she saw I was interested in work-related issues, she invited me to visit her husband in the hospital. I was happy to accept her invitation, for her husband had worked for Toyota Motors, and I thought it would be a good opportunity to learn more about the company.

Inside the hospital room that Mrs. Hara called her home, dried roses hung on the walls along with pictures of her once-healthy family. Holding back tears, she stood over her still husband, positioning him more comfortably on the bed. She said, "When my husband worked long hours at the company, he used to send me roses. Now I have hung them on the wall as a reminder of our relationship together."

As a sales manager for Toyota Motors, Mr. Hara had been forced to work for twelve hours a day, often seven days a week. The constant stress contributed to gout attacks. For years, he suffered painful attacks. At first, his attacks would occur once in a while, but as the years passed, they came more often until they occurred every month. Mrs. Hara pleaded with him to go to the hospital for a checkup, but since his work schedule was so busy, he couldn't find the time to go. Toward the end, his pain was so extreme, he had to use a cane to walk.

Hara's responsibilities required him to put in long hours almost every day of the year. Mrs. Hara explained, "The branch was new, and the managers wanted to be on top of the sales charts so everyone was worked very hard, especially at the beginning and the end of the month. It was typical for the company to force him to work thirty-five days in a row without one day off to spend some time with his family." Hara would spend so many days absent from his home that at times his wife and son would spend Sunday at work with him.

After thirty-five days of work, the company would give him a day off, but the very next day he was required to return to work for another long two- or three-week shift. The only time he had more than one day at a time off from work was when the company was closed during the national holidays. "We would often spend our holidays in the countryside, but the holidays were always too short."

Then came his collapse. In the fall of 1991, during an ordinary workday, he suddenly fell ill with meningitis and was rushed to the hospital. He never regained consciousness.

After the incident, Mrs. Hara was impoverished for many years, not knowing how to receive compensation for her husband's lost salary. At the time, she didn't know that her husband could receive workman's compensation for his injuries. The company union did nothing to help her with her claim. Not a single person in the union even contacted her about the issue. Luckily, a friend introduced her to the Open Society and they made contacts with the local Zenroren federation of unions. They helped her find a lawyer and apply for workmen's compensation. It took four years before her claim was accepted.

When she finally received her husband's workman's compensation, it was not enough to cover basic medical expenses so she was forced to sue. Her motives were not entirely monetary. "I wanted to show the rest of the world how badly Toyota treated my husband."

One of the first obstacles in her pursuit of justice was proving that her husband had been overworked, "I couldn't prove that my husband had to work so many hours because managers in Japan do not fill out time cards." The only way to prove her case was to ask her husband's colleagues to testify on his behalf, but they all refused to speak. "I was deeply hurt by their refusal," she said. "I had known some of them for years, we were close, they knew the intimate details of my husband's work. All they said was 'please understand'—that was it."

She suspected that her husband's superiors had ordered everyone to refuse to testify. The union was equally disengaged. "The union at Toyota is worthless, it doesn't do anything to improve worker's rights or working conditions. Most company unions in Japan are like that. After all the requests I sent for help, I didn't hear from them, not one word, until one day I received a letter from them. I held the envelope in my hands, elated that they finally had come around to help me—but when I opened the envelope, I saw a flyer asking me to support a Toyota Motors candidate in the national election! It had nothing to do with my husband's case."

Remembering the moment, she fought to hold back tears. "I just ripped up the letter and threw it into the garbage."

Mrs. Hara received national attention with her fight against Toyota, but she knew that to pursue her case she had to seek grassroots support. The Zenroren local, the Open Society, and other activist unions worked with her in battling Toyota. "They made me feel that I was not alone in my struggle. Members of the various unions and groups would come to court with me, to sit with me and show Toyota that many people were watching." Her supporters also helped her get many signatures to petition Toyota to end the case quickly.

In court, managers from Toyota defended their position. Without proof of his hours, what could Mrs. Hara do? Then she discovered that some company employees used a security card to enter and leave the office. If she could receive information from the security company, she could prove that workers were being forced to stay at the company late into the night. She tried to find her husband's card, looking frantically through his clothes. But she could not find it, so her lawyers asked the judge to obtain the information. When the court finally received the security records, they provided striking evidence of how long employees at Hara's branch were forced to work—on an average of twelve to sixteen hours a day, seven days a week.

The government commission investigating her case concluded that Hara had indeed suffered from overwork. The judge forced Toyota to settle the case, and they agreed to pay compensation. During the deliberations, however, Japan's number-one company tried to get out of paying for trivial items such as mattresses for the hospital bed and Mrs. Hara's commuting costs. Her lawyers rejected their request and demanded that Toyota pay for all expenses. After several long years, Mrs. Hara finally received full compensations for her husband's tragic fate. Yet she is still angry with Toyota. "The company refused to admit they did anything wrong." Fortunately, she continues to receive emotional support from the Open Society and has made several friends who are helping her raise her son.

The one-toothed drunk stumbled out of the bar, and moments later Shirai strode in. We all sat at the table on the tatami mat. *Shochu* flowed into glasses and beer caps hissed open. We huddled around the table, laughing, joking, and talking about the community. Erberto was in his element. Shirai turned to the owner and asked him to play us a tune. Koizumi picked up his guitar and began playing and singing with surprising passion. Others joined in, and soon we were all singing Japanese folk songs.

RULES THAT UNDERMINE DEMOCRACY

Bit by bit, I began to understand how Nizumi was undermining the democratic process. Ehime, a local lawyer and activist I met through the Open Society, was especially helpful in this regard. He invited me to his new office to talk about Japanese political campaigns. We sat together at one end of a long table, and he began to talk. "In the 1920s, campaigning door to door was outlawed in Japan, and voting rights were limited to men over twenty. The government wanted to control the voting base, and they didn't want grassroots movements to undermine their policies." After the war, the political system was restructured, and voting rights were extended to women, but the law banning door-to-door campaigning remained in effect to this day.

Ehime picked up a large textbook on Japanese law, and we began to discuss the factors that undermined Japanese democracy. "The government does not officially announce the candidates until one week prior to the day of the election," he said. "This dramatically limits all public debate. Campaign organizations distribute most of their information in the week before elections." During election week, a set of laws restricts the distribution of political tracts. The candidate cannot personally distribute information, the political organization cannot distribute information with photos, and only two versions of the campaign material can be distributed. Furthermore, all distributed material must receive an official stamp from the city campaign office.[3] Another law limits the candidate to using only two vehicles during the campaign.

According to Ehime, "These laws restrict citizen participation in political elections and suppress grassroots organizations." However, there are ways to get around the laws. "The political organization can publish special issues about the candidate in their newsletter or newspaper for distribution during the week of the election. For example, the Japanese Communist party can distribute information through their national newspaper, the *Akahata,* since they have a wide readership. The problem is most small grassroots organizations don't have a well-known newspaper. They suffer most from these backward laws." Ehime continued, "Another way to get around the laws is to distribute information about political policies without mentioning the candidate's name, but this also has a limited affect."

According to Ehime these laws were passed in the early 1970s when the Japanese Communist party carried out an effective campaign strategy called the "paper bomb." This saturated local communities with information on their candidates and it began to undermine the political power of the Liberal Democratic party.

The overall effect of these laws is to undermine the entire democratic process and make a charade of political campaigning. Political candidates have little choice but to ride around town speaking of their policies through loud bullhorns on the roofs of their vans. During election week, whether you are walking on an isolated street, exiting the subway station after a long day of work, or napping on a Saturday afternoon, you cannot escape the blaring sounds of dozens of candidates campaigning. Election week is highly unpleasant, and it contributes to the present cynicism about the political process.

No wonder employees at the company felt so disenfranchised. Not only did they not have the power to make changes at the company, they had very little power to make political changes, either.

---

[3] An official stamp is required by the city campaign office before the political party is allowed to distribute the campaign material. These stamps must be put on all campaign materials and the number of stamps a candidate receives depends on the number of voters in the district and the political organization to which he or she belongs.

FEAR OF OSTRACISM

One December morning when I arrived at the office, I saw that Hirama had been moved to a desk in front of Kurata's section. Now all the employees on the floor could see Hirama, sitting there all alone near the director.

I asked Kurasawa why management was being so harsh, and he explained, "Hirama does not have a place anymore at the company." In a society that placed a high value on being a group member, Hirama was being publicly humiliated as a man without a group. It was an extreme form of harassment, designed to force him to follow the hidden rule of early retirement. After forty years at Nizumi, this was how he would remember his final days: sitting by himself under the scornful and pitying eyes of his fellow workers.

Kurasawa said that those who are isolated are called *mado giwa zoku* (members of the window watching gang), as if they are indolent and lazy. I asked him if Hiraga was a *mado giwa zoku,* and he just laughed. We both knew that for all of his cigarette smoking and ostentatious boredom, old Droopy Eyes was extremely knowledgeable about the product and often made important technical contributions at meetings. Hiraga was, after all, a graduate of Tokyo University, so although it sometimes seemed like he was on Planet Mars, he was still a valued engineer.

The conversation with Kurasawa reminded me of a time when I met with Suzuki and Higuchi to talk about the drag reducer project. We met in a new office that was not quite ready to be occupied, so there was much open space. I had become accustomed to living and working in cramped, congested quarters, so it was quite a treat to relax in the large, open space. During a short break I leaned back in my chair, turned to Higuchi and said, "Wouldn't it be great to have a desk over there in the corner by the window."

He laughed as if I had made a good joke.

Suzuki, however, looked puzzled. He said, "Why would you want to sit *there?*"

I said, "It's got great light. And it's nice and private here."

Higuchi explained to Suzuki that Americans like to be isolated and away from other people. "They even have their own offices," he said in mild surprise. Suzuki pointed to the window space I had been coveting. He said, "That is not a desirable place to sit at Nizumi. That's where the company puts employees when they want them to leave."[4]

---

[4] Ostracism has historically played an important role in work in Japan. According to John

This in turn reminded me of another discussion I'd had with Higuchi about where the company puts lazy employees. We had just left a conference with a number of foreigners, one of whom remarked that Japanese never leave work at five o'clock like Westerners. Higuchi said, "That's not true. I know of a guy who leaves at 5 o'clock. He goes home to coach soccer for his kids." Thinking of what I still endured on the days I left at five-thirty, I wondered how his colleagues reacted to this early departure. Higuchi said, "They don't care, because he works in a section for those who don't like to work. The section is the copying section and all they do all day is make copies of drawings for employees."

"That's all they do?" I asked. "Make photocopies?"

"Yes, that's it, nothing but make copies," Higuchi said. "The company will shift lazy or incompetent employees from one section to another, hoping they will finally start improving. If they don't—they end up at the copying section."

"Get out of here!"

"It's true. And they're completely inept! Go ask for ten copies of a document. You might get two back—or twenty."

BECOMING THE DOGS OF TOYOTA

That week Uno announced the latest restructuring plan. The Design Division had been told to cut twenty people from the computer-aided engineering section. Ten would be let go, and ten would be transferred to another department—perhaps to work in sales. But engineers don't have a knack for selling products, and many would choose to retire early instead. It was Oda's feeling that the company was deliberately pushing engineers into early retirement by these transfers to sales—which were always considered a demotion.

The next week, Uno announced that Toyota Management was discussing the possibility of transferring Nizumi technology to the parent company. Toyota's technical development policy is that basic research is conducted at

---

Owen Haley, in order for agrarian communities to maintain smooth relations with the Tokugawa shogunate in producing the proper rice yield "the community itself had to develop mechanisms of control. The most prominent included the psychological sanction of collective community displeasure as well as more severe forms of community coercion, such as ostracism and expulsion." See John Owen Haley, *Authority without Power* (New York: Oxford University Press, 1991), 61.

their company and then handed over to the group company, typically a parts manufacturer, for further development. For example, if a Toyota parts manufacturer makes a pump for Toyota vehicles, the basic research will be conducted at Toyota, and when the research goals have been reached, the parts manufacturer will continue to develop the technology into design and production. This allows a small number of Toyota managers to control the technology.

When the men in my section heard of this technology transfer to Toyota, they worried that their jobs would be eliminated or that the entire section would be cut. But Uno reassured them, saying that since Toyota knew little about Nizumi technology, they would need to rely on Nizumi engineers. When Uno finished talking, Dr. Zombie reeled off a large number of research programs that would be cut back. None of the programs would be entirely cut, but all would suffer significant budget reductions. He also listed a number of new strategies to save money in the technical lab.

After the meeting, I approached Kurasawa and Mochida to ask them what they thought about Toyota controlling Nizumi. Kurasawa responded, "We will be the dog of Toyota."

"Worse!" said Mochida, standing up from his seat and continuing the animal imagery. "We will be like mice, afraid of what to say, and Toyota will be the lion, giving orders."

I was surprised with their response but later learned that Toyota is notorious for externalizing their costs to lower level group companies in the form of longer hours, less pay, and strict control of management and technology. Members of Erberto's group were uneasy about being consumed by Toyota because a hidden rule postulates that no employees in the Toyota industrial group can make more money than employees who work for Toyota Motors.

QUITTING THE COMPANY

Later in the week, an engineer named Iwata in our section announced that he planned to quit the company. "It is good that he is leaving," said Kurasawa. "The salary at Nizumi is so low, I am happy for him." Iwata was almost thirty, so he felt it was his last chance to change jobs. In the classified sections of all the major newspapers, companies often stipulated that applicants should be under age thirty-five, and it was generally understood that you had your best chance at getting a new job if you were still in your twenties. All the men were wondering where Iwata would be working, but he would not say.

His boss was apparently very angry because Nizumi did not plan to hire anyone to take Iwata's place. "We will be at a loss," he said. He would need to cut back on design projects, and without these, his own future prospects at Nizumi might be reduced. I observed the relationship between Iwata and his boss after Iwata announced that he was leaving. On the surface, the relationship between the young engineer and his boss remained as cordial as if nothing had happened. On both sides, mannerisms and expressions remained the same. The *tatemae* functioned as a lubricant to keep the relationship running smoothly in its final days. If the company had been American, I probably would have noticed at least a marginal shift in their relationship, or some displeasure from the boss. But I couldn't sense a thing.

Uno organized a good-bye party for the departing engineer. We stuffed ourselves into a small tatami room in a local *izakaya*. This *izakaya* was not the typical mom and pop joint but a part of a chain. The food was not nearly as good as at the local restaurants, and we ordered from a generic menu, but the men liked the place because it was cheap. The food quickly came to our tables along with the usual beer bottles. We all grabbed bits of the squid, tofu, and fried chicken that had been neatly placed in little dishes on the table and engaged in the usual good-bye party rituals. Uno gave a speech, and we all took turns talking about working with the departing engineer.

As the party came to close, the mystery remained: where would Iwata be working next? Finally, one of the boys popped the question. Iwata tried to avoid it, but at this point, he could not. He sat on his knees, looked downward, and confessed, "Honda." The silence lasted only a few seconds, but it was one of those times that seem to last forever.

When the men began to speak again, they seemed hurt. They asked him lots of questions about his job. They were particularly interested in his salary. At the time, although the Japanese auto market was not doing well, Honda was doing very well in the American market. Its annual bonus had become the highest in the industry, while Nizumi's was one of the lowest.

I could tell that everyone was jealous of Iwata and his job. Loyalty to Nizumi existed only in the world of *tatemae*. In reality, paycheck and benefits were what really mattered.

ENDURING WITH CLENCHED TEETH

Later that week, after Japanese language class, I bumped into Romone. As we walked down the dimly lit main street, we talked about work while the train rumbled in the background. Romone's outlook about Nizumi had soured, even though he was one of the few contract workers who was not let go but was offered a new contract. However, he was not a happy camper. "Since restructuring began," he said, "I am doing a job that three men used to do. The line speed is very fast, and the work is much more dangerous. Now there are no Peruvians on my line—they fired all of them except me. So it's lonely. I used to have a cousin and two close friends on the line, but now I'm by myself."

He told me that he intended to leave Nizumi to look for a job north of Tokyo. With the aid of a friend, he hoped to start a new life there—but he also dreamed about America. "I hate Japan," he said. "I really hate this country. I want to go to America. I heard life is good there."

Later in the year, economic conditions at the company grew even more dire, and more contract workers were asked to leave. Human Resources broke Romone's contract by forcing him to leave before his term was up. He was not alone. According to Romone, the entire group of temporary workers who had received extended contracts were forced to leave before their contracts had expired.

Since so many people were being downsized, I was naturally concerned about my own position at Nizumi. Higuchi was not encouraging.

"I don't know yet," he said, "but there is a chance that we will have to let you go. Abe told me unofficially today that the company must cut 30 percent of its remaining employees."

I was shocked, for the planned cuts meant that nine guys from our section of thirty would have to go. I pressed the issue, "What about me?"

Higuchi parried, "When did you learn about your contract last year?"

"The last week of March, just a few days before my contract expired. If they want me to leave, I'd like to know as soon as possible." My spirits were sinking. I remarked, "Japanese companies are known to fire foreigners before they consider putting out their own."

Higuchi agreed. "It is assumed that the job of a Japanese is more important than that of a foreigner."

I wasn't angry with Higuchi, for he was simply being honest. What bothered me was that I had no way to protect my job or my income. The company prohibited me from being part of a union, and as a contract worker, I did not have the option of taking a leave of absence, much less a *rifureshu* leave. Nor would I receive unemployment benefits.

I felt as though I had entered a four-sided rice paper box. I certainly wasn't going to move up. Nor would I move laterally. I would either get a pay cut or sink through the paper floor and be gone from the company forever. All foreigners—and about half the Japanese workers—were on contract and in the same position.

Later in the month, when Kurasawa was making a union announcement, I confronted him about the proposed fate of foreign contract workers. He seemed to be taken aback by my direct inquiry. Virtually none of the Japanese workers were as bold, for if they spoke up, they know very well their chances of promotion would be diminished. I suppose I felt I had nothing to lose.

Word of my confrontation went up the chain of command, and the very next day I heard about my future at the company. Uno, who in all of my time at Nizumi hadn't spoken more than a few sentences to me, came to my desk and said, "You need not worry about your job. Nizumi has never cut a foreign engineer."

Later on, Higuchi told me that Abe had intervened for me. Abe had heard that Human Resources was interested in firing the foreign engineers, and he had written a very strong letter in my support. Apparently, he had asserted that if my contract was not renewed, the entire drag reducer project would come to a halt. I was saved.

As long as I could provide Nizumi with a skill that no Japanese worker had, they'd keep me on—and get a bargain. For as Higuchi later told me, one reason Nizumi wasn't firing foreign engineers was because they were young and not especially well paid.

Foreigners were also cheaper on the line. At around this time, I noticed a large group of Thai workers being marched around company grounds in an orderly fashion. Two Japanese employees led at the front while another remained in the back, perhaps to guard workers from going astray. These were the latest recruits, for even amid the downsizing, Nizumi was still hiring foreigners at bargain rates, about $2.50 an hour.

It was February when the union negotiated with management about benefits. Kurasawa gave a brief speech to inform us that the company was doing even worse than had been predicted, so bonus pay would be further reduced and two divisions would be combined, to permit more job cuts. We turned to each other in alarm. The union leader continued. Managers would also get pay cuts, and the number of directors would be reduced from fifty to fifteen. But the technicians, office ladies, and temporary workers, many of them women, were the hardest hit. Those that were not being fired were receiving drastically reduced bonuses and no paid overtime work. On the average, a technician would now receive 160,000 yen ($1,400) a month, barely enough to pay the bills.

Later in the month, the union published an account of the initial union-management negotiation. The union confirmed that trouble lay ahead for the Japanese economy. They saw no improvement in sight and discussed the present hardships, such as cuts in overtime pay, cuts in the bonus, and extended service overtime. The union asked for an increase in wages and a reduction in working hours but wanted to "compromise while thoroughly negotiating" these issues.

Management responded by completely dismissing the union requests, "There is a recognition gap between the position of the management and the labor union, and we cannot make any concessions." As for bonus and overtime, management said, "We have no choice but to say that paying bonuses for working overtime is impossible." A discussion about the depressed condition of the Japanese market led into a list of initiatives to "get the company out of the deficit to survive in the twenty-first century." The "negotiation" ended with management saying that they would do their best to avoid further dismissal of workers—but they weren't making any promises.

I asked Shiina why the union and the workers were so passive about accepting management policies.

"What about this restructuring?" I prodded. "Why don't the workers try to fight it?"

"Because we will not win, and it will take too much energy," he said. "It is best to spend our energy finding a new job. Right now the economy is down, but when it goes back up, many will quit to find a job at another company."

I approached Higuchi to ask him about restructuring. He was very angry with both management policy and with how it had been disseminated. "What they are doing is dirty," he said. "They are leaking information to the press about company policy before they tell the employees!" These leaks had happened again and again.

At around this time, the union published the results of a survey they had taken. The response rate had been a high 88 percent: 7,247 union members had filled out the questionnaire and returned it. Almost all agreed that "life has become harder due to falling wages." To the question, "How much does your life depend on overtime pay?"[5] 70 percent of those surveyed said they could not make a living wage without overtime pay. An additional 20 percent could not save money for such things as housing and education without overtime.

Overtime was a crucial component of an employee's income, and it could be withheld at will by the section manager, who had absolute authority about which workers got overtime. This enforced worker obedience. If a worker broke company rules (even the hidden ones) or disrupted the power structure within the group or section, his or her wages could immediately be cut by approximately 30 percent.

It is often said that the Japanese worker is very loyal to his company—to the point of not using the paid vacations to which he or she is entitled. But according to the survey this is due to other factors. When asked "Did you use up your vacation days last year?" 52 percent of the respondents claimed they could not take all the days they were allotted. When asked why, 65 percent claimed that the "work environment and the workplace system made it difficult to use up holidays." For instance, Oda had a rule that no one in his section could take more than three consecutive days off. This angered Chen, since he wanted to take a week off to visit relatives in China.

The survey was intended to strengthen the position of the union during negotiations. However, it did not do much good—as proved by the results of the second round of negotiations. Although the union leaders presented a number of grievances, such as the need for wage increases and secure employment, they capitulated on all fronts. Management declared, "We have to endure with clenched teeth in order to save the company."

I asked Kurasawa at lunchtime one day about the labor-management negotiations. He always stretched out on his desk during lunch hour. "It's *tatemae*," he said, half asleep. "It doesn't have any meaning." Negotiations were a sham; management always got its way.

When I returned to my desk, I asked Shiina to elaborate upon Kurasawa's remark. "You must be careful here to understand the difference between the *honne* and the *tatemae*. It is very tricky. At times, it is even difficult for the

---

[5] The multiple choice responses included, among others, "I cannot make a living without overtime income" and "I can barely get by without overtime."

Japanese to understand." He held up a union newspaper and continued, "What is written here does not represent me at all. In Japan, the unions are enterprise unions, so they are weak and are not effective. Management-union negotiations are nothing but *tatemae*."

Shiina paused, then said. "People used to care about their work and the company. For example, when something happened that they did not like, say, the development of new technology, we used to engage in *nemawashi*."

"*Nemawashi*? What's that?"

Nemawashi was a collective action among employees who decided that a company decision or policy needed correction. The group, after many hours of discussion, would form a corrective policy and submit it to a high-level manager. If the manager agreed the new policy was a good idea, he would pass it up through the chain of command, and the new policy might well be implemented. *Nemawashi* typically occurred when subordinates felt a high-level manager was implementing an ineffective or destructive policy. "But not any more," Shiina said. "People just do not care."

A few days later, management announced a work-sharing policy as a way to soften the impact of the proposed layoffs. Unlike American work-sharing, however, the workers did not share jobs with each other; rather, companies in the *keiretsu* shared workers. So Nizumi would be sending redundant employees to group-related companies. The official policy was that it protected jobs and that it was a way for members of the conglomerate to support each other when the economy was down, but in reality this practice was a way for large Toyota companies to unload redundant workers onto lower companies.

I asked Kurasawa about the work-sharing plans. He said that the smaller group companies were already saddled with redundant employees from Toyota and other large group companies, so they had agreed only to accept a small number of workers from Nizumi—far short of what was expected.

WORKER UNREST AND LABOR-MANAGEMENT RULES

In mid January, Kurasawa sat at the center of the meeting table at the section, and a group of employees sat beside him as he announced the latest management proposal. When management proposed a new policy to the union for so-called negotiations, it was immediately considered company policy since the union never put up any resistance. Kurasawa announced that Nizumi needed to fire an additional four hundred employees and implement a severe pay cut.

An assistant manager sitting beside Kurasawa blurted out, "We can't even say anything!"

Shiga yelled, "I heard a couple of guys at the meeting saying there is going to be a strike!"

Mochida asked angrily, "Are the directors getting fired as well? Why can't we be part of the decision making?"

It was my first taste of labor unrest at Nizumi, but it soon subsided, and Kurasawa continued reading off the list of company proposals.

When the meeting was over, I spoke with a number of my colleagues, most of whom were angry that the union hadn't stood up for workers' rights. Shiina said, "We're on our way into hell."

That week, the union published the last labor-management negotiation of the fiscal year. An engineer who represented labor complained about working on a Toyota project. Several dozen had to work day and night to finish the project and had to sleep in the company dorms because they were working after midnight, when the trains stopped running.

Factory workers were also required to put in long hours, and many worked two consecutive shifts, from 8:30 A.M. until midnight. However, they were not offered a dorm room in which to crash. When the union objected to these long hours, management responded by saying that Toyota had increased competition in the group, and to compete, Nizumi's workers had to work harder and longer. Management ended by saying, "We must protect our company, so we don't want to fight against labor. We must share our pain together. Please trust us to protect your jobs."

An illustration of the "happy family" was published with the newsletter.

As restructuring continued, Toyota announced a plan to buy more of Nizumi. Toyota, however, remained silent about the details of their takeover plan. Many employees thought they would clean out redundant employees and managers, while others thought whole departments would be eliminated. From behind my computer, I saw Takanashi, in his bright fluorescent pants, sitting in his strange bird position. I asked him about how restructuring would affect the company. He said, "I think Toyota may buy all of Nizumi. Toyota is also cutting jobs, so they will send them here to work, putting out Nizumi employees. Only the very best guys will remain, and the higher-level positions will be replaced with Toyota managers."

I asked, "Does the union negotiate with management about jobs?"

"Not at all," Takanashi said, his face turning pink with anger. "When union leaders attend a meeting, they just sit and nod their heads to anything management says. If they speak out, they risk losing their own jobs."

To an outsider, the labor-management relationship in Japan seems based on consensus and harmony; policy is decided in a system in which each group negotiates until an equilibrium is achieved that satisfies the whole. Management always maintains a façade of cooperation, and the union always maintains a façade of independence. But in truth, the union is just a management arm.

The annual Spring Offensive was a telling illustration of how ineffectual the union had become. In the past, the Spring Offensive had consisted of protests and strikes to persuade management to increase benefits. But now it had devolved into people merely waving red banners and yelling "ganba-roo" in the street. Sometimes union members would demonstrate at the company entrance and hand out flyers to the employees, who showed no interest. At the end of the day, the trash would be filled to the brim with union flyers. At the end of the week, large garbage trucks would haul the entire heap (along with the company literature that was also continually distributed and trashed) to the dump.[6]

At first, I thought my reluctance to accept authoritarian rule at Nizumi stemmed from my being an American, with a different set of values from the Japanese, but then I realized it came from a simple sense of injustice. Why

---

[6] The employees were allowed to take company newsletters home with them. One newsletter had written at the top "for your family."

were so many employees so terribly unhappy? Why was it so hard to stand up to management? Why was there so much cynicism?

One day I opened the company manual that Shiina had mentioned many months earlier. This manual contained several hundred pages of company rules. The cover read, "The Labor Union Secretariat, who represents all workers at the company, has created the rules together with management." These rules applied to all workers, on the line or in the office, and included such subjects as working hours, holidays, overtime work, working breaks, family support, housing, business trip insurance, pay structure changes, rules that must be obeyed as a member of the labor union, rules for when an employee is sent to a subsidiary or abroad, and rules governing the acquisition of companies or the firing of employees.

An important set of rules governed the relationship between the company and the union. "Union activities must be held outside working hours," and "When a union activity is held after 7:00 P.M., the union must receive approval from Human Resources." Furthermore, "during a dispute, members of the union can only protest in designated areas as decided by the company."

The management enforced even more restrictive rules for union elections. "All workers running for an elected position in the union must obtain three to ten written recommendations from management, depending on the position." Another rule stated that if the number of candidates did not exceed the number of positions, no elections needed to be held.

As for union meetings, the rules stipulated that only union members could attend and that the chairman always had strict control of the meeting. Without the chairman's permission, union members couldn't voice their opinions, couldn't publicize union events, couldn't display posters to express their dissent—and couldn't even leave a meeting to show their displeasure. To show their "respect," members had to remain present until after the chairman had left.

It was common at Nizumi (and all Toyota companies) for the management and the union to choose candidates for union office in closed-door meetings. At Nizumi, since the number of employees running never exceeded the number of positions available, the election involved merely handing out ballots with the employees chosen for each union position, and the workers sending back the ballots after checking "yes" or "no." No one could remember the last time the slate had been rejected. As all aspiring managers had to first serve as union leaders, an "elected" candidate occupied a fused position—as union leader and potential company manager.[7]

As a result of these rules, there was a complete disconnect between the workers and the union, which was supposed to be there to support them. Every last person I interviewed, including the union leader Kurasawa, said that the union was weak and in no way represented the voice of the workers. It was universally acknowledged that the primary role of the union was to rubber-stamp management decisions.

Even if the employees had a stronger union, most workers thought that a strike would be self-defeating. Kume summarized the general feeling. "I think most employees at Nizumi want to strike, but what effect will this have? We will not get support from the general public. If the union of Japan Railway goes on strike, the whole country comes to a stop because the country depends on the railway. But if we go on strike, management will just get angry and cut our jobs and paychecks, and no one in the country will care."

RECEIVING A PROMOTION

One afternoon in mid March, I was told to go to Human Resources. Since I was a contract employee, my review came up before that of the regular employees. I knew my work had been assessed by Higuchi, Uno, and Abe. As I walked down the stairs, I wondered if I would be demoted or fired, despite Abe's efforts. Instead, I was asked to sign a new contract—which gave me a

---

[7] According to Shozo Sasaki of the Aichi Labor Institute, company policies are supported from the lowest levels because "the trade union collaborates and makes one body with the management." He further claims that at Toyota an employee seeking a union office must obtain up to fifty recommendations. If an employee received a recommendation from a person outside of the company-union collaboration, he or she would be subject to organized harassment from the company and union. Elections are a charade in which the "ballots are not kept secret. The workers vote by workshop, writing down the names of candidates on a table without partition, under the eyes of managers." See Shozo Sasaki, *Struggles against Toyotaism, from Worker's Rights, Human Rights, and the Democratic Control of Multinationals,* Asia Pacific Trade Union Symposium (Tokyo: Zenroren Press, 1994), 130.

In her study of the Japanese steel industry, Toshiko Kamata discusses the reasons for the pacification of workers within the context of the authoritarian hierarchy of the organization: "One's criticism of the Company or the union is reported immediately to one's superiors. Wary of informers, the workers cease to talk." The reason, she writes, is that the union officers are recommended by both management and labor and hence are "under the dual control of the company and union." See Toshiko Kamata, "Japanese Management and the Loaning of Labor," in *Global Japanization,* edited by Tony Elger and Chris Smith (New York: Routledge, 1994), 107.

promotion to assistant manager as well as a pay increase. At a time of drastic cutbacks, this was quite a surprise.

When I returned from Human Resources, Higuchi pulled me away from my desk to discuss my contract. Higuchi was unaware that I had just gotten a raise, so he began talking about the company's current compensation plans. "This year everyone is getting a pay cut," he said. "The company has been cutting back the yearly bonus. At its best, the yearly bonus used to equal six months' salary. Now it will be only three or four."[8]

In the previous system, employees' pay was based exclusively on their level. Everyone at the same level got the same pay. Under the present system, workers who performed better got a higher base paycheck. Higuchi said, "If someone at the same level as me gets the same promotion, my salary may be different than his, but I will not know how different—there is no information."

Higuchi said the reason he was speaking to me in detail about company policy (some of which I already knew) was that a Chinese engineer in the vehicle design section had been very upset when he'd received a pay cut, and Higuchi had been worried that I would also be angry. Higuchi wanted me to fully understand conditions at the company.

"But I didn't get a pay cut," I told him. "I got a raise."

He was shocked. *"You're* getting a pay raise—*what*? Everyone else is getting a pay cut!" He sat looking at me, dumbfounded. Finally, he said, "Well, then you're happy, I don't need to talk to you about this."

When Erberto heard about my pay raise, he, too, became very upset. He had received a large pay cut, and he felt his work was equal to mine. He spoke angrily, "I want to get back at them, I want unionization! Why are some workers getting more than others? Why are some getting raises while others are getting pay cuts? Why are some people being let go while others remain?"

I was starting to feel guilty. Had my raise been the result of favoritism? Or had I really made significant contributions to my section? I had produced excellent results on Abe's pet project—but Uno had been adamantly opposed

---

[8] Foreigners on contract typically do not receive a yearly bonus but were instead compensated by receiving an equivalent sum as part of their monthly paycheck. The advantage of not being on a bonus system was that when the company was not as profitable, paychecks remained constant. The disadvantage was that if the company was doing well, and bonuses increased, yearly salaries could rise dramatically.

to my working on it at all. I would never learn why I'd been promoted. They never showed me their evaluations, no one reviewed my performance, and I never received comments from anyone. The decision was made behind closed doors.[9]

It *was* unfair to Erberto, for he'd worked just as hard as I had and had gotten similar results to mine. Erberto said, "I know what they're trying to do. They want to pacify you because you spoke out at the union meeting. They're giving you money so you won't speak up anymore."

"Don't be silly, Erberto—they won't co-opt me like that, and you know it."

His anger did not subside quickly. A few days later, he discovered a trick that Oda was pulling on him and other employees in his group to keep them from being promoted. "None of the simulation I do has my name on it, so during evaluation, Human Resources has nothing to look at. The problem is Oda doesn't support me," he said. "Even if I have superb results, it doesn't matter anyway. You only rise in this company if your team leader likes you."

So much for the policy of evaluation based on performance. Other members of Erberto's team had also been punished after falling out of favor. "Two engineers from our division must be sent to Toyota," he said, "and guess what? They just happen to the two people Oda hates the most. God! This place is terrible! I can't wait to leave. Who will do the engineering simulation when I leave? No one can do it but me—and they will look like shit!"

This thought seemed to console him, and we were able to maintain our close friendship.

Shiina gave me some insider information that helped explain the draconian measures Nizumi was putting into place. He said that the reason for the severe downsizing and radical pay cuts was because Toyota had sent an ultimatum to the company. They would buy half of Nizumi's stock—but only if Nizumi would insure that it would be in the black the following year. If not, Nizumi would be expelled from the Toyota group.

---

[9] In *Japan Works: Power and Paradox in Postwar Industrial Relations* (Ithaca, NY: Cornell University Press, 1997), John Price reveals that Westerners misunderstand the Japanese seniority-based wage system. He claims that as early as 1949 employers in Japan played a large role in wage increases. Since management decided wage increases, the "Japanese system is best described as an incentive or performance based wage system. To be sure, workers do advance up a wage grid, but the rate of advancement is determined by management for the most part." I agree with Price's evaluation of the wage system. The opportunity for an employee to receive higher pay was determined by position and advancement, which was strongly determined by an employee's superior.

Soon, Nizumi announced the final result of the labor-management negotiations. They gave everyone a raise in base pay of 4,361 yen per month (about $36) but they also cut back the yearly bonus from 4.5 to 2.5 month's wages. It was a clever plan because the official story was that all employees had received raises, whereas in fact, everyone had received a 20 percent to 30 percent pay cut.

We were fast approaching the end-of-year promotion meeting, and it was rumored that Kurata was to be promoted one level up, to a higher-level management position. We all wondered who would fill his shoes. Many were eager for a new leader, for Kurata had been disappointing in providing new product development. The Advanced Design Project debacle ("We can do anything"—all words, no action) was directly attributed to him. His actions had contributed to Nizumi's reduced market share and the resulting punishment from Toyota. But was Kurata being demoted? On the contrary.

There was a lot of gossip around the office about who—among the half dozen men primed for the position—would get the job. Erberto and Chen would occasionally inform me about what was happening, because their boss Oda was privy to high-level gossip and was not shy about discussing the power struggle that occurred behind the scenes. We were all anxious about the outcome.

When they finally announced the promotions and transfers, we were all shocked to hear that an incompetent and spineless subordinate named Mori, a close associate of Kurata's, would become the new department manager. Mori was so inept that the standard joke about him was that he retired from the company a long time ago. "Kurata doesn't want to give up power," said Shiina. "He wants to have his puppet in place so he can keep pulling the strings."

Kurata's desire to continue to control the Design Division had a history. A few years back, the Research and Design existed in a division called R&D. Nakaya was a high-level manager in the analysis section while Kurata was a high-level manager in the research section. At that time, Shizumi *gikan* retired and a power vacuum developed. Nakaya attempted to gain control in the division by promoting his subordinates. Kurata became furious since he lost power and influence in a number of high-level positions. Kurata's appointment was to ensure that he would not again loose control over important positions. According to Shiina it was also "payback" and a signal to discourage those who would attempt to usurp his power.

The promotion of Mori was a learning experience for me. I had read about the seniority-based promotional system at Japanese companies, but I was learning that in most cases, promotion was based on power and connections.

Once Kurata was elevated to his new position, he moved up to the sixth floor and immediately made changes in the physical structure of his work environment. He tore down the walls of the office that Sasaki, the previous manager, had built. This had been the only enclosed office in the entire building. He also broke up one of the large engineering groups and scattered the managers into different positions so he could place his close subordinates in key positions. Erberto worked on the sixth floor and said that in the morning they were starting to have military-style drills similar to what we had observed at Toyota.

GETTING CANNED

I first met Kawasaki during my job interview—he managed my visit at Nizumi. He spoke fluent English and seemed very well educated. He was a drivetrain specialist so I thought he might be the manager of my section, but when I started the job, I discovered that Kawasaki worked directly under Abe, managing another group unrelated to his specialty.

During the job rotation meeting, Abe announced that Kawasaki was to be moved to a government research laboratory. The lab was a collective of the largest companies in the industry where they worked on joint projects to develop Japanese technology.

When I spoke to Shiina, he said that Kawasaki was being moved because upper management didn't like him. Shiina told me why Kawasaki had fallen out of favor. The company had initially decided to hire Erberto for a position in our section, as he had requested, but as they were enthusiastically preparing to accept him, Abe suddenly rejected him. Apparently Kawasaki had first introduced Erberto to Abe's boss instead of coming directly to Abe, breaking one of Abe's cardinal rules: all subordinates must talk to him before talking to his superior. Abe became very upset about being slighted by his subordinate and told Kawasaki that Erberto would not be allowed to work in the department—and possibly not at the company at all. Kawasaki, in panic, asked Kurata, to whom he was connected, for a big favor. Could Erberto work in

Kurata's division? If Nizumi couldn't offer Erberto a job at this point, it would be terribly embarrassing to the company. Kurata agreed to take on Erberto. This further angered Abe because he and Kurata had been rivals for years.

Kawasaki had made a grave mistake for which he would pay dearly. Soon after the incident, he was transferred out of the drivetrain section and given a menial job. Now, he was being sent for three years to the government research laboratory. By this point, I had learned that it was customary for managers to rid themselves of undesirable employees by moving them into other positions. Kawasaki's punishment was particularly severe since his new place of employment was four hours from his home and he would only see his family on weekends.

As soon as my conversation with Shiina ended, I raced over to Erberto. I had the inside scoop on his job assignment and wanted to share it with him immediately. He just shook his head in disbelief. After all these years, we had finally learned why he'd been diverted to the Design Division: because of Kawasaki's breech of etiquette.

A few days later, management distributed the "Communication Rules." It began with the insipid message: "April is a nice season and the time of warmth so let's think about the importance and pleasure of communication during business." The document discussed the transmission of information and how sound and intonation and gesture help communicate a message. It then presented an interesting developmental history of communication. "The person we initially communicate with is our mother," it read. "The way of communication is not by words but through physical intimacy [*skinship*]." The discussion about *skinship* ended by saying that it strongly influenced the personality development of children and that recent research revealed that physical intimacy with animals can "relax your mind." The document then discussed the three important aspects of business communication: receiving orders, sharing job instructions, and reporting and transmitting other information. In communicating, the employee must have a clear purpose. He must listen carefully and try to understand what the other person wants. It was important to try to understand what the listener was thinking (*kangaekata*) and to choose the best way to express the core meaning of the topic being discussed.

"Some humor including joking is also important in creating a good atmosphere for communication," it read. "When you order someone to do something, you should think of how to word it, and in many cases it is a good idea to use humor in your approach." Words, however, were not the only important aspect of communication. Feelings were also important, "You should understand the other person's feelings by closely observing their expressions, attitudes, and actions." The document claimed that the Japanese people do not typically express their feelings freely, so it was important to observe their body language. The document ended with a note, "If you can practice the above rules, communication will be easier and more enjoyable. Always remember—practicing and noticing feelings without words is very important."

Kawasaki's good-bye party was held in a Chinese restaurant in the neighboring town and was attended by a large contingent of the highest-level managers, including Nakaya. After the usual good-bye speeches, a moderator walked up to the podium and began a question-and-answer quiz about Kawasaki's life at the company. Kawasaki stood in the center of the room while the moderator posed a question to the audience. When an employee answered, the crowd laughed and Kawasaki interjected a few funny comments. Someone suddenly shouted a question about who was managing the section when the Irish engineer was at the company. Another responded, "Ask Mehri *san,* he must know!" I was hauled to the podium to a barrage of laughter. The moderator asked, "So, who was the *buchō* in charge when the company had to deal with the problem of the Irish engineer?"

A few years back, Sheila, the Irish engineer, had complained about overtime work to a diplomat at the Irish embassy.[10] The diplomat was upset with what he had heard and wrote a letter to the company asking them to pull back on overtime work requirements. The company was embarrassed and did not handle its response well. The Human Resources manager who was responsible for foreign engineers was caught in the crossfire, and she was blamed for the incident. As it happened, she was the only female manager at Nizumi, so pinning the blame on her alone created quite a stir. (You might think that after this incident, the company became more careful about inflicting overtime on its foreign engineers, but Nizumi's response was to refuse to hire any more Irish engineers.)

Now at Kawasaki's good-bye party, everyone was waiting for me to answer

---

[10]   At the time Irish government had an agreement with Japanese companies to hire Irish engineers who were finding it difficult to obtain jobs in Ireland because of the high unemployment rate.

the question, but I hadn't a clue about who the *buchō* was at the time. I made a few incorrect guesses, to bursts of laughter in the room, especially from the higher-level managers. In comic desperation, I suggested Dr. Zombie.

"Wrong," they yelled raucously.

The moderator finally had mercy on me and whispered, "It's Kurata."

"Oh, I know," I said, "It's the design director!"

Although this time I was right, they still screamed with laughter. The men were becoming very intoxicated.

Now the moderator was asking Kawasaki, "So who is your favorite office lady?"

Kawasaki named a few with whom he had worked, paused, then added, "And Miss Araki."

Someone shouted, "Oh, yeah, we know about *her*!" More laughter.

Then someone asked Kawasaki, "So now that you will be living so far away from home, will you visit your family on weekends?"

"Sometimes" he said "But not always."

"Ok, now, when you visit your family what do you plan to do: (1) Bring your laundry home, (2) Have your wife cook you some *real* food, or (3) Spend the weekend in Disney Land?"

The crowd was waiting for a jokey response. But Kawasaki just said quietly, "I think I'll spend time with my kids in the park." This had a sobering effect on us.

Then the moderator presented Kawasaki with an exquisitely wrapped present, saying, "It will be useful when you are lonely."

Kawasaki undid the wrapping, and out came a picture frame. The moderator said, "See? There are three places to put pictures, one for your wife and the others are for your two kids."

Then the moderator gave him another present—an iron. He would need one of his own, now that he would be living far away from his wife.

It was Kawasaki's turn to speak. He began by thanking those who had attended the party, and he gave a lofty talk about what technology would be important for the company in the future. Suddenly, he launched into a personal complaint about his new housing allowance. "I am only receiving 50,000 yen [about $420] to pay for my apartment," he said. "That's not enough for a studio in the worst part of town. How can my children come and visit when I can't make them comfortable?"

The party ended soon after that but some of us went on to a second drinking party with Kawasaki. When we sat down for a few drinks, Kawasaki told me, "My wife is a pharmacist, she's a very nice wife."

"Too bad she and your kids can't go with you," I said.

There are a number of institutional factors in the Japanese education system that prevent the family from moving to follow the husband. The first is that to ensure that children enter the proper university, which optimizes their chances of getting a good job, it is important for them to attend a well-known secondary school. Students and parents invest huge amounts of time and money on tutorial schools to prepare for the entrance exam to the high school of their choice, but acceptance is not transferable to another school.

Parents also feel that they will jeopardize their children's performance if they are suddenly switched to another school in which they do not have friends who can provide emotional support. A final obstacle is the location of the high-level schools, which are all in and around the major cities. But many of those transferred out of the company are relocated in the countryside, where the schools are not as good. In addition, it is difficult to transfer a mortgage from one house to another in a different town.[11]

Three days after his farewell party, Kawasaki came to our section and said good-bye by patting us on the backs and placing a cookie on each desk.

The next week, Erberto said, "Hey, let's get together with Kawasaki for dinner." Erberto gave him a call and he arranged a meeting at one of Erberto's favorite Indian restaurants. It was a quiet, classy place, without the loud chatter found in most *izakayas,* so we could talk easily. Kawasaki said the organization of the government lab was fundamentally flawed. "All of the patents or new technology developed are to be shared among all the companies involved," he said. But since all the companies were competitors, and some were fierce rivals for even the most minute market share, the engineers almost never shared information with each other. Many spent their days busying themselves with useless paper work or trivial hobbies. "I once asked a young engineer who worked at one of these labs what he did all day, and he responded, 'I spend most of my days at the bookstore reading comics.'"

We asked Kawasaki why he had agreed to leave Nizumi. "I was hesitant to accept the position," he said, "because it meant that I would have to live away

---

[11] From an interview with Yamato Kobayashi of the Research Institute of Democracy and Education, January 20, 2000.

from my family." His son and daughter were both young teenagers and were entering that critical stage in their lives when they had to study hard to enter well-known schools. Kawasaki's boss assured him that it would only be for three years, and his job would be secure when he returned. After much arm-twisting, he finally agreed and began preparing for his departure. Before leaving, however, he was told that his job was going to be extended to six years, with a strong possibility of another six years on top of that. If Kawasaki wanted to remain employed, he would have to accept the job, for he had little chance of obtaining an equivalent position at another company.[12] And so he had been tricked into going to exile for perhaps a dozen years.

ADMIRATION FOR THE UNITED AUTO WORKERS

Bridgestone was undergoing a restructuring similar to Nizumi's. One Bridgestone manager who lost his job took his life in a ritual suicide. Before he died, he distributed a chilling note to his colleagues. "[Bridgestone] is an excellent company that continues to expand its earnings every year, making a record 100 billion yen or more. This is made possible by sacking much of the workforce and by cutting wages for the rest, thus depriving us of the basic means of living. . . . We must stand up against executives who treat us like trash."[13] Many workers at Nizumi could relate to him, and he became a symbol of the misery restructuring was causing. My friend Mochida remarked, "He made a terrible mistake—he should have killed his boss, not himself."

Although this ritual suicide made the news, other deaths did not. It was becoming common for humiliated employees to throw themselves in front of evening trains, thereby saving face and providing their families with a life-insurance payoff.

I asked Higuchi if it was common in Japan for salarymen to kill themselves by way of *seppuku*.[14] "In the Edo period it was popular," he said. "People that do it today are usually on the extreme right. It's not the typical

---

[12]   An engineer with a specific skill would only be hired at the same seniority level by another automobile company that manufactures the specific product, but large Japanese companies typically do not hire full-time white-collar employees from a competing company. His only other alternative would be to quit and work at a parts supplier with lesser benefits and lower "name" status.

[13]   Atsushi Yamada, "Death of a Salaryman," *Japan Quarterly* (July–September 1999): 40–46.

[14]   Often referred to as *hara-kiri* in American literature, ritual suicide involves stabbing oneself in the stomach.

behavior of a Japanese businessman. I heard that in America when someone gets fired, the situation is quite different. The person who was fired will show up at work the next day and shoot his boss and the others responsible for his dismissal."

"It happens," I admitted. "But not often."

"What I find strange," said Higuchi, "is that they say in a few years the economy will be good again. But now that they are firing so many people, when the economy picks up we will have to train many new workers again."

In early April, those who had chosen to take refresh leave the previous year began returning to the company—but not for long. Most of them were fired, contrary to what Nizumi had promised. Shiina said, "I heard that when one person in the Design Division returned, he was forced to fill out a voluntary retirement form. They gave him a choice, either retire and accept an early retirement package, or be fired and receive no company benefits. He asked if he could be transferred to another section, but they said no and forced him to leave the company."

I thought about my former enthusiasm for refresh leave and marveled that I had been so naïve. My Japanese colleagues had known full well the consequences of taking refresh leave, which was why none of them had chosen to take it.

Later that month, Kurasawa called me to his desk. He said there would be a companywide union meeting open to all employees, and he wanted me to attend. I thought this was strange since in the past, as the union leader, he tried to hide union information from me. Union rules also forbade contract workers to attend meetings.

While I talked with Kurasawa, Mochida suddenly interjected, "The American will speak up!"

Kurasawa nodded and smiled.

Now I saw why they wanted me at the meeting. They valued my American antiauthoritarian stance. They needed a "trouble-maker" like me.

How ironic, I thought. Here I was in the supposed land of labor harmony, where employees and managers were supposed to solve disputes by consensus—yet the workers really long for a strong trade union like the UAW. I thought, "If only American workers could hear this!"

It was exciting. I intended to stir things up at the meeting, and this time, I had the men on my side. We entered the meeting room, where the tables and chairs had been arranged in a large square. Employees arrived, group by group, until the room was packed. The last to arrive were the union leaders. The senior leader sat in the center and his two subordinates flanked his side. They started talking about conditions at the company and why restructuring was necessary. They were taking the same line as management: if employees could persevere and be patient, they would be rewarded. The meeting was planned for one hour, and they spoke for a full fifty-five minutes without breaking for a moment. Finally, it was time for the workers to speak. One person asked a question about overtime pay and received a vague response. Another asked a question about bonuses and received a similar answer. A third asked about a leave of absence and was told to endure and he would be rewarded. Suddenly, the question period was over—before they had recognized me. Now I wouldn't get to speak. I was very disappointed, and I tried to get the question period extended—without success.

On my way back to my desk I bumped into Jimbo, who had also attended the meeting, and asked him why the question and answer session was so short. "The reason is that they do not want to hear anything that will surprise them," he said.

Later, I grumbled to Higuchi, "Why do they even bother having a meeting?"

"They have a meeting so they can say they had a discussion, but the reality is they only give a report on what they have decided. After they make a decision, there will be no change."

After the meeting, I went from person to person asking their opinions on the situation. Time and again, my colleagues spoke of the UAW as a good union that defended worker's rights, as opposed to the pacified Japanese enterprise unions. Kurasawa said, "In the U.S. the UAW is strong so they can strike—but Japanese unions are weak, we cannot strike, we are all robots."

I asked, "Why *don't* you just go on strike?"

Shiina shook his head, "Our situation is like that scene in a Western—you know the one—when the guns are drawn and the first person who moves gets shot. It's either move or die, but if we move we die, too."

"What do you mean?" I asked.

"If we do nothing, more and more of us will be fired. But if we strike, we will certainly be fired. If we want to put our ideals to good use, the only chance we have is to work for the community, like volunteer work for the handicapped or the homeless, that's all. We cannot strike, and everyone in the company knows this."

Technicians, who belong to a smaller, separate company called Nizumi Technical Staff, didn't even have an ineffectual union like ours. Kume said, "If we have a problem, we contact management, and they try to solve it, without much effect. The managers listen to us, but most of the time they do nothing to correct the problem." Although the Technical Staff did not have a union, the policy of the Nizumi Motors Union had a profound and deleterious effect on their benefits.

Kume said, "Everyone is angry about the union decisions. We all want to strike but it will not happen," he said. "We don't ever speak out. In Japan, many employees work for a lifetime at the same company, so speaking out results in a demotion later in one's career."

I asked, "Doesn't the union do *anything* to protect worker's rights?"

"Not really. If a union member speaks out against company policy, he will lose his job—it's that simple."

The facade of unionization meant you kept your eyes closed and your mouth shut.

All my friends who worked on the line had no job protection at all. They all lost their jobs. After Kofi left Nizumi, he worked at a few odd jobs but later got a good job at Nissan. Sanan went back to working as a waiter at a Thai restaurant. Nicholi quit factory life for good and found a job as a manager of a Mexican restaurant. Octavio was able to find a good job at a supplier company, while Jorge returned to Peru. The last I heard of Romone was that he had moved up north and got a job selling vegetables. Mehdi and Hossein continued to work at their company with only the remaining employees— the owner and his son.

GOOD-BYE, NIZUMI

On Christmas Eve, 1998, there was a fire in my parents' house in Connecticut. My mother was hospitalized, and my siblings begged me to come home and help rebuild the house. By then, I was feeling homesick, and I felt if I stayed in Japan any longer, I would lose touch with my family and friends

back home. Furthermore, as a foreigner at Nizumi, I felt permanently inse-
cure. I suspected that I did not have much of a future there.

When I told Higuchi I was leaving, I spoke only about my parents' situation. He had been such a kind boss—I didn't want him to feel that anything
at Nizumi had been unpleasant for me. A few days later, Higuchi told me that
Uno said I could take a leave of absence for six months and then return to
the company. I thanked him for the offer but refused. A couple of days later,
he approached me again. This time he said that Uno would save my desk for
me in the section for one entire year if I wanted to return. Obviously, Uno
wanted me to stay. The hundreds of colorful simulations I had produced,
whether they were accurate or not, had always added an extra "wow" to his
presentations.

It was only a matter of days before the men organized a drinking party for
me. We walked to an *izakaya* near the company, where a private tatami room
had been reserved. I sat next to Higuchi, and the others sat around us. Kurasawa was talking about how he thought the American economy was a bubble that would burst. Dr. Zombie told me about the early years of one of the
professors closely associated with the company. "During the first ten years of
his graduate school studies, all he did was play softball. But now look how famous he is!" He laughed his madman's laugh.

Higuchi turned to me and said, "When you leave, I will have a problem.
The drivetrain simulation will now be transferred to the Design Division." I
didn't know if he was trying to make me feel guilty about leaving or if he was
really troubled about handing responsibility over to our rival. Already, these
territorial issues were becoming less important to me.

The beer soon came, and Abe started the festivities by toasting me and
talking about his impressions of me when we first met. He said I was one of
the best engineers in the section and added, "I hope that others will follow
the steps of Mehri *san*."

I'd always liked Abe, and I appreciated his kind words, but they made me
feel a little uncomfortable. Performance had become a critical issue for the
men, and some, like Kurasawa, whom I now considered a friend, were not
high performers—nor would they ever be.

Then each man stood up and spoke about his relationship with me. Scarface said when I arrived at the company, he thought I was too serious, but
then he kept hearing laughter from the desks in my area, so he realized I must
be a fun-loving person. Jimbo spoke about having "the American" in the sec-

tion who was shaking things up. He thought my example might lead to a more independent way of thinking, "But, alas, things didn't change at all. However, I am thankful I have gotten to know Mehri *san*." Shiga joked about our wrestling match and said he was looking forward to the next one. I said I was looking forward to the next round on the karaoke stage. Kurasawa and Mochida joked about the International Adventure Club and how I went to the mountains to meet women. Higuchi gave a more conventional speech about my work and said he appreciated the progress I had made. Kume thanked me profoundly for introducing him to Rie, who was now his wife.

In recent years, several books have been written about the Japanese workplace, and some, particularly those written about transplants in America and Europe, have finally reported accurately about the Toyota Production System. However, the book that gets it best about Japan is still Kamata Satoshi's *Japan in the Passing Lane*—written more than thirty years ago. Kamata worked at Toyota for six months as a temporary worker and covertly documented his work experience. One of the many accidents that he documented was that of a worker who suffered a severe concussion when his hand touched an electric cord that was frayed. "Luckily the current passed through the base of his finger. If it had gone to his heart, he would have been killed instantly."

Kamata talks about a newsletter he received that discussed lengthening the workday. The workers were despondent. "They take it for granted that it will be decided by the top and sent down. Then again, many of them are thinking that whatever happens, it won't make much difference."

What has changed at Toyota in the last three decades? Not much. I experienced the same unsafe work environment, the same oppressive mechanisms of worker control, and the same power manipulations as Kamata chronicled. I wonder what will happen in the next thirty years. The Japanese I met at Nizumi were justifiably cynical about politics. Because they are denied access to a fair, democratic process in either the corporate or the political arenas, change will not come easily, nor soon.

After each member of the section had said a few words about me, I was presented with two gifts: a Nizumi T-shirt and a plastic model of the vehicle I had worked on. When I stood up to leave, all the guys stood up, too. They looked at me without saying a word. Abe put out his hand for a shake. Uno did the same, and so did Higuchi. I shook their hands warmly.

Everyone waited for some final remarks from me, but I was exhausted and had nothing more to say. I just gave them a smile. All my observations and assessments were confined to the journal I'd been writing from my first day at Nizumi to my last, a journal that testifies to my growing understanding of the Japanese culture and the bitter realities of the Toyota Production System.

From that journal has grown this book.

CHARACTER LIST

Abani	section office lady
Abe	manager of the Technical Research Division
Aizawa	engineer who works for Hoshino in the Advanced Design section
Akiko	a friend with whom Mehri did a home stay in the late 1980s
Baba	Nizumi worker who is transferred to Toyota
Bhanu	Indian factory worker whom Mehri meets in Japanese language class
Chen	mild-mannered, well-educated Chinese man who came to Japan after graduate school in England
Chiba	single man, colleague of Kurasawa's
Erberto	young Italian, best friends with Mehri
Fuse	dorm-mate, salesman
Genda	lazy competitor to Mehri in the Advanced Design group
Hans	engineer from Germany who came to work at Nizumi
Higuchi	Mehri's immediate boss
Hiraga, a.k.a. "Old droopy eyes"	lazy manager, heavy smoker
Hirama	short, stocky older man in charge of documenting competitor products and parts
Hoshino	manager in Advanced Design section
Hossein	Iranian who works at family-owned factory
Ienaga	quiet engineer, bullied by his group
Iida	tennis-playing female engineer at Nizumi
Inoue	the CAD clown, manager in the Design Division
Ishida	charismatic Nizumi candidate elected to local council
Ishii	effeminate engineer in Ebisawa's group
Jimbo	subordinate to Scarface

Jorge .... Peruvian who worked on the line, good friend to Mehri

Kado .... technician who worked in Erberto's group

Kawasaki ... previous manager of section who managed Mehri's interview

Kofi .... African factory worker, great friends with Mehri and Erberto

Koizumi ... owner of the Red Samurai pub

Kondo ...... middle-aged women who worked at Nizumi and loved punk rock

Kume ...... good-looking technician who works across from Mehri

Kurasawa ... union leader of Mehri's section

Kurata ...... director of the Design Department, tremendously important executive

Matsuki ..... Oda's copycat subordinate

Mehdi ...... Iranian factory worker, veteran of the Iran-Iraq war

Mochida .... young engineer who worked in same group as Kurasawa

Mori .... Kurata's inept associate

Nakaya .... high-level manager with commanding personality

Nicholi .... Romanian factory worker

Nishida .... Erberto's first boss, nice, mild-mannered employee

Octavio ..... Peruvian worker of Japanese descent who worked on the line, a good friend to Mehri

Oda .... Chen's boss, and Erberto's second boss, a confident, power-hungry manager

Ramone .... Peruvian factory worker of Japanese descent

Rie .... woman Mehri met at the city fair and introduced to Kume

Saiki .... handsome design engineer, Kurata's subordinate

Sanan ...... Thai ex–canoe maker who works on the line

Sawa .... crashes Baba's good-bye party

Scarface .... powerfully connected, a bully

Sheila ...... Irish engineer who was at Nizumi before Mehri arrived

Shiga .... subordinate to Scarface

Shiina ...... colleague who sat near Mehri and taught him much about Nizumi

Shirai ...... progressive activist in the Open Society

Shizumi ... very famous, charismatic older man, retired, former vice president
Gikan   of Nizumi

Steve .... American engineer from Ford

Suzuki ..... worked with Chen and developed mental health problems

Takagi ..... office lady who learned to be a skilled engineer

Takanashi ... antisocial engineer in Mehri's work group

Toyama .... law professor active in the Open Society, a progressive party

Uno .... strict section manager

Watanabe ... Suzuki's abusive boss

Yasui .... Oda's subordinate who tries to get information from Mehri

Dr. Zombie .. manager with maniacal laugh
  (**Takano**)

These are all last names, since in Japan only family and close friends use a person's first name.

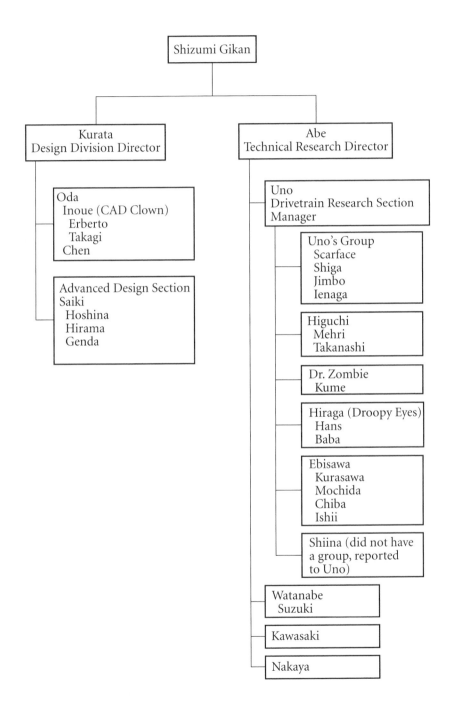

GLOSSARY

The Japanese words in this book have been transliterated using the Revised Hepburn System.

abunai: dangerous
buchō: upper-level manager
chōrei: morning drill at Toyota
chōshi warui: bad feeling
danchi: semipublic housing
dangō: bid-rigging
enka: Japanese country or blues, popular Karaoke selection
erai hito: upper-level manager
erai sensei: esteemed professor
gaman: to endure
ganbaru: "Let's give it our best," "Go for it!" used in many Japanese work rituals
gōkon: an informal meeting of single men and women
hachimaki: head wrapping
hai, wakarimashita: yes, I understand
hanchō: team leader, boss
hanko: Japanese signature stamp
henna gaijin: strange foreigner
hibachi: small charcoal grill
honne: what you actually feel or do (as opposed to *tatemae*)
ijime: bullying
izakaya: small pubs for businessmen
kachō: mid-level manager
kaiten sushi: budget restaurant where sushi passes in front of you on a conveyer belt
kaizen: continuous improvement for greater efficiency
kakarichō: assistant manager

kangaekata: shared way of thinking

kanpai: cheers

katachi: form, shape

katai: tough

keiretsu: industrial conglomerate

keiyaku shain: temporary worker

kōhai: subordinate

kokoro: how one feels and thinks

mado giwa zoku: an employee whose desk is placed by the window

mazui: tasteless, odious

nabe: traditional Japanese stew of vegetables and meat

natto: a sticky paste of fermented soy and sometimes mixed with raw egg

nemawashi: a collective action among employees who have decided that a company decision or policy needs correction

nijikai: second drinking party

obentō: a lunchbox

ojōsan: a spoiled, naïve woman

omiai: formal match-making

onegai shimasu: please, do me a favor

onsen bath: a hot spring

sabishii: lonely

sābisu zangyō: service overtime, or unpaid overtime

saoiryō rōdōsei: payment based entirely on performance and company bonus

sankon: marriages that result from company contact

shōchū: a relatively inexpensive rice wine

seishain: permanent employees of the company

senpai: teacher, mentor

shōji screen: a sliding door made of light wood and paper

tanshin funin: living away from one's home because of a job transfer

tatemae: what you are supposed to feel or do (as opposed to *honne*)

yakitori: grilled meat

yasashii: kind-hearted

yoshi: exhortation "Let's do it, let's work hard!"

REFERENCES

Abegglen, James. *The Japanese Factory: Aspects of Its Social Organization*. Glencoe, IL: Free Press, 1958.

Acker, Joan. "Hierarchies, Jobs, Bodies: A Theory of Gendered Organizations." *Gender and Society* 4, no. 2 (June 1990): 139–58.

Babson, Steve. *Lean Work: Empowerment and Exploitation in the Global Auto Industry*. Detroit: Wayne State University Press, 1995.

Berggren, Christian. *Alternatives to Lean Production*. Ithaca, NY: Cornell University Press, 1992.

Besser, Terry. *Team Toyota: Transplanting the Toyota Culture to the Camry Plant in Kentucky*. Albany: State University of New York Press, 1996.

Brenner, Mark, David Fairris, and John Russer. *Flexible Work Practices and Occupational Health and Safety*. Political Economy Research Institute, Working Paper Series, no. 30, 2002.

Brinton, Mary. *Women and the Economic Miracle: Gender and Work in Postwar Japan*. Berkeley: University of California Press, 1993.

Burawoy, Michael. *Manufacturing Consent*. Chicago: University of Chicago Press, 1979.

Clark, Rodney. *The Japanese Company*. New Haven: Yale University Press, 1979.

Cole, Robert. *Japanese Blue Collar*. Berkeley: University of California Press, 1971.

———. *Work, Mobility, and Participation*. Berkeley: University of California Press, 1979.

Cusumano, Michael. *The Japanese Automobile Industry*. Cambridge: Harvard University Press, 1989.

Dore, Ronald. *British Factory-Japanese Factory: The Origins of National Diversity in Industrial Relations*. Berkeley: University of California Press, 1973.

Elger, Tony, and Chris Smith. *Global Japanization? The Transnational Transformation of the Labor Process*. New York: Routledge, 1994.

Fucini, Joseph, and Suzy Fucini. *Working for the Japanese: Inside Mazda's American Auto Plant*. New York: Free Press, 1990.

Fujita, Kuniko, and Richard Child Hill. *Japanese Cities in the World Economy*. Philadelphia: Temple University Press, 1993.

Garrahan, Philip, and Paul Stewart. *The Nissan Enigma: Flexibility at Work in a Local Economy.* New York: Mansell, 1992.

Gordon, Andrew. *The Evolution of Labor Relations in Japan.* Cambridge: Harvard University Press, 1988.

Gottfried, Heidi. "Compromising Positions: Emergent Neo-Fordisms and Embedded Gender Contracts." *British Journal of Sociology* 51, no. 2 (June 2000): 235–59.

———. "Temp(t)ing Bodies: Shaping Gender at Work in Japan." *Sociology: The Journal of the British Sociology Association* 37 no. 2 (2003).

Gottfried, Heidi, and Laurie Graham. "Constructing Difference: The Making of Gendered Subcultures in a Japanese Automobile Plant." *Sociology* 27, no. 4 (November 1993): 611–28.

Gottfried, Heidi, and Nagisa Hayashi-Kato. "Gendering Work: Deconstructing the Narrative of the Japanese Economic Miracle." *Work, Employment, and Society* 12, no. 1 (March 1988): 25–36.

Graham, Laurie. *On the Line at Subaru-Isuzu.* Ithaca, NY: Cornell University Press, 1995.

Haley, John Owen. *Authority without Power: Law and the Japanese Paradox.* New York: Oxford University Press, 1991.

Hane, Mikiso. *Peasants, Rebels, and Outcasts: The Underside of Modern Japan.* New York: Pantheon, 1982.

Iwao, Sumiko. *The Japanese Women: Traditional Image and Changing Reality.* Cambridge: Harvard University Press, 1993.

Kamata, Satoshi. *Japan in the Passing Lane.* New York: Pantheon, 1982.

Kamata, Toshiko. "Japanese Management and the Loaning of Labor." In *Global Japanization,* edited by Tony Elger and Chris Smith. New York: Routledge, 1994.

Kawanishi, Hirosuke. *Enterprise Unionism in Japan.* London: Kegan Paul International, 1992.

Keeney, Martin, and Richard Florida. *Beyond Mass Production.* New York: Oxford University Press, 1993.

Kim, Suk, and Mahfuzul Haque. *The Asian Financial Crisis of 1997: Causes and Policy Responses.* Detroit: Multinational Business Review, 2002.

Kondo, Dorrinne. *Crafting Selves: Power, Gender, and Discourses of Identity in a Japanese Workplace.* Chicago: University of Chicago Press, 1990.

Krauss, Ellis, Thomas Rohlen, and Patricia Steinhoff. *Conflict in Japan.* Honolulu: University of Hawaii Press, 1984.

Lebra, Takie. *Japanese Patterns of Behavior.* Honolulu: University of Hawaii Press, 1976.

Liker, Jeffery, Jon Ettlie, and and John Campbell. *Engineered in Japan: Japanese Technology Management Practices.* New York: Oxford University Press, 1995.

Lo, Jeannie. *Office Ladies, Factory Women: Life and Work at a Japanese Company.* Armonk, NY: M. E. Sharpe, 1990.

Milkman, Ruth. *Gender at Work: The Dynamics of Job Segregation by Sex during World War II.* Urbana: University of Illinois Press, 1987.

Nakane, Chie. *Japanese Society.* Berkeley: University of California Press, 1970.

Ogasawara, Yuko. *Office Ladies and Salaried Men: Power, Gender, and Work in Japanese Companies.* Berkeley: University of California Press, 1998.

Okimoto, Daniel, and Thomas Rohlen. *Readings on Contemporary Society and Political Economy.* Stanford, CA: Stanford University Press, 1988.

Osterman, Paul. "How Common Is Workplace Transformation and Who Adopts It?" *Industrial and Labor Relations Review* 47, no. 2 (January 1994): 173–88.

Parker, Mike, and Jane Slaughter. *Choosing Sides: Unions and the Team Concept.* Boston: South End Press, 1988.

Perrucci, Robert. *Japanese Auto Transplants in the American Heartland.* New York: Aldine De Gruyter, 1994.

Price, John. *Japan Works: Power and Paradox in Postwar Japan.* Ithaca, NY: Cornell University Press, 1997.

Rinehart, James, Christopher Huxley, and David Robertson. *Just Another Car Factory: Lean Production and Its Discontents.* Ithaca, NY: Cornell University Press 1997.

Roberts, Glenda. *Staying on the Line: Blue Collar Women in Contemporary Japan.* Honolulu: University of Hawaii Press, 1994.

Rohlen, Thomas. *For Harmony and Strength.* Berkeley: University of California Press, 1974.

Sobek, Durward, Allen Ward, and Jeffrey Liker. "Toyota's Principles of Set-Based Concurrent Engineering." *Sloan Management Review* 40, no.2 (winter 1999): 67–83.

Sugimoto, Yoshio. *Introduction to Japanese Society.* New York: Cambridge University Press, 1997.

Tsuda, Takeyuki. "The Permanence of Temporary Migration." *Journal of Asian Studies* 58, no. 3 (August 1999): 687–722.

Womack, James P., Daniel T. Jones, and Daniel Roos. *The Machine That Changed the World.* New York: Harper Perennial, 1991.

Workers Rights, Human Rights, and the Democratic Control of Multinationals. Proceedings from the Asia-Pacific Trade Union Symposium. Tokyo: Zenroren Press, 1994.

Yamada, Atsushi. "*Death of a Salaryman.*" *Japan Quarterly* (July–September 1999): 40–46.

INDEX

Obedience, 28, 67–68

Obentō box, 56

Octavio (Japanese Peruvian worker), 104–5, 108

Oda (manager), 80, 90, 163–64, 198; competition with other divisions, 137–40; drinking parties and, 98–99

Office ladies, 11, 23–24, 28, 43, 148

Omiai information, 60

Onsen bath, 31

On-the-job training, 35

On the Line at Subaru-Isuzu (Graham), 8

Open office space, 9, 14–15, 21; seating hierarchy, 121–22

Open Society, 173–79

Ostracism, fear of, 184–85

Outsourcing, 112

Overstayers, 112–14

Overtime, 23, 34, 44–45, 190; foreign workers and, 202; service (*sābisu zangyō*), 94–97, 99, 124

Overwork, 53, 54, 67, 73–74, 76, 178–82

Oyabun-kobun relationship, 91n

Pamphlets on company goals, 19–20

Parker, Mike, 8

Patents, competition for, 141, 204

Patent submissions, 146–47

Pay-by-performance policy, 120–21, 198–99

Peruvians of Japanese descent, 13, 101, 103, 104

Politics, 125–27, 171–74; campaign rally, 127–29; city government, 174–78; getting out the vote, 132–36; opinions of the candidate, 129–32; rules that undermine democracy, 182–83

Pollution, 70–71

Posters, 15, 18, 79; contests, 116–17

Power groups, 89–92, 121

Presentations, 15, 163–64; harassment during, 41–42

Price, John, 5

Problem-solving, 35–38

Procurement process, 176–77

Production technology school, 5–6

Professors (*erai sensei*), 32, 89, 90

Promotions, 50–52, 157–58, 197–200

Pull manufacturing, 5

Quality control, 5, 101

Quality movement, 5

Quitting, 187–88

Race issues, 78–79, 101–3, 166–67

Refresh leave, 169–71, 206

Reischauer, Edwin, 29

Research department, 138–40

Restructuring, 123–25, 185–86; challenge leave, 162–63, 169; city government and, 177; contract workers and, 165–67, 188–89; pay cuts, 197–200; refresh leave, 169–71, 206; takeover plans, 192–94; work-sharing, 192–93

Retirement, early, 169, 184, 185

Rie (female worker), 104–5, 106

Rinehart, James, 8

Robertson, David, 8

Rolf (German consultant), 82–84

Romone (contract worker), 101, 103, 188

Rules: categories, 8–9; democracy undermined, 182–83, 210; for dormitories, 17; labor-management, 192–96; schools and, 95; service (*sābisu zangyō*), 94–97, 99; types, 9; unwritten, 8, 96–97

Safety and health issues: accident reports, 108–11; allergies, 55–56, 70–73; blame of worker, 106–7, 109, 119; contract workers and, 102, 103; cover-ups, 62; fatalities, 62, 103–4; injured workers, 52, 100–101, 108–11, 119–20; *keiretsu* businesses, 113–14; lack of training, 79–80, 108; line speed, 105, 118–19; manufacturing space, 7, 110, 119; overwork, 67, 75; pollution, 70–71

Israel Hospital Committee, some of the wealthiest people in town.

The effort to raise money and find a site for the new Jewish hospital was well underway when Louie Mayer met the Gordons in 1915. Louie, though ill at ease with Nathan, was comfortable with Sally Gordon. He told her what had happened to his mother, who spoke Yiddish but died in 1913 in a non-Jewish hospital in Canada. She had gone in for a routine gallbladder operation. Louie raced to Canada and saw her as she lay dying. Like the Jewish immigrants in Boston, Louie's mother could not communicate with the hospital doctors, nor could she eat hospital food. Louie was twenty-eight. Forever after he believed she was watching over him. He often had conversations with her and asked for her advice.

"Mayer was a man who dearly loved his mother and wasn't afraid to admit it," the film director Mervyn LeRoy said many years later. "Even though she died when he was in his twenties, he continued to speak about her as if she were still living."

Louie admired Sally Gordon, believed in what she was doing, and pledged money he didn't have to the Beth Israel Hospital. He became one of its first directors in 1915. As in all things Louie did, he was motivated both by his heart and by his eye for opportunity.

Here he was, a member of a board of directors made up entirely of millionaires. Banks in Boston did not look favorably upon Jewish men who wanted to borrow money. Beth Israel's board of directors could be a source of financing as reliable as any bank.

What Louie wanted to do was produce pictures. As an officer with Metro, he often visited the studios in New York where Metro pictures were put together. He loved those places—the director with his megaphone, the cameraman cranking his camera, the musicians playing sad music so the actors would cry, the beautiful young women in costumes. Not all of the men on the Beth Israel board listened to Louie's enthusiastic talk, but several did, and one, Colman Levin, asked Louie if he could visit a studio, too. "He knew Mayer had great ability," Colman Levin's son Myer recalled. Louie took Levin and his son Myer, then aged ten, to New York where they visited Francis X. Bushman's studio. Colman Levin was hooked. He and Louie became good friends and spent vacations together with their wives in Palm Beach.

Colman Levin's fortune came from carpet. He had come penniless to America from Lithuania at the age of seventeen. Now he was the exclusive distributor in New England of Congoleum-Nairn linoleum, as well as Mohawk and Bigelow carpets. Colman Levin was looking for a new risk. The amount of money spent annually in the motion-picture industry was far in excess of $500 million. More than half a billion admissions were paid annually to the box offices of motion-picture theaters. More than seventy-five thousand miles of film were manufactured and exhibited annually.

The new demand for American feature-length pictures encouraged the director D.W. Griffith to make a very long picture, a twelve-reel Civil War drama that was eventually titled *The Birth of a Nation.* By 1915 Griffith was already famous in America because of his work at the Biograph Studio, but he had never before tackled a project this big. He was compelled to make this movie despite all difficulties.

It was based on a novel, *The Clansman,* written by Thomas Dixon, of North Carolina, who was a member of the Ku Klux Klan, along with his father, a Baptist minister, and brother. Griffith's movie was originally called *The Clansman* and stayed that way until after it opened in Los Angeles. Thomas Dixon, who owned one-fourth of the company that profited from *The Birth of a Nation* openly discussed the reason he wrote his novel. He believed that the dominant passion of colored men was to have sexual relations with white women, and he said that one purpose of his book was to create a feeling of abhorrence in white people, especially white women, against colored men. His desire was to prevent the mixing of white and Negro blood by intermarriage. He believed that the National Association for the Advancement of Colored People was an "intermarriage society" that wanted to "lower the standard of our citizenship by its mixture with Negro blood." There was anti-intermarriage legislation on the books in ten states, but Dixon wanted it to be universal. He did not mention how often white slaveholders had mixed their blood with unwilling black women.

Thomas Dixon said that his solution to the "Negro problem" was to remove all Negroes from the United States. It would be quite a task to remove ten million people, but he was hoping his book and the film made from it would create public sentiment so a beginning could be made to get rid of all Negroes in a hundred years. He told reporters that Negroes themselves would cooperate because they would be able to see the advantage of moving back to Africa.

The Birth of a Nation played for forty-four consecutive weeks at the Liberty Theater in New York, at $2 admission, reserved seats, and souvenir programmes. When patrons entered the theater they were greeted by costumed men wearing the uniforms of Union and Confederate soldiers. The female ushers wore long dresses typical of young ladies in the South of 1860. The music, made up of classical pieces and popular songs arranged especially for the picture, was performed by an orchestra and chorus. Fashionable white audiences were moved to frenzies of praise and rose from their seats to applaud for half an hour.

Critics wrote accolades about the crowd and battle scenes. "The march of Sherman from Atlanta to the sea," wrote the critic of *Moving Picture World*, "made the audience gasp with wonder and admiration. Nothing more impressive has ever been seen on the screen, and I have to refer to *Cabiria* for a standard of comparison. . . . The photography is exceptionally fine."

Variety described the picture as "nicely cameraed" and predicted that "Many will see it twice, yea thrice, and still obtain much satisfaction and entertainment. It's there with a multiple of thrills."

The critic of the *Atlanta Journal* said, "There has been nothing to equal it—nothing. Not as a motion picture, nor a play, nor a book does it come to you; but as the soul and spirit and flesh of the heart of your country's history, ripped from the past and brought quivering with all human emotions before your eyes."

The story is the Reconstruction period from a southern point of view. In one of the opening scenes a white woman reaches out to hug a black child but draws back in disgust because the child smells so bad. Then the picture shows conditions in the South before the Civil War—how the slaves (most of them white actors in blackface) had easy hours, plenty of time for recreation, comfortable quarters, and kind masters. When the slaves are freed after numerous spectacular battle scenes, they proceed to lust after white women and humiliate their elderly former masters. To save themselves from the power-hungry and sex-mad Negroes, the white heroes form the Ku Klux Klan. A bugle blast from the theater orchestra announces the riders of the Klan, as they sweep across the screen saving white girls from the terror of the black mob. The final scenes are of an imaginary Utopia where the people, some looking like Koreans, others like early Romans, are blessed by Jesus Christ. The orchestra played "Gloria" from Haydn's Mass in C.

The picture had its debut in Los Angeles where black members of the audience became enraged. Before the picture opened in New York City, the NAACP tried to prevent its screening. After five weeks of pressure, Griffith did agree to cut a few of the shots of white girls being attacked by wild Negroes, and he cut most of the epilogue in which President Lincoln declares that he does not believe in racial equality and suggests that the solution to America's race problem is to send Negroes back to Africa.

The Birth of a Nation has gone down in history as the first movie ever shown at the White House. But it wasn't. *Cabiria* was. And *The Birth of a Nation* was not shown to President Wilson because it was so fine, but because its author, Thomas Dixon, was a former student of Wilson's at Johns Hopkins.

President Wilson had no idea what the movie was about and agreed to have the picture screened in the East Room as a courtesy to his former student on condition that there would be no publicity linking his name with Dixon's commercial efforts. President Wilson is said to have commented that the movie was like "writing history with lightning," but no one heard him say that except Thomas Dixon. Wilson allowed Dixon to show the picture again the the ballroom of the Raleigh Hotel to the members of the supreme Court, including the chief justice, and to several members of Congress.

Wilson would live to regret this decision. One week after *The Birth of a Nation* had its Boston premiere, five hundred angry demonstrators massed outside the Tremont Theater. The following Monday Governor Walsh promised to seek legislation to prevent screening *The Birth of a Nation* and all other movies that created racial or religious prejudice. The Boston branch of the NAACP, claiming the picture was "improper, immoral, and unjust," issued a booklet against it. Jane Addams of Hull House in Chicago said she was pained by the picture, which was seen as a deliberate attempt to humiliate ten million American citizens, to portray them as nothing but beasts. Rabbi Stephen Wise in New York described the picture as "this indescribably foul and loathsome libel on a race of human beings." Miss Lillian D. Wald said, "It is impossible to measure the potential dangers that threaten us if the production is allowed to go on."

Picket lines formed outside of box offices in every major city. Signs proclaimed "Fight Race Hatred," "This Film Panders to Depraved Tastes," and "Griffith Foments Race Antipathy." Naturally, everyone wanted to see what all the fuss was about. More than $15 million poured into the box office.

President Wilson's secretary wrote the following letter to two political leaders who were protesting the film in Boston:

It is true that *The Birth of a Nation* was produced before the President and his family at the White House, but the President was entirely unaware of the character of the play before it was presented and has at no time ex-

pressed his approbation of it. Its exhibition at the White
House was a courtesy extended to an old acquaintance.

Thomas Dixon admitted that he didn't dare allow the president to know the real purpose behind his film. While an active war raged in Europe, America used words to fight the
Civil War all over again.

In defending himself against the attack on *The Birth of a
Nation*, D. W. Griffith, son of a Kentucky colonel, said, "We do
pay particular attention to those faithful Negroes who stayed
with their former masters and were ready to give up their
lives to protect their white friends. No characters in the story
are applauded with greater fervor than the good Negroes
whose devotion is so clearly shown."

The British film critic Oswell Blakestone summed it all up
about fifteen years later in the magazine *Close Up*:

> As a spectacle Griffith's production was awe-inspiring
> and stupendous, but as a picture of Negro life it was not
> only false, but it has done the Negro irreparable harm.
> And no wonder, since it was taken from a puerile novel,
> *The Clansman*, a book written to arouse racial hate by ap-
> pealing to the basest passions of the semiliterate.

*   *   *

Be that as it may, to be in possession of such a picture seemed
to Louie Mayer like owning a golden goose. The whole country was talking about it, but only people who lived close to the
big cities had a chance to see it. When the picture finished its
run at major theaters it came up for sale. For $50 thousand
Louie could buy the distribution rights to it.

He had only $12 thousand of his own to invest, so he went
to his colleagues on the Beth Israel board. The men with
money told him he was wrong, the picture had played itself
out. But Louie still lived in Haverhill among hardworking
people who had no time to travel to Boston and who would
never dream of spending two dollars for "just a picture."

Louie convinced several of the Beth Israel directors to invest with him to purchase the New England rights to *The Birth of a Nation*. The men formed a company, Master Photoplays. Louie owned 25 percent. He distributed the film to towns in Maine, Connecticut, Rhode Island, New Hampshire, and Vermont. The picture had a long run at his Colonial Theater in Haverhill. Just as he predicted, those who had invested with him were handsomely rewarded.

Louie earned a quarter of a million dollars. He moved his wife and two daughters from Haverhill to Brookline, an affluent suburb of Boston where, according to his partner Colman Levin, the schools were good.

FOUR

Anna

By THE TIME that Louie was ready to become a producer, in 1917, almost everyone in the business realized that, for the most part, the public went to see stars not stories. The public did not feel loyalty to any particular director and didn't give a hoot at which studio their favorite player was working.

The first film star to capitalize on this realization was Mary Pickford, whose rise to fortune and fame was galling to every other film actress of the day. Though time has proved Mary Pickford to have had some enduring quality, in her day other film stars could not imagine why Mary should have a ton of money, her name plastered all over the place, and complete control over the films she made. She was cute, sure, but she wasn't *that* cute.

But time has shown that she *was* that cute, and anyone who sees her films today can easily understand why it was Mary Pickford who created the "star system." She was not especially

pretty, but she was adorable. She had a vigorous, healthy phy-
sique and a winning personality that was animated by an unusually active intelligence. Whether she was supposed to be a
rich girl or a poor girl, orphaned or secure, she was brave.
Maybe she cried and maybe she got knocked down but only
momentarily. Nothing could dampen her high spirits.
Blithely she headed off into trouble, very much like the intelligent "cartoon" monkey Curious George.

Billed as "Blondielocks" and "Goldielocks" and "The Girl
With the Curls," Mary soon realized her pictures were more
popular with audiences than other pictures produced at Biograph studio where she worked, on East Fourteenth Street in
New York City. She suggested to Biograph executives that
they capitalize on her drawing power by building her up in
the press. They refused. They believed that a motion picture's
success was based first upon the story, second upon the direction (D.W. Griffith worked for them), and third upon players
in general, as they all mixed together on the screen.

So when Carl Laemmle, who was struggling to make a success of his independent production company in the face of
the Patent Company's lawsuits and hoodlums, offered Mary
an increase in salary to $175 a week and promised to adver-
tise her as "Little Mary," she left Biograph and went to work
for Laemmle, who would one day change the name of his
studio from the Independent Motion Picture Company to
Universal Pictures. Laemmle promoted Mary Pickford's pictures to exhibitors in a series labeled "Little Mary IMPs," and
if an exhibitor wanted them he had to buy the rest of Laemmle's pictures, too. Most exhibitors, knowing they would earn
enough from Mary's pictures to pay back what they might
lose at the box office on IMP's other productions, were quite
willing to buy the whole line.

When the Patent Company goons arrived at the studio to
smash cameras and throw stones at the actors, Mary was
shipped to Cuba with the rest of Laemmle's top players and
remained there for three months. On the voyage to Havana
Mary confessed to her mother, sister, and brother that she had

secretly married Owen Moore, also a film actor. While in Cuba Moore fought so violently with one of the stage crew that the Cuban police were called. Before they could arrive, Mary, her mother, and Moore were on a boat back to the United States, and that was the end of Mary's tenure at Laemmle's studio.

Now known as "Little Mary," she returned to Biograph and insisted that her name appear at least on posters and hand-bills, if not on the screen. Mary's goal, frankly stated to her employers, was to earn $500 a week by the time she was twenty. After making about 150 one-reelers, she left Biograph to earn $200 a week in a play on the Broadway stage. She noticed that fans who knew her from the movies came to the theater to see her in person.

Adolph Zukor, now firmly in the business of buying plays and turning them into pictures, noticed the same thing. He bought the rights to *A Good Little Devil* and hired the entire cast, including Mary Pickford. She was offered a fourteen-week contract with Famous Players at a salary of $500 a week. She had reached her goal one year ahead of schedule. Within another year's time, "America's Sweetheart" was earning $1,000 a week and every other film actress in the country sat up and took notice.

Mary Pickford remained with Famous Players for five years. "I have no hesitation in calling them the happiest years of my screen life," she wrote in her autobiography. "I became one of Mr. Zukor's three children, the others being his own daughter Mildred and his son Eugene; and to the end of our association he was a loving and devoted father."

Zukor, Lasky, and W.W. Hodkinson joined together to form the distribution company Paramount Pictures, and that's when Mary Pickford's movies began to be released along with the output of other producers, like Bosworth and Morosco. Mary Pickford recalled:

I was driving up Broadway on my way home from the studio one evening when I noticed that a Famous Play-ers picture of mine, *Rags*, was showing at the Strand. I saw lines extending from both sides of the box office. The following week, on the same day at the same hour, I passed the Strand again. Another Famous Players picture was showing there, but it was not mine. No one was standing outside the box office. I bought a ticket and went inside. The theater was less than half-filled.

When contract time came around again, Mary insisted that her pictures be sold separately. Mary's mother, a talented businesswoman and Mary's best friend, negotiated with the Paramount executives. Mary's new contract, dated January 15, 1915, called for her to make ten pictures a year at a weekly salary of $2,000, plus half the profits of her productions. It was the first time a player was ever cut in on a percentage of the gross.

What Paramount planned to do was sell Mary's pictures separately and charge theater owners more for them. Mary Pickford pictures would be a kind of specialty line of Paramount's. A clause in Mary's contract provided that "all Pickford features must be sold at double the customary prices and that an exhibitor showing them must charge double admission." Paramount's plan was so successful Mary's mother demanded that Mary be paid $1,000 a day, every day, seven days a week.

In 1916, as Louie was moving from Haverhill to Brookline, Adolph Zukor in New York was taking over Paramount by acquiring the company's stock. He then merged his Famous Players with the Lasky Feature Play Company, which included Jesse Lasky, Sam Goldfish (Goldwyn), and Cecil B. De Mille. Famous Players and Lasky were two of the oldest companies producing feature photoplays, and it seemed a wise move to join together rather than compete for the same stories and the same stage actors. The new company, called Famous Players-Lasky Corporation, was incorporated with a capital stock of $12,500,000 and planned to release eighty-four pictures a year. Jointly, these two producing companies had controlled the largest number of the best-known stars of the stage and screen, including Mary Pickford, Geraldine Farrar, Marguerite Clark, Marie Doro, Pauline Frederick, Blanche Sweet, Mae Murray, Hazel Dawn, John Barrymore, Victor Moore, Donald Brian, Ann Pennington, and others whose names are more obscure today.

Famous Players-Lasky owned two well-equipped studios, one in New York and the other in California. Paramount became the distribution subsidiary of the new company. When Zukor completed his reorganization a year later, he had created the largest motion-picture company in the world, and the first one to control production as well as distribution.

Realizing how much Mary Pickford contributed to his prosperity, Zukor created a separate production unit called the Pickford Film Corporation. Her compensation was 50 percent of the profits payable at the rate of $10,000 every Monday during the life of the two-year contract. In addition Mary received $300,000 a year, plus a bonus of $40,000. "Mary, sweetheart," Adolph Zukor said, "I don't have to diet. Every time I talk over a new contract with you and your mother I lose ten pounds."

Charlie Chaplin, in his autobiography, describes a meeting with Mary, several years later, when they were organizing their partnership in United Artists. "I was astonished at the legal and business acumen of Mary. She knew all the nomenclature: the amortization and the deferred stocks, etc. She understood all the articles of incorporation, the legal discrepancy on Page 7, Paragraph A, Article 27, and coolly referred to the overlap and contradiction in Paragraph D, Article 24. On these occasions she saddened me more than amazed me, for this was an aspect of "America's Sweetheart" that I did not know." (It was easy enough for him to be critical of Mary. He had his brother Syd to look after all of *his* finances.)

Now that she was producing her own pictures Mary Pickford could choose directors, her supporting players, and stories. In advertising her name appeared alone and in large letters. She was given a studio for her sole use in New York, called Mary Pickford Studio, a private secretary, and parlor-car accommodations for herself, her mother, and her maid when they traveled to California to shoot during the winter. Thus did Mary Pickford set herself apart from all other motion-picture actresses of the time.

The only photoplayer keeping pace with Mary Pickford was Charlie Chaplin, who, like Mary, was surprised to discover how much the public wanted to see him. He was a British vaudeville comic and came to this country to perform on the stage in a production called "A Night in an English Music Hall." Chaplin stayed to make about thirty-five films in one year at Keystone, where he earned $175 a week, and had a lot of fun because Mack Sennett allowed him so much creative freedom. On a whim Chaplin dressed up in Fatty Arbuckle's gigantic trousers, put big shoes on the wrong feet, put on a jacket that belonged to a little boy, and discovered his tramp persona. Charlie Chaplin had every intention of returning to London and never imagined that his tramp character had attracted attention. In 1914 the manager of a Loew's theater on Seventh Avenue, a young man named Joe Vogel, wrote to Keystone in California to find out the tramp's name and to ask for more tramp pictures. Joe Vogel's audience kept asking him for more of those pictures. In Loew's sign shop Vogel had some three-sheet and one-sheet posters made, and he plastered them up in front of the theater the next time he booked a Chaplin picture. In those days there were no previews of coming attractions. Joe Vogel made up some slides advertising Chaplin's films and thus invented the first "trailer."

Charlie Chaplin left Keystone and went to Essanay in 1915 at a salary of $1,250 a week, plus a bonus of $10,000. After Charlie Chaplin's first year at Essanay, having created the film *The Tramp,* he renewed his contract at $5,000 a week. The next year, 1916, when Chaplin was twenty-seven, he moved to the Mutual Film Corporation, where he signed a $670,000 contract calling for twelve films yearly over which he would have complete creative control.

At the Vitagraph Studio in Brooklyn, a young actress was paying attention to all of this. She could rationalize the success of Pickford and Chaplin by telling herself that they were like athletes, had to strike it rich while young because they would soon be trapped by the roles they played: Mary could not go on playing a little girl, and Chaplin's tramp would soon grow tiresome to audiences.

Anita Stewart had to admit that the movie business had been good to her. She lived in a mansion on Long Island, with a closet full of furs, drove a fancy motorcar, and was the idol of millions of young girls, including Louie Mayer's own daughters, who carefully cut out the Anita Stewart paper dolls published in *Ladies World* magazine. Next to the tabs on the clothes were descriptions: "Miss Stewart favors this very attractive bathing cloak when she is on the sands," "This pretty fur-trimmed evening cloak is similar to the one worn in *The Combat,* and "A cunning hat and a light opera cape from her varied wardrobe."

What the girls who played with the paper doll knew was that Anita Stewart had to choose and pay for the clothes she wore in her films. All film actresses were responsible for the selection and purchase of their screen wardrobes. When films were only one reel long, fans saw the photoplayers in one outfit. Now that films were many reels long actresses had to appear in several different outfits appropriate to the various scenes. So audiences really saw an actress's taste in clothing. Anita Stewart's fashion sense inspired many imitators. People went to see her movies as much for the stories as for getting some ideas for their own wardrobes. Film critics were sure to let fans know what they could expect to see. *Variety* said:

> At the age of nineteen, Anita Stewart's dresses were charming. She looked very striking in a cloak of ermine tied shawl fashion round her shoulders. One frock worn was of silk lace, embroidered with daisies made in flounces, large roses sewn round the skirt. A one-piece dress of blue serge with a cape effect was very smart.

Her fans could identify with her because she was from a modest background, went to Erasmus High School in Brooklyn, and was not pushy. She never would have appeared in a motion picture if her brother-in-law had not been a director at the Vitagraph studio. He needed some extras and asked Anna, her real name, to pose in the background when she was fifteen. It was the public who picked her out after seeing her in three pictures. Fans wrote to Vitagraph saying that they wanted to see more of that pretty girl, so she was brought to the front of the screen. *Cosmopolitan* wrote:

> Anita Stewart stands second to none in popularity among the moving-picture stars. She is a true daughter of the films, for, unlike most of her rivals, she has never appeared in the spoken drama. With her talent for characterization, she has won an international reputation.

When her film, *The Girl Philippa*, opened at the Rialto Theater in New York City on New Year's day in 1917, people stood in line around the block. Records for a single day's receipts at any motion-picture theater in the world were broken when thousands were taken in at the box office. The theater opened at ten in the morning and played to capacity into the evening. Special policemen kept crowds in order around the entrance. Stewart's salary was $127,000 a year, plus a percentage of the box office. She was the sole support of her mother, her younger brother, and herself.

It angered her that Vitagraph was not giving her the recognition she felt she deserved. When she was starting out she expected to have second billing to the factory's name. Now she believed she was responsible for the factory's success and her name should be featured. But it never was. When Vitagraph gave away a calendar to advertise Anita Stewart's latest film, the words under the portrait of her were "The Girl Philippa." The poster for her popular serial *The Goddess*, released one reel at a time, showed a full-length photograph of the actress, dressed in long robes, surrounded by words— "Beauty, Hatred, Revenge, Love, Action, Suspense, A Continued Photoplay In Chapters, The Interest Increases Every Week." The biggest words on the poster were "The Vitagraph

Company of America." Anita Stewart's name appeared not at all.

She complained. The executives at Vitagraph agreed to release a story about her to the *New York Dramatic Mirror*. But the story only glorified the studio:

> In addition to a beautiful face and figure, Miss Stewart is the possessor of a pair of brown eyes of wonderful expression. As a child she attracted the atention of a number of American and European artists and posed for a number of their famous pictures, during which time she came under the notice of the shrewd Commodore J. Stuart Blackton, of the Vitagraph Co., who speedily contracted with her to appear in Vitagraph productions. . . . She has never appeared in films other than those made by the Vitagraph Co. . . . In the future evey success is possible to Miss Stewart, for in addition to being the possessor of extraordinary talent, beauty, and versatility, it is her good fortune to be associated with what is, in all probability, the greatest film producing organization in the world.

When Anita Stewart moved her family from an apartment in Brooklyn to an estate, "Wood Violet," on Long Island, Vitagraph reported her good fortune—"She comes to work at the Vitagraph studio every day in her machine."

When an actress colleague of hers at Vitagraph, Clara Kimball Young, was lured away from Vitagraph by Lewis Selznick and given the star treatment, including a production company named after her and her name in lights on Broadway, Anita Stewart began to feel deeply hurt.

Louie Mayer in Boston was paying attention, too. It was one thing for well-known producers to raid one another's stars, but it was quite another for an unknown person like Lewis Selznick to take Clara Kimball Young away from Vitagraph. A dark-haired beauty, famous on the stage before entering films, Young had been voted the most popular screen actress by the *Toledo Blade* in 1914. Lewis J. Selznick, a Russian immigrant from a family of eighteen children, was a jeweler from Pittsburgh who had no respect for the jewelry business. He thought jewelry was for suckers, but it was a lucrative business. He had no respect for the film industry either, but he figured he might as well make some money in it since making money in it seemed so easy. He founded a company called World Sales Corporation. World advertised its films as "Features Made From Well Known Plays by Well Known Players." Then he lured Clara Kimball Young away from Vitagraph by offering to put her name in lights, set up a production company for her, and give her a huge salary. Young's films made it possible for Selznick, his wife, and two sons to live in a twenty-two-room apartment on Park Avenue, eat choice food, sip vintage wines, employ many servants, and own four Rolls-Royces.

The story goes that in May 1915, Lewis Selznick heard a commotion in his outer office. When he rushed out to see what the matter was, he was told that the Germans had torpedoed the *Lusitania,* a transatlantic passenger ship. The British Cunard Lines vessel, which weighed thirty-one thousand tons, sank in eighteen minutes, killing almost two thousand people. "Oh, is that all?" Selznick is supposed to have said. "I was afraid Clara Kimball Young was breaking her contract."

After the *Lusitania* went down, Americans stopped singing "I Didn't Raise My Son to Be a Soldier" and started singing "Over There."

Lewis Selznick believed that he, and not Adolph Zukor, was the first producer to create a separate company for his star and that Clara Kimball Young, and not Mary Pickford, was the first player to attain such stature. Selznick published an open letter in the trade press congratulating Miss Pickford on her shrewdness in following an idea which he had originated:

Will you please express to my friend, Mr. Adolph Zukor, my deep sense of obligation? It is indeed delightful to encounter among one's co-workers a man so broad-gauged that neither false pride nor shortsightedness can deter him from the adoption of an excellent plan, even though conceived by another.

When Anita Stewart drove along Broadway she saw Clara Kimball Young's name blazing in electric lights. She read about Clara Kimball Young's new automobiles, about the fancy dinners she gave for politicians and business tycoons in her new mansion in Saratoga.

Then another colleague at Vitagraph, Norma Talmadge, who had been a classmate at Erasmus High in Brooklyn and who started at the Vitagraph studio at about the same time Anita Stewart did, was lured away from Vitagraph by Joseph Schenck, who made her the head of the Norma Talmadge Film Corporation.

Anita Stewart told the Vitagraph executives that she wanted more money and that she needed a rest. She had worked for them for six years straight without a vacation. They said she did not deserve more money; she was a star because they made her a star by using her in many pictures and keeping her before the public. As for a rest, if she wanted to rest she could retire for all they cared. They could easily replace her. Thousands of girls waited for a chance at every film studio in the country. Most of them would be willing to work free, just for a chance to be seen. Executives at Vitagraph admitted that there were three or four big stars earning fortunes but reminded Anita Stewart that the vast majority of photoplayers were content with modest salaries. The average five-reel photoplay earned between $50,000 and $75,000. How could Vitagraph pay their actress more than the picture would earn?

Vitagraph executives itemized for Anita Stewart the costs of an average photoplay production. "Incidentals," such as the weather, had to be figured in, and so did the efficiency of the director. If he wasted film, used more than the five thousand feet necessary to the picture, then the costs went up. A really careful director could bring in a five-reel picture for $9,500. The cost of an average production that took four weeks to complete and used a small cast was:

Star ($1,500 a week) $6,000
Leading man ($400 a week)....................1,200
Remainder of principals 1,300
Extras 300
Director ($750 a week).......................3,000
Assistant director ($75 a week)................300
Cameraman ($75 a week) 300
Assistant cameraman ($25 a week)...............100
Scenario and handling by studio staff 1,000
Transportation.................................500
Studio settings 1,000
Film stock for negative......................1,000
Renting locations 200
Costumes.....................................1,000
Incidentals....................................500

Total $17,700

—*New York Dramatic Mirror,* July 7, 1917.

One of Anita Stewart's duties was to appear every year at the Actors' Fund Fair in New York. She was expected to add glamour to the Vitagraph booth for no pay. She went from her work at the studio to the fair and had to stand on her feet and smile for hours. This particular year, 1917, she felt as if she weighed a ton, as if the men and women smiling at her and asking for her autograph were strangely distorted, like people in a fun-house mirror. She forgot why she was there and what she was supposed to be doing. When she began to speak in a random way, her mother took her home to Long Island.

But there was no rest for her. She had to go to Boston to make an appearance at Nathan Gordon's Olympia Theater in Scollay Square. Gordon's daughter Marion recalled:

We did entertain movie actors when they came through. I can remember having a big party for Anita Stewart. She was in Boston, for some reason. I can remember a big, big party and I can remember all the people going in to it. And my mother telling the cook to make little things in shapes. I remember we children weren't allowed to go to it and I remember all the excitement. I used to have a picture of Anita Stewart that she sent to my father.

Though Nathan Gordon did not usually socialize with Louie Mayer, he did invite him to that party. Both Sally Gordon and Louie were surprised by Anita Stewart's obvious ill-health. They expected a flashy, glamorous creature and saw, instead, an exhausted girl with dark circles under her eyes the color of bruises. Before the evening was over, Anita Stewart's mother had confided to Sally that instead of returning to Long Island they were going to Stamford, Connecticut, to check Anita into a sanitorium there.

The following week Louie took the train to Stamford and checked in at the Hotel Davenport. Then his nerve failed. How could he come before one of the greatest film stars of the day? What did he have to offer? Why would a star of her stature working for a big studio quit to work for a man who had never made a movie in his life? Louie worked up his courage by telling himself that he was going to visit Anita Stewart's mother, who must be very worried.

In bed in the sanitorium the young actress was inert, but now and then she sat up and plinked out some songs on a ukulele. She was as pale as an old memory. The nurses tried to feed her eggs and milk, and sometimes they sat on her bed and she tried to amuse them. Louie was surprised to see that there were no flowers in Anita Stewart's room, no boxes of candy, nothing that would show that she had international fame. Either everyone was ignoring her or no one knew she was sick. Aside from a handsome young man who was always in her room, and her mother, Louie saw no other visitors. Anita told Mayer that he was the only person in the entire film industry who had visited her.

Anita's mother informed Louie that while working on *The Girl Philippa* Anita contracted typhoid. Doctors said the actress should take six months off, but Vitagraph only gave her two weeks, saying that *The Girl Philippa* had to be finished while the leaves were still on the trees. After a rest of two weeks Anna returned to the studio and finished the picture.

"I didn't know what I was doing or why," she said.

It was in Vitagraph's interest to keep Anita Stewart's break-down a secret. Everyone working at the studio was asked to cooperate, told that it wouldn't do their friend's reputation any good to be known as an unreliable person. None of the executives from Vitagraph visited her, sent flowers, or expressed anything but annoyance at her collapse. The public assumed Anna was just fine, because they saw her moving around on movie screens.

Louie visited Anita several times in the sanitorium, brought her Margaret's chicken soup, and told her how much he admired her and how talented he thought she was. He told her all about himself, his boyhood in his father's junk busi-ness in Canada, his success in Haverhill, his success in Bos-ton, how he wanted to become a producer but didn't exactly know how. One thing he knew, the entire venture depended upon the star. "I go down on my knees to talent," he said. The star should be able to choose her own stories, her own direc-tor, and her costars. For instance, if he had a great star like her to work with he'd call his company Anita Stewart Produc-tions and give her mother a position on the board of direc-tors and a percentage of the profits. As for the young man who was in Anita's room every time Louie visited, Rudy Ca-meron, a stage actor who worked now and then at Vitagraph, if he wanted to work at Anita Stewart Productions he would be welcome.

Anita confessed that Rudy Cameron was her husband and said it was torture trying to keep that secret from the public. Vitagraph claimed her girlish appeal would be ruined if it became known that she was not a virgin.

Anita's husband Rudy listened to Louie's talk with special interest. Rudy Cameron was really Rudolph Brennan of the Connecticut Brennans, an old, wealthy family. He had defied his parents by taking up acting, and now he found himself in the humiliating position of not having made a success of it. He didn't know what else to do with himself; his dream was supposed to have come true. He had been on Broadway once, had not been asked to return, and was now trying to earn a living in pictures, something he thought a comedown. A graduate of Georgetown University, with a degree in civil engineering, he had so far been a disappointment to his family. That he had married Anita Stewart, a film actress, a girl with no education, no background, and a heavy Brooklyn accent, was too embarrassing.

Now here was a fellow from Boston offering to change Rudy's luck. As part of his wife's production company Rudy would be assured top roles. At the same time he would be a full-fledged businessman, as his parents had wanted. He would sit on the board of directors of Anita Stewart Productions and worry about profits.

As for Anita's mother, she was furious at the men who ran Vitagraph. She saw them as bloodsuckers. Maybe if Anita really could have a production company of her own, Anna's younger brother could also have a lucrative career in films. Both of Mrs. Stewart's children would be set for life.

Anita's contract with Vitagraph stated that she was to get 10 percent of the profits of all of her films. Both Anita and her mother felt that Vitagraph was not giving her a proper accounting of what was due her. Anita told Mayer that Albert E. Smith, president of Vitagraph, had given more than $50,000 to William Randolph Hearst's Star Company as royalties from Anita Stewart's *The Girl Philippa*. Payment of that sum was made without Anita's consent or knowledge and was more than she earned from the picture. When Anita objected, Albert Smith claimed that $50,000 was a fair price for advertising, that if it hadn't been for Hearst's favorable reviews, people would not have lined up outside the Rialto Theater. Smith reminded Anita that she was nothing more than a figment of publicity, that she was lucky to be working, since most studios would not touch a girl with such a high-strung, nervous temperament, who magnified "every trifling annoyance into an unsurmountable obstacle."

Louie visited Anita at the sanitorium for one month before suggesting that she join him in a new venture. In June Anita's lawyer told him to put up $10,000 to show he was sincere. Mayer did not have $10,000, but Colman Levin did, so they became partners. When Louie paid Anita's lawyer $10,000, Anita, in bed in the sanitorium, signed the following letter her lawyer had written to Vitagraph: "By reason of the continued violation on your part of my contract with you, I have severed my relation with your company." Letter mailed, Anita's lawyer told Louie that the actress was now a free agent and Louie could legally begin negotiations with her.

Anita left the hospital and went back to Long Island, and on September 1, 1917, Anita Stewart Productions was incorporated, with Colman Levin and Louis B. Mayer as chief executives.

Eleven days later Vitagraph went to the Supreme Court in Manhattan and secured a temporary injunction restraining Anita Stewart from fulfilling her contract with Louis B. Mayer. A month later, when Vitagraph sought to have the temporary injuction made permanent, the story burst into the newspapers.

> Anita Stewart, Brooklyn's best-known moving picture actress, five years ago received a salary of $25 a week when she first "broke into" the screen world. Today she is the central figure in an action in the Supreme Court in New York in an effort to compel her to accept a salary of $2,500 a week from the Vitagraph Company. The court action to compel her acceptance of this figure has been instituted because she has broken a contract which guaranteed her $127,000 a year. She broke the contract because she preferred to accept $10,000 a week—four hundred times what she received five years ago.
> —*New York Dramatic Mirror,* October 8, 1917.

In truth, Louie only offered to match her salary, but they inflated his offer to the press so that he would sound important and Anita Stewart could hold her head up with regard to Mary Pickford, Clara Kimball Young, and Norma Talmadge.

Referring to Anita's statement that she was "inadequately compensated," the lawyer who represented Vitagraph said,

"In one who was older and whose judgment was more mature, this claim would, in view of the fact that she is to be paid $127,000, be the extreme of audacity and impertinence."

Though she pleaded unkind treatment and the court heard her doctor testify about her continual exhaustion, Anita lost the suit. When the case was appealed she lost again and was told that she could not appear for Louis B. Mayer until after the trial set for October 31st.

Colman Levin was livid. He thought he was going to become a film producer, and here he was paying lawyers and seeing his name in the newspapers. Levin had to take time away from his carpet business in Boston to appear at the trial in New York. Vitagraph won and the decision made film history. "Vitagraph Co. of America v. Stewart et al." would be used as a precedent in holding movie stars to their contracts.

Vitagraph's lawyers showed that Anita Stewart's success was due to her schooling at the studio and to the "vast amount of money spent" in advertising her. Anita appealed the case and lost again. The appellate division of the Supreme Court issued an injunction restraining Miss Stewart from acting for any corporation or individual other than Vitagraph and Miss Stewart and Mr. Mayer were restrained from advertising or announcing that Miss Stewart was to work for any other company or individual. Louis B. Mayer was specifically enjoined from "enticing, inducing or causing the defendant, Anita Stewart, to refuse to work in the employ of the plaintiff."

Colman Levin said Mayer had tricked him and he would not pay another dime for legal fees. Metro Pictures became angry at Louie for trying to make a deal on his own, and he was shoved out. His name was mud.

Louie retreated to Haverhill, kibitzed with his brother Jerry at the New Orpheum, and found fault with the new manager of the Colonial. It was a bleak time. On Haverhill's streets women were sobbing as their sons and husbands marched to the train station on their way overseas to "Wipe Up the Earth With the Boches." No one wanted to go. They were drafted, their names drawn from a glass globe at the Senate office in

Washington. Haverhill protested that the city's population was six thousand less than Washington claimed and that the army was taking too many boys from Haverhill. But there was no getting around it. The local paper reported:

> Women sobbed frankly and unashamed, and there was hardly a dry eye among the hundreds of men, women and children who had gathered to press the hands of the soldier laddies for a last farewell. Even the children tried to be brave so that Big Brother, who was so brave himself, wouldn't leave Haverhill in an unhappy mood. They smiled courageously when Big Brother kissed them for the last time, and whispered, "Good Luck" in voices that hardly trembled at all. And after Big Brother was gone, they hid their heads and cried until eyes and noses were red and shiny. One mother, with two sons leaving, was inconsolable. She held first one, then the other to her breast, and seemed loath to allow them to board the train.

The boys arrived at boot camp: "Haverhill boys at Plattsburg learn to shoot. All but two have sore arms as result of recent vaccination." The recruits had to sleep on beds of hay because regular troops had run short of mattresses, thus the expression "hit the hay."

Mayer knew these boys. Many of them had been regular visitors at the Colonial Theater. Even if he couldn't produce feature pictures with Anita Stewart, he could still produce pictures. He asked Haverhill's mayor if he might take motion pictures of the boys setting off for war. Louie set up cameras in Haverhill and filmed the first lap of the boys' journey to the battlefields of France. The rookies assembled at City Hall; then, to the sounds of a marching band, they marched to the armory, then down Kenoza Avenue, Main Street, Merrimack Street and across the county bridge. Louie filmed them getting into the cars and trucks that took them away to Boxford, where they would be trained.

One of the boys wrote home to Haverhill from France:

We were obliged to wear gas masks all the way to the rear, and it was our first experience with gas. The next morning found two-thirds of our men overcome. Some were blind and speechless and badly burned from the fumes, while others suffered less and were merely unable to talk out loud. . . . A man from Battery A came back, overtaking us on a horse, and said that one of the men from the caissons of his battery was wounded and lying in the road. We went back for him. I leaped down and carried him to the car in my arms. I recognized the man was a friend of mine from Haverhill. Elvin Rice. I held him in my arms to save him the jolts; but when we arrived it was too late.

Our guns concentrated on the Boche reserve positions and we took care of the first defence, but at a terrible cost. One hundred and fifty men from my company were killed or wounded. . . . A hail of bullets tore through our ranks and I felt a tremendous shock in my right leg. As I fell there was another and then another in my left ankle. The men hesitated only for an instant and I put Corporal Thompson of Watertown in charge and yelled, "Give them hell, boys, and keep going." Three explosive bullets had mangled my right thigh terribly and one had smashed my left leg above the ankle. . . . I went to various hospitals, after being operated on at the first one. I am now waiting for my wounds to heal completely. There is still a hole clear through my right thigh.

Rudy Cameron was drafted, and the press photographed him leaving for action. The young woman sobbing at the depot was Anita Stewart, and the nation learned that their beloved wood nymph was actually a married woman.

Charlie Chaplin also wrote about the war:

We were caught in an avalanche of destruction and brutal slaughter that went on for four years to the bewilderment of humanity. We had started a hemorrhage of world proportion, and we could not stop it. . . . They said it was a war to make the world safe for democracy. As millions were mowed down the word "democracy" loomed up.

Americans at home tried to help. On the Boston Common there were barrels used to collect peach pits to dry for gas masks. Americans bought thrift stamps, used Karo syrup instead of sugar, and bought war bonds. While children went around chanting, "Beat the Hun!" Anita Stewart's contract with Vitagraph drew to a close. She said that when her contract expired she would go work for Louie Mayer.

Vitagraph insisted that her contract be extended because she had failed to act for them for twenty-nine weeks when she was sick. She refused. Vitagraph took her to court and won. In April 1918, Vitagraph charged Louis B. Mayer with conspiracy and took legal action: "As an aftermath of the controversy over the services of Anita Stewart," the press reported, "that was recently settled in their favor, the Vitagraph Co. has started legal action for $250,000 against Louis B. Mayer, Colman Levin, and J. Robert Rubin. Mayer is a well-known film distributor with headquarters in Boston. The case will be tried in Superior Court of Boston."

Anita Stewart went back to work at Vitagraph. Her publicity promised that she would wear "ever so many stunning gowns." She had been back at work less than a week when she was in a car accident. Two automobiles carrying Vitagraph actors to a location collided with a trolley car at Third Avenue and Sixteenth Street in Brooklyn. Anita Stewart was injured and missed more than a week of work.

By now Vitagraph was thoroughly sick of Stewart. If Louie wanted her, he could have her. In July 1918, an arrangement was reached by the attorneys representing Louis B. Mayer and Vitagraph whereby Anita Stewart could quit working for Vitagraph and begin working for Mayer. Vitagraph agreed to call off its $250,000 damage suit, for a certain fee. Vitagraph was so pleased by the cash settlement, and so glad to be rid of Anita, her mother, and the legal fees, that they told Louie he was welcome to use their studio to film his first movie.

Mayer had already chosen his first story. It had been published in *Cosmopolitan* and was entitled "Virtuous Wives." The story began:

When one realizes in the shifting tireless city of New York the disappearance of the old-fashioned home, the slight authority of the parent generation, the confusion of social standards, the relaxing of religious discipline, one can see that each marriage is to its participants a fact apart, wherein two bewildered mortals are suddenly compelled to establish for themselves, in their search for happiness and mutual respect, some code of standards, responsibility, and concessions, as though they were themselves creating the institution of marriage.

While paying Anita Stewart $5,000 a week to put together a motion picture from the story, Louie began a publicity buildup. The following appeared in *It* magazine:

Gosh! Anita Stewart is said to be the only professional woman in the world carrying life insurance in excess of $250,000. Louis Mayer has purchased for her a policy aggregating $300,000, for his own protection, since she is his star. The sum was too large for one company to underwrite, so it was split up between three of them.

Motion Picture Magazine ran a story in August 1918, entitled, "Ex-Tra! The Story of Anita Stewart's Hoodoo Year," in which executives at Vitagraph were shown to be careless of Anita Stewart's health when she had typhoid fever.

Production of *Virtuous Wives* began in Flatbush, and all seemed to be going well, except the soldiers who came home from overseas brought the Spanish Influenza along with them.

Only the Plague of Justinian and the Black Death can compare to it. The epidemic covered the globe. In the United States more than half a million people died from it, more than were killed in the war. The bug required only two days to incubate and then the victim came down with a three-day fever, headache, soreness of the joints, and, often, death.

By September 1918, ten thousand cases were reported at Camp Devens, Massachusetts; the young men were dying at a rate of seventy a day. The Red Cross pleaded for volunteers in advertising posters and magazine ads.

There is nothing in the epidemic of Spanish Influenza to inspire panic. There is everything to inspire coolness and courage and sacrifice on the part of American women. A stern task confronts our women—not only trained women, but untrained women. The housewife, the dietitian, the nurse's aid, the practical nurse, the undergraduate nurse and the trained nurse herself—all of these are needed. There are many things intelligent women can do to relieve the situation.

Public health officials published supposed methods of avoiding the flu: spray nose and throat with dichloride, keep windows open, bed rest, beware of shaking hands, don't use common towels. Everyone was required to wear a cotton mask over his or her mouth when going out on the street. "A gauze mask is 90 percent proof against Influenza." People were not allowed to congregate in bars, so beer was served in pitchers meant to be taken home. Police lurked, ever ready to arrest those who paused for a forbidden sip at the bar, just as they were ready to apprehend the new enemy of America, the "open-faced sneezer." Insurance companies advertised, "Spanish Influenza! Can you afford sudden death? If not, protect your Family & Business by Life Insurance." It became increasingly difficult to place a telephone call because so many telephone employees were out sick.

In Boston cemetery space ran out. Graveyards set up tents to hold the extra coffins that piled up day after day. Then coffins ran out. Furniture vans were commandeered to transport the influenza dead to the undertakers. One van overturned and spilled uncoffined bodies into the street. Governor McCall closed theaters, churches, and schools. Children chanted:

I had a little bird
And its name was Enza
I opened the window
And in flew Enza!

Theater closings were a disaster to the film industry. Cans of films piled up in factories. Shooting schedules were thrown off, and money ticked away with each second of the clock. Louie in Flatbush thought he would have no theater in which to show his first picture. As if that were not bad enough, coal and electricity were strictly rationed because of the war, so the studios in New York were cold and dark. Several film producers moved out of the city to California, where it was sunny and warm. Mayer had the star, he had the story and the studio, but the city was mad with panic, and there might be no place in which to show his finished work.

On November 11, 1918, New York City went wild with the news of the armistice. Whooping hordes thronged the streets, sirens shrieked, dozens of church bells bonged. People in offices tore up paper and tossed it from windows, along with slices of pamphlets, telephone directories, files, and wrapping paper. On the street people shuffled around ankle-deep in a blizzard of debris. They danced impromptu jigs. Business came to a halt. Shops closed. Automobile horns tooted and cars backfired. The march was merry but aimless; people banged tin plates, made drums out of buckets. At City Hall the mayor tried to make a brief address but was interrupted by everyone singing the "Star-Spangled Banner." Effigies of the kaiser were hung all over New York. And the flu bug had an orgy.

The flu attacked Mayer's twelve-year-old daughter Edith and almost killed her. He vowed that after the opening of *Virtuous Wives* in New York he would move his family to California and health.

The famous Strand Theater on Broadway stayed open. Louie's picture premiered there in December 1918. Uniformed ushers escorted patrons to seats and handed them a theater programme that was a work of art, a souvenir gift with a portrait of Anita Stewart on every page. On the cover were the words "And the Wise men shall secure unto their houses Virtuous Wives, sayeth the prophet." Inside, Louie promoted himself as well as his star.

Mr. Louis Mayer presents Miss Anita Stewart in a series of new productions designed for the better theaters. Miss Anita Stewart and her company will interpret only famous plays or widely read stories by well-known contemporary authors. Each subject's title will have a box office appeal at the better theaters second only to that of the star's name.

The *New York Times* was not too enthusiastic about Mayer's first attempt. The critic praised Anita Stewart as "a most attractive person with sufficient ability to express moods and meanings intelligently," and he praised supporting actress Mrs. DeWolf Hopper, who later became famous as Hedda Hopper. The critic said that the director deserved credit for extraordinary workmanship:

But the worthy efforts of everyone concerned are wasted on the play. It is based upon a story by Owen Johnson and is presented as a view of high society with a moral. If it is a view of any kind of society, its only moral is that men and women may break as many middle-class commandments as they please without injury to their characters. Some of the people in the play are unforgivably stupid and others are as vain and vicious as good respectable folk can imagine, but everybody is miraculously reformed at the last reel and becomes virtuous and intelligent—all because a little boy is nearly drowned. Some beautiful color pictures of Versailles, some good music, and the Topical Review repay one for going to the Strand this week, however.

Mayer moved his family to California and set up a studio on the grounds of Colonel Selig's zoo, thirty acres of caged animals used for adventure pictures supposedly filmed in Africa. Anita thought the working conditions at the Selig zoo quite primitive and missed the showers and luncheon facilities at Vitagraph. She rented a small house in Hollywood.

Hollywood proper was chiefly a residential district where hundreds of gallons of water were used daily by gardeners trying to coax grass to grow on the grounds surrounding the bogus Spanish haciendas of the stars, directors, and producers, and the box-shaped stucco dwellings of the technicians and extras who fed the growing factories. It was a small town where almost everyone knew everyone else, where gossip columnists weren't needed to spread rumors. On the hills there were forests of oil derricks. Entertaining was mainly confined to the home, because night spots were few. In Beverly Hills coyotes invaded the garbage cans, and sidewalks ran along and disappeared into open fields. Many of the white globes that adorned streetlights had been shot-up by revelers from the nearby roadhouses.

In the press Louie was referred to as "Anita Stewart's impresario." When writing the story of Anita Stewart's life, two years later, a reporter from the *New York Dramatic Mirror* said, "One day the announcement was made that her own company had been formed under the direction of Louis B. Mayer, the well-known producer."

Anita Stewart fulfilled her three-year contract with Mayer and then made pictures for other companies. She moved into a mansion with her mother and her dogs, divorced Rudy Cameron, and married George Peabody Converse, a New York millionaire and socialite, the son of a former president of U.S. Steel. Anita Stewart became known as one of America's best-dressed women. She advertised Lux Toilet Soap and wrote a novel. In 1935 she returned to New York and spoke to reporters. "We haven't been here since repeal," she said, "and I never saw such a change. The dirty old speaks have become sidewalk cafés or swanky bars. It's delightful. What a civilized place!" She divorced her second husband twelve years later.

In later life she said, "These stories about so many old stars being broke makes the girls of the silent days look so dumb. The Talmadges aren't broke. The Gishes aren't broke.

Look at Mary Pickford and Fairbanks. They certainly aren't broke."

She died in 1961. She was found unconscious in the bedroom of her Beverly Hills home by her sister, who lived with her. A fire department rescue squad worked on her for an hour. Anita Stewart's sister gave the actress's age as fifty-nine, but official records showed she was sixty-five.

FIVE

Marcus Loew

MARCUS Loew grew up among pushcarts in the days when New York City's skyline was lower. There was no Empire State, Chrysler, Woolworth, or Flatiron building. There was no Grand Central Station. The Waldorf-Astoria, St. Regis, and Plaza hotels had yet to be built. Tiffany's wasn't there, and neither was Radio City Music Hall, the Frick Mansion, Rockefeller Center or the New York Public Library. Cobblestone streets were crisscrossed with trolley tracks, dirt streets were dented by wagon wheels.

Times Square was known as Longacre Square, a place to avoid after nightfall. On a triangular plot between Forty-second and Forty-third streets was the eight-story Pabst Hotel. Marcus Loew was thirty-four years old when the Pabst Hotel was torn down in 1904 and the $2 million Times building was erected. The Times building, one of the tallest in the world, gave new life to the square. Theaters were built in its shadow, including Hammerstein's Victoria, the Lyceum, and the Lyric. Restaurants followed those theaters. Millions of people began to visit the square; they could get off the subway right under the new building. Longacre Square was renamed Times Square.

By the time Marcus Loew was forty he had seen New York City change entirely. "New York was essentially a place of big business," said Charlie Chaplin, recalling his arrival there in 1910. "The tall skyscrapers seemed ruthlessly arrogant and to care little for the convenience of ordinary people; even the saloon bars had no place for the customers to sit, only a long brass rail to rest a foot on, and the popular eating places, though clean and done in white marble, looked cold and clinical."

As far back as 1910 New York was in a hurry. Chaplin said:

I was alien to this slick tempo. In New York even the owner of the smallest enterprise acts with alacrity. The bartender serves a beer with alacrity, sliding it up to you along the polished surface of the bar. The soda clerk, when serving an egg malted milk, performs like a hopped-up juggler. In a fury of speed he snatches up a glass, attacking everything he puts into it, vanilla flavor, blob of ice cream, two spoons full of malt, a raw egg which he deposits with one crack, then adding milk—all of which he shakes in a container and delivers in less than a minute.

Then, as now, rents were outrageous. An unskilled laborer earned less than $9 a week but had to pay $15 a month for a four-room tenement flat in an immigrant neighborhood. Middle-class people complained that soon only the very rich would be able to afford to live in the city. The very rich complained, too. In 1879 William H. Vanderbilt paid $400,000 for a whole Fifth Avenue block between Fifty-first and Fifty-second streets, and thirty years later that sum only bought a few lots on upper Fifth. In 1906 a house on Fifth Avenue, built on speculation, sold for $510,000. A few months later the neighboring six-story townhouse sold for even more. A British wit of the day, when talking about Manhattan, remarked that "to live in New York it is well to take the precaution of being a millionaire."

A millionaire was no longer a person with a million dollars but a person who earned a million dollars annually. The ambitions of many immigrant boys were shaped by the vast fortunes of the new industrial aristocracy; Morgan, Vanderbilt, Astor, Carnegie, all of them were former immigrants. They were the men whose money was changing the city's skyline. In one year, 1906, there were plans for fifteen tall office buildings to be built in Manhattan with funds from that power elite.

They were the American superstars of the day, the incarnations of the American Dream. They set a standard of wealth for everyone, especially those with imagination living on the Lower East Side, a section dense with people, merchandise, garbage, and odors.

Many of the early movie men grew up on the Lower East Side. William Fox lived on Stanton Street between Columbia and Sheriff. Adolph Zukor spent several years of his youth working there, and his partner Jesse Lasky was steeped in the place. Marcus Loew's father was a waiter there.

Graduates of the Lower East Side were accustomed to a lot of visual stimulation: potatoes stacked in pyramids on a pushcart next to a cart of fish laid out on dripping ice, a mangy dog under the cart licking up the puddles. Fresh fruit, heaps of peanuts, colorful gumdrops, green beans, beets, and underpants, all sizes. Wooden barrels full of pickles under awnings, wooden barrels full of trash. On most of the iron fire escapes, mattresses were stacked up to air out. Girls at the windows; babies at the windows. People were arguing everywhere, about trade unions, about the prices at the pushcarts. "Pullers" came out of stores and pulled customers inside.

Bands marched down the street. There were German bands, Austrian bands, Polish bands. On street corners acrobats did flips, jugglers threw fiery batons. The organ grinder's monkey would smoke cigarettes. Opera singers and violinists went to the poorest of the poor and asked nothing of them except what they could afford, a coin or two. Perhaps some of the wide-eyed children standing on the streets watching the performers thought that there could be no greater mission in life than to entertain poor people.

There were no bathtubs in the tenements. There was no running water. Women had to lug buckets up from the pump in the courtyard so they could wash dishes and children. So many people lived in each room that most rooms looked like hospital wards with the beds lined up. The outhouse was in the courtyard, and all the families in the building used it.

Marcus Loew made sure that in Loew's theaters the lavatories were elegant and clean. Beautiful ladies' rooms were a trademark of his. It was said at one time that many women paid the ten-cents admission fee to his theaters simply to use the ladies' rooms. They were lavish. When asked why he made such a big deal over rest rooms, Mr. Loew remembered his childhood. "A lot of our customers still live like that," he said. "So it's a wonderful experience for them to visit one of my theaters."

He began with a penny arcade on East Fourteenth Street in 1905. For twenty-five cents customers could shoot a miniature rifle containing a magazine of sixteen cartridges. A mechanized gypsy nodded her head when a penny was dropped in her slot and pushed out a card revealing one's fortune. A penny bought horoscopes with a portrait of one's future husband or wife. Customers could stamp their name and address on an aluminum plate. They could hear, through two little insulators on a wire, the Floradora Sextet or Sousa's band, as transmitted by Edison's new invention the phonograph. They could peer into a black eye-piece and witness such tabloid silent dramas as *The Servant Girl's Dream* or *Fun in a Boarding School*.

The peep show was the most popular machine in the penny arcade. The dramas lasted as long as three-quarters of a minute, and on Saturday nights people lined up with pennies in their hands. Marcus Loew opened a "picture show"—admission five cents—on the floor above his penny arcade.

The founder of Loew's Theaters was a most undistinguished-looking man, barely five feet tall, a friendly gap between his two large front teeth. His moustache was bushy, his lips were generous. His voice was surprisingly deep for one so small. Like most soft-spoken men he was slow to anger. His whole attitude was one of humility and apology. The only thing about him that sparkled were his gold teeth. He stood tipped slightly backwards, as if waiting for his wife, who was a foot taller, to make sure he was all tucked in.

Those who worked for Marcus Loew reported that he never argued with his employees and that he spoke with reluctance when he had to correct them. People described him as the most fair and decent man in show business. His press agents were able to obtain top stars to go on tours for him because most of them wanted to repay some kindness of his.

That Sime Silverman, the editor of *Variety*, was eager to help Marcus Loew is an indication of Loew's character. Sime Silverman founded *Variety* in 1905, with $1,500 cash, to champion the rank-and-file worker in the theater, from stagehand to star. Sime Silverman loathed most vaudeville tycoons, like B.F. Keith, because of the way they pushed actors around. Sime hated dishonesty, hated phonies, and could spot one immediately. He thought Marcus Loew should succeed.

A few times a week Sime escaped from the midtown newspaper whirl in the backseat of one of his three chauffeur-driven motorcars. He stopped at roadhouses in Westchester and Long Island for dinner. As he motored along he noticed new housing developments. So that no other theater man would have a chance to discover the location, Sime published the news the next day. "Marcus Loew is developing a new realty project on the Grand Concourse, and a prime focal point will be a deluxer in the Bronx." Loew read this news in *Variety*, investigated the site, and built Loew's Paradise.

Or, "Loew toppers Nick Schenck, Bob Rubin, and prexy Marcus Loew were driving toward Long Beach when they were struck with the idea that Jamaica would be an up-and-coming residential development, and accordingly took an option on a corner site for a theater." Marcus Loew read this, took a look at the site, and built the Loew's Valencia, in Jamaica. Loew's Theaters, Inc., one of the greatest organizations in show business, was built up on friendship.

For several years, around the time that Mayer was moving out of Haverhill to Boston, Marcus Loew acquired theaters at a tremendous rate. The theaters weren't much more than a string of broken-down small-time vaudeville houses. Many of them needed as much renovation as Louie's Gem Theater did in Haverhill. Marcus Loew's first theater was, like Louie's, a reconverted burlesque house. There may have been a "store" show or two, but Loew's Theatre was the first bona fide movie theater in Brooklyn. Opening night he sold only one ticket. Gross receipts were ten cents. The customer was an old woman. Loew ran the picture, then gave the customer her dime back. His faith in motion pictures was badly shaken and remained so for a long time. His theaters would be devoted primarily to vaudeville, and movies would fill in between the acts.

Marcus Loew's original string of eleven theaters was located in or near New York City. By 1917 he had added houses in Quebec, Toronto, Hamilton, Ottawa, and Montreal. Then he opened houses in Cleveland, St. Louis, and Pittsburgh. He acquired theaters in Birmingham, Knoxville, Nashville, Memphis, New Orleans, and several other southern towns. Loew built the palatial Loew's State in Los Angeles and bought the Sullivan-Considine circuit of theaters in the West, which gave him coast-to-coast coverage. By 1918, when he was forty-three, he owned 112 theaters and had ten thousand people working for him with an annual payroll of $8 million. He hired talented, industrious employees, paid them well, and did not interfere with their work.

"The secret of success?" he asked. "That's easy. Give people what they want, give them their money's worth, and they'll stand in line at your door."

Whenever a new theater opened, no matter where it was, it

was treated as a gala event worthy of publicity. What the stunt
would be was left up to the theater managers, because it was
assumed they knew their community best, and if they needed
help they called upon Loew's publicity staff. Usually when a
theater opened in some down-in-the-heels neighborhood,
Loew and his uptown friends were invited to appear in tuxe-
dos and ballgowns. In a theater on Avenue B that was failing,
Loew's publicity staff instituted amateur shows for the neighborhood residents and built a pool on the stage so local girls
in bathing suits could have diving contests. His staff got music publishers from Tin Pan Alley to send song pluggers to his
theaters so audiences could vote for their favorite new song.
Beauty contests for local girls were held at Loew's theaters,
and professional showgirls from *Ziegfeld's Follies* danced on
the stages of theaters in the poorest neighborhoods. Flo
Ziegfeld tried out new dance numbers on the Loew's stages to
polish them before bringing them to his famous theater in
Manhattan.

"We study a neighborhood before we assign a program to
it," Loew said. "In some places we find that the people want
only a motion picture show. . . . In other localities—and these
spots appear to be increasing—the folks want vaudeville
sandwiched in between the films. We haven't any particular
brand of entertainment—we just aim to entertain, that's all."

Marcus Loew inaugurated children's shows on Saturday
mornings, charged the children less, and presented motion
pictures and the kind of live acts that children like: magicians
and animals. He booked Singer's Midgets into his theaters, a
troupe of eighteen Hungarian and Austrian midgets who
traveled with two baby elephants, a couple of ponies, and
about twenty dogs. (The troupe was organized by Baron Leo
Singer, who thirty years later was asked to find 124 midgets to
play Munchkins in *The Wizard of Oz*). When Loew's Orpheum
on Eighty-sixth and Third Avenue opened, he had the entire
cast of the featured picture arrive in limousines, one to a car,
and the parade up to the front door blocked traffic for miles.
Monster sunlight arcs, recently developed for motion-picture

use, were set around the front of the theater, and they lighted the whole neighborhood. Cameramen, newspaper people, and a parade of celebrities made it a night for the books. It set the pattern for all big theatrical openings.

Marcus Loew refinanced his Loew's Theatrical Enterprises. He issued seven thousand shares on the market, formed Loew's Inc., and was listed on the New York Stock Exchange. In 1919 his board of directors included the president of Liberty National Bank, the president of General Motors, and the vice president of Bankers Trust.

Despite his success—he was president of a $25 million company—Loew was dissatisfied with the quality of most of the pictures shown in his theaters. He agreed with the British reporter who wrote the following tongue-in-cheek article about America on movie screens:

> America is a large country entirely surrounded by sin and sentiment. It is inhabited in the East by unscrupulous but enormously successful business men, who devote their nights to squandering in cabarets their ill-gotten gains of the day before. In the West "bad men" rob stage coaches and banks and shoot sheriffs and their partners in crime and spend a good deal of time rolling on the ground in attempts to gouge each other's eyes out. The North is peopled by bearded scoundrels who go there to escape from the law, to steal mining claims and to menace lonely girls snowbound in log cabins. The South is notable for cacti and half-breeds. The last-named have no particular vice; they are just bad. The rich women of the East are notable for the scantiness of their costumes, their uncharitable attitude toward other women and for their remarkable bedrooms. These are of enormous size and have at least one telephone and an easy way of egress for the heroines and ingress for the heroes.

Marcus Loew wanted to be able to control the content of the films he showed as well as the price he paid for them. His former partner, Adolph Zukor, was already doing that. Zukor was not only producing pictures in his Famous Players-Lasky studio but also distributing them through his Paramount company. Loew's rival, William Fox, was making a fortune producing cowboy movies starring Tom Mix, who never drank, smoked, used profanity, or killed his enemy.

Several theater men who owned smaller chains than Loew's were already producing pictures by pooling their money. The First National Exhibitors Circuit, with Nathan Gordon in Boston, offered Charlie Chaplin $1 million for eight two-reel pictures. Mary Pickford signed on for three pictures at $250,000 each. Then the Talmadge sisters signed. With America's top stars and a national chain of first-run theaters, First National came onto the scene full-blown.

Marcus Loew decided to shop for a production company of his own. Metro Pictures, which Mayer had nothing to do with by this time, had moved from New York to the west coast. The studio was overstocked with war dramas, and everyone was tired of war. Weekly income dropped from $108,000 to $6,000, while a weekly payroll for the distribution system alone ate up $30,000 a week. The company needed financing and a theater chain to showcase its films.

Marcus Loew came to the rescue by purchasing Metro Pictures for $3 million. He pumped money into the studio so it could produce fifty to seventy-five pictures a year at an average cost of $200,000 a picture, ten times what Metro had been spending before.

Luck pursued Marcus Loew. No sooner had he bought the failing studio when executives there hired an unknown dancer, an Italian named Guglielmi, who used the stage name Rudolph Valentino. Metro paid Rudolph Valentino $350 a week and cast him in *The Four Horsemen of the Apocalypse*. Valentino's sensual appeal to women was unprecedented, and Metro became known as the miracle studio. Money poured in.

Marcus Loew began to feel crowded in his office in the Heidelberg Building at Forty-second Street and Broadway, where he rented the entire second floor. Forty booking agents

at forty desks supervised the scheduling of vaudeville and picture shows in all the different districts of the country. At the
other end of the floor the auditing department tabulated receipts and expenses of all Loew's theaters. Telephones jan-
gled and typewriters clacked. There were three waiting rooms
packed with hopefuls, one for ladies, another for gentlemen,
and another for agents. A sign in the ladies waiting room said
"This room is for the use of ladies only; this means YOU."
Aspiring performers, writers, and agents were filtered
through several secretaries. News about whether or not one
had made the grade was shouted through a megaphone: "Not
interested in the Sulzer film" or "No room for airplane exhi-
bitions." A lucky few were conducted through three doors
and down a corridor to Marcus Loew's office.

There were only three big buildings in Times Square at
that time; the Times building, the Astor Hotel, and the
Claridge Hotel. Times Square had an open feeling; theaters
and stores sported awnings. Social activity was centered in
the Astor and the Claridge, which almost faced each other
across Broadway. Theatre men like Flo Ziegfeld, George M.
Cohan (who sang "Remember me to Herald Square," not
Times Square), William A. Brady, and David Belasco could be
found at the Claridge. Motion-picture people like Marcus
Loew, Nicholas and Joe Schenck, Adolph Zukor, William Fox,
W.R. Sheehan, Goldwyn, and the Warner brothers dined and
talked shop across the street in the Astor's Hunting Room.
Loew wanted his offices to remain in Times Square, where
the action was.

He could walk to Shanley's Grill, located in the Putnam
Building at Forty-third Street and Broadway, where New York
movie men also met to talk about their work. "From half a
dozen to a dozen of us would gather between eleven o'clock
and midnight," Adolph Zukor recalled, "to eat and sit up to
all hours building castles in the air. Table rules allowed a man
to talk about his dream. My dream was to make feature-length
pictures to replace the one- and two-reelers. But no one took
me very seriously." Marcus Loew's dream was to build a the-

ater and office tower right on Broadway, in the middle of the legitimate theater district.

Near Loew's office, at the corner of Forty-fifth Street and Broadway, was the Bartholdi Inn, a rendezvous for actors and chorus girls out of work, and for prostitutes. At the top of a wide staircase leading up from the street sat Mama Bartholdi, a kindhearted, overweight woman with a moustache. She collected a dollar a night from any actor or actress who arrived with a suitcase. If the performer was out of work but trying, she never asked for the dollar and knew she'd collect when the actor got a break. Men who arrived without suitcases paid a different fee.

Jimmy Durante, who was playing the piano in speakeasies at that time, made jokes in later years about the Bartholdi Inn: "I'm in a hotel room, and there's a knock on the door, and a voice says, 'This is the house detective; you got a woman in your room?' And I says, 'No.' So he t'rows one in."

When the Bartholdi Inn came up for sale, Marcus Loew negotiated for two years, bought the property, tore the inn down, and built a sixteen-story office building. On the ground floor was the 3,500-seat vaudeville and picture palace, Loew's State Theater, his 104th playhouse. It cost $1 million. "In his office in the new theatre building yesterday," reported the *New York Times*, "Mr. Loew declared that the State was probably the last theatre that he would build for a considerable period. He will open no new houses at all for months, he said, and then he will slowly increase his circuit by adding theatres already in existence, rather than by building new ones."

The Loew's State Theater had its gala opening in August 1921. Huge arc lights on the sidewalk sent corridors of white into the night sky as if Broadway were a landing strip. Police had to hold back the crowds. A limousine arrived and Theda Bara stepped out dressed in a vampy black gown with a fillet of gold in her black hair. The crowd shouted to her and applauded. Buster Keaton arrived to watch himself on the screen that night in *Hard Luck*. He escorted his wife, Natalie

Talmadge, who wore a flame-colored velvet evening coat. Monte Blue, David Warfield, Lillian Gish, George Arliss, Clara Kimball Young, Marion Davies, Dorothy Dalton, Sophie Tucker, and William Randolph Hearst—everyone who was anyone—descended from limousines and entered an unusually large lobby decorated with imported sienna marble wainscoting and ornamental cast-iron grills. Under crystal chandeliers was an ornate fountain, water tinkling into a marble basin. Women in the balcony were allowed to smoke, an innovation that some said meant the end of the world. The audience watched five hours of vaudeville and pictures before the final curtain fell. Marcus Loew, tiny on stage, accepted applause while surrounded by the entire cast of sequined girls from the *Ziegfeld Follies*.

Adolph Zukor, not to be outdone by his former partner, arch rival, great pal, and now relative, since their children had married and given them a mutual grandchild, built an office tower and movie theater across the street on the site of the old Shanley's Grill. The Paramount Building cost $17 million, was a thirty-three story edifice, headquarters of Famous Players-Lasky and Paramount. Zukor's office was on the ninth floor and the entire ground floor was the vast Paramount Theater. Thomas Edison attended the dedication of the building. Zukor said:

> To me it was not simply a mark of success of the movie industry or of myself in it. It was a symbol of the opportunities in America, and my mind was less on that great structure of stone and steel, than on my life in Hungary and the journey to the United States with a few dollars sewn in my vest.

Meanwhile, at Mr. Loew's Metro studio on the west coast, Rudolph Valentino asked for a hundred-dollar raise. Metro executives offered him fifty, so the Latin Lover walked out and went to Adolph Zukor.

Valentino's first picture for Zukor's Famous Players-Lasky studio was *The Sheik*, a film that earned millions and influenced fashions for months. Young men grew sideburns, slicked their hair straight back, and wore wide-bottomed trousers. The important windows on Fifth Avenue suggested the interior of a harem: oriental carpets, leather hassocks, billowing curtains, patterns on the ceiling. Women, so reports said, fainted in the aisles while watching Valentino on the screen. Thousands of fan letters on scented paper arrived for him every week.

Zukor began to buy up the legitimate theaters on Broadway, including the Criterion, New York Theater, Rivoli, Rialto, Empire and Lyceum. Altogether he owned four hundred theaters in the United States and Canada. He owned producing companies in Great Britain, France, Belgium, Spain, Scandinavia, and Poland, and a $3 million production and distribution organization in India. He had branch offices in twenty-eight of the principal cities of the United States and Canada, in London, Sydney, Mexico City, Havana, Tokyo, and Manila. He owned 140 subsidiary corporations engaged in either producing, distributing, or exhibiting motion pictures. He distributed more than thirty thousand films every week throughout the United States.

The Federal Trade Commission issued a formal complaint against Famous Players-Lasky, charging that the acquisition of many of the Paramount theaters was accompanied by coercion and intimidation. The commission further charged that independent producers could not get a showing for their films because Zukor controlled most first-run theaters. In Cleveland alone he controlled six. In Missouri, seventeen were owned by Zukor, who played only his Famous Players-Lasky pictures. The FTC estimated that sixty-seven cents of every dollar spent in the United States by motion-picture audiences went to Zukor's organization. The commission stated:

> The theatres owned, controlled or operated by Famous Players-Lasky Corporation are permanently closed to all competitors. The producers of many prominent artists, who are not affiliated with Famous Players-Lasky Corpo-

ration are denied a showing of their pictures in the first-run downtown theatres in New York City, where three of the five first-run theaters are owned by the Famous Players-Lasky Corporation and the remaining two first-run theatres are owned or controlled by competing producers, who likewise exhibit their own productions exclusively.

To compete with Zukor, other producers and distributors began to join together. Vitagraph swallowed up Kalem, then Selig, Lubin, and Essanay. Zukor got even bigger by absorbing Selznick. The Lincoln & Parker Film Company of Worcester, Massachusetts, bought Thomas Edison's studio in New York City, all its equipment and scenic accessories, as well as over a million feet of film negative and the Edison Plant in Orange, New Jersey. The "Big Four," as Charlie Chaplin, Mary Pickford, Douglas Fairbanks, and D.W. Griffith were known, merged their interests and formed United Artists. They issued stock and owned all of it themselves. First National Pictures merged with Associated Producers Company.

After Valentino walked out, the head of Metro quit, and the man who replaced him had no talent for organizing people. Loew did not know whether to try to build up Metro or just abandon the studio. Some Metro pictures were good. Lillian Gish's *The White Sister* ran for six months on Broadway. Rex Ingram directed *Scaramouche* and cast Ramon Novarro, who was supposed to replace Valentino as a Latin Lover. Metro had Buster Keaton and the beautiful child actor Jackie Coogan under contract. But most of Metro's films—they cranked out a picture a week—were mediocre. Loew's program consisted of Metro pictures during the first half of the week, Paramount and independent product at the end of the week.

At the same time that Metro Pictures was failing, other companies were producing smash hits. *The Last of the Mohicans,* produced by Associated Producers and starring Wallace Beery, was hailed by critics as "a truly exceptional picture." Douglas Fairbanks produced and starred in *The Mark of Zorro,* and audiences flocked to see it. First National scored a triumph with Charlie Chaplin and Coogan in *The Kid. Nanook of the North,* produced by Robert J. Flaherty, showed audiences the possibilities of turning the camera on nature itself. From Europe came *The Cabinet of Dr. Caligari,* a surreal horror film.

Marcus Loew began to worry that he was letting down his stockholders, ordinary people who had trusted him. He had a heart attack. His doctor sent him to Florida, saying that if Loew didn't rest he'd die.

At the same hotel in Florida, recovering from frazzled nerves, was Frank Joseph Godsol, the chairman of the board of Goldwyn Pictures. Joe Godsol, usually full of confidence because he was tall, handsome, rich, and ruthless, was worried and deflated. It was beginning to dawn on him that he had made a mistake squeezing Sam Goldwyn out of the company that Sam had founded. Sam Goldwyn was the only person at the Goldwyn studio who knew anything about making motion pictures, and now, four years after his ouster, the product had become inferior.

The weakness of the Goldwyn corporation had always been that it lacked sufficient outlets for its product. Though the company did control the Ascher theater chain in the Midwest, Bishop Cass Theaters in the Rockies, and the Miller Amusement Company's theaters in Los Angeles, those houses were not first-run. The Goldwyn corporation owned halfshare in the Capitol, the biggest theater in New York City, seating over four thousand.

As for players under contract, Sam Goldwyn believed that the story was the important element in movies. He thought Mary Pickford's huge salary was ridiculous. Arguments over it caused him to leave Famous Players-Lasky to start his own company. Goldwyn refused to pay large salaries to players and therefore had few stars under contract.

At the time that Sam Goldwyn was ousted, the company was producing *Ben-Hur.* Now, four years later, the picture was still not finished. The whole cast was on location in Rome, and money was being gobbled up. It was worry over *Ben-Hur* that required Joe Godsol to rest on the beach in Florida.

The strength of the Goldwyn corporation was its modern and efficient plant in Culver City, a facility that cost Sam Goldwyn $14 million. Sam was convinced that California, not New York, was the best place for photoplay production. "We find that we can take just as good photographs in California sunlight on our own fifty-acre plant, the biggest in the world," he said, "as New York can turn out in any of its cramped little halls. We can build big sets in our big lot and leave them standing as long as we please."

There were forty-two buildings on the property, from the large administration building to the small bungalows used as dressing rooms. Magnolia trees perfumed the air, fir trees lined the entrance drive. There was an entire miniature city almost a half-mile long, with streets that duplicated avenues in Russia, Spain, France, China, Alaska, and New York.

On the beach in Flordia, Marcus Loew and Joe Godsol defied their doctors and talked business. Loew had theaters and some big-name stars; Godsol had the studio facility.

News that Loew was thinking of acquiring Goldwyn Pictures filtered across the country to Louie Mayer in California. The person who was chosen to run the combined studios would be one of the most powerful men in the film industry. He would control the finest studio facility, some of the best stars, directors, and writers, and the product that would be shown all over the world in Loew's Theaters, the best theaters. Mayer knew that there was no one at Metro Pictures with enough skill to organize two previously rivalrous companies. With Sam Goldwyn out of Goldwyn Pictures, there was no one there who could do it either. Within the Loew's organization, Marcus Loew's health would not allow it, and his chief lieutenant, Nicholas Schenck, had his hands full administering Loew's theater empire.

The head of the new studio would have to be a consummate politician, able to meld the artistic temperaments of creative people from two separate companies. He would have to organize thousands of employees into various departments:

executives, writers, directors, players, cameramen, scenic designers, film editors, unit managers, prop people, painters, carpenters, plasterers, electricians, transportation people, location scouts, special-effects experts, budget estimators, accountants, studio police, fire department, doctors, barbers, teachers, wardrobe people, makeup artists, seamstresses, script girls, cooks at the commissary, a publicity staff, and still photographers.

Marcus Loew was familiar with Louis B. Mayer but could not have been very impressed. Louie produced four pictures for Metro, and three of them were not at all socko at the box office.

But the fourth picture, *Pleasure Mad*, starring Norma Shearer, was a hit. It was produced by Irving Thalberg, a young man Louie had hired away from Universal Pictures. "No picture can be considered a success," Thalberg said, "unless it appeals to the matinee trade. When you've got a picture women want to see, the men will have to go along. A woman can always keep a man away from a picture that attracts only him." Louie gave Thalberg free rein, and the Louis B. Mayer Film Company began to produce decent product.

But there were a lot of small-time producers making good pictures. There was no reason at all for Marcus Loew, who had money and experience enough to hire the best of the best, to hire Louie to head the new Culver City studio. Only now and then was Louie's name in the newspapers, and then he was referred to as Louis B. Mayer "of Boston." Louie would need something spectacular to gain the respect of Marcus Loew.

SIX

What Louie Brought to the Table

JUST AS Mayer had seen Anita Stewart's nervous breakdown as an opportunity for himself, he now heard opportunity knocking again in rumors that there was trouble between William Randolph Hearst, the publishing tycoon, and Hearst's mistress Marion Davies.

Davies was threatening to leave Hearst. This was not an idle boast. She had enough money, hundreds of friends, and an intensely independent spirit. Hearst was old enough to be her father, had scant sex appeal, and was plagued by jealousy. He adored Marion Davies, describing her as the best friend he ever had.

At fifty he was a big, oafish, awkward man, boyish, shrewd, kind, ruthless, and natural in his manner. Like many people of bulk, he was extremely light on his feet and could dance the Charleston with teenage energy. Charlie Chaplin said that of all the people he ever met, William Randolph Hearst made the deepest impression. "It was the enigma of his personality that fascinated me."

Hearst's empire consisted of hundreds of publications, large holdings in New York real estate, mining, and vast tracts of land in Mexico. Hearst's enterprises were worth about $400 million. While Rockefeller felt the moral burden of money, and Pierpont Morgan was imbued with the power of it, Hearst spent millions nonchalantly, as though it were weekly pocket money.

The problem between Hearst and Davies was more professional than personal. William Randolph Hearst wanted to turn Marion Davies, who had been a *Ziegfeld Follies* girl, into a film star. He could not offer her marriage—he was already married and the father of five grown sons—but he could offer her fame. He set up a studio in the Bronx, named his company Cosmopolitan Pictures, and starred Marion in all of the productions. Her stardom was a matter of personal vanity. He wanted the whole world to see the treasure he possessed in Marion. In his many newspapers and magazines he publicized Marion's personality and praised her film performances. He sat alone in his projection room and ran her movies again and again, loving every pretty close-up. But only the public can make a star, and the public did not take to her. Hearst's publicity was so overdone, Marion's face on so many pages, that her name became something of a joke to people in the film world. Her films lost money and her career went nowhere.

William Randolph Hearst selected the roles she played, and they were always the same, the innocent virgin. Marion Davies knew that her talent was as a comedienne and that she should play brassy dames. She was beginning to believe that she might make more progress without Poppy, as she called Hearst.

Born Marion Douras in Brooklyn and educated in a convent, Marion declared at a young age that marrying for love was a ridiculous thing to do. She intended to marry for financial comfort, or not at all. At the age of sixteen she went to dance on the Broadway stage and was soon accepting diamond bracelets from stage-door Johnnies. Hearst had been a stage-door Johnny for years, but when he saw Marion in the *Ziegfeld Follies* (she was nineteen), he fell in love.

His wife Millicent was an ex-showgirl, but she had shed her past and was now a respectable matron in New York society. Though her sons thought Marion Davies a whore and felt hurt for their mother, Millicent was quite resigned to her husband's infidelity. "If it weren't Marion it would be someone else," she said. She had a satisfying life of her own in New York and thought it amusing how her husband pretended there was nothing wrong between them. She said:

> He acts as though Marion doesn't exist. He is always sweet and charming, but never stays more than a few hours. And it's always the same routine: in the middle of dinner the butler hands him a note, then he excuses himself and leaves the table. When he returns, he sheepishly mentions that some urgent business matter needs his immediate attention in Los Angeles, and we all pretend to believe him. And of course we all know he returns to join Marion.

Despite Millicent's philosophical attitude, Marion Davies was a pariah in New York society. So Hearst moved his Cosmopolitan Pictures from the Bronx to California, where he arrived with Marion aboard his 284-foot cruiser. From then on the film colony enjoyed an era of fabulous dinner parties with hundreds of guests: actors, senators, polo-players, chorus boys, foreign potentates, and writers. Hearst set Marion Davies up in a house on the beach in Santa Monica, with seventy rooms, a dining room that could seat fifty guests, and suites to accommodate twenty guests. Recalled the writer Anita Loos:

> The enormous compound in Santa Monica, which Hearst modestly called the Beach House, was ablaze with lights. It looked like a country club; a main building of "sea-shore Colonial" and a wide veranda overlooking

two swimming pools, one heated, the other at air tem-
perature like certain wines. A tall hedge separated the
grounds from the beach, beyond which gleamed the
phosphorescent surf of the Pacific. The Hollywood elite
was gathered in a ballroom decorated by a collection of
portraits; Rembrandts, Van Dykes, Goyas, and Titians.
But hanging next to a masterpiece of Goya was a portrait
that had been painted by Howard Chandler Christie for
the cover of *Cosmopolitan* magazine, and showed Marion
in the cute boy's outfit she wore in *Little Old New York*.

Hearst built himself a huge chateau, San Simeon, on four
thousand acres and populated the grounds with lions, mon-
keys, and bears. Signs on the five-mile driveway warned "Animals have the right of way." Hearst and Marion Davies were
the king and queen of Hollywood, but the problem between
them did not go away.

Thomas Ince, the studio chief of Cosmopolitan Pictures,
cast Marion in the roles that Hearst specified. Then, in November, 1924, Ince suddenly died of a heart attack brought
on by acute indigestion. Ince had ulcers and had been drinking at a party aboard Hearst's yacht. Rumors spread that Ince
had been shot by Hearst in a jealous rage. Ince's widow called
the rumors, "weird and silly," Hearst's nephew said they were
"absurd," and Charlie Chaplin said the rumors "were completely untrue." Ince's body was examined by his own physi-
cian, by the District Attorney of San Diego, by the Chief of
Homicide of Los Angeles County, and by mortuary physi-
cians, all of whom agreed he died of heart failure.

Marion valued her career largely because she felt it over-
came the stigma of being a "kept girl." She attended very few
parties outside of her own home, where she felt guests
wouldn't walk out on her. "When I get among strangers," she
confided to Anita Loos, "I never know. . . ."

Cosmopolitan Pictures were distributed by the Goldwyn
Corporation. Marion saw the merger of Metro and Goldwyn
as her chance to get her career out from under Hearst's mis-
management. She thought that some of the writers and direc-

tors at Goldwyn and Metro might help her persuade Hearst
to let her express the comic side of her nature. But Hearst,
upon hearing about the impending merger, announced that
he was going to start a company of his own to distribute Marion's pictures, and he intended to buy his own theaters in
which to show them. Marion threatened to leave Hearst, and
Mayer heard the news as opportunity knocking.

Louie, smug with the orderliness of his own household, did
not approve of a man who lived with one woman while married to another. It was 1924 and he was proud of his marriage
to Margaret and of the way they were rearing their daughters.
That Hearst, a father of sons, would flaunt a mistress seemed
to Mayer beneath contempt. Nonetheless, he made an
appointment.

Hearst's down-to-earth manner, his high-pitched voice, and
his genuine pain about the rift with Marion disarmed Mayer.
Hearst said that if he could divorce his wife he would, that he
would marry Marion in a minute if he were free. But he did
not believe in divorce. Hearst thought the marriage vows
were sacred and that his marriage to Millicent was eternal.
Hearst did not want Marion parading around like a harlot on
the screen, and he could not understand why she wanted to.
Louie realized then that Hearst was jealous of Marion and
feared losing her to a younger man.

Mayer said there was no reason for Hearst to lose control
of Marion's pictures, that he was right to want to guide her
career. On the other hand, an independent young woman
like Marion should be put on a salary, not given an allowance
as she was now. Louie said he thought that Marion had great
talent and that she should be able to work with the best directors and supporting players. He suggested that Hearst merge
Cosmopolitan with Goldwyn and Metro and that Hearst set
up quarters for Marion right on the grounds of the Culver
City studio, where Louie, if he were put in charge of the studio, could keep an eye on her when Hearst was away on business. If Louie were put in charge of the combined companies,
he would make sure that Marion was treated like a queen and

that none of her pictures would have anything dirty-minded in them. Hearst liked the theatrical way Mayer spoke, his lively disposition, his histrionics. He called him "son." Mayer called Hearst "Chief." As for Marion Davies, Louie, like most people, was enchanted by her.

Louie took the train to New York to apply for the job of managing Metro-Goldwyn. He offered Marcus Loew not only his enthusiastic self, a proven showman who believed as Loew did that family entertainment was the key to success, but also Cosmopolitan Pictures and the backing of William Randolph Hearst's publishing empire, which included the *New York Mirror*, and the *Los Angeles Examiner*. Hearst could splash articles about Metro-Goldwyn's pictures and players all across his newspapers. He would order his columnist Louella Parsons to discuss Metro-Goldwyn players "helpfully," and to ignore the actors of other companies. Hearst had promised that he would build a fourteen-room bungalow for Marion on the Culver City lot, *if* his friend Louis B. Mayer was put in charge.

The *New York Times* reported on April 18, 1924:

> One of the largest mergers in the history of the motion picture industry was consummated yesterday by Marcus Loew, who heads the consolidated interests which will be operated under the name of the Metro-Goldwyn Corporation. The corporations included in the merger are Metro Pictures, Goldwyn Pictures, and the Louis B. Mayer Company. Their combined authorized capital stock is approximately $65 million. Distribution of Cosmopolitan Productions is included in the merger.

It bothered Louie that his name was not part of the new corporate name. Right and left, small producers were getting obliterated by the companies that bought them, their names disappearing from letterheads. It happened to Selznick when Zukor bought him out and changed the name of Selznick Enterprises to Select. Louie demanded that each picture produced by Loew's new company include his name on the main-title card, "Louis B. Mayer Presents a Metro-Goldwyn

Production." He further demanded that "in all advertising and paid publicity the name Louis B. Mayer shall be prominently mentioned as the producer of said motion picture photoplays." All contracts with stars, directors, and writers would be made in the name of Louis B. Mayer, but they all had to be approved by the home office in New York.

Mayer was hired as vice president in charge of all production activities of the Metro-Goldwyn Corporation, with a salary of $1,500 a week; Thalberg was named second vice president and supervisor of production at a salary of $650 a week. Mayer, Thalberg, and their lawyer J. Robert Rubin would get 20 percent of the profits earned by Metro-Goldwyn. The new company, a subsidiary of Loew's, Inc., would have its headquarters in the Loew's State building on Broadway. All major financial decisions would be made in New York, and no picture could be produced in Culver City without approval from the home office.

Marcus Loew said to the *New York Times:*

Every other business has experienced the same difficulties in its beginnings and has come to realize the economic necessity of centralization. In the railroad business, for instance, this was brought about by the Union Pacific, the Southern Pacific, the Central Pacific and the Illinois Central, who gradually achieved the amalgamation of all the Western roads. They were centralized as they are today, yet all retain their individuality.

On the theatre pages of newspapers across the country the headlines proclaimed: "Metro, Goldwyn, Cosmopolitan and Louis B. Mayer in Giant Motion Picture Merger Headed by Loew;" "Huge Film Merger Links Three Great Movie Companies;" "Metro-Goldwyn Merger Excites Entire Industry;" "Metro, Goldwyn Firms Combine;" and "$65,000,000 Movie Merger Completed." Marcus Loew told Louie that their policy would be great star, great director, great play, and great cast, and that he, Mayer, was authorized to get these without stint or limit. "Spare nothing, Louis," Loew said, "neither expense, time, nor effort. Results only are what I am after. Simply send me the bills and I will okay them."

Mayer presided over the gala opening of his new studio in Culver City in 1924. A Navy band blared marches while five hundred guests, including Admiral Samuel Robinson, commander-in-chief of the Pacific fleet, gathered on the square lawn between the actors' dressing rooms and a row of attached one-room bungalows, which served as offices for writers and directors. On a flag-draped rostrum Mayer sat with civic dignitaries and movie stars. Mae Murray wore yellow to match her canary-yellow Pierce-Arrow parked in front of her dressing room. Lon Chaney sat perfectly still soaking in the atmosphere like a lizard. Francis X. Bushman arrived in a lavender Rolls-Royce driven by a chauffeur in lavender uniform. The star stepped out of the car smoking a lavender cigarette and holding the leash of a harlequin Great Dane. Clara Bow drove up in a flame-red Kissel convertible painted to match her hair and surrounded by two chows whose coats had been dyed the same shade. Rudolph Valentino came over from the Paramount studio in a custom-built Voisin tourer with specially designed silver coiled cobras for radiator caps. Buster Keaton's vehicle was the ultimate. Built for him by the Fifth Avenue Bus Company, it was a yacht-like thirty-foot land cruiser complete with bunks for six, two drawing rooms, a gallery, and an observation deck. He drove it himself wearing a cocked hat and an admiral's uniform borrowed from Metro's costume department.

People went to the rostrum to congratulate Mayer, who was dressed immaculately in suit and vest. He kept jumping out of his chair to reach down to shake hands, then he settled sideways into his chair just to leap up again. A large portrait of Marcus Loew, who was too ill to attend, decorated the raised platform. Mayor Loop of Culver City made the first speech then read congratulatory telegrams from President Calvin Coolidge and Secretary of Commerce Herbert Hoover.

Mayer, who was taking elocution lessons and had allowed

someone else, for the first time, to write his speech, stood up, accepted a floral key to the studio, and spoke in a booming voice that was supposed to mask his terror. "I hope that it is given me to live up to this great trust. It has been my argument and practice that each picture should teach a lesson, should have a reason for existence. With seventeen of the great directors in the industry calling this great institution their home, I feel that this aim will be carried out. . . . This is a great moment for me." He enunciated every word so that he could hide his Yiddish accent. "I accept this solemn trust, and pledge the best I have to give." A group of pretty starlets released colorful balloons into the sky.

All this, the hundreds of people, the bands, the opportunity, the incredible amount of work it would be, and his name was not to be the big one on the letterhead. He put his prepared speech aside and added his name then and there. "I have been warned that this new company starts off with a handicap, that its pictures will bear a name that can never become easy to say, a Metro-Goldwyn-Mayer picture. That we should have a short name, crisp and able to become familiar, like other studios. I can only tell you fellow workers this—if we all do our jobs as I know we will, within a year, wherever you go, when someone asks where you work, you can simply say, not three long words, but three short letters: M-G-M. And everyone will know you're connected with the foremost movie studio in the world."

SEVEN

What's Funny About the Lion Logo

METRO Pictures' trademark was a parrot on a circular perch, its head down and mouth open in an inexplicably vicious way. Goldwyn's logo was much more attractive, so Marcus Loew decided to keep on using it.

The lion trademark was created in 1917 by a young Columbia University dropout named Howard Dietz. He was working for an advertising agency in Manhattan that specialized in promoting coat and suit manufacturers. One of the Phillip Goodman Agency's clients had been Sam Goldwyn, when Sam was in the glove business. Phillip Goodman, a fat man, enjoyed talking about the fat men of literature, like Balzac and Thackeray. When Goldwyn separated himself from Jesse Lasky and Cecil B. DeMille, after they joined Adolph Zukor, he set up his own motion-picture production company in Fort Lee, New Jersey. He remembered Phil Goodman fondly and hired him to design a logo.

Goodman, like every other New Yorker, had seen motion-picture production companies come and go. Goldwyn Pictures, with no product, no stars, no nothing, was not a major client. Goodman gave the job to his twenty-year-old assistant Howard Dietz.

Howard Dietz had many talents but staying in school wasn't one of them. He never graduated from his high school in the Bronx. During the summer of his junior year he crammed for the entrance exams to the Columbia University School of Journalism, passed, and was accepted. But once there he cut as many classes as he attended. "I wasn't conscientious in my studies," he wrote in his autobiography. "It wasn't that I couldn't grasp the essentials. It was that the class was at nine o'clock, and I got to bed at dawn and imagined that I could melodiously snore my way to a degree." The students he partied with were writers, and he joined them in contributing to the campus humor magazine, *The Jester*.

Using an animal in a motion-picture company trademark was not original to Dietz. There were not only Metro's parrot, but Bison Film Company's buffalo and Pathé's rooster as well. Perhaps he had a touch of nostalgia for his pals still in school because he decided to use a lion, which was the trademark of Columbia's humor magazine, a laughing lion that satirized Columbia University's straight-faced lion symbol. The founders of Columbia took their lion from the crest of Kings College in England.

Sam Goldwyn's instructions were to create something that would make his company seem high-class. He had decided to do something unprecedented. He was going to advertise in a general magazine, *The Saturday Evening Post*, rather than in the trade press. All other producers advertised to theater owners and never thought of going directly to the public. The words above Goldwyn's new logo on his fullpage ad would be: "Pictures built upon the strong foundation of intelligence and refinement."

A lordly lion in profile was certainly strong and refined. To make the lion seem to represent intelligence, Howard Dietz decided to surround it with Latin. But Howard Dietz didn't know Latin. He didn't know that it is not only impossible to say "Art for Art's Sake" in Latin, because such a conception would have been foreign to the Romans, but also that the words *Ars Gratia Artis* make no sense when put together.

"For some reason people think things are cooler if they're in Latin," said Brian Krostenko, a Harvard University Latin scholar. "I don't know why, but we get a lot of calls from people who want to have, for instance, "Save the Whales" translated because it sounds better in Latin. This is a perfect case of somebody knowing that "art" is related to the Latin word *ars* and kind of fudging it on there and hoping that it'll sound authentic to the unwashed masses who don't know Latin. They will see *artis* up there and think it must be a snazzy company."

In Latin, the word *ars* means art as in the art of baking bread, a practical way of doing something, a set of principles for producing something specific. The "art" of public speaking, for instance. "In order to say 'for its own sake' in Latin," Mr. Krostenko said, "you actually say 'for its own sake.' You don't repeat the noun."

Art for its own sake is an idea that never would have occurred to the Romans. Roger Ceraglioli, another Harvard Latin scholar, said:

There's a funny thing with the whole issue of Latin mottos, which is that people attach them to their own cultural predispositions and aren't really interested in what the Romans thought. The true origin of this phrase is not in Latin but in English. It's not a Latin thing. Romans never would have cultivated it as an ideal. Roman society worked on a patronage system. Basically, rich guys took care of poor guys, and artists were poor and beholden to the people who paid their bills. Often these people showed up in the poems because they paid the bills. You don't do that today. If you get a National Endowment for the Arts grant you don't necessarily have to write in praise of the United States government. But for a Roman you would. It would obligate you. Art for its own sake would make no sense.

The phrase "art for art's sake" first appeared in 1818 in a work of French philosophy written by Victor Cousin. "We need religion for religion's sake, morality for morality's sake, art for art's sake." The French concept of *l'art pour l'art* became popular in England where it was known as "art for art's sake." In Latin, *Ars Gratia Artis* is gibberish.

"It's an interesting question which I hadn't really thought about before," said Mr. Krostenko. "I've probably seen that logo a million times, and I never thought about it. It's film trying to create a past for itself, trying to sound noble. That's something the Romans would have appreciated because they did that themselves."

It seems fitting that the most famous motion-picture company logo in the world, a logo representing the art of illusion, is itself illusion.

EIGHT

The Home Office

Howard Dietz's flare for ballyhoo was so exactly suited to the motion-picture business, Sam Goldwyn hired him to be head of publicity for Goldwyn Pictures. After the merger Marcus Loew inherited Dietz and made him head of Metro-Goldwyn-Mayer publicity.

The publicity department in New York was in close contact with the studio staff in Culver City and pushed movie news in trade papers, magazines, newspapers, and syndicates. Dietz arranged the appearance on city streets of pretty girls in bathing suits in open limousines. The advertising department, also located at 1540 Broadway, contracted out for press-sheets, showmen's manuals, and other tools useful to exhibitors. Then there was the sales promotion department, which used a direct-mail campaign to the public and to exhibitors and helped the latter find ways to exploit each particular picture. And there was the ad sales department, which was re-

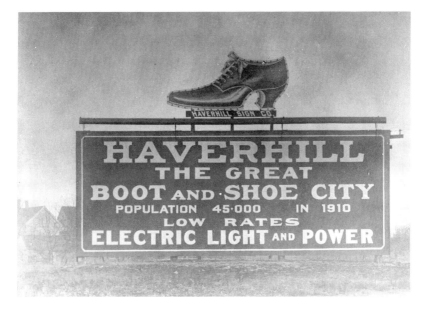

Haverhill, Massachusetts, a thriving city known for its leather goods, is where Louis B. Mayer started his film career. The shoe is framed in electric lights which glowed at night. [COURTESY OF THE TRUSTEES OF THE HAVERHILL PUBLIC LIBRARY]

Temple Street, Haverhill. In 1910, Mayer, age twenty-six, lived on the middle floor of the third house on the right, with two preschool daughters, his wife, his wife's brother who worked as a projectionist in Louie's theater, and a servant girl from Canada. He lied to the census taker that he was born in New York City, not Russia, and that his father's place of birth was Germany, another fib. This picture was taken in 1938 when Temple Street was on its way down. In Mayer's day, the neighborhood was new and attractive, a short walk to the center of town and to the train depot. [COURTESY OF THE TRUSTEES OF THE HAVERHILL PUBLIC LIBRARY]

(Above) The staff of the Cozy Nickel, one of four movie halls in Haverhill in 1908. Only two of these ushers can be identified: Arthur Roma, on the far right, and next to him, Fred Moore, who became a mill worker. Notice how the policeman looks like a Keystone Kop. [COLLECTION OF BEATRICE MALBON]

(Right) Louie Mayer and his wife of forty-eight years, Margaret Schenberg, on vacation in Palm Beach in 1915. His mother liked Margaret so much she once kissed the hem of her daughter-in-law's skirt. [COLLECTION OF EDNA GRACE]

Colman Levin, a wealthy Boston carpet merchant, believed in the unknown Louis Mayer and invested in his film ventures. Unfortunately, Levin was dragged into court when Vitagraph sued to get its star, Anita Stewart, back.

Theda Bara (1891-1955), the first film star to have a bogus private life created for her. Her appearance in *A Fool There Was* (1915), in which she played the screen's first vamp, made her a star. Bara's wickedness was hype. In truth she did not sneer at virtue and was often pained by her screen image. But when she attempted more sympathetic roles, her fans stayed away. Fritz Leiber, the noted Shakespearean actor, is the Caesar here to Bara's 1917 Cleopatra. [COLLECTION OF TODD LUSPINSKI]

Mary Pickford (1893-1979), a star of international popularity, was the first to demand a huge salary and control over her pictures. She proved that the public cared more for photoplayers than for screen stories, directors, or the studio when the film was produced. [COLLECTION OF TODD LUSPINSKI]

Anita Stewart (1895-1961) was Louis B. Mayer's first star. He lured her away from Vitagraph in 1917 by creating a production company for her and by offering her husband, Rudy Cameron, her leading man here in *Rose o' the Sea* (1922), a position on the board of Anita Stewart Productions. Known for her good taste in clothes, she and other actresses had to select and pay for their own screen wardrobes. [COURTESY OF THE BOSTON PUBLIC LIBRARY, PRINT DEPARTMENT]

Adolph Zukor (1873 1976), founder of Paramount, was modest and unassuming despite his great wealth and power. With him in this 1929 photo, is his wife, Lottie Kaufmann. Contrary to popular belief, the early film magnates were not promiscuous but enjoyed long and satisfying marriages. [COURTESY OF QUIGLEY PHOTOGRAPHIC ARCHIVE, SPECIAL COLLECTIONS DIVISION, GEORGETOWN UNIVERSITY LIBRARY]

Samuel Goldwyn (1882-1974) believed that it was the story, not the star, that made a picture great. "Brains write them. Brains direct them. Brains are responsible for their wonderful perfection," was his advertising motto in 1916 when he became a producer. "See These Stars in These Plays by These Authors." [COLLECTION OF ALVIN H. MARILL]

William Fox (1879-1952), the most innovative of all the early film men, scorned personal publicity and trusted no one except his wife, Eve, to whom he was married for fifty-two years. Fox's attempt to take over Loew's, Inc., in 1929 brought him financial ruin. Notice the crooked finger on the hand holding the paper; that arm was paralyzed from a childhood accident. Despite this, Fox became a champion one-arm golfer. [COURTESY OF QUIGLEY PHOTOGRAPHIC ARCHIVE, SPECIAL COLLECTIONS DIVISION, GEORGETOWN UNIVERSITY LIBRARY]

Marcus Loew (1870-1927), founder of Loew's Theaters and Metro-Goldwyn-Mayer, believed in inexpensive family entertainment. "More people have a dime than a dollar." The ladies' rooms in his theaters were lavish and immaculate because he knew that many of the women in his audience still had to trudge downstairs to outhouses in tenement courtyards. [COURTESY OF QUIGLEY PHOTOGRAPHIC ARCHIVE, SPECIAL COLLECTIONS DIVISION, GEORGETOWN UNIVERSITY LIBRARY]

Pembroke, Marcus Loew's mansion next to the sea in Glen Cove, Long Island. Loew's son, Arthur, ordered the house razed in 1968. All that remains are rubble and weeds and the beautiful wrought iron gate at the entrance. [COLLECTION OF THE GLEN COVE PUBLIC LIBRARY]

Loew's State Building and Theater, 1540 Broadway, home office of M-G-M until about 1960. At the time of this photo, 1921, Marcus Loew did not own Goldwyn Pictures or Mayer Film Company, just Metro Pictures. The marquee announces Viola Dana starring in Metro's *The Match Breaker*. Louis Selznick's film company is advertised on the billboard to the left, and the Camel sign in Times Square does not puff yet. Until the mid-1980s, this historic building stood opposite the hideous new Marriott Hotel but now it's gone. [COURTESY OF THEATRE HISTORICAL SOCIETY ARCHIVES LOEW'S COLLECTION NYC]

Lobby of the 3,500-seat Loew's State Theater. Long after other picture houses had stopped live shows, in the 1940s vaudeville still graced its stage. [COURTESY OF THEATRE HISTORICAL SOCIETY ARCHIVES LOEW'S COLLECTION NYC]

Al Altman (1898-1965), Metro-Goldwyn-Mayer's New York talent scout, with Joan Crawford, his first "discovery." Crawford's screen test was made in New York by Altman who noticed her dancing in a 1924 Broadway revue. [COLLECTION OF THE AUTHOR]

Nicholas Schenck (right) is congratulated, insincerely, by Louis B. Mayer. Marcus Loew had died and Schenck has become president of Loew's, Inc, making him Mayer's boss. Next to Schenck (1881-1969) is J. Robert Rubin, Loew's corporation counsel, and Pansy Wilcox, the new Mrs. Schenck. [COURTESY OF QUIGLEY PHOTOGRAPHIC ARCHIVE, SPECIAL COLLECTIONS DIVISION, GEORGETOWN UNIVERSITY LIBRARY]

sponsible for posters, lobby displays, music cues, slides, and novelties used for particular pictures.

Loew's Inc. was Metro-Goldwyn-Mayer's parent and was responsible for everything that the studio produced, the number of pictures made, which pictures, and how much each would cost. All story ideas were okayed by the home office, as were all casting suggestions. Hollywood was a pretty face, so to speak, but New York was the heart and lungs.

The lifeblood of the industry was distribution. Getting films to about eighteen thousand theaters at home and several hundred abroad was so complicated it was a business in itself. Metro-Goldwyn-Mayer's distribution company was another of Loew's subsidiaries with headquarters at 1540 Broadway.

It is commonly believed that the excitement of the motion-picture business came from the glamour of the stars. A case could be made that the excitement, which set this industry apart from every other in America, was generated by every member of the industry not because of his proximity to, or identification with, celebrities but by his very own job. There was an unusual amount of freedom inherent in what each person did, whatever his particular function. If the industry was a pulsating, glittering machine it was because each cog believed that the whole outcome depended upon him, and in most instances he was right. It can be seen how right he was by following the progress of a silent movie from its birth in the film laboratory in California to its appearance in a theater.

Two negatives were made of each film, one for use in foreign countries and the other for use in America and Canada. About two hundred positive prints, sometimes more, sometimes fewer, depending upon how popular the film was expected to be, were taken from the American negative. Each print had a life of only about fifty-nine showings. The instant a movie came out of the laboratory it began its rapid decline, not only because the public was fickle and wanted new pictures all the time, but also because the stuff the print was made of was fragile; every time it was projected it was damaged slightly.

First a print was sent to New York, where the heads of all departments concerned with distribution viewed it in the projection room. The question was, how much money would this picture earn? Approximating what a picture would bring in was not an exact science. If the heads of the various departments could not agree, the movie was placed in some small theaters, in two or three large ones, and in a few medium-sized towns, and the public's response to the picture was determined. The only correct appraisal of a motion picture was the public's opinion of it. The men in distribution were good at figuring out how much revenue to expect.

The sum that they determined was checked with the sales statistical department, which kept a record of the history of all accounts for about nine years. The records of each theater were checked to see if the revenue expected from a particular film was realistic.

For the purpose of selling, the film industry divided the United States into three territories: eastern, central, and western. The total revenue expected from a picture was divided up between the territories. Each territory was supervised by a division manager, one for the eastern states, another for the central states, and a third for the western states. Each accepted his proportionate responsibility of the total amount that was expected from the films. Each territory, under the supervision of the division manager, competed with the other territories. Sometimes east would bring in the most money, sometimes west. It was a game played every year, and salary bonuses depended upon the outcome.

The three territories were further divided into districts. The eastern territory, for instance, was divided into four districts. The first district included Boston, New Haven, and Maine. There was a district manager who supervised the sales activity in those three states. Another district manager in the eastern territory was in charge of Philadelphia, Washington, and Wilkes-Barre. Yet another district manager of the eastern territory watched over Atlanta, Memphis, Charlotte, and Jacksonville. The fourth district manager was in charge of New York, New Jersey, Brooklyn, Albany, and Buffalo. The central and western territories were similarly divided into smaller chunks.

Each chunk was further divided into branches, and each branch had its own manager. The four districts in the eastern territory were divided into fifteen branches. It was from the branches that the salesmen spread out. There were about forty eastern salesmen, fifty central-territory salesmen, and about seventy salesmen working in the west.

Selling films was entirely different from selling another product. First, there was nothing concrete to show when the sale was made. The picture had not yet been produced. The sale was made on the company's reputation, on the drawing power of a particular star, on the popularity of a well-known story, on the appeal of an expensive spectacle, or on the basis of how well a similar picture had done the year before. Second, there was no fixed price for the film. It all depended upon the salesman's imagination. If he could invent a clever sales plan, he might convince a theater man to pay more for a picture. Depending upon a salesman's skill and his ability to show an exhibitor how to get the most from a particular picture, the price for a film could vary by as much as a thousand dollars. Third, the pictures were leased, not sold, sometimes for a flat rate, sometimes for a percentage of the box office.

Pictures were often leased to exhibitors in a block, which might be a dozen, two dozen, or more pictures. Exhibitors who bought a company's whole line received a substantial discount. This infuriated exhibitors who did not want to buy a block but only wanted, say, the Clark Gable picture. Though some exhibitors wanted to abolish block-booking, others saw the advantage of it. They needed a constant supply of product, and the cut in price they received for buying a block was passed on to their customers. The studios were churning out a picture a week, so the product was mostly pedestrian and only occasionally great. Block-booking assured the studios that even the duds they produced would be sold. And block-booking, flawed though it was, allowed producers to take chances. They could try offbeat projects knowing the film would have a showing and that the financial loss, if there happened to be one, would be cushioned by the system. Block-booking gave the studios confidence to spend money vigorously in order to bring forth a steady flow of pictures.

The film *Freaks*, produced by M-G-M in 1932, could only have been created in such an atmosphere of confidence. It was produced to compete with Universal's *Frankenstein*, which was breaking box-office records. The director of *Freaks* was brought up in the circus and had been a contortionist and clown by the age of sixteen. Tod Browning, who had just made *Dracula* for Universal, cast real "show folk" in his picture, including the beautiful Siamese twins Violet and Daisy Hilton, who, though joined at the base of the spine, had been performing in public since the age of four. By the age of seventeen the Hilton Sisters earned thousands a week as a two-person band in vaudeville. Browning cast the pinheads Schlitzie, a forty-year-old woman exhibited in sideshows as "Maggie, the Last of the Aztecs," and sisters Elvira and Jenny Lee. He hired Prince Randian, "The Living Torso," known also as "The Caterpillar Man," who had to move by inching along because he was armless and legless. He could roll a cigarette with his lips and was, offstage, a married man with five children. Browning also employed Johnny Eck, "The Living Half-Boy," who had no legs but used his hands to dance, run, and walk a tightrope; the bearded Lady Olga, whose whiskers hung down to her chest; and the famous midgets Harry and Daisy Earles.

Freaks was thought to be a sickening picture and was never released in England. Several American exhibitors refused to show it. Today it is considered a classic. The film cost $316,000 and lost $164,000.

Though block-booking has gone down in history as the infamous practice of greedy producers, the facts are that exhibitors were not pressured to buy in blocks and no decisions were made at the time of the salesman's visit. Salesmen left contract applications with the exhibitor, who had ten days to decide if he wanted to accept or reject the deal. The deal was strictly on a cash basis—no credit extended. Just as the exhibitor charged cash to the customer at the box office and extended no credit, so did the home office expect cash three days before the print would be delivered to the theater.

When a picture was "sold," the salesman brought the contract in to his branch manager who then sent it to the branch booking manager who set the dates and sent notice of those dates to the exhibitor. The booking then went on the shipping list, and the date of shipment was fixed. The contract then went to the accounting department so that the exhibitor could be billed and notice of the booking sent to the ad sales department, which created everything in the way of advertising novelty. The branch managers had in their offices all the articles used to make up theater displays and had them on hand, so that the exhibitor could advertise a week prior to the screening.

The two hundred prints made from the American negative at the laboratory in California were shipped directly to about forty branch offices. Part of a branch manager's job was educating theater owners in the proper handling of projection equipment so that the print would not be damaged. After a print was shown it was examined by an inspection department and repaired, if necessary.

Getting the prints from one place to the next was the responsibility of the shipping department. The shipping clerks in every branch office had to know how to ship a picture to a given point, allow it to remain there for one day or two or a week, get it back on the first train, give it time for inspection, and make the next train to the next exhibitor, all on an exact schedule. Sidney R. Kent, who was in charge of distribution for Famous Players-Lasky, said:

> The success of our business is determined right in this department. The booking department comes first and then the shipping department, with the inspection de-

partment functioning between them. The percentage of booking efficiency against your prints is the formula for your ultimate revenue on any given picture. . . . One of our problems is to get the maximum booking time out of a print so that print can turn in as many dollars as possible while it is still in good condition.

Selling pictures abroad required an altogether different organization, which in the case of Loew's Inc. was yet another subsidiary company with headquarters in New York. The film distributor abroad had to be first a diplomat and second a salesman, because, by the middle to the late twenties, there was a great deal of resistance to American movies in foreign countries for two reasons. First, American movies broadcast American values and were seen as propaganda for American clothes, cars, and luxury. Second, foreign governments wanted to protect their own film industries by keeping American movies out. Nonetheless, American movies were distributed in Portugal, Spain, Ireland, Belgium, China, Mexico, Egypt, Algeria, Morocco, Tunis, Palestine, India, Argentina, Japan, Korea, and about fifty other countries.

So much of the film industry in America depended upon the exhibitor. If he were a showman and had a gregarious personality, his theater was bound to be a success. Theaters were licensed to operate by local city halls, so theater men were directly responsible to the people in their towns. If an exhibitor showed something offensive he was subject to a barrage of abusive telephone calls. The fire chief might decide to visit and find enough hazards to revoke the license. Grassroots censorship organizations, and church-sponsored ones as well, did not hesitate to picket on the sidewalk under the theater marquee. Theater men conveyed what they knew about the people in their town to those who sold films, and the word sprayed upward to those who made films. Ultimately it was the American populace that decided what it would pay to see.

Time has exaggerated the power of the old studio heads. Louis B. Mayer, for instance, did set a tone of luxury for his studio, from the lunch room to the dressing rooms, but the kinds of pictures Metro-Goldwyn-Mayer made were determined not by him but by executives in New York.

Louie's team of producers in California submitted budgets to the top brass in New York. A film budget included money for director, story, screenplay, cast, props, extras, cameramen, cutters and projectionists, producers and their assistants, stills and still photographers, wardrobe, makeup and hairdressers, auto and truck hire, meals and lodging, travel and transportation, location fees and expenses, on-set musicians who played sad songs so actors would cry, and a hefty sum for that indefinable something called overhead. A daily log for every picture shot at the studio or on location was submitted to and reviewed by "the boys at the home office."

Salary checks to all Metro-Goldwyn-Mayer employees, including Louis B. Mayer, originated in the New York accounting office and were signed by New York executives. Their bonuses were figured out, life insurance paid, and sick benefits determined. In the same building on Broadway was the vaudeville booking staff and a maintenance department responsible for the upkeep of all the Loew's theaters. Carpet had to be replaced, walls repainted, and plumbing fixed.

In the basement of the Times Square building was the employees' restaurant. Elderly actors who had once been big in small-time road shows, but who now described themselves as "resting," knew that Marcus Loew would feed them free in that restaurant.

Those who worked at the home office felt themselves to be right on the pulse. If anything, they felt sorry for people who were stuck living in California, where there was almost no night life and shopping was hopeless. Rumor had it that the motion-picture people of Los Angeles, which was a tenth the size of New York City, spoke of nothing but movies and had no other interests. Though Sam Goldwyn extolled the virtues of making pictures in the California sun, many of the producers who fled New York during the flu epidemic now returned.

They claimed that electric light was better for filming than sunlight, because actors did not suffer from sunburn while standing under it, that sunshine was useless at noon, and that the morning sun put too much red and yellow into the film. Electric lights were dependable and did not move across the heavens, making it impossible to retake a piece of film. "Some of the cinema men so much prefer artificial sunlight to the natural product," said one report of the day, "that they bar the sun from doing any more work around their studios." New York studios became known as "sunless temples."

World Film Company opened a studio in Fort Lee, New Jersey; Famous Players-Lasky opened one in Astoria. D.W. Griffith returned, set up business offices at the corner of Forty-second Street and Broadway, and invested a million dollars in a studio near Mamaroneck. Asked how long he intended to be absent from California, he replied, "Forever."

Griffith told a reporter:

> The territory around Los Angeles has been filmed to death. Here in the East are all the properties and the background, interior or exterior, that we require for luxurious settings. New York is the metropolis and the home of wealth. Also it is the home of much of the best brains in the country. It is the home of the best actors, the best artisans, the best and newest in theatrical production. In the future I can't see any other center possible for the picture producer who seeks the best of everything to score artistic successes.

Broadway was where prestige was, not Hollywood. "For me," said Edward G. Robinson about his days as an actor on Broadway, "New York was the center of the world—glamorous, filled with gorgeous women, paradise for a young bachelor with a featured part in a successful play." Humphrey Bogart played on Broadway during the twenties, as did James Cagney, Spencer Tracy, Fredric March, and Clark Gable. Lynn Fontanne was in *Pygmalion,* Roland Young in *The Last of Mrs. Cheyney,* Leslie Howard in *Berkeley Square,* and Gertrude Lawrence and Noel Coward in *Private Lives.* Cecil Beaton, the fashion photographer, said about New York, "In the blaze of midnight the moon is given no chance."

There was not only the Great White Way but the Great Black Way, too. The clubs in Harlem stayed open long after Times Square had gone to sleep. Fifteen major bands, including Duke Ellington's orchestra, played there. Ethel Waters sang and earned more money than any other black female entertainer in the world. The Harlem clubs were segregated, and mixed couples were welcome at none of them. The famous Cotton Club was for white people only. Prohibition was scorned all over New York.

Prohibition changed New York nightlife forever, opening the door of the entertainment industry to racketeers. Famous restaurants like Rector's, run by respectable restaurateurs, went out of business when they couldn't serve beer or wine. A new violent type, a ruthless breed, took over the wining and dining industry and operated in the most unlikely places. About thirty-two thousand speakeasies cropped up in back rooms, up flights of stairs. People who had never before had a cocktail now drank rotgut gin that would have burned away their throats without the orange-juice mixture that made it relatively smooth. Tired of war, Americans were did not have the energy to fight Prohibition.

Girls bobbed their hair, took off their whalebone corsets, and wore short skirts. They could now vote, had seen something of the world during the war, and were not content to be confined. Stockings, which had been black, brown, or white, became beige. Respectable girls, much to the horror of their mothers, put on lipstick and rouge.

Bootleggers took over New York's nightlife, because they were the only ones with enough money to open nightclubs where people could watch a show of gorgeous girls and hilarious comics and drink at the same time. Those plush saloons not only provided a good place for gangsters to invest their money, but also provided a profitable market for their product. Patrons paid a cover charge at the door, then were served watered-down liquor. Anyone who had anything to do with floor shows—dancers, comedians, singers, impresarios—all had to do their bargaining with gangsters; it was impossible to avoid contact with the mob. Comics, chorus girls, and workers in the vineyards were all mixed up with the gangsters, whether they liked it or not.

Silent picture star Louise Brooks said:

> When I worked in nightclubs, and in the theatre, I knew all the real gangsters. Men like Capone. They were the most disgusting, idiotic boors. But, oddly enough, they had one great talent. During Prohibition, they owned a lot of nightclubs and they would hire people for these clubs that nobody else would have. A girl like Helen Morgan for instance; nobody wanted her. She had a delicate little voice, she had very long legs, she had a large bosom, which wasn't fashionable then; she wasn't very animated, and she sat on the piano and wouldn't use a microphone. The gangsters loved her. They put her in a nightclub called the Backstage, and all of a sudden Ziegfeld "discovered" her.

Most of the clubs in New York City, the Silver Slipper, the Hotsy Totsy, LaVie, Club Rendezvous, the Fifty-Fifty, ended when their owners died violent deaths. Two speaks survived, the 21 Club and the Stork Club.

*   *   *

William Fox returned from his California studio to New York and built a second studio, in 1920, at Tenth Avenue and Fifty-fifth Street, a section of the city known as Hell's Kitchen. His New York studio was the home of Fox's newsreels, and after the merger of Metro-Goldwyn-Mayer it was rented by Loew's as a studio for screen tests.

The facility, a massive, four-story brick factory, cost Fox about half a million dollars. By 1924 William Fox was the foremost producer of newsreels in the world. His cameramen were everywhere. At first, starting in 1914, Fox produced his newsreels not for profit but to add to the prestige of the new

Fox Film Company. A letter he received from President Wilson did a great deal to advertise his company:

> I'm interested and deeply gratified to learn that the Fox Company is intending to devote its news-weekly to the promotion of universal and lasting peace. It can render the greatest service. The motion picture industry as an educator and as a power for good can be made of the greatest service to the nation and to the world and I congratulate the company on its public-spirited plan.

By 1922 more than a thousand Fox newsmen were cranking cameras in Russia, Africa, Australia, Peking, Hong Kong, Tibet, Liverpool, Borneo, Paris, Madrid, Canada, and New Guinea. In Sicily they caught the eruption of Mount Etna. The films were silent, of course, the scenes identified and explained by captions. The subjects covered were all-encompassing: the collapse of Honeymoon Bridge at Niagara Falls, the crown prince of Germany in exile after World War I, Ku Klux Klan meetings, the bandit Pancho Villa, earthquakes, authors, planes, trains, science, fads, entertainment, coronations, and fashions. Fox News, "Mightiest of All," issued two newsreels a week, each about fifteen minutes long.

On the first floor of Fox's New York plant were the stages used for the production of fashion stories. Fashion shows were the most popular segment of newsreels. Models displayed hats made entirely of feathers, fur coats meant to be worn at the beach, and the fad of leg-painting. Broadway dancers modeled the latest swimsuits. Fashion coverage was worldwide: "Fraüleins Display Newest Pretties. Berlin Mannequins Let You Have an Intimate View of What the German Girls Wear in Their Sleep." Audiences saw what women were wearing in San Francisco and what the latest was from Paris. "Elegance and simplicity are the hallmarks of fashion today," said one of the captions.

The second floor of Fox's building was devoted to filming short subjects about music, travel, transportation, adventure, technology, sports, and urban and rural life. The short-subjects department maintained a staff separate from the news division, with its own cameramen and film cutters.

The news department, comprised of cameramen, editors, and contact men, was housed on the third floor and was open twenty-four hours a day, seven days a week. On the fourth floor was the library, where all of the newsreels, past and current, were housed, as well as all index cards, "dope" sheets, and various cross-referenced clipping files arranged alphabetically, numerically, and by subject matter.

*   *   *

Metro-Goldwyn-Mayer's New York screen tests were directed by Al Altman, who was head of the New York talent department at 1540 Broadway. One of the first Metro-Goldwyn-Mayer stars to pose for a test at Fox's studio was Joan Crawford.

She was far from being a star at the time. Al Altman spotted her in 1924 when she was dancing in the chorus line at the Winter Garden Theater on Broadway, in a revue, *Innocent Eyes*, starring the French music-hall performer Mistinguett. In Paris, Mistinguett sang and danced in lavish spectacles at the Folies-Bergère and the Moulin Rouge. Her stage partner in Paris, by the way, was a young dancer she had discovered, Maurice Chevalier. Mistinguett was reputed to have the most beautiful legs in the world, and they certainly were the most highly insured. Louie Mayer thought to capitalize on that idea. He wired New York, asking Altman to go to the show to see if Mistinguett might care to launch a movie career in America.

Innocent Eyes was Mistinguett's American debut. At almost fifty, she lacked some of her former vitality. She was backed up by forty-five young chorus girls who danced to Sigmund Romberg's music while dressed in extravagant costumes of feathers and sequins. The chorus was exceptionally precise and animated, the girls arranged according to size, with the shortest at the ends of the line. Much as Al wanted to pay attention to Mistinguett, his eyes were drawn to the showgirl at the end of the line, a very short, chubby, roundfaced girl with enormous eyes and a kind of frantic energy. She danced as if electrically generated and seemed to Al to be the only person on the stage.

After the show, when the girls came out of the dressing room transformed from sparkling showgirls into just anyone's daughters in street clothes going home after work, he introduced himself to Lucille Le Sueur, who said she had no interest in a movie career. Her dream was to dance on Broadway, and she was in the middle of it.

Innocent Eyes was panned by the critics and had a short run. The night it closed Al returned to Lucille's dressing room. She said she was a dancer, not an actress. Dancing required music, and she would look like an idiot flailing around on a silent screen. She assumed that when Al said screen test he meant a film like the one she had made in Detroit, dancing naked. She had no intention of ruining her career on Broadway. But Lucille Le Sueur liked Al, and he liked her. They were both from poor backgrounds, were young, attractive, and ambitious, and loved show business. They were new in New York, from small towns, and were happy to be living in Manhattan. Lucille was from Texas, Al from Massachusetts. The friendship that lasted the rest of their lives began.

Al Altman had worked for Louie Mayer in Boston at the office of Gordon-Mayer. Fresh out of college, he was hired by Louie as an accountant. He was too energetic and restless for that sedentary job, but was trying it because his mother said accounting was a reliable profession. Al's father sold secondhand furniture in Clinton, Massachusetts, a mill town where everyone knew everyone else. Rather, Al's *mother* sold furniture; Al's father gave it away if the customer was too poor to afford it. The eldest of six, Al was like Louie in the way he felt financially responsible for his parents and siblings. Al had many traits in common with Louie—a devotion to his mother and a horror at hearing anything bad said about mothers in general, a belief in the power of finely tailored clothes and polished shoes, and an abhorrence of dirty jokes. Most of all they shared a love of show business.

Al was an amateur magician who personally knew most of the great professional magicians. As a child, having pored over Professor Hoffman's book *Modern Magic* and practiced all the moves, Al went backstage in a vaudeville theater in Worcester to introduce himself to the great Howard Thurston, whose *Wonder Show of the Universe* boasted eighteen large-scale illusions. Thurston was the magician who levitated the "Princess Karnac" and made Beauty, an Arabian horse, disappear into thin air. Al became a friend of Houdini, Harry Blackstone, and Cardini.

Mayer put Al in charge of booking talent for Gordon's theaters, and, when Louie went out to the west coast, he asked Al to move to New York to find potential movie talent on the Broadway stage. In New York, Houdini was organizing the Society of American Magicians. Al joined immediately and became an officer of the club.

Al and Lucille Le Sueur often went together to Harlem clubs, where Lucille earned extra money by winning Charleston dance contests. The other patrons dancing in the club stepped back like seas parting and gave her the floor. The owners of the clubs welcomed her because she sparked the places up for the other patrons. They liked Al because he was always taking coins out of the waiters' elbows.

When *Innocent Eyes* closed Lucille went to work dancing in a speakeasy that was owned half by the mob and half by Nils Granlund, Marcus Loew's press agent, whose office was at 1540 Broadway. Granlund agreed with Al that Lucille had something special, and he encouraged her to try a screen test. Finally, because she was broke, she agreed. It was unheard of at that time to test an unknown chorus girl for a part that did not exist. Nicholas Schenck, vice president of Loew's, told Al that it was a waste of film and that he would not approve the expenditure. Only experienced actors took tests to see how they fit a specific part. When Mayer heard that Schenck was interfering with Al Altman, a Metro-Goldwyn-Mayer employee, he was furious. He wired Marcus Loew and said that Al was to be given a free hand. If Al thought the dancer was worthy of his time, then she was. Just where Metro-Goldwyn-Mayer left off and Loew's Inc. started was confusing right from the start.

On Wednesdays the first-floor stages at Fox's studio in Hell's Kitchen were made available to Metro-Goldwyn-Mayer. Al Altman directed screen tests there using Fox's experienced cameramen, electricians, set designers, and wardrobe people. Some of the most famous Hollywood stars—Jimmy Stewart, Henry Fonda, Bob Hope, Ava Gardner, Celeste Holm, Dinah Shore, John Forsythe—posed for screen tests in Fox's newsreel factory in New York. The stages were fully equipped, even including a small swimming pool for underwater shots.

Silent screen tests were somewhat standard: walk toward the camera, stop where the mark was on the floor, then turn full-face to the camera, profile right and left, then look sad, mad, questioning, and wistful and, if possible, weep. Sometimes a dramatic recital of lines from a play was included. Lucille LeSueur's test was turned down by the casting directors in Culver City. None of them could see anything special about her and wired Al, "She doesn't have what we're looking for." Al made another test, and that was turned down, too, "No good." Al just couldn't believe he had been so wrong. So he organized a third test.

In Lucille Le Sueur's third test, Al tried something different. He invented the idea of an ad-lib test, one in which the actor responds in a natural way to what the off-camera director says. Al wanted his test to show how interesting Lucille was to watch when she was off-guard. Al communicated with the cameraman by making a sign at the end of a take. If it was no good, Al held his hand out like a traffic cop. If good, he made the O.K. sign with finger and thumb. Later, the cameraman had to go into the laboratory and break his material down into the print takes, keeping the good ones and discarding the rest, then splicing the former together. The test showed Lucille Le Sueur talking, chewing gum, and doing her wild Charleston. Instead of leaving the decision up to the casting directors on the West Coast, Al phoned Louie and asked him to look at the test.

Lucille wrote years later when she was famous as Joan Crawford:

> I didn't know what to do first, but Al told me, "I'm going to stand next to the camera. Just talk to me and forget about the camera." I got through the test with Al coax-ing, cajoling, reinforcing, encouraging, and getting the most from me on film. That test belonged to Al and to his confidence in my latent talent.

Anita Stewart was the first film star who had had no acting experience before appearing on the screen, and Joan Craw-ford was the second. Theda Bara as the first film star to be "created" by her studio, and Joan Crawford was the second. Some say that it was because of Crawford, her extreme desire to be a star and go along with the studio's ballyhoo, and the immediate attraction the audience felt for her, that Louie Mayer came upon his revolutionary idea of building a stable of stars. His was a remarkable notion.

He would pay talented new photoplayers to wait around until the right part came up for them. While they waited they would receive "grooming" and then be introduced to the public in movie magazines and on personal tours. Before Joan Crawford ever appeared in any movie she attended the-ater and sales conventions, where she paraded around in shorts with a Metro-Goldwyn-Mayer sash across her chest. "Authorized" biographies about her private life were in-vented by the publicity department, highlighting pitiful sto-ries of her childhood. Dates were arranged for her with famous playboys. She was told whom to invite to the parties she gave, and where to seat them at the table. She was advised to get into the gossip columns. When her mother, whom she hated, arrived in Hollywood to mooch off her, Crawford was instructed by Mayer to buy a house for her and never to say a bad word about her. A publicist was assigned to handle Joan's interviews and supervise her choice of clothes, makeup, and house furnishings. That a studio could take an inexperienced player, hired for no particular role, and turn her into a star was new to everybody. Behind Mayer's freedom to do that was Marcus Loew, who gave his employees plenty of money to work with and complete freedom. "Spend" was his philosophy. "Spend and send the bills to me."

If Joan Crawford, whose very name was invented in a contest, a girl from a poor background with no acting experience, could become a film actress, then anybody could. The talent department at 1540 Broadway was inundated with hopefuls who waited outside Al Altman's office door. Thursdays were open-door day. Anyone who wanted to be in pictures could come in for an interview. Men who had been corset manufacturers showed up in search of a new career. The sale of corsets was no longer lucrative; modern girls refused to be bound up. Men who had been in the textile industry waited outside Al's door for a chance to change careers. They were not selling as much fabric as they used to, because skirts were so short.

Al became a night wanderer, prowling the city after-hours, seeing every play on Broadway and Off-Broadway, believing that a star might be found anywhere, dancing in a cabaret or selling cigarettes in a speakeasy. Whereas Al previously thought of himself as a "talent finder," he now saw his job as a much more aggressive one. A great fan of Buffalo Bill, the Indian scout-turned-showman, Al coined the phrase "talent scout." He was the film industry's first.

Metro-Goldwyn-Mayer became known for its many movie stars, "More Stars Than There Are in Heaven." Al helped to find them, and Mayer polished them, a perfect partnership that demonstrated how fruitful relations between the home office and the studio could be.

NINE

The Merger Succeeds

O<small>F ALL</small> the headaches that Marcus Loew inherited from Goldwyn Pictures, the most costly was *Ben-Hur*. The production was bogged down in Rome, where Mussolini and his Socialist Workers were staging strikes. Construction of the sets had come to a halt; thirty full-scale Roman galley ships to appear in sea battles were half finished; a coliseum facade was no more than a foundation. Director, actors, everything was in chaos.

It was considered a coup when Sam Goldwyn managed to buy the movie rights to *Ben-Hur*, because the book was so famous. When it came out in 1890, it broke all publishing records. Its author, Lew Wallace, spent five years writing it and achieved the largest single sale of any book apart from the Bible. *Ben-Hur* was the first work of fiction to be blessed by the Pope, which assisted sales. The novel was turned into a play in 1899 at a cost of $71,000. The scale of the Broadway production was immense; elaborate crowd scenes and vast choruses, intricate lighting effects, a sea rescue (with stage-hands positioned in the wings shaking lengths of cloth to simulate waves) and a chariot race, using two horses pounding a treadmill while a painted panorama of the Circus Maximus revolved behind them. The play ran for a year on Broadway.

Ben-Hur set a precedent in the movie world when Kalem Company was sued in 1907 for stealing it. There was no such thing as "movie rights" then. Kalem decided to film Lew Wallace's story in "sixteen magnificent scenes with illustrated titles." The famous chariot race was staged with a ready-made background--the annual fireworks display at Manhattan Beach. Kalem's director added some interior scenes shot at Kalem's studio at 131 West Twenty-fourth Street, then circulated leaflets proclaiming *Ben-Hur* to be "Positively the most superb moving picture spectacle ever made in America."

Kalem was sued by both Harper and Brothers, the book's publisher, and Klaw and Erlanger, producers of the Broadway play. The suit was fought through to the United States Supreme Court. Kalem said that the production on the screen was "merely a series of photographs" and that the movie was a good advertisement for the book and the stage play. The final decision against Kalem was handed down in 1911, and Kalem had to pay $25,000.

Eventually, motion-picture rights to the book did come up for sale. About 1920, Goldwyn Pictures won the prize and was, thereafter, stuck with the huge bills. To get out from under Goldwyn's mistake, Marcus Loew sent Mayer to Europe to see what could be done. It was the first time Louie had ever gone to Europe, and it must have felt like quite an accomplishment to go with all expenses paid. He took Margaret and their two daughters. After inspecting the production in Rome, Mayer decided that the entire operation had to be scrapped, along with all personnel, including the stars and director. The production had to be moved from Italy back to Culver City. It was because of the expense of this second filming of *Ben-Hur* that Hollywood producers, for many years afterwards, shied away from shooting pictures on location.

Marcus Loew went to Rome to fire everyone, saying it wouldn't be fair if he made Louie do that unpleasant work.

While in Europe, Mayer went to Berlin to meet Mauritz Stiller, the great Swedish director, who was working there. Stiller's beautiful and sophisticated films had catapulted Swedish cinema into a leading position in Europe. He showed Louie his latest movie, *The Saga of Gösta Berling*, and there on the screen was Greta Garbo. Stiller, who was twice her age, was the actress's mentor, teacher, and companion. Friends called them Beauty and the Beast, because Stiller was very tall, had huge feet, a craggy face, and an eye that was disfigured. "I immediately noticed how easily one could dominate her," Stiller wrote in his diary before life taught him better, "by looking straight into her eyes."

Mayer knew he could make a star of Greta Garbo and signed her to a contract. He invited Stiller to bring her to the United States with promises that Stiller would become a great director in America, too. But Mayer loathed Mauritz Stiller, not because Stiller was openly homosexual, but because he was *Jewish* (Moshe Stiller) and openly homosexual. That a boy who had attended Hebrew school should turn out that way, no. Absolutely not.

Back in Culver City, Irving Thalberg took charge of *Ben-Hur* and supervised the construction of a $300,000 coliseum on a field near the studio. The coliseum was supposed to have huge statues decorating it, but *huge* was too expensive. Instead, the carpenters made the statues man-sized, out of plaster, and Thalberg hired midgets to stand near them so the audience would be fooled. The casting department enlisted almost four thousand extras to fill the stands during the chariot race, which was filmed by many cameras. The stuntmen drivers were told that the winner of the chariot race would get $150, second place would get $100, and third, $50. The race on the screen was, in fact, a real race with real wheels coming loose. Camera cars sped before the onrushing teams, an innovation in filming. *Ben-Hur* was completed at a cost of $4 million.

The picture opened at the George M. Cohan Theater in New York on December 30, 1925. It was Metro-Goldwyn-Mayer's first major offering to the public. All the stars, the director, and the producer came to New York to attend the gala opening. For the first time in picture history, a blasé Broadway audience forgot itself and cheered madly during the chariot-race scene.

"*Ben-Hur* is not a flat picture upon a screen," the critic from *Photoplay* wrote. "It is a thing of beauty and a joy for ten years at least. This is a truly great picture. No one, no matter what his age or religion, should miss it."

Mussolini banned the picture in Italy because the Roman general was shown defeated. The picture was banned in China, too. "*Ben-Hur* is Christian propaganda decoying the people to superstition, which must not be tolerated in the present age of revolutionary enlightenment."

Even though *Ben-Hur* was a success, it was really Sam Goldwyn's picture. The first one produced entirely by Metro-Goldwyn-Mayer was *He Who Gets Slapped*, the story of a scientist who begins a new life as a circus clown. It starred John Gilbert, Norma Shearer, and Lon Chaney. It was a feather in M-G-M's cap that the great Lon Chaney signed a contract with the studio. He knew everything about the art of pantomime, having grown up with deaf parents. Because he could imitate anything, the joke in Culver City was "Don't step on a spider. It may be Lon Chaney."

The success of *He Who Gets Slapped* could have been credited to Lon Chaney's brilliance, but when the studio brought out its next film, *The Big Parade*, the industry had to admit that Metro-Goldwyn-Mayer was capable of superior work. Considered a classic today, the film was directed by King Vidor and starred John Gilbert, who became America's heartthrob. It was during the production of *The Big Parade* that the home office and the studio got into the first of the hundreds of arguments that would eventually mark their relationship.

The Big Parade was about the futility of World War I, but no battle scenes had been written into it. When Thalberg saw the completed film he insisted that battle scenes be put in. The picture had to be reshot, an unheard-of idea. Loew's salesmen had promised exhibitors one "John Gilbert picture," and here it was. To spend more money on it made no sense at all. The picture would easily fulfill the contract with theater men. Loew's vice president, Nick Schenck, said Thalberg's request was outrageous and proved that Louis Mayer had no consideration for the Loew's stockholders, that he was spending like a spoiled child. After Nick saw the film in the projection room in the Loew's building, he said it was just fine as it was. But Marcus Loew disagreed. He had hired Louis Mayer to be chief of production and intended to allow him to function in that capacity. Loew told his chief lieutenant to leave production to the boys at the studio. If they said the picture needed to be redone, it did.

The army supplied five thousand troops, two hundred trucks, and a squadron of airplanes, and King Vidor shot twelve more reels of film. Night battle scenes added another $40,000 to the cost. *The Big Parade* opened at the Astor Theater in New York and played there for ninety-six weeks. The picture cost $250,000 and earned $15 million. One critic wrote, "*The Big Parade* is not properly to be compared with most other motion pictures, it is related to the very best that the theatre, legitimate or cinema, can offer as drama of a moving and important kind. Yet it is as a motion picture that it is astounding, that it renews faith in the cinema form and creates an enthusiasm for its destiny. . . . By all means procure your tickets of admission."

Many people who did that were in for a surprise. Accidents were happening in theaters all over the city. A fire broke out in the basement of one theater, and the audience had to be evacuated. Another evening, in a different theater, a water pipe broke, and the audience had to file out to the street. Whole audiences stood on New York sidewalks wondering what was going on.

It was the mob. The mob that controlled New York's nightlife had found a way to muscle into the movie business. They realized that the movie industry was dependent upon the projectionists in the theaters. If the mob could organize the men who operated the movie machines, then they could control the industry. Projectionists all over the city began to hear through the grape-vine that the projectionist in the theater across the street was getting more money and working fewer hours. Theater owners who did not increase a projectionist's wages found their furnace bursting or water pipes breaking, or someone in the audience would have an accident. All over New York projectionists began to grumble. They wondered why they hadn't realized before what long hours they worked, imprisoned in that hot cramped booth, and they began to agree that there should be a union to protect them, a Moving Picture Machine Operator's Union.

Once organized they threatened to call a strike that would shut down more than four hundred theaters in New York. The demand was for a thirty-percent wage increase, at least two projectionists in every theater instead of one, and work shifts that lasted no longer than six hours.

Hundreds of men who had been wanting to become movie machine operators formed the Reel Club and alerted theater owners that they were willing to work as scabs. Theater owners, including Marcus Loew, said that union projectionists would not dare strike because their places would be filled immediately. Applications were pouring in. Negotiations between the Moving Picture Machine Operators Union, the Theater Owners Chamber of Commerce, and the Vaudeville Managers Protective Association broke down, though there had been a wage increase offered.

The union projectionists met at Beethoven Hall on Fifth Avenue and voted to take an enforced vacation, all one thousand of them at once. They would take a trip up the Hudson River to spend a day at Bear Mountain. The projectionists marched to the pier and boarded a sight-seeing boat.

Scabs were brought into the theaters, but they didn't know

how to run the machines. Projectors had to be cranked, and the focus did not lock and had to be adjusted continually. The machines back then were not threaded automatically, so audiences had to wait while the scabs tried, shut off the machine, tried again. Dissatisfied audiences complained, saying they wanted their money back.

The Vaudeville Managers Association met the union's demands and agreed that there would be two operators in each theater, each working a six-hour shift and each with a 5 percent pay increase. Because Prohibition was keeping the mobsters rich and busy, they crawled back under their rocks.

*   *   *

Mauritz Stiller and Greta Garbo arrived in New York to no fanfare at all. Al Altman met them at the pier and escorted them to the modest Commodore Hotel after one photographer snapped a picture of Garbo leaning against the railing of the ship. No one photographed the great director. Mayer wanted to show Mauritz Stiller that in America Stiller was less than nothing. Howard Dietz visited the Commodore and remembered his first impression of Greta Garbo:

> You had to stare to latch onto her beauty, but once latched on, you lost your poise in her presence. She didn't speak except when necessary and you found yourself talking nonsense to make conversation. She used no makeup, and we weren't used to natural coloring in those days. Her hairdo was casual as a drunken driver's. She wore a comfortable stained suede suit, the same suit every day.

Greta Garbo and Mauritz Stiller were, finally, released from neglect at the Commodore Hotel and put on a train for California. At the studio, Greta Garbo refused to pose in scanty silk trunks for publicity photos, would not parade around at sales conventions, and refused to grant interviews because she was ashamed of her English. Louie told publicity to leave her alone. Clarence Brown, who directed her second picture at M·G·M, said:

> Greta Garbo had something that nobody ever had on the screen. Nobody. I don't know whether she even knew she had it, but she did. And I can explain it in a few words. I would take a scene with Garbo—pretty good. I would take it three or four times. It was pretty good, but I was never quite satisfied. When I saw that same scene on the screen, however, it had something that it just didn't have on the set. Garbo had something behind the eyes that you couldn't see until you photographed it in close-up. You could see thought. If she had to look at one person with jealousy, and another with love, she didn't have to change her expression. You could see it in her eyes as she looked from one to the other. And nobody else has been able to do that on the screen. Garbo did it without the command of the English language. For me, Garbo starts where they all leave off. She was a shy person; her lack of English gave her a slight inferiority complex. I used to direct her very quietly. I never gave her a direction above a whisper. Nobody on the set ever knew what I said to her; she liked that.

Her second film, *Flesh and the Devil*, exploded box-office records with its sizzling love scenes and made Garbo a star. What she learned from her costar John Gilbert was that she could demand a higher salary. Louie refused to meet her demands, so she quit working. She went to her hotel and refused to come out.

She was in the middle of filming a costly production called *Love*, which was a rewrite of the book *Anna Karenina*. Work on the set came to a halt. The money lost was enormous. No one knows whether it was Louie's original idea or whether he was in such a frantic state that he was susceptible to lunacy, but he announced that he would find a Garbo look-alike so production on *Love* could continue.

In New York, Al Altman was instructed to find someone who not only looked like Greta Garbo but also could act exactly like her, including her relationship with the camera. When Al suggested to Louie that the idea was absurd, Louie accused Al of not loving him.

Because Garbo was not yet a household name, Al ran an announcement in the tabloids that Metro-Goldwyn-Mayer was seeking someone who looked like the girl John Gilbert loved in *Flesh and the Devil*. Win a free screen test!

About a hundred young women showed up at the Roosevelt Hotel on the appointed day. A few of them misunderstood who Greta Garbo was and thought the contest was to win a meeting with John Gilbert. Others thought it was a call to anyone who wanted to be in the movies. Some thought makeup could change them entirely. After an hour or so Al stopped being polite and greeted each candidate with "Nope. Next!" Mayer insisted that Al run the contest again, saying he had everyone in the country looking for a Garbo look-alike. It was the least Al could do for him.

At the end of the second contest Al went out of the hotel discouraged. He was approached by a big, awkward, phlegmatic person with droopy eyes, angular body, sunken chest, world-weary manner, pencil eyebrows, substantial nose with a prominent crevice under it, and a thin mouth, the top lip almost annoyingly narrow. The main difference between this Greta Garbo and the real one was that the real one was not such a sad person. Al said, "Why didn't you come in?" She hunched her shoulders. Her name was Rhoda. After Al disarmed her by taking a coin out of her chin and hearing the familiar surprised "Hey!" he invited her to dinner.

To attract customers away from speakeasies, restaurants made themselves exotic. One of the most popular was on Christopher Street in Greenwich Village, the Pirate's Den. A peglegged pirate held open the door of a smoky cellar hung with maps, toy ships, fish skeletons, whale vertebrae, and nets. The waiters, dressed up like eighteenth-century pirates, were blandishing their cutlasses at each other and dueling between the tables. "Marvelous!" said Rhoda, "Ha! Ha!" And she crossed her large hands at the wrists and pressed them to her flat chest and kept them there like a corpse. She ate as if she were starving. With each new taste of food she said, "Marvelous!" and showed Al a small, guilty smile.

The waiters staged a mock storm. There was a flash of lightning and the sound of thunder and ship's bell as pirate voices came from various parts of the restaurant: "All quiet on the main deck, sir!" and "Forward light burning bright!" and "Prisoners safe in the brig!"

Rhoda agreed to meet Al at his office the next day. Al asked her to read a scene from a play. She did not read well. The real Greta Garbo had been in seclusion for several months. Metro-Goldwyn-Mayer salesmen across the country had to appease exhibitors who wondered when their Garbo/Gilbert picture would arrive. The child actor who was to play Anna Karenina's son was getting bigger by the day, John Gilbert's next picture was being thrown off schedule, and ads for *Love* had already appeared—"Gilbert and Garbo in Love!"

Al hired drama coaches, modeling coaches, and voice coaches who all said there was something strange about Rhoda. Nevertheless, Louie was thrilled when he saw Rhoda's test. She did look just like Greta Garbo!

Rhoda, her face covered with a veil, went to Grand Central Station with Al. She was so scared her breathing had a catch in it. Al reminded her of the money she would earn as he escorted her to the train. He knew that it was inevitable that Louie would give in and pay the real Greta Garbo what she wanted. Rhoda would try to get work in the movies, but she would never find it because she looked too much like Garbo. With a more intelligent and resourceful girl Al wouldn't have worried.

About a week after Rhoda arrived in Culver City, Al received a telephone call from one of Mayer's producers. He accused Al of trying to make a fool of him. Al phoned Louie, who explained what had happened.

The outraged producer was one who took advantage of his position to seduce young women at the studio. Joan Crawford began to get good roles after she agreed to sleep with this man. If she had not, she later said, she would have had to "hang around all the time watching Norma Shearer make the most of her three expressions."

The producer promised to advance Rhoda's career. She refused his advances. He insisted. They wrestled and the producer discovered that Rhoda was a man. Everyone at the studio was sworn to secrecy about Rhoda. "She" was driven to downtown Los Angeles and dumped. What became of Rhoda no one knows.

Mayer agreed to pay Greta Garbo $5,000 a week, and the picture *Love* went into production. To publicize it, Howard Dietz got a professor at Columbia University to do an experiment to determine which women were most easily aroused, blondes or brunettes. It became a subject of vital concern to the press across the nation. The publicity department in New York filled the Embassy Theater with girls in their twenties, mostly from the chorus, and had several interns in white jackets pass down the aisles with bloodpressure gauges. As the young women watched erotic scenes from the Garbo and Gilbert film, interns listened to their hearts and took their blood pressure. The stunt was a great success, and all seven of New York's daily newspapers shouted out the news that blondes were hotter than brunettes. Redheads challenged the blondes, but the stunt had served its purpose

At the end of Louie's first year as head of production, M-G-M made a profit of more than $4 million, more than any other studio except Paramount. Irving Thalberg that first year supervised the creation of more than thirty pictures, and none of them lost money. Mayer and Thalberg attracted the greatest film actress of the day, Lillian Gish, to their studio. She signed a long-term contract. Her first role was Mimi in the film *La Boheme,* directed by King Vidor. *Tess of the d'Urbervilles,* starring Blanche Sweet, was a great hit even though Mayer made the director change the tragic ending of the story into a happy one. The studio's motto became, "Make It Good . . . Make It Big . . . Give It Class!"

TEN

The God of Talk
Wakes Up

THE SAME year that Marcus Loew built his office tower in Times Square, a crowd in Madison Square Garden heard President Warren Harding speak from Arlington, Virginia, where he dedicated the Tomb of the Unknown Soldier. His speech was transmitted by telephone lines from Virginia over a newfangled divice called a "loud-speaking telephone." When the device became more familiar, people called it a loudspeaker.

Conventional telephones were now commonplace. Almost all middle-class homes had one. Poles had been planted in meadows where cows grazed, wires crisscrossed the country. Electrical engineers devoted themselves to finding ways to amplify the weak current that carried conversation so that people could speak long-distance.

By 1922 Western Electric public-address systems had become a standard item of commerce. They replaced the film

139

director's megaphone, allowing him to give simultaneous instructions to thousands of extras in crowd scenes.

Radio, formerly a tool of the navy, came into the home.
Instead of going to the movies, families sat around the radio.
They listened to Samuel "Roxy" Rothafel, broadcasting on
WEAF from the Capitol Theater on Broadway: "Good night,
pleasant dreams, God bless you."

Marcus Loew bought a Brooklyn radio station in 1922. The
sending apparatus, which was about the size of an office desk,
and the generator, which could be carried by one man, were
moved into the Loew's State building, and an antenna was
raised on the roof above Times Square. A studio was parti-
tioned off at one end of an office and hung with flannel
drapes. The windows and all the doors except one were
sealed. The studio was just large enough to hold a small orchestra and an announcer. With all the windows and doors
sealed, it was suffocating to work in the studio longer than
fifteen minutes at a time, so programs were designed in fifteen-minute intervals, a custom which persisted for a while.

Loew's station put out its programs on a feeble five-hun-
dred watts. The idea was that vaudeville players performing
in Loew's theaters would advertise their own acts on WHN—
Al Jolson, Eddie Cantor, Mae West. But there was a lot of air-
time to fill. People who wanted to try performing on the
radio were invited to walk in. "Anyone who came in and said
he was a singer or a comedian," said Nils Granlund, who ran
the station, "or played something, we put him on without further question." An acrobatic dancer named Ruby Stevens,
who dreamed of becoming an actress, recited poetry on the
station. The movies turned her into Barbara Stanwyck. Ethel
Merman, when she was a young stenographer, first sang for
the public on WHN and was so popular she broadcast regu-
larly every Tuesday and Thursday for a year. *Ethel Merman
Time* was the first regular fifteen-minute time segment ever
plugged on WHN. By the end of the second year of broadcasting, WHN had inaugurated the first amateur show, the first
audience-participation show, the first newscast, the first com-

mercial, and the first remote-control broadcast from a night-club and from a political forum. WHN became a major asset for Loew's Inc. and grew into the popular WMGM, a fifty-thousand-watt radio station that entertained New Yorkers for more than thirty years.

Motion pictures began to talk, in a way, before anyone could hear them. In 1910 only eighty feet of titles were used per reel, and those titles were clipped from stock rolls—"the next day," "ten years elapse," and "happily ever after." By 1925 screen stories had such complicated plots they could not be told by the camera alone. Audiences were reading as fast as they were watching, talking inside their own heads.

Motion pictures were never meant to be silent. There was always musical accompaniment, sometimes an orchestra, sometimes a single piano. In many theaters sound effects were created by a person who stood behind the screen with blocks of wood, a pistol, bowls of water, and whatever else was needed. The man in charge of sound effects at Louie Mayer's Colonial Theater in Haverhill, William H. Murphy, spoke all the film dialogue, male and female, through a megaphone and did not stop doing that until 1925. Motion pictures were not thought of as "silent" until promoters of sound systems began to describe them in that way. By the middle twenties most thoughtful people realized that films were a new art form and accepted the motion picture as something more than an inferior kind of stage drama. Crowds and pageantry could be handled on a larger scale in film; the scene could shift in place and time, scale and distance. The scene could be dimmed or brightened, whipped up or slowed down. Animals, a storm-tossed ocean, a flooded river, a wagon train, all could appear in the same play. And film acting, at its best, brought the art of pantomime to new heights. It was because motion pictures were so articulate that the world loved them.

Yet the idea of making them audible fascinated inventors right from the start. In 1903 Bert Whitman in New York invented Cameraphone, a rudimentary talkie device. In 1907 Adolph Zukor experimented with talking pictures. "I simply put live actors behind the screen," he said. He hired a writer to study the photoplays and prepare scripts that would synchronize dialogue with the action. The actors, five or six of them, took their cues from watching the pictures in reverse on the back of the screen, and they shouted their lines through megaphones. Zukor and Marcus Loew, partners at that time, promoted their scheme as Humanova. The following year the French Gaumont company exhibited the Chronophone at the World's Fair in St. Louis. There were Webb's Talking Pictures and Vivaphone (not Vitaphone) Talking Pictures.

Thomas Edison had brief success with his Kinetophone in 1913, but told the world there was no future for motion pictures that made noise. The vice president of Vitagraph agreed with him. "Music is the only medium which is of value and which helps motion pictures. The voice is a detriment to almost all styles of pictures. Why have words when any well-made picture tells the complete story?"

Carl Laemmle tried a German device called Synchroscope. D.W. Griffith showed a picture called *Dream Street* in 1921 which contained some dialogue. Dr. Lee De Forest demonstrated his invention, Phonofilm, the first sound-on-film talking picture, at the Rivoli Theater in New York in 1923.

In 1924 an Englishman, Claude H. Verity, arrived in New York to demonstrate the synchronization of music and speech with motion pictures. He had found a way of recording sound onto film after the negative had been developed. "He declares," reported the *New York Times*, "that in his opinion it is not possible to make a picture of players simultaneously recording sound, emphasizing the idea that the question of continuity has to be considered after a negative of possibly 50,000 feet is cut down to the show length of, say 8,000." Mr Verity was quoted:

> To my mind there is a great future for the film industry in the coming development of the sychronized picture. I don't think that talking and singing pictures have really much entertainment value, but the picture with synchro-

nized sounds, be it voices or music, will enhance the worth of productions. Such productions should be arranged with specially edited and composed orchestrations, together with spoken words to eliminate titles, and, if necessary, songs—and these sounds to be recorded to synchronize exactly with the action on the screen. Here, I firmly believe lies the further evolution of the film, which would also enable selections from operas or musical comedies, music-hall sketches and comic songs, or stage successes to be produced. Would it not cause a new interest in the industry if such productions were created?

But American theater owners were not impressed. There were twenty thousand motion picture theaters in the United States. A device had to be of proved efficiency to justify the enormous cost of remodeling those theaters to accommodate sound equipment.

During the middle twenties, having made great strides in recording and amplifying sound for telephones, electrical engineers working at the Western Electric Company turned their attention to making talking pictures. Film men had not asked them to do this. It was a scientific challenge they set for themselves, and their first "star" was an engineer at the laboratory singing "How Dry I Am."

Sam Warner, of the two-year-old company Warner Brothers, was the first producer to act on reports that a new sound motion picture system had been perfected by the Western Electric Company. He saw a demonstration of the system and convinced investors to back him. The Western Electric Company licensed Warners to produce sound pictures under its patents, and the Vitaphone Corporation was formed to promote the invention. That pictures would talk was not the intention of the Warner brothers, Sam, Harry, Jack, and Albert. They did not see any advantage to hearing photoplayers talk. Sound pictures, as they conceived of them, would be feature-length motion pictures, with built-in musical accompaniment, and short subjects that would replace live vaudeville acts.

The Warner brothers, four of twelve children, had come to New York from Ohio, where their family owned a few nickelodeons. They understood the small theater owner and believed that most of them would be eager to install sound equipment, because it would save them money on live musicians and vaudeville acts and would enable their patrons to see expensive performers who might never visit their community. Vitaphone Corporation's stated aim was to make available to motion-picture theaters large or small, located anywhere, "the music of the greatest symphony orchestras and the vocal entertainment of the most popular stars of the operatic and theatrical fields."

At the time Sam Warner began to investigate sound, Warner pictures were shown in lowclass houses. The brothers did not have enough money to buy first-run theaters. Their biggest star was the dog Rin Tin Tin. "He was the only leading man who never gave a bad performance," Jack Warner said. "He faced one hazard after another and was grateful to get an extra hamburger for a reward."

Sam Warner hoped that audiences would like sound pictures so much they would only go to theaters where sound equipment was installed, equipment that theater owners would have to purchase from the Warner brothers.

Vitaphone was a system that recorded sound vibrations on a wax disc that looked like a huge phonograph record, while a camera, in a soundproof booth, filmed the performer. The projection machine synchronized the film with the sound, which was reproduced by loudspeakers placed behind the motion-picture screen and operated from the projection booth. There was one wax disc for every ten minutes of film. The Warner brothers spent the fall and winter of 1925 experimenting with soundproofing and microphones in the old Vitagraph studio in Flatbush and at the Manhattan Opera House. Reports of their slow progress circulated in the industry.

Marcus Loew did not pay much attention. His company was still counting the profits from *Ben-Hur, The Merry Widow,* and *The Big Parade*. Adolph Zukor said about sound, "It's a fad, it won't last." William Fox, of course, saw the future. He thought that any sound system that depended upon synchronizing a wax disc with film was primitive. The wax discs had a short life, maybe twenty playings, and the sound had a gurgly, underwater quality.

In 1926, as if responding to the impending explosion of talk, Rudolph Valentino died. His death seemed to symbolize the death of those screen stars who relied too heavily upon pantomime. Their day was over.

Valentino's manager arranged for the body to lie in state at Campbell's Funeral Home and announced that the public would be allowed to view it. A crowd of thirty thousand gathered, mostly women. The crowd stretched for eleven blocks, and as police tried to form orderly lines some women became so overwrought they had to leave in ambulances. Windows were smashed, and mounted policemen charged into the crowd again and again. After one retreat of the crowd, twenty-eight women's shoes were gathered up. Women then rubbed soap on the pavement to make the police horses slip. The funeral home was barred to the public, but some people got in and nearly wrecked the place snatching souvenirs.

On the day of the funeral one hundred thousand people lined the streets near the church where services were held. Many women wept as if their own husbands had died. They clutched a book of poems, *Day Dreams*, written by Valentino. The screen idol believed in "automatic writing" and claimed that his book was written by his "Power." Here is a sample poem, entitled "Your Kiss:"

> Your kiss,
> A flame
>   of Passion's fire,
> The sensitive Seal
>   of Love
> In the desire,
> The fragrance
>   of your caress;

Alas
   At times
      I find
         Exquisite bitterness
In
Your kiss.

*   *   *

In August 1926, the first fruits of Vitaphone were shown at Warner's Theater at Fifty-Second Street and Broadway. Instead of the live vaudeville acts that typically opened major picture shows and the musicians who normally accompanied the silent films, there was machinery in the theater—large acoustic horns connected to electrical loudspeakers linked by wire to amplifiers, phono cartridges, and turntables in the projection room. The feature picture, *Don Juan*, the story of a sex fiend who falls in love at last, had been produced as a silent and converted to sound at a cost of $110,000. There were thirteen reels of John Barrymore synchronized with discs of music especially composed for the movie and played by the New York Philharmonic Orchestra. There were sound effects on the disc, too, the clinking of swords during a duel.

Far more impressive to the crowd were the six short subjects that preceded *Don Juan*. The first was a speech by Will Hays, the popular and diplomatic president of the Motion Picture Producers and Distributors of America, the industry's self-regulating organization. Hays was short and lightweight, and his ears stuck out far enough to make him the brunt of many jokes. Using elaborate hand gestures which he thought would make his appearance on the screen more dramatic, Will Hays presented his 325-word speech before the Vitaphone cameras at the Manhattan Opera House, where recording equipment was set up.

"Because it was not only my first experience but the first speech ever recorded for talking pictures, I remember every detail," he wrote in his memoirs. "At dinnertime I rehearsed

it. Wanting to guard against any possible slip-ups, I telephoned Kirk Russell of our own staff and asked him if within
two hours he could copy the speech in inch-high letters on
big cards so that it could stand on two easels where I could
see it while speaking. This he did. In the recording room that
evening I stood in front of a microphone and camera and
said my piece—with gestures:"

> My friends, no story ever written for the screen is as dra-
> matic as the story of the screen itself. Now we write an-
> other chapter in that story. Far, indeed, have we
> advanced from that few seconds of shadow of a serpen-
> tine dancer thirty years ago when the motion picture
> was born—to this public demonstration of the Vi-
> taphone synchronizing the reproduction of sound with
> the reproduction of action. The future of motion pic-
> tures is as far flung as all the tomorrows, rendering
> greater and still greater service as the chief amusement
> of the majority of all our people and the sole amusement
> of millions and millions, exercising an immeasurable in-
> fluence as a living, breathing thing on the ideas and
> ideals, the customs and costumes, the hopes and ambi-
> tions of countless men, women, and children. In the pre-
> sentation of these pictures, music plays an invaluable
> part. The motion picture is a most potent factor in the
> development of a national appreciation of good music.
> That service will now be extended as the Vitaphone shall
> carry symphony orchestras to the townhalls of the ham-
> lets. It has been said that the art of the vocalist and in-
> strumentalist is ephemeral, that he creates but for the
> moment. Now, neither the artist nor his art will ever
> wholly die.

People could hardly believe their eyes and ears. "The synchronization was so perfect," one critic wrote, "that one had
to pinch oneself now and then to realize that this was a mechanical reproduction rather than the original."

The audience saw and heard the New York Philharmonic
play the overture to *Tannhauser*, Mischa Elman play Dvorák
on the violin, Roy Smeck play the ukulele, Marion Talley sing

an aria from *Rigoletto,* Efrem Zimbalist and Harold Bauer play Beethoven's "Kreutzer Sonata," Giovanni Martinelli sing an aria from *I Pagliacci,* and Anna Case sing an opera solo assisted by Spanish dancers. Such was the taste of the audience back then. Warners stock went from almost nothing to quite a lot the very next day.

A reviewer in a Dallas, Texas, newspaper wrote:

> Nothing has happened in New York this summer which is more important for Dallas than the opening of the new Warner Motion Picture Theatre. It means that before long the greatest artists will be available to the remotest village, in a form so lifelike that the very personality of the artist seems to be present, and it is easier than not to believe he is actually before you.

The Warners continued their steady production of Vitaphone synchronized-sound shorts and features through the 1926–27 season, releasing as many as five new shorts a week. George Jessel delivered a monologue and sang an Irving Berlin song, Al Jolson sang "When the Red, Red Robin Comes Bob, Bob, Bobbin' Along" and "April Showers," and George Burns and Gracie Allen did their funny routines. Now and then, in the theater's projection booth, the machine operator got his talkie records mixed or the needle on his phonograph skipped a groove or two, and a man's voice came out of a woman's mouth or a woman opened her mouth and out came dog barks.

Producers wondered what deaf people would do for entertainment if movies talked. Western Electric Company began to experiment with an earphone device that would be attached to the seats in theaters. "It has been successfully used in a number of theaters during an experimental period. In the meanwhile there are many silent pictures in circulation." This was the company's response to concerned citizens.

Producers wondered what would happen to America's lucrative film-export trade if pictures spoke English. Silent film titles were translated into thirty-six languages, including

Gaelic, Siberian, Hebrew, Javanese, Estonian, Hindu, Malay, Croatian, Ukrainian, Siamese, Armenian, Latvian, Greek, Arabic, Korean, Flemish, Syrian, Lithuanian, and Chinese. Would films for export have to be produced first in one language and then entirely again in another language? Would talkies be entitled to the same degree of free speech as the stage and the novel?

William Fox thought that the best sound system was one that recorded sound right on the film itself, a system he had first seen demonstrated at his studio on Tenth Avenue. Fox thought that there was a ventriloquist present or some other trickery and demanded that the invention be demonstrated at Fox Hall, his estate in Woodmere, Long Island. The patents to the system were owned by its inventor, Theodore Case, who had been experimenting since 1911 at his laboratory in upstate New York. Case had managed to change sound waves into electrical vibrations, which in turn were changed into light variations that were photographed onto the edge of film. When the film was projected the process was reversed, and the recreated sound waves were transmitted to the audience from amplifying speakers behind the screen. Case had tried to sell his sound-on-film system to Western Electric and others, but no one was interested except William Fox. Fox bought Case's patents and called his system Movietone.

He also bought the American rights to the patents of a German sound system which used a photoelectric cell to reproduce sound. The invention was called Tri-Ergon. William Fox recognized the genius of this German system and bought the American patent rights to it for $60,000. As early as 1922, Fox established the American Tri-Ergon Corporation, himself owning 90 percent of the stock.

Fox first demonstrated his Movietone system to the press in February 1927. About fifty reporters arrived at his studio. When all were assembled, they were photographed singing "Oh, Susannah." Then each one had to introduce him- or herself, name and newspaper. That was it. The reporters went away to have lunch. Four hours later the reporters returned to the studio and climbed the stairs to the projection room. There, on the screen, they saw themselves singing, talking, and moving in perfect synchronization. Mr. Fox then showed several sound shorts, a banjo-and-piano act, a comedy sketch, and three songs by a popular cabaret singer. Next day the papers were full of William Fox's achievement, sound right on the film itself.

Like the Warner brothers, William Fox's desire for a workable sound system had nothing to do with making talking feature pictures. He wanted a lightweight, portable system so he could record the events of the day while they were happening for his newsreels. He needed a compact system that his newsreel cameraman could tote to the remotest village in Tibet. Perhaps because a botched operation in his childhood paralyzed one of his arms, he wanted to help medical students by documenting correct surgical procedures. One of Fox's first ventures with Movietone was recording a surgical operation in a Chicago hospital, the first time in history that an operation was filmed and simultaneously explained by the surgeon. Fox, who never had a chance to go to school, hoped to introduce audiovisual teaching in the areas of science and mathematics and to make film libraries available for home use.

He said to a group of students at Harvard College:

> Just imagine professors of this college coming to our studio and delivering lectures on subjects they have studied for years and that they hope to present to this body of students. We photograph the speaker and at the same time on the same celluloid we photograph his voice. That lecture can simultaneously be shown, not only in Harvard, but in all the universities of the world, so that the speaker's voice may be heard in a thousand classrooms at one time. The Movietone or the Vitaphone or whatever talking apparatus the public will ultimately adopt will be one of the greatest factors for education that it is possible to conceive.

Early sound newsreels had no commentator. They recorded only natural sounds: traffic, people crossing the street, the sounds made by a newly hatched bird. Fox never imagined that sound newsreels would make new demands on politicians accustomed to speaking on street corners and to convention crowds. The intimacy of the sound camera quickly resulted in a new political speaking style. Politicians began to speak to invisible audiences rather than to the ones right in front of them.

The one drawback of the Movietone system was its speakers. The sound was weak. William Fox was compelled to make a deal with the telephone company to obtain the superior amplifiers developed by their Bell Laboratories. Thus, the telephone company had its thumb in both the Movietone and Vitaphone pies right from the start. Western Electric formed a new subsidiary, Electrical Research Products Incorporated (ERPI), to assume Western's sound-picture and other nontelephone business. Every theater that converted to sound installed ERPI speakers and paid that company a monthly fee for upkeep. ERPI hired and trained hundreds of installation and service personnel, established networks of regional offices across the country, and redesigned equipment for easier installation. Bell Laboratories built a new office building in New York exclusively for sound-picture development.

Instead of depending upon exhibitors to voluntarily convert to sound, and tired of having his films kept out of Loew's and Zukor's theater chains, Fox began a campaign of buying theaters. "My object," he boasted, "is to build up a chain of theaters that will cover the forty-eight states of the Union. From Maine to Illinois, from California to Illinois, and some day the chains will meet." To finance his Fox Theaters Corporation, Fox developed close ties with Harold Stuart, president of the Chicago investment house of Halsey, Stuart & Company, a connection Fox would come to regret.

But he was up and flying on January 21, 1927, when he exhibited the first Movietone sound films at the Sam Harris Theater in New York City. He then brought Movietone to the

Roxy Theater, the 6,000-seat "Cathedral of Motion Pictures," which Fox had just purchased. The entire program at the Roxy was Movietone features, newsreels, and short subjects. In May, when Charles Lindbergh took off alone for his thirty-three hour flight to Paris, cameramen from Movietone News were there. That very night at the Roxy, audiences heard smiling "Slim" Lindbergh say a few cheerful words before getting into his single-prop one-seater to cross the Atlantic Ocean. When the airplane on the screen roared off into the black-and-white yonder, six thousand people stood up in the theater and cheered for nearly ten minutes.

The following month Movietone News cameramen recorded President Coolidge welcoming Lindbergh home and the tumultous welcome that awaited Lindbergh in New York City.

Five years later there was more news of Lindbergh, but this time it was sad. His baby son had been kidnapped. Missing for two months, the ransom money paid, the baby was found mutilated and dumped in New Jersey. The great news photographer Sammy Shulman was sent to Swazey's undertaking parlor to take a shot of Lindbergh when he came to identify the body. "I took a shot of Lindbergh there the next day when he came to identify what was left of his poor baby," Sammy wrote in his memoirs. "I got him going in. When he came out I put my camera to my eye and looked through my finder at him. Then I put the camera down without making the shot. You know how it is."

When Warners' *The Jazz Singer* opened in New York the night of October 6, 1927, the audience was thrilled to hear not only the sound of Jolson's singing but the sound of his speaking voice, too: "Wait a minute, wait a minute, you ain't heard nothin' yet!" The film's director, after seeing the rushes, wanted to cut the dialogue, but the coproducer, Darryl F. Zanuck, author of the Rin Tin Tin dramas, insisted on leaving it in and adding several more scenes of Jolson speaking. Harry Warner worried. "What if they laugh when they hear that guy talking? God, we'll be ruined!"

It was *The Jazz Singer* that showed America the potential of sound pictures. The *New York Times* critic wrote: "Not since the first presentation of Vitaphone features more than a year ago at this same playhouse has anything like the ovation been heard in a motion-picture theater." Long lines formed day after day at the Warner Theater, and exhibitors in other cities began hastily raising money to install Vitaphone equipment in their theaters so they could take advantage of the Jolson film's popularity.

The Warner brothers were released from obscurity. Everyone in the industry was talking about them. Oscar Levant, the musician and wit, said he was walking down the street with his little girl, age five. They passed a pair of identical twin boys, age three. "Daddy? Are those the Warner brothers?"

Vitaphone salesmen visited theaters across the country and left promotional brochures with exhibitors:

At last, pictures that talk like living people! Vitaphone Talking Pictures are electrifying audiences the country over! For Vitaphone brings to you the greatest of the world's great entertainers. Screen stars! Stage stars! Opera stars! Famous orchestras! Master musicians! Vitaphone recreates them all before your eyes. You see and hear them act, talk, sing and play—like human beings in the flesh! Do not confuse Vitaphone with mere "sound effects." Vitaphone is the ONE proved successful talking picture—exclusive product of Warner Brothers. Remember this—if it's not Warner Brothers Vitaphone, it's NOT the real, life-like talking picture. Vitaphone climaxes all previous entertainment achievementts. See and hear this marvel of the age—Vitaphone!

Sam Warner was ill when the *The Jazz Singer* made its debut, and he died a few days afterwards. His brother Harry went to Washington to speak before the League of American Penwomen. He was asked how he felt being the leader in the field of sound pictures. Wearing the Jewish symbol of mourning, a slashed black ribbon in his lapel, Harry said, "We have been very successful, but most of the joy has been taken out of it."

Irving Thalberg, at the Metro-Goldwyn-Mayer studio in Culver City said, "The talking picture has its place, as has color photography, but I do not believe it will ever replace the silent drama any more than I believe color photography will replace entirely the present black-and-white."

Adolph Zukor went into the talkie business with a sound-on-film system called RCA Photophone, which had been developed by the General Electric Company and sold to David Sarnoff at the new Radio Corporation of America. Famous Players-Lasky used the RCA Photophone in 1927 for their picture *Wings*, a World War I drama that brought Gary Cooper to prominence. Even before fame he was the heart-throb of the secretarial pool at the studio.

Photoplay magazine offered a $500 prize for the best name for talking pictures. Some of the entries were: soundies, speakies, squawkies, pictovox, photophone, phonise, cinophone, vocafilm, photovoice, audies, and audifilm.

Now came a new tyrant to the movie studio: the sound engineer. Directors, authors, actors, and cameramen stepped to one side, completely baffled. The sound experts, heavily armed with blueprint designs of monitor rooms and sound-proof stages, elbowed their way into the center of motion-picture stages and intimidated everyone.

No one thought of a movable microphone. The sound engineer placed the microphone in one spot on the set, hidden by a bouquet of flowers or an ashtray, and all the actors had to gather around and speak into it. Actors whose graceful or animated way of moving was part of their charm now looked as if they'd seized-up. Tap dancers had to be sure to tap in a small area around the mike on the floor. Photoplayers had to learn to talk dialogue and play it. They could no longer make faces and look camera left, camera right, up, down, and do what the director told them to do and hope that he could put it together into a performance. Verses appeared in the press making fun of the actor's plight.

Little Miss Starlet in ermine and scarlet
Getting a thousand a day.

Along came the talkies
Revealing her squawkies
And put poor Miss Starlet away!

Or,

If you can speak, and not call birdie boidie,
If you can laugh and make it sound like fun,
If you will not refer to poifect loidy,
Hey, hey! You'll be in talkies yet, my son!

And,

I cannot talk, I cannot sing
nor screech nor moan nor anything.
Possessing all these fatal strictures
what chance have I in motion pictures?

The consternation among silent players when sound arrived was naturally very great, because the microphone helped some voices and took away from others. Many stars who were on their way down anyway blamed their slipping on sound. But most of those with real ability and determination adjusted to the new medium—Jean Arthur, William Powell, Adolphe Menjou, Gary Cooper, Greta Garbo, Joan Crawford, and so many others.

As for the great directors of the silent screen, they could no longer run out in the morning with a camera and shoot something here and something there. Formerly, stories might begin with a line written on the back of an envelope. Or the director would see a cliff, throw a dummy off, and film the scene. "There's the heavy," he would say. "Now why did we throw him off the cliff?" With the coming of sound directors had to learn to read scripts, digest characterization, and pace a story that was written. Title writers had to change into dramatists and learn how to write dialogue.

Producers had to change their studios, supervise the construction of soundstages, hire new technical talent, listen to the pleas of those who couldn't survive the cataclysm, and convince the men with money to keep on investing. Ernst Lubitsch, who directed Greta Garbo in *Ninotchka*, recalled those days of transition and said, "You could name the great stars of the silent screen who were finished, the great directors, gone, the great title writers who were washed up. But remember this as long as you live: the producers didn't lose a man. They ALL made the switch! That's where the great talent was."

Theater musicians were set adrift. Having played for hundreds of films, both good and bad, the accompanists were sure they could act as well as most of the performers they had seen on the screen. One organist's claim to fame was that he looked like Francis X. Bushman. Al Altman sent his test out to the west coast, but the response was "Looks too much like Francis X. Bushman."

It was because William Fox converted his Tenth Avenue studio to Movietone that Metro-Goldwyn-Mayer's eastern screen tests became talkies before the M-G-M studio in California was wired for sound.

Now screen-test shooting began at five in the morning to avoid the noise of New York traffic. The studio floor was covered from wall to wall with thick spongy carpet. Acoustic plaster and many layers of balsam wood covered all the walls. Trusses supported many pounds of soundproof insulation on the high ceiling. The door was so heavy with soundproofing it was difficult to budge. A big sign on it said "SILENCE!" The installation of sound made every minute of studio time so expensive that formerly good-natured technicians were nervous wrecks. They resented the sound man. What this scientist from MIT or Cornell said was law. None of the crew was allowed to wear shoes. They had to walk around in their socks. Chewing gum was forbidden—it crackled. What the cameraman thought would be a good angle the sound man said would be impossible. Actors had to move carefully, so they looked wooden.

Because microphones picked up the whir of the camera, cameras had to be enclosed in soundproof booths known as "greenhouses" ten-feet tall and eight-feet wide. Two cameras were set up on a table inside the booth, and the cameraman and his assistant almost suffocated, wedged in there shooting through a pane of optical glass. It took four men to move the camera two inches. Electric fans, which had formerly taken away the heat from the spotlights, now were forbidden because they made noise. Windows had to be shut tight. If one of the crew sneezed the test had to be shot again. Gone were the musicians who had once played so that actors could get into weepy moods. No music, no visitors, no walking around, no chatting, and definitely no sipping soda through a straw or showing off one's loud belch.

Meyer Mishkin, the Hollywood talent agent, began his career at the reception desk in Fox's New York studio.

> I ran errands and took actors up to the dressing rooms. Sound had only just come in and they needed to find people who could talk so they took them from the hit shows. Every day I used to hear the Gettysburg Address coming out of the sound room. Every day. Finally, I got up the nerve to go in there and ask the engineers why the Gettysburg Address all the time. They told me they were trying to get rid of the sibilant "s" sound. Four-score and seven years ago. . . .

Mary Lewis, the Metropolitan Opera singer, was given a screen test at the Fox studio. Wearing a purple evening gown and manipulating an orange fan, she swept across the tiny stage in front of the camera booth. Directly in front of the camera a huge signboard was placed which had written on it, in chalk: "Mary Lewis, height 5 feet 6 inches, color of eyes, blue, color of hair, brown." The signboard was photographed then quickly removed.

Miss Lewis took her place at the red chalkmark on the rug. She complained of a slight cold and frequently ran to the piano to spray her throat with a purplish liquid. The piano, with the accompanist ready at the keyboard, had been moved out of focus, and a huge, thick black velvet curtain placed behind it to keep the sound within the limits of the microphone.

Al Altman leaned forward in his chair and cued Miss Lewis's entry. The pianist struck the opening bars of "Vilia" from *The Merry Widow*. Miss Lewis crossed from behind a black screen and walked forward until she had reached the prescribed spot on the carpet. Nodding as if to a great stage audience and smiling and pirouetting for a moment, she began to sing a song from the part she had played in *The Merry Widow* in Paris.

After the song was finished she walked to the backdrop, picked up her fan from a chair, waltzed around the stage for a few moments, and then returned to the chalk spot again. Her second song was a waltz from the same opera. After the second piece she stood still for a moment and then said: "I suppose I ought to tell you who I am. I am Mary Lewis, late of Ziegfeld, the Opera Comique in Paris, and the Metropolitan Opera Company. Besides singing in English, I can also sing and speak as well in German and French. I have been asked to demonstrate this by reciting a few lines from *The Merry Widow*. I shall recite in French the speech of the heroine when she tells what love is—*L'amour, l'amour est la vie—c'est courte—c'est—*"

Miss Lewis broke off in the middle of the speech to continue in German. After that she stood still until the cameras stopped grinding. "Thank you very much, Miss Lewis," Al said. A blue smock was brought to the singer to throw over her expensive gown, and then Al and his crew went into the recording room to hear a playback of what Miss Lewis had just sung. There were some flaws in the recording so a new test had to be taken. Miss Lewis went through exactly the same paces as before, doing the scene as if it were her first. Again Al thanked her, and she left the scene after bowing and shaking hands with the young woman who was to have the next test.

"Let me out of here!" yelled the cameraman, bursting from the booth, and he ran outside for some fresh air.

The Fox and the Schenck

THE MOTION-PICTURE industry had become so respectable by 1927 that its leaders were invited to speak at Harvard University's Graduate School of Business Administration. Adolph Zukor, Jesse Lasky, Cecil B. DeMille, Marcus Loew, William Fox, Harry Warner, and eight others gave a series of lectures telling their own stories in their own ways. "Here we have a fully developed industry," said the dean of the school, "that has gone through its stages of development in such a short space of time that its pioneers are still in active control of its destiny." The film industry was a living case study.

There were three lectures a week in a course that was required for a degree. About three hundred students attended. How each of the industry pioneers introduced himself is revealing of personality. Here's what Zukor said:

It is indeed a privilege to have the opportunity to address a class in Harvard College. You gentlemen living

here and developing your ideals and ambitions here are
so close to the institution that I do not believe you can
appreciate the opportunities you have. To a man like myself who never had the chance of a college education,
this is a great opportunity, and if I am a bit nervous it is
not because I am not glad to be here. Even if it should be
an ordeal to talk to you I do it with pleasure and I hope
that it may do some good.

Here's what William Fox said:

More than twenty years ago I learned very promptly that
I never could earn a livelihood as a speaker, so that the
first chance I got some years afterward to go into a profession that did not require any talking but depended
entirely on the camera, I took, knowing it was silent. I
had really no other choice if I wanted three meals a day.

Marcus Loew, whose past as a paperboy was ennobled
when he was introduced as a "former newspaper man," said:

I cannot begin to tell you how it impresses me, coming
to a great college such as this to deliver a lecture, when I
have never even seen the inside of one before. But Mr.
Hays persuaded me that it was my duty to come, and I
finally promised I would, provided the doctor permitted
it. Yesterday morning before I left, the doctor thought I
shouldn't, but I persuaded him that he was wrong and
got his permission in that way. Of course, he still feels
that he was right and that I was wrong, but I do not think
so, because I have been compensated for my trip. I do
not know what I should ever have done if I neglected
this opportunity.
    It was very hard sailing when I first started in the mo-
tion picture business. At that time, if you were seen in a
motion picture theatre your reputation was gone, and I
did not like that at all.

Six months later at age fifty-seven, he was dead. Sime
Silverman, the editor of *Variety*, said his pal was "burned out
worrying for his stockholders."

Five thousand people attended Loew's funeral at Pembroke, his forty-six acre estate on Long Island Sound. Two thousand mourners were allowed into the mansion, an eighty-room manor house built in about 1918 by a Captain De Lamar, whose fortune came from silver mines. There were twelve master bedrooms, twelve baths, and stained glass globes designed by Louis Comfort Tiffany, who lived nearby. A large French Renaissance mantel dominated the main hall, and on the landing of the gigantic staircase was a pipe organ hidden behind an elaborate fretwork panel. All the rooms on the main floor were large and laid out for entertaining hundreds of guests. There was a paneled billiard room, with ornamental cornices and parquet floors, and a breakfast room with an unusual lead-glass ceiling.

More than two thousand mourners stood outside the arched wrought-iron gates and looked in at Japanese gardens with reflecting ponds connected by lacy wrought-iron bridges, a mosaic tile swimming pool seventy feet in circumference, a garage that could hold twenty cars, and a stable that could accommodate twenty horses and twenty cows. Loew's yacht, the *Caroline*, its flag at half-mast, was docked at the landing.

Services were held in the marble reception hall where Loew's slight body, looking like a figure from Madame Tussaud's Wax Museum, lay in its coffin surrounded by thousands of floral tributes. Though Loew had been reared an Orthodox Jew and looking upon the dead is forbidden in that faith, Catholic etiquette had somehow taken over, and the mourners marched past the coffin to peer down on Loew's waxy features and say something like, "He looks good," to his grieving wife Caroline. His twin sons David and Arthur, thirty years old, stood near the open casket.

"To know Marcus Loew was to love him," the rabbi said, and a general murmur of assent hummed in the room. "He was a man without an enemy."

Sophie Tucker, the singer, was overcome. She had performed on the stage of Loew's first theater. She said that he

paid $20 a week for an act with one person, $40 for two people, and a three-person act didn't get on. Charlie Ebbets, who
owned Ebbets Field, was there. "Marcus Loew used to say to
me, if you want to make good, never grow tired of your
shop."

The pallbearers were David Warfield, the actor who had
been in partnership with Loew since the penny-arcade days,
Nick Schenck, whose perpetual smile was temporarily absent,
Dave Bernstein, Adolph Zukor, Lee Shubert, and Loew's lawyer J. Robert Rubin. The coffin was fitted into the hearse,
against a backdrop of ocean. Limousines followed by a parade of motorcars drove toward the cemetery, passing the
Woolworth mansion, J.P. Morgan's estate of eighty acres, and
the Pratt estate of over one thousand acres with eight mansions, one for each son.

The sad parade drove by Mountainview Farm, a thousand-
acre tract which Adolph Zukor had turned into a family compound, complete with an eighteen-hole golf course, a
clubhouse that contained a movie theater, a guest house, a
children's house for the families of his two married children,
a swimming pool, and a filling station where guests could
tank-up free. There was an up-to-date dairy on the property
which produced enough milk to keep a nearby orphanage
supplied. As for being Marcus Loew's neighbor, "This was
pleasant," Zukor said, "because we could sit on the veranda
and make fun of each other's pictures. Our company had
starred Enrico Caruso in a film titled *My Cousin*. The great
opera star's voice naturally could not be used, and Marcus
claimed the picture was the greatest bust in all history. I was
never able to argue him down on that point."

At the cemetery in Brooklyn, David Warfield tried to throw
himself into the grave. Nils Granlund, Marcus Loew's press
agent, was heartbroken and said, "I was devoted to this wonderful guy."

All motion-picture studios and motion-picture film ex-
changes in the United States and Canada observed the occa-

sion of Marcus Loew's funeral by ceasing operations for five minutes at two o'clock that day.

Years later Adolph Zukor said, "The mogul has been played up as a kind of lavish potentate surrounded by flunkies. Now I suppose Marcus Loew would come under the mogul heading. He put together a theater empire and in due course the Metro-Goldwyn-Mayer producing company. But, frankly, I always thought of Marcus as more of a tennis mogul. He nearly always beat me."

Marcus Loew's will had been drawn up in 1912. It began: "In the event that the net value of my estate exceeds $200,000 . . ." At the time of his death a conservative estimate valued his estate at $30 million.

He left 400,000 shares, one-third of the outstanding shares of Loew's Inc., to his wife and his sons. And he left them to wonder if the company could have any future without him.

Caroline Loew did not believe that anyone could run her husband's company. She had watched him build it from nothing on the strength of his personality and imagination. Her sons agreed. Now was the time to sell their stock, while Loew's Inc. was on top. They asked Nicholas Schenck to find a buyer.

Far from being hurt at their lack of confidence in his ability to run Loew's empire, Nick Schenck was delighted. His commission on the sale would amount to about $10 million, more than he would ever earn as an executive at 1540 Broadway. He had worked for Loew's Theaters since 1912. $10 million would buy him everything he wanted right then, which was simply to have the leisure to spend his days with his new bride, the vivacious and congenial Pansy Wilcox, an exshowgirl. Nick Schenck had been stuck for years in a loveless, childless marriage. Now, at age forty-six, he was happily in love at last.

It did not occur to him that Louis B. Mayer might feel betrayed if the company were sold. He hardly knew Mayer. The theater end of the business was so much older and so much more profitable than the Culver City studio that it would have surprised Nick to discover that Mayer felt proprietary about that particular subsidiary. Nick saw Mayer simply as an employee of Loew's, an important one, true, but replaceable. Nick Schenck often showed a lack of imagination in his business dealings.

In 1913, he bought the southeastern states' rights to one of Adolph Zukor's pictures. Because Schenck was in charge of managing Loew's theaters, he had a ready-made outlet. Each time he booked *Queen Elizabeth* into a Loew's theater he made a commission from Zukor. When Marcus Loew found out what his chief lieutenant was doing, he forced Schenck to sell his interest.

In 1923, Schenck again used his connection with Loew's to further his own interests. He bought a theater in Peekskill, a small city thirty-nine miles north of New York City on the Hudson River. Peekskill was surrounded by little towns, like Tomkins Cove, West Haverstraw, and Verplanck, where there were no theaters. Close by was Bear Mountain, which drew hundreds of tourists, and the West Point Military Academy. Though Schenck's theater was not part of the Loew's chain, it got all the privileges of the chain—publicity, expensive carpet, the best pictures.

Another theater opened in town, but the owner found it impossible to book decent pictures. Distributors told him that they were afraid of renting top pictures to him because, if they did, Nick Schenck would cut them off from the Loew's chain. The independent owner had to book stupid pictures, and his new theater was getting a bad reputation. The theater owner went to see Nick Schenck and complained. Schenck said that there was not room in Peekskill for two theaters, and he offered to sell. The other exhibitor refused to buy, so his theater was vandalized. Posters were ripped off his entrance. Someone telephoned and asked the exhibitor if he had changed his mind about buying Schenck's theater. The exhibitor said no. That night a stink bomb was left in his theater, and everyone ran out saying they would never return.

The exhibitor, thinking that Marcus Loew was behind all this, wrote a letter to Loew complaining. The exhibitor also complained to the Motion Picture Theater Owners of America, an organization of independent theater owners like himself with no connection to production. The organization wrote a formal complaint to the Federal Trade Commission, and the case was taken to court in New York City. The judge, in a stinging order directed at Nick Schenck, threatened to resort to criminal law if intimidation of the independent exhibitor continued. The judge said that this skulduggery was just one more example of the low morals of motion-picture people and called upon Federal authorities to investigate the whole motion-picture industry.

Schenck closed his Peekskill theater. Loew apologized to the other exhibitor, paid to have all the seats in his theater reupholstered, and made sure he received first-run movies.

As he secretly looked for buyers, Schenck assumed the presidency of Loew's Inc. He announced that 15 to 20 percent of all the pictures to be made at Culver City in 1928 would contain sound and that $3 million would be spent to wire Loew's theaters with the Movietone sound-on-film process, at a cost of about $20,000 per theater. Only about a thousand movie houses in the country were wired for sound. Mostly they showed short subjects. The bulk of sound films in 1928 were filmed vaudeville acts. Vaudevillians quickly realized that they were hurting their drawing power by doing their regular acts for Vitaphone and Movietone, so they refused to appear except with substitute material. Which is unfortunate now, because those acts which made the performers famous are lost.

By the fall of 1929, two years after *The Jazz Singer*, only about one-fourth of the theaters in America had managed to change to sound. One of the major problems in theaters was where to situate the amplifying horns, because the area behind the screen was needed for the vaudeville presentations still popular at most theaters. The whole film industry was in a tizzy.

There were at least $1 million worth of silent pictures in company inventories. If talking pictures won out the public would no longer pay to see silent pictures, and those remaining would become junk.

Installing soundstages at the studios was vastly expensive. And suppose producers discovered they had installed an obsolete process? Through 1928 and 1929, producers went from adding synchronized sound tracks to already completed silent films and grafting a few scenes of dialogue or song onto those films, to planning their first all-talking features and announcing that in the future they would make only sound pictures. Similarly, each went from remodeling existing studios for sound to building completely new studios designed for sound work.

King Vidor, the director of *The Big Parade,* wanted to make a singing and talking picture, *Hallelujah,* with an all-Negro cast, something unheard of. Irving Thalberg was excited about the picture, but Nick Schenck ordered production of the picture to stop. He did not want to show an all-Negro picture in Loew's theaters, because black people would attend and that would drive white people away. King Vidor, used to having complete freedom from Marcus Loew, traveled to New York. He told Schenck that for every dollar the company put into the picture, he, Vidor, would match it from his own salary.

The picture was shot in Tennessee and in Culver City on the new soundstages. Irving Berlin wrote a song for it. *Hallelujah* received rave reviews.

> Rarely has a film been so moving, so awakening to our own responsive inner experiences; the plantation becomes the world and its characters become ourselves. In many ways it is an astonishing picture, it is also prophetic for it hints of a nobler form of motion picture for the future, a maturer concept of what motion accompanied by sound can bring to the screen.
> —*From Quasimodo to Scarlett O'Hara*, Stanley Hochman

But the picture lost money just as Nick Schenck said it would. White people did stay away. Though Irving Thalberg said that Metro-Goldwyn-Mayer could afford to lose money now and then, Schenck did not agree. He sent a spy from the home office, Eddie Mannix, out to the west coast to report on Louis B. Mayer, who Nick believed to be financially irresponsible.

Greta Garbo's first talkie, *Anna Christie*, in which she says, "Gimme a visky with chincher ale on the side and don't be stingy, baby," made up for whatever money Metro-Goldwyn-Mayer lost on *Hallelujah*. But now everyone at the studio suspected that with Marcus Loew gone the studio would have to constantly justify itself to the home office. Eddie Mannix, come to spy, stayed on at the studio and became one of Louie's closest friends.

* * *

It came as a surprise to film executives that audiences rushed out to music stores to buy sheet music of the songs they heard on the screen. A whole new field had opened up since Al Jolson sang "Sonny Boy" in *The Singing Fool*. The movie industry was talking about the "theme song."

Suddenly there was money to be made in publishing movie music. Film executives began acquiring already established music publishing companies, all located in New York City, the center of American popular music. Warners paid $10 million for three houses—Harms, Witmark, and Remick—which were assembled into one giant organization, Music Publishers Holding Corporation. William Fox bought Red Star Publishing Company. Metro-Goldwyn-Mayer acquired Leo Feist, Robbins Corporation, and one or two lesser firms. After becoming a subsidiary of M-G-M, Robbins became the foremost publisher of talking-picture music, with more than half the hits of the nation, including "You Were Meant for Me" and "Singin' in the Rain," from the 1929 picture, *The Hollywood Revue*.

Money began to pour down on previously impoverished New York songwriters. They traveled by Pullman coach out to California, where studio executives told them the type of ma-

terial needed for specific productions and set strict dead-
lines. Directors were now afraid of any silence in their
movies. Heroes and heroines burst into song at incongruous
moments. Some producers included as many as eighteen
songs in a single film, hoping that the audience would choose
at least one to play on the piano at home. Composers and
lyricists, much as they disliked the pressure of movie work,
did not return to New York. Tin Pan Alley vanished.

Talkies and radio shortened the life of a popular song.
Time was when a hit would last through a season. It was carried by a leading vaudevillian over his circuit; it was played by
the bands. Talkies and the radio abolished time and space.
The radio, in a single hour, reached more people than any
headliner of vaudeville reached in a year. By 1929 total radio
sales amounted to more than $800 million, an increase of
more than 1,000 percent over sales just five years before. The
talkie, by the system of virtually simultaneous presentation,
achieved the same effect. A hit in New York became, overnight, a hit in Los Angeles. This speeded up competition.
Where formerly there had been ten songs struggling for recognition, now there were fifty. Out with the old hit, in with
the new.

To insure a steady supply of music, motion-picture producers bought the motion-picture rights to Broadway musicals and operettas, including *Rio Rita, Show Boat, Animal
Crackers, Hit the Deck, New Moon, No, No Nanette, The Vagabond
King,* and *The Desert Song.*

Amid this flurry of activity and confusion, word got around
that Nicholas Schenck was planning to sell Loew's Inc. and all
its subsidiaries, including the studio in Culver City. Warners
wanted to buy and so did Paramount. But William Fox was
the only one who seemed able to raise sufficient funds. When
asked if he was contemplating selling out to William Fox,
Schenck lied. "Were it not for the fact that such reports are
apt to do harm, this newest rumor would be the most ridiculously amusing gossip that I have heard in years."

Louis B. Mayer, in the grip of a higher cause, was oblivious.

He was campaigning for Herbert Hoover. Mayer saw in Hoover a perfect American. Hoover was an orphan who put himself through school and went from rags to riches. Hoover believed in self-reliance, did not believe in welfare or labor unions, and thought businesses were capable of arbitrating labor disputes themselves. When Hoover was secretary of commerce he staunchly refused to let the federal government censor motion pictures. When asked by members of the film industry to arbitrate the thousands of controversies that arose between theater owners and distributors, Hoover held back federal interference, insisting that the industry police itself.

In 1927 Louie founded the Academy of Motion Picture Arts and Sciences, not only so artists could be recognized with Oscars but also to keep labor unions out of Hollywood. Mayer hoped disputes could be negotiated by the academy, which was composed of actors, directors, and producers.

Mayer had donated plenty of money to the Republican National Committee and had become a favorite afterdinner speaker at Republican functions. He imagined that with the right publicity he could turn Herbert Hoover into the biggest star of them all.

Louie neglected the home front. He became so absorbed in Hoover's presidential campaign that he became unavailable to the people at the studio. Irving Thalberg complained that he was bearing the entire burden of production and it wasn't fair, considering Louie was earning twice as much.

Complaints about Mayer reached New York. Nick Schenck, a Democrat, had contributed $25,000 to Al Smith's campaign. That the head of his studio was supporting Hoover only strengthened Schenck's resolve to get out of Loew's.

William Fox offered to pay double the price that Loew's Inc. stock was selling for on the open market. This was a deal hard to refuse. The actor David Warfield added his 38,000 shares to the pile. The Shuberts put in their 17,000 shares, and Nick Schenck threw in his and all the shares owned by his relatives. The sales price for the entire block was about $50 million.

In an effort to Movietone the entire world, Fox was buying theaters fast. He bought twenty houses in New England and put together a circuit of one hundred thirty theaters in New York. He spiraled his holdings into a formidable chain of eight hundred houses. Profits in three-years' time for Fox Theaters Corporation rose to $10 million, and the new corporation's estimated value at the time of the anticipated merger with Loew's was $50 million. Fox also bought the Gaumont chain of three hundred theaters in Great Britain for $14 million in cash plus notes for $6 million due in six months.

Fox imagined himself becoming king of a global entertainment empire. All he needed was $50 million and he would own the giant Loew's, which that year had earned a profit of $12 million.

Fox borrowed some of the money from the Western Electric Company. The telephone company knew that William Fox owned the patents for the German Tri-Ergon system. They told Fox that the patents were worthless. He wasn't sure if the patents were valid or not. Nobody could really be sure since the field was so new. But Fox was sure of one thing. If the telephone company wanted his patents and fought him in court to get them, they could ruin him because they could afford to fight for years. He decided to cooperate. He allowed telephone scientists into his laboratory to investigate the photoelectric cell system.

The telephone company, in the person of John E. Otterson, agreed to lend William Fox money to buy Loew's. Fox said about Otterson:

> When he shakes your hand, you can feel the muscular development throughout the entire arm, and he makes sure to grip you so that you do feel his muscular development. He never allows you to forget that he is speaking for the great and mighty Telephone Company. He is not a man who uses either tact or diplomacy; he does all things by brute force. He will give you his promise and

word of honor again and again, and without a wink of an eyelash deny that he ever said so. He is as cold as ice, and feels that because he represents the Telephone Company he is privileged to break his word at will.

Otterson loaned Fox $15 million to help in the purchase of Loew's, and he helped Fox borrow $3 million more from the Chatham & Phoenix bank. Then Otterson asked to buy the Tri-Ergon patents. Fox agreed to sell for $25 million. The price was rejected.

Fox raised money from other sources, too. The investment banking company of Halsey, Stuart & Company loaned him $10 million for a year, as did the Banker's Securities Company of Philadelphia, which took part of the Loew's shares as collateral. The Fox Theater Corporation raised $16 million by selling new shares of stock. Fox raised a total of $57 million.

William Fox was aware that the federal government might squawk at the merger of two such giant corporations as Loew's Inc. and Fox Film Corporation. But he, like Mayer, believed himself responsible for Herbert Hoover's victory at the polls. Fox had put his newsreel staff at Hoover's disposal and had photographed Hoover in a favorable light.

With a pal in the White House, Fox figured he had nothing to worry about. Nonetheless, to make sure he was safe, Fox went to the man he was sure Hoover would appoint as attorney general, William Donovan, who was then the assistant attorney general. Donovan suggested that Fox write a letter in support of the merger. Fox wrote:

A survey was made of the situation during last year and when the figures were compiled, there was a clear indication that the Loew Company and the Fox Company were wasting seventeen million dollars a year by duplication of their work. Fox Film and Metro-Goldwyn-Mayer are running two sets of executives; two sets of studios are competing for the purchase of stories, for the price of the performer and director; and when pictures are completed, we rent them to the exhibitors. We have some two hundred offices throughout the world in which is carried on the rival business. Great economies are required in the motion picture business. From our records it is clear that of the gross money we receive for the pictures we make and release, at least forty percent comes from other countries. Fox Film has a rental agency in every country in the civilized and non-civilized world other than Russia, and it has come into my mind, what is going to occur when an English-speaking picture is going to Czechoslovakia or to Hungary or to Rumania or China or Japan, from which countries we are receiving substantial revenues from silent pictures? It is clear we cannot make talking pictures in every language, and I can see no reason why these obscure countries will change their language to suit the American producer. I reached a conclusion that it will be necessary to reorganize our entire business so as to meet this new condition. I feel there is a responsibility to retain for our country the well-earned position that it has in the making and distributing of motion pictures throughout the world. I feel that if the picture companies are deprived of a great part of their foreign revenue, we might get to a place where we cannot carry on. I hope to be able soon to make foreign language pictures to hold our business abroad.

Donovan studied Fox's proposal, and Fox understood him to say that the Justice Department would not turn its antitrust guns against the merger.

So Schenck summoned Arthur Loew, Marcus's son, home from London where he had gone to attend the opening of the company's new Empire Theater. Arthur Loew, hearing that Fox had managed to put together temporary financing, sailed home immediately. On February 24, 1929, in a banking office in New York, Arthur Loew turned over his family's stock certificates to William Fox, and the deal was concluded.

A few days passed. Harry Stuart, of Halsey, Stuart & Company, telephoned William Fox and said that the 400,000 shares that Fox had purchased did not represent control of Loew's, and without control of the 1.35 million outstanding shares Fox really had no power over the company. Harry Stuart advised Fox to go into the open market and buy more shares of Loew's in the names of various individuals. Stuart said, "For goodness sake, own the majority or you will be wiped out here. You can see your danger." He arranged for Fox to buy on the open market $14 million more of Loew's stock on a 50 percent margin.

Soon after, a representative of the telephone company called and told Fox to buy more shares so he would be sure to control Loew's. Fox bought 260,900 additional shares in individual names. He stripped his companies of all the cash they had, acting entirely on the advice of his bankers and his so-called friends at AT&T. Altogether, his plan was to own 660,900 shares of Loew's stock at a price of about $73 million.

Nick Schenck made the merger known to the public. He announced that Loew's Inc. would continue in operation as an independent entity. The Fox Corporation and M-G-M, once rivals, would now make their plans with full knowledge of each other's commitments.

Louie was the last to know. He and his family were on a train bound for Herbert Hoover's inauguration in Washington. Louie's train stopped in New Orleans, where he had dinner with some Louisiana theater owners at the Montmarte Hotel. The front desk paged him; he picked up the phone and heard from his lawyer that Schenck had sold the company to William Fox. There was a long silence, as if Louie had been knocked unconscious. Then he said, "Well, Nick is president of the company. He can do what he wants with it."

A few days later, in the *New York American,* a Hearst newspaper, there was a full column about Louis B. Mayer and his family, the first informal guests entertained by the Hoovers in the White House. There were pictures of Mayer, Margaret, Irene, and Edith with the new president of the United States. Louis B. Mayer must have been amazed that he, an immigrant boy from Russia, was being entertained at the White House.

Mayer's daughter Irene remembered that visit to the White House for quite another reason:

> Seated around the Hoover dinner table was a handful of people. Midway through the meal appeared a perfect stranger, who had entered quietly and stood there about ten feet from the President. It was immediately obvious that the room was unguarded. We sat frozen in an awful silence. After "Who are you?" the thing uppermost in Hoover's mind was "How did you get in?" Equally unguarded, apparently, was the front door, through which the man had strolled; and, it would seem, so was the front gate as well. The man was quite polite; he had come a considerable distance to tell the President he needed a job because of the "terrible unemployment." Then the room filled with people. What is notable about the occasion is that from the next day on, March 13, 1929, the Secret Service was put in charge of the White House police by Presidential order.

While visiting Washington, Louie found out that Hoover had not appointed William Donovan attorney general, as Fox had assumed, but William Mitchell, a man dedicated to eradicating monopoly in American business. When Mayer told Mitchell about the merger of Fox and Loew's, Mitchell promised to investigate.

Two federal investigators showed up at William Fox's office in New York. They wanted to know exactly how many shares of Loew's stock Fox owned and where the money came from to buy those shares. Soon after, a letter arrived from the Department of Justice asking William Fox to divest himself of all Loew's shares.

Fox went to Washington and laid his case before Herbert Hoover at the White House. He reminded Hoover of how favorably Hoover had appeared in Movietone newsreels. Fox recalled:

> After we had adjourned to his smoking room, I frankly told him of my great embarrassment. He listened to it

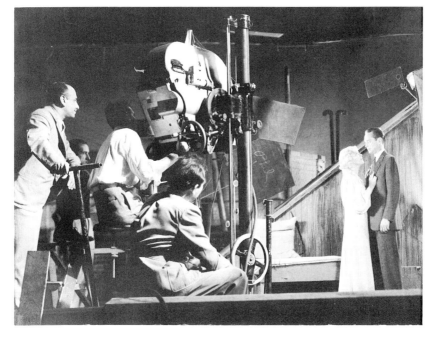

Franchot Tone's screen test directed in 1932 by Al Altman at the Fox
Studio on Tenth Avenue and Fifty-fourth Street. Tone's test was not
accepted by "the boys on the coast" because he and Jean Muir seemed so
stiff together. Before retaking the test, Altman told both actors that the
other was infatuated. That sparked things up. Jean Muir ultimately signed
with Warners and Franchot Tone with M-G-M. [COLLECTION OF THE
AUTHOR]

Microphones on movie sets picked up the whir of the camera in the early
sound movies so cameramen had to seclude themselves inside soundproof
booths. Here an unidentified Vitaphone cameraman poses with a Bell
Telephone Laboratories sound engineer. [COURTESY OF THE BOSTON PUBLIC
LIBRARY, PRINT DEPARTMENT]

Louis B. Mayer, with General Douglas MacArthur, Chief of Staff of the United States Army, in 1930, had such a sincere appreciation of talent and so loved personal publicity that he went out of his way to make his Culver City studio attractive to statesmen and celebrities from all over the world. [COLLECTION OF THE AUTHOR]

Mayer, his star Norma Shearer, and his top producer, Irving Thalberg, Shearer's husband, at the 1931 opening of *Strangers May Kiss*. [COLLECTION OF THE AUTHOR]

Louie's daughter, Edith, marries William Goetz, 1930. The designer
Adrian dressed Edith and her bridal party. Except for Edith's sister, Irene,
and her mother, the women are all stars of the silent screen. From left:
Marion Davies, Irene Mayer, Mrs. Mayer, Louie, Edith Mayer, William
Goetz (later to become vice president of 20th Century-Fox), Carmel
Meyers, May McAvoy, and Bessie Love. [COLLECTION OF THE AUTHOR]

Greta Garbo, with Beulah Bondi and Cecilia Parker, in 1934 filming
a scene from *The Painted Veil*. On the right are Garbo's personal
cameraman, William Daniels, and director Richard Boleslavsky.
[COLLECTION OF THE AUTHOR]

Arthur Loew (1897-1976), Marcus's son, headed Loew's International from 1920 to 1936 when he became president of Loew's for a brief time. "I despised the job of having to answer to stockholders," he said. "It kept me awake nights and literally made me sick." He was married three times and claimed to have invented jockey shorts. [COURTESY OF QUIGLEY PHOTOGRAPHIC ARCHIVE, SPECIAL COLLECTIONS DIVISION, GEORGETOWN UNIVERSITY LIBRARY]

When David O. Selznick (1902-1965) married Irene Mayer, he became a producer at M-G-M which occasioned the mocking phrase, "the son-in-law also rises." He left to start his own company and in 1939 produced *Gone With the Wind*. but never again achieved the success he enjoyed at age thirty-seven with that picture. Selznick lived to see M-G-M credited with producing the film, though it merely distributed it and had its star, Clark Gable, under contract. [COURTESY OF PHOTOFEST]

Fred Waller (1886-1954), once head of special effects at Paramount's Astoria studio, invented Cinerama, the three-dimensional film process for which he received an Oscar in 1953. Waller, who lived on Long Island, also invented water skis. [COURTESY OF QUIGLEY PHOTOGRAPHIC ARCHIVE, SPECIAL COLLECTIONS DIVISION, GEORGETOWN UNIVERSITY LIBRARY]

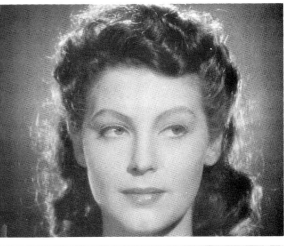

Ava Gardner, the sultry M-G-M star, at age seventeen when Al Altman made her screen test in New York. Ava is a prime example of what was good about the studio system. A poor, uneducated Southern girl could learn how to walk, dance, speak, and sing — all free of charge. [COLLECTION OF THE AUTHOR]

Nick Schenck and Dore Schary after they ousted Louis B. Mayer from Metro-Goldwyn-Mayer in the early fifties. Schary (1905-1980) headed the M-G-M studio from 1951 to 1956 but without much success. [COURTESY OF QUIGLEY PHOTOGRAPHIC ARCHIVE, SPECIAL COLLECTIONS DIVISION, GEORGETOWN UNIVERSITY LIBRARY]

Joseph L. Tomlinson (right), a Canadian road builder who started the first proxy fight in film history. [PHOTO BY BARRETT GALLAGHER FOR *FORTUNE*, JUNE 5, 1957]

Willie Bioff extorted $2 million from the movie corporations in the late 1930s by threatening to pull projectionists from the theaters. He split his take with what remained of Al Capone's gang and then squealed on its members at his trial. [COURTESY OF QUIGLEY PHOTO-GRAPHIC ARCHIVE, SPECIAL COLLECTIONS DIVISION, GEORGETOWN UNIVERSITY LIBRARY]

1955: Willie Bioff's gang finished serving prison time for racketeering and were released. Bioff himself was blown to smithereens when he got into his truck one November day that year. [COURTESY OF PHOENIX NEWSPAPERS, INC.]

Joseph Vogel (left) (1895-1969), president of Loew's, Inc., with Howard Dietz (1896-1983), Loew's top publicity executive, who also simultaneously had a second career as a noted lyricist. Dietz created the company's Leo the Lion trademark and invented the phony Latin of the logo, *Ars Gratia Artis*. [COURTESY OF QUIGLEY PHOTOGRAPHIC ARCHIVE, SPECIAL COLLECTIONS DIVISION, GEORGETOWN UNIVERSITY LIBRARY]

Joe Vogel (right) with his noted attorney, Louis Nizer, after winning the battle in 1957 for control of Loew's, Inc., by an overwhelming vote of the stockholders. [COURTESY OF QUIGLEY PHOTOGRAPHIC ARCHIVE, SPECIAL COLLECTIONS DIVISION, GEORGETOWN UNIVERSITY LIBRARY]

attentively; he was vitally interested. The reasons for his interest were apparent—I had claimed that an injustice had been done to me by the Department of Justice. Before I had left, he had requested that my attorney go back to the department sometime later and have another talk.

Mayer went to New York after Hoover's inauguration to confront Nick Schenck not only for his lack of loyalty to the company but also for not letting him get in on a great stock deal. Louie could have sold his Loew's shares, too, for twice their worth. He accused "Mr. Skunk" of selfishly trading a company that he had helped to build. Loew's gross income before the merger of Metro, Goldwyn and Mayer was about $19 million. Since Louie had become production vice president, the company's worth had risen to more than $100 million. Mayer felt he was entitled to some of the $50 million that Fox paid for the company. Nick said that Louie's contract was secure and that all would remain the same. Fox Films would make low-budget pictures, and M-G-M would continue to make classy pictures. To ease Mayer's hurt, Schenck offered Louie $100,000 which was refused.

Word got back to William Fox that perhaps the source of his troubles with the Justice Department was Louis B. Mayer, now a power in Republican politics. Mayer, in 1929, was far from famous. To Fox, Louie was just a competent studio employee. "It was my job now to make him my friend if I could," Fox said. Fox telephoned Mayer and requested that they meet at Fox Hall. Louie accused him of all kinds of underhandedness and refused to call him Bill. Fox told Mayer that he bought Metro-Goldwyn-Mayer because of Louie's ability. "I have reconsidered this transaction," Fox said to Mayer, "and I have reached the conclusion that you have not been treated properly. If we can merge these two companies, I am willing to recommend to our company to pay you and your associates $2 million. We will pay you $2 million if and when this consolidation is made." They would also negotiate a new contract that both parties would think fair.

According to Fox, Mayer replied:

You must have known that I have moved heaven and earth to prevent this consolidation. Surely you felt that someone used his influence to have the government change its opinion with reference to the acquisition of these shares. I was responsible for that, and it was a perfectly easy matter. But now you have given me a difficult task. How am I going to get them to change their opinion back again?

The treasurer of the Republican National Committee came to visit William Fox some weeks later and told him that everything was all right as far as the Justice Department was concerned. The only problem was that there were connections between Loew's and Paramount that had to be cleared up. Marcus Loew's son had married Zukor's daughter, so an alliance existed between the two companies. The Department of Justice wanted that alliance abrogated because it would look as if Fox were absorbing Paramount as well as Loew's. If William Fox could make sure that all ties between Loew's and Paramount were broken, he could go ahead and take control of Loew's Inc.

Fox liked to talk business on the golf course. He would discuss the matter with Nick Schenck that Wednesday at the Lakeview Country Club on Long Island.

It was in July of 1929 when Fox, in the backseat of his Rolls-Royce, was being driven to the golf course to meet Schenck. "I was dreaming of the perfect conclusion," he recalled. "Life had just begun, and this was to be the greatest stepping-stone of my career. At fifty-one, I was to be the head of the largest company of its kind in the world."

Fox's chauffeur took a wrong turn. A Ford car came speeding toward them over a hill, and the head-on crash sent the Rolls spinning into the air. When it landed, Fox crawled out from underneath, blood pouring from his head. His chauffeur was dead. The woman who had been driving the other car was severely injured. Fox was carried to the hospital where he had several blood transfusions. He was near death for ten days. Then he was taken to Fox Hall where he remained inert for three months. His business affairs fell into disarray.

It is ironic that it was a Ford that helped to cause Fox's downfall. Fox had taken on Henry Ford in the early twenties, threatening to ruin him in his newsreels if Ford did not stop publishing anti-Semitic articles in Ford's newspaper, the *Dearborn Independent*. Fox had discovered that more people died in car accidents involving Ford cars than in any other cars. He planned to have his newsreel men photograph accidents, interview grieving relatives, and then have an automobile expert explain which part of the Ford car was defective. Millions of people would see this footage, so Fox warned Henry Ford. The derogatory article Ford was planning to write about Fox never appeared, and Ford did tone down his anti-Semitic diatribes.

In bed at Fox Hall after his nearly fatal accident, Fox was visited by one of his business associates, Harley L. Clarke. A wealthy man from Chicago, Harley Clarke had gone into the business of manufacturing movie projectors. His company, National Theatre Supply, made about 85 percent of all projection machines used in America. Fox used those machines in his theaters. But Fox was also experimenting in his laboratories with projection machines that would throw big images upon a wide screen. Clarke realized that if Fox perfected the experimental machines, Clarke's movie-projector manufacturing business would be ruined. So he suggested they go into business together. Fox and Clarke formed a corporation known as the Grandeur Company, which they owned fifty-fifty. The Grandeur system was being developed on 80 mm film for wide screens, and *The Big Trail*, with John Wayne, was already in production for showing on the huge Roxy screen.

Harley Clarke said he wanted to buy Fox's voting shares in Fox's companies. William Fox found this an odd request and said he wasn't interested in selling. Then he heard that rumors were circulating that his brain had been damaged in the

car accident. On the advice of his publicity director, Fox
called a news conference. Thirty reporters showed up at his
estate on Columbus Day in 1929, and Fox met them on his
boat landing, where they could see his impressive yacht loll-
ing in the water. His publicity director Glendon Allvine
recalled:

> Fox began the press conference by referring to himself
> in the third person. William Fox has invited you to his
> home today to tell you something of his plans for the
> next twenty-five years. When a man reaches fifty, three
> courses lie ahead. He may dream of his past accomplish-
> ments, he may rest on his oars, or he may make ambi-
> tious plans for the future. The latter of these possibilities
> appeals to William Fox.

Fox reminded the reporters that he was the president of
Fox Film Corporation, owned 53 percent of it, and was the
president of Fox Theaters, owning 93 percent of that. His
sound-on-film pictures were far ahead of competing sound
films, and his Roxy theater earned $100,000 a week. He
owned the patents to the Tri-Ergon sound process. His Movietone newsreels were so successful he was able to open his
own newsreel theater, the Embassy, on Broadway. He announced that he would produce films for teaching science in
high schools and colleges and that he would make his sound-
on-film system available to clergymen. Next morning the
newspapers carried word that William Fox was not debili-
tated at all.

On the evening of October 24, 1929, Fox was well enough
to go into Manhattan. He ventured out to attend a banquet
for a newly appointed officer of the national committee of
the Republican party. Several members of Hoover's cabinet
were at the dinner as well as several members of the Senate
and House. The heads of every large financial group were
there, including the Rockefellers and the Morgans.

Hoover's secretary of commerce made a speech. He said to
the assembled bankers of America that the country was in a

grave condition because people were refusing to buy bonds. He said that all great nations were built on the public's willingness to buy bonds, and that unless a market could be created for bonds, and the current speculation in common stock terminated, the nation was threatened. "He drew a picture so black," Fox said, "that I trembled at the thought of what would occur the next day when these hundred bankers would reach their offices, and when the bell would ring at ten o'clock on Wall Street. No one could have listened to him that night without wanting to sell every share of stock he owned the next morning."

Which is what William Fox did. And so did almost everyone else. Word went out by telephone and telegraph that the bottom was dropping out, and sell orders redoubled in volume. There was a stampede to get out of the market. Leading stocks went down, down, down. The roar of voices that rose from the New York Stock Exchange became a roar of panic. Brokers from all over the country, their customers standing frightened before them, tried to reach the Stock Exchange in New York to find out what was happening, but telephone lines were clogged, and few could get through. Over sixteen million shares of stock were thrown on the market by frantic sellers. The panic, which lasted several days, was felt by the entire nation.

Because it was necessary only to put down a fraction of a stock's cost in order to own it, like buying a house, even those with moderate incomes owned stock. Now people lost their stocks before they had even paid for them. In every town there were families that dropped from showy affluence into debt. Day by day the newspapers reported suicides. The Loew's shares that Fox had purchased for $73 million fell until they were worth less than half that much.

Fox's brokers began to call his margins. The Loew's shares dropped to a point where Fox's margin was short $10 million. Bank after bank refused to lend him money. The federal government began an action against Fox requiring him to divest himself of the Loew's shares.

Herbert Hoover made cheerful speeches, saying good times were just ahead, that only the lunatic fringe of specula-tors had been driven out of the stock market. Workers lost their jobs, farmers lost their farms. Migrant workers fleeing the Dust Bowl went to Los Angeles and set up shacks on the edge of the city. Hoboes traveled the rails. On the streets of New York men sold apples to passersby.

The public grew tired of sound pictures after the novelty of them wore off, and box-office receipts declined. Those stars who had been with the studios since the silent days and were commanding huge salaries were phased out and new players hired at half the price. John Gilbert, who made $250,000 a picture, was replaced in 1931 by Clark Gable, who earned $350 a week.

In New England, independent theater owners started price-cutting. To lure customers they offered two feature pictures for the price of one, an expensive picture and one cheap B picture. The big theater chains refused to follow the example set by independent exhibitors, but soon they were forced to because the public began to demand a double bill. Audiences could now expect to see two features, a newsreel, a short sub-ject, and a cartoon. A double bill required twice the product, so the talent department in New York had to find twice as many new faces as before. Talent scouts combed Broadway, Off-Broadway, little theaters, colleges, acting schools, stock companies, opera, musical revues, and ballet. They looked for foreign-speaking actors, because movies would be made in two or three languages, usually English, German, and Spanish. The *New York Times* wrote:

> Since the vastly increased popularity of talking films, stage and screen players and also singers are constantly having tests made in NY of their voices and their per-sonal appearance. These tests, which cost from $100 to $250, according to the length of the film used, are sent to Hollywood, where the producing executives decide whether or not the player is suited to work in any forth-coming productions. Even John McCormack, the well-

known Irish tenor, who last week signed a contract to appear in a talking and singing picture for the Fox Film Corporation, "made a test," as it is alluded to.

Youngsters who previously would have been considered too green for a contract now had a chance to gain experience in low-budget pictures. Drama coaches, singing teachers, and dancing masters were hired by the studios to get the novices up to par. A youngster with potential did not have to pay one cent for the lessons that might one day make him a star. The B movie served as a training ground for directors, producers, and writers, too.

While other film producers were busy with matters pertaining to their studios, William Fox was scrambling to keep himself from bankruptcy. Wall Street was full of rumors of the impending collapse of Fox Film and Fox Theaters. Stockholders began to believe that William Fox had managed his companies badly. Word came to Fox from a Wall Street insider that a pool had been organized and a raid on Loew's was to begin, which is to say that the price of Loew's shares was going to be driven down even further. Will Hays visited Fox.

It was upon Fox's recommendation that Will Hays got his $250,000-a-year job with the movie industry. At the beginning of their friendship Fox had told Hays of his ambition to manage the greatest moving-picture organization in the world, and Hays had told Fox that he had a right to that ambition, because no one in the entire industry was more competent. Now Will Hays suggested that Fox sell his companies. He had a friend willing to buy. Was there someone Will Hays thought more competent than William Fox? The mysterious buyer turned out to be Fox's partner in the movie projector business, Harley L. Clarke, a man who knew nothing about film production.

"I gave Hays the price that night," Fox recalled. "I told him that before the market crash, Clarke once inquired if my voting shares were for sale, and I told him then that I had no intention of selling them, but if I did the price would be $100 million." Now Fox offered to sell for a third of that price.

Harley Clarke took control of Fox's companies and ran them into the ground.

Legal wrangling continued. In 1932 a Senate committee accused Fox of deliberately wrecking his own companies, and the Fox Film Corporation instituted a suit against him. Then Fox was accused of income-tax evasion. Then a lunatic threatened to kidnap his grandsons and left notes demanding $5 million. The police found the culprit to be a chauffeur Fox had once fired. Fox's lawyers' fees were in the millions. The Loew's stock Fox had acquired, more than 600,000 shares, was sold on the open market, making Loew's Inc. the most widely held of all the movie stocks. Because so many citizens owned Loew's stock the public felt more interested in and involved with Metro-Goldwyn-Mayer's activities than with those of any other studio.

In October 1936, when the government demanded $3 million in back taxes, William Fox declared bankruptcy. He estimated that in 1930 he was worth "about one hundred million," and now he was penniless. The bankruptcy judge, J. Warren Davis, told Fox that he, the judge, needed $15,000 for his daughter's wedding. Fox sent the money to him in an unmarked envelope. Then Judge Davis said that he needed $12,000 more. Fox came through with that money, too. The federal government traced the money to Judge Davis's daughter in Florida, and Fox was indicted on a charge of conspiracy to obstruct justice through bribing a federal judge. He pleaded guilty and was sentenced to a year in prison and fined $3,000.

He was sent to Lewisburg Penitentiary in Pennsylvania's rolling valleys, where Amish people keep pristine farms. Bucolic roads led to a chilling sight, a massive red-brick building shaped like a Florentine palace with a high tower in the middle. The use of the building could not be mistaken. There were guard towers and high walls. Pheasants pecked in the grass near small houses that were government housing for the prison employees. They pecked in the fields of corn and hay and near the pigpens and henhouses where William Fox was forced to work.

William Fox's visitor, used to being greeted by a butler, was now greeted by a metal door that opened by itself, then clanked shut. An unseen man's voice said, "Do you have any alcohol, drugs, or weapons?" Fox's visitor entered not a foyer hung with expensive paintings but a concrete yard where a door marked "Control Center" opened. A maid did not take the visitor's hat and coat. Instead, a guard frisked the visitor and relayed his name on an intercom. In Fox's art collection there were fifty-two paintings, including the work of Gainsborough, Van Dyck, Tintoretto, Murillo, and Rubens. Now his visitor passed walls decorated with oil paintings done by prisoners. The images were conventional, a covered bridge or a farm scene, but the atmosphere in the paintings was gloomy, and the style was dead. At the end of a corridor was the infirmary, some offices on either side of the hall, and a room with a table and a few chairs. Women waiting to see their husbands were explaining to small children that Daddy was "in the army." Down below, a courtyard full of inmates, some lying around, others standing in groups, others by themselves just sitting. From the bars on the windows hung string bags of food from home.

William Fox was thin, weak, and embarrassed-looking in drab prison clothes. Only his expensive shoes showed his former life. "I would have been wiser," he said, "to work with Jewish financiers like the others in the industry do. I was not wise to trust Episcopalians."

He languished in prison for six months. Upon release he tried to get going again by setting up an office on Fifth Avenue. "Now there is nothing to stop me," he told a reporter from the *Times*, "from putting my name on a new company. I started with nothing, and I'm not afraid to try again. Imagination and courage are still the essential elements for success in this business." He took an option on a 1,500-acre site in Los Angeles where he planned to build a studio. He planned to produce pictures and distribute them and give writers, directors, and stars a percentage of the profits. But no one would lend him the money to start again. He sank so deeply into obscurity that the *New York Times* referred to him as "the late William Fox" while he was still alive.

TWELVE

The Mob Muscles In

IT SEEMS strange that William Fox was in Lewisburg Penitentiary at the same time as Willie Bioff. There should be one place for great men to go when they make a desperate mistake, and another place for worms.

"We had about twenty percent of Hollywood when we got in trouble," Willie Bioff bragged after he was sentenced to ten years. "If we hadn't got loused up we'd of had fifty percent. I had Hollywood dancin' to my tune."

Willie Bioff from Chicago found himself with nothing to do when Prohibition was repealed. He was a tiny tributary of Al Capone's bloody river and was pals with those who enjoyed smashing the legs of merchants who wouldn't pay up. Bioff was in business for himself, but the mob didn't cash in because his profits were so small. What he did was organize meat peddlers. Butchers who had stores resented those peddlers standing outside their doors selling on the sidewalk and harassing them. Willie Bioff organized them, divided Chicago into territories, and for a fee protected each peddler's territory.

He went into this business having failed as a pimp, an occupation he was later to repudiate by calling it a "youthful indiscretion." He was fond of saying he was only twenty-three when he did time for pandering, but court records prove he was thirty-six. He was sentenced to six months in jail but stayed there only eight days. No one bothered to care until years later.

He was arrested for burglary as "Morris Bioff," for loitering as "Henry Martin," and for trying to break into the Chicago Poultry Union Hall. He had such a record of arrests the Chicago police branded him a public enemy in 1933.

Bioff was about five-feet-six, weighed two hundred pounds, and had powerful shoulders, no neck, a muscular torso, moon face, double chin, muddy eyes, and an ugly scar under his lip. His walk was a swagger, and he poked the person he was talking to with a stumpy index finger. To make himself appealing he splashed on lilac after-shave. He was proud of his hard past. He said:

> Don't let nobody hand you the bunk that I wasn't born in Chicago. There's been talk that I'm a foreigner. There was a lot of kids, like in most poor families. When I was eight, my old man tossed me out on the street to shift for myself. I peddled papers, run errands, and so on, and met a lot of people. I got wise to the trick of stealin' hams from Swift's warehouse back a the yards. Some weeks I wouldn't have nothing but ham to eat, except maybe apples that I would sneeze from peddlers' carts on South Halsted Street.

Bioff did not come into his own surname and see that it pointed the way to his future occupation as an extortionist until he met George Browne.

Georgie had been a stagehand and must have been likeable because he was elected business agent of the local stagehand's union in Chicago. He hefted around scenery in one of Barney Balaban's theaters. Barney Balaban, who eventually became the president of Paramount in 1936, was the son of an immigrant grocer. With his brother Abe and his friend Sam Katz he built a theater empire from a start with one nickelodeon in Chicago. The Balaban and Katz chain of theaters was nationwide and was the first, in 1917, to introduce air-conditioning. After talkies arrived and replaced live performances, stagehands who had set up scenery for vaudeville acts in Balaban's theaters found themselves unemployed.

Georgie Browne and Willie Bioff saw how they could feed off the distress of the members of the stagehands' union in Chicago, where, in the early thirties, two hundred and fifty out of four hundred members were out of work. They set up a soup kitchen where unemployed stagehands could get free meals and where employed stagehands could get a meal for only thirty-five cents. The soup kitchen was financed by local politicians who expected Bioff and Browne to campaign for them among the stagehands. If a local politician wanted to share a meal with the brethren so he could shake some hands, it cost him from twenty to fifty dollars. Bioff and Browne made a small profit but not enough to attract attention.

The stagehands began to look to Bioff and Browne as benefactors. That made them feel strong enough to go right to the top to shake down Barney Balaban. They reminded Balaban that he was the cause of hardship to previously loyal employees and told him that it cost $7,500 a year to run a soup kitchen. Barney Balaban said he would be glad to contribute that amount. Willie Bioff came into his name on the spot. "Then we might as well make it fifty thousand" he said. Balaban was appalled. He refused. Bioff knew that if he told the stagehands that Balaban did not want to help them he could make them strike. The stagehands' union included projectionists. Bioff told Balaban that if he didn't pay up, the projectionists in his Chicago theaters would walk out. This was a serious threat, because projectors were complicated to run even before sound, but now with discs to synchronize they required even more skill. To save himself from losing millions, Barney Balaban agreed to buy off Willie for $20,000.

Imagine the delight of Bioff and Browne, who now had more money for themselves than they had ever had before in their lives. They kept all of it and went to celebrate their easy victory at a gambling resort run by a big-time gangster, Nick Circella. It was hard not to notice two lively bumpkins who spent $300 drinking and bragging. Nick Circella reported what he had seen to his colleagues in what was left of Al Capone's gang.

Bioff and Browne were contacted by a man they knew not to mess with. He presented them with an invitation to a meeting. Attending the meeting was Frank Nitti, considered the brains behind Al Capone and known to hoodlums as "the enforcer." (He ended up shot dead and tossed like garbage on the railroad tracks.) Louis Compagna, alias "Louis Cook," "Lefty Louis," and "Little New York," an early bodyguard of Capone's, was at the meeting. Paul DeLucia, alias "Paul Ricca," who was involved in the killing of a Chicago newspaperman, was there, and so was Francis Maritote, alias "Frank Diamond" and known as "the Immune," because of his freedom from conviction and the frequency of his arrests on charges ranging from larceny to murder. Also attending were Charles Gioe, alias "Cherry Nose Joy," Frank Rio, and Harry Hochstein.

The wealth of the motion-picture industry was fascinating to everyone in America, and it was constantly played up by industry executives who wanted to impress investors and fan-magazine writers who wanted to delight readers. Hollywood was the third largest news source in the country, after Washington and New York. There were at least three hundred correspondents responsible for sending out news of the studios to the world. Money was almost always the focus of stories. Millions were spent on movie-star salaries, story properties, elaborate sets, and theater decoration. Actually, if the size of the industry were measured by dollar volume of business, the motion-picture industry was not even among the first forty richest. It was surpassed by such industries as laundries, hotels, restaurants, loan companies, investment trusts, liquor, tobacco, and musical instruments. There were forty-four other industries that reported a larger gross income in 1937 than did the combined motion-picture producing and exhibition corporations.

Photoplay, Silver Screen, Screen Book, Screenland, Modern Screen, Motion Picture, and dozens of other fan magazines reported on the wealth of the stars, all of whom, so the stories went, deserved every penny because of their hard childhoods and their current sacrifices. Even though Marion Davies had gold faucets in her bathroom and Will Rogers kept polo ponies, they wished they could live a simple life because the price of fame was so high. "In Hollywood, health, friends, beauty, even life itself, are sacrificed on the altar of terrible ambition." Money was pouring into Hollywood, supposedly, at a time when men on the streets of New York were selling apples. Readers at beauty parlors getting their marcels, married to men who had lost their jobs or taken a pay cut, felt inspired, not envious, and escaped from the worries of the day by reading about how Clark Gable's fabulous success was ruining his marriage.

The mob understood that the entire motion-picture industry could be tied up by controlling the "boothmen." Since the motion-picture business was nationwide, the mob set about organizing all projectionists across the country.

The target was the five major film companies that dominated the industry in the thirties, three old and two new. Paramount, Loew's, and Warners had grown large with time; Twentieth Century-Fox and RKO were giants at birth.

Though the feelings between Mayer and Nick Schenck were poisoned after Marcus Loew's death, and the uneasiness of the truce they made permeated both the home office and the studio, they did come together in 1933 for the creation of a new film company, Twentieth Century Pictures. Nick, who continued as president of Loew's after Fox's downfall, invested in Twentieth Century to help his older brother Joe, who had been a successful producer in the early years. Nick's brother had decided to go into partnership with Darryl F. Zanuck, who quit his job as chief of production at Warners to start his own company.

Mayer invested in Twentieth Century to help his daughter Edith's husband, William Goetz. Some said that William Goetz deserved to be vice president of Twentieth Century; others said Louie bought him the job.

For the sake of a daughter and a brother, Louie and Nick wanted Twentieth Century Pictures to succeed, so they loaned the new studio some of Metro-Goldwyn-Mayer's top players. Twentieth Century did so well that in 1935 it was able to acquire the enfeebled Fox Film Company, getting not only all of Fox's theaters but also the star who kept Fox Films alive, Shirley Temple. The number-one box-office draw said in later life that of all the famous laps she had to sit on, her favorite belonged to J. Edgar Hoover, who did not jiggle his knees and bounce her.

The fifth major film company in America at the time that the mob muscled in was RKO. Born in 1928 with $80 million of working capital, three hundred theaters, and four studios, RKO represented the merger of three companies: the Radio Corporation of America, the Film Booking Office of America, and the Keith-Albee-Orpheum theater chain.

The Radio Corporation of America was created by General Electric and Westinghouse to control patents essential to radio broadcasting. General Electric scientists, like those at the telephone company, came upon a way to make movies talk. David Sarnoff, RCA's general manager, was assigned the task of exploiting the new sound method, Photophone. After failing to interest Loew's and Paramount in Photophone, Sarnoff decided to buy a movie company. For $500,000 he bought controlling interest in Joseph Kennedy's Film Booking Offices, which had not only a production studio but also a system of national distribution.

Now Sarnoff needed theaters that he could wire with the Photophone process. In 1928 the Keith-Albee vaudeville chain took over the Orpheum chain. The Keith-Albee-

Orpheum circuit had three hundred vaudeville houses. Sarnoff approached the owners of the new Keith-Albee-Orpheum company, who gave up trying to make vaudeville big again and gladly sold out. Sarnoff became president of a new vertically integrated company, the Radio-Keith-Orpheum Corporation, or RKO. Alfred Hitchcock used Photophone in his first talkie, *Blackmail*.

All of the "Big Five," as the major film companies were called, produced motion pictures, operated worldwide distribution outlets, and owned chains of theaters. Though competition between them was fierce, they cooperated by loaning each other movie stars and by showing each other's pictures in their theaters.

Loew's Inc. spent about $28 million a year on pictures. It was Nick Schenck in Times Square whose job it was to divide that amount among A and B movies. The distribution department in New York determined how many stories in each cost category would be made.

Stories were selected on the basis of previous financial success, either as a play, novel, or short story. Most movies had proven their worth in some other form before reaching the screen. To find further material, dozens of "readers" hired by the M-G-M story departments in Hollywood, New York, and Europe, sifted through novels, plays, and short stories and submitted reports on everything they read: "Only one word describes this book, S-E-X. If it isn't performed it's talked about, chapter in and chapter out. And the talk gets pretty rough. The Stanley character is a plain boor, as uncouth as they come. And as for Boris' mother . . . ugh. Take the bed out of the story, no story." Or "screamingly funny film could be made," or "story could stand more incident." The selection was determined by which stars were to be showcased, and what kinds of stories the distribution department thought would sell. Exhibitors exerted a conservative influence upon American films.

Once a property was selected the project was turned over to a producer at the studio. In Culver City, Irving Thalberg

was in charge of assigning the property to one of ten associate producers, each a specialist in a particular kind of picture: comedy, action film, animal story, love story. Each
associate producer had to make about six pictures a year,
which meant they supervised the writing of the screenplay,
assigned a director and cast, and helped organize the various
departments involved in the film—the art department, costumes, makeup, and editing. Because production revolved
around stars, publicity and promotion were involved right
from the start. If a war picture was about to be produced, the
public began to hear months in advance about the heroic war
record of its male star.

*   *   *

This, then, was the industry that the mob decided to hold up.
George Browne wanted to be elected president of the International Alliance of Theatrical Stage Employees (IATSE), the
labor organization that negotiated for projectionists. Browne
said that he had once run for president but had been defeated. The syndicate asked Browne who it was who had not
voted for him. Browne replied, New York City, Jersey City,
Cleveland, and St. Louis. The syndicate called upon their connections to help convince local unions to support Georgie
Browne. Abe ("Longy") Zwillman in New Jersey, Lucky Luciano in New York, Al Palizzi in Cleveland, and Johnny
Dougherty in Missouri were assigned that task. Louis "Lepke"
Buchalter, Lucky Luciano's right-hand man, was ordered to
take to Luciano this message from Nitti: "Local 306, New
York projectionists, is to vote for Browne."
    Buchalter replied, "I don't have to see Lucky on that,
Frank. I can handle that myself. I'll also see Kaufman of New
Jersey and see that Longy delivers that outfit."
    IATSE held its annual convention in Louisville, Kentucky.
Half a dozen dangerous men known as the "educational com-
mittee" circulated among the crowd of mostly honest family
men, glad to be employed during the Depression, and let it be
known that Browne was to be elected. George Browne was

elected without opposition. There was no violence. Browne became president and he appointed Bioff as his representative. Nick Circella was appointed by the syndicate to spy on George Browne and Willie Bioff to be sure they gave the syndicate 50 percent of their take. They would take from both ends of the industry. Union dues paid by thousands of workers would be pocketed, and a hefty sum would come from producers for protection against strikes.

Circella cautioned Bioff and Browne against "getting caught wrong" by the mob. If they needed help they were to call upon Frank Costello, the "slot machine king," and Lucky Luciano, who controlled projectionists in New York.

Willie Bioff went back to Chicago and called together the Chicago Exhibitors Association. He pointed out that only one projectionist was employed in each of the Chicago theaters. Bioff said that elsewhere in the country two men were employed in each projection booth. Bioff told the theater men that the union was going to demand a two-man booth in Chicago. A projectionist in Chicago earned about $95 a week, working five hours a day, six days a week. Barney Balaban warned Willie Bioff that the employment of an extra man in each booth would cost $500,000 and would bankrupt the theaters. Bioff said, "You'll have two men, or else. If that is going to kill grandma, grandma is going to die." But, if Balaban wanted to save a lot of trouble for himself, he could pay Bioff $100,000. Balaban paid. The mob took half.

The syndicate then said to Bioff, "We got a big family so we'll need more dough. You and Georgie now get one-third, not half." Bioff and Browne objected. Then a pal of theirs, Tommy Malloy, who had been extorting money from movie-theater operators in Chicago, was murdered for failing to share his spoils with the syndicate. Then another pal who was trying to organize apprentice motion-picture operators was rubbed out. Willie and Georgie decided that one-third was better than death.

The film industry had previously managed to operate without strong unions. IATSE had no power in Hollywood.

Hollywood worked on the "call system." Workers registered for jobs at the union hiring hall on Santa Monica Boulevard. When the studios were at the peak of production, most of the technicians, laborers, carpenters, and painters were busy. But there were many weeks when men and women had to sit at the telephone waiting for a call to work. Most were not engaged on a regular weekly or monthly salary, and very few worked fifty-two weeks a year. There were a great many days of leisure but no vacations, because nobody could afford to risk being away from the telephone. If a worker wasn't right there to take the call, the job was given to someone else.

When the workers decided to organize, they did so based on their line of work. There was the United Studio Technicians Guild, made up of 7,500 prop makers, nurserymen, miniature makers, set electricians, and special-effects men who made snow, rain, earthquakes, and shipwrecks. There were the Associated Actors and Artists of America and the American Federation of Actors, headed by Sophie Tucker. There were the Screen Actors Guild, the Screen Publicists Guild, and the Federated Motion Pictures Crafts Guild, made up of hairstylists, studio painters, makeup artists. Musicians had a union and so did carpenters.

The production of one picture required the services of a microphone man, recorder, two sound grips, makeup man (with up to nine assistants), hairdresser (with up to twelve assistants), costume designer, head electrician (who had up to thirty-two on his staff), cameraman, second cameraman, two assistant cameramen, still cameramen, actors, stand-ins, director, and others, all belonging to separate organizations.

Louis B. Mayer, like many self-made men, detested unions. He believed trade unions would ruin America. But the National Recovery Act of 1933 encouraged labor to organize and required that management recognize labor's demands. The federal government encouraged workers to demand shorter hours and better wages. Hollywood producers were obliged to bargain with dozens of different classifications of workers. Bargaining went on day in and day out.

Willie Bioff convinced labor leaders in Hollywood that one union, IATSE, could bargain with producers better than dozens of unions and that, if the various Hollywood locals would come under the IATSE umbrella, he would guarantee a 10 percent pay hike within the first year.

The Hollywood unions were reluctant to hand over power to Willie Bioff. To show Hollywood workers that he could make good his boast, Bioff called a strike in Chicago, and four hundred theaters went dark for two days. Theater executives agreed to give Chicago projectionists a 10 percent pay increase. Hollywood workers were impressed. They voted to put their unions under the control of Willie Bioff's parent organization. More than twelve thousand workers began paying 2 percent of their salaries to Willie Bioff so that he would represent them with management. No accounting was made for that 2 percent assessment, which gave Bioff and Browne $2 million a year, nor were any union meetings ever held. But Willie Bioff did what the separate unions were unable to do. He did get pay increases for the workers, because he controlled the lifeblood of the industry, the projectionists.

There were studio workers in Hollywood who wanted nothing to do with Willie Bioff. They kept their unions independent and tried negotiating with producers on their own. But when they went out on strike, as was their right, and formed a picket line outside the offices of management, gunmen from Chicago, fortified by longshoremen from New York, suddenly showed up and began clubbing and kicking picketing workers. This happened every time an independent union went on strike. Management, said Bioff, was trying to smash the unions. Management would rather bludgeon picketers than pay higher salaries. Newspaper cameramen who photographed the melee saw their plates destroyed and were warned to shoot no more pictures. Producers tried to convince workers that it was Bioff calling in the roughnecks, but workers blamed management, and Bioff's reputation was enhanced every time a picketing worker was injured.

But there were men and women working at the studios who

saw the situation clearly. Ed Wentworth, a carpenter at
M-G-M, withdrew from the carpenters' union when Willie's
organization took it over. Wentworth had belonged to the carpenter's union for forty years, starting in New York where he
had once been president of his local union. Seven of his fellow workers withdrew from the union with him. "I will tell
you, gentlemen, if you want an old man's candid opinion, you
have no more chance of doing anything here, you seven men,
than a snowball would have in hell for the simple reason that
there isn't a producer in Hollywood who would dare produce
a picture without the IATSE jurisdiction over it, for it
wouldn't be shown in any theater in the country." Ed
Wentworth lost his job because he would not join IATSE.

At Warners, a capable electrician named Francis Harrison
Black was dismissed for speaking out against Willie Bioff.
Many workers tried to oppose Bioff, and many lost their jobs.
Because most of them had families to support, they had no
choice but to crawl back to Willie and agree to join IATSE.
They were allowed to join but only if they signed the follow-
ing apology:

> I, the undersigned, an expelled member of the IATSE
> who has appealed this expulsion, being cognizant of the
> fact that this expulsion is the result of my activities dur-
> ing the past three or four months, which were detrimen-
> tal to the interests of the IATSE, do hereby sincerely
> apologize to the Alliance, its members, and particularly
> to the international officers, for all derogatory state-
> ments made by me against them. I am profoundly sorry
> now that I made these statements and committed these
> actions, which I admit and now realize have caused a
> vast amount of trouble, expense and unrest in the affairs
> of the Alliance and have seriously jeopardized the wel-
> fare of the Alliance and its members. I have reached the
> conclusion that my activities were wrong. . . . I am willing
> that I be placed on probationary status for a period of
> two years, and during this probation I agree not to be a
> candidate for any office, either elective or appointive,
> and if during this period of time I engage in any acts in

violation of the constitution of my local union or the IATSE, I agree voluntarily to surrender my membership card. I further pledge that I will be loyal to the IATSE. . . . I am grateful for this opportunity extended to me and solemnly promise that my conduct in the future will be such that the officials of the Alliance will never regret their leniency extended toward me.

"Them producers," Bioff bragged after securing another pay increase, "would like to see me dead in every room in this building."

Bioff took himself to New York, the heart of the artichoke. At 1540 Broadway he marched into Nick Schenck's office and introduced himself. "Now look," he said, "I'll tell you why I'm here. I want you to know that I'm the boss. I elected Mr. Browne, and I want two million dollars." Nick told Willie he was crazy. Bioff said, "That's what it has to be, and you have to come through with it." Nick asked how he was supposed to get $2 million. Bioff said, "Stop this nonsense. It will cost you a lot more if you don't do it."

Accidents began to happen in Loew's theaters. Pictures were run backwards, newsreels appeared in the middle of feature attractions, pipes burst. One manager reported an outbreak of bedbugs in his theater. The accidents seemed random, at first. Joe Vogel, who was in charge of Loew's theaters in New York, heard of accidents from fourteen of his theaters. Then Nick Schenck realized that Willie Bioff had orchestrated the chaos. A phone call from an unidentified person informed Nick that $100,000 would stop the accidents. Nick called in Dave Bernstein, Loew's treasurer. Bernstein fiddled with the books, manipulated expense vouchers, and came up with $100,000 in cash, which Nick took to the Waldorf-Astoria in an envelope and handed to a man he described as "one dog whose bite would be as bad."

"I've found out that dickering with these picture producers goes about the same all the time," Willie Bioff said to a reporter who visited him in his suite at the Waldorf-Astoria, where he was posing as labor's best friend. "You get into a room with them and they start yelling and hollering about how they're bein' held up and robbed. That goes on and on. Me, I'm a busy man and don't get too much sleep. I always go to sleep when that roaring starts. After a while it dies down and the quiet wakes me up. And I say, 'All right, gentlemen, do we get the money?'"

Nick spoke to his brother Joe and found out that Joe had been buying off Willie for months. Joe had so far paid Bioff $100,000 out of petty cash and phony expense vouchers.

Nick spoke to Albert Warner in his office on West 44th Street, Warner Brothers headquarters. Albert Warner, vice president and treasurer of Warner Bros. Pictures, said he had refused to pay Willie Bioff $50,000 a year but was so scared he had hired two bodyguards to follow him everywhere. His brother Harry, at the studio in California, had done the same. Finally, unable to stand the strain, Albert Warner agreed to pay Bioff $50,000 in $10,000 installments. Warner left the $100 bills in a sealed envelope with his secretary.

Earl Allvine, a director for Fox Movietone News, was shooting a short subject in Chicago when he was visited by Willie Bioff's men, who told him he needed more workers on the payroll. Allvine declined to hire anyone else and was visited personally by Willie Bioff, who called him a fresh punk and warned that if he wanted to take his pretty face back to New York he had better put six Bioff men on the payroll. Earl Allvine still refused, so he was beaten and left for dead in an alley. When he recovered he did what Willie had asked.

Bioff held a meeting in Nick Schenck's office. Albert Warner was there, and so were representatives from Twentieth Century-Fox and Paramount. Bioff said he had changed his mind. He would not demand two million from the industry. He would accept one million. Having stated his demand, he left the office so the film men could figure out how the industry would come up with $1 million a year. They decided it was in their best interest to fiddle with their books and give in to Willie's extortion. Losing one million was better than losing hundreds of millions.

There was a strange silence in the press about labor unrest in Hollywood. Normally, everything that went on at the studios was reported in the *Hollywood Reporter*, a pro-worker trade paper published daily in Los Angeles. About the rumors of extortion payments, about the studio strikes that were busted by gunmen, and about the workers who had lost their jobs because they would not join IATSE, the newspaper was mum. Circulation of the *Reporter* was small, but its influence was great. Franklin Delano Roosevelt had it delivered to the White House and read it every day.

William R. "Billy" Wilkerson, who founded the paper in 1930, once boasted to Mayer that the *Reporter* was more effective in propagating information about the motion-picture business than any wire service. To prove his point, Wilkerson had Louie supply a phony story about Clark Gable which was printed in the *Reporter* the following day. That one story generated more than five thousand clippings around the world.

The *Hollywood Reporter* was not the only enterprise that Billy Wilkerson owned. A dapper little man, he owned the Vendome, the most fashionable lunchtime restaurant in Hollywood, and the Trocadero, one of the most popular nightclubs. The Vendome and the Trocadero complemented each other because, since one was open only for lunch and the other only for dinner, the same staff could service both. Billy Wilkerson also owned Larue's, Humphrey Bogart's favorite restaurant, where spaghetti was served in huge, silver tureens.

Willie Bioff told Wilkerson that if he printed stories unfavorable to IATSE his waiters would walk out on strike, stink bombs would explode in the kitchen of Larue's, customers would get food poisoning at the Vendome, and bugs would show up in the food at the Troc. Billy Wilkerson, who had operated a speakeasy in New York before moving to Los Angeles, knew firsthand that a gangster's threat was serious. Instead of printing news of labor unrest at the studios, he sent fine wine to Willie Bioff. When Wilkerson went to Europe, he returned with gift handkerchiefs embroidered with Willie Bioff's name.

But Mayer was a tougher adversary. Louie told Willie Bioff that he would bury him alive. Willie Bioff said that if anybody was going to die it would be Louie. The argument was about the purchase of filmstock.

The duPont film company wanted to sell raw filmstock to Metro-Goldwyn-Mayer. The company was offering a 7 percent commission, about $50,000 a year, to anyone who could convince M-G-M to change from Kodak film to duPont. Willie Bioff wanted that $50,000. Eastman Kodak raw film was better than duPont, and for fifteen years Louie had been buying it from the same salesman. That Kodak salesman supported his family on the commission he made from selling his product to Metro-Goldwyn-Mayer. Nick told Louie to cancel all orders for Kodak film and buy only duPont film. When Mayer asked what he was supposed to say to his friend, the salesman at Kodak, Nick replied, "Just handle it, Louis." When Louie objected Nick said, "I want you to give that duPont commission to a friend of Willie Bioff's. Because he can make us plenty of trouble. But I don't want you to argue. Just do it."

Willie Bioff appointed his brother-in-law, an unemployed stonemason, as the subagent. Bioff paid him $125 a week for stopping at the duPont office to collect the commission. In selling raw filmstock to M-G-M, duPont would earn about $10,000 a month. Nick Schenck hoped that the $50,000 commission on film would satisfy Bioff and release Nick from coming up with $50,000 a year from the books of Loew's Inc.

Bioff, bloated with confidence, went to the Walt Disney studios to interfere with the cartoonists' strike. He told the cartoonists that if they affiliated with IATSE he would bring the powerful projectionists' union to side with them against management. As Hollywood actors had already done, the cartoonists rebelled and refused to allow Willie Bioff to represent them in any way. Bioff withdrew from the fight and retired to a deck chair in his lemon grove.

Bioff now lived on an eighty-acre San Fernando Valley estate that he called Laurie A. Rancho, after his wife Laurie. Nearby were the estates of Tyrone Power and Annabella, Clark Gable and Carole Lombard, Robert Taylor and Barbara Stanwyck, and Louella Parsons. Bioff's estate was surrounded by adobe walls four-feet thick. Visitors had to announce themselves over a private telephone system at the entrance. An electric switch at the house opened the gate, which then closed automatically. Bioff, who now dressed in expensive, well-tailored but unobtrusive clothes and wore no jewelry, was proud of his ranch and enjoyed showing it off to visitors. The ancient house had been fully renovated. There were two bedrooms with a bath between, a large den done in knotty pine, and an ornate living room with costly Louis Quinze furniture. A Kermanshah carpet, eighteen by twenty-six, covered the entire floor. The dining room was furnished in mahogany. "It's a good deal too fancy for Laurie and me," Bioff was proud to say. "We live on the porch and in the den. I see it's been said that I chiseled our furniture from the movie studios. It ain't so. All of those fancy-lookin' chairs and sofas and statues and whatnots were wedding gifts from my wife's family. They're in the furniture-manufacturing business in Chicago."

In comfortable chairs on the porch, Willie and his carefully screened visitors could survey eighty acres of alfalfa while being served cold beer by a maid in uniform. "I call my ranch the Laurie A. for my wife," Bioff said. "It's comfortable, but not swell. If alfalfa goes as high as ten dollars a ton, I make my living expenses out of the five to seven cuttings a year and fifty dollars a month clear on top of that. I got a Mexican couple to work the land, and one maid in the house." Rumor had it that each olive tree on his property cost $600 and that the cedars, palms, and other trees, which Willie bought and had transported to his property, were equally expensive. Bioff claimed that his landscaping cost $2,800, no more. "My wife is nuts about flowers," he said, "and so am I. We grow all our own fruit and vegetables. I'm building a playhouse, so I can have a place to entertain my pals."

To buy his ranch, Bioff "borrowed" $100,000 from Joe Schenck, president of Twentieth Century-Fox. Rumors began to spread. A studio craftsman, Jeff Kibre, spokesman for the Motion Picture Technicians Committee, charged that Joe Schenck paid Willie in an effort to bribe him and bring the four locals of IATSE and their membership of twelve thousand under the control and dominance of producers. Joe Schenck was accused of trying to block collective bargaining. Bioff was accused of being in the pay of the producers, not that he was extorting money but that he was being "bent" by it.

The rank and file refused to listen. Bioff was their hero. Union members said that under Bioff they had received pay raises and benefits, and they regarded the controversy over Bioff as something trumped up by management.

Mayer decided to launch an investigation of Willie Bioff. He hired private investigators to poke around in Chicago. He learned that Willie had been a bartender and handyman in a Chicago house of prostitution owned by Jack Zuta, a notorious vicemonger. Jack Zuta died, gangland style, and Willie was sent to jail for perjury and pandering. He served only eight days of his six-month term. The man who represented Bioff at the trial was Morris I. Green, now disbarred, who testified that efforts to fix the case had been made by Bioff's mentor, Jack Zuta, who was shot to death in 1930 in Wisconsin.

When Bioff in California heard that people had been digging up his record in Chicago, he went to the Mayer home and said, "There is no room for both of us in this world, and I will be the one who stays here." Badly frightened, Mayer realized he had little time to let Willie's crime record leak out. News of it had to pour out.

He told everything he had found out to Arthur Ungar, editor of *Daily Variety*, the west-coast branch of New York's *Variety*. Though Ungar was not pro-worker, he had noticed that his rival, Billy Wilkerson, printed nothing about Willie Bioff in the *Hollywood Reporter.* "Me?" explained Bioff. "I ain't an important guy. I only work for our president George E. Browne. I do what I'm told and go where I'm sent. There was a situation here in Hollywood that needed cleaning up, and Browne put me on the job."

Daily Variety blasted away at Bioff five times a week, stories about Willie's posh ranch, about the lavish landscaping. Editor Ungar called on the Los Angeles police for a bodyguard, and his office and home were watched for bombs. "Bomb Ungar?" Bioff guffawed. "Why, that's the last thing I'd think of. . . . The guys I work for don't pay no attention to what he writes anyway." Another journalist, Westbrook Pegler, a syndicated columnist known as journalism's "angry man," was writing about trade unions, and his investigations took him to Hollywood. Arthur Ungar gave Westbrook Pegler what information he had, and "Westy" began an in-depth investigation of the pudgy czar of the movie unions. Westbrook Pegler eventually won a Pulitzer prize for his exposé of labor racketeering.

The Illinois state's attorney's office sent for Willie Bioff, who was arrested and told that he had to finish serving his sentence. He said to the press:

I would call my plight persecution. Maybe I have been doing too much for the working man. I think the big interests are after me. I represent thirty-five thousand people who are fighting for better wages, conditions and hours. Who would be interested in going back all these years to dig up a skeleton and make an issue of it? This was all brought up at a time when it would cost producing companies a lot of money in increases. The money interests want to see me out of the picture. So do the C.I.O. and the Communists.

Bioff offered to resign, but union members wouldn't let him. They gave him a vote of confidence and said he would remain their leader even if he had to conduct labor negotiations from his jail cell. The unions criticized the California governor for granting Bioff's extradition to Chicago. Bioff's lawyer, State Senator Abe Marovitz, said that if Bioff had to serve time in Bridewell prison "it would leave him broken in spirit and health, and when he came out he probably would have to go on relief." The state sentator went on to say, "Bioff was raised with murderers and thieves, in one of the toughest neighborhoods of Chicago. It is a credit that he has raised himself to amount to something. He has completely rehabilitated himself."

The judge in Chicago set Bioff's bail at $5,000 and gave him permission to leave the state until his case was decided. Upon his return to Los Angeles, Bioff barged into Louie's house late at night and accused him of being the man behind the trouble. His goons surrounded Mayer in the front hall. They played a game of shoving Louie from one to the other, laughing like maniacs, until Bioff snapped his fingers and called them off. Louie fled to a health resort in Santa Monica where he received no telephone calls or visitors. He communicated with Nick Schenck via telegram.

Bioff rested comfortably at his ranch. He laughed at the idea that the union had made him wealthy. "It's the union that's rich," he said, "not Willie Bioff. We got four and a half million dollars in our war chest and we're ready for anything." His prized possessions were three gold, diamond-studded union-membership cards presented to him by union members in Cleveland, Chicago, and Hollywood. "Since I come to Hollywood," he bragged, "I've cost the producers six million dollars a year."

Willie's respite at his ranch was short-lived. He lost his case in Chicago and was sent to Bridewell prison where he remained for five months, from April to September. From his prison cell he continued to represent thirty-five thousand workers who rose to their feet and cheered when George Browne said Willie's "only unpardonable offense was that he had fought for the unpaid worker." Browne continued:

This man had walked the streets of Chicago for fifteen years, nothing was ever said or done to indicate to him that this old charge had not been officially dropped. The evidence presented showed that his lawyer had informed him eighteen years ago that he had won his case and, thinking nothing more of it, the matter was forgotten. It takes no great mental ability to discern what was back of all this persecution of this one man, when they have to go back eighteen years to dig up an unsettled misdemeanor in order to keep this leader of our studio members out of circulation. Let us hope that from now on he will be able to enjoy the peace he so richly deserves and that this persecution by his and our enemies will cease forever.

Westbrook Pegler investigated George Browne. In Chicago he located a hospital record showing admission of Browne for a gunshot wound and interviewed the patrolman who signed in the patient and the doctor who operated on him. Browne was revealed to have been a two-bit gunman before gaining respectability as a union leader.

At Twentieth Century-Fox, Joe Schenck's lavish "business expenses" attracted the notice of the Internal Revenue Service. Examining his books, federal agents noticed that $50,000 a year seemed to dribble away mysteriously. Joe Schenck was charged with income-tax evasion. On the stand he was asked about the mysterious $50,000. Under oath Joe Schenck told the whole country how he and other film producers had fallen victim to extortion. He said that he had a responsibility to stockholders to protect their investments, and that he had no choice except to go along with Willie Bioff because "in labor matters and other things they were running matters by force and fear and intimidation, and there was no limit to which they would not go if people did not do what they wanted."

"I never extorted a dime from anybody," Bioff told the press. "You can say for me that I am completely surprised."

Joe Schenck's secretary was called to the stand in federal court. She said that one day in June, three years earlier, she was summoned to Joe Schenck's office, and there sat Willie

Bioff. She said that the labor leader was a frequent visitor, that he and Mr. Schenck were always holding conferences. Miss Nolander saw a lot of money. She said that Mr. Schenck was counting it, and it amounted to $100,000. He handed it to her, and she put it in a manila envelope and tucked it into the little tin box that usually contained office petty cash. She was scrupulous about receipts and presented several in court. For instance, Joe Schenck purchased a luncheon for heiress Doris Duke for sixty cents and flowers for Shirley Temple for $25. The price for gold-plating the household silver was $364; one grocery bill came to over $500; and rental on a house in Palm Beach came to $400, all charged-off to business. As to why the grocery bill was so high, Miss Nolander said that Mr. Schenck had changed cooks three times during the month, and each new cook wanted to buy a lot of special spices to suit her own culinary whims. A note to Mr. Schenck in the tin box said, "Your laundry bill is high because you had Harpo and Mrs. Marx's laundry in there, too." Just before leaving for Europe, Joe Schenck took some of the $100,000 out of the box. Miss Nolander was asked how Mr. Schenck instructed her to enter the $100,000 transaction in the books. "He didn't," she said.

IATSE had to pay the legal fees of Willie Bioff and George Browne because one of the bylaws of the union stated that the union must provide legal protection for its officers. That particular bylaw was new and had been rushed through the annual convention by George Browne.

In federal court on charges of racketeering, Bioff was asked if he ever used an alias. He replied, "No."

"Did you ever use the name 'Link?'"

"The fact is, I was called Link."

"Ever use any other names?"

"I signed the name 'Berg' on a lease one time to save some money."

"Ever register at hotels under names other than your own?"

"I used the name 'William Bronson' at hotels and on airplane registrations to escape newspapermen."

"Did you ever use the name 'Joe Schenck'?"

"No."

"Did you ever use the name 'Harry Martin'?"

"I don't remember."

Executives from the major studios testified against him. The vice president of Paramount said, "I regarded the making of these payments to Mr. Bioff, and to such others as were associated with him in receiving these payments, as necessary to preserve my company against possible and very probable financial disaster." Albert Warner said that he paid Bioff $50,000, and Bioff was back the next year for another sum. "I told him that I thought the first $50,000 completed our arrangement. He said no, that I would have to pay and pay." The defense counsel asked Albert Warner if he "really believed that a man like Bioff could walk into your office and threaten personal violence." The witness replied, "Yes, sir." Albert Warner added that his company could not have stood the financial strain of a strike of theater projectionists. Nick Schenck testified that Bioff said, "You pay us or else we'll wreck your business." Mayer went on the stand and told how he was forced to give Bioff the duPont commission on raw film stock.

Bioff was sentenced to ten years and Browne to eight. Bioff's sentence was shortened to two years because he turned state's evidence and testified against the gangsters who backed him. Mention was made of Fred Blacker, whose nickname "Bugs" grew out of his habit of throwing bedbugs into theaters of nonpaying movie men. He could not be called into court because he had recently been murdered. Eight of Al Capone's gang were called into court, and Willie Bioff pointed his finger at each of them. That was when union members learned that the 2 percent of their salaries that they paid each year in dues went to enrich the pockets of the eight Capone men. All eight were sent to the federal penitentiary at Lewisburg, Pennsylvania.

Willie Bioff got out of jail in two years, moved to Arizona with his wife Laurie, and lived a quiet life as William Nelson.

Ten years went by, and the men he had fingered finished serving their time. One day Willie Bioff got into his pickup truck, turned the ignition key, and was blown to smithereens. "I don't know whether this was a professional gangster job or not," said Lieutenant Edmundson of the Phoenix sheriff's office. "But it certainly was an effective one." The blast threw Bioff twenty-five feet and scattered wreckage over a radius of several hundred feet. The garage door was blown out, the roof shattered, and windows broken. The blast rattled windows a mile away. It left only the twisted frame of the truck, the motor, and the wheels.

THIRTEEN

New Faces

IRVING Thalberg produced many of Metro-Goldwyn-Mayer's great movies—*The Big Parade, Anna Christie, Freaks, Strange Interlude, The Barretts of Wimpole Street, Mutiny on the Bounty, A Night at the Opera*—and was often given more credit than Mayer thought he deserved for the success of the studio. "Irving was my ideal for what I wanted to become," said Arthur Freed, the great producer of M-G-M musicals. "First of all, he had great taste. Second of all, he had a great sense of women."

When Irving Thalberg died in 1936, at age thirty-seven, in the middle of producing *Camille*, starring Greta Garbo, Mayer said, "Every son of a bitch in Hollywood is waiting for me to fall on my ass now that Irving has gone." What he probably meant was not everyone in Hollywood but Nick Schenck at the home office. Nick seized the opportunity of Thalberg's death to show his lack of faith in Louie. He sent a New York executive, Sam Katz, out to the west coast to help Louie with administrative duties. "He'll be like another arm to you, Louis," said Nick. "I don't need another arm," was the reply.

Though Mayer could see how Thalberg made the best use of stars, he believed himself to be the one who groomed glamour out of raw talent. That ability of his would not be dimmed by Thalberg's death. "I'm going to fool them," he said of Nick and his other detractors. "I'm going to build up the biggest collection of talent so that this studio can't fail." He told his staff on both coasts, "I want you to help me. If you come across any actor, director, or writer who looks promising, let me know and I'll sign them up." Mayer called his plan "strength in depth." There were scouts at every beauty contest, college play, Broadway opening, and modeling agency. He kept steady pressure on the New York talent department.

Hollywood's search for talent, which was, in fact, painfully sincere, produced dozens of publicity gimmicks. Twentieth Century-Fox took cameras into the Stork Club "searching for talent." Debutantes, saying it was "such fun," swarmed into the club on Sunday nights. Cameramen made tests, two silent reels, and showed them twice during the night at the club.

Paramount invited theater owners across the country to find the most beautiful girls in their communities. One girl would be chosen from all the local winners to receive a Paramount contract. Hundreds of photographs poured in. Overwhelmed, the man who was supposed to choose the winner told his assistant, "Just throw the pictures up in the air and when they land facedown, eliminate them. When you get down to the last ten, let me know." But the last ten were all so beautiful he threw them up in the air again and eliminated those that landed facedown. Finally, only one picture landed on its back. "I've been on my back ever since!" Ann Sheridan said. She made twenty films of no consequence for Paramount then went to Warners, where she was billed as the "Oomph Girl" and became a star.

The editor of the *Brooklyn Eagle*, in an effort to boost circulation, telephoned M-G-M's New York office asking if he might offer a screen test to the winner of a beauty contest he planned to organize. Al Altman met with the editor of the *Brooklyn Eagle* and stipulated that the contest be called a "Personality Poll." He wanted the contest open to girls who might not be beautiful but might have some spark of life.

Al described screen tests as they were in 1936:

> The purpose of the screen test is to show the movie directors and producers at the M-G-M studios in Culver City how you will look when you are magnified thirty to sixty times. The chances are one thousand to one that any defects you may have will be magnified. That is why I suggest suitable preparation long before you attempt your career in the movies.
>
> The cost of tests ranges from five hundred dollars up. After the test is completed and if it is satisfactory to the New York production executives it is sent to the West Coast studio where the M-G-M producing personnel view it. These tests may be run off in the same projection room and at about the same time as the rushes of a Joan Crawford, Shearer, or a Garbo production.
>
> Due allowance is made for inexperience, but, unless there is a marked individuality, unless you have something that is a little different from the rest and unless you show an understanding of acting principles or, as we call it, "showmanship," then in that case your Western colleagues refer to the Eastern talent executive in terms which I cannot describe in this genteel newspaper.
>
> The screen test director, after preliminary conversations with the applicant, decides tentatively the personality which he will attempt to create on the screen. In most instances this is the personality known to the close friends of the applicant herself and not the one she has on display for certain occasions. Once you become a star in the movies you may be given an opportunity to display your versatility, but for the test you will be asked simply to be yourself.
>
> Here's a tip: Never tell a motion picture executive that you want to duplicate any star's work. Having conferred with the director and having selected scenes which he

suggests best suited to your personality, you will then be
expected to memorize your scenes. A conversational
style of delivery is better than any attempt to project
your voice as though you were on the stage. Read your
lines just as though you were talking to your mother and
father, but pretend that your mother and father are busy
and that you have to impress them. So color your statements a little more than you normally would.

Two more important tips: Watch your hair and your
clothes. Study the smart magazines for suggestions.
Study various ways of doing your hair before a mirror.
For purposes of tests, makeup experts do not usually
evolve original coiffures, but they will co-operate so that
you may be assured that the proportion of hair to face
will be effectively balanced. Cameramen advise staying
away from white clothes, unless you are a very little girl.
Black form-fitting clothes are said to be best, particularly
when splashed with white. If you look like a million dollars when you face the camera for the first time, there is
a good chance that you will look that way on the screen.

The starting salary of an M-G-M contract player is usually around $75 a week. That is the salary at which Joan
Crawford started.

Everyone in America knew that the studios were looking
for a child to compete with Shirley Temple. Mothers who
loved the movies and wanted to be in them or near them
pushed their children to perform. An army of photographers
made a living off those women, promising them "clear, sharp
natural portraits of kiddies so essential for casting. Plenty of
proofs to choose from. There is no pull like a good photograph." Desperate mothers bought space in *The Casting Director's Album of Screen Children* and prayed that their child's
photograph would be noticed by some casting director. A typical description next to a photograph was "Danny Whitmark,
two years old, height thirty-two inches, weight twenty-nine
pounds. Try me as a girl!" The mothers thought that they
could make their child talented by feeding them candies in
exchange for memorizing lines, or by spanking them if they

refused to dance. The estimate was that one hundred children poured into the Hollywood marketplace every fifteen minutes. Only one child in fifteen thousand ever earned a weekly wage.

Al Altman said:

> There's something wrong somewhere when so many mothers run around from studio to studio fighting for the chance to exploit childhood and advance their own selfish ends. My assistants are polite but firm. They know I don't encourage the parents of these "wonder kiddies." Whenever we need children in pictures we can find all we want among the professional children who have been brought up in the theater.

One of M-G-M's most famous child stars, Margaret O'Brien, when asked to cry for the camera at age four, said, "When I cry, do you want the tears to run all the way, or should I stop them halfway down?"

Al made about fifty tests each year and had about twenty-one of them accepted by the studio. Sometimes the first test of a person who later became famous was not accepted, as in the case of Franchot Tone. One of Al's staff first saw Franchot Tone in Buffalo, where he played the romantic lead with the Gary-McGary Players, then saw him again in a small part with Katharine Cornell's company on Broadway. Franchot Tone had no desire to be in pictures or to leave Manhattan. His dream was to be a star on Broadway. Al spent a year persuading him to take a screen test. In the test Franchot Tone was cold and unappealing. His heart was not in it. The young woman who played opposite him in the test was cold, too. "After watching his screen test, I just couldn't see how I could be that wrong. I decided to use a little psychology and make another test, mostly for my own professional satisfaction," Al said. "I went privately to Franchot and told him that the girl who played opposite him in my screen test thought he was marvelous. 'What did you do to her?' I asked. 'She's hard to impress.' Then I went to the actress and told her Franchot thought she was marvelous. 'What did you do to him?' I asked her. 'He doesn't fall easily!' They agreed to make another test and played up to each other to the limit. It was swell. Franchot Tone was signed by M-G-M as a result of that test and so was the girl." Franchot Tone went on to be nominated as best actor in 1935 for *Mutiny on the Bounty.* The girl was Jean Muir, whose promising career was stopped by the blacklist during the "red scare."

When Franchot Tone married Joan Crawford in 1935, they invited Al to their wedding in Fort Lee, New Jersey. Their honeymoon was at the Waldorf-Astoria. "Thank God I'm in love again," Joan told the press. "Now I can do it for love and not for my complexion."

That same year Al made a test of James Stewart. One of the New York scouts first saw him in a Princeton University Triangle Club show. A tall skinny kid, Jimmy danced in a chorus line of other boys dressed like showgirls. The other boys accentuated their ridiculous appearances with excessive mugging and gestures. The tall skinny kid played it straight. Then he did a solo with an accordion, a funny bit in which the song and the accordion were out of sync. The boy was a senior, son of a hardware storeowner in Pennsylvania. A couple of years later Jimmy Stewart had a bit part on Broadway. Then he became a member of a stock company in Locust Valley, Long Island, the Red Barn Theater. The play Al went to see was *Divided by Three*, starring Hedda Hopper. Al visited Jimmy Stewart backstage to ask if he would consider going to Hollywood. It turned out Jimmy Stewart could do card tricks, too.

"How did your parents feel about your decision to give up architecture?" Al asked him.

"Waal, they weren't too pleased. I told them acting was something I really wanted to try. Mother, bless her heart, said she'd back me up. Dad was sore as heck. He kept shaking his head. 'No Stewart has ever gone into show business.' Then he lowered his voice and whispered, 'Except one who ran off with a circus. And you know what happened to him? He wound up in jail.'"

With the cameras rolling, Al said to Jimmy, "Imagine that I have a large horse in the palm of my right hand. I'm going to release him so that he can gallop up to you. He goes obediently, but the path he chooses is to go up the wall, across the ceiling, and down the other wall. After that he will come back to me and climb into my hand." Jimmy Stewart's screen test showed a baffled, tongue-tied, good-natured character.

Meyer Mishkin was working at the reception desk. "I remember one day Al came over to me and said, 'Get this fellow Stewart on the phone. Tell him I want to take some long shots of him. Tell him to bring a brown suit and a gray suit.' So I called this kid up and said, 'Mr. Altman wants you to get over here and bring a brown suit and a gray suit.' He says, 'A brown suit and a gray suit? That's all I got!'"

A discouraging aspect of a talent-scout's job was testing young women that men who were influential in the film industry wanted to seduce. For the most part, the men were financiers rather than movie men, because movie men knew the cost of film and personnel. Every screen test required the presence of a producer, director, cameraman, assistant cameraman, electricians, sound men, makeup men, a hairdresser, carpenters, grips, et al. When Al Altman complained about the "must-tests," Nick Schenck said, "How do you know she don't got talent? So-and-so tells me he discovered she's got talent and we should give her a chance. Goes under the head of goodwill."

"The interviews usually go like this," Al said in an interview with the *New York World-Telegram.* "We exchange how-de-dos. The tongue-tied hopeful sits down. I usually begin by saying, "So you'd like to go into pictures, eh?"

"Oh, yes, Mr. Altman!"

"Hm! Well, tell me about yourself. What have you done?"
    (long pause)

"Well . . . er . . . nothing, really. Yes, nothing, I guess."
    (Short, puzzled pause)

"You've gone to school haven't you?" (brief pause)

"Oh, yes, Mr. Altman. I've been to school."

"Why do you want to go into pictures?"

(Very long pause, indicating deep thought)

"Well . . . er . . . I guess because I think it would be sooo interesting."

(absolutely no pause)

"Have you had any experience?"

(bewildered pause)

"What do you mean, Mr. Altman?"

"I mean have you ever been on the stage? Have you ever done any acting, singing, dancing, pantomime?"

(very short pause, indicating partial comprehension)

"Well . . . no, I haven't; that is, not in public. I sing for myself. Sometimes for my friends . . . only my close friends, you know. (Brightly) But they all think I should be in pictures. That's why Mr. Doakes sent me in."

"It seldom varies," said Mr. Altman, "except that some are dumber than others. For ten minutes, perhaps, I have to go through that kind of tongue-tied dialogue, while Louis B. Mayer is on the wire from Hollywood, with a pressing casting problem affecting a picture with $300,000 already invested in it. I think of these persons coming in, taking up valuable time, being literally pushed through opportunity's door and I think of the way some kids have to work themselves to death to get a break. I've come to the conclusion the city makes most people pretty helpless, and that the kids who make their opportunities go farther than those whose opportunities are created for them."

Al directed Celeste Holm's screen test when the actress was only sixteen. Eventually she won an Oscar as best supporting actress for her third film, *Gentleman's Agreement,* in 1947. In an interview in her apartment overlooking Central Park, beautiful in a red turtleneck and black trousers, Celeste Holm, now in her early seventies, said:

> I remember being shy of all of it. I am still self-conscious unless I know what I'm doing. Sixteen is awful enough, and then just to be put in front of the camera. I think what they did was just interview me, just to see what I

would do. What would she do if you put a light on her. I wore my mother's dress because it made me look slender. [The test, she recalls, was successful.] Then you see, I had dinner with Colonel Rubin [J. Robert Rubin, M-G-M executive], and he kept looking down the front of my dress, and I didn't like that. I had the feeling I was being looked at like a piece of meat; how are her tits. I said to my mother, I don't want this. I don't want to have to learn with those men. I don't like their attitude. I don't think they know anything about artistry, and I don't know that much myself and I want to learn from an audience. You see, when you first start doing pictures, it's so hard because, I mean unless you know what an audience will do you're flying blind. But if you know what an audience will do when you do go forth, well, then you're ready for pictures, I think. They offered me something but it didn't interest me. I knew they'd come to me again, and they did.

She did fifty-four parts on Broadway before going to Hollywood at the age of twenty-four.

Louis B. Mayer came to see me in *Oklahoma*, and he was very impressed. I thought he was a pompous little man. I did not see the best of him. He said, 'I understand you're not interested in making pictures.' I said, 'On the contrary, I'm very interested in making pictures, but I'm interested in my own input. I mean I have decided what to do which has lead me to here, so I want to be able to keep on deciding because I think I know what's best for me.' He said, 'I have no interest in anyone who doesn't appreciate a great opportunity.' 'Well,' I said, 'it all depends on what you think is a great opportunity,' and he got up and left. That's all right. I signed with Twentieth Century-Fox. See, he was used to bluffing and pushing people around. Nobody pushes me around. I think you either had to be a kid who trusted him or you had to be an idiot who trusted him. But I don't think he was necessarily to be trusted. He showed me no respect. I mean did he think I'd arrived where I was overnight? He was dealing with an intelligent woman. Then what happened was after I made *Gentleman's Agreement* he was so sweet to me, oh dear, oh my, every time I saw him he'd kiss me. So there.

Mayer asked Mervyn LeRoy, a film director at Warners, to come to M-G-M and take over Thalberg's job as chief of production. At a salary of $6,000 a week, LeRoy would be responsible for selecting story material, assigning supervisors, selecting writers and directors, thrashing out scripts with writers, casting films, approving costumes and sets, making changes in cutting, previewing films and ordering retakes, and overseeing publicity and advertising campaigns. Mervyn LeRoy's first film for M-G-M was *The Wizard of Oz.*

"*The Wizard of Oz* was a very shaky proposition then," said producer Arthur Freed, "because Nick Schenck in New York didn't like it at all."

Once Nick was convinced, the search for Munchkins began. Leo Singer, whose vaudeville troupe of midgets called him "Papa Singer" and were chauffeured in his seven-passenger Lincoln limousine, signed a contract to organize the search for 124 proportionately correct little people. Almost all of the Munchkins chosen were seasoned performers either in midget troupes or on their own. Jeane LaBarbera, known as Little Jeane, was just over twenty-four inches tall. She was a comedian who also played the violin in the London Palladium, the Hippodrome in New York, and in several Broadway productions. She and her husband, who was six-feet tall, did a comedy act together for years. Murray Wood, four-foot-two, began his career by singing onstage in New York with Kate Smith.

Some of the midgets who played Munchkins felt that stage careers had been forced upon them. Meinhardt Raabe, who played the Munchkin coroner, had a bachelor's degree in accounting from the University of Wisconsin and a masters in business administration from Northwestern University. "Years ago," he said, "the public conception was small body, small mind. The door was slammed shut in my face as far as an accounting career." The man who played the mayor of

Munchkin City, Charley Becker, trained for a career in engineering. "Nobody takes an engineer seriously these days," he said. "I mean if he's also a midget."

The New York talent department was asked to help find Munchkins. A casting call brought hundreds to the Loew's building on Broadway. Very few were perfectly formed. Mothers with sad faces held child dwarfs by the hand. Twin boys with long mule faces danced around Al's office. A tiny black man, whose carnival name was "Little Richard," came into Al's office with a gigantic snake coiled around his neck. A tiny woman with a wrinkled face lifted up her tiny skirt to show Al tiny ruffled underpants, then climbed on his desk and sat by his inkwell. They came from every state east of Illinois—little people with Maine accents, little people with Rochester, New York, accents, nice ones, nasty ones, ambitious ones, lazy ones dragged there by a relative, lewd ones, prudish ones.

All of them lived in a world that was too big, full of inconveniences, from the huge beds and bathtubs in other people's houses to the tall stools at soda-fountain counters. When the men went to the barbershop they had to sit in the children's chair. When they went to the theater they had to raise their voices at the box office or the ticketseller wouldn't notice them, and once inside they couldn't see over the heads of the people seated in front of them. Almost all their clothes had to be made-to-order, especially shoes. One man told Al he had been arrested in the subway for not putting his coin in the turnstile slot. He couldn't reach it, and the other people in the crowd were in such a hurry they failed to notice him, and he was swept along under the turnstile arm. The judge presiding over his case gave him a suspended sentence.

Twenty-eight midgets went from New York by bus to the west coast to appear in *The Wizard of Oz*. They earned less money than the cairn terrier who played Dorothy's dog Toto.

M-G-M musicals required an endless supply of pretty background girls. Young women from chorus lines and modeling agencies took tests on the stage at the Fox studio. Dozens appeared in the same test. Each girl had to enter wearing a ballgown, walk toward the camera to the tune of "A Pretty Girl Is Like a Melody," pause, look right, look left, then look directly into the camera and smile. As one finished the next entered, one right after the other, a stream of girls floating toward the camera. Then they changed into costumes that revealed their legs, midriffs, and shoulders, and then changed into a third costume. Each girl had to speak at the camera, introducing herself by citing name, height, and experience. Those tests were each about fifteen minutes long.

Of the hundreds of girls who answered casting calls, almost none were beautiful. Most of them were just pretty. A beautiful girl, Al maintained, was a freak. One day an M-G-M messenger boy brought a photograph to Al of an eighteen-year-old woman who was from a tobacco farm in South Carolina. The messenger boy had seen the photograph in the window of a photographer's studio and thought he would like to take that girl on a date. So he went inside and spoke to the photographer, who turned out to be the girl's brother-in-law. She was an exceptional beauty, with a cleft in her chin, a sultry smile, and green eyes. With her older sister, who lived in New York, the girl came to see Al. He could not understand one word she said, her southern accent was that thick. Al's solution was to make a silent test of Ava Gardner. Wearing a long gown, she walked across the stage toward the camera. Al told her to look down, look up, smile, then go to the vase on a table and pick it up. Al thought the test a hopeless failure until he projected it on the screen. It was on the screen that Ava Gardner's sexiness came out. Louie phoned Al after seeing the test and said, "She can't act, she can't talk, she's terrific!"

At the studio she was taught to speak, sing, and move in an aristocratic way. Everything she learned she learned free-of-charge from the best teachers in the business. Before she went out to the west coast she said that even if she didn't get any good roles she could succeed by marrying the biggest star in Hollywood. Mickey Rooney was the biggest star, and Ava did marry him. He called her "Mummy." He called all of his wives "Mummy," but Ava was the first.

Americans sitting in darkened movie theaters saw not only Hollywood's new faces but also newsreels full of Hitler reviewing S.S. troops marching with swastika banners. Movietone News filmed the 1936 Olympics held in Berlin. The world should have realized something was out of kilter when Nazi paratroopers, fully dressed in uniforms, pistols strapped to their hips, and helmets on their heads, dove off high diving boards in unison, their arms straight up. On the newsreel screen, Goering and Goebbels watched through binoculars as the soldiers landed in a swimming pool. Two years later the screen showed Premier Mussolini passing his military might before Hitler in the grand finale of a Rome spectacular.

Fashion, as seen on the newsreel screen, was influenced by the war. Parisian models showed off hats decorated with airplanes, tanks, and battleships. One hat was designed like a gas mask. Real gas masks were issued to British civilians during the Munich crisis, and all Londoners were warned to always carry their gas masks. So when British youngsters gave dances they called them masked balls and twirled for the Movietone cameras wearing their gas masks.

Warners' top salesman, Joe Kauffman, was trapped in an alley in Berlin by Nazi thugs and clubbed to death. The German government banned all pictures showing Jewish actors. Nazi propaganda accused the Jews of "controlling" the American film industry. Soon all American movies were banned, first in Germany, then in Austria, France, and the other countries that Hitler invaded. While the costs of production in Hollywood were soaring because of the advent of sound, foreign markets were shrinking because of fascism.

Charlie Chaplin said that he would never have made *The Great Dictator,* his spoof on Hitler, if he had known what went on in the Nazi concentration camps. He initially thought Hitler was just another fool:

> The face was obscenely comic—a bad imitation of me, with its absurd mustache, unruly, stringy hair and dis-

gusting thin little mouth. I could not take Hitler seriously. The salute with the hand thrown back over the
shoulder, the palm upward, made me want to put a tray
of dirty dishes on it. "This is a nut!" I thought. But when
Einstein and Thomas Mann were forced to leave Germany, this face of Hitler was no longer comic but sinister.

In New York the renowned fashion photographer Cecil
Beaton revealed himself to be an anti-Semite in 1938 when he
decorated the margins of a *Vogue* magazine article with min-
uscule sketches and writing. In the margin of a piece entitled
"The New Left Wing in New York Society," he sketched symbols of old money—a manor house, portraits of ancestors,
sounds of classical music, volumes of Shakespeare and
French poetry—and in the other margin he drew satirical
nightclub scenes. In tiny handwriting he wrote, "M.R. Andrew ball at the El Morocco brought out all the damn kikes in
town." He drew a cartoon of a society page and wrote, "Party
darling Love Kike." In an illustration legible only by turning
the magazine upside down Beaton wrote, "Why is Mrs.
Selznick such a social wow? Why Mrs. Goldwyn? Why Mrs.
L.B. Mayer?" Cecil Beaton was fired from *Vogue*, and his work
was banned from the pages of all Conde Nast publications for
three years.

This was a difficult time for Louis B. Mayer, not only because he knew he was working for a man who distrusted him
but also because his home life was falling apart. His wife had
changed. In 1933, when she was forty-eight, a hysterectomy
left her seriously depressed and in pain. She suffered a break-
down. On the advice of doctors, Margaret moved to a small
beach house where she was attended by nurses. Doctors, re-
peating the wisdom of the day, said that after a hysterectomy
a woman must never engage in sexual intercourse again. Margaret's depression deepened, so Louie took her to the Austin
Riggs Sanatorium in Stockbridge, Massachusetts.

He returned to California and wandered around his big,
empty house, alone. "L.B. asked me to move in with him," said

producer Mervyn LeRoy. "He was lonely, I guess, and wanted companionship. I didn't, and I've always wondered whether I made a mistake. Maybe he needed me." When Margaret was released from Austin Riggs her condition had not improved. Louie was technically married, but not really. His male friends suggested that he go out with other women.

Shirley Temple claims that Mayer tried to make love to her mother at this time. In 1940, when Shirley was twelve, she was interviewed at M-G-M by Arthur Freed, who, she says, exposed himself to her in the privacy of his office. Shirley's mother, meanwhile, was being interviewed in Louis B. Mayer's all-white office. Shirley wrote in her autobiography:

> Ushering Mother to an overstuffed couch, Mayer returned behind his desk and mounted a long-legged chair, a vanity which gave him increased stature while seated. Wiping his eyeglasses on a silk handkerchief, he recounted how admiringly he regarded her. Every child should be so lucky to have such a mother, he purred, a real mother, yet someone sexy and refined. Usually solemn, his eyes glinted. Surely she could recognize real sincerity when she saw it. Never forget, he continued, at M-G-M we are a family. We take care of our own. Slipping down off his chair, he approached the sofa and sank down beside her, uttering a contented sigh. Surely she was the most unique mother in the world, he said. Someone who should be a star in her own right. He grasped her hand, pulling her toward him.

Shirley Temple has, unwittingly, recorded a most lonely and confused seduction scene. Mayer was, by the account of many who knew him well, clumsy when it came to expressing genuine sexual interest in women. Basically he was a prude. His mother, he believed, was watching him from Heaven, and her instructions had been very clear when he was a boy: only do it to make babies.

FOURTEEN

Coming Apart

THE FILMING of the Japanese sneak attack on Pearl Harbor was the result of happenstance. Movietone cameraman Al Brick was in Hawaii shooting a documentary short subject on the United States Navy, *Filming the Fleet*. He was the sole newsreel man there. His footage of sinking ships, billowing smoke, and drowning men was so horrible most of it was not shown to the public.

What Americans wanted to see were Andy Hardy movies. This was a series of nine films starring Mickey Rooney as a small-town boy who loved and respected his mother and father and whose adventures were innocent. Rooney became the most popular male star in America. Several young women who later became stars had early roles as the girl next door to Andy Hardy—Lana Turner, Esther Williams, Judy Garland, and Kathryn Grayson. To show his gratitude to Mickey, Louie gave the actor a racehorse as a twenty-first birthday gift.

The Munchkins remember Mickey Rooney, who is not much over five feet, as a rather nasty boy-next-door. Recalled Tommy Cottonaro, a midget cast as a Munchkin villager:

> Back then, I drove a 1934 Pontiac every day. One day we got out early, and it was raining cats and dogs. I had the privilege of parking on the lot. Mickey Rooney, who was on the lot that day visiting Judy [Garland], had jacked up the rear end of my car. It was raining so hard that we all jumped into the car. I started it, put it into gear, and, of course, nothing happened. Mickey Rooney and some others were looking out a window at us laughing.

The Andy Hardy pictures outgrossed releases that cost ten times as much. The top brass in New York told Mayer to produce another series. Studio screenwriters came up with the popular Max Brand character Dr. Kildare for a series about hospital doctors starring Lionel Barrymore as Dr. Gillespie and Lew Ayres as Dr. Kildare.

During the war years it seemed as if Mayer could do no wrong. His dream that he could produce successful pictures without Irving Thalberg was coming true. *Mrs. Miniver*, starring Greer Garson, won seven Oscars in 1942, including best film, best actress, and best director. Like Greta Garbo, Greer Garson was an unknown actress when Mayer first saw her. He was in London in 1934 and happened to see her on the stage. He brought Garson to Hollywood and made her a movie star.

Metro-Goldwyn-Mayer produced several popular animal pictures, including *National Velvet*, which starred the twelve-year-old Elizabeth Taylor. The film was shot in Arizona during the year that its young star was developing womanly charms. The late Helen Deutch, who wrote the screenplay from Enid Bagnold's original novel about a horse-crazy girl who pretends to be a boy so she can ride in the Grand National horse race, recalled that there were many delays in filming. With each week that went by, Elizabeth Taylor looked less and less as if she could ever pass for a boy. "When we started filming," Miss Deutch said, "Elizabeth wore a shirt and trousers. By the time we finished shooting we had to put her in ruffles and a loose-fitting jacket. Everyone involved kept talking about Elizabeth's bosoms. Poor little thing!"

The year before, when Elizabeth Taylor was eleven, she played a supporting role in *Lassie Come Home*, the first of a series of Lassie pictures. Lassie was really laddie, a male collie named Pal. The Lassie pictures not only introduced the most popular dog since Rin Tin Tin but also were proof that B pictures could make money. *Lassie Come Home* cost $400,000 and grossed $4 million.

The Lassie pictures did much to enhance the reputation of the man in charge of B pictures, Dore Schary, one of the few men Mayer misjudged.

Except for the loneliness caused by his wife's illness, Louie was at the top of his game in 1941 when he promoted Dore Schary from the screenwriters' pool. Here was an ambitious young man who believed that B pictures could be quality pictures. Dore Schary kept proving that Mayer's belief in him was justified. In three years Schary produced about twenty-four lowbudget pictures, and none of them lost money.

Dore Schary was a New Yorker whose chatty, casual manner masked an outrageous sense of his own importance. When asked by a trade paper to write about his life, he began: "The subject of this case history is six feet one inch tall, weighs 186 pounds, and has dark brown hair more than slightly gray at the temples, and blue eyes. He is an American and a Jew by birth, devotion, and conviction, and a Democrat by choice."

When Dore Schary produced *The Next Voice You Hear*, about a married couple who hear God's voice coming over their radio, he could find no actor suitable to read God's lines. He cast himself. His voice sounded like God's, to himself. His view of Mayer was unusual. Though other so-called intellectuals saw Mayer as a yahoo, few in the industry thought of themselves as his equal. Most people appreciated his contribution to the formation of the American film industry. Dore Schary's contempt for Louie was unbounded, though it was Louie who took Schary out of the screenwriters' pool and gave him a chance to be a force.

In 1943, full of his own marvelousness, Dore Schary did an unheard-of thing. He asked the home office to side with him against Mayer. The argument was about *Bataan*, a war picture. Mayer had a personal interest in this picture. The wife of its star was having an affair with Louie's son-in-law, David Selznick. Louie thought that if the picture were a boxoffice success its star, Robert Walker, would gain status at home, and his wife would return to him. Walker's wife was Phylis Isley, who, as Jennifer Jones, had just won an Oscar. Louie thought it might be Robert Walker's lack of success that made Jennifer Jones lose interest in him and turn to David Selznick, who was producing her pictures and had fallen in love with her. Louie's daughter Irene, now a mother of two boys, was on the brink of divorce. Selznick and Jones eventually got married, but at that time Louie was hoping to save Irene's marriage by making a success of Robert Walker, later cast by Alfred Hitchcock as the charming psychopath in *Strangers on a Train*.

When Mayer saw the rushes of *Bataan* he blew his top, because the screen was full of black soldiers. He said Dore Schary could use one black soldier, because white people stayed away from pictures which had a lot of black people in them. Schary thought it was only fair to show black soldiers on the screen, since in real life black soldiers were dying for America in the war. Dore Schary went to New York to plead his case at the home office. Schary could not see Mayer as anything more than a company employee, as he himself was.

Nick Schenck reminded Schary of the dismal boxoffice failure of *Hallelujah*, so Dore Schary cast only one black soldier. The picture was a success anyway.

In 1943 Louie gave Dore Schary a chance to produce an A picture. Dore Schary chose to tell the story of Hitler as a western. He thought that if he made it simple Americans would get the point. Hitler, Goebbels, and Goering were to be three escaped convicts. Hitler would be named Hygatt; Goering,

Gerrett; Goebbels, Gribbles; Mussolini, Mollison; Stalin, Slavin, etc.

When Mayer read the script he knew it would be a flop, but to appease Schary and give the work one more chance he sent the script to Nick Schenck in New York. Schenck nixed the picture. Dore Schary got so angry he quit. No one cared. Without him, in 1944, Metro-Goldwyn-Mayer grossed $166 million and won two Academy awards with *Gaslight*, starring Ingrid Bergman.

When the war ended and Americans stored their blackout shades in attics and basements, new, strange words came into the language: Auchswitz, Treblinka, Dachau. Refugees from Europe, wearing foreign-looking overcoats, wandered bewildered among hurrying New Yorkers. Under some sleeves were tattooed numbers.

Displaced persons who had been successful entertainers in Europe waited outside Al Altman's office door. During their long journey to America they had been telling themselves they were better off than other refugees because at least they had talent to sell. Song and dance was a universal language. Soon they would be basking in Hollywood next to a kidney-shaped swimming pool. They had been taught in school that French was the international language, but in America no one could understand them. Their performances made no sense to casting directors.

"Gable's Back and Garson's Got Him!" was M-G-M's pitch, but the cheerfulness sounded ridiculous. While Esther Williams swam to music in lavish turquoise swimming pools on the Metro-Goldwyn-Mayer lot, other studios took note of the prevailing mood and gave free rein to their European directors. At Paramount the Viennese-born Billy Wilder, who had lost his mother and other members of his family in concentration camps, directed *The Lost Weekend*, a drama about alcoholism which won Oscars in 1945 for best picture, best director, and best actor (Ray Milland). That same year Joan Crawford, working at Warners under the direction of Hungarian-born Michael Curtiz, won best actress for *Mildred*

Pierce, the story of a rigid matron who cares for nothing but the success of her chain of restaurants and her selfish daughter. Two years later a film that dealt directly with anti-Semitism won an Oscar, Elia Kazan's *Gentleman's Agreement.*

There was a feeling of alarm at Metro-Goldwyn-Mayer as profits began to slide. Everything had been going along well when heavy war production gave citizens a lot to spend at the box office, and the studio's penchant for escapist themes was welcomed by war-weary audiences.

In 1947 M-G-M received no Academy awards, and few of its pictures amounted to much at the box office. As one theater man said, "Most of us were thoroughly spoiled by the war years when all we had to do was open the door and get out of the way."

Panic set in. Mayer was blamed. Nick had never forgiven him for ruining Nick's chance to sell out at a terrific profit to William Fox so many years before, and now was his chance to express his anger.

Mayer's philosophy, shared by Marcus Loew, was that money is made by spending it, not saving it. While he did, in fact, spend a great deal on star salaries, story properties, and sets, he was scrupulous about budgets, and every penny spent had to bring in a penny. He knew that Americans respect nothing more than wealth and that it enhanced the reputation of his studio by claiming that millions were spent there in an effort to bring forth the best. He liked to brag about the size of his salary check, saying it was the biggest check paid in America. The check was about $1 million. Louie wanted people to believe his salary was the highest in America, which was, of course, ridiculous. He did not earn more than other top film executives, and his salary was a fraction of what the very wealthiest men, like Rockefeller, earned. But he knew people loved to be impressed.

Nick Schenck knew that Louie's bragging about money was exaggeration. "Louis likes that," Nick said. Now, though, to get the heat off himself, he claimed that Louie was the reason the company was losing money. Too much was being spent.

And now he turned against Mayer for something he had always liked, his love of racehorses. Nick Schenck loved horse racing so much he owned a house in Saratoga and spent every racing season there. Mayer, in 1945, with thorough-breds raised at his farm in California, was the leading money-winning owner in the country, earning $533,150. He had to pay 10 percent of his purses to his jockey and 10 percent to his trainer, but he kept 80 percent. When employees at the studio complained that Mayer was spending too much time at the racetrack, Nick was of two minds. He respected Louie's dream of proving that California was as good a place to breed racehorses as Kentucky. But he was also looking for a scape-goat. Just as the studio began to lose money, Mayer finally bred a champion at his farm in California.

Her name was Busher. Her sire was War Admiral, the 1937 Triple Crown winner, and her grandfather was Man o' War. As a two-year-old Busher had seven starts and five victories. In 1945, when she was three, she was named Horse of the Year. In the history of racing only four fillies have ever won that title, and two of them were four-year-olds. As a three-year-old Busher won ten out of thirteen starts and earned $273,735. In 1947 Nick scolded Mayer and told him to spend more time at the studio. He said that Mayer was making the wrong kind of pictures.

Louie was sixty-three, grieving over the death of his brother Jerry, and in the middle of a divorce from his wife of forty years. To soften Nick's criticism and because he needed money for his divorce settlement, Louie put all his horses on the auction block. His dream of owning a Kentucky Derby winner vanished.

Mayer was not to blame for Metro's poor showing. America had changed. War-weary young people wanted to settle down, buy homes, and raise a family. Veterans, their tuition paid by the government, went back to school and spent their nights studying, not going to the movies. Women who had been working in factories gave their jobs to the returning soldiers and had babies. Some were content with the change, others resented it. The ideal became not an apartment in the city but a house in the suburbs. Armed with lowcost veterans' mortgages, thousands of families moved away from the cities, where most of the theaters were. Families with babies preferred to stay home and listen to the radio rather than drive into the city, fight traffic, park, and then pay the high admission prices theaters had to charge to make up for lower attendance.

Radio had something new to offer, the disc jockey. This new breed of entertainer turned the disks and made a sales pitch in just the right ratio, which gave radio a new intimacy. Disc jockeys plugged the songs they liked, and record sales soared. The long-playing record was invented at this time, and so was the 45 rpm. Music lovers saved their money in order to afford the new three-speed record machines. Music from movies now came out not only on sheet music but also on records, so movie companies bought up record companies.

Americans discovered bowling and spent an estimated $250 million a year on equipment and fees. Photography became a popular hobby, and so did boating. The National Association of Engine and Boat Manufacturers calculated that twenty-five million people were involved with recreational boating. Anglers, table-tennis fans, hunters, bicyclists, and archers multiplied by the millions. Miniature golf, a fad in the thirties, became popular again. Americans read Alfred C. Kinsey's *Sexual Behavior in the Human Male*. In the winter of 1947 people in New York could practice what they read when twenty-eight inches of snow kept them indoors.

Shopping centers were built to service the new suburban population, but shopping center owners refused to rent space to theater companies. They considered movie theaters to be such special buildings and so expensive that they were afraid if the theater failed the shopping center would be stuck with an empty store that no one else would rent. Few of the new shopping-center owners imagined that a movie theater would draw in customers.

The only theaters that were thriving were drive-ins, which

first made their appearance in 1933 in Camden, New Jersey. In 1946 there were about 342 car palaces in the country, and ten years later there were almost five thousand. Food and drink concessions yielded as much as 50 percent of the profit. Drive-in impresarios catered to basic needs by providing bottle-warmers for the infants, playgrounds for the kids, and laundromats that would finish washing and drying by the time the movie ended. This so-called by-product income accounted for a greater profit margin than the basic show business, and film distributors complained, saying that they were entitled to a percentage of the popcorn and allied profits.

Television sales soared after the war. Practically any bar that could boast television found itself deluged with customers. The joke was "Help Wanted, Bar Tender Who Can Fix Television." The invention had been around for years. In 1938, RCA-NBC produced the first televised drama, "The Mummy Case" and telecast regular five-hour weekly shows beamed from studios in the Empire State Building. At the opening of the New York World's Fair in April 1939, David Sarnoff, head of RCA, made his first commercial telecast with "Now, at last, we add sight to sound." After the war millions of receivers were sold, and movie men began to refer to television as the "Monster."

The World Series was first telecast in 1947. Set owners complained of neighbors who barged in to watch. Hostesses complained that the art of conversation was dying because guests left the table to sit transfixed in front of the screen. Wives complained that their husbands neglected them to watch sporting events, and parents wondered how to tear their children away from the set, which at that time had a screen ten-by-eight inches. In 1948, ten million Americans saw President Truman on television when he took the inaugural oath of office.

The careers of vaudeville and radio performers were stimulated by television. Jimmy Durante, Eddie Cantor, Arthur Godfrey, Jack Benny all flourished. Producers of live stage plays and ballet now had a new stage on which they could reach millions of viewers. But "Closed Until Further Notice" was what played on many small-town movie-house marquees. A shuttered movie theater made a neighborhood look decayed. In some towns theaters were allowed to operate rent-free, and in others contributions from neighboring businessmen kept the movie house going.

In March 1956 *Business Week* reported that of the 19,200 active theaters in the United States, 27 percent were operating at a loss. Roughly 30 percent were just doing better than breaking even. According to the *Motion Picture Newsletter*, in 1956 over half the theaters were hardly worth keeping open as far as their owners were concerned.

Perhaps Loew's Inc. would have done better if Wiliam Fox had taken over. He understood the impact of television years before other movie men did. "The new medium," William Fox said in 1935, "will put a stadium, amusement park, theater, and university into every home. The modern home will be built around the television room. Rooms designed by interior decorators will arrange the family in concentric half-circles in front of the television screen."

In the three years following the war, the number of television sets in homes increased from 14,000 to 172,000 to one million. Ten years later almost every home had one. Television did to the movies what the movies, in their youth, did to the legitimate theatre. Almost overnight it cut motion-picture theater attendance in half.

It used to be that people went to the movies two and three times a week no matter what was playing. Now the picture had to have some merit before people would get up off their couches. Pressure was on all the studios to produce blockbusters, to score with every effort. "We've got to give them big pictures," William Fox said years before the wide-screen concept entered anyone else's head, "or people will stay home and look at little pictures on radio beams."

Mayer urged Nick Schenck to get involved in television, but Nick insisted that television was a nuisance that would pass. He could not see that television shows—produced on shoestring budgets, lacking technical polish, and scorned by major stars—were exactly like the early flickers. David Sarnoff, head of RCA, realizing that television had a voracious appetite for talent and stories and needed films to fill in between live shows, tried to persuade Nick to put Loew's into a fifty-fifty partnership with RCA. Nick refused, telling Sarnoff to spend a little more of his own money before trying to get Loew's money. While other film companies sold their old films to television and rented studio space to television production crews, Metro-Goldwyn-Mayer did not.

Good news came, at first, from overseas. When the ban on American films imposed by Hitler was lifted, American films flooded Europe. Europeans couldn't get enough of American product. Though Americans were beginning to appreciate European films, the trade was not equal, so foreign governments balked and the joyride came to an end. Claiming that Americans were taking out too much European currency, foreign governments froze the amount of money that film companies could convert to United States dollars. American film companies could take out $17 million annually. Americans could earn all they wanted in Great Britain, France, Italy, and Germany, but the money had to be spent in those countries. So most of the major American film companies built studios abroad. Producers now began to notice how much cheaper it was to make pictures in Europe than in Hollywood. They could fill whole stadiums with people willing to work for almost nothing. As for scenery, it was already there—real castles, cathedrals, and chateaus and beautiful countryside. To encourage Americans to produce pictures on their soil, foreign governments gave American companies tax breaks.

Movie people began to run to Europe for another reason—the Communist witchhunt. Under the leadership of J. Parnell Thomas, the House Committee on Un-American Activities began to pick on Hollywood. Parnell, knowing that his name would be front-page news if coupled with the names of movie stars, announced he was going to "expose and ferret out" Communist sympathizers in Hollywood.

But what really gave the deathblow to the American film industry as it existed then was the government's insistence that production/distribution companies be divorced from theater companies. Loew's Inc., the government said, could no longer own Metro-Goldwyn-Mayer.

Declared Thurman Arnold, the United States attorney general in 1938:

> The danger in this country is the private seizure of power. It is subject to no checks and balances, it is subject to no elections every four years, it is subject to no criticism and no attacks because no one even knows about it. It is private seizure of power which the Sherman Act prevents. If we are to maintain an industrial democracy we must stop the private seizure of power and that is exactly what we have in the film industry.

After the war the cry was taken up by America's new attorney general, Tom Clark. His mission was the destruction of all monopolies. The "Paramount Decree," as it has come to be known, was a civil antitrust action against eight major motion-picture distributors, the five major companies and three lesser ones: Columbia, Universal, and United Artists. The old way was dead. The new way was this: each picture had to be rented on a separate basis, theater by theater, without regard for other pictures or exhibitor affiliation, and existing companies had to be split into separate theater and producer-distributor companies with no interlocking directors or officers. The five divorced circuits were prohibited from acquiring additional theaters unless they established to the satisfaction of the district court that such acquisitions would not unreasonably restrain trade.

Independent exhibitors, and there were about ten thousand of them classified as small business operations, hailed this decision. Time would prove to the independent theater owners that block booking, while it guaranteed them a large number of turkeys, also allowed them to buy a single film for a very low figure. Soon they would face producers who had to sell every single one of their pictures as hard as they could. Producers, instead of renting for a flat fee, would demand a percentage of the box office, rarely less than 50 percent. And theaters in the same vicinity could find themselves playing the same feature. "It's easy to say one of us ought to back down," said a theater man a few years after the Paramount Decree, "and take an inferior picture just to offer the area some variety, but would you do it if you were one of the three competitors? Why should you let the other two guys clean up on your generosity?"

Independent producers now came into their own. They were able to show their films in first-run houses, and that brought in enough money for them to hire big names. The victory of the Department of Justice and the independents had disastrous effects on the film industry, which had been built on vertical integration, the spine of its self-confidence. Now the studios, with their huge overhead, could not be sure they had an outlet for their product, and the theater companies, with *their* huge overhead, could not be assured of a steady flow of quality merchandise. Nonetheless, most of the film companies got on with the business of cutting loose their theater chains and began to concentrate on finding innovative ways to keep their studios solvent.

Loew's and Metro-Goldwyn-Mayer found divorcing so difficult the federal government gave them almost ten years, until February 1957, to work things out. Loew's Inc. had an outstanding long-term debt of $31 million to the Metropolitan Life Insurance Company and several banking houses. How that debt was to be divided between the Loew's theater company and the Metro-Goldwyn-Mayer production-distribution company was the issue. The loans were to run until 1965 and bear an interest rate of 3 percent. The theater company thought it should assume less than a third of the debt and did not want to compromise.

All the major studios had to cut costs drastically. A picture a week was out of the question. Studios could no longer support a stable of stars and writers. Soaring labor costs and income taxes made the maintenance of huge payrolls disadvantageous from the standpoint of both the studios and the stars. Only the best story properties were bought and produced. Small-scale pictures were eliminated, so new talent no longer had a training ground. Talent scouts could no longer promise a long-term contract to youngsters willing to study hard. Gone were the free dancing, singing, and drama lessons.

Movie stars discovered the percentage deal and refused to sign long-term contracts. They began to sign contracts for one film at a time. They demanded a high fee as well as a percentage of the box-office take.

Actors' agents, who used to sit hat in hand in the casting director's waiting room, now had their turn on the throne. From posh offices they called the shots. Agents put together package deals in which producers were forced to sign a lesser actor, or a particular screenwriter or director, in order to get the famous actor. Audiences began to see films in which the star and the costar were mismatched, teamed only because they were both clients of the same agent.

All the major studios except Metro followed the lead of independent producers and offered their stars percentage deals. The profits to the actor were deemed capital gains and subject to only 25 percent tax. Soon stars were not content with a percentage of profits but demanded a percentage of gross receipts. Artists began organizing their own production corporations and taking long-term payments from their own companies, as well as capital-gains profits from the venture. Actors were no longer embarrassed to admit they worked free-lance.

Nick Schenck was bewildered. "By what right do they claim to become owners of the property? Did they finance the production? Did they take the risk if there is a loss? Did they concern themselves with the huge overhead of the studio? Did they develop the Metro trademark? Who is he? He's nobody. We took him from nobody, we lavished him with lessons and publicity, and now he's the most desired man in the world. Who taught him how to walk? Who straightened his teeth and capped them into that smile? Who taught him how to pronounce words and improve his voice? We taught this dumbcluck how to depict great emotions. And now he wants a piece of the action? No! Never! What ingratitude! What are we, just a mere financing oranization?" So more and more stars left the company payroll.

Any small entrepreneur, who acquired an important script and who was willing to give up 50 percent or more of his profit to the star and cast, could lure stars away from their old employer and arrange bank financing on the strength of his package. Previously unknown companies like Allied Artists raided M-G-M stars with attractive partnership deals.

Nick Schenck, weary of reporting bad news to his stockholders, suggested to Mayer that Dore Schary might be able to produce pictures that made money and instructed Louie to hire him back again as vice president in charge of production, Irving Thalberg's old job.

In June 1948, Dore Schary, age forty-three, signed a seven-year contract with Metro-Goldwyn-Mayer at $4,000 a week. He would be allowed to choose his own stories, directors, stars, and producers. Nick invited Schary to New York to give a press conference outlining plans for getting the studio out of the doldrums. Always before it was Mayer who told reporters what future pictures the studio would produce.

When Dore Schary arrived in New York he was treated to theatre tickets, a limousine, and a lavish suite at the Sherry Netherland. Nick Schenck turned over his office to Schary, who received reporters there. Sitting in the president of the company's chair, Dore Schary said to the press, "Pictures, in addition to their basic function which is to entertain, have a responsibility to keep that entertainment on a certain level. Entertainment can not be a static word. It changes. What was entertainment fifty years ago can not be looked on as entertainment today." He went on to say, "Films must provoke thought as well as entertain. They must educate and inform *as* they entertain. . . . We all of us live in dread of the A–bomb and the H–bomb. We must believe deeply that the biggest force—the biggest hope for the future—is the overwhelming bomb of courage that lies in the heart of man."

It became evident that Dore Schary and Louis B. Mayer defined a successful picture differently. To Louie, the box office was the final answer. If it made money a picture was successful. There was a factory to run, and its fuel was money. Dore Schary, on the other hand, was haughty about profits. What did profits have to do with great art?

He pronounced Mario Lanza's pictures "trifling" though they brought in millions. Critics were hailing Lanza as the new Caruso. He couldn't appear in public without being ripped apart and had to wear padding under his clothes to protect his flesh. Mario Lanza's fan mail was full of nude photographs of women who claimed that if he didn't sleep with them they'd kill themselves. Lanza believed his body contained the voice of God. He often said, "This is God's voice. It passes through here," and he'd grab his throat. Dore Schary had no patience with him. He thought Lanza was arrogant and foulmouthed.

Mayer had tolerance for all kinds of big babies if they had talent. He advised Mario's friends not to leave the singer alone for any longer than they would a little child. He was subject to black moods.

Dore Schary went around saying that Mario Lanza was just an ex-truckdriver. In truth, Lanza never drove a truck. The publicity department made up the idea so the singer would seem approachable. Before signing with Metro, Lanza was a successful concert singer, who had sung opera to 125,000 paying customers in an open-air concert in Grant Park in Chicago, appeared with the NBC Symphony Orchestra, and received a fifteen-minute standing ovation when he sang in the Hollywood Bowl, and was a married man with a child. But he did have an earthy way of talking. Lanza was fond of saying that singing, for him, was all sex. "When I'm singing, I'm scoring. That's me. It comes right out of my balls."

For Mayer there was no argument, because he was a strong

believer in the power of gonads. He said to Lanza at their first conference, "Mario, I'll tell you what makes a star. When every woman in the theater, regardless of age, wants you for herself, and every man wants to be you."

Now Dore Schary, as vice president in charge of production, had to supervise a Mario Lanza picture. Dissatisfied with his leading lady, Lanza said to her, "You've got to be more sexy. Push up to me; let me feel your pussy next to my cock." The leading lady ran off the stage. Schary sided with the lady and had it noised around that Mario Lanza was temperamental.

The Toast of New Orleans was screened for Dore Schary. "We have a three-million-dollar lemon on our hands," he said to Mayer. Louie watched the movie and loved it. He phoned Nick in New York. "What the hell is Schary talking about?" he said. "What's he got against Lanza and [Kathryn] Grayson?" Box-office receipts proved Louie to be right.

During the filming of *The Great Caruso*, a picture that eventually grossed $19 million, Mario Lanza felt the need of some more praise. At that time he was as much a recording star as he was a movie star. His song, "Be My Love," was at the top of the charts. *The Great Caruso* had twenty-seven vocal segments. In nine operatic scenes Lanza was joined by stars from the Metropolian Opera.

Lanza was tired of hearing about how fat he was. He wanted people to love him fat or skinny. When he went to Schary with a complaint, instead of praising his talent Schary reminded Mario that Metro-Goldwyn-Mayer had a long list of stars who had preceded him. "I told him," Dore Schary was later proud to report, "that the studio through all its years had had to survive, despite the loss of Jean Harlow, Wallace Beery, Marie Dressler, John Gilbert, Edward Arnold, Lionel Barrymore, and a host of others, if it came down to it, Metro would have to get along without him. That sobered him up."

Lanza said:

Mayer knew how to deal with people. When I got mad I'd go into his office and I'd say what I was mad about and I'd call him a Jew sonofabitch and Mayer would burst into tears and say, "Mario, I thought you loved me." I'd say I didn't dislike him but he and the studio were making me unhappy with their demands on my life and he'd say he'd do something about that and exactly what was I talking about. I'd explain it to him and he'd say again he'd do something about it and I'd leave feeling a little better. Most of the time nothing ever was done about it but he knew how to handle me. I'd go in to see Dore Schary and I'd call him a Jew sonofabitch and he'd throw me out of the office. Now you can't work for a man like that.

Dore Schary made a list of all of Lanza's faults; his sexual escapades, his drinking, his eating, and read it to him. "I have a list here," Schary said to him, "of all your misdeeds. And look at you—you dress like a bum. M-G-M has a star image to maintain. You don't even look like a star." He suspended Mario from the studio.

"I'm doing as the studio says," Lanza said in defense of himself, "but how can anyone cure a broken heart? Can Dore Schary remake me? What am I supposed to do? Take water and become a Boy Scout? If I did all those things expected of me then I wouldn't be singing."

In the film, *The Student Prince*, Schary replaced Lanza with Edmund Purdom and dubbed Lanza's singing voice. Fans in the audience were supposed to tolerate their darling's voice coming out of another man's mouth. Lanza's RCA Red Seal album of *The Student Prince* sold in the millions even though he wasn't in the picture.

The tension between Schary and Mayer began to build. Schary's attitude was that he asked the older man's advice simply to be nice, not because he needed it. But others at the studio bypassed Schary and went, as they were accustomed, to Louie when they had a problem. "What became apparent as the weeks sped into months," Schary wrote in his autobiography, *Heyday*, "was that Mayer was eager to demonstrate to Schenck that he was still in charge."

Mayer and Schary disagreed about making the 1949 movie *Battleground*. Louie said it would be a failure. Nick Schenck asked Schary if he were sure of the project. "Not wanting to have a continuation of debate on the subject," Schary recalled, "I told Schenck that if he wished me or ordered me to take the picture off the schedule I would immediately resign. That settled the issue."

Battleground was made and Louie was proved wrong. The screenplay won the Academy award, and the picture made money at the box office. Nick Schenck began to think Schary was another Thalberg, but this "boy wonder" was his, not Mayer's. Schenck said the name Dore with the same tenderness one might say the word *lovely*. He called him "my boy" when speaking on the phone to him. In his first year as vice president in charge of production, Dore Schary supervised the production of thirty-eight pictures, many of them very successful.

Nick Schenck gave Schary undue credit. All of the successful pictures except *Battleground* were the work of producers who had been at the studio with Mayer for years. *Father of the Bride*, for instance, was produced by Pandro S. Berman. Jack Cummings, Louie's nephew, produced *Three Little Words*, starring Red Skelton and Fred Astaire. As for the now-classic *Annie Get Your Gun,* Arthur Freed produced it. He had produced about twenty-seven musicals for Metro-Goldwyn-Mayer before Dore Schary showed up.

In 1950, when Dore Schary decided to make the novel *The Red Badge of Courage* into a movie, there were many who thought it a bad idea. Howard Dietz, vice-president in charge of advertising, publicity, and exploitation for Loew's on the third floor of 1540 Broadway, said, "A novel is a novel. A poem is a poem. And a movie is a movie. Take the Wordsworth poem 'I wandered lonely as a cloud' and make a movie about it. What can you show visually? 'I wandered lonely as a cloud / That floats on high o'er vales and hills / When all at once I saw a crowd, / A host of golden daffodils.' We might have a cloud, some vales and hills, and then a batch of daffodils." Dietz went on to say, "Two things sell tickets. One, stars. Two, stories. *Red Badge* has no stars, no story. Can't sell [John] Huston. Directors don't sell tickets, except DeMille."

Mayer knew that the picture would be a financial disaster.

This is *thoughts*. How are you going to show the boy's thoughts? Nobody will go in. A million and a half. Maybe more. What for? There's no story. I am against it. No women. They want to make it. No love story. John Huston. Now he wants *The Red Badge of Courage*. Dore Schary wants it. All right. I'll watch. I don't say no, but I wouldn't make that picture with Sam Goldwyn's money.

The director, John Huston, cast Audie Murphy, the most decorated GI in World War II, twenty-four decorations including the Congressional Medal of Honor, in the lead. The choice of Audie Murphy was odd. In *The Red Badge of Courage* he would have to play a coward. Audiences would not enjoy seeing their hero acting like a wimp on the screen even though, at the end, he becomes braver.

Dore Schary again went over Mayer's head and asked Nick Schenck to intervene. "That's Nick" Louie said. "He always has to be the big I am, the big cheese. All he knows about movies you could stick in a cat's ass." Louie begged Gottfried Reinhardt, the producer chosen by Dore, not to make the picture. "Twenty-six years with the studio!" Mayer said. "They used to listen to me. Never would Irving Thalberg make a picture I was opposed to. I had worship for that boy. He worked. Now they want cocktail parties and their names in the papers."

When Louie advised Dore Schary to avoid the press, to be like Irving Thalberg and put his name on nothing, Schary responded, "L.B., I'll make a deal with you. Change the name of the studio to Metro-Goldwyn-Mayer-Schary, and I'll never put my name anywhere else."

At the preview of *The Red Badge of Courage* the audience began filing out before the end. The preview cards said,

"Slow," "Lousy," "Stinks," "Burn It," "Forget It." Instead of being contrite, or saying that he should have listened to Mayer, Dore Schary said, in an interview with Lillian Ross of *The New Yorker:*

> I love the problems inherent in show business. I love the risks, the excitement in the work, and all the people who are problems. The only thing I miss is the time to study. I love to read a lot. In about ten years, I want to get out of the industry. I've been in show business for eighteen years, and when I retire, I want to write books about it and teach and lecture. I love to teach the youngsters who are just coming up in show business.

He said he was going to add narration to the film.

> I want to get more of the text of the book into the picture. I want to tell the audience the narration is from the book. A lot of people don't know this is a book. I want to be blunt with them. Put them in a more receptive mood. I want to tell them they're gonna see a classic, a great novel. . . . The voice of the narrator must be warm, intimate, and dignified. I may have to do it myself.

At this time, the contracts of several executives came up for renewal. Louie recommended to Nick that the contracts be supplemented by options to buy Loew's stock within a period of six years at the then current market value. Nick did renew the contracts, including Dore's, and he bestowed stock options on everyone except Louie.

Mayer was embarrassed by *The Red Badge of Courage,* thought it stunk, and refused to release the picture. He said that as long as he was head of the studio it never would be. He wrote a letter to Nick and told him to choose between him and Schary.

Then, King Lear-like, he thought to test Dore's loyalty to him by suggesting that he might retire. "What would I do with myself?" he said. "What would you do if you were me if you wanted or had to retire. Be honest." The answer he wanted to hear was, "You? Retire! I'd be lost without you! Never do it! I beg you!"

Dore said, "It's impossible for me to know or to guess what I would do if I were you." Louie insisted Dore tell him. "Well," Dore responded, "I don't know how much you've got, but I assume it is in millions. I think, in your place, I'd travel, write, set up a foundation, and administer it to provide ego satisfaction, then I'd set up a fund for destitute people in the industry and do something on behalf of an industry that helped me become successful."

"First," Mayer replied, furious, "you say that because you're a pauper. Second, don't spend my money. And I don't owe this industry or this company a goddam cent. I got what I got because I deserve it. Nobody gave me anything. Screw the company and screw the stockholders. And, furthermore, I've been everywhere so I don't want to travel."

The Red Badge of Courage was released and received the praise of some critics, but audiences didn't go for it. Metro-Goldwyn-Mayer lost money, and many of the people who worked on the picture said they should have listened to Mayer in the first place. Nick Schenck said, lighting a cigarette and smiling in a fatherly way, "Dore is young. He has not had his job very long. I felt I must encourage him or else he would feel stifled. It would have been so easy for me to say no to him. Instead, I said yes. I figured I would write it off to experience. You can buy almost anything, but you can't buy experience. Now he will know better. A young man has to learn by making mistakes."

Nick considered the letter Louie sent him. Nick looked at company records, and they showed that, in the two years that Dore had been in charge of production, losses had been reversed. Instead of a deficit, Metro-Goldwyn-Mayer now showed a profit, the result of great pictures like *An American in Paris, King Solomon's Mines,* and *Father of the Bride.* Nick Schenck sided with Dore Schary.

Mayer sent his resignation to Nick, thinking that Nick would never accept it. But Nick immediately let the press know that Louis B. Mayer was "retiring." Within weeks the name Metro-Goldwyn-Mayer was officially changed to "M-G-M" to remove all traces of Mayer. "He's an old man," said Dore Schary. "He's rich. He's healthy. Let him enjoy himself now. I don't know what the hell he got mad about. He could have been so happy here."

Dore Schary said that just because he thought L.B. was "reckless, tough, rough, and mean as a polecat," it didn't mean that he did not respect him. Schary said he did respect Louie, that Mayer reminded him of his father. Dore Schary's father ran a small catering business.

FIFTEEN

Staying Afloat

MAYER let the press know he had not retired. "I am going to remain in motion-picture production, God willing," he said. "I am going to be more active than at any time during the last fifteen years." But he was crushed and thought of nothing but revenge. At first he believed success would be the best revenge and put his hope of regaining dominance in Cinerama, an entirely new motion-picture technique.

That movies would have to offer audiences something television could not seemed obvious to everyone. Thirty million people were staying home to watch *I Love Lucy*. In their panic few movie men saw the simple truth: People will always want to get out of their houses, and movies offer an inexpensive chance to do that and to be with others. But in the early fifties it seemed as if Americans might stay in their TV dens forever, so the film industry devoted its energies to improving color and utilizing big screens and three-dimensional effects.

Color was controlled by the Technicolor Corporation, which owned most of the patents on color film. When a studio contracted to use Technicolor, it received not only a Technicolor camera but also a cameraman who understood color cinematography and a color consultant who worked with the art director, set decorator, and costume designer. Technicolor processed the film in its own laboratories and was always overburdened with a backlog of work. In 1948 the government stepped in with an antitrust action and ordered the Technicolor Corporation to release ninety-two of its basic patents to all producers on a no-royalty basis, and twelve others for a "reasonable" royalty. The system under which studios had been forced to contract with Technicolor for the supply of stock, processing, and cinematographic staff was also outlawed.

Eastman Kodak introduced Eastman Color, an easy to use color system. Color became the rage. The number of features produced in color jumped from around 20 percent to more than 50 percent.

Not that Eastman Kodak color development was asleep until 1948. The company dramatized the effectiveness of color pictures taken with its Kodachrome film at the New York World's Fair in 1938. To help develop a show, Eastman Kodak asked the help of Fred Waller, a New York inventor. He worked in what would be called today the "special effects" department of Paramount's Astoria studio. Back then he worked in the "trick film department." For the World's Fair, Fred Waller devised a panoramic arrangement of eleven screen projections of Kodachrome slides. The effect was so successful the Hall of Color drew larger crowds than any other commercial exhibit there.

For the Hayden Planetarium's exhibit Waller came up with a rounded screen surface, in the "Time and Space" show, which gave the effect of travel through space. He used both motion and still pictures to get a three-dimensional effect.

For the World's Fair Corporation he produced motion pictures of people on the inside of a Perisphere. The figures marched in time to the theme song of the Fair.

It was during the period of the New York World's Fair that Waller built his first model of the Cinerama process, hoping to sell it to one of the Fair's exhibitors; but his invention was considered too radical.

Waller, who eventually held patents to more than fifty inventions, including water skis, was fascinated that wide-angle pictures seemed more three-dimensional than standard pictures. He invented a wide-angle lens but could find no screen of sufficient angle to show what dramatic improvement could be made with the use of peripheral vision. At his home in Huntington, Long Island, he experimented by closing off portions of his sight to find out which parts of his eyes were needed to keep him from bumping into chairs and children. He drove his car around his driveway using only his peripheral vision to guide him and concluded that it was that vision that gave a sense of realism and depth.

His first apparatus was sixteen cameras put together on a single frame and driven by a single motor. He photographed people on his lawn and then mounted the camera on his car and took a running shot down the roads in Huntington. He used eleven projectors for showing the pictures on a six-foot radius spherical screen set up in a potato barn. Word of his work circulated, and a year later he demonstrated his progress to about a hundred people. Laurence Rockefeller attended the showing and was so impressed he became Fred Waller's partner in the Vitarama Corporation and gave Waller a garage on West Fifty-fifth Street and Sixth Avenue in which to continue his experiments. Waller worked on the Cinerama cameras, the screen, and a new sound process that would be stereophonic.

Though the war interrupted his work on Cinerama in 1940, the military showed him a new application for his invention. A friend of his who majored in gunnery at Annapolis said that the Cinerama screen had all the essential qualities needed to simulate a moving target for a flexible-gunnery trainer to teach machine gunners to shoot down aircraft. The result was the Waller Gunnery Trainer, which used films of moving planes projected on a spherical screen to imitate battle conditions for airplane pilots in combat. The air force said the Waller Gunnery Trainer saved over 350,000 lives.

In 1949, in the indoor tennis court of an estate in Oyster Bay, Long Island, Waller gave his first private demonstration of Cinerama. Lowell Thomas, the legendary broadcaster and narrator of Movietone newsreels, invested heavily in Fred Waller's invention and formed the Cinerama Productions Corporation.

Mayer became a major stockholder and chairman of the board of Cinerama Corporation even though he had doubts about the future of the invention. To convert a single theater to Cinerama cost from $50,000 to $100,000. Bankers Trust loaned the company about $1 million to convert theaters in Detroit, Chicago, Los Angeles, Pittsburgh, and a few other cities. But when all was said and done only two hundred theaters in the world were able to show the product.

Cinerama was launched at the Broadway Theater in New York in September 1952 with *This Is Cinerama*, a two-hour travelogue which included a gripping roller-coaster ride and an airplane trip through the Grand Canyon. Stereophonic sound was something entirely new to audiences—the screech of airplane wheels, the sound of water on a rather sickening gondola ride in Venice, and music that was everywhere all at once. Cinerama, after one year, grossed $10 million. It played in New York for 122 weeks to an audience of 2.5 million, the longest run in the city's history.

Film industry executives recognized that the day of the big screen had arrived. The problem was finding lenses that could project large images. An independent producer, Arch Oboler, came out with a 3-D picture that required audiences to wear Polaroid spectacles to get the 3-D effect. In 1952 audiences ducked as spears were thrown, seemingly right at them, in the African adventure *Bwana Devil*. The success of *Bwana Devil* convinced Warners to try 3-D. Audiences ducked again the following year when chairs came toward them in *House of*

Wax, a thriller that grossed $1 million for Warners in its first week.

Spyros P. Skouras, who started with theaters in St. Louis and became president of Twentieth Century-Fox in 1942, got his company out of its slump with CinemaScope in 1953, a wide-screen process that essentially reversed the federal divorcement decree, because every theater that installed wide screens had to buy the big films to go along with it, and those films were produced solely by Twentieth Century-Fox. No other films would fit. The studio went from a failing company to a thriving one with *The Robe,* a biblical story shown in CinemaScope with stereo sound. That audiences preferred big screens was proved when films were brought out in both regular and wide-screen formats. The box-office take at the big-screen theater was always more. Twelve CinemaScope pictures were released in a year and grossed $40 million.

"We cannot overemphasize our belief," Spyros Skouras told reporters, "and conviction that CinemaScope is the only remedy to combat the ravages of television at the box office and recapture lost audiences. Astrolite and Miracle Mirror screens are best for showing CinemaScope, sharper pictures, improved color brilliancy and they distribute light evenly to all seats not just light in the center of the screen."

Warners came out with WarnerScope, Paramount came out with VistaVision, and Michael Todd, the independent producer who married Elizabeth Taylor, introduced a 65mm process called Todd-AO. His first wide-screen stereo-sound effort was *Oklahoma,* and his second was *Around the World in 80 Days,* both smash hits.

The day of the gimmick had arrived: Vectograph, Variascope, Vitascope, AmpoVision, Bolix 3-D, Glamorama, Moroptican, Naturama, Perspecta Sound, and even Smell-o-Vision.

Small theater owners did not want to spend money on big screens and lavish sound systems. Some succumbed to pressure from the majors, but others refused and found themselves without product to show. In desperation they turned to

European films. Much to their amazement, they discovered that there was a segment of the American population that did not mind reading subtitles in foreign-language films. Many Americans, in the early fifties, were tired of the domination of the Catholic Legion of Decency and other church-related film-censoring organizations which put their moralistic stamp on almost all American movies. European films were more adult. The small theater owners called their shops art theaters and played up the films' smallness and sexual daring, and audiences lined up to see films by Fellini, Vittorio De Sica, and Ingmar Bergman.

As for Cinerama, its second production, *Cinerama Holiday*, was just as successful as *This Is Cinerama*. But the following year, *Seven Wonders of the World* did not make much profit. Audiences were tired of the novelty. Mayer, discouraged and bored, ignored at parties where he was once the center of attention, fighting with his daughter Edith, and cranky with his new young wife, snapped on his television set in 1954 to watch Ed Sullivan's *Toast of the Town*.

Ed Sullivan, who invariably opened his show by saying, "Tonight we have a really big *shew*," had decided to devote one of his shows to saluting the accomplishments of the greatest movie studio in the world, Metro-Goldwyn-Mayer. Ed Sullivan asked Dore Schary to narrate the program. The salute to Metro-Goldwyn-Mayer lasted an hour, and Mayer's name was hardly mentioned. The spotlight was on Dore Schary, and to him went all the credit for the studio's success. Even *Gone With the Wind* came across as Dore Schary's creation, though he had nothing to do with it nor was it produced by Metro-Goldwyn-Mayer.

It was as if Louis B. Mayer never existed. Dore Schary blamed the "oversight" on Ed Sullivan's writers. He said he was sorry if L.B. had been slighted.

That powerful energy that was Louie's gift at birth and had been unused since his ouster now found another outlet. He pledged his fortune to revenge and vowed to destroy his enemies and return in triumph to the company that bore his name. He was driven now, in the last years of his life, not by a passion to create but by hatred.

Mayer's fury was justified. He had, indeed, been replaced by a lesser man. Dore Schary's 1955 film *The Prodigal* lost $1 million and alienated Lana Turner, one of the company's biggest box-office draws. She was mortified by her role in the picture as a half-nude high priestess of the Temple of Love. Released two years earlier *Bright Road*, starring the relatively unknown Harry Belafonte and an all-black cast, was another financial disaster. Schary blamed the poor tastes of the public on the failure of his films.

The problem, Nick Schenck and Dore Schary agreed, was that there were not enough new faces. The stars who had once sparkled in the Metro-Goldwyn-Mayer firmament were too expensive and too old. Clark Gable was cast off from the studio after twenty-two years of loyalty and fifty-four pictures. Greer Garson was let go. Joan Crawford came back to M-G-M for one last try, *Torch Song*, which didn't do well at the box office. She married Alfred Steele, an executive at Pepsi-Cola who brought her full-circle back to her miserable childhood by beating her up and leaving her in debt.

A headline in *Variety* reported: "Hollywood Fears New Face Famine for Future Films." It was the bleakest period for fresh faces in the annals of the screen, according to the paper. Contract rosters were cut to the bone. Production had been curtailed by doing away with B pictures, which were the training ground for new players. Independent producers cast one picture at a time because that was all that they could finance. They did not keep stables of stars on long-term contracts.

The major studios blamed theater owners for the new face famine, saying that the first thing the exhibitor asked was "Who's in it?" and when the name was unfamiliar they refused to buy the film. Under the system of block-booking, theater owners had to show films with new faces in them. Now they wouldn't take the chance. Theater owners were blaming the studios, saying that Hollywood wasn't giving fledgling stars enough buildup. Studios replied that players refused to sign long-term contracts, so it was impossible to invest money in their training and in worldwide publicity.

Many of the promising young players were more interested in television than in films. "Time was when a talent scout's excursion to Broadway swamped him with calls from agents and players," the press reported. "Not so today, at least with those young players who are in TV."

Dore Schary was asked to take a look at the screen test of a young woman named Grace Kelly. He pronounced her drab, with a "rather ordinary Irish accent." In her role as Gary Cooper's wife in *High Noon*, Dore Schary thought she had been overshadowed. John Ford, a director working at M-G-M insisted that Grace Kelly be hired to star in his film, *Mogambo*. Schary managed to sign Kelly to a long-term contract. She was nominated for best supporting actress in *Mogambo*, and everyone began to notice her. Schary proceeded to offer her such inane roles that she refused to fulfill her contract and was suspended from the studio three different times. While Schary was busy suspending her, she went over to Paramount, starred in *The Country Girl,* and won the Academy award for best actress. Alfred Hitchcock understood her appeal and cast her in *Dial M for Murder, Rear Window,* and *To Catch a Thief.* Made famous by other studios, she returned to M-G-M when she was offered *High Society* and *The Swan.* Though he did nothing to further her career, Dore Schary gave himself credit for Grace Kelly's success. "I take a small bow for signing her up on contract, a rare stunt in 1953."

Loew's executives blamed theater managers for the decline in profits. "Our plan," said Charlie Reagan, Loew's general sales manager, "focuses on the local community and theater, not on the glorification of Hollywood. Our motto is 'There's More Fun at the Movies.'" The managers of Loew's theaters across the country were subjected to a barrage of criticism— they didn't vacuum the floors fast enough, they didn't replace the carpet when it got worn, they didn't advertise enough in local papers, they didn't innovate with stage shows, they didn't join the local chamber of commerce and get to know everyone in town.

Dore Schary produced a picture in CinemaScope and Eastman Color called *Bad Day at Black Rock*, and it was such a success that his name was redeemed. He bought the rights to Evan Hunter's best-selling novel, *The Blackboard Jungle,* thinking he would wake up America to its failing educational system.

The Blackboard Jungle was the story of an idealistic white teacher (Glenn Ford) in a boys' vocational school who faces insubordination and violence from his students (all of them white except a thirty-year-old Sidney Poitier playing a teenager) and apathy from his fellow teachers. The students were to be played basically by unknown actors from New York. A casting call went out that M-G-M's talent department on Broadway was looking for boys to play juvenile delinquents. Notes were kept on each candidate—good-looking but can't project, not sure enough of himself, a little too soft or too cute, academic type, possibility but requires a year's coaching.

After eight hundred boys had been given individual auditions without announcements of results, cynics began to whisper that the talent search was just promotion, that when the final production date was set the studio would quickly round up the necessary quota of players from California's own juvenile-stock rosters.

"The company's sole objective," Al Altman told the *New York Times*, "is to hunt for boys who have talent and are waiting for the opportunity to show it. We are hunting everywhere." From eight hundred boys Al had to choose nine for screen testing.

Paul Mazursky, actor, director, screenwriter, and producer, recalled:

> I was working in a restaurant called the Salad Bowl. It was on Seventh Avenue across the street from where the Stage Delicatessen is. It's no longer there. I was like a counterman. This was one of the first health-food restau-

rants in New York. One day John Cassavetes came in and said they're looking for juvenile-delinquent types over at M-G-M. I was already an actor. I had already been in a movie called *Fear and Desire,* but it was tough so John said, "Well, let me take you over there; I know the guy, Al." So we finished work and John Cassavetes took us over and there was Al sitting up there at M-G-M. I'd never been to a thing like that in my life. I didn't know what the hell was going on. Al said to me, "What have you done, kid?" So I lied like mad, said I'd been in *Mister Roberts.* Everyone in New York at that time who was a young actor said they'd been in some company of *Mister Roberts.* Al said, "Are you a tough guy?" I said, "I'm from Brownsville. Yeah, I'm tough." He said, "All right. Come in Friday. I want to test you." So I said, "For what part?" He said, "I'm just going to give you one of those tests where I ask you questions."

I showed up that day. I wore one of those teenage jackets, and I talked with a Brooklyn accent. I remember Al as being a delightful and open guy, you know, to take a guy who was working behind the counter. So I did the test. I sat on a stool and answered a lot of questions.

In Al's ad-lib tests he asked hopefuls if they played any sports, if they ever did any writing, how often they went to the movies, or what they would do if they couldn't have a career in pictures. He asked were any of their relatives in the theatrical profession, did they have a personal philosophy about acting, who was their favorite actor, what was their opinion of Hollywood, what was their favorite motion picture, what was their favorite role, had they ever had any unusual adventures, did they govern their lives by any rules, what was their most treasured possession, did they have any superstitions, did they play a musical instrument, did they have any pets, any phobias, any hobbies, what was their childhood ambition?

"Then I go back to work," Paul Mazursky recalled, "and I'm working behind the counter squeezing carrot juice when the owner says there's a phone call for you and I told you I don't want you getting any phone calls. So I answer the phone and it's Al. He says, 'you got the part.' And I ripped the phone, I almost threw it out. I took the apron off and threw it against the wall. I went crazy! It was a great thing for me. It changed my life."

Another actor who made his debut in *The Blackboard Jungle* was the talented Vic Morrow. He came to see Al without an agent and without enough money for lunch. He was cast as a vicious kid who tries to rape the sexy woman teacher and pulls a switchblade on Glenn Ford. He went on to star in *Portrait of a Mobster, The Bad News Bears* and many other films. He had many television credits, including starring in the ABC series "Combat." In 1982, while filming John Landis's *Twilight Zone—The Movie,* Vic Morrow was killed. In the scene he and two child actors were running from a helicopter which was firing at them from about thirty feet off the ground. The helicopter spun out of control and crashed. Both children were killed, and Vic Morrow was decapitated.

When *The Blackboard Jungle* was released in 1955 it caused a furor. Clare Boothe Luce, the United States ambassador to Italy, refused to attend the Venice Film Festival unless the movie was withdrawn. She said her attendance at the festival would mean she agreed with the portrait of American youth as shown in the film. Dore Schary protested that she was taking advantage of her position to censor artistic creations. She said American producers had to take some responsibility for the image of the United States in foreign countries. She said that most European people never travel to America to have their views properly adjusted by reality, and she certainly was not going to sanction a picture that showed American youth as stupid and violent. It was bad enough that Europeans believed Chicago was full of gangsters, New York full of fat capitalists, Los Angeles full of Hollywood tarts, and the land between was the "Grapes of Wrath." The sponsors of the Venice Film Festival dropped *The Blackboard Jungle* from the program and that made the picture front-page news.

The Catholic Legion of Decency gave the picture a B rating, which meant it was morally objectionable. The Canadian province of Alberta banned the picture altogether, and in England it was classified "X," which meant no children were allowed even accompanied by adults.

The film opened on Broadway at the Loew's State Theater, following the Oscar-winning *Marty*, the story of a sweet and lonely fat man who finds love at last.

The *New York Times* found that *The Blackboard Jungle,* directed by Richard Brooks, was sensational, exaggerated, and would discourage teachers from working in city schools. It was an antipublic-school picture and would give the United States a bum rap overseas. Young boys might imitate the foul behavior they saw on the screen.

The New York *Daily News* called it good entertainment, that it "gave the honest, slam-bang lowdown on the junior punks and electric chair candidates who have been permitted to make shambles of some U.S. high and vocational schools."

The film was banned in Memphis, where Lloyd Binford said it was the vilest picture he had ever seen in his twenty-six years as chief censor. Dore Schary accused him of banning the film because it showed black and white students in a classroom together. Mr. Binford replied, "When the picture first started, I thought we were going to pass a picture showing Negro and white students together. It was so bad we banned it and not because of the Negro students."

The film was also banned in Atlanta. Mrs. Christine Smith Gilliam, censor, found it immoral, obscene, and licentious. Loew's threatened to sue, saying that Mrs. Gilliam's charges were too vague and that the ban violated freedom of the press. The Atlanta Board of Review took another look at the picture and told Loew's to go ahead and sue. They wouldn't show that picture in Atlanta theaters. When the picture was shown in RKO theaters it appeared with a disclaimer saying that it was not about schools in that area. There were debates on radio and television about the picture. Educators said that the incidents were stacked, that many isolated violent acts were put together for the sake of melodrama.

Senator Estes Kefauver went to Hollywood to investigate.

He set up hearings to determine if the studio had acted responsibly when making *The Blackboard Jungle*. The first witness called was Dore Schary, who presented the senator with two huge volumes of news clippings that reported the crimes of juvenile delinquents.

M·G·M made more money from *The Blackboard Jungle* than from *Mogambo* or *Seven Brides for Seven Brothers*, but audiences came away feeling agitated, unsafe, and wronged. Louie Mayer was sickened by the film. It was exactly the kind of picture he loathed. It was violent and it lectured. His life, he believed, was a monument to the opposite kind of picture, family entertainment that allowed people to escape from their woes. He agreed with Mary Pickford, who said, "I don't believe in taking advantage of someone who comes to the theater by teaching him a lesson. He can go to church, he can read the newspapers. But when people go to a motion picture they want to be entertained."

Now Louie began to feel that it was not only for his own satisfaction that he cause the downfall of Schary and Schenck, but also that it was his patriotic duty to rid "his" studio of men with such bad taste. He began to marshal his forces.

M·G·M was the only major production company that had not made alliances with independent producers. Other companies, to cover their overhead, were not only buying the products of independent producers to distribute, but also renting their soundstages, wardrobe departments, property departments, and scenery to independent producers. All of the five majors except M·G·M were also allowing television producers to rent their facilities.

Nick Schenck realized he had to put a toe into the future and arranged to distribute Sam Goldwyn's film of the Broadway smash *Guys and Dolls*. Sam Goldwyn felt as Mayer did, that the new vogue for realism in films was misguided. "People don't want to pay good money to see somebody else's kitchen," he said.

It was one of the rare times Loew's Inc. had ever agreed to distribute an independent producer's picture. "This distribution agreement," Schenck told the press, "represents a significant step for us in our new policy of joining with the leading independent producers in the marketing of outstanding films." Sam Goldwyn's picture, shown in all the Loew's theaters, did over $13 million in business, becoming the number-one box-office attraction of 1955.

Loew's executives now began to believe that it was more profitable to distribute other companies' pictures than to produce their own in Culver City. Loew's stockholders continued to be alarmed.

Investigation showed that Loew's Inc. was riddled with nepotism. Nick Schenck's nephew was vice president and director of Donahue & Coe, the advertising agency that did most of Loew's work and billed the company $4 million a year. Two of Nick's nieces controlled the People's Candy Company, which owned the popcorn and candy concessions in all the Loew's theaters. Nick had an interest in the company that sold carpet to the theaters. The Loew's board of directors suggested that Nick Schenck, now in his seventies and having served fifty years as president, retire.

He was replaced by Marcus Loew's son Arthur, who did not want to be president. Arthur Loew was fifty-six, close to the age when his father died, and he had no intention of worrying himself into an early grave. But to soothe stockholders he agreed to serve briefly.

Arthur Loew had inherited some of his father's pioneering spirit, which inspired him to develop the international possibilities of motion-picture distribution and theaters. He was president of Loew's International Corporation, a Loew's subsidiary. Noted for business acumen and skill, he had been working for his father's company since the day he graduated from college. He supervised the international distribution of M-G-M pictures and was in charge of one hundred thirty sales offices in thirty-eight countries. Overseas distribution was vitally important to M-G-M, as foreign revenues had come to make up almost 50 percent of the company's gross.

Something of a ladies' man, Arthur Loew was married

three times, first to Adolph Zukor's daughter Mildred, then to Oscar Levant's exwife Barbara Smith, who charged that he was a cheapskate. "I had no money when I married him," Barbara Smith said to the press at their celebrated divorce. "He tried to make sure I should never have any while I lived with him. I am a cast-off wife without money or support. I appeal for justice while he laughs and brands me as a gold digger and money gouger." The night before the wedding, she claimed, she was induced to sign an agreement giving up all claims to his fortune.

In 1935, when he was between wives, a young French woman arrived in America and accused Arthur Loew of being the father of her child. She sued him for $100,000 in damages, claiming that he had met her when she was sixteen-years-old during a cruise on the liner *France*. She said he promised her a career in the movies and enticed her to the Hotel Majestic in Paris, where he seduced her. The case was settled out of court. She and her mother went back to Paris satisfied.

Used to spending a lot of time in Europe as well as playing tennis, sailing his yacht, and flying his plane, Arthur Loew gritted his teeth and turned to his new task. He went to Hollywood to act as a liaison between the home office and the studio. He engaged the management-consulting firm of Booz Allen and Hamilton to make a four-week survey of operations at the studio in order to recommend ways to cut costs. He called his investigation "Operation Self Probe."

Wall Street caught the scent of a lucrative liquidation operation. Dreyfus & Co., Hirsh & Co., and the Leon Lowenstein Foundation controlled about 250,000 shares of Loew's common stock and thought that Loew's Inc. might be better dead than alive because of its real-estate holdings and its valuable film library. There began to be rumors of a takeover.

To support his position, Arthur Loew turned to two Wall Street houses that had lately acquired substantial blocks of Loew's stock, Lehman Brothers and Lazard Freres. Both companies placed representatives on the Loew's board.

Arthur Loew decided to eliminate all executive profit sharing and announced that no money at all would be paid into the retirement fund for the next year. M-G-M's library contained one thousand sound feature films and over a thousand sound short films. Arthur Loew decided to lease 770 feature films and 900 short subjects and cartoons, produced from 1929 to 1949, to television. The representatives on the board from Lehman Brothers and Lazard Freres believed Arthur Loew should not lease but sell outright the pre-1949 film library to TV. A $50-million offer had come in, but Loew refused. He planned to announce at the annual stockholders' meeting that the company would acquire an interest in or purchase television stations and that M-G-M would produce programs for television.

Loew, remembering how intimate his father had felt with those who owned stock in the company, decided to attend a stockholders' meeting. His predecessor, Nick Schenck, had never attended one. Usually about a hundred and fifty folks showed up out of the more than thirty thousand who owned stock, few enough for everyone to fit comfortably into the projection room at 1540 Broadway. After what was always a convivial meeting, the stockholders were shown the studio's latest movie, then they went to the restaurant in the basement for the annual free lunch.

But in 1956 Loew's earnings were down about $3 million and stock was worth only five cents a share. So many stockholders returned their invitations that the annual meeting had to be held in the Loew's State Theater. About eight hundred people filed into the theater and sat down quietly. When Loew got up to speak someone began stamping his feet, and soon half the room was stamping, and the crowd began to boo and shout questions. One man stood up and demanded to know why only three M-G-M pictures out of fifty-two had made money in the last eighteen months. A woman demanded, "What about television?"

Appalled, Arthur Loew sat down. When the stockholders calmed down, he told them about his plans to lease old films to television. The titles would include: *The Yearling, Mrs. Miniver, Gaslight, National Velvet, Goodbye Mr. Chips, The Wizard of Oz, Grand Hotel, Mutiny on the Bounty, David Copperfield,* and *Treasure Island.* A stockholder shouted, "Long overdue!" Loew reported that he had cut costs—abolished all profit-sharing contracts for executives, eliminated retirement-plan payments for everyone making more than $500 a week—and that earnings would be up enough to cover a twenty-five-cent quarterly dividend. Loew said he planned to buy pictures from independent producers and was working on a contract with the British producer Sir Michael Balcon, who created *The Lavender Hill Mob* starring Alec Guinness, to make six pictures a year for M-G-M to distribute. A stockholder stood up and shouted, "These directors are big-salaried old windbags!"

The rental of old M-G-M pictures to television brought $20 million in fresh revenue and gave aging stars a new life. Joan Crawford and others were young again for a new generation of fans. But now they had to compete against their own selves as they had once been. No one wanted to see a wrinkled Joan Crawford in a current movie when they could sit at home and see her in her youth on the television screen. She called it a "living death when Hollywood sold out to television."

Arthur Loew resigned. This was not his cup of tea. The Loew's board of directors called upon Joseph Vogel to be president. He didn't want the job either. But there was no one else as competent. "We believe," wrote the editor of *Boxoffice,* "that Joe Vogel is the man who can keep Leo roaring, proudly, from theatre screens around the world."

Joseph Vogel, age fifty-five, had worked for Loew's since 1914. He was a kid then, an usher in a Loew's theater in Harlem. He stayed to become manager of that theater, where his creative promotion of upcoming pictures brought him to the attention of his boss, Marcus Loew. Eventually, Vogel was put in charge of New York City theaters, then general manager of all Loew's theatres at a salary of $3,000 a week. Under his direction, over a period of ten years, Loew's Theatres earned a profit of $75 million. He had a modest demeanor, a soft voice, and light blue eyes, and everyone liked him.

"You mention Joe Vogel," said trade-press publisher Martin Quigley, Jr., now in his seventies.

> I remember once flying on one of their junkets to London and when he got to London airport, whichever one was being used then, Joe Vogel had taken off his shoes for the flight and he couldn't get them on. So here he was met by his people in a fancy car to take him wherever he was going and there he went off in his stocking feet with one of his associates holding his shoes. He was a very well-regarded person and the theater operation he ran for many years was very successful.

Pressure was put upon Vogel to fire Dore Schary. Wall Street blamed Schary for the company's decline, believing that Dore Schary was part of the old Schenck regime. If it was going to be business as usual, Wall Street intended to start a proxy fight.

Schary's contempt for the popular and his accent upon the serious led to the gibe "We used to be in the entertainment business, but have sold our souls for a pot of message."

The *Wall Street Journal* reported:

> The studio division has shown little, if any, profit under his management although it represents the area of greatest investment for the company. . . . Despite the management's oft-repeated statements of support for Mr. Schary, it had increased the number of independently produced films and distribution arrangements for non-Schary supervised units using the Metro lot, thus shearing away some of Mr. Schary's authority.

Joe Vogel was no fan of Dore Schary's. That there would be a top executive working for Loew's who did not want to give his entire life to the company was something that Joe Vogel could not understand. Schary, from Vogel's point of view, spent too much time on politics. Vogel and most of the Loew's board members were ardent Republicans. They wore their "I Like Ike" buttons proudly. Dore Schary campaigned for Adlai Stevenson and was a delegate at the Democratic convention in Chicago. Schary produced an hour-long documentary, on the history of the Democratic Party during the Roosevelt and Truman administrations, which was shown at the convention. When Vogel asked Schary to defend the time he spent pro-ducing a political movie, Schary claimed that he didn't use one penny of company money and that he worked on his film only at night and on the weekends. To someone like Vogel, who worked all day for Loew's *and* at night and on weekends, who watched and evaluated every picture produced by the major studios, about four hundred a year, so that he could better exploit M-G-M's competing product, and was accus-tomed to total dedication from men who had been with the company as long as he had, Dore Schary's excuse sounded lame. Schary asked to be taken off the M-G-M payroll for the week he was away in Chicago.

His film was telecast directly from the convention by NBC and ABC, but it didn't do Adlai Stevenson a bit of good. Eisenhower won by a landslide. The film did not do Dore Schary any good either. When asked by reporters if he was about to be sacked, Schary said, "There's no battle about me. I would have been the first to hear about it and I haven't." He said that he had inherited tremendous financial overhead. There were too many contract players for the number of films produced. Four thousand employees created only twenty-nine films. "L.B. insisted upon maintaining a large staff of producers and stars on long-term contracts," Schary said, "to provide what L.B. called 'strength in depth.'"

Joe Vogel fired Dore Schary a year before Schary's contract was due to expire. He said that Schary had a lot of enemies on the board of directors, among the stockholders, and in the studio. Nick Schenck turned against Dore Schary, too, saying it was the worst mistake he ever made giving Schary authority to run the studio. "The dismissal of Mr. Schary," the *New York Times* said in December 1956, "which came as a climactic turn in a long series of dramatic unseatings of executive personnel at Loew's Inc. and Metro-Goldwyn-Mayer, and is essentially another indication of the inexorable change in big studio operations happening in Hollywood."

SIXTEEN

Proxy Fight

Loew's Inc. was a quarter-of-a-billion-dollar industrial empire. For almost forty years it was the preeminent motion-picture company in America, the only great film combine to escape the Depression unharmed. It produced motion pictures under the trade name Metro-Goldwyn-Mayer. Its studio was known as the Tiffany of studios. It owned 129 theaters in the United States, three in Canada and 39 abroad, as well as music-publishing companies, a recording company (which manufactured phonograph records under the M-G-M label and produced continuous hit songs), a radio station, interests in television stations, and a motion-picture studio in Elstree, England.

Loew's Inc. employed almost 14,000 people, 8,500 in the United States and 4,900 in forty-seven other countries. It had valuable real-estate holdings, including theaters and office buildings in large cities. In Culver City it owned 185 acres, some found to be oil-producing, on which there were twenty-eight buildings containing production stages, laboratories for developing film, a building for the manufacture of cartoons, prop rooms with thousands of costumes, scene docks, dressing-room buildings, office buildings for writers, directors, and administrators, and machine shops and woodworking shops staffed by workers who could build everything to look like anything. There was a dubbing studio for rerecording pictures in foreign languages. Gross receipts derived by Loew's Inc. from its worldwide activities averaged about $178 million a year. Its management had been so successful that its stockholders contentedly endorsed whatever it desired.

Now the mood was sour. Though Dore Schary had been fired, and the company had made distribution deals with independent producers and had launched into television production, Loew's stock was way down. There was talk of a proxy fight. It would be the first proxy fight in the history of the film industry.

Just who instigated the fight is moot. Some say it was Louis B. Mayer, age seventy-two. Others say Louie was brought in as a prop by Stanley Meyer, age forty, a citizen of Hollywood with ambitions beyond his abilities. His name began to appear in newspapers. Louis B. Mayer hailed him as "a bold, aggressive man, tough as a bull." When Louie was asked by reporters if he really believed Stanley Meyer was competent to run M-G-M, Louie said, "I'd bet you $100,000 he could *not* do it—but give me a year to teach him what *I* know, and I can make him the most gilt-edged property in Hollywood today."

Stanley Meyer was the son of an executive at Twentieth Century-Fox and son-in-law of the chairman of the board of Universal Pictures. His only professional accomplishment was that he coproduced the popular television series *Dragnet*. Mayer had invested money in that program. Stanley Meyer was so fond of Mayer he made him godfather of one of his children. When Meyer sold out his 25 percent interest in *Dragnet*, he found himself with a million dollars to spend and nothing to do. He asked Louie for advice. Louie suggested that Stanley become president of Loew's Inc., an idea which at first seemed preposterous but began to grow on Meyer the more Louie flattered him. Some say that idea came from Meyer himself, who saw the iron was hot at Loew's Inc. and asked Louie to back him.

To gain control of the company, Stanley Meyer and Louie Mayer went to Joseph Tomlinson, who owned three-and-a-half million-dollars' worth of Loew's stock. Joe Tomlinson never imagined getting involved in the management of the company. He didn't know the first thing about making movies or running theaters, but he owned more Loew's stock than any other individual shareholder.

A Canadian citizen, a 1932 graduate of MIT, with a degree in business management, Tomlinson made millions building roads in Canada. He was president of Consolidated Truck Lines, Ltd. Mayer described Tomlinson, whose greeting was a hard slap on the back, as "a real two-fisted guy." Tomlinson, age forty-seven, was a huge, broad-shouldered man with matted-down hair, a gruff face, a long nose, and a thick reddish-brown mustache. A chain-smoker, he used a cigarette holder to cut down on the ill-effects of nicotine. He was not above illegal activities: His firm pleaded guilty to defrauding the Ontario government of $360,000 in connection with highway contracts and had to pay a fine of $100,000, one of the toughest penalties of its kind in Ontario legal records. Tomlinson now lived in Fort Lauderdale, where he kept his yacht.

Some say Louis B. Mayer contacted him. Others say Stanley Meyer contacted Tomlinson and together they convinced Louie to back them. Whatever the truth, the three men teamed up.

Mayer told Tomlinson that it might be possible for him to become the head of the greatest entertainment empire in the world and that the decline of the company could be reversed. Tomlinson was flattered, honored, and sincerely believed that with Louie behind him giving advice he would learn enough about the motion-picture business to be at least chairman of the board, or maybe chief executive at the studio.

The first thing Joe Tomlinson did was hire an attorney, Ben Javits, brother of Jacob Javits, the United States Senator from New York. Ben Javits organized a small group of Loew's stockholders who made phone calls to other stockholders to ask if they were happy with the management of Loew's. Did they know that Louis B. Mayer, the man who made the company great in the first place, was no longer employed there? Many stockholders were surprised to learn that Louis B. Mayer was no longer chief. They began to equate the recent loss of profits with his absence.

Joe Vogel, Loew's new president, received the following letter from Joseph Tomlinson:

> Dear Mr. Vogel: I have come to the conclusion that it is necessary for me to communicate with my fellow stockholders in our mutual interest. Specifically I intend to seek the election of a Board of Directors, truly representative of the stockholders' interest and capable of directing the affairs of the company free from the inherited blight of mismanagement, waste and nepotism, which the present board perpetuates, and which you, under the present board are incapable of escaping. Let me also say that I believe that the hope of not only the United States but the world lies in winning the great struggle through which it is passing in dealing with "isms" and adverse forces around the world. The winning force to do that is the managerial corps of American business, in fact the managerial corps of all business. Nobody can or will do it as much as they. If this group should lose the confidence and support of the American people, all is lost for all of us. Therefore stockholders in American corporations, particularly, are the strongest bulwark to protect and defend what we hold dear. It is this which motivates me in what I have to say. The company has been operated in a way that seems to serve the special interests of the managers, their relatives, their friends, their lackeys. The evil relationship is insidious and far-reaching throughout the company. Only a new and sound directorate, uncontaminated by misguided loyalties and habit patterns can hope to cope effectively with

the problem of cleaning house.

Vogel hired an attorney of his own, Louis Nizer. "I have a lawyer's prayer," Nizer once told some young law students. "Please, O Lord, give me the good health and vitality to be able to perform my duties in the most arduous of professions." Louis Nizer had many famous clients, both entertainers and society people. He was known for his discretion. Joe Vogel wanted to keep the internal struggles of his company out of the public eye. Vogel was mortified that the company he had known in the days when Marcus Loew's generous spirit pervaded it was now involved in an ugly fight.

The Tomlinson faction let the press in on its every move. In December 1956 the *Wall Street Journal* reported that Joseph Tomlinson had arrived in New York from Fort Lauderdale to open headquarters in a midtown hotel in order to "mobilize nation-wide sentiment to effect reforms in the management of Loew's." Tomlinson hired a professional proxy-soliciting concern on a standby basis and asked for and received a list of Loew's stockholders. "He reiterated yesterday that he would 'prefer' to avoid a proxy fight. His statement added that if differences with the management cannot be settled 'internally' then 'we are ready to nominate our own slate of candidates for the board of directors. And we are prepared to elect them. The continuing deterioration at Loew's Inc. must be stopped.' "

Tomlinson and his attorneys met with Joe Vogel and his attorneys. Tomlinson's demands included a new board of directors, the reinstatement of Louis B. Mayer as consultant to the studio, and the appointments of Tomlinson as chairman of the board and Stanley Meyer as president of the company. Joe Vogel rejected these demands, especially the one about Stanley Meyer, who was qualified in no way at all to become the president of anything.

Vogel sought the support of the bankers who controlled hundreds of thousands of shares in Loew's, Lazard Freres and Lehman Brothers. They agreed with Vogel that Tomlinson and Meyer had no knowledge of the industry. On the other hand, the bankers were not crazy about Joe Vogel. They thought he was a Schenck man, part of the old management.

Tomlinson courted the bankers, too. While Vogel and his counsel were meeting late one evening with Tomlinson and his lawyer, Vogel's secretary announced that one of the top men at Lazard Freres was on the phone for Tomlinson. The call appeared to confirm what Tomlinson had been telling Vogel, that he had the bankers on his side. Actually, the Lazard Freres man was just returning Tomlinson's call. But Joe Vogel got scared, foresaw open warfare at the next stockholders' meeting, and decided to compromise. He said he would agree to a new board of directors, thirteen in all, made up of six who supported Vogel, six who supported Tomlinson, and one neutral person they could both agree upon.

The six directors named by Tomlinson were himself, Stanley Meyer, Ray Lawson, who was a pal of his from Canada, and three friends of Mayer—Louis Johnson, once Louie's attorney and former secretary of defense; K.T. Keller, former president of Chrysler Corporation; and Fred F. Florence, chairman of the executive committee of the Republic National Bank of Dallas.

The six directors proposed by Vogel were himself; George A. Brownell, a partner in the John W. Davis law firm; William A. Parker, chairman of the board of Incorporated Investors, Inc.; John L. Sullivan, once secretary of the navy; George L. Killion, president of the American President Lines, Ltd.; and Frank Pace, Jr., executive vice president of General Dynamics Corporation and a former secretary of the army. The thirteenth director Vogel and Tomlinson chose together was Ogden Reid, president and editor of the *New York Herald Tribune*.

When the annual meeting of the stockholders took place three months later, with Joe Vogel presiding for the first time, a "harmonious" slate of thirteen directors was presented and was elected by 4,567,000 votes. One of the stockholders who held proxies for 14,000 votes stood up and said:

I think management should be complimented on the fact that there was no proxy fight. I also think the opposition who placed some members on the board are also to be complimented on that score. I wonder if Joe Tomlinson, who has made some public statements in the course of getting these various men on the board would get up and say something which would help the other stockholders.

Tomlinson, who was sitting at the dais with Joe Vogel, rose and replied:

I would be very happy to say a few words. My effort in the first place was to see that the stockholders of this company got a fair break. When it became apparent, in my opinion, that a satisfactory reconciliation could be made and save the company the vast expense and waste which would take place if a proxy fight was carried out, I was very happy to sit with Mr. Vogel.

But after the meeting Tomlinson called a private caucus of directors and proposed that Vogel be removed as president and Stanley Meyer be designated in his place.

Tomlinson, now a director of the company, was within his rights to demand that the corporation provide him an office on its premises, free. He moved into 1540 Broadway with three attorneys and several accountants. Every day he went to his office on the twelfth floor and proceeded to make life uncomfortable for Joe Vogel. He thought that if he became enough of a nuisance Vogel would get fed up and quit. Vogel, like so many soft-spoken men, did not seem like a fighter, but he was.

Tomlinson demanded the expense and entertainment accounts of all officers and executives, interoffice correspondence of all kinds, production costs on motion pictures that had lost money, the write-off cost of stories that had never been used, and all contracts with producers, stars, or executives. He demanded production and distribution schedules and costs, records of advertising expenditures, television contracts, music-recording contracts, and tons of vouchers and documents. The whole building was in a turmoil. Men and women who were busy doing their jobs had to stop to find records for Joe Tomlinson. Work ground to a halt as all departments were flooded with demands to produce documents long stored in warehouses. When people objected to Tomlinson's demands, he said he was only acting to ferret out wrongdoing.

"If he can find anything wrong," Joe Vogel said, "I want to know about it, too. I'm not responsible for what the prior regime did, and I don't want to give the impression that I am shielding it. I want everybody to know that I am trying to do the right thing. All that I want is for a stockholder to come up to me someday and say, "Gee, Joe, this is a great company!' "

From the pile of documents delivered to him, Tomlinson did find some grievances, and these he put into letters addressed to Joe Vogel with copies sent to all the directors. Every twenty-four hours Tomlinson sent a letter to Vogel. Then Tomlinson increased that number to two letters every day stating serious charges against the current management. An example:

> Dear Mr. Vogel: I understand that you plan to transfer the pre-1949 film library to a Liberian Corporation. The purpose of this letter is to request that all steps looking toward putting the program into effect promptly be halted. In my view, the new directors should pass specifically on the question of whether the corporation would incur the risk of placing $60,000,000 worth of assets in a foreign corporation. They should certainly review the decision to enter into this transaction without prior clearance from Internal Revenue, in view of the fact that the consequences could be severe, amounting to an immediate liability of as much as $15,000,000 if the ultimate ruling is adverse. I am so strongly of the view that no further action should be taken on this matter until the new board has been fully informed of the proposal and the problems which it raises, that I hereby request that you inform me by letter by the end of the current week, what your plans are in this regard. I am taking the

liberty of sending a copy of this letter to the other members of the Board.

Vogel countered by saying the sale of the $60-million film library to the Liberian firm would save the company money, because the capital-gains tax would be less than income tax. Then Tomlinson accused Vogel of purchasing a television station that was bankrupt. Vogel wrote back that the television station was solvent. None of the charges Tomlinson brought against Vogel could be made to stick.

The energetic Tomlinson found it something of a chore to sit behind a desk couped up in a New York office while his yacht waited in balmy waters. He lasted a few months, then packed up his staff and departed. But now the men and women who had worked at 1540 Broadway for years who had previously concerned themselves with their own jobs and seldom had anything to say about the way the company was run, began to say that it might not be such a bad idea after all if Joe Vogel steps down. Louis Nizer was on Joe Vogel's side. Let Stanley Meyer take over. Meyer doesn't know much, but L.B. would be there to help him. The man who made this company great in the first place is the best man to turn the company around now.

Behind the scenes, every time Joe Vogel was about to sign a contract for a package—story, star, and director—Louie found out about it and convinced the star that it was the wrong vehicle for him or her. When Vogel did manage to bring a package to the board of directors for approval, he was continually shot down by Tomlinson and Stanley Meyer. Vogel began to acquire a reputation in the industry as a man who could not put deals through.

Meetings of the board became Vogel directors against Tomlinson directors. There was a lot of whispering and private little groups meeting in one corner while other little groups met in another corner. One of Joe Vogel's board members, Frank Pace, the executive vice president of General Dynamics, suggested that a mangement-consultant firm be called in to recommend ways of getting the company moving again. He said that when he was secretary of war, Robert Heller & Associates had performed such a task for the War Department and they also had reorganized the Chrysler Corporation.

So a representative of Robert Heller began to investigate both the home office and the studio in Culver City. Much to the amazement of everyone, he recommended that Joe Vogel be replaced as president, Louis B. Mayer be elected chairman of the board, and Stanley Meyer be hired as assistant to the president.

Joe Vogel refused to resign. Instead, he stopped being discreet and announced to the press that Louis B. Mayer was trying to regain control of the company. A headline in *Motion Picture Herald* read: "Vogel Challenges Tomlinson to Open Battle for Loew Control." The story continued:

In a dramatic move believed to be without precedent in the corporate annals of the motion picture industry, Joseph R. Vogel, president of Loew's Inc., Monday of this week brought out into the open the long-threatened showdown between Loew's management, headed by him, and the Joseph Tomlinson-Stanley Meyer-Louis B. Mayer group for control of the company. Mr. Vogel issued a call for a special meeting of Loew's stockholders September 12 for the express purpose of removing Mr. Tomlinson and Mr. Meyer from the board of directors.

Variety reported:

Louis B. Mayer has hit back at charges that he was master-minding a "plot" to seize control of Loew's from the administration led by Joseph R. Vogel. Mayer called Vogel "a fool who doesn't know what he's talking about" and contended that if he wanted control of Loew's he never would have left his job as studio head. "I don't think he's capable of filling the post," he snapped. "I'm told he was a fool to accept it." Mayer admitted he was giving advice to Joseph Tomlinson and Stanley Meyer, but added he's also giving Vogel advice.

News of the impending proxy fight was shouted in the *New York Times, New York World-Telegram and the Sun, Boxoffice, Film Daily, Motion Picture Exhibitor, Independent Film Journal, New York Journal-American, New York Post,* and *Wall Street Journal.*

Vogel, now more furious than embarrassed, wrote to the stockholders:

> On behalf of Loew's Inc., I am calling the stockholders into a special meeting to remove Joseph Tomlinson of Canada and his associate Stanley Meyer from the Board of Directors. Tomlinson and Meyer with the constant guidance of Louis B. Mayer have been actively attempting to seize control of this great public company and against the interests of the stockholders. The stockholders and the entire motion picture industry are well aware of Mayer's record when he was in supreme command of the studio. During his term of 27 years he received over twenty million dollars in compensation. In the last three years of Mayer's sole authority as the studio's head, in 1947, 1948, 1949 the pictures released lost about nine million dollars. This is the man who at the age 72 is attempting to recapture his position through the Tomlinson-Meyer machinations. At the special meeting which is being called, the stockholders will also be asked to enlarge the Board from 13 to 19 seats, and to fill the new and vacant posts so that an effective working majority of independent directors can be given to management. A full slate of candidates of the highest standing in their respective fields will be presented.

Ben Shlyen, the editor of *Boxoffice,* the trade magazine for theater owners, wrote an editorial in July 1957 in favor of Joe Vogel:

> After showing the patience of Job, Joseph R. Vogel, president of Loew's, Inc., has decided to come to grips with two dissident stockholders and directors whose reported actions have interfered with the management's well-stated efforts to bring the company back to its former

pre-eminence.... Through his long experience in the management of Loew's Theaters, in which he served as executive vice-president in charge of this successful circuit's operations, and later as its president, Mr. Vogel is unusually well qualified to carry out his duties as president of the parent organization. He has long since proved to be one of the industry's most astute theatre operators and his knowledge of films and their evaluation, from the standpoint of what the public will pay to see, is a tremendous asset.

The management consultant from Robert Heller & Associates reversed his report and said that Joe Vogel should remain as president. If he could unite the board he would be the best man for president. "It is our view that Mr. Vogel is a very competent executive and were it not for the conflict in the Board we would have recommended unqualifiedly his retention as president and chief executive officer."

Two of Vogel's directors tired of the fighting and resigned from the board. So did Ogden Reid, the neutral director. Joe Tomlinson now had six directors, Vogel four. Under the bylaws directors were empowered to fill vacancies on the board and could do so by a mere majority. Tomlinson immediately called a meeting of directors so he could put three more of his own men on the board. Joe Vogel was in California attending to studio business, and the meeting was called to coincide with Vogel's absence.

On the day of Tomlinson's special board meeting, sirens shrieked and a police escort accompanied a long black limousine to the door of 1540 Broadway. Out of the car and into the glare of popping flashbulbs stepped Louis B. Mayer. A crowd had been assembled on the sidewalk to cheer as he entered the building.

Surrounded by reporters, Louie stepped out of the elevator on each floor and greeted Loew's personnel. Even at the age of 72 he radiated power. He said to the assembled crowd of executives and secretaries, "I have come back because I am lonely for Leo the Lion."

Mayer was made a director, and Joe Vogel, who wasn't there to defend himself, was removed from office. When the meeting was over Louie held a press conference announcing the demise of the old regime and the beginning of a return to greatness. A photo of Mayer entering the Loew's building appeared in the newspaper. "I am home again," the caption read. "I am here to restore Loew's to the top again. I have decided to take back the company I built."

When Vogel returned from Hollywood, where he was arranging for the new production of *Ben-Hur*, this time with Charlton Heston, he wrote a letter to the stockholders: "The Tomlinson-Mayer faction held a rump meeting of five directors out of the thirteen elected by the stockholders. The meeting, of course, was illegal. A quorum of seven is required by the bylaws. Only five attended. Louis B. Mayer's program has simply shifted from obstruction to usurpation."

The battle was taken to court, and during the months that it took to resolve the dispute the film industry rallied behind Joe Vogel. He was named "Pioneer of the Year" by the directors of Motion Picture Pioneers, an organization made up of men who had served the industry for more than twenty-five years. When he heard he had been named for the honor, Vogel said, "From a corporate point of view we are going through a stormy period, but we will win out over the forces of destruction. I realize that while I am the personal recipient of the honor, it is primarily an acknowledgement of the part the Loew company has played as a service to the industry and the public."

Several Loew's stockholders got together and formed a unit to back Vogel. They called themselves the Loew's Stockholders Protective Committee and elected as their chairman Harry Brandt, a theater-circuit operator and president of the Independent Theatre Owners of America. Membership in the committee was about one hundred, including actor Burt Lancaster, the producer Michael Todd, Leo Lindy of the famous Lindy's restaurant in Times Square, and others representing the motion-picture, financial, and industrial fields.

Brandt hoped the committee would control a million shares of Loew's. Sam Goldwyn and Frank Sinatra joined the fight against Mayer.

Theater owners organized to support Vogel. In August 1957, Harry C. Arthur, Jr., chairman of the board of the Southern California Theater Owners Association, wrote a letter to all members urging that they buy as much Loew's stock as they could to back Joe Vogel in the upcoming proxy fight with the Joseph Tomlinson combine. "We urge you to retain the stock, so that Loew's will be owned, if not actually, then substantially by the exhibitors of America."

Independent theater owners in Ohio agreed to vote their association's Loew's stock for Vogel management. It was the first time the Ohio exhibitors' group ever voted its film-company stock.

Mayer's rump meeting was declared illegal, but that was not the end of the fight. Only the stockholders had the power to determine who would run Loew's Inc. Each individual stockholder heard from both sides. Tomlinson hired a staff of telephone callers to contact as many stockholders as they could in every state. They telephoned from morning to night. Hello, Mrs. so-and-so? I'm a Loew's stockholder and I know you are, too, and that's why I'm calling. I'm worried about the company. I think it's gone downhill since Mr. Louis B. Mayer was ousted. Yes, there is something you can do. Have you sent in your proxy vote yet?

On October 15, 1957, more than a thousand Loew's stockholders filed into the Loew's State Theater on Times Square for the big showdown. There were so many stockholders the theater was closed for regular business that day. Joe Vogel, who had attended the gala opening of that theater, when Marcus Loew had stood on the stage surrounded by girls from the *Ziegfeld Follies*, and had once been in charge of keeping that theater shipshape, must have been saddened to notice that the maroon velvet stage curtain was worn and the carpet needed to be replaced.

On the stage, instead of marvelous performers there were

the drabbest of the drab, people known as "computers." They had been supplied by Bankers Trust Company, and their job was to count the millions of votes cast by the stockholders. Ushers with microphones were stationed in the aisles. Their job was to act like hosts of a TV talk show and hurry with the mike to the stockholder recognized by the chair.

In front of the orchestra pit a long table was set up with chairs for Vogel and his advisers and a stenotypist who had been working at Loew's for years. Words flew into her ears and out through her fingers. Next to the main table was a smaller one for two officers of Bankers Trust, who were to act as inspectors of election and who had filed their statutory oaths to conduct the election properly. They had to determine all questions that arose from conflicting proxies. A stockholder could change his or her mind many times, but the last vote before time was up was the one that counted.

In almost every section of the theater, especially in the first twenty rows, were men and women with megaphones. They intended to be heard even if not recognized by the chair. And sprinkled among the stockholders were the kooks. A woman wrapped in a beach towel said through her megaphone that, since some of the directors had just returned from their yachts on the Caribbean, she wanted to represent the poor stockholders, who could only go as far as Miami Beach.

In the front row of the orchestra sat the men Joe Vogel was going to propose as candidates for the board of directors: General Omar Bradley, who was then chairman of the board of a division of Bulova Watch; Bennett Cerf, the publishing executive, entertainer, and writer; the president of the board of education of the city of New York; a tax specialist; a former attorney general of the United States; a vice president of an advertising agency; the head of a diamond company; and Robert O'Brien, who had worked for years as an attorney with the Securities and Exchange Commission and was an assistant to the president of Paramount.

As usual, the meeting started with a showing of the company's latest movie. This year it was the comedy *Don't Go Near the*

Water, starring Glenn Ford and Anne Francis, a zany tale about United States Navy press officers on a Pacific isle miles away from battle in World War II. When the houselights went up, the stockholders were served box lunches. Then the official meeting began. A spotlight from the balcony lit up the front table. Joe Vogel stepped to the microphone and began reading his formal opening statement—a stockholders' list had been duly filed, the officials of Bankers Trust Company would act as inspectors of election, and other routine statements. Someone near the front shouted, "Mr. Chairman, I raise the question of the absence of a quorum."

Vogel said, "Please let me finish, and you can bring that objection up when I finish."

Then dozens of people in the first twenty rows began to talk at once. "Mr. Chairman!" one shouted. Another said, "Don't interrupt. He has the floor." Another said, "If there is no quorum, there is no meeting." There was shouting all over the place.

Stockholder: "Mr. Chairman—"

Vogel: "You are out of order, Sir."

Stockholder: "No, Sir. It is a point of order. I am not out of order."

Vogel: "I have ruled."

Stockholder: "You have ruled and you may be wrong."

Another stockholder: "I don't see why you don't give that man a chance to speak."

Vogel: "I will give him a chance."

Stockholder: "You want everybody to be as brief as possible, but you do all the talking."

This bedlam continued for a while. Vogel called upon his lawyer to rule on whether or not a quorum was present. Louis Nizer read the legal rule then said, "It is one thing for a stockholder to insist upon asserting his rights. Right or wrong he has the right to speak. It is another thing to obstruct a meeting by having men placed throughout the meeting in such a way as to cause confusion and prevent the meeting from taking place."

But the bedlam continued. Tomlinson and Vogel had a confrontation. "I don't want control of the company!" Tomlinson shouted. "I want good management! You cannot get it until the old guard is rooted out! You, Mr. Vogel, are not capable of rooting them out."

"Are you through, Mr. Tomlinson," said Vogel. "I want to give you every opportunity."

"Get the boxing gloves!" an excited stockholder shouted.

"Would-be speakers popped up and down so fast," reported *Motion Picture Herald*, "that Mr. Vogel had to interrupt those already recognized and promise they would be heard. His patience seemed inexhaustible."

Louis Nizer said to the assembled stockholders, "This has been a bitter contest through many courts, and the opposition has had its fair opportunity to present all of its arguments and has the same opportunity again today if they wish it. That is their privilege; but the president has appealed to you to conduct this meeting in an orderly manner, and when he has ruled on a point of order it is no use having five people stand up and scream."

Then followed a debate—should the board be increased to nineteen members or kept at thirteen. Everyone had something to say on the matter. Then the meeting was adjourned so votes could be tabulated. The meeting was reconvened an hour later. The amendment to enlarge the board to nineteen directors was carried by about two million votes.

The Vogel slate for new directors was then nominated. Tomlinson proposed new directors of his own and expressed his lack of faith in Joe Vogel. The debate was vigorous and below the belt. Someone accused Tomlinson of being a crook; someone else accused Vogel of not being able to get along with Culver City. Back and forth it went until seven thirty that night. An adjournment was taken to tabulate the votes, and an hour later the meeting reconvened. The entire slate of Vogel's directors was elected.

Vogel was radiant. "I can't say how much I thank you all for your confidence, and I want you to know that I am going to do everything in my power to merit that confidence. All my associates will break their necks to do a job for you, I promise you." The meeting which had started at ten that morning ended at eight that night with Vogel victorious.

Word arrived in New York that Mayer was seriously ill. On October 29, 1957, a week after the stockholders of the company had voted against him, he died.

"I liked these men," said Louis Nizer thirty-five years later when he was asked what he remembered about Louis B. Mayer and Joe Vogel. "They were very talented. My general impression was that these were all brilliant men who headed these enterprises." Ninety-years-old, his gaze turned more inward than out, sitting in a dark suit and bright yellow tie behind a huge desk in an office with walls of windows overlooking Manhattan, author of ten best-selling books, and attorney for so many clients his law firm takes up three floors of a swank building on West Fifty-second Street, Louis Nizer said, "Rarely do you find the genius of an uneducated man heading a great enterprise today. The motion-picture industry grew up in the hands of unsophisticated people, untrained men who had no background as scholars or in the arts, yet they founded a new art form. That to me is the great surprise."

Epilogue

THE Loew's State building in Times Square, that monument to an era, was demolished in 1988 to make room for a glass skyscraper. The hyphens are gone from MGM's name, the letters no longer stand for people who can make any difference, and headquarters are in Hollywood.

Louis B. Mayer lived to see his name removed from the studio logo, a name he had pushed forward with the relentlessness of a stage mother. When he died in 1957, he left most of his money to the Louis B. Mayer Foundation which was to be headed by his daughter, Irene.

During the last days of his battle with leukemia, Louie was attended in a California hospital by Dr. Sidney Farber, who in 1947 earned international renown for achieving the first remissions of childhood leukemia through the use of chemotherapy. "Dad was uplifted by Farber's presence," the late Irene Mayer Selznick recalled. "Farber was his symbol of hope, and Dad attributed godlike qualities to him. . . . I spent hours with the doctor. He was a quiet man with a rare inner quality, a truly inspiring human being."

In 1948 Dr. Farber discussed the urgent need for funding blood research with a friend of his who owned a chain of theaters in Boston. The friend suggested that Dr. Farber speak at the monthly luncheon-meeting of the Variety Club of New England, an organization of motion-picture theater own-ers and managers who met for companionship and to orga-nize philanthropic projects.

Dr. Farber's speech about children dying of cancer was so moving and hopeful that the members of the Variety Club decided to help him by collecting money in their various the-aters. Radio host Ralph Edwards wanted to help, too, so he invited Dr. Farber to speak on the radio show "Truth or Con-sequences." Ralph Edwards discussed baseball with a boy dying of cancer, calling the boy "Jimmy." Famous baseball players spoke with the child, and radio listeners began to send money in to help all the little "Jimmys" out there. Would a little "Jane" have been as appealing?

It doesn't matter. Girls and boys have benefited equally by the Jimmy Fund, which was founded in 1948 by the Variety Club of New England and is now one of the most popular charities in the world. Dr. Farber's dream of a comprehensive cancer institute was realized in the late 1960s, when the Charles A. Dana Foundation donated a multimillion-dollar grant to help fund the construction of a new facility. The Dana-Farber building in Boston was completed in 1978. The Dana-Farber Cancer Insitute is now a teaching affiliate of the Harvard Medical School and is formally affiliated with thir-teen hospitals in Maine and Massachusetts. Its reputation for cancer research is international.

Irene Mayer Selznick claimed that Louie's dying wish was to use foundation money to honor Dr. Sidney Farber. If that was her father's dying wish it is strange that she waited thirty years to follow his instructions. But wait she did, and the results have put her father's name in lights again.

In 1988 she donated $5 million to the Dana-Farber Cancer Institute for a new building in Boston to be called the Louis B. Mayer Research Laboratories. At the dedication of the building, in which scientists in state-of-the-art laboratories spend their days in white lab coats sorting cells in high-powered machines, Irene Selznick, in her eighties, said, "It was a great relief to me that my father's dream actually came to pass. I like to think my father's name will be best remembered for the miracles that will be achieved in the fine new building that bears his name."

The building, which represents the efforts of theater men in the Variety Club who raised much of the rest of the money needed to build it, is right down the street from the Beth Israel Hospital, whose founders got Louis B. Mayer started in the first place.

Bibliography

Ackerman, Carl W. *George Eastman*. Boston: Houghton Mifflin Company, 1930.

Allen, Frederick Lewis. *The Big Change*. New York: Bantam Books, 1961.

———. *Only Yesterday*. New York: Harper and Row, 1931.

Allvine, Glendon. *The Greatest Fox of Them All*. New York: Lyle Stuart, 1969.

Balio, Tino, ed. *The American Film Industry*. Madison, Wisconsin: the University of Wisconsin Press, 1976, 1985.

Bandy, Mary Lea, ed. *The Dawn of Sound*. New York: the Museum of Modern Art, 1989.

Baxter, John. *Sixty Years of Hollywood*. Cranbury, New Jersey: A.S. Barnes and Co., Inc., 1973.

Beaton, Cecil. *Cecil Beaton's New York*. New York: J.B. Lippincott, 1938.

Behlmer, Rudy, ed. *Memo From David O. Selznick*. New York: Viking Press, 1972.

Berg, Scott A. *Goldwyn*. New York: Alfred A. Knopf, 1989.

Berle, Milton. *B.S. I Love You.* New York: McGraw-Hill Book Company, 1988.

Black, Shirley Temple. *Child Star.* New York: Warner Books, 1988.

Bluem, William, and Jason E. Squire, eds. *The Movie Business, American Film Industry Practice.* New York: Hastings House, 1973.

Bogle, Donald. *Toms, Coons, Mulattoes, Mammies and Bucks.* New York: Viking Press, 1973.

Boller, Paul F., Jr., and Ronald L. Davis. *Hollywood Anecdotes.* New York: Ballantine Books, 1987.

Brooks, Louise. *Lulu in Hollywood.* New York: Alfred A. Knopf, 1983.

Brownlow, Kevin. *The Parade's Gone By . . .* New York: Alfred A. Knopf, 1969.

———. *Hollywood, the Pioneers.* New York: Alfred A. Knopf, 1979.

Cary, Diana Serra. *Hollywood's Children.* Boston: Houghton Mifflin, 1978.

Chaplin, Charles. *My Autobiography.* New York: Simon and Schuster, 1964.

Chaplin, Lita Grey, with Morton Cooper. *My Life With Chaplin.* New York: Bernard Geis Associates, 1966.

Coblentz, Edmond D., ed. *William Randolph Hearst, a Portrait in His Own Words.* New York: Simon and Schuster, 1952.

Cohn, Lawrence. *Movietone Presents the Twentieth Century.* New York: St. Martin's Press, 1976.

Cox, Stephen. *The Munchkins Remember.* New York: E. P. Dutton, 1989.

Cripps, Thomas. *Slow Fade to Black—the Negro in American Film.* London: Oxford University Press, 1977.

Crowther, Bosley. *Hollywood Rajah.* New York: Henry Holt, 1960.

———. *The Lion's Share.* New York: E. P. Dutton and Company, 1957.

Dietz, Howard. *Dancing in the Dark.* New York: Quadrangle/The New York Times Book Co., 1974.

Drimmer, Frederick. *Very Special People.* New York: Amjon Publishers, 1973.

Eames, John Douglas. *The MGM Story.* New York: Crown, 1979.

Erens, Patricia. *The Jew in American Cinema.* Bloomington, Indiana: Indiana University Press, 1984.

Ewen, David. *The Life and Death of Tin Pan Alley.* New York: Funk and Wagnalls, 1964.

———. *Panorama of American Popular Music.* New Jersey: Prentice Hall, 1957.

Ewers, Carolyn H. *Sidney Poitier.* New York: New American Library, 1981.

Fairbanks, Douglas. *Laugh and Live.* New York: Britton Publishing Company, 1917.

Farr, Finis. *Fair Enough, the Life of Westbrook Pegler.* New Rochelle, N.Y.: Arlington House Publishers, 1975.

Field, Alice Evans. *Hollywood, U.S.A.: From Script to Screen.* New York: Vantage Press, 1952.

Finch, Christopher, and Linda Rosenkrantz. *Gone Hollywood.* New York: Doubleday and Company, 1979.

Flamini, Roland. *Ava.* New York: Coward, McCann and Geoghegan, 1983.

Fowler, Gene. *Schnozzola: The Story of Jimmy Durante.* New York: Viking Press, 1951.

Freeburg, Victor Oscar. *The Art of Photoplay Making.* New York: Macmillan Company, 1918.

Friedman, Lester D. *Hollywood's Image of the Jew.* New York: Frederick Ungar Publishing Co., 1982.

Gabler, Neal. *An Empire of Their Own.* New York: Crown, 1988.

Gardiner, Harold C. *Catholic Viewpoint on Censorship.* New York: Imagine Books, 1961.

Goldberg, Isaac. *Tin Pan Alley.* New York: John Day Company, 1930.

Goodwin, Doris Kearns. *The Fitzgeralds and the Kennedys.* New York: Simon and Schuster, 1987.

Grady, Billy. *The Irish Peacock.* New Rochelle, N.Y.: Arlington House, 1972.

Granlund, Nils Thor. *Blondes, Brunettes, and Bullets.* New York: David McKay Company, 1957.

Green, Abel, and Joe Laurie, Jr. *Show Biz, from Vaude to Video.* New York: Henry Holt and Co., 1951.

Griffith, Richard, Arthur Mayer, and Eileen Bowser. *The Movies.* New York: Simon and Schuster, 1957.

Grun, Bernard. *The Timetables of History.* New York: Simon and Schuster, 1975.

Hampton, Benjamin B. *History of the American Film Industry.* New York: Covici, Friede, 1931. Reprint. New York: Dover Publications, 1970.

Hays, Will H. *The Memoirs of Will H. Hays.* New York: Doubleday, 1955.

Hayward, Brooke. *Haywire.* New York: Alfred A. Knopf, 1977.

Higham, Charles. *Hollywood at Sunset.* New York: Saturday Review Press, 1972.

Hochman, Stanley. *From Quasimodo to Scarlett O'Hara.* New York: Frederick Ungar Publishing Company, 1982.

Irwin, Will. *The House That Shadows Built.* New York: Doubleday, Doran and Comapny, 1928.

Jacobs, Lewis. *Rise of the American Film.* New York: Harcourt Brace, 1939.

Johnston, Alva. *The Great Goldwyn.* New York: Random House, 1937.

Kanin, Garson. *Hollywood: Stars and Starlets, Tycoons and Flesh-Peddlers.* New York: Limelight Editions, 1984.

Katz, Ephraim. *The Film Encyclopedia.* New York: Thomas Y. Crowell, 1979.

Katz, Jacob. *From Prejudice to Destruction.* Cambridge, Mass.: Harvard University Press, 1980.

Kennedy, Joseph P., ed. *The Story of Films as Told by Leaders of the Industry.* Chicago: A. W. Shaw Company, 1927.

Kirkpatrick, Sidney D. *A Cast of Killers.* New York: E. P. Dutton, 1986.

Kracauer, Siegfried. *From Caligari to Hitler.* Princeton, N.J.: Princeton University Press, 1947.

Lasky, Jesse L., Jr. *Whatever Happened to Hollywood?* New York: Funk and Wagnalls, 1973.

Lee, Albert. *Henry Ford and the Jews.* New York: Stein and Day, 1980.

Leff, Leonard J., and Jerold L. Simmons. *The Dame in the Kimono.* New York: Grove Weidenfeld, 1990.

LeRoy, Mervyn. *Mervyn LeRoy: Take One.* New York: Hawthorn Books, 1974.

Levant, Oscar. *Memoirs of an Amnesiac.* New York: G. P. Putnam's Sons, 1965.

Levin, Martin, ed. *Hollywood and the Great Fan Magazines.* New York: Arbor House, 1970.

Linenthal, Arthur J. *First a Dream: the History of Boston's Jewish Hospitals 1896 to 1928.* Boston: Beth Israel Hospital, in association with the Francis A. Countway Library of Medicine, 1990.

Loos, Anita. *Kiss Hollywood Good-By.* New York: Viking Press, 1974.

Mankiewicz, Joseph L. *More About "All About Eve."* New York: Random House, 1972.

Marx, Samuel. *Mayer and Thalberg, The Make-Believe Saints.* New York: Random House, 1975.

Menjou, Adolphe, and M. M. Musselman. *It Took Nine Tailors.* New York: McGraw Hill Book Company, 1948.

Nizer, Louis. *My Life in Court.* New York: Doubleday and Company, 1961.

Norman, Barry. *The Story of Hollywood.* New York: New American Library, 1987.

Partridge, Helen. *A Lady Goes to Hollywood.* New York: Macmillan, 1941.

Peary, Danny. *Close-Ups: The Movie Star Book.* New York: Simon and Schuster, 1978.

Peiss, Kathy. *Cheap Amusements.* Philadelphia: Temple University Press, 1986.

Pickford, Mary. *Sunshine and Shadow.* New York: Doubleday, 1955.

Pilat, Oliver. *Pegler, Angry Man of the Press.* Westport, Conn.: Greenwood Press, 1963.

Ramsaye, Terry. *A Million and One Nights.* New York: Simon and Schuster, 1926.

Randall, Monica. *The Mansions of Long Island's Gold Coast.* New York: Hastings House, 1979.

Reynolds, Debbie. *Debbie, My Life.* New York: Pocket Books, 1988.

Robinson, David. *Hollywood in the Twenties.* New York: A. S. Barnes, 1968.

Robinson, Edward G. *All My Yesterdays.* New York: Hawthorn Books, 1973.

Rooney, Mickey. *i.e., an Autobiography.* New York: G. P. Putnam's Sons, 1965.

Ross, Lillian. *Picture.* New York: Limelight Editions, 1952.

Runyon, Damon. *On Broadway.* London: Constable and Co., Ltd., 1950.

Schary, Dore. *Case History of a Movie.* New York: Random House, 1950.

———. *Heyday.* Boston: Little Brown and Co., 1970.

Schatz, Thomas. *Hollywood Genres.* Philadelphia: Temple University Press, 1981.

Scherman, Bernadine Kielty. *Girl From Fitchburg.* New York: Random House, 1964.

Schulberg, Budd. *Moving Pictures.* New York: Stein and Day, 1981.

Schulman, Sammy. *"Where's SAMMY?"* New York: Random House, 1943.

Schumach, Murray. *The Face on the Cutting Room Floor.* New York: William Morrow and Co., 1964.

Seldes, Gilbert. *The Movie Comes From America.* New York: Charles Scribner's Sons, 1937.

Selznick, Irene Mayer. *A Private View.* New York: Alfred A. Knopf, 1983.

Sinclair, Upton. *Upton Sinclair Presents William Fox.* Los Angeles: by the author, 1933.

Sklar, Robert. *Movie-Made America.* New York: Random House, 1975.

Skolsky, Sidney. *Don't Get Me Wrong—I Love Hollywood.* New York: G. P. Putnam's Sons, 1975.

Slide, Anthony. *Aspects of American Film History Prior to 1920*. Metuchen, N.J.: Scarecrow Press, 1978.

———. *The Big V: a History of the Vitagraph Company*. Metuchen, N.J.:
Scarecrow Press, 1976.

Stone, Jill. *Times Square*. New York: Collier Books, 1982.

Strait, Raymond. *Lanza, His Tragic Life*. New York: Prentice Hall,
1980.

Swanberg, W.A. *Citizen Hearst*. New York: Charles Scribner's Sons,
1961.

Tauranac, John, and Christopher Little. *Elegant New York*. New York:
Abbeville Press, 1985.

Taylor, Deems. *A Pictorial History of the Movies*. New York: Simon and
Schuster, 1943.

Thomas, Bob. *Thalberg, Life and Legend*. New York: Doubleday and
Co., 1969.

Tornabene, Lyn. *Long Live the King: A Biography of Clark Gable*. New
York: G. P. Putnam's Sons, 1976.

Wayne, Jane Ellen. *Crawford's Men*. New York: Prentice Hall Press,
1988.

Wilk, Max. *The Wit and Wisdom of Hollywood*. New York: Atheneum,
1971.

Woodman, Bertha. *From the Hill to Main Street*. Haverhill, Mass.:
Trustees of the Haverhill Public Library, 1987.

Zierold, Norman. *Garbo*. New York: Stein and Day, 1969.

———. *The Moguls*. New York: Coward-McCann, 1969.

Zukor, Adolph. *The Public Is Never Wrong*. New York: G. P. Putnam's
Sons, 1953.

Index

294